Know who work w/
grp people – roles
assign
purpose of leader/coord

diff styles –
talker w/o think
instigator
counter-attacker
listener – holistic

in mind – 3 people in room want to be in small grp –
        why?
        get to know –
2 O's   red/blue   face – 60sec – hobbies
                                    bkgrnd – family
                                    where school
                                    what study

not mean → bosom buddies / but can at least work w/'em

Social Psychology

Social Psychology

A SOCIOLOGICAL PERSPECTIVE

Arthur G. Neal
Bowling Green State University

▲▼ Addison-Wesley Publishing Company
*Reading, Massachusetts • Menlo Park, California • London
Amsterdam • Don Mills, Ontario • Sydney*

Library of Congress Cataloging in Publication Data

Neal, Arthur G.
  Social psychology.

  1. Social psychology. I. Title.
HM251.N358 1983   302   82–11336
ISBN 0–201–05361–6

ISBN 0–201–05361–6
ABCDEFGHIJ-DO-89876543

Preface

The primary distinguishing feature of this text is that it offers social psychologists a text with a sociological focus. There are two major problems with the existing texts: (1) that most are written by psychologists who ignore the research of sociologists; (2) those who attempt to combine psychology and sociology do not provide an adequate treatment of either. The major advantage of this text is that it gives comprehensive treatment to the sociological side of social psychology.

Sections of the book are organized around unit ideas that emphasize symbolic meanings, status and identity, group processes, and psychological modernity. The guiding assumption is that the core ideas of social psychology can be summarized around a limited number of theoretical perspectives and applied to the topics of concern to most social psychologists. The advantage of developing unit ideas is that the material is organized to provide cumulative contributions to understanding and knowledge.

The writing style is oriented toward students, and a serious attempt was made to present subject matter in a jargon-free fashion without sacrificing scientific or technical accuracy. Three to eight boxed inserts are included in each chapter to enhance student interest and to show the applicability of social psychology for understanding social and personal problems. The boxes are directed toward summarizing a theme, providing findings from a recent research article, applying and elaborating a concept, or drawing upon an illustration from the news media. The boxes were carefully constructed to provide a close integration with the textual materials.

The illustrations and research materials were drawn primarily from journal articles and major monographs that have been published since 1970. A concerted effort was made to present up-to-date materials, research findings, and theoretical perspectives. Out-moded theories are deemphasized or ignored, and most of the references to publications prior to 1970 consist of classical studies that have a special contemporary relevance. The advantage to both students and instructors is that the subject matter is contemporary and reflects the current interests and research of social psychologists.

About a third of the book is devoted to the emerging concerns of the field as reflected in recent journal articles and book titles. Specific chapters are included on the meaning of work and leisure, on authority relationships, on family violence, on mass society, and on the quality of life. These chapters were designed to provide students with an appreciation of the varieties of life styles and experiences in contemporary social living. The guiding assumption in these and other chapters is that an adequate treatment of social psychology should contribute to an understanding of modern culture and the historical uniqueness of our time and place.

The social construction of reality has been emphasized as the unifying theme. This theme was developed by drawing on theoretical perspectives from symbolic interactionism, exchange theory, role theory, ethnomethodology, and phenomenology. By emphasizing both a unifying theme and a variety of theoretical perspectives students will be able to develop an appreciation of the many theories and methods used by social psychologists for predicting and explaining human behavior. The multiple theories and methods converge in an emphasis on the process by which realities are constructed out of social relationships.

There were many people who made important contributions to the production of this book. Rachael Graham served as an editorial consultant on early drafts and taught me a great deal about the English language. Jim Tudor introduced me to the excitement of photography; Howard Cotrell stimulated my interest in visual sociology; and Jack Ward was very helpful through supervising the photographic reproductions. Ron Hill was super as the editor at Addison-Wesley, and I recommend him highly to any sociologist thinking about writing a textbook. Susan Middleton served as copyeditor and contributed to making this book more readable than it otherwise would have been.

The present book was not completed with the publisher that initially suggested the idea. As a result, I am unable to acknowledge my indebtedness to many of the anonymous reviewers who responded to early drafts of several chapters. Some will be able to recognize the use made of their suggestions; other will not. The known reviewers that I owe a special indebtedness are: John P. Hewitt (University of Massachusetts, Amherst), Dona Eder (Indiana University), and Richard Felson (SUNY, Albany). Their perceptive insights proved very useful, although none of them should be held responsible for any of the present defects. The limitations rest solely with the author.

In some respects the writing of this text was exciting and fun; in other respects it was a frustrating experience. The multiple methods and theoretical perspectives of social psychology posed a major challenge. Hopefully, some degree of theoretical unity and coherence has been achieved through emphasis on the theme of reality construction as a social process. Only time will tell if we have succeeded or failed in this venture. The promise of social psychology is to offer explanations of human behavior on the basis of the best available research evidence.

Contents

> **Boxes:**
> 3.1   The normative ordering of life events   75
> 3.2   Perceptions of "most people"   78
> 3.3   The problem of selecting a career   80
> 3.4   Stressful life events   83
> 3.5   The myth of social class and criminality   92
> 3.6   Justifications for a deviant sport   97
> 3.7   On the use of disclaimers   100

> **Boxes:**
> 4.1   Increasing alienations during the 1960s   117
> 4.2   Two sources of opposition to the Vietnam war   120
> 4.3   Reference groups   121
> 4.4   A measure of powerlessness   123
> 4.5   The value of children   126
> 4.6   Attitudes toward hippies   131
> 4.7   Fear of decision making   134

Boxes:

Boxes:

Boxes:

12　Family Violence　　379

Boxes:

Boxes:

Boxes:

INTRODUCTION AND ORIENTATION I

1

What to look for in this chapter:

What is social psychology?
How do the two social psychologies differ?
What theories of human behavior prevail in social psychology today?
What methods do social psychologists use in their studies of human behavior?

Social Psychological Inquiry

Social psychology is a legitimate child of the twentieth century. Its parents are respectable, genderless, and of equal status: each contributes to the qualities and attributes of the child, but the child has its own distinctive identity. The sociological parent makes a contribution through its emphasis on social structure, group membership, and social change. We are all a part of the structures studied by the sociologist, and the qualities of our lives are shaped by them. The psychological parent emphasizes thought processes, cognition, conditioning, and reinforcement. Psychology provides images of ourselves as thinking, minded, information-processing creatures. The field of social psychology can be thought of as representing the overlap between sociology and psychology; it draws on the characteristics of the two without being a carbon copy of either.

While social psychology has clearly established its legitimacy, it is also an oddity. Some say that social psychology has "a split personality"; others say that there are really two social psychologies rather than one (Stryker, 1977). A good deal of evidence could be assembled to support either view. That social psychology is a divided field is suggested in several ways. Many colleges and universities offer two courses bearing the identical label of social psychology but offer them in two separate departments. The faculty member who thinks of himself or herself as a social psychologist could have received graduate training exclusively in either a psychology or a sociology department. Sociologists and psychologists have their own separate journals in social psychology. The psychologists publish in the *Journal of Social Psychology* and the sociologists publish in the *Social Psychological Quarterly*.

The divisions in social psychology are an outgrowth of the compartmentalization that has occurred in the modern university. Knowledge has become fragmented, broken down into small units, and extensively elaborated. There are both advantages and disadvantages to this process. The advantages are

that one can explore topics in depth, that one can develop high levels of expertise in limited areas, and that one can direct resources toward solving specific,
identifiable problems. The main disadvantages are that compartmentalization
tends to draw boundaries, to generate vested interests, and to produce schisms
within the academic community. Problems develop in communication across
departmental boundaries; sociologists and psychologists fail to interact with
each other; and researchers working on related problems frequently fail to
exchange ideas or to share the excitement of their research. Students are also
affected by the compartmentalization process. Knowledge is packaged in bits
and pieces and frequently contained within the boundaries of a specific course
and its requirements. If knowledge is to be integrated at all, the responsibility
is left entirely up to the student.

We may understand the development of social psychology during the
twentieth century as an outgrowth of the desire for insights into many facets
of human behavior. Why do people do the things they do? Are there identifiable qualities underlying human nature? Are humans unique in the animal
kingdom? Why do people go to war? What is the basis for human aggression?
How do people differ in their personality characteristics? Is human behavior
predictable? Why do people respond differently to similar situations? These
are among the many questions still associated with social psychology in popular thinking. They are not among the basic questions social psychologists
raise today, although these questions did receive a great deal of attention in
the historical development of the field. We now know that many of these questions are unanswerable, or that we can give credible answers to them only
through highly qualified restatements of the questions.

We have rejected many of the early theories in social psychology because
they presented static models of human behavior. Today we recognize that
social life is always in the process of change and development. What we see
and do in the world around us is shaped by interactions with the many people
in our lives, and these interactions continue throughout the life course. The
study of social psychology today begins with an appreciation of the diversity
of human behavior and with a recognition that humans construct their realities from their relationships with one another.

The unity of social psychology as a field lies in the objectives of inquiry.
The overriding concerns are with understanding group processes and the many
ways in which groups influence individual thought and behavior. Both psychologists and sociologists are concerned with relationships between the individual and society, with thought processes, with social learning, and with
the situations in which social behavior occurs. We can clarify each of these
major concerns through a comparison and contrast of some of the major theoretical perspectives within psychology and sociology.

The diversity within the field stems from variations in theoretical perspectives, in agendas for research, and in levels of analysis. Some social psychologists place primary emphasis on cognition and thought processes, while

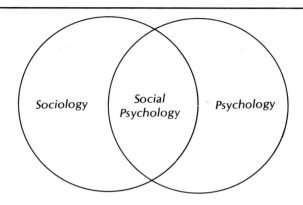

The psychological version of social psychology bears an affinity to biology with its emphasis on physiological responses to environmental stimuli. In contrast, the sociological version of social psychology bears an affinity to history and anthropology with its emphasis on social organization and culture. The common domain of the two social psychologies lies with the overlapping interests in environmental context, cognitive processes, and social learning.

FIGURE 1.1
The Two Social Psychologies

others emphasize behavior and the learning process; some prefer to concentrate on small groups, while others like to deal with broader social structures; some prefer the methods of experimental research, while others choose naturalistic observations or survey research. But whatever the differences among them, social psychologists are oriented toward describing, explaining, and understanding human behavior. The research of social psychology should enable us to see more clearly the social influences that guide and shape our own behavior as well as the behavior of those with whom we interact.

A. THE FACES OF SOCIAL PSYCHOLOGY

Thomas Kuhn (1970) emphasized the importance of paradigms for the growth and development of the various sciences. According to Kuhn, a **paradigm** is a constellation of assumptions, beliefs, values, theories, and research techniques shared by the members of a scientific community. In effect, "a paradigm is the fundamental images of a subject matter within a science" (Ritzer, 1975: 7). The paradigm identifies the topics for investigation, specifies the kinds of questions to raise, points to the rules or methods to follow, and suggests what will be found and why it is important. The conduct of research is thus a social enterprise that is guided by a set of principles based on consensus within a scientific community.

Social psychology is not comprised of a single scientific community but of several subcommunities. There is no single paradigm to serve as a guide to inquiry; instead, there are multiple paradigms and theoretical perspectives shared by some but not all social psychologists. As a multiple paradigm science, social psychology is characterized by multiple and overlapping theoretical perspectives that vary in degrees of compatibility with each other. The differences in paradigms are why we have at least two social psychologies rather than one. Even within psychology and sociology there are substantial variations in assumptions and topics for investigation. We can note the multiple theoretical perspectives by drawing on the topics that have emerged as the central ones for social psychological inquiry. These topics include concern for cognition, social learning, and social situations.

1. Cognitive Theories

Cognitive theories place emphasis on mental processes and on the content of ideas. Humans are regarded as information-processing creatures that orient their behavior by drawing on the knowledge at their disposal. **Cognition** refers to the process of "mapping" one's environment: developing ideas about what exists, how events are organized, and what lines of action are possible. In effect, cognitions are reflected in consciousness or awareness and comprised of reality definitions or "mental dictionaries" of the world. Sensory inputs from the environment are coded, processed, stored, and recalled when the need arises. In emphasizing the cognitive process, we regard people as responding to their environments by thinking about objects and events and shaping the lines of action they follow.

Sociologists and psychologists agree that the individual's images of reality are not photographic representations of the actual world or of stimulus objects. Reality as the individual knows and understands it is a highly selective process. As Krech, Crutchfield, and Ballachey (1962: 24) noted several years ago, "there are no impartial facts." The physical world does not have a logic of its own that results in the same cognitions for all people. The army general may see mountains as obstacles to tank warfare, rather than as objects of scenic beauty; the physicist may see solid objects as comprised mainly of empty space; and the artist may see colors, shadows, and light variations that most of us ignore or overlook. What we see in the world about us is shaped by a symbolic process in which we classify objects, store information, and interpret events.

Several theories have been elaborated by social psychologists to clarify the cognitive process. These include symbolic interactionism, attribution

Parking Buildings and Skyscrapers
The construction of parking buildings and skyscrapers cannot be understood as a direct response of humans to their environments. Skyscrapers and parking buildings are realities created through patterns of human interaction.

theory, and cognitive consistency theory. Symbolic interactionism is one of the major cognitive theories in sociology, while attribution theory and cognitive consistency theory have commanded a great deal of attention among psychologists. Each emphasizes the social construction of reality as an underlying theme, although there are substantial differences among them in basic assumptions, in topics for investigation, and in views on the process by which cognitions operate to shape behavior.

Symbolic interactionism may be illustrated by drawing on Herbert Blumer's (1969) view of objects as units for social psychological analysis. Other aspects of symbolic interaction theory will be saved for later discussion as the topics of the course are developed and elaborated; but for now, let us consider the view of objects as developed by a symbolic interactionist. Blumer rejects the notion of objects as having a reality in their own right. In the final analysis, the literal meaning of an object is a human creation. Such a view of an object may become clearer by drawing on Kurt Riezler's observation on the pieces in a game of chess.

Chess has its king and queen, knights and pawns, its space, its geometry, its laws of motion, its demands, and its goals. The queen is not a real queen, nor is she a piece of wood or ivory. She is an entity in the game defined by the movements the game allows her. The game is the context within which the queen is what she is. ... The game is a little cosmos of its own (cited in Goffman, 1961: 27).

It is perhaps obvious that the objects used in playing a game are symbolic creations, but a similar process operates in the course of everyday life. Grades, diplomas, degrees, and job titles are socially created resources, and as objects with social meaning they orient and structure our lines of action. We do not respond to an environment of things, but to objects that are known and understood. Objects are designated, created, or defined, rather than being "just things that are there."

Attribution theory (Jones and Davis, 1965; Kelley, 1971) is compatible with the basic assumptions of symbolic interactionism. Attribution theorists view reality construction as a symbolic process and place emphasis on the organization of experiences and the perception of events. According to attribution theory, a close relationship exists between the observer and what is observed. Perceptions of friends, lovers, the poor, racial minorities, and other people stem from an attribution process. The qualities observed are not so much "what is really there" as they are imputations, judgments, or evaluations made by an observer.

A major concern of attribution theorists is the process observers use to make causal explanations. How are events organized and how did they happen? The attribution of cause is not an objective statement about what really happened, but a perception of cause and an explanation that a social actor makes. For example, poor people may be viewed as poor because of "the lack of opportunities," or they may be viewed as poor because of "personality defects." The

---

BOX 1.1
The Functions of Attribution

Donelson R. Forsyth catalogued and described four basic types of attribution: explanatory attribution, predictive attribution, egocentric attribution, and interpersonal attribution. These attributions are creations of meaning that serve as a basis for understanding and action.

Explanatory attributions are based on assumptions about how and why events occur. The physical and social worlds become understandable through the efforts of individuals to impose order on their environments.

Predictive attributions are judgments about the likely occurrence of future events. Such predictions are oriented toward active intervention by individuals in shaping events and in achieving desired goals. The quest for understanding is accompanied by the practical desire for personal mastery and control.

Egocentric attributions occur in those situations in which realities are created out of self-serving motivations. These attributions are based on seeing oneself at the center of events and reflect a blending of wishful thinking with reality perception. Egocentric attributions would not be made by individuals if their evaluations were based on strictly rational considerations.

Interpersonal attributions are forms of communication by which individuals attempt to clarify their actions to each other. People exchange information and offer explanations to avoid being misunderstood or to prevent others from drawing the wrong conclusion.

These forms of attribution serve several interrelated functions: they permit prediction and control; they facilitate understanding and action; they link individuals to their environments; they enhance the prospects for harmonious social relationships. Attributions are not statements about the real world in an objective, scientific sense. Instead, they are forms of cognition that humanize the external world and reflect the reality construction process.

Source: Donelson R. Forsyth, "The Functions of Attributions," *Social Psychological Quarterly* 43 (June, 1980): 184–189.

---

failure of students to learn in the public schools may be attributed to "bad study habits," or to "an unfavorable school environment." Whether causal explanations are based on environmental factors or on the personal qualities of individuals has a great deal of bearing on the decisions and actions of the observer toward the events in question. (See Box 1.1.)

While attribution theory assumes the importance of causal explanations in human affairs, **cognitive consistency theory** emphasizes the quest for balancing and harmonizing perceptions of the world. Consistency theorists hold that humans seek orderly and coherent views of their environments,

vs cog. dissonance?

of themselves, and of the important people in their lives. Problems emerge when individuals face contradictions in their perceptions. Leon Festinger (1957) calls this **cognitive dissonance**, a state of tension that occurs when a person holds two incompatible or contradictory perceptions at the same time. Dissonance is not so much the "objective" contradictions in a given situation or the person's incompatible beliefs that may be noted by an outside observer; instead, dissonance results from the individual's experience with the absurdity of the contradictions that he or she perceives.

The dissonance may be between two or more beliefs or between self-attitudes and behavior. For example, the observation that "I smoke cigarettes" may be incompatible with the observation that "cigarette smoking causes cancer." A state of dissonance exists if I believe each of the above statements to be true and if I think of myself as a sane, reasonable person (Aronson, 1980). Under such circumstances, according to cognitive consistency theory, the individual would seek to work out some resolution to the contradiction. To stop smoking would be a simple solution to the problem of dissonance, but if this solution is not acceptable, adjustments are then required in beliefs and attitudes. For example, the person may regard the linkage of cigarette smoking to cancer as a statistical relationship that does not apply in all individual cases. Or the person may switch to filter-tipped brands, or the individual may justify continued smoking on the grounds that an enjoyable life is preferable to a long life.

Although many experimental studies have documented the process of reducing dissonance in given situations, several social psychologists do not accept the theory as a general statement of the cognitive process. Stability, harmony, balance, and consistency may be desirable, but for most people under most circumstances they are problematic. For example, Alfred Schutz (1960) has observed that knowledge in everyday life is only partially clear, frequently inconsistent, and not at all free from contradictions; and Viktor E. Frankl (1965) has noted that the quest for consistency in modern social life is not nearly so important as developing the capacity to live with contradictions. However, the consistency issue is an important one in social psychology, and its implications will be developed and explored more fully in the chapters on norms, attitudes, the social self, and role relationships. Rather than locating the consistency problem in the area of cognition alone, this text will develop the many facets of the consistency issue as concerns growing out of social relationships in specific situations.

2. Learning Theories

The contrast between cognitive and learning theories may be drawn on to illustrate the general use of theory in social psychology. Theories elaborate specialized concepts to serve as guides to inquiry. The complexities of human thought and action are necessarily reduced in drawing boundaries around the topics for investigation. Theories necessarily simplify because it is not possible to take into account all of the many facets of human behavior in any given study. Accordingly, psychologists and sociologists have elaborated several theories of learning. In general, psychologists have placed greater emphasis on the principles of conditioning and reinforcement, while sociologists have placed primary emphasis on the socialization process. This text will not attempt to specify the central concepts and assumptions of each of the learning theories in social psychology but only to give a general outline of the alternatives available and to indicate the approach of the present book.

The major variations in social psychological theories consist of the contrasts between cognitive and learning theories. Learning theories in psychology developed out of the tradition of behaviorism and directed attention toward behavior stimuli

Principles of Learning
We can apply certain principles of learning to interactions between humans and non-human animals.

objects within the environment that serve as stimuli for behavior. Behaviorism assumes that the investigator must develop learning principles out of observing events and should omit or ignore mental processes. Behaviorists have argued that the basic principles of learning can be established using nonhuman animals (dogs, rats, pigeons, and so forth) and that cognitive variables can be disregarded. For example, B. F. Skinner (1971) has argued that, because behavior can be predicted directly from the principles of conditioning and reinforcement, such subjective variables as beliefs, attitudes, and values are unnecessary. Fortunately, there are few learning theorists today who would fully agree with Skinner's radical position, but many who conduct their research within a learning theory tradition still downplay the importance of subjective variables.

Conditioning theories of learning have an intellectual indebtedness to the early experimental work of Pavlov on stimulus objects in the environment. Pavlov studied the digestive system of dogs and discovered that salivation was produced not only through the smell and taste of food but also through the stimulus objects that were associated with eating. The sound of the footsteps of the animal caretaker elicited the production of saliva. Further experiments indicated that dogs could be conditioned to respond to several stimulus objects. The ringing of a bell prior to feeding conditioned the dogs to respond by salivating. The sound of footsteps and the ringing of a bell then became stimulus objects that the experimental animals associated with the positive reinforcement of food. Several basic principles of the learning process were subsequently established in psychological research that manipulated environments and rewards.

Reinforcement theories elaborate the principles of learning by concentrating on the contingencies of rewards under controlled experimental conditions. These studies have demonstrated that behavior can be modified by manipulating rewards and punishments: desired behavior can be strengthened, while undesirable behavior can be extinguished or inhibited (Skinner, 1971). However, only some of the studies of conditioning and reinforcement in psychology fall within the scope of social psychology. These include the theories that take into account humans' greater learning capacities over other animals and the importance of group influences in the learning process. The psychological theories of current relevance to social psychology necessarily include the cognitive elements of the learning process.

The growing emphasis on **exchange theory** in recent years (Beniger and Savory, 1981) draws on several aspects of learning theories in the concerns with human decision making and with the social transfer of valued resources. Social psychologists emphasize two central themes in exchange theory: utility theory concentrates on the process by which individuals make choices and decisions, while distributive justice emphasizes the underlying rules by which society allocates desired resources. In the first case the social psychologist is concerned with the rationality of human choices, while in the second with the fairness rules that operate in social relationships.

Exchange theory draws on assumptions from learning theories by placing emphasis on the manner by which objects and events take on special value because of prior conditioning. Actions that have been rewarded in the past are likely to be repeated and with increasing frequency, while previous behaviors that turned out to be unrewarding are likely to be avoided (Homans, 1974). Drawing on these principles, the character of social reinforcements become important to exchange relationships. The utilities associated with objects, events, and relationships depend on such positive reinforcements as winning approval, gaining acceptance, and being liked, while patterns of avoidance rest on such negative reinforcements as rejection, ridicule, and punishment. Subjective meanings enter into exchange relationships: the importance of tradeable objects is based on the values social actors attribute to them.

According to the utility component of exchange theory, decision making is based on a type of cost-benefit analysis. Individuals assess the advantages, disadvantages, and relative value of one course of action compared to another. The utilities are the benefits relative to the cost in the exchange of desired resources. Drawing on economic models of consumer choice, exchange theorists view individuals as seeking to increase their rewards and to reduce their costs in the pursuit of valued goals. Exchange theorists assume human behavior to be motivated by the pursuit of pleasure, by rational evaluations, and by the promotion of self-interests.

We derive most of our important rewards from social relationships, and we obtain these rewards at some degree of cost. Exchange theory focuses attention on the importance of perceived fairness and justice in social transactions. If we feel that we have not been treated fairly in an exchange relationship, we are likely to become angry. Under such circumstances, we may seek retribution, withdraw from the relationship, or avoid involvement in similar situations in the future. Fairness and justice are important concerns in social relationships. There are certain resources we have under our control, and if we give them up, we expect to receive benefits of equal or greater value in return. Getting what we deserve, incurring obligations, and paying our debts are among the many negotiations involved in social living. These concerns will be elaborated as we progress through the subject matter of the course.

Socialization is the central focus of learning theories among sociologists. Socialization refers to the process by which social relationships and social interactions shape group values, norms, attitudes, and behavior patterns. The overriding assumption is that social learning is a continuous, developmental process. Sociologists place particular emphasis on the importance of the self as an outgrowth of social relationships. Learning how to belong, learning what is necessary for the playing of social roles, and learning how to achieve the goals of personal interest are among the many tasks individuals must confront as members of social groups.

Individuals come to terms with basic facts about social life through the process of socialization. Throughout the life course, we can fulfill most of our personal needs only through interactions with others. We are dependent on others for most of the food we consume, for the medical services we receive, and for the transportation that enhances our freedom of movement. And out of this dependency, we are bound by social constraints on what we can or cannot do, on the rules we must follow, and on the range of behavior that others around us will permit or tolerate. Impulses, desires, hopes, and aspirations are held in bounds by social norms and by the constraints of social control.

The duality of society and the individual is exhibited throughout the socialization process. The group's concerns are with promoting orderly and predictable social relationships; the actor's concerns are with asserting mastery and control over his or her environment (Dawe, 1970). Social order is sustained through shared conceptions of the normal state of affairs, through the rules that prevail as the regulators of conduct, and through the shared understandings that give form and coherence to the activities of everyday life. The actor's control over his or her environment is facilitated by selecting goals from the alternatives available and by knowing what must be done to attain the goals of interest.

Men and women live in immediate acts of experience, and they orient their behavior toward the objects and events that have the highest priority of the moment (Weigert, 1981). Immediate concerns often involve such concrete matters as writing a term paper, preparing for an exam, paying the bills, scheduling next semester's classes, preparing for a date, getting a summer job, or repairing the car. The concerns of the moment, however, tend to have cumulative effects that develop into attitudes and values persisting through time and extending across a variety of situations. These relatively enduring frameworks of understanding involve some blending of a sense of coherence with perceptions of complexity and chaos; some mixture of feelings of membership and belonging with those of personal loneliness and isolation; and some combination of feelings of personal mastery and control with feelings of helplessness.

The assumptions that a person holds about the predictability of social events are of special relevance for making personal plans. If the person feels that the course of social events lacks predictability, then planning does not appear to be feasible, and the individual's personal life takes on a pattern of aimlessness and drift. Making plans for the future may proceed with confidence only if the individual feels that the goals selected are appropriate and attainable. Yet, the outcome of events often fail to support initial intentions. For example, intended love affairs fail to develop as expected, vacations turn out to be unrewarding, and children fail to measure up to the hopes and aspirations of their parents. Such unexpected occurrences require reflection on the rules and rational properties underlying the conduct of orderly social life (Garfinkel, 1967).

B. SYMBOLIC INTERACTIONISM

This text takes the position that an application of the core ideas of symbolic interactionism can encompass most of the central concerns in social psychological inquiry. The appeal of symbolic interactionism lies in the scope of the topics covered. It is a theoretical perspective that integrates the concerns of social psychologists with cognition, behavior, and social environments. This perspective holds that humans live in a world of symbolic meanings, that realities are constructed through social interaction, and that behavior occurs in a situational context. Symbolic meanings, social interactions, and social situations provide the contextual framework for social psychological inquiry.

The major tenets of symbolic interactionism have come to be associated with the social thought of George Herbert Mead (1934) and his notions about the linkages between mind, self, and society. He stressed the quality of awareness as being the central feature of the mind, and viewed both self and society as social constructions of reality. Mead maintained that a self is not present at birth but develops as an outgrowth of social interaction. We have selves because we think we have selves; but in the final analysis the self is a product of social influences. The qualities of social interaction also provide the basic reference points from which images of society are developed. Notions about society are extended from experiences with the important people in an individual's life and include pondering the qualities of casual acquaintances, the attributes of strangers, and the characteristics of "most people." From these considerations, symbolic interactionism is a cognitive theory that holds that social relationships supply the content for our thought processes. The primary objective of the present inquiry will be to clarify the place of symbols and social relationships in individual thought and action.

1. Reality Construction

The term *symbolic* in symbolic interactionism places emphasis on systems of meaning we create from our experience (Blumer, 1969). We do not live in a world of objective reality or solid facts, but in a world that we have organized into sets of meaning. These meanings consist of our notions about the attributes of objects, persons, places, and events. Such sets of meaning give content to our thoughts and shape our behavior. They enable us to answer the questions of who we are, where we belong, what we are to do, and what we are to become. Here the basic assumption is that we tend to act on the basis of our understanding, regardless of how incomplete or inadequate that understanding may be.

As we go about our daily activities, we are aware of the reality of our own existence, the reality of other people, and the reality of the objects and events

Interpersonal Communication
We seek verification of our own ideas about reality through communication with others.

that enter into our consciousness (Holzner, 1968). These realities as we know them are constructed from our experiences with others and organized into systems of meaning through the use of symbols. For organizing experiences we draw our primary symbols from our language, which permits us to use vocabularies to characterize objects, to think about events, and to make plans for the future.

In the course of everyday behavior, most of us proceed in a practical, utilitarian manner in the pursuit of an immediate set of objectives (Garfinkel, 1967). We organize our daily goals around a set of assumptions about the predictability of social relationships, and we tend to act with some level of confidence about the adequacy of our understanding of the events in which we are engaged. We hold some level of probability for mastery and control over the outcomes we seek, and we assign some degree of reward value to the social relationships we have established with others. These components of social life may be understood as our constructions of reality, and they reflect the symbolic meanings we attach to the events in which we are engaged.

Because our experiences, imaginations, and life circumstances differ, we do not share the same realities but live in a world with a diversity of meaning. Our own understanding of events is not fully congruent with the perceptions of others. For example, the realities of the classroom are not the same for the professor as for the students. The professor has control over the available learning resources, already knows what the students are expected to learn, and speaks with authority in delivering lectures and in directing class dis-

---

BOX 1.2
Multiple Realities of the Classroom

Professors frequently seek student evaluations of teaching effectiveness to obtain some cues on how to improve the learning environment of the classroom. From these evaluations it becomes clear that students, however, frequently have mixed and contradictory reactions. Students apparently do not share the same reality. Consider, for example, the following selected but unedited comments from students who presumably listened to the same lectures, read the same assignments, and took the same examinations (or did they?):

Sociology is interesting in a weird way. It's really different, for sure. The discussions were pretty neat most of the time. I feel that I learned quite a bit in this class, if I can only remember it all. I really liked the professor and think that he is super. Not only did he make a not-all-that-thrilling subject interesting, but he has a cute way about him. I think that he did a good job. Sometimes the lectures got a little boring, but how fascinating can you make social stratification, anyway?

Somehow the relevance and importance of this course, rather the whole subject, escapes me. I feel that it is a cold, hard, impersonal way of looking at life with no real purpose other than making cold, bland observations. At times the information was interesting, but usually it was depressing, reinforcing my conviction that I am a barbarian living in a barbaric society.

The lectures were a pure waist [sic] of my time as they were very incoherent and rarely covered material which was covered on tests. Speaking of tests, what a joke! The questions were very, very ambiguous and in many instances didn't cover any of the reading or lecture material. I really wish I hadn't signed up for this course (from this Professor anyway). I'm going to make a point of it to forewarn my friends about this guy, what a jerk!

The one redeeming element of this course was the instructor, who stimulated thought in often thoughtless discussions, and exhibited an enthusiastic and dedicated approach to his subject.

cussions. The aims and objectives of the students and the professor may be similar in several respects, but the perspectives brought to bear on the situation are likely to differ. The students themselves are varied in the intensity with which they listen; they hear different things; and they give different interpretations to what the professor and other students say. (See Box 1.2.)

The notion of reality construction is an uncomplicated idea, but its implications for our understanding of human behavior are very great indeed. How strange it now seems that early psychologists and sociologists were searching for a unified reality lying in back of human conduct. Some saw humans as hedonistic and pleasure-seeking; others saw them as basically competitive and engaged in struggles over scarce resources; still others viewed humans as cooperative and altruistic. We now recognize that the concerns with a unified human nature raised unanswerable questions and gave oversimplified answers. The conclusions about a unified human nature turned out to be reality constructions of the early investigators. They emphasized only the evidence supporting a point of view and ignored, disregarded, or discounted contradictory evidence.

Modern social psychologists recognize that humans do many things in their relationships with one another. They take each other into account and modify their behavior accordingly; they exchange valued resources and become dependent on one another; they compete for scarce resources and become hostile to their competitors; they create and enforce rules in attempts to regulate conduct and to promote orderly social relationships. In effect, humans construct their social realities through the decisions they make and through the lines of action they follow. Because of the capacities of humans to make many different kinds of decisions and choices, the realities they construct are richly varied.

The theme of reality construction requires rethinking some of the questions popular thinking associates with social psychology. For example, students who enroll in a social psychology course frequently expect to receive answers to the question of why people do the things they do. Surely the question is clear and direct enough for an unequivocal answer from the social psychologist. The question, however, is much more complicated than it appears. In the history of social psychology several attempts were made to specify the grounds for human motivation. Early theorists emphasized the importance of basic needs and concentrated on such drives as hunger, sex, and physical comfort. They directed efforts toward specifying within a social psychological framework "the energizers" or "the triggering mechanisms" of human behavior. If a person is hungry and if food is available, it is somewhat obvious that he or she will be motivated to eat. But how, when, and what people eat are determined by a series of social definitions. Both cultural conventions and personal definitions determine the number of meals per day, the equipment used in eating, and the foods consumed. Many of us do not think of grubs, grasshoppers, or snails as suitable for human consumption, but other people at other times and places have regarded these foods as delicacies. The reality construction perspective does not view motives as the actual causes of behavior, but as the perceived causes or as the subjective views on why people do the things they do.

In recent years, social psychologists have reformulated the basic questions about human motives. Rather than asking, "Why do people do the things they do?" questions are directed toward the conditions under which a concern for motives arises, toward the accounts actors give for their conduct, and toward the social acceptability of the explanations that are offered. In effect, people use language to conceptualize their motives, to explain their behavior, and to repair social relationships that may have been damaged. The language of motives then becomes a reality constructed to make sense out of human experiences and to promote harmonious relationships. Within this framework, motives are not so much the literal or objective grounds of human conduct as they are explanations that people offer for their conduct. The study of motives in social psychology then becomes a study of the process of reality construction.

In the world of daily life we act on the basis of our reality definitions. We assume the firmness of our knowledge and the dependability of the things we know (Holzner, 1968). But from a social psychological perspective the firmness of a reality construction grows out of a relationship between the observer and what the observer observes. We see the world from our own vantage point, and the meanings we give to what we see are shaped by our previous experiences. Imagine how the qualities of your life would differ if your parents had been very rich or very poor, if at birth you had been a member of the opposite sex, or if you had decided not to attend college after graduation from high school. If any of the above conditions had prevailed, the important people in your life would not be the same, your present social attachments would differ, and your major life goals would have taken a different shape.

The multiple realities of modern social life are reflected in the diversity of lifestyles among segments of the population (Feldman and Thielbar, 1975). A *lifestyle* refers to an overall design for social living that characterizes a subgroup in society. The design includes a world view, established ways of doing things, a set of aspirations for the future, and other attributes of social life that are shared only by some members of a larger population. Similarities in lifestyles derive from shared life circumstances, values, attitudes, and behavior patterns.

In our society the variations in lifestyles are perhaps greatest in the contrast between "the super rich" on one hand and those caught up in the culture of poverty on the other. Because most of us think of ourselves as members of the American middle class, we do not share the orientations of "the jet set"; we do not have memberships in country clubs; we do not plan long vacations in expensive resort areas; and we do not own new and expensive, "gas-guzzling" automobiles. At the same time, we do not share in the culture of poverty. We

do not perceive serious restrictions on our life chances; we do not take a fatalistic view of the world; we do not feel seriously hemmed-in; and we do not see
the lack of opportunities as preventing us from achieving most of the things
we want out of life. The similarity in social and economic circumstances has a
major influence on patterns of social attachments and constitutes the primary
basis for developing shared lifestyles for any given group of people.

Variations in lifestyles occur over time as a result of different degrees of
exposure to changing historical circumstances. Young adults presumably
have greater receptivity to changing norms, values, and attitudes than do
older people who continue with lifestyles shaped during an earlier period of
time. We may note, for example, the different circumstances of growing up
during the conditions of scarcity and hardship of the Great Depression of the
1930s as compared to growing up during the times of prosperity and material
well-being of the 1950s and 1960s. Patriotism and national pride were prominent among young people during World War II, and this stands in contrast to
the hostile attitudes toward war and militarism that developed among many
young people during the Vietnam War. Thus orientations toward numerous
aspects of social life are likely to vary according to historical circumstances
and reflect different viewpoints according to age and generation level.

2. Social Interaction

The above considerations suggest that the primary sources of meaning for
individuals develop out of social relationships. The meanings assigned to
various aspects of social life emerge through the process of communication.
We adjust our ideas and actions to take into account the cues we receive from
others. We turn our attention outward to observe the behavior of others, and
in doing so we derive ideas about ourselves, about other people, and about the
organization of social life in general. These ideas about self and society become central to our usual manner of thinking and are expressed in our subsequent patterns of interaction.

The influence of society in the thoughts and actions of individuals is
most clearly evident in the definitions we give to specific social situations.
The situation consists of the immediate sphere of social experiences, encompassing our locations in time, place, and a set of social relationships. The definition of the situation also includes a set of notions about the social rules for
regulating behavior, and this permits us both to make predictions about the
conduct of others and to evaluate the likely response of others to our own
course of action. Since individuals differ in their images of social life, social
interactions are oriented toward bringing our own goals and understanding
into alignment with the goals and understanding held by others.

Under ordinary circumstances we are inclined to assume that our own understanding of the world is also shared by others. These notions about shared

understanding provide us with orientations that we bring to bear on specific situations. We usually base interactions on such definitions as the role identities of those involved, the focus of the activity, the attributes of the social setting, and the proper rules for regulating conduct. These definitions may be regarded as setting the stage for interactions to occur, and transactions proceed in an orderly fashion if the coparticipants can verify their expectations as being correct.

Such everyday activities as attending class, going to work, eating lunch, playing tennis, or going on a date are organized into routine patterns of mean-

Unfocused Gathering (Status and Identity)
At weddings, funerals, and other ceremonial occasions, those in attendance experience shared realities only to a limited degree. Variations in social characteristics, personal identities, and other life circumstances give different meanings to the events in question.

ing and coherence. For example, we can make purchases in a store because we know something about the exchange rules for transferring the ownership of desired resources. We hold notions about what to use money for, how to select the objects for purchase, what constitutes the proper demeanor in relationships between customers and clerks, what the sales tax will be, and what are appropriate ways to package or wrap the purchased items.

Although a great deal of social life proceeds in a routine and orderly fashion, our knowledge in given situations is frequently incomplete and contradictory. We are not always clear about the identities of those with whom we interact, just as we often lack an understanding of how our own qualities and attributes are being perceived by others. We respond to the illusions and appearances of others, just as we too engage in performances designed to have an effect on those with whom we interact. These qualities of social relationships suggest that there are dramatic and theatrical dimensions to the manner in which humans interact with each other (Goffman, 1963; 1967). (See Box 1.3.)

Role relationships are central to our personal identities and to the attain-

---

BOX 1.3
Social Life as Theater

The writings of Erving Goffman represent a variation on the symbolic interaction approach to social psychology. The starting point for Goffman is a recognition that many aspects of social behavior resemble theatrical performances. Appearances, illusions, social settings, and audience responses are among the important components of social life. People play roles in public places as well as within the intimacy of friendship and marriage.

The theatrical analogy is useful for explaining a great deal of human behavior. The model calls attention to the ways in which people separate perceptions of illusion from those of reality, seek authentic experiences, communicate availability for social interaction, and negotiate for the use of space. The model is general enough to explore the many facets of social encounters, yet specific enough to examine social behavior in elevators and negotiations for the use of space on urban sidewalks. The details of social interaction are brought under close scrutiny.

Because the analogies are drawn between theatrical performances and everyday life, we should not conclude that social life is not to be taken seriously. To the contrary, social drama is basic to the human condition as a result of the need to limit behavior to specific lines of action. Who does what, when, where, and why are central questions to an understanding of social behavior, and these are among the concerns of dramaturgical analysis. Performances, pretenses, and illusions are among those aspects of human behavior one should recognize in separating what is genuine from what is spurious.

Sources: Erving Goffman, *Behavior in Public Places*, New York: The Free Press, 1963; and *Interaction Ritual*, Garden City, N.Y.: Anchor Books, 1967.

ment of our basic life goals. As a matter of fact, many aspects of our personal lives are unthinkable apart from the ways in which the roles we play mesh with the roles played by others. For example, a person cannot be a wife without a husband, a teacher without students, a clerk without customers, or a parent without children. From our relationships with others, we refine our notions about ourselves and our position within the social system. We come to identify ourselves as having some degree of social effectiveness, and we develop an awareness of what others expect of us as a result of our age, sex, religion, socioeconomic status, and other social categories within which we are located. By knowing where we stand in the broader scheme of social affairs we are able to relate to others in a meaningful fashion.

From our selective involvement in society, we orient ourselves toward some degree of order and stability in social life. But we also experience the chaos inherent in social living. We encounter the unexpected happening, the frustration of human effort, and the limits of our capacities for attaining the goals we value. Social interactions are orderly when we were able to make reasonably accurate predictions about the behavior of others and when others are able to make adequate predictions about our own behavior. Under conditions of order, we assume that social life as we know and understand it will continue into the future (Schutz, 1967; Schutz and Luckmann, 1973). Such an assumption permits us to make personal plans with some degree of confidence that we can carry them out. There is a loss of order under those conditions in which the consequences of events become uncertain and the behavior of others becomes undependable.

In the study of social psychology, we can examine the dual themes of order and conflict form the vantage point of individuals in given types of situations. We cannot correctly assume that conditions of order prevail, nor that conflict and struggle are inherent in social relationships. Both order and conflict are outcomes of social relationships, and there are many conditions under which individuals may cooperate or become antagonistic toward each other. In some cases individuals do cooperate, but in other cases interactions take a hostile form. Looking at social life in general, we may conclude that social relationships usually involve a mixture of both order and conflict.

The study of conflict concentrates on the antagonistic forms of social interaction. Social conflict is evident in family life and in the political sphere when individuals engage in acts of physical violence. Increased awareness of child abuse and the battered spouse has provided us with new ways of thinking about family relationships, just as reports on terrorism, hijackings, and political assassinations have provided us with new perspectives on the political process. Violence is one of the more dramatic expressions of conflict, but social conflict is not limited to overt acts of violence. Conflicts also occur in the stresses and contradictions that are deeply embedded in the organization of daily life. Racial minorities, women, and other segments of the population must deal with negative stereotypes, discriminatory practices, and perceived injustices in the course of everyday life. Social interactions and personal histories are shaped not only by the course of action selected by the individual, but also by the collective events of the larger society.

Within the framework of reality construction, this text will emphasize the themes of order and conflict in social relationships. These themes are implicit in the human condition, and an adequate understanding of them requires firmly locating individual thought and action within the context of specific historical situations. Living in a particular historical epoch, living in a specific society, being born into a specific family, becoming involved with a particular group of social friends, and having a specific set of plans and aspirations for the future are among the many conditions that determine both who we are and what we subsequently will become.

C. RESEARCH METHODS

The study of social psychology indicates that the content of human thought and action is richly varied. Through the creation and use of symbols, humans are able to adapt effectively to a wide variety of environmental circumstances. Through their interactions with each other, people are always in the process of creating new meanings and realities. As a result of the diversity in human experiences, social psychologists are required to think clearly about ways to derive dependable knowledge about social behavior. The concern with methodology is at the center of social psychological inquiry. While theories serve as guidelines on what to study, methods provide frameworks for making observations and drawing conclusions.

Some of the concerns with methods in social psychology stem from problems unique to the study of human behavior. The ways in which chemists, geologists, and physicists think about their subject matters differ in several respects from the image of science from the viewpoint of social psychology. The physical sciences see their subject matter as relating to "objective" principles that exist independently of human perceptions and intentions. Their research is oriented toward the study of impersonal events and solid facts. In the final analysis, however, the scientific study of the physical world is a human enterprise, and the conclusions of research are an outgrowth of cognitive processes. Scientific facts turn out to be the conclusions accepted as facts within a scientific community. The validity of truth claims is based on the consensus of those who are socially recognized as competent to decide.

The problems unique to social psychological inquiry derive from recognizing that the research enterprise is a cognitive process. The social psychologist is a thinking, acting, feeling human being studying the thoughts and the behavior of other human beings. Human awareness and consciousness is the very subject matter for investigation. In some way or another, the social psychologist necessarily enters into the worlds of the people being selected for study, and this intervention has both advantages and disadvantages. The primary advantage is that the social psychologist can employ methods that would be inappropriate or nonapplicable in the physical sciences. The major disadvantage is that the interaction process influences human behavior, and the responses that subjects give to the researcher may shape the findings of the research.

There are several ethical issues that further separate social psychology from some of the other sciences. For example, biologists may dissect organisms for scientific purposes, and chemists grind, heat, combine, or destroy substances. In contrast, social psychologists have ethical obligations to the subjects selected for study and limits are imposed on what the researcher can or cannot do. The subjects should not be harmed or injured; their participation in a research study should be voluntary; they should potentially benefit from the research; and deliberate deception by the researchers should be kept to a minimum or avoided altogether. These and other ethical considerations document the special human character of social psychological inquiry.

Rather than making direct truth claims in social psychological analysis, observations are usually regarded as tentative and conditional in nature. The conclusions of research are based on the problem selected for analysis, the sample drawn on for study, and the procedures used in data collection. Systematic modification of any of these may alter the results of research. Thus in social psychology, as in scientific research more generally, conclusions are dependent on the methods employed. If researchers ask the wrong kinds of questions, if the sample they select is not representative, or if the subjects are not permitted to express their true point of view, the conclusions of the research are likely to be inadequate. An implied statement in social psychological research is that under some specified set of conditions, utilizing some specific set of methods, some specific set of results has been obtained.

Social psychologists use several research strategies. Some prefer descriptive studies based on observing social behavior in natural settings, while others prefer using statistics and computers to analyze data collected on large samples. Some social psychologists prefer to work with small groups in an experimental setting, while others prefer to study the distribution of attitudes and behavior through survey research and carefully selected samples. There are strengths and weaknesses to each of the several methods, although in any case researchers are concerned with deriving valid information about some aspect of social behavior.

1. Participant Observation

Data collection in social psychology proceeds from the assumption that to know about social behavior we must observe social life directly. We may gain insights into behavior by turning our attention outward and examining the meanings people give to the events in which they are engaged. To some extent, we all take the role of the observer in what we see and hear in everyday life. Through mentally putting ourselves in the position of others, we are able to develop some understanding of feelings, thoughts, and motives. Such a procedure is refined in social psychological inquiry through the use of participant observation.

Using the **participant-observer technique** the researcher becomes involved in the activity under study and as a participant makes observations about the social forces that are operating. This method requires the investigator to take on a social role while operating among those being studied, to select major informants as sources of information, and to gain access to desired vantage points for making observations. For example, while working at some particular job—as a cabdriver, as a cocktail waitress, as a newspaper reporter, or as a factory worker—the social psychologist may gain insights into the multiple meanings that are given to the world of work. The researcher may deliberately seek to become involved in a street corner gang, in a social movement, in a religious ceremony, or in some other aspect of social life as an objective of the research. Involvement permits social psychologists to make observations both as an insider and as an outsider. As an insider the researcher can have firsthand knowledge of the events the researcher is studying. As an observer the researcher can collect descriptive data and can refine and modify plausible explanations through successive observations.

The advantage of this method stems from the closeness of the researcher to the subject matter under investigation. The social psychologist is able to develop a sympathetic understanding of the phenomenon he or she is studying by drawing on personal experiences as well as by collecting information on the experiences of others. The researcher can make recurrent observations and can verify the correctness of the interpretations through checking them out with the people being studied. The major disadvantage to participant observation is that its success depends on the skills of the researcher to such a degree that an independent replication of the findings is often difficult to obtain. In specific instances, the researcher may note selectively the unusual or the exotic, rather than the typical case; the presence of the observer may modify the context of the behavior being studied; or the researcher may become overly involved in the subject for analysis. Studies of religious cults have been known to result in a conversion experience and a loss of objectivity for the researcher. Thus the personal experiences and biases of the investigator can have important influences on the conclusions of the research.

To minimize the problems of involvement and intervention by the researcher, some social psychologists prefer to emphasize naturalistic observation rather than active participation. In some natural settings investigators can study social behavior with only a minimal level of participation. The researcher is required only to conceptualize a problem for study and a selective vantage point for making observations. The investigator can observe the flow of traffic, the play of children, the patterns of nonverbal communication, and the breaking of social rules without intervention. The degree of involvement in the activity being investigated depends in part on the preferences of the researcher and in part on the problem under investigation. The study of deviant lifestyles, for example, is likely to require greater personal involvement than is the study of everyday behavior in public places. In any case, the techniques of both participant and nonparticipant observation are useful in collecting data on topics that do not readily lend themselves to other methods.

2. Experimental Methods

Because there are many variables influencing behavior in natural settings, some social psychologists prefer to use **experimental methods.** Under the controlled conditions of the laboratory, the investigator can manipulate variables systematically in order to observe their effects on the behavioral outcome of concern. The researcher has control over the sequence of events he or she is investigating and through these controls is able to demonstrate the causal effects of one variable on another. The investigator can precisely measure the effects of a manipulated variable, can test hypotheses, and can replicate and extend the results of other investigators. The primary advantages of experimental methods derive from the ability of the researcher to create the conditions in a laboratory setting that he or she wishes to investigate.

Experimental methods have been used in the study of such topics as how people interact in conferences, how patterns of avoidance and attraction develop in social relationships, how people go about making choices and decisions, and how people mobilize resources to attain their goals. A large number of concerns in social psychology lend themselves to investigation in the small-group laboratory. For example, hypotheses on conformity, interpersonal attraction, persuasive communication, and group problem solving can be studied under experimental conditions. Through the use of laboratory methods, the researcher derives basic knowledge on such processes as communication, interpersonal influence, cooperation, and conflict.

The critics of the experimental approach maintain that social behavior under laboratory conditions tends to be artificial and that the behavior of individuals is highly influenced by the very fact that they are being studied. For example, if students are participating in an experiment, their behavior may be oriented toward pleasing the researcher; if workers are being studied, they may increase their industrial output, regardless of the effects of experimental variables; and if patients are receiving what they think is medication, they may show physical improvement regardless of the properties of the pharmaceutical agent. Because awareness shapes behavior and because human conduct is influenced by situational variables, the findings of experimental studies may not apply to natural settings. The uncertainty of generalizing from the laboratory to the external environment has led some social psychologists to recommend the use of **field studies** to approximate the experimental design.

In conducting field research in a natural setting, the investigator frequently does not attempt to influence or control behavior but only to make observations on the unfolding of events. For example, the social psychologist does not create or instigate riots on a college campus, but if a riot is occurring the social psychologist may very well take advantage of the situation to make a study of collective behavior. Social psychologists obviously do not manipulate natural disasters such as floods, tornadoes, or earthquakes; but they may be interested in developing research teams to observe the ways people respond to sudden and unexpected devastation. Field studies have provided several new insights into the ways communities respond to conditions of stress and emergency. Such studies may be regarded as natural in that researchers investigate the effects of some occurrence in a "real world" setting.

3. Survey Research

Survey research is another procedure in which the investigator does not attempt to influence behavior but rather to obtain information on the distribution of attitudes and behavior within a general population. From data collected on samples the researcher can make fairly accurate predictions about rates and trends within larger populations. For example, data collected by means of survey research on national samples indicate that during this generation, as compared to previous ones, a larger percentage of high school graduates are deciding to attend college; more people are living together without getting married; young people are postponing marriage to a later age; married couples are having a smaller number of children; and a larger percentage of women are employed in the labor force. Such data reveal the changing values, choices, and actions of a very large number of people. Researchers can use survey research to tap the new forms of reality that people are constructing in response to changing environmental circumstances.

Survey research consists of using questionnaires and interviews to collect data from randomly drawn samples. Sampling methods have been refined to permit collecting information that will be representative of a larger population. Refinements in methods for sampling, for data collection, and for data analysis have contributed to the emergence of survey research as the research strategy many social psychologists prefer. The development of computers for data processing now permits the use of statistical techniques in hypothesis testing that was not possible only a few years ago. Electronic data processing has vastly increased the speed for coding questionnaires, for tabulating frequency distributions, and for analyzing responses. The speed with which data can be collected and analyzed is contributing to a rapid expansion of social psychological knowledge about both community-wide and national populations.

One of the major advantages of survey research is that it permits a linkage of decisions made at individual levels with overall rates and trends in the larger society. For example, we can view the population growth for any particular country as an overall outcome of the intentions, motives, and decisions of a vast number of individual couples. A given couple is not likely to make a decision to have a child or an additional child by considering the impact this will have on the world's population growth or by pondering the market value of the world's resources that will be consumed by the average child born in the United States today. But the additive effects of the fertility behavior of individual couples result in the population growth rate for any particular country and have implications for how the country makes use of the available resources. Rates and trends are the consequences of the actions of a large number of people that converge to produce some overall effect within a social system.

The growth of survey research in social psychology and in other academic areas has been prompted in part by the usefulness of information on attitudes and behavior for planning purposes. Through survey research we can establish the feasibility of one policy compared to another; we can identify specific problems; and we can enhance decision making on the basis of carefully collected information. Further, we can identify variations in the quality of life among the different segments of the population. To what extent are men and women satisfied with their jobs? Do people generally find their uses of leisure to be rewarding? What level of optimism do people hold for the future of their country? How do people feel about their health? These are among the many questions social psychologists can answer through the use of survey research. Variations

	TABLE 1.1 **Multiple Methods in Social Psychology**
Data Collection Procedures	Unstructured interviews Participant-observation Laboratory experiments Field studies Survey research
The Research Enterprise	Forming concepts Developing hypotheses Sampling subjects Operationalizing variables Constructing questionnaires Processing data Drawing conclusions
Research Goals	Description Prediction Explanation Understanding

in responses to these questions can be related to differences in such social characteristics as education, occupation, gender, race, and community of residence.

The critics of survey research maintain that collecting data in the standardized format of a questionnaire does not permit tapping the nuances that surround the attitudes and behavior of specific individuals. Further, some see survey research primarily as a static form of research. Data usually are collected at a single point in time (cross-sectional collection), thus precluding the study of group dynamics or the causal sequences that are possible in the experimental study. The criticisms are valid, but they also indicate that there is no one method that can be used to investigate all topics of concern to social psychologists. Participant-observation techniques cannot determine the distribution of attitudes in the general population; survey research cannot effectively handle the dynamics of social interactions; and experimental studies in small-group laboratories will not permit us to draw conclusions about the nation as a whole. The implications to draw from these observations are that the methods of social psychology complement one another; the strengths of one set of methods are the weaknesses of the others. All are needed to investigate the many kinds of problems of concern to social psychologists. (See Table 1.1.)

The underlying assumption of social psychological inquiry holds that there are basic uniformities and regularities in social life that we may identify and make a part of our awareness. These uniformities are the **empirical generalizations**, or the hypotheses that research studies have confirmed. As such, empirical generalizations constitute the substantive knowledge of the field. The social psychologist is concerned with drawing on a series of cases for making overall predictions that are better than chance. Rather than being concerned with predicting an individual's behavior or describing a unique event, the social psychologist is typically oriented toward discovering recurrent patterns in social behavior. Most social psychologists hold a certain amount of disdain for an emphasis on absolutes or certainties in explaining human behavior. A special reason for the distrust of absolutes grows out of the subject matter for investigation. Men and women act on the basis of their awareness, and the character of this awareness is highly variable by time, place, and social circumstances.

SUMMARY

The field of social psychology can be thought of as representing the overlap between psychology and sociology; it draws on the characteristics of the two fields without being a carbon copy or duplicate of either. The overriding concerns of social psychology are with understanding group processes and the many ways in which social interactions shape individual thought and behavior. The relationship between the individual and society, the social construction of reality, and the situational basis of human behavior are among the topics encompassed in the overlap between the two fields.

Social psychology is a multiple-paradigm science, in which several theoretical perspectives have been elaborated to serve as guides to inquiry. The major theoretical approaches, however, deal with some aspect or another of cognition, social learning, and social situations. Social psychologists are concerned with describing, predicting, and explaining human behavior. Cognitive theories emphasize mental processes and the content of ideas, while learning theories emphasize the contingencies of conditioning and reinforcement. The field of social psychology today is dominated by cognitive theories, both in psychology and sociology, although there are still many social psychologists who place primary emphasis on theories of learning. Symbolic interactionism is the major cognitive theory in sociology, while attribution theory and cognitive consistency theory occupy prominent places in psychology. Although there are major differences among them, each theory concentrates on reality construction as a major theme.

Social psychology offers a major set of perspectives on the multiple aspects of reality construction in social relationships. The scope of inquiry is broad enough to encompass the processes by which people form self-identities, by which they develop social attachments, by which the behavior of individuals results in rates or trends within the larger society. Through communication and interaction, individuals become both the producers and the products of social life in its varied forms.

Investigators use a variety of methods in social psychological inquiry. In each case, however, they emphasize systematic observation as a basis for drawing dependable conclusions about human behavior. Using participant observation, the researcher observes social life directly in natural settings, and obtains information through active involvement. Experimental studies, by way of contrast, use the laboratory to create the social conditions of concern and to test for the effects of variables on each other. Through survey research the social psychologist taps the distribution of attitudes and behavior in the general population by carefully drawing representative samples and using questionnaires. There are advantages and disadvantages to each of these methods, but all are directed toward clarifying some of the basic principles in the social construction of reality.

BASIC TERMS

Paradigm
Cognition
Symbolic interactionism
Attribution theory
Cognitive consistency
   theory
Cognitive dissonance
Conditioning theories
Reinforcement theories

Exchange theory
Socialization
Participant-observation
   technique
Experimental methods
Field studies
Survey research
Empirical generalizations

REFERENCES

Aronson, Elliot
    1980 *The Social Animal,* San Francisco: W. H. Freeman.
Beniger, James R. and Laina Savory
    1981 "Social Exchange: Diffusion of a Paradigm," *The American Sociologist* 16 (November): 240–250.
Blumer, Herbert
    1969 *Symbolic Interaction,* Englewood Cliffs, N.J.: Prentice-Hall.
Dawe, Alan
    1970 "The Two Sociologies," *British Journal of Sociology* 21: 207–218.
Feldman, Saul D. and Gerald W. Thielbar
    1975 *Life Styles,* Boston: Little, Brown.
Festinger, Leon
    1957 *A Theory of Cognitive Dissonance,* Stanford, Calif.: Stanford University Press.
Forsyth, Donelson R.
    1980 "The Functions of Attributions," *Social Psychological Quarterly* 43 (June): 184–189.
Frankl, Viktor E.
    1965 *Man's Search for Meaning,* New York: Washington Square Press.
Garfinkel, Harold
    1967 *Studies in Ethnomethodology,* Englewood Cliffs, N.J.: Prentice-Hall.
Goffman, Erving
    1967 *Interaction Ritual,* Garden City, N.Y.: Anchor Books.
    1963 *Behavior in Public Places,* New York: The Free Press.
    1961 *Encounters,* Indianapolis: Bobbs-Merrill.
Holzner, Burkart
    1968 *Reality Construction in Society,* Cambridge, Mass.: Schenkman.
Homans, George C.
    1974 *Social Behavior: Its Elementary Forms,* New York: Harcourt, Brace, and World.
Jones, E. E. and K. E. Davis
    1965 "From Acts to Dispositions: The Attribution Process in Person Perception," in Leonard Berkowitz (ed.), *Advances in Experimental Social Psychology* (vol. 2) New York: Academic Press.
Kelley, Harold H.
    1971 *Attribution in Social Interaction,* Morristown, N.J.: General Learning Press.
Krech, David, Richard S. Crutchfield, and Egerton L. Ballachey
    1962 *Individual and Society,* New York: McGraw-Hill.
Kuhn, Thomas
    1970 *The Structure of Scientific Revolutions,* Chicago: University of Chicago Press.
Mead, George Herbert
    1934 *Mind, Self, and Society,* Chicago: University of Chicago Press.
Ritzer, George
    1975 *Sociology: A Multiple Paradigm Science,* Englewood Cliffs, N.J.: Prentice-Hall.

Schutz, Alfred
  1967 *The Phenomenology of the Social World* (trans. by George Walsh and Frederick Lehnert), Evanston, Ill.: Northwestern University Press.
  1960 "The Stranger," in Maurice R. Stein, Arthur J. Vidich, and David M. White (eds.), *Identity and Anxiety,* Glencoe, Ill.: The Free Press, pp. 98–109.
Schutz, Alfred and Thomas Luckmann
  1973 *The Structures of the Life-World* (trans. by R. M. Zaner and H. T. Engelhardt, Jr.), Evanston, Ill.: Northwestern University Press.
Skinner, B. F.
  1971 *Beyond Freedom and Dignity,* New York: Knopf.
Stryker, Sheldon
  1977 "Developments in 'Two Social Psychologies': Toward an Appreciation of Mutual Relevance," *Sociometry* 40 (June): 145–160.
Weigert, Andrew J.
  1981 *Sociology of Everyday Life,* New York: Longman.

THE II
REALITIES OF
EVERYDAY LIFE

2

What to look for in this chapter:

What is social reality?
What is the importance of symbols for human behavior?
How do people develop an understanding of events under conditions of uncertainty?
How and why do self-fulfilling prophecies operate in human affairs?

Constructing Social Reality

Social reality refers to the meanings that people give to objects and events through the process of human interaction. Without social relationships, without communication, there is no social reality that is known or knowable. Whatever the other forms of reality may be, a basic fact about the human condition is that reality as any given group of people knows and understands it is a socially constructed process. This basic fact is the starting point for social psychology, and to understand the construction of reality as a social process is to understand a great deal.

Symbolic communication is the primary means by which those who are trying to make sense out of their environments or trying to understand what is happening to them share knowledge and information. In effect, through symbolic communication we create a social order and impose it on the physical world. We may understand this order as systems of meaning by which people, objects, and events are defined, classified, and evaluated. The created order is always fragile because both physical and social environments fail to conform to what men and women come to expect of them. People must do a great deal of repair work as they respond to the changes occurring within themselves, as they adapt to the changes in their environments, and as they negotiate with each other.

Within a given society, the construction of reality is evident in the process of developing plausible explanations about the unfolding of broader social and political events. We tend to form images about the causes of crime, inflation, unemployment, and other problems that are of concern to us. Through modern means of mass communication we are aware of many more events than we experience directly, and the assessments we make of these occurrences reflect the qualities of our personal lives and our relationships with others. When we regard the news available as incomplete or untrustworthy, we tend to fill in the gaps with our own constructions of social reality through discus-

Symbolism in Art (Reality Construction)
*Sculpture, architecture, and other art forms frequently have symbolic meanings that
are not self-evident to the untrained observer.*

sions with friends, neighbors, and relatives. Through filling in the gaps of
missing information, we in effect become newsmakers by forming opinions
about occurrences in the broader society.

The two overriding concerns in the construction of social reality are
those of meaning and action. How do we go about making coherent the events
in which we engage, and how do we go about attaining the goals of interest?
In our everyday life, these kinds of problems have usually been settled in advance by others and ourselves, but in some situations it becomes necessary to
reflect on the meaning of events and their implications for our futures. We
may become uncertain about the worth of what we are doing, or we may have

doubts about our abilities to achieve the goals we are seeking. These are the conditions of crisis in the personal lives of individuals in which their thinking is directed toward creating new forms of meaning in order to give stability and purpose to their lives (Holzner, 1968).

The process of reality construction is one of creating meanings, designs, and vocabularies for describing the external environment and incorporating them into personal spheres of thought and action. Although the cumulative experiences of a given group of people shape their basic design for living, it is the individual's definition of the situation that shapes the immediate course of action he or she is likely to follow. We live in immediate acts of experience, and on these experiences we impose a wide variety of symbolic meanings. In the ordinary course of events we are able to draw on the meanings others provide to us, but in many types of situations communal forms of understanding are not readily available. These circumstances require us to reflect on the meaning of social life and its practical implications for our own existence.

Our constructions of social reality tend to be pragmatic in orientation because they specify the range of alternatives available to us. As such, we develop notions about what is necessary to attain the goals we value and what the consequences likely to follow are if we pursue one course of action compared to another. Since we are not islands unto ourselves, the meanings we attach to events and occurrences in our daily lives become important for our self-images and for our relationships with others. The selective manner by which we construct our own versions of social reality plays an important part in the overall qualities of our personal lives.

The theme of reality construction emphasizes that individuals are active creators of their social worlds (Manis and Meltzer, 1972). The images of human behavior this theme conveys do not limit creative acts to scientific discoveries, works of art, or other celebrated achievements; instead, this approach views the ongoing activities of everyday life as creative and practical accomplishments. We construct images of places we have never seen, we organize our daily schedules into predictable patterns; we establish goals and work toward their attainment; we create self-images; and we develop ideas about the men and women that prevail in our society. Humans create and shape their physical and social worlds through decision making and action.

A. SYMBOLIC MEANING

The central concern in the study of symbolic meaning is with the process by which we as individuals develop an understanding of the events and situations in which we are engaged. Symbols are the raw materials from which we construct meanings in social life, and as such they consist of words or gestures we draw on to identify objects and events. Symbols are arbitrary; there is no necessary or inherent reason for a particular symbol to represent any particular object or event. We construct meanings through the symbols we use because it is practical and expedient to do so, and we must have some level of agreement on what our words and gestures will mean if we are to communicate successfully with others. The responsiveness of individuals to each other in given situations is possible only through some degree of shared understanding of the messages being transmitted.

1. *Reality Perceptions*

Language is the primary vehicle humans draw on to create and maintain their social worlds. Our uses of language shape our reality perceptions, permit us to identify and classify objects in our environments, give meanings to our experiences, structure our social acts, and enable us to communicate with others. In these processes we notice only a small portion of environmental events; most of them we ignore or give only slight attention in passing. Through naming and labeling we create a symbolic universe, and the symbols we use become the central aspects of reality as we know and understand it. In the conduct of human affairs, the symbols that are used and the objects they represent become blended inseparably in reality perceptions, in communication, and in social action.

The classical research of Edward Sapir (1956) and Benjamin Whorf (1956) emphasized that there are as many different realities as there are languages, and that the organization of experiences by any given group of people is a highly selective process. Learning a particular language provides us with a set of lenses, so to speak, through which we are able to see and conceptualize the world around us. We give our experiences coherence and meaning through using vocabularies we have learned from our relationships with other people. We seldom create entirely new words to describe what we see and experience; rather we draw on ready-made interpretations to give form and content to what we see and experience.

The established ways of doing things for any particular group of people are shaped by the vocabularies they use for describing reality. The aspects of objects and events in need of elaboration vary from one society to another, and this basic principle of language may be illustrated by citing some classical examples from anthropology. For example, in Arabic countries, there are more than 6000 separate terms for describing aspects of a camel and its equipment, and the Hanunoo of the Philippines have separate terms for identifying each of ninety-two varieties of rice (Thompson, 1975). Here in the United States both our rice and our camel vocabularies are highly limited because these two objects have low degrees of meaning for us. Among some Eskimo groups, there are more than a hundred separate terms for distinguishing such aspects of snow as its wetness, its looseness, its portability by the wind, its suitability for cutting into blocks, or whether it is falling or on the ground. The Eskimo would regard the use of a single term as inadequate because detailed and precise knowledge of snow is important for survival in a hostile environment. In America our snow vocabulary limits our perception, since we see only snow or sleet, while the Eskimo see a variety of different types of snow.

Although our camel, rice, and snow vocabularies are limited, a safe bet would be that our car vocabulary greatly exceeds that of most other peoples of the world. We have extensive vocabularies for describing numerous varieties of cars, such as *convertibles, hard tops, subcompacts, intermediates, hatch backs, corvettes, lemons, clunkers,* and *gas-guzzlers.* The importance of the automobile is reflected in the ease with which Americans are able to identify such aspects of cars as *fenders, hub caps, bumpers, disc brakes, automatic shift,* and *power steering.* Such vocabularies permit identifying objects of interest, and they suggest the importance of reality construction as an ongoing process. Our great grandparents did not share our car vocabularies, but they did know a great deal about blacksmithing, horses, buggies, apothecaries, and phonographs.

The process of reality construction never ends. It is always ongoing, always developmental, always in the process of refinement and modification (McHugh, 1968). New realities are created in response to changing environmental circumstances. For example, countries during times of war and preparations for war develop elaborate military vocabularies. *Tanks, bazookas, submarines, atomic bombs, fall-out shelters, intercontinental ballistic missles, nuclear warheads,* and *nuclear blackmail* are among the forms of "war talk" in the twentieth century that provide us with new images of the possibilities and limitations of the world we live in. The activities of people, both individually and collectively, are shaped by the vocabularies they use for conceptualizing events and planning lines of action. In this respect, symbols serve as aids to perception and reflect the fears and aspirations of any given group of people.

Language, then, is a shared framework through which a group of people order their perceptions of the world around them. The process is guided not so much by a concern for defining what is actually out there as for extracting relevant elements from the environment and giving meaning to them. For example, some people use a vocabulary for describing birds that lumps many different species together on the basis of color. Some people see only blue birds, yellow birds, red birds, or black birds, rather than many different varieties and aspects of birds. A serious bird watcher, however, would view the placing of different species into the same linguistic category as vulgar and unsophisticated. Crows, cow birds, starlings, and grackles are distinct and qualitatively different varieties of birds; bird watchers would regard it as an error in perception to think of them as "black birds." I know this to be the case because I have observed the indignation among my bird-watching friends when someone identifies birds only on the basis of color.

Because of the high degree of selectivity in extracting meaning from the objects that enter into our field of vision, we ignore and distort several of the dynamic forces in our environment. The classical writings of Benjamin Whorf (1956) on the importance of language in thought and behavior illustrate this process well. From his experience with a fire insurance company, Whorf recognized the potentially hazardous implications of the language we use in defining given situations. He noted that men working around gasoline drums that were full were aware of the dangers involved and refrained from smoking. They were less cautious, however, about smoking around empty gasoline drums, because the term *empty* conveyed the sense of "a void," "being inert," "nothingness." Yet, empty gasoline drums are even more dangerous because of the explosive vapors they contain. Smoking under these conditions, then, is based on incomplete knowledge of the situation and constitutes a linguistic error in perception. Our selectivity in using language for our construction of reality may very well lead us to ignore attributes of situations that are important to us. We use words to define reality and then act on the basis of these definitions.

Reality perceptions do not stem so much from naming, listing, and describing a world of solid facts as from subjective interpretations we impose on environmental stimuli. Humans may endow mountains, rivers, and stones with extraordinary qualities and sacred meanings, as they have at many times and places, or they regard these aspects of the environment as prime examples of mundane and uninteresting things. The notions about what exists are in effect ideas or cognitions of what is real, what is possible, and what lines of action are appropriate. Peter L. Berger (1969) has described these cognitive processes in terms of the human tasks of **world construction** and **world maintenance.** We create the world through our perceptions of it, and then seek to maintain the world in a style and manner consistent with our beliefs about it. (See Box 2.1.)

2. *Specialized Vocabularies*

The ideas of world construction and world maintenance are important in modern, industrialized societies. Extensive scientific and technological vocabularies are being elaborated for naming things and the attributes of things. The English language now has more than 600,000 words and is continuing to expand at a rapid pace. Decisions on what is real, what is valid, and what is possible increasingly depend on judgments by experts and specialists. We do not all share the same realities because we employ different languages, and we are limited in our capacities for grasping all of the many realities important to us.

The limitations of personal knowledge stem from the fact that modern societies are large and heterogeneous. Most of the meanings conveyed by the English language are understood only by subgroups and small segments of the larger population. A lawyer, for example, may readily understand the specialized vocabulary another lawyer uses, but those outside the legal profession probably will not. And the medical terminology doctors use is so far removed

> **BOX 2.1**
> ## The Concepts of World Construction and World Maintenance
>
> Peter L. Berger has described the cognitive process in human behavior as involving the dual tasks of world construction and world maintenance. Berger does not mean that humans literally construct or maintain the world, but that they face the problem of making sense out of their experiences and out of the conditions of their existence.
>
> The concept of *world construction* refers to the realities created by humans through the invention of language, tools, social norms, values, and other aspects of culture. These realities are constructed out of the activities in which humans are engaged. But, once created, these realities become endowed with factual qualities; they are experienced as objective; they are defined as the natural state of affairs. As social influences impinge on thoughts and actions, the worlds constructed at the individual level become two steps removed from the physical world. The first step involves constructing the realities at the collective level, while the second step consists of the efforts of individuals to make sense out of their personal experiences.
>
> *World maintenance* consists of the social influences, controls, and supports by which people uphold definitions of reality in any given social context. A great deal of repair work is required because both societies and individuals always remain unfinished products: people frequently pursue self-interests at the expense of the group's well-being; human efforts lead to frustration and failure; people sometimes make mistakes and do stupid things. In efforts at world maintenance, the social definitions of reality come to be defined as the ultimate realities of the universe and as the basis for order in human affairs.
>
> *Source:* Peter L. Berger, *The Sacred Canopy*, Garden City, N.Y.: Anchor Books, 1969.

from everyday speech that the physician sometimes has difficulty explaining the results of medical diagnosis in a language the patient can understand (Glaser and Strauss, 1964). Sometimes college graduates who can engage in lively conversations about the ideas of Shakespeare or Camus have a great deal of difficulty grasping the language of an income tax form or the provisions of an insurance policy. The uses of specialized vocabularies by subgroups of the population provide grounds for mutual understanding and shared meanings within the group, while at the same time they exclude all who are nonmembers.

From the vantage point of the individual, however, it is not necessary to develop a grasp of all the technical vocabularies that shape and influence our lives. This would not be possible. Instead we tend to orient our daily lives around a general understanding of the events in which we are engaged and to regard precise and detailed knowledge on the inner workings of things as the task of specialists (Berger and Luckmann, 1967). For example, it is not necessary for us to develop a grasp of the terminology needed to understand the principles on which the telephone works; it is only necessary to know how to call the repair person when the phone is out of order.

3. Internalization

From the standpoint of the individual, reality construction reflects the process of internalizing aspects of social life into personal thought and action. **Internalization** is the process in which an individual incorporates shared symbols into his or her system of thinking about persons, objects, and events. Internalization is important because it not only facilitates using language to exchange information in social relations but also to provide a vocabulary for thinking and reflection. Individuals introduce and maintain order in their experiences through a linguistic mapping of their environments (Turner and Edgley, 1980). People emphasize only selective aspects of their social and physical environments; others they ignore.

Internalizing a language serves a dual set of functions for the individual: **denotative meanings** provide for communicating with others and **connotative meanings** allow for personal reflections on events. The denotative meanings are those shared by the members of a social group. They are dictionary definitions, scientific definitions, legal definitions, and other definitions that reflect realities perceived by a given group of people. Such definitions facilitate problem solving and the sharing of information as people interact with one another. (See Figure 2.1.)

While denotative meanings reflect the shared frameworks for defining reality, connotative meanings refer to the variety of emotions, evaluations, and actions associated with social objects. The connotative meanings are subjective in character and constitute the qualitative assessments individuals employ in creating order and stability in their personal lives. Nuances of personal style express connotative meanings as individuals modify, alter, and refine symbols by putting them to use.

The way in which connotative meanings enter into social thinking and the organization of our everyday experiences may be illustrated by examining our conceptions of time. The measurement of time by the ticking of a clock is representative of the mechanical world view that is built into modern society. It is a notion of time as successive events moving in a linear direction through fixed and identifiable intervals. Time does not have an existence of its own but is a social creation for the purpose of establishing intervals, organizing events, and coordinating the schedules and activities of an extremely large number of people.

While we agree to conceptualize time in terms of the ticking of a clock, we have experiences with time that contradict our notion of time as a fixed set of intervals. "Time flies," "time moves on," or we do not have "enough time" when we are engaged in activities rewarding to us. On the other hand, "time drags" when we are required to endure a boring lecture, and we have "time on

$$\overline{X} = \frac{\Sigma x}{n} \qquad s^2 = \frac{\Sigma x^2}{n-1}$$

$$t^2 = \frac{(n-1)\ (\Sigma D)^2}{n\Sigma D^2 - (\Sigma D)^2}$$

$$\chi^2 = \frac{(fo - fe)^2}{fe}$$

$$r = \frac{\Sigma XY - (\Sigma X)(\Sigma Y)/n}{\sqrt{\Sigma X^2 - (\Sigma X)^2/n}\ \sqrt{\Sigma Y^2 - (\Sigma Y)^2/n}}$$

Symbols in statistics are based on the use of numbers as an aid to logical thinking. Mathematical symbols do not reflect reality directly, but are representations of what exists in the real world to some extent. As with other forms of social life, meanings are based on some degree of consensus on the referents for symbols and what constitutes an appropriate use of them.

FIGURE 2.1
Statistical Symbols and Reality Construction

our hands" while waiting to catch a bus or a plane. Our ideas about "saving time," "wasting time," or "doing time" are purely artifacts of our own creation. We utilize symbols as a way of imposing order on the world around us and then respond to these symbols as though they had a reality all of their own.

The research of Osgood, Suci, and Tannenbaum (1957) suggests that there are numerous connotative meanings that surround any social object or event. The connotative meanings are important because, as Turner (1976) has suggested, "people are not just miniature reproductions of their society." As a way of determining the subjective meanings associated with social objects and events, Osgood and his colleagues developed and refined the **semantic differential technique.** This measurement technique consists of using a series of polarized adjectives for locating social objects within the individual's realm of meaning and experience. (See Box 2.2.)

From numerous studies utilizing the semantic differential technique, three major dimensions of connotative meaning have been identified (Snider and Osgood, 1969). These dimensions consist of evaluation, potency, and activity. Evaluations relate to the assessment of social objects in terms of *good-bad, clean-dirty, happy-sad, fair-unfair, beautiful-ugly,* and similar de-

BOX 2.2
Attribution of Qualities to a Political Leader

Listed below is a set of polarized adjectives for locating the qualities of President Reagan as you see them. For each pair of qualities please circle the point that represents where between the two extremes you see President Reagan as being located.

PRESIDENT REAGAN

weak	.	.	.	.	.	.	.	.	.	strong
clean	.	.	.	.	.	.	.	.	.	dirty
small	.	.	.	.	.	.	.	.	.	large
warm	.	.	.	.	.	.	.	.	.	cold
greedy	.	.	.	.	.	.	.	.	.	generous
safe	.	.	.	.	.	.	.	.	.	dangerous
lax	.	.	.	.	.	.	.	.	.	dedicated
soft	.	.	.	.	.	.	.	.	.	loud

The above is an application of the semantic differential technique developed by Osgood, Suci, and Tannenbaum (1957). By assigning numbers to the scale positions ranging from negative to positive, we can derive summary scores from the specific items for characterizing your overall impressions of President Reagan. Your score on the semantic differential should predict the degree to which you are basically in favor of the policies initiated during President Reagan's administration.

Note: For a sourcebook on the measurement of meaning, see James G. Snider and Charles E. Osgood (eds.), *Semantic Differential Technique*, Chicago: Aldine, 1969.

scriptive terms. The potency aspect of meaning incorporates such descriptive terms as *large-small, strong-weak, heavy-light,* and *thick-thin.* The activity variables include such polarized adjectives as *fast-slow, active-passive, hot-cold,* and *sharp-dull.* The investigator may take the pattern of scores across these three sets of bipolar adjectives as an index of positive and negative orientations. As such, the bipolar scores may be used by a researcher to predict behavior toward the social object in question. The use of adjectives as a way of measuring the constructions of meaning appears to correspond to the frameworks we draw on for evaluating people and events on a daily basis.

B. SYMBOLIC CONTROL

While the use of symbols in the creation of meaning relates to the understanding and predictability of events, the use of symbols in the assertion of control relates to the concern with problem solving and mastery. The detached student of language may note that symbols are abstractions, substitutes, or vicarious meanings that stand for something else. The situation is quite different, however, when we look at symbols from the vantage point of those who use them. The separation between a symbol and its referent—the object it represents—is a distinction we tend to lose sight of in the course of our daily lives. We tend to blend the symbol and its referent into an inseparable pattern. Symbols make up a very large part of the stimulus environment for any social group, and we come to perceive symbols as having an existence in their own right. The perceived reality of symbols is clearly evident in the numerous forms of magical practices throughout the world.

1. The Use of Magic

The classical studies by Sir James Frazer (1915) remain the definitive work of the logic of magical practices. Frazer noted the widespread view of a sympathetic relationship between symbols and their referents. Magicians assume a relationship to be sympathetic when they regard manipulating a symbol as having an effect on the symbol's corresponding referent. Frazer described an underlying assumption of magical practices as the law of similarity: like tends to produce like and an effect resembles its cause. The magician assumes that he or she can produce the desired effect by creating an imitation of it. Thus the magician may build a ritualistic fire during the winter solstice to induce the sun to return and permit the days to become longer. In word magic the user assumes that the manipulation of a verbal symbol can have an effect on the person or event it represents.

It would be easy to dismiss magic as an error in thinking, but to do so would overlook important social psychological functions for its practitioner. The use of magic is situational in character and generally found under circumstances in which individuals are involved emotionally in a set of events surrounded by uncertainty. In Bronislaw Malinowski's (1954) study of the Trobriand Islanders, he noted that they did not use magic when fishing in the calm and safe waters of the lagoon, but that on fishing expeditions out in the ocean there was an extensive elaboration of magical practices. Expeditions on the high seas were always surrounded by uncertainty over the prospects of a storm and over the emergence of other troubles that could neither be adequately foreseen nor circumvented.

Malinowski theorized that magical practices involve the use of symbols for seeking additional mastery and control over events after practical, utilitarian knowledge has been fully exhausted. (See Box 2.3.) For example, he noted that the Trobrianders were fully aware of agricultural practices and knew that the planting of seeds and the cultivation of crops were necessary. But having used the full scope of agricultural knowledge, they still had no guarantee that the crops would be successful. The crop might be destroyed by

BOX 2.3
Love Magic as Indirect Communication

Love magic is a symbolic activity designed to win a desired sex object. The practice may consist of wearing a love charm, giving a special gift, singing a special chant, decorating the face with cosmetics, or any other form of symbolic activity designed to increase the intimacy of a relationship. Drawing on anthropological data from twenty-three societies, Paul C. Rosenblatt made a study of love magic as a form of indirect communication. His central thesis was that love magic is employed to express an interest in another person, to reduce anxiety, and to avoid the possible embarrassments associated with direct and open communication.

Direct communication of a love interest may have several undesirable consequences: the suitor may be rejected, refused, or ridiculed; barriers may be created to the further development of a relationship and desired options may be closed off. Rosenblatt observes that, because of the risks involved in open communication, love magic is employed as an indirect means of expressing the desire to build an intimate relationship. Indirect communication has the advantage of being ambiguous, requiring the intended love object to make use of his or her imagination. Since the initiator didn't make a firm offer, there is no direct proposal for the love object to reject. Options that could have been closed to the suitor through a direct approach stay open, and prospects remain for the further development of a relationship.

In some societies, a go-between or a third-party negotiator is employed to avoid the potential risks in communicating a love interest. In such cases, love magic is unnecessary, since face-saving devices have been institutionalized. Thus, magical practices in love encounters may be understood as sending messages under conditions of uncertainty in order to manage impressions and to avoid the possibility of failure or embarrassment.

Source: Paul C. Rosenblatt, "Communication in the Practice of Love Magic," *Social Forces* 49 (March, 1971): 482–487.

insects, or the weather conditions might not provide an adequate growing season. These possibilities were beyond the control of the Trobriander, and as a result, they used numerous forms of protective magic, such as sacred rituals and amulets and they recited prayers during the planting of seeds. Magic served as a tonic of reassurance that they would obtain their desired outcomes.

The research of Paul Blumberg (1963) on hazardous occupations in the United States provides support for Malinowski's thesis on the use of magical symbols for coping with conditions of uncertainty. For example, in coal mining the accident rate is about seven times as great as for general industrial work. In the course of their daily work, miners face the recurrent dangers of

Forecasting Personal Futures
Reality constructions take many forms. Palmistry, tarot cards, and astrology are among the many techniques of forecasting the future. People who have difficult decisions to make and who have a strong desire to reduce the uncertainties in their lives sometimes seek the services of a fortune teller. If you are one of these people and happen to be in downtown Manhattan, Mrs. King may be able to help you. What do you think?

cave-ins, mine explosions, getting lost, or personal accidents. Blumberg notes an extensive set of magical lore surrounding the dangers of mining as an occupation. Some miners believe that rats have an intuitive knowledge of dangers in the mine, and as a result when rats head toward the shaft, it's time for the miner to leave also. There is a taboo against whistling in the mine, since this may set up vibrations that cause the earth to move. Returning to the mine after completing a day of work some believe to be bad luck. Many companies will exempt the miner from his last day of work before retirement because of the widespread belief in "the fatal last shift."

People use magical beliefs and practices as a means of symbolic control in numerous other occupations that involve a high degree of uncertainty. These include gambling, competitive sports, acting, and farming. In each of these occupations there is a fairly high degree of uncertainty about the attainment of desired outcomes. In the movie industry, for example, an actor's success obviously depends on acting ability, but the actor also faces uncertainty about getting a desirable part and unpredictability in audience responses. As a result, Hollywood stars and other entertainers elaborate magical beliefs and practices as a way of supplementing practical knowledge and acting talent.

2. Taboo Topics

The use of symbols becomes clearly evident in our emotional involvements with such positive events as love making, as well as in our experiences with such human tragedies as those of death and dying. The realities we construct in connection with these events have implications for the ways in which we attempt to assert control over them. People sometimes think that talking about certain events will cause them to happen, and as a result they look on numerous topics as being unsuitable for free and open discussion.

There are certain topics people avoid to reduce the uncertainties and potential embarrassments associated with them. These have been described by Norman L. Farberow (1963) as **taboo topics**, and they consist of all those forms of reality that we avoid talking about because of their sensitive character. Farberow observed that several aspects of sex and death are taboo topics for many Americans, and several research studies bear out his observations. (See Box 2.4.)

The research of Lee Rainwater (1960), for example, indicates that many married couples within the working class have difficulty in discussing such emotion-laden topics as sex, contraception, and family planning. In many cases the avoidance of free and open discussion of sexual topics stems from feelings of personal insecurity and from a concern that the cohesiveness of the relationship may be affected. The apparent inability of many couples to communicate with each other on the topics of sex and contraception often results in the lack of family planning and the consequent occurrence of unwanted pregnancies (Mukherjee, 1975). The numerous moral concerns and anxieties surrounding sexual conduct also make it difficult for many parents to provide sex information for their children, even though the parents may regard such basic knowledge as being important.

Numerous anxieties in our own society also surround the topic of death, and the research of Glaser and Strauss (1965) indicates that this tendency to avoid the topic of death occurs among medical personnel as well as among

> **BOX 2.4**
> **Unplanned Pregnancies among Teenagers**
>
> In a review of numerous studies of teenage contraceptive behavior, Scales (1977) has noted some of the consequences of low levels of communication about contraception among youthful partners. Among sexually active people, teenagers constitute a special risk category of unintended pregnancy because of their failure to use any method of contraception or to adequately adhere to the requirements if a method is used.
>
> There are several variables implicated in the low levels of contraceptive use among sexually active teenagers. Among them is the question of whether the responsibility falls primarily on the male or on the female. While there are generally low levels of knowledge about sexuality and reproduction among teenagers, males usually receive even less sex education than females, especially from parents. For teenage girls, using the more effective contraceptive methods (such as the pill) requires planning in advance and admitting to herself an intention to be sexually active. These requirements stand in contrast to the fact that teenage intercourse tends to be sporadic and unplanned.
>
> Because of the social constraints on free and open discussion of the topics of sex, contraception, and reproduction, teenagers are often misinformed about their own sexuality. Many females do not use any method because they think they cannot get pregnant unless they really want to, and many males do not use any method because they believe it makes sex less attractive. While many teenagers do fear pregnancy, contraception is often not used because "it makes sex seem planned," and others simply "trust to luck" that a pregnancy will not occur.
>
> *Source:* Peter Scales, "Males and Morals: Teenage Contraceptive Behavior and the Double Standard," *Family Coordinator* 26 (July, 1977): 211–224.

friends and relatives of a dying person. While physicians and nurses are able to talk freely to one another about technical aspects of health care that is related to life and death, they are seldom able to talk openly about the process of dying itself. Consequently, those in the medical profession are prone to avoid telling a terminally ill patient that the patient is dying. Family members are also inclined to refrain from informing a patient of impending death, even though many who are terminally ill may very well prefer such a disclosure. Apparently most Americans have difficulty discussing the death process beyond the factual conditions pertaining to when and how the death of a particular person occurred.

We can observe a related phenomenon in the research of social psychologists on the **MUM effect**, which refers to the general reluctance to communicate negative information to the affected person (Conlee and Tesser, 1973). We withhold bad news from a friend, a co-worker, or a spouse because we assume that the potential recipient of bad news does not want to be told about it. By way of contrast, we generally assume that the potential recipient of good news has a desire to know, and we tend to comply with this assumption by transmitting positive information without hesitation (Rosen and Tesser, 1970). The uncertainty surrounding the transmission of undesirable information was evident in the accounts from ancient Sparta in which the messenger who brought bad news was sometimes put to death. Thus the manner in which news is processed becomes an important concern in social relationships.

C. NEWS EVENTS AND REALITY CONSTRUCTION

In contrast to the inherent constraints on discussing sensitive topics, certain kinds of disruptive situations emerge to promote a quest for information and a readiness to engage openly in a discussion of events. This especially occurs during times of public crisis, and may be noted in social reactions to political assassinations, civil strife, natural disasters, or unsolved mass murders. Under these conditions, everyday social life becomes disrupted, and people make a collective attempt to arrive at an adequate understanding of the events in question. Individuals verify and modify their assessment of events through engaging in conversation with others.

On a daily basis, listening to the evening news or reading a newspaper is a means of obtaining verification of how social life is organized and how it operates. The primary character of news, as noted by Robert E. Park (1940), derives from its interruption of our activities. The quest for news is greatest when a person feels a need for a sense of direction in a rapidly changing situation, or when ambiguous situations develop that need clarification. News becomes relevant while events are in process, when outcomes are uncertain, and when normal routines need adjustment. Ordinarily, after the outcome of events is settled, our interest in obtaining further information is diminished, and we return to the pursuit of business-as-usual.

1. Disruptive Events

One of the important features of the context of news in modern society is that of the speed with which remote national and international events directly impinge on the life-world of individuals. Approximately 90 percent of all Americans heard about the assassination of President Kennedy within two hours after the event occurred. We experience such a disruptive event as a crisis when it appears to threaten and invalidate the usual assessments of social reality. Under such conditions, doubts emerge about the future as an extension of the present, and we perceive social events as discontinuous. Forces are operating that we can neither clearly understand nor control, and it becomes difficult to integrate the problematic part of social life with the organization of everyday behavior.

The assassination of President Kennedy provided an occasion for intense individual and collective involvements with a historical event of crisis proportions. The expressions of grief over a three-day period temporarily halted routine activities, and most people remained in continuous contact with the news media. All over the country, in small groups usually made up of close friends and relatives, people centered discussions on a variety of topics related to the importance of the event.

The research of Gilbert Abcarian and his associates (1966) identified some of the prominent themes that emerged from these discussions. People exchanged notions about why the assassination had occurred and who was responsible. Was the assassination a result of a conspiracy, or had a mentally deranged individual killed the president? They also directed concerns toward ways in which others were responding to the event. At the forefront of the deliberations were the implications for the individual's personal life as well as for the future of the country. Even those people usually disinterested in political events became emotionally involved with historical circumstances.

Although immediately there was a great deal of discussion in the news media as to why the assassination had occurred, the reasons remained sufficiently obscure to generate widespread discussion for weeks and years following the event. The research of Sandra J. Ball-Rokeach (1973) has characterized such a condition as one of "pervasive ambiguity," which refers to the inability to establish meaningful links between given events and the total social situation. The emotional impact of the presidential assassination generated a need for information that could not be met by the news-gathering agencies. The simple notion that a single individual, acting as an individual, had killed the president was insufficient for many people who had become emotionally involved with the event. In the ensuing months and years following the Kennedy assassination, numerous books and magazine articles were written to offer alternative explanations to the official government investigation. Many people regarded the conclusion of the Warren Commission that Lee Harvey Oswald had killed the president as inadequate and incomplete.

One of the special problems of news reporting is that of presenting objective information under conditions in which the unfolding of events is characterized by uncertainty. Gaye Tuchman (1973) has observed that news journalists refer to developing news as a type of event in which the amount of available information is highly limited. This occurs under conditions in which newsworthy facts are still in the process of emerging. In constructing reality under conditions of uncertainty, newsmakers draw on a variety of standardized techniques in order to meet deadlines and publish plausible accounts. (See Box 2.5.)

Tuchman (1972) notes that in processing unexpected events, newspaper journalists are able to sustain the illusion of being objective by presenting conflicting possibilities and leaving it up to the reader to make his or her own

BOX 2.5
Routine Treatments of Unexpected Events

Concentrating on the process of making news, Tuchman (1973) addressed the question of how an organization can routinely process unexpected events. The suddenness of disruptive events generates the problem for news reporters of developing an account that will satisfy the desire of their readers for current and dependable information. This is achieved by drawing on the following ready-made categories of newsworthy events:

Hard news—factual information of general interest, such as the State of the Union Address, the train-car accident, the bank holdup, "the fire that will occur tomorrow."
Soft news—human-interest stories, such as an account of a lonely female bear, a feature on a friendly big-city bus driver, or a story on how some individual survived a blizzard or a tornado.
Spot news—a subclassification of hard news that deals with some specific episode of short duration, such as a robbery, a murder, or an accident.
Developing news—another subclassification of hard news that refers to events that are building up in an unpredictable manner, such as the emergent events surrounding a political assassination.
Continuing news—a series of stories on the same topic that are presented over a period of time, i.e., coverage of the activities of the state legislature.

These classifications relate not only to news as events, but also to the procedures news reporters follow in the development of a story. The forms of news that are "urgent and timely" require speed in gathering facts and meeting deadlines, while other forms of news involve judgments on what constitutes newsworthy materials. The classifications given here are not discrete categories, but a practical set of guidelines for the organization of the work involved in reporting on one kind of happening as compared to another.

Source: Gaye Tuchman, "Making News by Doing Work: Routinizing the Unexpected," *American Journal of Sociology* 79 (July, 1973): 110–131.

assessment of the situation. The information presented may be based on interviews, rather than on firsthand knowledge. The judicial use of quotes frees the journalist from having to defend what is printed as a truth claim in its own right. An additional strategy of reality construction, as Tuchman notes, consists of placing the available information in an appropriate sequence to give the appearance of being plausible and accurate. The use of these techniques derives from the dual attempts of journalists to provide a news service for their clients on a regular schedule and at the same time to report on what can be defended as factually correct information.

The construction of reality is a continuous process in our everyday lives, and in this respect we are all newsmakers (Molotch and Lester, 1974). Through news encounters we extend our awareness beyond the range of experience available in our immediate environment. Remote events become a part of our understanding of the organization of social life in general. Events occurring in the broader society are of practical importance to us, and our concern is not so much with really knowing what happened "out there" as it is with establishing reference points for orienting our own lives.

One illustration of this process is the social game in which individuals recall the routine activities of their lives when they were interrupted by some major event of societal importance. For example, the game took the following forms for your parents and grandparents:

"Where were you when you heard about _____ ?
— the Japanese attack on Pearl Harbor?
— the assassination of President Kennedy?
— the resignation of President Nixon?"

Such games reveal more than interesting conversation. We tend to draw on news events as benchmarks for linking the past with the present in our personal lives. Important occurrences are useful in demarking social time in pretty much the same way that birthdays, anniversaries, getting a job, being promoted, changing place of residence, and attending funerals are used by individuals as reference points for assessing the general qualities of their life circumstances. Such events are used creatively for constructing the meaningfulness of past experiences and anticipating the future (Molotch and Lester, 1975).

In emphasizing the theme that individuals are newsmakers, the research of Tamotsu Shibutani (1966) has clarified some of the mechanisms for constructing reality under conditions of crisis. Drawing on crosscultural and historical examples, Shibutani stressed that **improvised news** is a form of rumor that derives from ambiguous situations. Improvised news arises from situations in which people are concerned with the outcome of events that are neither predictable nor immediately manageable. For rumor to develop, it is necessary to share with others an emotional involvement in a set of events and for the official news sources to be inadequate in their coverage or regarded as untrustworthy.

Improvised news derives from communication patterns that develop in those situations in which something out of the ordinary has happened, and people pool their intellectual efforts to make events coherent. Imagine, for example, the bewilderment that occurred among the Japanese-Americans living in the San Francisco Bay area on December 7, 1941, who suddenly found themselves suspected of being enemy agents, or the confusion among residents of Hiroshima on August 6, 1945, in their encounter with the first atom

BOX 2.6
Spiders in Bubble Yum and Worms in Hamburgers

In recent years Americans have directed a great deal of concern toward the safety and nutritional value of many widely consumed foods. Within this context, two rather interesting rumors emerged in the public schools and spread rapidly. One rumor held that spider eggs were used in making Bubble Yum, while another maintained that ground worms were used in making hamburgers.

The rumor about spider eggs in bubble gum surfaced in the spring of 1977 and spread rapidly throughout the public schools on the East Coast. A front-page article in the *Wall Street Journal* (March 24, 1977) reported that "within the past month, rumors have swept like a prairie fire among school children in the Greater New York area (and a few other places as well) that the product causes cancer or has spider eggs in it, or both. And many kids believe it."

To counter the rumor, the manufacturer of Bubble Yum placed full-page ads in several newspapers in the New York area. One of the ads proclaimed "Someone Is Telling Your Kids Very Bad Lies about a Very Good Gum." The grotesque character of the rumor would appear to reflect the anxieties many people have about quality control and regulation in the food industries.

In 1978, a similar rumor arose and spread throughout the public schools. This rumor held that red earthworms were ground and added to hamburgers to increase their protein content. To counter the reduced sale of hamburgers, McDonald's held a news conference to refute the rumor and to read a letter from the Secretary of Agriculture on the inspection procedures of the USDA. Other franchises, such as Wendy's and Burger Chef, also issued public statements that the meat in their hamburgers was 100 percent beef and nothing else (*Wall Street Journal,* November 15, 1978, p. 15).

bomb. These are examples of dramatic events that people cannot understand in terms of past experiences. Under these conditions, individuals react not as separate entities but in collaboration with others in the quest for understanding and action. Insofar as possible, they seek information from others who share similar social characteristics and who share a similar stake in the outcome of events (Ball-Rokeach, 1973). By deliberating on the events in question, a pattern of agreement tends to emerge for the construction of plausible explanations of events and their implications.

The popular view that rumor is false news needs to be qualified. People create plausible explanations under conditions of uncertainty, and in some cases, rumors provide more accurate information than official news sources. Because rumors are closely linked with crisis situations, we cannot adequately understand them if we view them as erroneous or pathological. Since we must act everyday on the basis of unverified reports, the central feature of a rumor is not its accuracy, but its credibility as an informational basis for action. As

Shibutani (1966) noted, in many cases we act on the basis of rumors not because we believe them but because we cannot afford to ignore them. (See Box 2.6.)

Rumors are often short-lived phenomena. As responses to unexpected and unpredictable events, they temporarily reflect the stresses and hopes of a particular group of people and then recede into the background of everyday life. Their importance as a form of social behavior lies primarily in the ways in which they manifest human efforts toward creating order and stability.

In the title of its publication the Disaster Research Center at Ohio State University has characterized disruptions of social life as *Unscheduled Events.* These disruptions are unscheduled in the sense that they are unplanned and un-

Cooling Tower of a Nuclear Power Plant

For several days in the spring of 1979 one of the major topics in the news consisted of the events surrounding "a nuclear accident" at Three Mile Island, near Harrisburg, Pennsylvania. The mishap at the nuclear power plant involved a leakage of radiation and the failure of the cooling system to function properly. Several people in Harrisburg evacuated the area, while others proceeded with business-as-usual. One interesting response consisted of holding "an end-of-the-world party" at one of the bars nearby. In other parts of the country, the cooling towers of nuclear power plants took on new symbolic meaning for many people.

anticipated. Through collective deliberations on what has happened and what needs to be done, people's responses to such disruptions as tornadoes, hurricanes, and earthquakes usually result in the emergence of new forms of organization that had no existence prior to the crisis (Quarantelli and Dynes, 1977). Temporary groups emerge to do the work that needs to be done, and this may range from the forming of search-and-rescue teams to the sharing of resources and providing welfare-types of services.

D. DEFINITION OF THE SITUATION

Whether individuals pursue the routines of everyday life or encounter disruptive events, their behavior is shaped by the definitions that are given to social situations. The **definition of the situation** is a symbolic construction of the realities that are present in a specific environmental setting or social context. Such a definition is in effect a set of reality perceptions, and it serves to structure and regulate social action: using definitions of the situation, people give environments human meaning, evaluate possible lines of action, and predict likely outcomes. In everyday situations, social definitions are taken for granted; behavior proceeds in a routine and orderly fashion, and most of the problems connected with reality construction have been settled in advance. In disruptive situations, by way of contrast, the usual predictive frameworks are no longer operative, something unusual has happened, and remedial action or repair work becomes necessary. Under these circumstances people require reflections on situations, objects, and events as guidelines to social action.

1. The Self-Fulfilling Prophecy

The meanings constructed in everyday life provide the individual with a framework for orienting his or her behavior in a practical, utilitarian direction. We tend to act on the basis of our understanding of the events in which we are engaged, and the outcomes of doing so are usually adequate for the purposes at hand. Recognizing the importance of the meanings individuals impute to the situation, W. I. Thomas (1928) formulated his well-known theorem on the **self-fulfilling prophecy.** This theorem holds that if someone defines a situation as real, it tends to become real in its consequences. The definition of the situation results in a self-fulfilling prophecy in those cases in which a particular course of action provides support for the initial assessments. We tend to orient our behavior toward obtaining verification for the ways we define the situations of which we are a part. To some degree the responses of others who share similar views provide such verification, and to some degree the outcomes of our own behavior validate our initial assessments.

In Robert Merton's (1957) clarification of the self-fulfilling prophecy, he limits the concept to instances of false definitions of the situation and to

Trusting Banks

Banks are currently among the most trusted of American institutions. Even banks located in urban areas where rioting and looting took place during the 1960s were not the objects of attack or hostility. We must assume that banks are trustworthy in order to use them for the deposit of our weekly paychecks or as a place for keeping our savings. We can imagine the problems that would result if bankers decided to keep for themselves all of the money placed in their care by depositors.

patterns of behavior that make the original false conceptions come true. Merton uses the run on banks that occurred during the 1930s in the United States as an example. There were several instances of people rushing to a bank to withdraw their savings in response to hearing that the bank had become insolvent. In many cases, the banks were in a sound financial position but limited in the cash on hand, since most of their money had been loaned out to customers. After a run on banks by depositors withdrawing their savings, many banks were forced into defaulting on payments. In effect, banks became insolvent because they were defined as being insolvent; defining banks as unsound led to a course of action that soon resulted in the closing of banks, although at the outset they had been financially sound.

In a critique of Merton's view on the self-fulfilling prophecy, Daya Krishna (1971) explores the implications of individual consciousness and awareness in conjunction with the realities of social life. While the operative effects of the

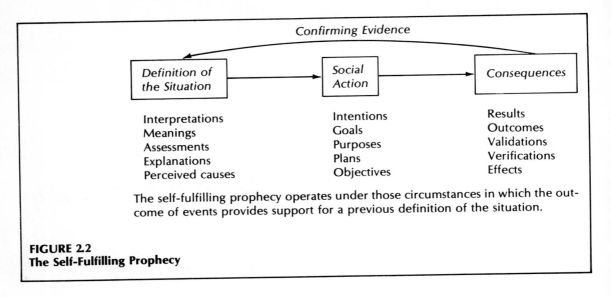

Confirming Evidence

Definition of the Situation	Social Action	Consequences
Interpretations	Intentions	Results
Meanings	Goals	Outcomes
Assessments	Purposes	Validations
Explanations	Plans	Verifications
Perceived causes	Objectives	Effects

The self-fulfilling prophecy operates under those circumstances in which the outcome of events provides support for a previous definition of the situation.

**FIGURE 2.2
The Self-Fulfilling Prophecy**

self-fulfilling prophecy are more clearly evident in those cases in which the initial definitions are false, he notes that we tend to act on the basis of our beliefs about situations without actually knowing whether they are true or false. Thus in Krishna's view the operative effects of the self-fulfilling prophecy are not dependent on false definitions of the situation. If those who interact with each other in a given situation are in agreement on their definitions, this constitutes an essential part of the social reality for any given group of people. (See Figure 2.2.)

Situations are defined from the social actor's point of view, but the source of the definitions consists of ideas, meanings, and categories of thought the actor draws on from interactions with others (Perinbanayagam, 1974). The knowledge received from others is used for interpreting events and for determining the course of action to follow. For further illustration of the self-fulfilling prophecy, let us take the health care field and note the importance of patient attitudes for recovery from illnesses and injuries.

During both World War II and the Korean War, members of the medical staff observed some soldiers dying from relatively minor battle wounds; these deaths could not be fully explained on physiological grounds. In other cases soldiers receiving serious battle wounds demonstrated remarkable recoveries, although the medical odds were clearly against them. The underlying variables seemed to be one's attitudes toward one's physical condition and assessments of the prospects for recovery (Ackerknecht, 1942; Frank, 1964). Thinking that one will die may very well act as a self-fulfilling prophecy. Extreme attitudes of fear may produce a condition of shock and set physiological processes in motion that result in rapid deterioration and death.

Some surgeons recognize the important part the patient's attitudes play in the success of an operation. In some cases, they will not perform surgery if the patient holds a dim view toward the likely outcome. The technical skills of the surgeons may not be enough; they must be reinforced with the patient's favorable attitudes toward the prospects for recovery. Doctors recognize that physical well-being is intimately connected with self-attitudes as well as with actual physiological conditions. Some paraplegics, for example, think of themselves as being physically and vocationally disabled, while Franklin D. Roosevelt as a paraplegic went on to become president of the United States.

2. The Placebo Effect

In the area of medicine, one of the more prominent forms of the self-fulfilling prophecy occurs with the **placebo effect.** A placebo is an inert substance which, when taken as medication, results in an improvement for the patient. The success of a placebo primarily depends on the patient's definition of the situation as one in which the taking of medication will help (Frank, 1964). The desire for relief from the symptoms of illness is usually a strong one among patients, and this combines with a basic faith in the ability of physicians to provide help. Prescribing a placebo is not so much an act of dishonesty on the part of a doctor as it is a recognition that under certain conditions an active medication may be unwarranted.

A. K. Shapiro (1959) noted that the history of medicine up until recent times has been primarily a history of the placebo effect. Most people recover from illnesses whether they take anything or not, and the improvements following the taking of medication may lead to the patient's conclusion that the "medicine" helped. Today we would regard the medicine shows that our great-grandparents saw at county fairs as a form of quackery, but in their times, such performances were defined as consumer education. Previous generations relied on Lydia Pinkham's compound, hadacol, and other patent medicines claimed to have impressive healing powers. Such medicines were packaged for immediate use by the purchaser, instructions were included for proper dosage, and exaggerated claims were made for their curative properties. From the modern standpoint, we know that the patented medicines did not have the curative properties that they were claimed to have, but the compounds did contain enough alcohol to make our great grandparents feel better, whether they were cured or not.

Historical evidence that many of the medicines in the past were actually placebos has not reduced levels of confidence in the medical profession. To the contrary, medicines serve as tonics of reassurance, and people seek out medical experts when they are faced with health problems that they feel they cannot handle themselves. They expect to improve, and the use of what is socially defined as a symbol of healing has important implications for recovery from many types of illness. The optimal condition for bringing about the self-fulfilling prophecy is when neither the patient nor the doctor is aware that the substance prescribed is in fact a placebo.

In recognition of the placebo effect, the empirical testing of new pharmaceuticals often consists of using a double-blind research technique. In this method the researcher minimizes the physician's power of suggestion by keeping knowledge about which substance is active and which substance is a placebo from the physician as well as from the patient. A careful comparative analysis of physiological responses may then indicate the degree to which the outcomes are due to the patient's pharmacological reactions to a particular drug rather than to social psychological factors.

These examples show that attitudes play an important part in the control

---

BOX 2.7
Dip in Deaths Before Ceremonial Occasions

The research of Phillips and Feldman (1973) suggests that people die less often than expected before their birthdays, presidential elections, and certain religious holidays. Apparently, they "postpone" death in order to fulfill obligations and to derive a set of rewards from participating in ceremonial occasions. Involvement in the celebration of ceremonies reflects an integration into a meaningful set of social relationships. Such celebrations are designed to emphasize shared values, to reinforce relationships, and to commemorate special events.

In testing their "deathdip" hypothesis, Phillips and Feldman used biographical information on birth and death rates for 1333 famous people. Results of the study indicated that significantly fewer deaths occurred in the month preceding birthdays than would have by chance. A disproportionate increase in deaths occurred within the three months following birthdays, suggesting that the previous deathdips were a result of postponement. Famous people are likely to be the focus of the deathdip phenomenon for numerous reasons. Famous people tend to celebrate their birthdays publicly and frequently receive many gifts and tokens of appreciation.

Similar findings on the dip in deaths before ceremonial occasions were found in analyses of other celebrations. For example, Phillips' and Feldman's study of death rates for the United States between 1904 and 1968 indicated a statistically significant dip in deaths before presidential elections. They also noted that deathdips occurred among certain subgroups around the celebration of special religious holidays. Thus, the subjective meanings given to important ceremonial occasions frequently result in the postponement of death until after they are over.

Source: David P. Phillips and Kenneth A. Feldman, "A Dip in Deaths Before Ceremonial Occasions," *American Sociological Review* 38 (December, 1973): 678–696.

and management of illnesses. A more surprising set of findings is the research of David P. Phillips and Kenneth A. Feldman (1973), who show the importance of social definitions in the timing of death. Postponement of dying until after the celebration of birthdays and other ceremonial occasions demonstrates the importance of situational definitions for the functioning of individuals. People faced with both a terminal illness and a strong reason for living simply postpone dying until after some important event has occurred. Cognition, emotionality, and physiology are sufficiently interrelated that notions about the proper time for dying may serve as a self-fulfilling prophecy. (See Box 2.7.)

3. Aligning Actions

A recurrent problem in the health care field, as in many areas of social life, is that of bringing one's own goals and interests into alignment with the goals and interests of others. The construction and maintenance of reality requires a great deal of repair work, not only because the relevant aspects of situations frequently are changing, but also because those interactig do not share the same concerns and interests. For example, in the diagnosis and treatment of illness, the realities constructed by the physician and the patient differ in fundamental ways (Tessler and Mechanic, 1978). The patient tends to have a *global* orientation toward health problems: something has occurred that interferes with normal functioning so the patient seeks remedial action. The physician, by way of contrast, is trained to think in terms of *specific* maladies for which there are specific remedies.

The physician is able to perform effectively his or her expected role if able to identify specific problems. In many cases, however, the linkage between a specific malfunction and a specific remedy cannot be established. The physician may not be able to locate any specific problem, or may identify a specific problem for which there is no known cure. In either of these cases, several outcomes can occur: the physician may prescribe a placebo rather than an active medication; the physician may refer the patient to a diagnostic center for further testing; or the physician may suggest to the patient the lack of any apparent medical problem. The realities defined by the doctor may be unacceptable to the patient: the patient may become angry with the doctor; the patient may seek the services of another physician for "a second opinion"; or the patient may seek remedies that lack endorsement by the medical profession.

The basic process of arriving at a definition of the situation has been described by Randall Stokes and John Hewitt (1976) as one of **aligning actions.** The alignment of social action involves the resolution of two basic problems the actors in given situations confront. The first involves the efforts of participants to align their actions with each other in order to get on with the business of attaining the goals and outcomes of interest. Under most circumstances, the alignment of actions is easy to achieve, but in situations of doubt, stress, and uncertainty, alignment may become highly problematic. The second form of alignment is where individuals make their joint actions compatible with social norms. The interacting individuals may agree on their definition of the situation, but their plan of action may involve ethical risks if it violates social norms.

Aligning the actions of individuals stems from the special difficulties people face in their efforts to deal with each other. Stokes and Hewitt (1976: 844) observe:

People fail to hear each other correctly; they want to do valued things that can't be done simultaneously; their tools won't work properly; they are forgetful; they play by the rules and don't win; and so the list could go on to cover the multitude of experiences in everyday life in which a particular problem has to be dealt with.

In such cases, the alignment of conduct is often necessary for joint efforts to proceed smoothly in the desired directions. People usually achieve alignment through verbal exchanges that permit people to develop some level of agreement on how to proceed in solving the problems of mutual concern.

The problem of aligning actions is evident in the creation and management of the sick role in our society. Illness involves much more than a physiological malfunction; interacting individuals also define the existence of a health problem and respond to the definitions they have created. In some cases, their claims of illness may not appear to be convincing. The person who claims to be ill may be regarded as "pretending," or the person's health problems may be looked on as "a figment of the imagination." If individuals in contact with the person regard the claims of illness as valid, they will align their actions in several ways. For example, if they define a person as sick, then they do not hold that person responsible for the existing condition, especially if they view the illness as being caused by "microorganisms" or by "something that is going around." But if they define the person as sick, then the sick person incurs both rights and responsibilities. The sick person is exempted from such routine duties as going to work or performing normal household chores. At the same time, the sick person has the responsibility to seek professional help and to try to get well (Wolinsky and Wolinsky, 1981).

If medical professionals validate the claims of sickness, the sick individual is granted preferential status and permitted to play roles denied to those who are well. He or she receives special treatment and is exempted from the performance of tasks that are usually expected in everyday life. The enactment of sick roles involves new alignments of the actions of the ill person with the actions of family members, friends, and employers. How all parties involved achieve these alignments reflects the kind and severity of sickness accorded to the individual. There are sufficient variations in the negotiation and management of illness at all stages of its development that we cannot adequately understand illness by considering its physiological attributes alone. How people define and react to problems of illness are matters of social definitions and symbolic constructions for establishing social supports in an interactional framework (Segall, 1976).

Further, the definitions of pain or pleasure depend to some significant degree on an interactional framework. For example, in cases of a normal childbirth some women describe the experience as pleasurable, while others describe the experience as very painful. The research of Doering, Entwisle, and Quinlan (1980) suggests the social supports expectant mothers receive influence the differential definitions of childbirth. The quality of the birth experience may be enhanced through adequate training and preparation for the delivery. Individuals may take classes in a hospital setting to assist them in defining child delivery in positive terms. The presence of the husband in the delivery room also seems to help, since there is a sharing of experiences and the mother receives social support. If the expectant mother has not prepared adequately or if social supports are lacking, childbirth is likely to be a painful experience; but if the positive definitions of childbirth are worked out in advance and supported in social relationships, the delivery of a baby can be a pleasurable experience.

The alignment of action is important not only in problematic situations but also in the routines of everyday life. Our sense of social support on a daily basis is related to our assumptions about the correspondence between our own assessments and the assessments made by others. If we did not make such assumptions, a great deal of social life as we know it would not be possible. For example, approximately 95 percent of Americans in the labor force utilize private automobiles as a means of getting to work on a daily basis. Cars moving in opposite directions pass within two feet of each other at speeds of 55 miles per hour or more. We necessarily assume that approaching automobiles will drive to their right side of the road, that they will stop if the light is red, and will go if the light is green. Without such a coordination of driving behavior, the private automobile would lose its feasibility as a practical means of transportation. The automobile is in many ways symbolic of American life; the assumptions about driving behavior are somewhat representative of the many other assumptions we make about the correspondence between the way we define situations and the way others define situations.

SUMMARY

The raw materials for the social construction of reality derive from the use of symbols embedded in the language and culture of any particular group of people. The meanings people give to objects and events vary as a result of differential locations in time and space. Social agreements on the proper ways to order and organize objects and events in the environment give symbols specific meaning. This is achieved primarily through the process of communication and social interaction. The specialized vocabularies which have developed in modern societies reflect the experiences and concerns of subgroups within a larger population. Variations in the uses of language are primarily important because of the differences they imply in styles of social thought and action.

From the standpoint of the individual, reality construction is surrounded by connotative meanings that express the variety of emotions, evaluations, and actions associated with objects and events. The language that is internalized facilitates problem solving and a sense of mastery and control over events. This is clearly evident in the assumption of a close correspondence between symbols and the objects and events they represent. Magical practices and the avoidance of sensitive topics reflect efforts to control the outcome of events in which there is a strong emotional investment.

In contrast to the avoidance of sensitive topics, certain kinds of disruptive events emerge to promote open discussion and a quest for information. This especially occurs in times of crisis in which news events become of central relevance for our understanding of the organization of social life. News-making is a form of reality construction that derives from concern over disturbing events that have intruded into our everyday activities. When the outcome of social events appears to be uncertain, we tend to fill in the information gaps by improvising news through deliberation and discussion with others.

We act on the basis of our understanding of the events in which we are engaged, and the outcomes of doing so usually provide verification of the initial assumptions we made. This is the principle of the self-fulfilling prophecy, which holds that if the situation is defined as real, it tends to become real in its consequences. The run on a bank by depositors may result in a bank's defaulting on payments regardless of its initial solvency, and the taking of a placebo often does result in improved health for the individual. The self-fulfilling prophecy usually operates when individuals align their own actions with those of others to attain the goals they seek. Our own definitions of reality generally need verification from the opinions and responses obtained from others.

BASIC TERMS

World construction	Taboo topics
World maintenance	MUM effect
Internalization	Improvised news
Denotative meaning	Definition of the situation
Connotative meaning	Self-fulfilling prophecy
Semantic differential	Placebo effect
technique	Aligning actions

REFERENCES

Abcarian, Gilbert, H. Theodore Groat, Arthur G. Neal, and Sherman M. Stanage
  1966 "Crisis, Charisma, and the Imputation of Motives: Student Responses to the Assassination of President Kennedy," *Revista Mexicana de Orientacion* 1, no. 1: 46–67.
Ackerknecht, Erwin H.
  1942 "Problems of Primitive Medicine," *Bulletin of the History of Medicine* 11: 503–521.
Ball-Rokeach, Sandra J.
  1973 "From Persuasive Ambiguity to a Definition of the Situation," *Sociometry* 36 (September): 378–389.
Berger, Peter L.
  1969 *The Sacred Canopy*, Garden City, N.Y.: Anchor Books.
Berger, Peter L. and Thomas Luckmann
  1967 *The Social Construction of Reality*, Garden City, N.Y.: Anchor Books.
Blumberg, Paul
  1963 "Magic in the Modern World," *Sociology and Social Research* 47 (January): 147–160.
Conlee, Mary Charles and Abraham Tesser
  1973 "The Effects of Recipient Desire to Hear on News Transmission," *Sociometry* 36 (December): 588–599.
Doering, Susan G., Doris R. Entwisle, and Daniel Quinlan
  1980 "Modeling the Quality of Women's Birth Experiences," *Journal of Health and Social Behavior* 21 (March): 12–21.
Farberow, Norman L.
  1963 *Taboo Topics*, New York: Atherton Press.
Frank, Jerome D.
  1964 *Persuasion and Healing*, New York: Schocken Books.
Frazer, Sir James
  1915 *The Golden Bough: A Study in Magic and Religion*, London: Macmillan.
Glaser, Barney G. and Anselm L. Strauss
  1965 *Awarness of Dying*, Chicago: Aldine.
  1964 "Awareness Context and Social Interaction," *American Sociological Review* 29 (October): 669–679.
Holzner, Burkart
  1968 *Reality Construction in Society*, Cambridge, Mass.: Schenkman.
Krishna, Daya
  1971 "'The Self-Fulfilling Prophecy' and the Nature of Society," *American Sociological Review* 36 (December): 1004–1006.
McHugh, Peter
  1968 *Defining the Situation*, New York: Bobbs-Merrill.
Malinowski, Bronislaw
  1954 *Magic, Science and Religion*, Garden City, N.Y.: Anchor Books.
Manis, Jerome and Bernard Meltzer
  1972 *Symbolic Interaction: A Reader in Social Psychology*, Boston: Allyn and Bacon.
Merton, Robert K.

1957 *Social Theory and Social Structure*, Glencoe, Ill.: The Free Press.

Molotch, Harvey and Marilyn Lester

1975 "Accidental News: The Great Oil Spill as Local Occurrence and National Event," *American Journal of Sociology* 81 (September): 235–260.

1974 "News as Purposive Behavior," *American Sociological Review* 39 (February): 101–112.

Mukherjee, Bishwa Nath

1975 "The Role of Husband-Wife Communication in Family Planning," *Journal of Marriage and the Family* 37 (August): 655–667.

Osgood, Charles E., George J. Suci, and Percy Tannenbaum

1957 *The Measurement of Meaning*, Urbana: University of Illinois Press.

Park, Robert E.

1940 "News as a Form of Knowledge," *American Journal of Sociology* 45: 669–686.

Perinbanayagam, R. S.

1974 "The Definition of the Situation," *Sociological Quarterly* 15 (Autumn): 521–541.

Phillips, David P. and Kenneth A. Feldman

1973 "A Dip in Deaths Before Ceremonial Occasions," *American Sociological Review* 38 (December): 678–696.

Quarantelli, E. L. and Russell R. Dynes

1977 "Response to Social Crisis and Disaster," *Annual Review of Sociology* 3: 23–50.

Rainwater, Lee

1960 *And the Poor Get Children*, Chicago: Quadrangle Books.

Rosen, Sidney and Abraham Tesser

1970 "On Reluctance to Communicate Undesirable Information: The MUM Effect," *Sociometry* 33 (September): 253–263.

Rosenblatt, Paul C.

1971 "Communication in the Practice of Love Magic," *Social Forces* 49 (March): 482–487.

Sapir, Edward

1956 *Culture, Language, and Personality*, Los Angeles: University of California Press.

Scales, Peter

1977 "Males and Morals: Teenage Contraceptive Behavior and the Double Standard," *Family Coordinator* 26 (July): 211–224.

Segall, Alexander

1976 "The Sick Role Concept: Understanding Illness Behavior," *Journal of Health and Social Behavior* 17 (June): 162–168.

Shapiro, A. K.

1959 "The Placebo Effect in the History of Medical Treatment," *American Journal of Psychiatry* 116: 298–304.

Shibutani, Tamotsu

1966 *Improvised News*, Indianapolis: Bobbs-Merrill.

Snider, James G. and Charles E. Osgood (eds.)

1969 *Semantic Differential Technique*, Chicago: Aldine.

Stokes, Randall and John P. Hewitt

1976 "Aligning Actions," *American Sociological Review* 41 (October): 838–849.

Tessler, Richard and David Mechanic
   1978 "Psychological Distress and Perceived Health Status," *Journal of Health and Social Behavior* 19 (September): 254–262.
Thomas, W. I.
   1928 *The Child in America*, New York: Knopf.
Thompson, David S.
   1975 *Language*, New York: Time-Life Books.
Tuchman, Gaye
   1973 "Making News by Doing Work: Routinizing the Unexpected," *American Journal of Sociology* 79 (July): 110–131.
   1972 "Objectivity as Strategic Ritual: An Examination of Newsmen's Notion of Objectivity," *American Journal of Sociology* 77 (January): 660–679.
Turner, Ralph H.
   1976 "The Real Self: From Institution to Impulse," *American Journal of Sociology* 81 (March): 989–1016.
Turner, Ronny E. and Charles Edgley
   1980 "Sociological Semanticide: On Reification, Tautology, and the Destruction of Language," *Sociological Quarterly* 21 (Autumn): 595–606.
Whorf, Benjamin L.
   1956 *Language, Thought and Reality* (ed. by J. Carroll), New York: John Wiley.
Wolinsky, Fredric D. and Sally R. Wolinsky
   1981 "Expecting Sick-Role Legitimation and Getting It," *Journal of Health and Social Behavior* 22 (September): 229–242.

3

Social Norms

Social norms enter into the awareness of individuals as attributes of social life that they must confront as a basic part of the realities of group living. The social norms are the rules for regulating behavior that specify the obligations of individuals in their various roles and in the patterns of their interaction with each other. People have an obligation to pay income tax when due; parents are obligated to provide for the care of their children; children are obligated to go to school; and if one is driving an automobile on a public highway there is an obligation to comply with the traffic laws of the state.

Creating social norms is not an option available to most people; instead, norms are a part of the social givens that individuals must accept as the basic realities of social life. The suggestion would seem strange to us that we sit down and attempt to work out a policy statement on whether cannibalism, in-group murder, or incest should be permitted within our society. These are among the issues that have been settled in advance, and the moral solutions are transmitted in the social heritage we have received from our remote ancestors. Since social norms are created and enforced through group living, the matter of choice for the individual primarily centers around the decision of whether to comply with norms or to disregard them in the pursuit of personal goals and objectives.

The norms that have the highest level of support within a social group are those to which the group assigns sacred qualities and which the group views as being related to the ultimate conditions of the human existence. The sacred qualities of social norms are to be found in the attitudes that the group holds toward the rules of conduct. Norms become sacred in character if they are treated with a high degree of respect, if they are regarded as having supernatural support, and if they are deeply embedded in notions about what is necessary for sustaining order and stability in one's personal life. If norms are held to be scared, their violation has a belittling effect, and self-punishment is likely to occur even if others do not detect the violation or bring it forward for any kind of official action.

We may think of sacred norms as being internalized in the sense that they are deeply embedded in notions about reality and the manner in which serious mistakes may be made. Such norms often take the form of taboos, which consist of rules prohibiting us from engaging in certain lines of action. For example, the norm prohibiting the eating of human flesh is nearly universally understood as binding on conduct, although from a purely dietary standpoint human flesh may be suitable for consumption. The norm prohibiting cannibalism is so deeply embedded in moral judgments that we can understand violations only when survival needs or mental derangement are involved. Consuming the flesh of a deceased friend or relative is unthinkable, and if it did occur we would automatically associate it with abnormality. No sane or reasonable person could commit such an act unless the alternative was starvation, and even in survival situations the eating of human flesh would have serious emotional consequences for most people.

Because the norm prohibiting cannibalism is so deeply embedded in social morality, enactment of formal laws making such behavior illegal is unnecessary. On the other hand, most social norms are mundane in character and mainly reflect standardized operating procedures for promoting the coherence and stability of group living. In contrast to cannibalism, many regard the law that sets a maximum speed of 55 miles per hour on interstate highways as being so mundane and secular that they may violate it with impunity. Nevertheless, the laws regulating the speed of automobiles do constitute social norms since they are enforceable and are oriented toward standardizing behavior. The final source of authority on what constitutes a social norm does not rest with the individual but with the group sanctions by which the group enforces the rules of conduct.

By growing up in a given society, we become aware of many norms that specify what we must or must not do in specific situations. We are clearly aware of the norms prohibiting murder, kidnapping, armed robbery, having sex with genetic relatives, and excessive drinking of alcoholic beverages. But, there are numerous social norms that lack clarity as guidelines for conduct. The complexity of modern society includes such a diversity of experiences with group living that there is often widespread disagreement on what the norms actually are and on what kinds of punishment are appropriate if norms are violated.

Because of the diversity in modern society, the orderliness of social relationships frequently becomes problematic. We often find ourselves in situations in which we cannot assume that others share our own understanding of events; we sometimes have difficulty in making plans with confidence that we can effectively carry them out; and we frequently enter into social relationships with some degree of suspicion and distrust of the motives and behavior of others. The study of social norms should enable us to see more clearly the basis for the orderliness of everyday life, as well as to identify some of the basic reasons a combination of order and conflict exists in social relationships. These topics relate to the normality of everyday life and the meanings we give to the events in which we are engaged.

In this chapter, we will examine the dual themes of normality and devi-

Normal Flow of Pedestrian Traffic
Traffic signals are important symbols of authority and social norms in urban areas. Without them the coordination of pedestrian and automotive traffic would be difficult. Most of the people in this picture are complying with social norms, but some are not.

ance. While normality relates to shared understanding about the basis for order in social life, the theme of deviance suggests that all people do not share a single reality. Instead, we hold multiple notions about the conduct of human affairs. The interactions that occur between deviants and enforcers of social norms are essentially transactions that clarify the rules of conduct. These interactions are important because they demonstrate the obligations people have to each other, the ways people make mistakes, and justifications for problematic conduct.

A. THE NORMALITY OF EVERYDAY LIFE

The normality of everyday life is based on a set of assumptions about the overall organization of social relationships. **Normality** implies predictability and orderliness in our personal lives and in our relationships with others. Our lives proceed in a normal, routine fashion if there are clearly defined rules for regulating our conduct and if we experience our relationships with others as living up to what we have come to expect from them. The generalized views of social life as orderly and predictable have been described by Alfred Schutz (1971) as "the assumptions of everyday life." According to Schutz, these include:

1.   that social life as it is known up to this point will continue into the future;
2.   that knowledge derived from social relationships is dependable, although its origin or its true meaning may not be clearly understood;
3.   that it is sufficient to know something about the general style of events in order to manage and control them; and,
4.   that the same assumptions we hold are likewise accepted and applied by those with whom we interact.

To the degree that our experiences verify the correctness of these assumptions, we may proceed with confidence in the normal pursuit of our daily objectives. But if we fail to find support for any one of these assumptions, we face some degree of crisis. We are required to develop an alignment of our own thoughts and actions with our perceptions of the general rules that regulate social behavior (Stokes and Hewitt, 1976).

1. Social Continuity

The everyday assumptions about social continuity relate to notions about social time as durable and continuous. From our experiences with social life we can predict the outcomes of numerous events with a reasonable degree of certainty. For example, students seeking a college education must necessarily assume that the college will award them a degree after they complete the requirements as set forth in the catalog. We can predict with a reasonable degree of confidence that presidential elections will be held every four years, that Christmas will be celebrated this year, and that a movie we are going to see will start at approximately the stated time. The regularities of the shifts from night to day and the regularities of the seasonal variations are examples from our environmental experiences that time is continuous and predictable.

Many of the regularities of social life derive from the dependability of scheduled events. The workday for most industrial workers begins and ends at a predictable time, classes in our universities begin and end according to a prearranged schedule, and we make payments on bank loans at regular intervals. We make other kinds of predictions from our experiences with the ways social events usually emerge and develop. Children go to school, grow up, buy cars, enter the labor force, get married, and perpetuate the life cycle through their own subsequent reproduction. The stability of our personal lives is in large measure dependent on our experiences with and anticipation of social continuity. We assume that the social conditions surrounding the events in which we have acquired a deep emotional investment will continue to continue. (See Box 3.1.)

BOX 3.1
The Normative Ordering of Life Events

Drawing on a national sample of more than 33,000 men aged 20 to 65, Hogan (1978) made an analysis of the normative sequence of life events during the early years of adulthood. Approximately 70 percent of American males order their life events so they can first complete their schooling, then take on their first full-time job, and subsequently enter into first marriage. We look on such a sequence of life events as the natural or appropriate one within the context of American values. "Being out of step" occurs when one has full-time employment prior to completing one's schooling, or when one gets married prior to getting a job.

The level of educational attainment is one of the major variables associated with a disorderly sequence of life events. Hogan's results indicated that among men with a high school education or less, only 5 percent married before completing their education. By way of contrast, among men with one or more years of graduate or professional schooling, 57 percent married before completing their education. Military service also tends to be disruptive, since it often delays the completion of schooling and increases the probability of marriage prior to full-time employment.

One of the consequences of a disorderly sequence of life events is that it increases the probability for an unstable marriage. Marriage prior to employment or prior to the completion of one's schooling results in significantly higher rates of divorce or separation. Departure from the normative sequence produces some degree of stress, since it implies discord or disharmony with the approved order in which major life events are expected to occur.

Source: Dennis P. Hogan, "The Variable Order of Events in the Life Course," *American Sociological Review* 43 (August, 1978): 573–586.

Cues to the normal ways of doing things are provided by an individual's social heritage. By growing up in a particular society we learn that it is appropriate for weddings and funerals to be performed in a church or temple, that we may reasonably expect to receive greetings and gifts on our birthdays, and that professors will turn in grades to the registrar if we have satisfactorily met the requirements for completing our courses. Such shared frames of reference provide a practical set of assumptions about how social events are organized and what constitutes the proper sequence for their occurrence.

2. Dependability of Knowledge

An additional assumption of everyday life is that a general knowledge of events in which we are engaged is sufficient for us to act meaningfully in relationship

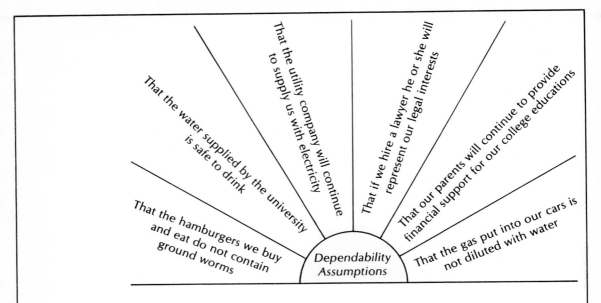

Because of the specialization that has developed in modern society, we become highly dependent on the integrity of others for the many services we receive. The above are examples of the implicit assumptions about the normality of everyday life. If we didn't make such assumptions, our social worlds would become unpredictable and we would become incapacitated.

FIGURE 3.1
Dependability Assumptions in Everyday Life

to them. We make purchases in a store without knowing how the merchandise is produced. The workers who produce the commodities we buy do not enter our field of vision, and we only rarely think about the human labor or the technology that produces the objects we use. In this respect, we tend to draw boundaries around the objects of concern to us. We typically think of steak as an item obtained from the supermarket and seldom reflect on either the manner in which beef is produced or the imagery surrounding the slaughter of animals. (See Figure 3.1.)

Most of us drive automobiles without knowing very much about how they operate mechanically. We are aware of the proper steps and procedures to follow in driving a car, and for most of us this is adequate. It is usually sufficient for us to know that if we flip a light switch the light will come on. In doing so, we are unlikely to ponder the nature of electricity, how it is produced, or the technical principles on which it works. Our daily lives are then oriented toward the objects of interest and guided by a general knowledge of the procedures to follow in achieving the objectives we seek. The dependability of knowledge permits us to proceed in a matter-of-fact fashion in those situations we clearly understand to be normal, routine, and standardized.

3. Shared Symbolism

In the pursuit of routine activities we also assume that others share our own understanding of the world. As humans we are dependent on each other, and this requires us to use common frames of reference as a basis for interaction. We share a common language as a form of communication; we agree on the value of money as a medium of exchange; we understand the procedures to follow in making a purchase; and we share a common knowledge on how to determine the time of day.

We can imagine the difficulties we would encounter if we started speaking different languages, if money were to lose its economic value, if store owners decided to keep rather than to sell their merchandise, if the mail carrier refused to deliver our mail, and if the hands on all of our watches and clocks were suddenly to start moving in random and unpredictable patterns. Social life as we know it would be seriously disrupted, to say the least, and we would confront the problem of reorganizing our daily lives and our relationships with other people.

From these assumptions of social continuity, of the general adequacy in our knowledge of events, and of the correspondence between our own understanding and the understanding held by others, we are able to proceed with a reasonable degree of confidence in our everyday life. We are aware of the alternatives available to us in given situations, and we know what to expect from the pursuit of the outcomes we seek. But as Schutz pointed out, if any of these assumptions fails to be sustained, we then face a stress situation. Confusion, bewilderment, and disbelief are prominent among our responses to social situations in which our assumptions about everyday life fail to be supported by the unfolding of events.

We may consider the assumption of shared symbolism as the individual's conception of society. Every man and woman has at least some minimal conception of society, and the degree of correspondence between one person's view and that of another is in part a reflection of the degree of complexity built into any given social system. Since there are multiple vantage points for viewing a heterogeneous society such as our own, the variety of realities individuals may construct is very broad indeed. We do not have an official label for describing the totality of modern society, nor is it necessary for the person on the street to struggle with an overview of the social system. Instead, notions about the attributes of most people, especially those we have to deal with on a daily basis, are generally adequate.

George Herbert Mead (1934) coined the concept of the **generalized other** to refer to the individual's internalized conception of society. The generalized other includes the individual's perception of "most people," the imper-

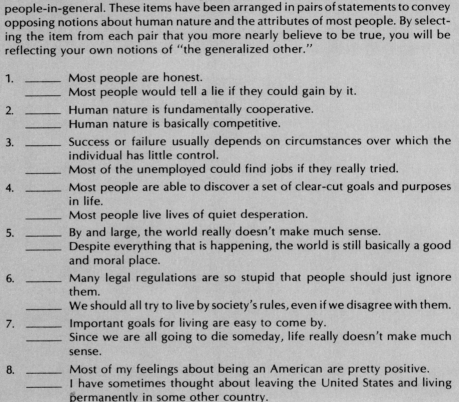

BOX 3.2
Perceptions of "Most People"

Listed below are several items designed to illustrate some of the perceptions of people-in-general. These items have been arranged in pairs of statements to convey opposing notions about human nature and the attributes of most people. By selecting the item from each pair that you more nearly believe to be true, you will be reflecting your own notions of "the generalized other."

1. _____ Most people are honest.
   _____ Most people would tell a lie if they could gain by it.

2. _____ Human nature is fundamentally cooperative.
   _____ Human nature is basically competitive.

3. _____ Success or failure usually depends on circumstances over which the individual has little control.
   _____ Most of the unemployed could find jobs if they really tried.

4. _____ Most people are able to discover a set of clear-cut goals and purposes in life.
   _____ Most people live lives of quiet desperation.

5. _____ By and large, the world really doesn't make much sense.
   _____ Despite everything that is happening, the world is still basically a good and moral place.

6. _____ Many legal regulations are so stupid that people should just ignore them.
   _____ We should all try to live by society's rules, even if we disagree with them.

7. _____ Important goals for living are easy to come by.
   _____ Since we are all going to die someday, life really doesn't make much sense.

8. _____ Most of my feelings about being an American are pretty positive.
   _____ I have sometimes thought about leaving the United States and living permanently in some other country.

sonal "they," and the collective "we." Our notions about the generalized other emerge from the accumulation of social experiences, and in this respect our particular conceptions of society are shaped by our own vantage points within it. (See Box 3.2.)

Our ideas about society are necessarily selective and involve reducing the complexity of social life in order to deal meaningfully with it. Accordingly, our views of the generalized other serve to simplify events, to make them coherent, and to provide us with a rough approximation of the actual state of affairs. The generalized other, then, constitutes a series of assumptions for constructing a collective portrait of society. The collective portrait of most people, or the impersonal "they," sets the boundaries on what is permitted, what is tolerated, and what is prohibited within the social system. It also provides us with guidelines for whom to trust and when to trust.

Drawing on Mead's notion of the generalized other, C. Wright Mills (1963) views the process of thinking as a form of conversation between the social actor in any given situation and his or her internalized conception of society. The generalized other takes the form of an internalized audience that provides for an interplay of meanings and this serves as a mechanism for testing out the validity of ideas. Conversing with the generalized other allows the individual to derive conclusions about the sources of approval, rejection, or opposition. It also enables the person to determine the need to reformulate a set of plans or the need to abandon a course of action altogether. The proneness to act impulsively becomes socially regulated by taking others into account and modifying his or her behavior accordingly.

B. STABILITY, CHANGE, AND CONFLICT

While everyday assumptions are oriented toward social stability, our experiences require confronting the changes that occur in the conditions under which we live. William James (1890) developed the idea of "the stream of consciousness" as a way to describe the processual character of social life. He referred to the fundamental reality of change in the human condition. Modifications are always occurring within the intricate networks of social life. Our own life circumstances are continuously being altered by changes in the external environment as well as by changes within ourselves.

While changes are always occurring, perceptions of the normality of everyday life are highly variable among individuals and across situations. Some people view modern social life as proceeding in a routine and coherent fashion, while others regularly experience everyday life as highly complex, confusing, and bereft of purpose. For those who find social life to be difficult, there are two major forms a crisis of meaning may take. One kind emerges on a situational basis, as with an unexpected pregnancy, the breakup of a love affair, or the accidental death of a friend. The second kind is more pervasive and occurs in conjunction with one's feelings about the enduring forms of chaos in modern social life.

1. Crisis of Meaning

A **crisis of meaning** occurs under those conditions in which the individual feels that he or she is lacking in an adequate understanding of the interrelatedness of events (Seeman, 1959). This may be expressed in several ways. Individuals may become uncertain about what they ought to believe, about how they ought to act, and about what goals are worth pursuing. The core component of a crisis of meaning is uncertainty, and this may be expressed in the perceived complexity of events, in the problems of having too much to choose from, and in the feeling that social life as it is known and understood is unlikely to continue into the future.

In his classical writings, Emile Durkheim (1964) viewed a crisis of meaning as deriving from the mass-like character of modern society. Historically, social organization has vastly increased in scale: modern societies now consist of millions of individuals and extend over vast geographical areas; the division of labor has increased social differentiation; and remote events impinge on the life-world of individuals without the cushioning effects of local forms of social

---

BOX 3.3
The Problem of Selecting a Career

The research of Janis and Wheeler (1978) suggests that selecting a career is one of the more consequential decisions the young adult in our society will ever have to make. Yet it is a decision we often make in a hasty manner and on the basis of inadequate information. Many people regret their career choices, but regard their work as an "irrevocable commitment" and are unwilling to pursue job alternatives. Getting trapped in an unwanted job frequently stems from a failure to think clearly about career choices earlier in life and from simply moving haphazardly from one job to another.

An effective way of approaching career decisions consists of seeking information on career alternatives, evaluating the conditions of work in different occupations, and examining the implications of a particular type of employment for one's life plans and preferences. Janis and Wheeler recommend the use of a balance sheet for listing the advantages and disadvantages of job possibilities. The evaluation should include anticipating the costs and benefits for oneself and for one's significant others, as well as the job implications for self- and social approval. In effect, the selection of a career should be compatible with the results of self-evaluation.

In implementing career decisions, minor setbacks should not lead to overreaction, since all lines of work involve numerous obstacles that one must confront. Effective decision making requires what Janis and Wheeler have called "stress innoculation." This consists of anticipating problems before they emerge and being prepared to deal with them as a necessary part of career development. Thinking clearly about career choices also requires some concern with contingency plans, because if a particular job does not work out satisfactorily one can then make changes without major disruptions occurring.

Source: Irving Janis and Dan Wheeler, "Thinking Clearly about Career Choices," *Psychology Today* 11 (May, 1978): 67f.

organization. The limited vantage point of the lone individual often prevents him or her from understanding the events occurring in the broader society.

If the individual's minimal standards for clarity and understanding are not being met, then planning the numerous facets of one's life become very difficult indeed (Toffler, 1971). Conditions of uncertainty often occur in situations in which the individual is making consequential decisions, such as selecting a career, making major consumer purchases, getting married, becoming a parent, and changing place of residence. If the broader social environment is experienced as chaotic and unpredictable, then one may refrain from making a set of life plans, emphasizing instead the hedonistic view of "living for today and letting tomorrow take care of itself" (Srole, 1956). The lack of confidence in one's decisions or the failure to make long-range plans altogether may eventually result in the feelings that one's personal life is drifting, being shaped by forces that one can neither adequately understand nor control (Parenti, 1978). (See Box 3.3.)

While many people in modern society may routinely experience conditions of uncertainty, feelings of meaninglessness reach their highest level of intensity under those conditions in which everyday life is seriously disrupted and people call into question their prior assumptions about social continuity. The orderliness of social life is dependent on a correspondence between people's understanding of events and the outcomes that follow. In many situations, however, the orderly progression of social events fails to develop (Parsons, 1972).

The discrepancy between expectations and occurrences may be illustrated by the case of the premature death of a college student in an automobile accident. A college student is likely to have deferred numerous gratifications in the pursuit of an education. Parents often make extensive sacrifices in helping to prepare their sons and daughters for a career. To have this life and all this human effort end in an automobile accident fails to correspond to what one may reasonably expect from socially shared conceptions of justice, fairness, merit, and reward.

While some degree of crisis always characterizes the death of a friend or a close relative, there are shared conceptions of socially appropriate times to die—when one becomes very old, after having a long and useful life, or as relief from a prolonged and painful illness. The meaninglessness of death reaches its greatest intensity when it seems out of place—when it manifests a lack of congruence between what we have come to expect and what actually occurs. Social groups offer rewards and incentives in promoting expenditures of energies in socially desired directions. However, what we get and what we deserve may be out of alignment in terms of the standards of the social system itself.

The death crisis is only one of several crises of meaning that are implicit in the human condition, and these can never be completely eliminated, regardless of how effectively a society organizes or manages itself. The recognition that collective solutions have developed for dealing with numerous types of crises in social relationships facilitates adaptability to the conditions of one's existence. These solutions constitute the normative order, and they provide a basic design for living, a framework for assessing what is proper and improper, a set of notions about what one must or must not do under certain circumstances. Commitments to social norms provides the individual with perspectives by which the self and others may be evaluated.

The normality of everyday life is shaped by the agreed-on rules for regulating our own conduct and the conduct of others. Conditions are normal if we can make a reasonable set of predictions about the outcomes of the events in which we are engaged and if these outcomes make sense to us in terms of our own ideas about social purpose and meaning. These predictions are possible because of our internalized notions about the rules that guide the decision making and conduct of most people in given types of situations (Davis, 1972). They manifest our ideas about both what does exist and what ought to exist in the conduct of human affairs.

2. Stressful Life Events

The orderliness of everyday life may become problematic for us if we are not able to develop an adequate understanding of the motives and behavior of those with whom we interact. We are confronted with a crisis of meaning if we are not able to develop an adequate understanding of the events in which we are engaged, if we are not able to make adequate predictions about the behavior of others, or if we come to feel that our lives are empty as a result of pursuing goals that have lost their purpose. The experiences of social life as normal and meaningful require that we have a clear set of ideas about ourselves and our relationships to the broader social order.

The stability of social relationships tends to be undercut if a large number of changes in life circumstances are occurring within a short period of time. The changes in question consist of any major type of life event, such as starting or finishing school, getting married or divorced, becoming a parent, taking on or losing a job, or experiencing the death of a friend or a family member. A series of studies over the past several years has concentrated on the impact of stressful life events, with particular emphasis on the importance of abrupt changes in social status for the physical well-being of the individual (Dohrenwend and Dohrenwend, 1974).

The onset of numerous forms of illness has been found to be associated with the number of changes in life circumstances during the preceding year. If extensive changes take place within a limited time frame, the probability increases for psychosomatic illness, such as sleeplessness, nervous tension, and the experience of pain in various parts of the body (Myers et al., 1972). Psychosomatic illnesses are those forms of physical impairment deriving from the attitudes held by the individual. Even the more organically based illnesses, such as those of the cardiovascular and respiratory systems, are likely to be precipitated by the exposure of the individual to a large number of stressful life events. Apparently, the stresses induced by social changes weaken the capacity of the body to resist the disease-producing organisms that are always present in the environment. (See Box 3.4.)

The thrust of these studies has been to show that the onset of physical illness is related to the scope of the disruptions individuals experience. In clarifying the nature of these disruptions, Thomas H. Holmes and Richard M. Rahe

BOX 3.4
Stressful Life Events

In an analysis of the variable properties of stressful life events, Ruch (1977) concentrated on three overlapping dimensions of social change: (1) the degree of disruption, (2) the social desirability of the change, and (3) the area of social life affected. The following examples illustrate some variations in the level of disruption:

LEVEL OF DISRUPTION

Extreme	Moderate	Minor
Death of a spouse	Pregnancy	Going on vacation
Divorce	Trouble with in-laws	Christmas
Jail term	Changing jobs	Change in school
Marriage	Son or daughter leaving home	Traffic ticket
Retirement	Outstanding achievement	Trouble with boss
Major injury or illness	Change in residence	Change in eating habits

Ruch argues that the desirability of life events is important for our understanding of the effects of social change on stress and illness. Her analysis indicates that the more disruptive events are likely to be socially undesirable, while the moderate and minor changes may provide sources of pleasure (vacations, Christmas, outstanding personal achievement) along with some degree of stress. The effects of desirable life events on illness are less clear than are the effects of socially undesirable changes.

Stressful events also differ in terms of the areas of social life they affect. In general, the more stressful changes are those related to aspects of family relationships, the moderate stress ranges are associated with employment and financial affairs, and the lower levels of stress derive from changes in personal habits and lifestyles.

Source: Libby O. Ruch, "A Multidimensional Analysis of the Concept of Life Change," *Journal of Health and Social Behavior* 18 (March, 1977): 71–83.

(1967) developed a system for measuring the amount of adaptive behavior generally required to cope with specific changes in social status. The system of weighted scores was a more refined measure than a simple count of the number of stressful events that had occurred. Barbara Snell Dohrenwend (1973) made further refinements by taking into account whether the stressful events are desirable or undesirable in character. Socially undesirable events, for example, include divorce, loss of a job, and death of a spouse, while the desirable events include such changes as marriage, job promotion, and vacations. In general, but not exclusively so, the more negative events consist of breaking social

Marriage as a Stressful Life Event
While marriage usually is regarded in positive and rewarding terms, it also is stress producing. In the Social Readjustment Rating Scale developed by Holmes and Rahe (1967), a stress score of 50 was assigned to marriage. Other life events were measured on a scale up to 100, with the magnitude of the score depending on the readjustments generally required relative to those that accompany getting married.

bonds, while the more positive ones consist of some new form of social attachment, such as the birth of a child or a new job.

Utilizing the weighted scores of the Holmes and Rahe (1967) readjustment rating scale, Dohrenwend's (1973) findings indicated that how much change occurred was a better predictor of psychosomatic illnesses than whether or not the change was undesirable or desirable. Thus illnesses that impair functioning are based more closely on the scope of the required adjustments to change than on the negative or positive evaluations of the life events. From this it follows that success in goal attainment may have disruptive effects that are similar to those of failure. Each requires adjustments in relationships between the self and the broader social environment. Apparently, the stability of one's social world is important for the psychological well-being of the individual, and the psychosomatic symptoms that develop are a reflection of the social disruptions that have occurred.

Drawing on a community-wide sample of 720 adults in a metropolitan area, a study by Myers, Lilienthal, and Pepper (1975) indicates that the relationship between life events and psychosomatic illness is modified by social status characteristics. Experience with only a few changes in life events had a severe impact on subjects characterized by lower levels of social integration, such as the unmarried, the unemployed, or those dissatisfied with their jobs. On the other hand, subjects who were more fully integrated into the social system, such as those with higher levels of income and education, were able to tolerate a wider scope of change in life events without manifesting psychosomatic symptoms. Thus people who have access to more integrative social relationships and who are more fully satisfied with their work activities are able to cope more effectively with stressful life events.

The degree of comfort one derives from belonging to social groups is related to the predictability of social relationships and the willingness to accept social norms as binding on one's own conduct. Conformity to group standards may be a basis for self-esteem and for earning prestige and respect from others. But if one lacks valid knowledge about what the norms are, or if one deliberately engages in risk taking through the violation of social norms, others may invoke extreme pressures to preserve the integrity of the group itself.

3. Multiple Norms

In large and complex societies such as our own, individuals belong to a wide variety of groups, and each of these groups has its own set of standards for regulating the conduct of members. This diversity contributes to an overall system that may be characterized as one of multiple norms and multiple sources of authority. Multiple norms result in part from the separation of institutions (Wiebe, 1975), in part from the pluralism reflected in a large number of organized groups (Presthus, 1978), and in part from the variety of informal associations that serve as sources of social attachment and personal meaning (Akers, 1973).

Since we live in a multigroup society, we are often confronted with competing loyalties and conflicting social norms (Yinger, 1965). For example, the norms pertaining to work commitments and career advancement often conflict with the values and interests of family life. Business executives sometimes receive opportunities for job advancement that require giving up leisure time, spending less time with the family, or moving to another part of the country. If only the norm for regulating conduct in the work sphere were of concern, decision making in such cases would be less difficult. But loyalties to family and to the local community are also frequently involved. As a result of multiple and overlapping group memberships, individuals are required to re-

Conflict among Norms
The conflict between norms promoting militarism and those emphasizing humanistic values became evident during the summer of 1980 with the reintroduction of registration for the draft. The army recruitment poster became a symbol that evoked a sensitive response for many young people faced with the possibility of compulsory military service.

solve the conflicts among norms, and the manner in which they do has consequences for the alignment of loyalties and priorities.

Because organized subgroups set norms for regulating member conduct, individuals very often find themselves in situations in which compliance with one set of norms requires violating another. Elective abortions may be permitted by the state, but prohibited by the Catholic Church. Compulsory military service may be required by the state, but normatively prohibited by certain religious groups that look with disdain on the taking of human life under any circumstance. The resolution of such normative conflicts becomes urgent under conditions in which individuals are required to take some specific line of action. Women do become accidentally pregnant and must decide whether or not to have an abortion, and conscientious objectors do sometimes receive notices to report for military service. Under these circumstances individuals must resolve for themselves the conflicts inherent in the loyalties to both church and state.

Many norms are specific to the organizations within which individuals carry out their daily activities (Pollis and Pollis, 1970). All large-scale organizations develop their own systems of norms for dealing with types of situations and cases, and these procedures sometimes conflict with the collective norms of the broader society. While much may be said for the claim that "what's good for General Motors is good for the country," there are also important qualifications. Profit making is a major objective of the modern business corporation, and this goal is often in conflict with the interests consumers have in product safety and dependability. The goal of profit making may very well lead the modern business corporation to compromising generally understood principles of normative conduct and even to violating the law outright (Schrager and Short, 1978).

The numerous rules for regulating member conduct in small and intimate groups may add additional complexity to social norms. Delinquent gangs often develop their own special rules that stand in conflict with the norms of the broader society (Cloward and Ohlin, 1960). The use of obscene language, excessive drinking, taking drugs, acting tough, and holding hostile attitudes toward law enforcement are among the means that delinquent gangs use to promote group solidarity and that serve as sources of status and recognition (Cohen, 1955). Thus small and intimate groups may develop norms that stand in opposition to the general value system of the broader society.

Because of the multiple norms in modern society, individuals are often confronted with divided loyalties and competing demands on their behavior. The conflicts among norms may result in feelings of uncertainty about what to do in given situations, or it may result in a general tendency to orient oneself in an expedient direction by selectively drawing on norms to justify a line of action one wishes to undertake for personal reasons. The consequences of having competing norms are those relating to disorder and lack of predictability, since it is often unclear what guidelines for behavior are operating in the conduct of others.

C. NORMLESSNESS

Conditions of **normlessness** occur in those situations in which social norms are ineffective as regulators of conduct. Individuals may ignore or violate rules of behavior under a variety of conditions and for a variety of reasons; however, the basic component of normlessness is a generalized expectancy that socially unapproved behavior is necessary for goal attainment (Seeman, 1959; 1975). Such a view goes beyond the factual observation that deviant behavior does sometimes occur. Instead, normlessness implies that rule violation is prevalent and symptomatic of the way the system works. Those who hold these attitudes make moral judgments on society and regard social controls as inadequate for regulating the conduct of society's members.

People frequently express such cynical attitudes toward the political realm in a variety of notions about public officials (Finifter, 1972). These include the views that candidates for public office make promises they do not intend to keep, that those running the government serve special interests, and that public officials are unresponsive to the needs and concerns of the people they are supposed to represent. Attitudes concerning normlessness in government also extend over into the business realm (Neal and Rettig, 1967). People frequently view business corporations as institutions maximizing their profits by engaging in coercive and fraudulent practices.

As a result of attitudes of normlessness the individual enters into social relationships with some degree of suspicion and distrust. The person tends to look behind verbal statements for the hidden motive and expects to be taken in—by the repair person, by the sales person, by false campaign promises, or by misleading advertising. Such notions imply that uses of force and fraud are prevalent within modern society and that the individual must rely on his or her own resources, rather than be interdependent with others and share with them a sense of moral community.

1. Blocked Opportunities

Robert Merton (1957) presented the theory that the violation of social norms stems from a contradiction inherent in the organization of modern society. He argued that within American society the emphasis on success goals and status attainment (money, fame, power, and so forth) are pervasive, while opportunities for gaining access to such goals are blocked for those at the lower socioeconomic levels. In his view, people at these levels have internalized monetary values and status attainment as personal goals but do not have the necessary resources (such as education and family sponsorship) for achieving them through the use of socially approved means. (See Table 3.1.)

As a result of blocked opportunities, individuals may turn to the use of illegitimate means for the attainment of goals that are widely held and accept-

TABLE 3.1
Success Goals in Book Titles

The cultural emphasis on success goals may be noted readily in the titles of numerous books that suggest the desirability of wealth and power. Listed below are several titles that reflect some aspect or another of the success theme.

The Joy of Money
Think and Grow Rich
How to Prosper from the Coming Bad Years
Solid Gold
Happiness Is a Stock that Doubles in a Year
Do You Sincerely Want to be Rich?
How People Get Power

A prominent counter-theme reflects the normlessness associated with an emphasis on the success goals of money and power. Here are some titles that suggest the failure of norms to regulate conduct adequately.

The Dark Side of the Marketplace
False Promises
The Wreck of the Penn Central
Responses of Presidents to Charges of Misconduct in Office
Confessions of a Stock Broker
The Wall Street Jungle
Culture Against Man
The Politics of Lying
The Seamy Side of Democracy

able within society. This explanation of normlessness would seem to be especially applicable to many of the crimes people at the lower socioeconomic levels commit, such as prostitution, burglary, auto theft, and armed robbery. Attaining "the good life" becomes more important than adhering to the social rules for regulating conduct. For such people, the manner of obtaining desired resources is not nearly so important as the fact of having access to them.

The research of Richard A. Cloward (1959) suggests that many individuals at the lower socioeconomic levels lack access even to "illegitimate means" for the attainment of success goals. These are cases that involve a "double failure" by the standards of the social system: the success goals that the society at large promotes are not attainable by either approved or disapproved means. One pattern of response to such a situation is to become "an outsider" (Becker, 1963), withdrawing from the way of life that is normal or typical for most people within society. This pattern of response is one of retreatism and withdrawal.

Retreatism refers to the rejection of both the success goals emphasized in the broader society and the social norms designed to standardize behavior.

The individual assigns a low reward value to the basic design of living typical of his or her society. When this occurs, the normative order turns upside down, so to speak, as the individual develops behavior patterns that are socially unacceptable. This may take such forms as alcoholism, drug addiction, or mental illness. In such cases those in the mainstream of social life withdraw their emotional support, and the individual places a special value on one or more forms of deviant behavior.

Conditions of normlessness are expressed not only in perceptions of the broader society but also in self-attitudes. The level of normlessness in personal commitments becomes intensified under those circumstances in which the individual comes to place a high reward value on deviant behavior. The normative order turns topsy turvy in the thinking of the individual (Durkheim, 1964), and behavior the community regards as deplorable serves as a guideline for personal thought and action. Thus the concept of normlessness includes the value the individual places on his or her own deviant acts as well as the perception that deviant behavior is prevalent within one's own society.

2. Unrestricted Opportunities

If blocked opportunities in the attainment of success goals are a major factor in normlessness at the lower socioeconomic levels, the lack of constraints and the overabundance of opportunities may be a major factor in the occurrence of normlessness at the higher socioeconomic levels. Professionals and businessmen have a much clearer awareness than others have of how norms actually work in the regulation of conduct. Because of this they become much more highly skilled in covering up violations of social norms and in evading the sanctions by which social norms are ordinarily enforced. Ralph Wahrman (1970: 229) has noted the preferential treatment of higher-status individuals as follows:

...The higher one's status the more reluctant is the group to define him as deviant. Severe sanctions occur only when the actor is perceived to have not only technically violated a norm, but also to have no acceptable justification for having done so. The higher one's status, the more willing is the group to find or invent an acceptable justification or set of mitigating circumstances for the behavior. They may even deny that the act took place. These responses make necessary only the mildest of sanctions or no sanctions at all.

Social deviancy may be defined as behavior that departs from normative standards in a disapproved direction and that exceeds the tolerance limits of the broader community (Clinard, 1968). From a social psychological standpoint, we should not think of people as being deviants, but instead limit the concept of deviance to behavior that departs from community standards in an unacceptable direction. Any society will tolerate some degree of norm violation, and those who engage in specific acts of deviancy may or may not accept the value system of the larger society. Behavior becomes deviant only when the failure to comply with social norms becomes unacceptable and constitutes a basis for the application of group sanctions.

William Simon and John H. Gagnon (1976) make a distinction between deviancy that occurs under conditions of scarcity and deviancy that is accompanied by abundance and affluence. For those who have easy access to desired goals, a major problem is to derive a sense of gratification and self-fulfillment from one's commitments. The attainment of specific goals may not be gratifying unless individuals perceive some set of limits to what is possible. Since conditions of abundance greatly extend the range of the possible, individuals may face the problem of insatiable desires: the more they have the more they want and the less satisfying the obtained benefits become at any given time (Durkheim, 1964).

The problems of normlessness in business, government, and the professions derive not from blocked opportunities, but from readily available opportunities for attaining goals by means other than thrift, hard work, and job dedication. Though people often associate the crime problem with the offenses committed by lower-class individuals, Edwin H. Sutherland (1949) chose to direct his attention toward the numerous offenses committed by those in middle-class occupations. These are forms of normlessness that occur among individuals who are highly respected and looked up to in their communities and in their society. These offenses do not evoke responses of indignation as do those involving crimes of violence, such as armed robbery and rape, but they do have the effect of undermining public confidence in the basic institutions of society (McCaghy, 1976). (See Box 3.5.)

Normlessness among white collar workers typically consists of offenses involving some form of deception, misrepresentation, or violation of a position of trust. Since most middle-class individuals carry out their occupational functions within the confines of a large-scale organization, there is a moral imperative that their efforts be directed toward advancing the interests of their employers rather than themselves. Deviance within this context derives from enhancing one's own personal interests at the expense of a variety of constituents. These include offenses against one's employer (embezzlement and company theft), against one's clients (deceptive advertising, price fixing), against one's community (environmental pollution), and against the state (income-tax evasion).

The normlessness that occurs among the middle and upper classes derives not only from access to resources and opportunities, but also from the development of skills for neutralizing the effects of social norms. Gresham Sykes and David Matza (1957) regarded **neutralization** as the process by which individuals develop justifications for deviant acts. The following are examples of arguments intended to deflect the stigma attached to being caught violating a social norm:

> **BOX 3.5**
> **The Myth of Social Class and Criminality**
>
> Drawing on official statistics, numerous criminologists until recently emphasized the importance of social class as a major predictor of variations in crime rates. Numerous studies indicated that crime rates were higher at the lower socio-economic levels, and that the city areas characterized by high crime rates were disproportionately comprised of lower-class individuals. However, conclusions from data on high-crime areas tend to be misleading and unwarranted. Crimes have a high visibility in the inner city, and they are often committed by transients in the area rather than by the people who live there.
>
> The research findings indicating that the lower classes commit more crimes were in part a function of the decade in which the studies were made. More recent studies of court records show fewer differences in crime rates by social class than was the case in the 1950s and the early 1960s. The recent convergence in the crime rates across social classes in the official statistics probably does not reflect any historical change in behavior but rather an increased awareness of the legal rights of the underprivileged and a change in the manner in which the criminal justice agencies deal with the members of different social classes.
>
> Studies of self-reports on criminal conduct reveal very few differences in crime rates by social class level. From an analysis of the results of thirty-five separate studies, Tittle, Villemez and Smith (1978) concluded that the overall evidence in support of a relationship between social class and criminal behavior is negligible. Recent crime statistics show little difference in overall crime rates by social class, and studies of self-reported crimes show even less.
>
> *Source:* Charles R. Tittle, Wayne J. Villemez, and Douglas A. Smith, "The Myth of Social Class and Criminality: An Empirical Assessment of the Empirical Evidence," *American Sociological Review* 43 (October, 1978): 643–656.

"It really wasn't my fault" (denial of responsibility).
"I didn't really hurt anyone" (denial of injury).
"They had it coming to them" (blaming the victim).
"Everybody's picking on me" (condemning the condemners).
"I didn't do it for myself" (appeal to higher loyalties).

Sykes and Matza (1957) regarded these kinds of arguments as working within the dominant normative system rather than creating opposing values. The techniques of neutralization draw on the patterns of thought that are prevalent within society, and people use them for evading the sanctions by which social norms are enforced. Although one may find such techniques at all social class levels, they become much more convincing and persuasive when they are presented by individuals who hold positions of authority and respectability within the community.

3. Societal Reactions to Deviance

To adequately understand the place of social norms in modern social life requires that we examine the societal reactions to deviance as well as the numerous causes of rule violations. The societal reactions to deviance include a wide range of attitudes and behavior on the part of those who have an awareness that social norms have been violated. Those who read newspapers, those who become victims of crimes, and those who make judgments about the manners and morals of our times are reacting to the problems of deviance and social control. The societal reactions that are official, however, are vested within the criminal justice system. These include the societal reactions of those who are authorized to make the laws as well as those who have the authority to impose legal sanctions in cases where violations have occurred.

Social control agencies select cases to clarify social norms and to demonstrate the kinds of sanctions that can be invoked if rules are violated. In this respect, Kai T. Erikson (1962) has suggested that deviance is a "vital resource" in human organization, since it establishes the moral boundaries within which socially acceptable conduct is located. Society tolerates some deviant activities and absorbs them into the mainstream of social life. Many aspects of rule violation receive little or no attention among social control agencies, and as a result a selective process operates to designate only certain individuals as deviants.

is this always effective?

We can derive evidence for the selective enforcement of social norms from several sources. Studies of self-reports on criminal conduct indicate that most violations of the law are never detected or reported to the police. Among the crimes known to the police, very few ever result in an actual arrest. Among those persons charged with crimes, many are never prosecuted or convicted. And among those who are convicted, very few actually serve prison sentences. Thus a highly selective process operates in the criminal justice system through the choosing of cases to prosecute for the enforcement of social norms. This process is one of designating and labeling certain individuals as deviants, and is controlled by several factors.

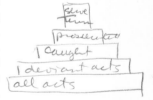

In part, the selection of specific individuals as deviants depends on the clarity of the evidence that a violation has occurred and that a conviction can be obtained. However, numerous other considerations enter into the readiness of the police and the courts to invoke legal sanctions. These include several aspects of the process of social interaction between the accused and the agencies of the criminal justice system. For example, juveniles who oppose police authority by resisting arrest are more likely to receive harsh treatment by the courts, somewhat independently of the alleged deviant acts (Bernstein *et al.*, 1977). Thus the demeanor of the accused and the level of hostility the accused expresses toward the criminal justice system have an effect on the harshness of the punishment invoked.

The selective enforcement of social norms also derives from the discretionary powers that have been given to the courts in the disposition of given cases. Since the more privileged segments of society create and maintain the criminal justice system, there is a tendency for poor people and members of minority groups to receive harsher treatment than their more privileged counterparts in the middle and upper classes (Chambliss and Seidman, 1971). For example, the research of H. A. Bedau (1965) indicates that in states with capital punishment, the death penalty is applied disproportionately to males and to those who are poor and uneducated. Other studies have shown similar effects of socioeconomic status in the disposition of cases involving grand larceny and assault. Members of the lower classes are overrepresented among those charged with these offenses as well as among those who receive a prison sentence (Nagel, 1969). (See Figure 3.2.)

The well-educated and privileged members of a society have the resources necessary for justifying their conduct and for defending themselves against the deviant label. They are likely to be respected by their neighbors and acquaintances, and to share many values and interests with their communities,

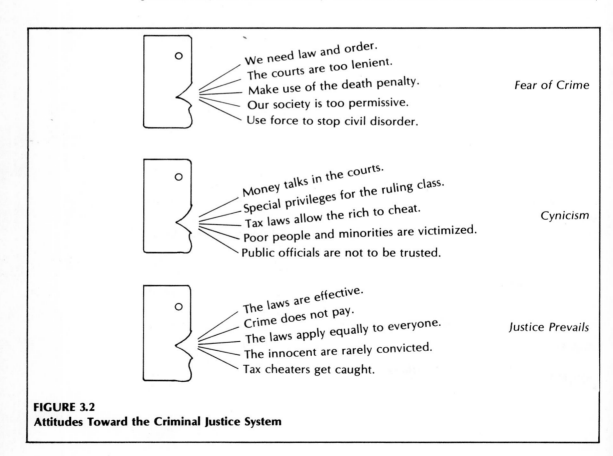

We need law and order.
The courts are too lenient.
Make use of the death penalty.
Our society is too permissive.
Use force to stop civil disorder.

Fear of Crime

Money talks in the courts.
Special privileges for the ruling class.
Tax laws allow the rich to cheat.
Poor people and minorities are victimized.
Public officials are not to be trusted.

Cynicism

The laws are effective.
Crime does not pay.
The laws apply equally to everyone.
The innocent are rarely convicted.
Tax cheaters get caught.

Justice Prevails

FIGURE 3.2
Attitudes Toward the Criminal Justice System

and to have powerful and influential friends that may provide help when needed. If troubles with the law do develop, higher status individuals have the resources necessary for securing the services of lawyers who may draw upon the intricacies of the law for obtaining delays, dismissals, or acquittals.

The harsh treatment the less-privileged members of society often receive derives in part from social attitudes the general public has toward the characteristics of those who are more likely to commit certain kinds of offenses. The research of J. L. Simmons (1965) on public stereotypes indicates that several varieties of deviants are often looked on as "maladjusted," "insecure," "weak-minded," "irresponsible," "frustrated," "impulsive," "aggressive," "abnormal," and "dangerous." Such folk attitudes toward the attributes of deviants has a bearing not only on the selective process by which certain individuals are designated as deviants but also on societal reactions to those labeled deviant.

Initial violations of the law may occur for a wide variety of reasons, and the objectionable behavior may be only a small part of the total life organization of an individual. But, if a youthful offender is designated as a deviant by the criminal justice system, this can influence the responses by friends, peers, and significant others. It may make it more difficult for the person to get a job; former friends may shun or avoid the offender; and to obtain social support and understanding, the offender may drift toward others who are also designated as deviants.

While the designation of deviants primarily serves the function of clarifying the nature of the norms and the potential consequences of their violation, the labeling of certain individuals also has the effect of producing what has been called **secondary deviance** (Lemert, 1967). This occurs as a result of altered social reactions to individuals who have such labels bestowed on them as prostitute, child molester, burglar, or embezzler. Since people tend to respond to others on the basis of their definitions of the situation, the label of deviant becomes a type of self-fulfilling prophecy in the production of subsequent deviance. From the expectations and role definitions a person receives from others, a pattern of deviance may take on increased social significance and become a major part of the individual's total life organization.

D. EXCUSES AND JUSTIFICATIONS

In everyday life, social norms involve much more than a set of enforceable rules for the regulation of conduct. Norms are used to organize experience and to maintain orderly sets of social relationships. Social rules may be clear enough as an abstract set of principles, but their applications in everyday life frequently are surrounded by uncertainty. The practical accomplishments of everyday life involve much more than using norms as a blueprint for behavior. People also draw on norms for making sense out of their own actions as well as out of the actions of other people.

The concern about normative conduct in interpersonal relationships grows out of problematic situations. When confusion develops over something that has happened, a person's behavior becomes subject to evaluation inquiry. This takes the form of a *why* question: others request or demand an explanation for the behavior in question. Explanations are required under those conditions in which the person has been caught in a socially unacceptable form of conduct, there has been a failure to conform to "the rules of the game," someone is being required "to pay up," or the person is "having his (or her) day in court." Under these circumstances, the person in question seeks to find a justification for his or her conduct that will be socially acceptable. The concern is with "getting off the hook," and the degree of success in doing this depends on the plausibility of the explanation offered.

1. Offering Accounts

Marvin Scott and Stanford Lyman (1968) describe the process of explaining or justifying behavior to relevant others as one of offering an **account.** They define an account as a verbal statement made by a social actor to explain unanticipated or untoward conduct. Since explanations of an individual's behavior are usually called for in a face-to-face relationship, the actor is likely to create an excuse or a justification the person perceives to be both socially acceptable and compatible with his or her own self-image. This involves an attempt to align motives, responses, and performances with self-evaluations as well as with the shared frameworks of meaning in given societies and subgroups (Stokes and Hewitt, 1976).

Some questions about the reasons for conduct are not asked because they have been settled in advance through the commonly held expectations of everyday life. These types of taken-for-granted behavior consist of what Harold Garfinkel (1964) calls "the routine grounds of everyday activities." Such behavior is taken for granted because it has not occurred to either the actor or the coparticipant to make it problematic.

If this behavior *is* made problematic, the response is likely to be one of anger and hostility, as Garfinkel and his students have demonstrated in several empirical studies. This response in part results from the perceived inappropriateness of probing too deeply into the grounds of everyday activities and in part results from the lack of understanding and acceptable justification for what is taken for granted. For example, in the exchange of the greeting, "How are you?" we do not really want to know the respective details of the physical and mental well-being of the other person, nor do we consider it socially appropriate to inquire why the other person asked the question or what kinds of information the other person seeks. The verbal exchanges are at a superficial level, and the individual who probes deeply into their hidden meaning is behaving inappropriately.

Explanations may be required or demanded, however, when the behavior appears to fall outside the boundaries of acceptable conduct. Under such a circumstance, as Scott and Lyman (1968) note, a person may offer two major types of accounts: excuses and justifications. An **excuse** is an account that admits to the inappropriateness of the conduct but denies full responsibility for its occurrence. On the other hand, a **justification** consists of accepting respon-

---

BOX 3.6
Justifications for a Deviant Sport

Despite its illegality, cockfighting persists as a widespread practice throughout the United States. As a martial sport, cockfighting consists of matching gamecocks in an arena for a battle that ends in the death of one or the other of the combatants. The central issues that cockfighters face are those of the "riffraff" images of participants and the alleged cruelty of the sport. McCaghy and Neal (1974) have identified a series of arguments cockfighters present to neutralize the stigma of the sport. Some of the ethical embellishments of cockfighting consist of the following:

1. Historical precedent—Cockfighting is one of the oldest known sports. It was very popular in the early seats of civilization, including ancient China, Greece, Rome, and early England.
2. Notable participants—Interest in cockfighting as a sport was held by some of the most famous men in history. Allegedly, famous breeders and fighters of gamecocks included George Washington, Thomas Jefferson, John Adams, Henry Clay, Andrew Jackson, and Abraham Lincoln. Other notables included Alexander the Great, Caesar, Hannibal, and Ghengis Khan.
3. Model to emulate—The gamecock is seen as emblematic of courage, commitment, and a variety of other virtues that are worthy of human emulation.
4. Altruism—The very existence of the gamecock is dependent on the breeding and special care received from the cockfighter. Through genetic selection, conditioning, and survival of the fittest, the intrinsic qualities of the gamecock are continuing to be enhanced.
5. Naturalism—Gamecocks are natural-born fighters that enter into battle voluntarily and with enthusiasm.
6. Self-actualization—Through being victorious in battle, gamecocks attain their highest possible level of accomplishment.

From acceptance of the above assumptions, it follows that cockfighting may not be appropriately viewed as a form of cruelty. Instead, cockfighters view the activity as one of the most humane and exemplary of sports.

Source: Charles H. McCaghy and Arthur G. Neal, "The Fraternity of Cockfighters: Ethical Embellishments of an Illegal Sport," *Journal of Popular Culture* 8 (Winter, 1974): 557–569.

sibility for an action while denying the claim that there was anything wrong with it. (See Box 3.6.)

In developing excuses, the individuals draw on socially approved vocabularies to explain why they are not accepting responsibility for the action in question. Scott and Lyman noted that excuses very often take on the form of explaining how the conduct was not one's own fault: it was the result of an accidental happening; or it was caused by uncontrollable biological urges; or one failed to be fully informed; or one came to be used as a scapegoat. In the accident, one is not personally responsible because the event was neither intended nor subject to personal control. An individual may also attempt to excuse an action on the grounds that certain relevant information was not available, and if it had been, his or her behavior would have been different. A more complex disclaimer consists of some variation on the notion that one is a victim of scapegoating. Here the emphasis is on the view of being falsely accused and selected out to bear the brunt of the responsibility for a happening that was actually caused by someone else.

In the emphasis on biological explanations, the individual considers his or her behavior to be motivated by drives and urges that are uncontrollable. This line of excuses is especially applicable to sexual misconduct. In excuses for premarital and extramarital sexual behavior, the accounts within cultural subgroups invoke some variant of the notions that "it's human nature," "men are like that," "she was asking for it," "there is something biological that causes it," or "something just happened." These accounts embody the view that the mysterious inner working of biological forces produced the socially unacceptable outcomes, and as a result the actor is relieved of full responsibility. The extent to which such accounts are acceptable depends on their compatibility with the generalized values and interpretations held in common by the actor and his or her audience.

2. Honoring Accounts (Justifications)

In admitting responsibility for one's conduct, the individual may attempt to disavow any implication that the behavior was wrong or inappropriate. This may take a variety of forms, such as maintaining that the behavior was actually of a positive rather than of a negative character, that a particular act was permissible because no one was injured, that the victim deserved to be injured, or that the conduct was actually praiseworthy because it was motivated by a sense of loyalty to others. These arguments are clearly recognizable in the accounts that accompany the occurrence of political scandals, as well as the numerous disruptions that occur in daily life.

Whether or not any of these explanations are honored as being justified in any particular case depends on the qualities of the social relationship. The acceptability of an account is closely related to negotiating the identities of

In Jail

Those visited in jail are men and women who have failed to give socially acceptable accounts of their conduct.

both the actor and the viewing audience since this has implications for the continuation of a social relationship. The processing of accounts is fraught with potential embarrassment, and as a result the transaction becomes one of devising ways to save face to maintain the poise and stability of the relationship (Ho, 1976). The offering of accounts and their acceptance or rejection help to clarify what people do, who they are, and where they are located in their relationships with one another.

The normalcy of individuals in any society depends on their capacity to offer acceptable accounts for overt performances. Serious and repeated breaches of social expectations are very often associated with mental illness if the individuals do not present adequate explanations. In this connection, Philip Blumstein (1974: 565) has observed, "It cannot be overstated that people respond to our symbolic restructuring of our deeds, much more so than to the deeds themselves." The symbolic restructuring of our deeds involves the use of socially approved vocabularies for neutralizing the problematic character of conduct and its consequences. Success in doing this requires an awareness of the strengths and weaknesses of one's own position in relationship to that of others, as well as being sensitive to the kinds of persuasive arguments and explanations that are likely to be honored in any given case.

Blumstein (1974) has found that the honoring of an account depends on the perceived integrity of the individual as well as on the credibility of the account the individual offers. The usual sense of social responsibility on the part of an actor may suggest that the offensiveness of the behavior in question was

---

BOX 3.7
On the Use of Disclaimers — *accts used before theaction*

Hewitt and Stokes define a **disclaimer** as "a verbal device employed to ward off and defeat in advance doubts and negative typifications which may result from intended conduct" (1975:3). These are devices used in the hope that one's plan of action will not disrupt a set of social relationships through an undesirable definition of the situation. Among the types of disclaimers Hewitt and Stokes identify are the following:

Hedging—a qualification of an opinion or an intended line of action by expressing uncertainty about its adequacy. The language of hedging is expressed in preface statements such as "I could be wrong on my facts, but...."; "I'm no expert, of course, but....."; "Just off the top of my head, it seems....."; "I'm not sure this is going to work, but let's....." Such qualifiers permit the testing out of one's ideas or plan of action without having to fully defend them in the face of opposition from others.

Sin Licenses—paying due respect to social rules for the regulation of conduct, while at the same time establishing the conditions under which they may be violated. Examples of this type of disclaimer may be found in such comments as "I realize that you may think this is the wrong thing to do, but...."; "This is technically against the law, however....."; "I know this is against the rules, but....." Such disclaimers announce in advance one's intent to violate a rule while presenting the justification for doing so.

Appeals for the suspension of judgment—a plea for others to withhold their anger or dismay over some particular act until an adequate or "correct" explanation has been given. The request for a suspension of judgment is expressed in such phrases as "don't react until I have had time to finish"; "hear me out before you explode"; "don't get me wrong, but....." The request for a suspension of judgment is oriented toward permitting the listener to have all of the relevant information before arriving at a conclusion.

The use of these and other disclaimers are interaction tactics employed by individuals faced with upcoming events that are recognized as having potentially disruptive effects on a set of social relationships. The concern is for minimizing the consequences of problematic conduct.

Source: John P. Hewitt and Randall Stokes, "Disclaimers," *American Sociological Review* 40 (February, 1975): 1–11.

out of character and that the person is not likely to repeat it. In such cases the individual is expected to recognize the offensiveness of his or her actions, to offer some form of apology, and to promise that such conduct will not happen again. The acceptability of an account also depends on its adequacy and its credibility. The responding audience must find the explanation believable in order for all involved to repair the damage and restore the qualities of the relationship. (See Box 3.7.)

While accounts are essentially verbal statements to explain the grounds for problematic conduct, they are not always expressed in face-to-face situations. Instead, one often invents and refines excuses and justifications while thinking about embarking on a particular course of action. One may anticipate in advance the questions others might raise about what one is doing or about to do. In this respect, social justifications and excuses tend to serve as social control mechanisms. If one cannot develop an adequate explanation for a course of action that will be compatible with one's identity, or if the plans appear to be unacceptable to others, the person may abandon the line of action altogether. Here the implication is that the internalized conceptions of self and society shape the boundaries around which the gamesmanship and the theatrics of social life are enacted. The anticipated reactions of others serve as constraints on one's proneness to act impulsively in a socially unapproved way.

SUMMARY

The normality of everyday life is dependent on the degree to which we are able to make predictions with a reasonable degree of accuracy about the outcomes of our relationships with other people. These predictions consist of assumptions about the continuity of social life as we know and understand it, about the adequacy of our knowledge to manage and control events, and about the correspondence between our own understanding of events and the understanding of others.

If these assumptions are sustained, social life proceeds in an orderly fashion. A failure to receive support for these assumptions may result in a crisis of meaning. The central component of a crisis of meaning is uncertainty, and this may be expressed in the form of the perceived complexity of events, in the problem of exposure to competing social pressures, and in the feeling that social life as one knows and understands it lacks a clarity of direction and purpose. Conditions of meaninglessness are associated with a lack of confidence in the making of plans for the future and with the feeling that one's life is drifting and being shaped by forces one cannot adequately control.

Predictions about what most people are likely to do in a given situation reflect notions about the rules that guide decision making and conduct. Social norms tend to lack effectiveness in regulating conduct if they are in conflict with each other and if individuals are blocked in their opportunities for attaining cultural goals through the use of socially approved means. Normlessness is also likely to occur under those conditions in which individuals are able to avoid the sanctions by which social norms are enforced. People frequently violate social norms, but society selects and designates only certain individuals as deviants. The societal reactions to deviance consist of some degree of emphasis on the use of punishment to establish the moral boundaries of socially approved conduct. After individuals are labeled deviant, a self-fulfilling prophecy often results, which increases the probability for further deviant acts.

The normalcy of the individual in any society is dependent on his or her capacity to use socially approved vocabularies for justifying conduct. The social group will require or demand explanations when the behavior of an actor fails to measure up to the group's standards. Offering an account becomes a means of saving face when a person's behavior is subjected to evaluative inquiry. Individuals offer accounts as either excuses or justifications. If the explanations given are adequate, the individual avoids embarrassment and the integrity of the social relationship is maintained. Social norms are thus vocabularies for talking about personal experiences and motives, as well as agreed-on rules for the regulation of conduct.

BASIC TERMS

Normality	Neutralization
Generalized other	Secondary deviance
Crisis of meaning	Account
Normlessness	Excuse
Retreatism	Justification
Social deviancy	Disclaimer

REFERENCES

Akers, Ronald L.
    1973 *Deviant Behavior,* Belmont, Calif.: Wadsworth.
Becker, Howard S.
    1963 *Outsiders,* New York: The Free Press.
Bedau, H. A.
    1965 "Capital Punishment in Oregon, 1903–64," *Oregon Law Review* 45: 1–37.
Bernstein, Ilene Nagel, William R. Kelly, and Patricia A. Doyle
    1977 "Societal Reactions to Deviants," *American Sociological Review* 42 (October): 743–755.
Blumstein, Philip W.
    1974 "The Honoring of Accounts," *American Sociological Review* 39 (August): 551–566.

Chambliss, William J. and Robert B. Seidman
  1971 *Law, Order, and Power*, Reading, Ma.: Addison-Wesley.
Clinard, Marshall B.
  1968 *Sociology of Deviant Behavior*, New York: Holt, Rinehart, & Winston.
Cloward, Richard A.
  1959 "Illegitimate Means, Anomie, and Deviant Behavior," *American Sociological Review* 24 (April): 164–176.
Cloward, Richard A. and Lloyd E. Ohlin
  1960 *Delinquency and Opportunity*, Glencoe, Ill.: The Free Press.
Cohen, Albert K.
  1955 *Delinquent Boys*, Glencoe, Ill.: The Free Press.
Davis, Nanette J.
  1972 "Labeling Theory in Deviance Research," *Sociological Quarterly* 13 (Fall): 447–474.
Dohrenwend, Barbara Snell
  1973 "Life Events as Stressors," *Journal of Health and Social Behavior* 14: 167–175.
Dohrenwend, Barbara Snell and Bruce P. Dohrenwend
  1974 *Stressful Life Events*, New York: John Wiley.
Durkheim, Emile
  1964 *The Division of Labor in Society*, New York: The Free Press.
Erikson, Kai T.
  1962 "Notes on the Sociology of Deviance," *Social Problems* 9 (Spring): 307–314.
Finifter, Ada W.
  1972 *Alienation and the Social System*, New York: John Wiley.
Garfinkel, Harold
  1964 "Studies of the Routine Grounds of Everyday Activities," *Social Problems* 11 (Fall): 225–250.
Hewitt, John P. and Randall Stokes
  1975 "Disclaimers," *American Sociological Review* 40 (February): 1–11.
Ho, David Yau-fai
  1976 "On the Concept of Face," *American Journal of Sociology* 81 (January): 867–884.
Hogan, Dennis P.
  1978 "The Variable Order of Events in the Life Course," *American Sociological Review* 43 (August): 573–586.
Holmes, Thomas H. and Richard M. Rahe
  1967 "The Social Readjustment Rating Scale," *Journal of Psychosomatic Research* 11: 213–218.
James, William
  1890 *Principles of Psychology*, New York: Holt.
Janis, Irving and Dan Wheeler
  1978 "Thinking Clearly about Career Choices," *Psychology Today* 11 (May): 67f.
Lemert, Edwin M.
  1967 *Human Deviance, Social Problems, and Social Control*, Englewood Cliffs, N.J.: Prentice-Hall.
Light, Ivan
  1977 "The Ethnic Vice Industry, 1880–1944," *American Sociological Review* 42 (June): 464–479.
McCaghy, Charles H.

1976 *Deviant Behavior*, New York: Macmillan.

McCaghy, Charles H. and Arthur G. Neal
1974 "The Fraternity of Cockfighters: Ethical Embellishments of an Illegal Sport," *Journal of Popular Culture* 8 (Winter): 557–569.

Mead, George Herbert
1934 *Mind, Self, and Society*, Chicago: University of Chicago Press.

Merton, Robert K.
1957 *Social Theory and Social Structure*, Glencoe, Ill.: The Free Press.

Mills, C. Wright
1963 "Situated Actions and the Vocabularies of Motive," in Irving L. Horowitz (ed.), *Power, Politics, and People*, New York: Ballantine, pp. 439–452.

Myers, Jerome K., Jacob L. Lindenthal, and Max P. Pepper
1975 "Life Events, Social Integration, and Psychiatric Symptomatology," *Journal of Health and Social Behavior* 16:421–427.

Myers, Jerome K., Jacob L. Lindenthal, Max P. Pepper, and David R. Ostrander
1972 "Life Events and Mental Status," *Journal of Health and Social Behavior* 13: 398–406.

Nagel, Stuart S.
1969 *The Legal Process from a Behavioral Perspective*, Homewood, Ill.: Dorsey Press.

Neal, Arthur G. and Salomon Rettig
1967 "On the Multidimensionality of Alienation," *American Sociological Review* 32 (February): 54–64.

Parenti, Michael
1978 *Power and the Powerless*, New York: St. Martin's Press.

Parsons, Talcott
1972 "Religious Perspectives in Sociology and Social Psychology," in William A. Lessa and Evon Z. Vogt (eds.), *Reader in Comparative Religion*, New York: Harper & Row, pp. 88–93.

Pollis, Nicholas P. and Carol A. Pollis
1970 "Sociological Referents of Social Norms," *Sociological Quarterly* 11 (Spring): 230–242.

Presthus, Robert
1978 *The Organizational Society*, New York: St. Martin's Press.

Ruch, Libby O.
1977 "A Multidimensional Analysis of the Concept of Life Change," *Journal of Health and Social Behavior* 18 (March): 71–83.

Schrager, Laura Shill and James F. Short, Jr.
1978 "Toward a Sociology of Organizational Crime," *Social Problems* 25 (April): 407–419.

Schutz, Alfred
1971 *Collected Papers 1: The Problem of Social Reality*, The Hague: Martinus Nijhoff.

Scott, Marvin B. and Stanford M. Lyman
1968 "Accounts," *American Sociological Review* 33 (February): 46–62.

Seeman, Melvin
1975 "Alienation Studies," *Annual Review of Sociology* 1: 91–124.

1959 "On the Meaning of Alienation," *American Sociological Review* 24 (December): 783–791.

Simmons, J. L.

1965 "Public Stereotypes of Deviants," *Social Problems* 13 (Fall): 223–232.

Simon, William and John H. Gagnon

1976 "The Anomie of Affluence: A Post-Mertonian Conception," *American Journal of Sociology* 82 (September): 356–378.

Srole, Leo

1956 "Social Integration and Certain Corollaries," *American Sociological Review* 21 (December): 709–716.

Stokes, Randall and John P. Hewitt

1976 "Aligning Actions," *American Sociological Review* 41 (October): 838–849.

Sutherland, Edwin H.

1949 *White Collar Crime*, New York: Holt, Rinehart & Winston.

Sykes, Gresham M. and David Matza

1957 "Techniques of Neutralization," *American Sociological Review* 22 (December): 664–670.

Tittle, Charles R., Wayne J. Villemez, and Douglas A. Smith

1978 "The Myth of Social Class and Criminality: An Empirical Assessment of the Empirical Evidence," *American Sociological Review* 43 (October): 643–656.

Toffler, Alvin

1971 *Future Shock*, New York: Random House.

Wahrman, Ralph

1970 "Status, Deviance, and Sanctions," *Pacific Sociological Review* 13 (Fall): 229–240.

Wiebe, Robert H.

1975 *The Segmented Society*, New York: Oxford University Press.

Yinger, J. Milton

1965 *Toward a Field Theory of Behavior*, New York: McGraw-Hill.

What to look for in this chapter:

What are the major components of an attitude?
How are attitudes formed?
Why do people differ in the attitudes they hold?
What are the relationships between attitudes and behavior?

Attitudes

The effectiveness of social norms in regulating conduct is dependent to a very large degree on the distribution of attitudes within a social group. If people look on social norms favorably, they are likely to obey them. But if social norms fail to align with the perceptions and evaluations of individuals, then people are likely to ignore or violate such norms. Social norms are realities residing outside the individual, who must confront them as an aspect of group living. By way of contrast, attitudes fall within the subjective domain. They are realities that social actors construct in their attempts to make sense out of the world around them.

Def norm

The study of attitudes has provided one of the more important contributions of social psychologists to the study of human behavior. Since individuals tend to act on the basis of their own understanding and evaluations, the explanation of numerous aspects of social behavior is dependent on knowing how attitudes are distributed within a population. Over the past several decades, the refinements in measuring and sampling techniques have enhanced greatly the value of survey research. The measurement of attitudes and the study of their distribution within a population has had both theoretical and applied implications.

For an adequate understanding of the dynamics of modern social life, we need to take into account the assessments of events that individuals make. The attitudes of consumers shape the potential markets for the products of modern industry. The preferences for one type of television programming compared to some other determine the boundaries within which the major networks develop their schedules. The planning of the successful political campaign is often dependent on information about the public attitudes toward major political problems and their proposed solutions. Understanding of numerous aspects of social behavior is then dependent on knowing why individuals differ in the intensity with which they hold certain attitudes and how social attitudes enter into decisions to follow one course of action compared to another.

The primary assumption of attitude research is that people themselves are an important source of information about social life. The researcher, rather

TABLE 4.1
Selective List of Attitude Scales

Some attitudes measured by social psychologists

Religiosity	Authoritarianism
Sexual permissiveness	Dogmatism
Occupational prestige ratings	Machiavellianism
Social distance	Powerlessness
Job dissatisfaction	Normlessness
Community solidarity	Social isolation
Marital happiness	Anomie
Militarism-pacifism	Status-concern
Life satisfaction	Intolerance of ambiguity
Self-esteem	Radicalism-conservatism
Self-acceptance	Personal values inventory
Self-estrangement	Social responsibility
Internal versus external locus of control	Misanthropy

Sources: Charles M. Bonjean, Richard J. Hill, and S. Dale McLemore, *Sociological Measurement: An Inventory of Scales,* San Francisco: Chandler, 1967; Delbert C. Miller, *Handbook of Research Design and Social Measurement,* 3rd edition, New York: David McKay, 1977; John P. Robinson and Phillip R. Shaver, *Measures of Social Psychological Attitudes,* Ann Arbor: Institute for Social Research, University of Michigan, 1973.

than guess the kinds of meaning individuals ascribe to social events, can assess the definitions of given situations from the standpoint of individual actors. The investigator can determine the distribution of attitudes within a given population through scientific sampling techniques and questionnaires. We may realize the importance of using attitude scales by noting the results of a study by Charles Bonjean, Richard Hill, and Dale McLemore (1967) which concentrated on measures sociologists employ. Their analysis indicated that over a twelve-year interval, the measures reported in the four leading sociology journals (*American Sociological Review, American Journal of Sociology, Social Forces,* and *Sociometry*) included about 2000 different scales, most of which consisted of the measurement of attitudes. These results suggest that the tasks involved in the analysis of attitudes rank pretty high among the priorities of contemporary social psychologists. (See Table 4.1.)

The importance of attitudes in the study of social behavior derives from the correspondence between evaluations we make about aspects of social life and the lines of action we pursue in relationship to these evaluations. This is not to imply that there is a one-to-one relationship between the attitudes we hold and the course of action we follow. To the contrary, there are numerous constraints inherent in social living that lessen the likelihood for action in a direct and forthright manner that is consistent with the attitudes we hold. Attitudes are meanings we construct to serve as general orientations toward events, while our behavior is grounded in immediate and specific situations.

In observing the separability of attitudes and behavior, we should not infer that one is necessarily of greater importance than the other in the overall character of social life. Instead, we may regard attitudes and behavior more appropriately as equally important but separable dimensions of social reality. Overt behavior has a direct bearing on social relationships in immediate situations, while underlying attitudes relate to the overall qualities assigned to social life. The degree of comfort we feel toward our life circumstances is in part dependent on the extent to which we are able to act in a fashion that corresponds to our understanding and evaluation of events.

attitude vs behavior

An Extremist Attitude
This billboard, located near Angola, Indiana, expressed an extremist attitude in the summer of 1980. It was a response to the national frustrations that resulted when Americans were taken hostage in Iran during the fall of 1979.

A. THE NATURE OF ATTITUDES

Because the attitude concept is so central to social psychological inquiry, many definitions have been presented as guides to research. In the history of social psychology, researchers tried out and rejected several specific definitions either because the definitions rested on false assumptions or because the definitions were too narrow and limited. In the early days of attitude research, investigators defined **attitudes** as "the energizers of behavior," as constituting "an implicit readiness to respond" or as "a predisposition to behave" in a particular fashion, or as "the triggering mechanism" that intervenes between understanding and action. The guiding assumption of these definitions was that the study of attitudes would greatly increase the prospects for predicting human behavior. These early researchers were overlooking the important gaps between what people think and say and what they actually do (Deutscher, 1973). Today we are aware that the linkages between attitudes and behavior are more complicated than earlier investigators imagined.

From several decades of research on attitudes, we now know that attitudes have limited effectiveness in predicting the behavior of specific individuals in specific situations. We do know, however, that attitudes can be effective as predictors of behavior trends when we draw on large samples and have information on the distribution of attitudes within a population. We also know that there are several components to take into account in defining and analyzing attitudes. An attitude involves much more than "the immediate nexus," "the trigger," or "the energizer" of behavior. There is now general consensus that an adequate analysis of attitudes must take into account the components of cognition, affectivity, and behavior tendencies. In combination, these components represent the scope and boundaries of attitude research.

The **cognitive component** of an attitude refers to perceptions and beliefs about the qualities and attributes of an object, situation, or event. Cognitions are reality perceptions—knowledge and information about what exists. They can be thought of as mental pictures for mapping the environment. People differ in their reality perceptions, and such differences help to explain the variations in attitudes. For example, differential religious attitudes are based on differences in beliefs about the realities of God, human immortality, and the sacred grounds for moral conduct. Some believe in the existence of God and life after death, while others do not. Such reality perceptions are important for attitudes toward the church as a social institution and are likely to influence the kinds and degrees of religious participation.

The **affectivity component** of an attitude refers to the feelings, sentiments, and emotions associated with reality perceptions. Such emotions as fear, hate, love, anger, sympathy, envy, and contempt are among the varied responses an individual can have to persons, places, objects, and events. The affectivity side of attitudes is expressed through such verbal statements as "I like Christmas," "I despise TV commercials," "I hate my boss," "I sympathize with the poor," "I am afraid of snakes," and "I envy the good tennis player." Such displays of sentiment and emotion reveal important aspects of an individual's attitudes. While the investigator can separate affectivity and cognition analytically, they frequently occur together because people are seldom neutral or indifferent to their experiences and environments.

The **behavioral component** refers to the intentions and action tendencies associated with objects, situations, and events. It is important to recognize that this aspect of an attitude relates to intentions or predispositions, rather than to actual behavior. Many of our attitudes do not contain any direct plan of action, and our inclinations frequently are inconsistent with our actual behavior. For example, our attitudes toward the morality (or immorality) of public officials usually do not serve as guidelines for any specific course of political action. Regardless of our attitudes toward the morality (or immorality) of public officials, we continue to pay our taxes, obey most enacted laws, and may or may not vote when an election is held. Many eighteen year olds who strongly oppose war and military preparation as a national policy still registered for the draft when legally required to do so. As a result of the gap between what people think and what they do, it is important to separate the behavioral from the cognitive and affective components in the study of attitudes.

From this discussion of components, we can define an attitude as the interplay between the cognitions, the emotional evaluations, and the action tendencies the individual associates with persons, objects, situations, and events. In effect, an attitude is a social orientation that expresses an inclination to respond, in some way or another, to reality perceptions and evaluations. The three components of an attitude serve to structure the social world for the individual and to give a sense of direction and purpose to the course of life events. Virtually any aspect of social life (motherhood, religion, authority, public officials, Christmas, marriage, and so forth) can be studied from the vantage point of the orientations that individuals bring to bear on these situations and events.

From this definition, we can think of attitude formation as expressing the process of attribution. Our attitudes do not emerge directly from the inherent characteristics of objects and events. Instead they derive from the meanings we construct from our experiences. For example, one way to attribute meaning to societal events is by pondering such causal questions as, How did it come to be so? or, Why did it happen? Why do nations prepare for war? Why is the rate of unemployment so high? Why is the cost of living going up so fast? Why are millions of Americans living under conditions of poverty? The actual causes as expressed by expert opinion or as determined by objective evidence may not correspond very well to the assessments any given social actor makes. Yet the evaluations people do make about the qualities and attributes of objects and events have a bearing on the level of support one type of public policy receives compared to another and on whether people pursue individual lines of action with vigor or avoid them altogether.

An Intensely Held Attitude
The person who holds an attitude with a strong level of conviction may feel obligated to share it with the rest of the world.

The communication of attitudes through interaction constitutes a very important part of the dynamics of social life. Communication provides a basis for testing the correctness of our own assessments by matching them with the evaluations that others make. Since many of our attitudes require social supports, we modify and refine them after receiving messages from social relationships. In other cases individuals hold attitudes with strong convictions and wish to promote particular points of view. This may take the form of public displays, in which the individuals express not only how they feel but also what they regard as the appropriate views for others to hold.

Attitude displays are public expressions of personal convictions about some social issue. One form of such displays is the use of bumper stickers. These frequently consist of slogans, which attempt to dramatize a personal concern for a social issue or call attention to some problem area being neglected.

TABLE 4.2
Bumper Stickers as Attitude Displays

A casual list of attitude displays recorded from bumper stickers:

WARNING: I BRAKE FOR ANIMALS
WARNING: I BRAKE FOR JOGGERS
HONK IF YOU LOVE JESUS
CHRIST IS THE ANSWER
DON'T BE GROUNDED...WHEN THE RAPTURE COMES
NO NUKES
NUCLEAR POWER PLANTS ARE BETTER BUILT THAN JANE FONDA
THERE IS NO FUTURE IN NUCLEAR POWER
WHO KILLED KAREN SILKWOOD?
BAN THE NEUTRON BOMB
THE SHOT HEARD AROUND THE WORLD WAS FIRED FROM AN
     UNREGISTERED GUN
GUNS DON'T KILL PEOPLE, PEOPLE DO
SUPPORT YOUR LOCAL POLICE
DON'T BE FUELISH
REAL AMERICANS BUY AMERICAN CARS
BUY A FOREIGN CAR AND PUT EIGHT AMERICANS OUT OF WORK
NEVER BEFORE HAS SO FEW FED SO MANY—FOR SO LITTLE
     THE AMERICAN FARMER
DON'T COMPLAIN ABOUT FARMERS WITH YOUR MOUTH FULL

The slogans listed in Table 4.2 reflect a variety of concerns with such issues as nuclear power plants, the protection of animals, Christianity, and gun-control legislation.

B. ATTITUDES IN SURVEY RESEARCH

The display of attitudes in public campaigns and demonstrations clearly indicates the concerns of vocal segments of the population, but such displays may not reflect majority sentiment. Currently the most frequently used methods for studying attitudes are those of survey research. These methods include the use of questionnaires, the selection of random samples, and the development of scales for measuring attitudes. Researchers have refined these methods over the past several decades to provide reasonably accurate information on the overall distribution of attitudes within a population. Survey research has become increasingly important in recent years as a method for planning and evaluating several aspects of social life.

1. Units for Analysis

Survey research emphasizes several aspects of social attitudes. The central units for analysis include the direction, the intensity, and the generality of attitudes. Most of the reports in professional journals employ one or more of these units in studies of attitudes. In combination, they reflect the variations in social commitments, the overall behavior tendencies of a population, and the predispositions to support or oppose a particular policy.

The **direction** of an attitude refers to whether the evaluations are positive or negative, whether the general tendency is to agree or disagree with a set of items, or whether the scores of specific subgroups as compared to others are high or low. The overall direction of attitudes is very often of special concern in the formation of public policies on such sensitive issues as sex education, pornography, capital punishment, protection of the environment, and energy depletion. The initiation of policies that are not in alignment with the direction of public sentiment is likely to meet with a great deal of resistance and hostility from the American population.

Direction is also reflected in the changes in social attitudes over time. For example, successive surveys on public attitudes toward crime have indicated that the crime problem is a major concern of the American people. The view of crime as a major societal problem is accompanied by the belief that the crime rate is increasing and by the fear that, as an individual, one is likely at some time or another to become a victim of criminal conduct. These specific attitudes tend to coincide with the individual favoring a public policy that invokes severe punishments for criminal offenses. Those who perceive crime to be increasing are more likely to favor the use of the death penalty for certain criminal offenders than are those who regard crime as less of a problem (Thomas and Cage, 1976).

While the direction of an attitude refers to whether the evaluations are positive or negative in character, the **intensity** of an attitude refers to the strength of the conviction with which a position is taken. Some attitudes are casually held, while others reflect high levels of emotional involvement. We can illustrate variations in the intensity of attitudes by examining survey research on responses to nuclear power plants. A plurality of Americans favor the development of nuclear power plants to meet the nation's growing needs for electricity (Pokorny, 1979). The prevailing sentiment seems to express a practical concern with developing technological solutions to an identifiable problem. About a third of Americans, however, are opposed to nuclear power plants, and they hold this conviction strongly. As a result of the intense feelings over nuclear power plants, further developments along these lines are likely to face organized opposition.

The intensity of an attitude can be measured by determining the level of agreement with specific questionnaire items. The format of answers frequently consists of responses along a continuum ranging from "strongly agree,"

"agree," "disagree," to "strongly disagree." By summing responses to a series of interrelated items the researcher can determine the intensity with which the attitudes are held. Individuals with more extreme scores (either high or low) are more likely to back up their attitudes with some overt line of action than are those whose attitudes fall in the middle or the neutral range of the distribution. More intensely held attitudes are also more resistant to change in the face of persuasive arguments to the contrary (Rokeach, 1968).

The **generality** of an attitude refers to the range of beliefs and evaluations that are organized into a coherent set of identifiable responses. Attitudes that have a high degree of generality are those that provide consistent orientations toward a broad series of events. For example, the attitude of cynicism is generalized when it incorporates a distrust of politicans, business people, advertisers, newspapers, and used-car dealers. In reality, the level of cynicism seldom goes this far, although the distrust of government does tend to accompany a distrust of big business (Neal and Rettig, 1967). The suitability of attitudes for measurement is in part dependent on the generality of the attitude in question among the subjects selected for study. Some beliefs are highly specific and situational in character and thus lack sufficient scope and stability in the life-world of individuals to be important variables for analysis.

2. The Measurement of Attitudes

The measurement of attitudes has been one of the major concerns of sociologists and psychologists for the last four or five decades. Many scales have been developed for measuring such attitudes as religiosity, authoritarianism, cynicism, powerlessness, belief in a just world, social distance, and sexual permissiveness. Such measures are designed to tap not only the direction, intensity, and generality of attitudes, but also the variations in attitudes among subgroups of the population and the consequences of attitudes for behavior.

In developing an attitude scale, the researcher usually proceeds by constructing a large pool of questionnaire items in order to discard those that do not work out. The researcher may construct a set of items that on purely logical grounds appear adequate to measure the attitude of concern; later some of the items prove useful, while others do not. The final selection of items depends on the responses of the subjects for study. Refinement of an attitude scale requires that the items be clear and accurate and that they form a coherent pattern in the life-world of the population selected for study. For these reasons, researchers are concerned with the reliability and validity of an attitude scale.

The **reliability** of a scale for the measurement of an attitude consists of the degree to which responses to a set of item statements follow an internally consistent and predictable pattern. This may be determined through the use of the split-half technique for determining reliability. This procedure consists of summing the scores on the even-numbered items and correlating them with the sum of the scores on the odd-numbered items; or it may consist of summing the scores on the first half of the scale and correlating them with the sum of the scores obtained on the second half. One method of increasing the reliability of a scale consists of correlating the specific items with the total score and discarding those items that reveal the lowest correlations.

The concern with the problem of reliability is with the coherence among responses to a series of items. If responses to several of the items lack consistency, the reliability of the test scores will diminish accordingly. When this happens, the obtained data may suggest that the attitude the researcher has identified lacks centrality in the belief system of individuals or that more than one attitude may be involved. The researcher then has to make a decision on how to best use the information available. The decision may consist of limiting the analysis to only those items that cluster into a general pattern, or the decision may be to work with a series of specific attitudes. For example, if the researcher is studying life satisfaction, he or she may wish to separate attitudes toward work from those relating to the uses of leisure, family life, health, and finances. In general, attitudes in these separate areas tend to interrelate, but the obtained correlations are usually low enough to suggest that there is variation in the levels of satisfaction in aspects of a subject's social life (Campbell, 1981).

Thus, there are choices researchers make in the selection of items for measuring particular attitudes, but their choices are limited by the requirement that they establish statistical criteria to show the reliability of the measure. While reliability relates to the obtained consistency in scores among items, the issue of **validity** is directed toward the question of the degree to which a scale actually measures what it claims to measure. Here the obligation of the researcher is to provide an accurate label to describe the item content of a scale.

To provide evidence for the validity of a set of items that is independent of the researcher's own judgments, the research can apply the technique of consensual validation. This procedure consists of submitting a set of items to a series of judges for independent evaluations of what the items are measuring. The level of consensual validity can then be determined through an analysis of the level of agreement among a set of judges on the underlying content of a set of items. Since this method of validating a scale is time-consuming, many social psychologists prefer to use the technique of discriminant validation.

Here the assumption in using discriminant validations is that if a scale is measuring what the researcher claims it measures, the scores should provide a basis for differentiating known groups. For example, if religiosity is the attitude of interest, the researcher may correlate the obtained scores on a set of items with the frequency of church attendance. In this case, the test for validity is based on the notion that a valid measure for tapping degrees of religiosity (high versus low) should discriminate subjects who are regular churchgoers from those who attend church infrequently or not at all. Thus an attitude scale

BOX 4.1
Increasing Alienations During the 1960s

Neal and Groat (1974) conducted a study to determine the correlates of stability and change in levels of alienation (powerlessness, meaninglessness, normlessness, and social isolation) over an eight-year interval. The authors collected survey data from more than 300 recent mothers in 1963 and again from the same subjects in 1971. Since identical items were included in both surveys, the authors were able to determine the stability and change in scores.

The results indicated that high degrees of stability characterized the alienation scores. Subjects who were alienated from the surrounding society in 1963 were also alienated in 1971. The findings suggest that conditions of alienation are deeply embedded in basic world views, which have high degrees of stability and persistence for individuals. The stability of scores occurred over a relatively long period of time and was not significantly affected by changes in family size, employment status, or marital duration.

Within the context of relatively stable scores, changes did occur in levels of alienation for the total sample. Scores increased for the total sample on each of the alienation variables, but without much of an effect on the relative placement of specific individuals. The overall changes were greater for feelings of normlessness (e.g., perceived immorality of public officials) and powerlessness (e.g., "this world is run by the few people in power") than for feelings of social isolation (loneliness). These changes appeared to represent emergent attitudes of despair during the 1960s in responses to a protracted war, civil strife, environmental crises, and such economic problems as unemployment and inflation.

Source: Arthur G. Neal and H. Theodore Groat, "Social Class Correlates of Stability and Change in Levels of Alienation: A Longitudinal Study," *Sociological Quarterly* 15 (Autumn, 1974): 548–558.

has discriminant validity if the obtained scores differentiate known groups in the expected direction.

An additional concern in the measurement of attitudes is with the **stability** of scale scores. This may be determined through the test-retest method, in which the investigator administers the same scale to the same subjects after an interval of a week, a month, a year, or longer. For example, the research of Neal and Groat (1974) on levels of societal alienation (feelings of powerlessness, meaninglessness, normlessness, and isolation) was based on questionnaire data collected in 1963 and again from the same subjects in 1971. The results indicated that subjects who scored high on each of the alienation scales in 1963 also tended to score high on the same scales eight years later. The scores for most subjects were relatively stable, but the changes that did occur tended to follow a pattern of increases in levels of alienation over this historical time period. (See Box 4.1.)

3. Subjects for Study

The degree of weight assigned to the place of attitudes in the prediction and explanation of social behavior remains a controversy, both within the scientific community and within segments of the general population. However, it clearly appears that the concerns with the study and measurement of social attitudes will persist in the foreseeable future (Miller, 1977). The general acceptability of attitude research is reflected not only in the increased importance placed on surveys for use in social planning, but also in the readiness of a large proportion of the population to take the time and effort to respond to questionnaires.

A general recognition of the importance of sensitive information for planning purposes has facilitated the accessibility of subjects for survey research (Sudman, 1976). In many cases, the researcher is seeking information on very intimate aspects of the personal lives of individuals. The information of concern to the researcher may very well be of the type that subjects previously have not revealed in their social relationships (Derlega and Chaiken, 1977). Subjects are willing to disclose private attitudes because they assume social psychologists have ethical commitments to maintain the confidentiality of the responses, to identify a completed questionnaire by code number rather than by the name of the subject, and to report the findings in terms of group rather than individual responses.

The anonymity of respondents is maintained through close control over the names of those who participate in the survey; the researcher has an obligation to refrain from public disclosure of any obtained information that would permit identifying a specific respondent. Further safeguards are built into survey research through the emphasis on the principle that participation in a study is voluntary, and hence those individuals who regard the topics for investigation as being too sensitive will exclude themselves from the sample. Yet, while survey researchers generally emphasize voluntary participation, the accuracy of the findings is in part dependent on the representativeness of the sample.

The basic principle in the selection of subjects is that of **random sampling**, which refers to the procedure of selecting subjects in such a fashion that each individual within the population has an equal probability of being chosen (Kish, 1965). One of the variations in the use of this technique is that of taking an interval sample (each "nth" case) from a complete listing of the members of an organization. If the study is community-wide, a sample may be drawn from the city directory or some other complete listing of the residents.

While the use of a purely random sample provides the ideal way of selecting subjects for maximizing accuracy, in reality researchers often depart from this ideal because of concerns with costs and feasibility. However, the subjects who are included in an attitude survey should not be atypical of the population of interest. In community-wide surveys, there is often a departure from random sampling because of the low accessibility of certain subjects for survey research. Low-access subjects are more often found at the two ends of the stratification system. Those with limited education often find it difficult to understand the questions and the purposes of research, while those at the upper echelons are often inaccessible because of the time commitments required in responding to a questionnaire, their low regard for attitude research, and a general tendency to distrust social psychologists (Daniels, 1967). As a result, the sentiments of those at both the upper and the lower echelons of our stratification system are frequently underrepresented in the results of survey research.

C. THE FORMATION OF ATTITUDES

One of the primary reasons for the collection of survey research data is to enable the researcher to determine the sources of differential attitudes within the general population. Specific attitudes are often an outgrowth of generalized lifestyles that are shaped by such variables as group memberships, socioeconomic status, and age and sex roles. Since most individuals have multiple group memberships in modern society, it is important to know which ones are of most importance in the formation of specific attitudes.

1. Social Determinants

The social basis for attitude formation may be determined through the study of grouped responses from a relatively large number of people. The researcher is interested in the sources of attitudes, which requires identifying the major variables that may account for why individuals differ in the attitudes they hold. Analysis of the sources of attitudes are important, since individuals may reveal similar attitudes in survey research but differ substantially in their reasons for having the attitudes. (See Box 4.2.)

One of the major sources of variation in attitudes derives from the **pluralism** of modern society. Such memberships as political party affiliation, organized religion, and special interest groups are important sources of specific attitudes. For example, Catholics differ from non-Catholics in their attitudes toward birth control, Democrats tend to differ from Republicans in their attitudes toward social welfare legislation, and members of labor unions differ from business people in their attitudes toward wage costs as a major cause of inflation. Thus groups differ in their patterns of linkage into the broader social system, and these differences at the group level are expressed in the different evaluations that individuals make.

A second major set of variables in the formation of attitudes consists of the multiple aspects of **socioeconomic status.** Educational attainment, occupational status, and family income have been demonstrated in numerous

BOX 4.2
Two Sources of Opposition to the Vietnam War

Drawing on data from several sources, including student samples and national surveys, Howard Schuman (1972) made a study of attitudes toward American involvement in the Vietnam War. His analysis indicated that similar levels of opposition derived from two different sources. One consisted of condemning American actions on moral grounds, while the second consisted of opposing the war because of our failure to win it.

Early opposition to American involvement emerged on college campuses. The first campus protests occurred in 1965 with the initiation of bombing attacks on North Vietnam. Few people expressed doubts about the prospects of the United States winning the war. Instead, they based their opposition primarily on moral concerns. These included questioning the purposes of American involvement there and of the destruction American military technology was wreaking on the Vietnamese people.

Public opposition to the war came later and was based on a widely different set of concerns. Schuman's research indicated that the shift in public opinion was not based on moral concerns, but on the lack of military victories. A sharp drop in the level of public support occurred during 1968 when the escalation of military efforts turned out to be unsuccessful. Since the war could not be won easily by stepping up military operations, many people arrived at the conclusion that we should get out.

The confusion about the moral and practical aspects of the war often results in errors in thinking about the sources of mass opinions. Schuman's research suggests it is an error to assume that "the public slept until awakened by college protest." Many who eventually came to oppose the war on practical grounds also held negative attitudes toward students who had engaged in social protest.

Source: Howard Schuman, "Two Sources of Antiwar Sentiment in America," *American Journal of Sociology* 78 (November, 1972): 513–536.

studies to be important sources of variation in attitudes (Rothman, 1978). Variations in life experiences and opportunities provide individuals with vantage points from which they perceive and evaluate social events differentially.

The research by Joan Rytina, William Form, and John Pease (1970), for example, indicates that numerous aspects of attitudes toward the American opportunity structure are closely linked to one's own position within the stratification system. The higher the level of income, the greater the perceived equality of opportunity for obtaining a college education, for getting ahead in one's occupation through hard work, and for having an influence on the political process. Thus the greater one's own position of privilege, the greater the perceived opportunities that are available for everyone else. Those at the lower income levels, by way of contrast, not only see few opportunities, but also regard the basic institutions of society as being partial to the wealthy and influential. (See Box 4.3.)

Overlapping the stratification variables, generational levels constitute an additional source of variation in attitudes. A generation may be thought of as comprising those within an age category who have encountered similar historical events during the course of their formative years. Examples of studies of such generational units are Stephen Ward's (1975) historical analysis of the World War I veterans and Glenn Elder's (1974) analysis of the children of the Great Depression. Several observers have noted that the life circumstances of those achieving maturity in the United States during the rising economic prosperity of the 1960s differed in several important ways from those who were socialized during the hard times of the depression in the 1930s. Basic values and life interests are likely to take a different form for those growing up under conditions of scarcity compared to those entering adulthood during times in which the standards of living are relatively high (Simon and Gagnon, 1976).

BOX 4.3
Reference Groups

Since individuals are involved in multiple sets of social relationships, there are many sources of specific attitudes. Occupations, church affiliations, political party memberships, age levels, and gender roles provide numerous vantage points from which individuals may take a stand on social issues. Because of multiple and overlapping group memberships, research on attitudes is directed toward finding out which reference groups individuals draw on for the assessment and evaluation of social events. A **reference group** is a social category or organizational membership that exerts an influence on the formation of specific attitudes among individuals.

While reference groups are frequently based on actual group memberships, a variety of other considerations can also shape attitudes. For example, plans and aspirations for the future frequently have more of an influence on attitudes than do present status characteristics. Aspiring to membership in certain groups (e.g., becoming a doctor or a sociologist) may lead individuals to develop attitudes they presume to be appropriate for a future social status.

Attitudes may also be based on making comparisons of one's own situation with that of others. For example, middle-class individuals may hold attitudes toward their own situations by making comparisons with the super-rich or with those living in conditions of poverty. Their assessments of well-being are likely to be shaped by which of these alternative references they draw on. If they compare themselves with those at the poverty level, middle-class individuals are likely to regard themselves as being well-off. But if middle-class individuals compare themselves with the very rich, they may see themselves as being deprived.

2. Learning Experiences

While one may identify the general pattern of attitude formation through the study of the effects of group membership, socioeconomic status, and generational levels, one needs to examine the more immediate conditions for the development of attitudes from the standpoint of the learning experiences of individuals. The formation of individual attitudes is primarily an outgrowth of positive and negative reinforcements that accompany experiences with social objects and events.

The learning theories of attitude formation hold that positive and negative evaluations primarily derive from the kinds of rewards people associate with prior experiences. Individuals tend to repeat actions for which they have been rewarded (Klinger, 1977), and if rewards are consistently associated with a particular type of event, the attitudes toward that event are likely to be positive in character. In contrast, if experiences with some type of event have been negative ones, the expected outcomes from subsequent occurrences of that event are likely to be regarded as unfavorable. Learning theory holds that attitudes emerge from prior experiences and are generalized to encompass new events or similar situations.

The development of attitudes provides much greater degrees of freedom than do direct lines of action. We may form attitudes about places we have never seen, about events we have never experienced, and about achievements and failures we have not yet known. The development of attitudes enables us to generalize about the attributes of objects, persons, events, and situations in the world around us. The raw materials that enable us to form such imagery, however, derive from the concrete aspects of our experiences.

From the numerous activities in which we have been engaged (at home, at play, at school, at work, and so forth), we develop notions about the differential value of the goals we may pursue. Many of the goals, however, that offer the potential for high rewards we may not see as being accessible to us, or we may consider the costs in their attainment too great. As a result, the experiences we hold for the probability of success or failure in a particular line of action are likely to influence the vigor with which we pursue a given set of desired goals. If we expect to fail at some particular task, we are likely to behave in such a fashion that failure will in fact be the outcome (Jones, 1977).

Several lines of research converge in emphasizing the importance of the attitudes of personal mastery and control for human thought and action. One of these research traditions derives from the work of Julian Rotter (1966), which emphasizes the variable of **internal versus external control of reinforcements.** Here the emphasis is on a sense of internal control, which refers to expectancy for success in obtaining desired outcomes through one's own behavior. By way of contrast, external control refers to the view that forces outside oneself determine the outcome of events. Beliefs in external forces include beliefs in luck, in taking chances, in the workings of fate, and in "the hand of destiny." (See Box 4.4.)

BOX 4.4
A Measure of Powerlessness

This is a survey to find out what the public thinks about certain events that we face in our society. Each item consists of a pair of statements. Please select the one statement of each pair (*and only one*) that you more strongly believe to be true. Be sure to check the one you actually *believe* to be more nearly true, rather than the one you think you should check or the one you would like to be true. This is a measure of personal belief; obviously, there are no right or wrong answers. Again, be sure to make a choice between each pair of statements.

1. _____ I think we have adequate means for preventing run-away inflation.
   ___*___ There's very little we can do to keep prices from going higher.

2. ___*___ Persons like myself have little chance of protecting our personal interests when they conflict with those of strong pressure groups.
   _____ I feel that we have adequate ways of coping with pressure groups.

3. _____ A lasting world peace can be achieved by those of us who work toward it.
   ___*___ There's very little we can do to bring about a permanent world peace.

4. ___*___ There's very little persons like myself can do to improve world opinion of the United States.
   _____ I think each of us can do a great deal to improve world opinion of the United States.

5. ___*___ This world is run by the few people in power, and there is not much the little guy can do about it.
   _____ The average citizen can have an influence on government decisions.

6. ___*___ It is only wishful thinking to believe that one can really influence what happens in society at large.
   _____ People like me can change the course of world events if we make ourselves heard.

7. ___*___ More and more, I feel helpless in the face of what's happening in the world today.
   _____ I sometimes feel personally to blame for the sad state of affairs in our government.

Note: Score is based on the total number of choices of the powerlessness statements (*).

Source: Arthur G. Neal and Melvin Seeman, "Organizations and Powerlessness: A Test of the Mediation Hypothesis," *American Sociological Review* 29 (April, 1964): 216–226.

A related theme is emphasized in the research of Martin Seligman (1975) on the experimental effects of learning in highly controlled compared to uncontrolled environments. The key concern in his research is the variable of **learned helplessness**, which refers to a pattern of reinforcements leading one to the conclusion that the outcome of events cannot be voluntarily controlled through one's own efforts. The learning experience is such that one obtains rewards and punishments independently of one's own behavior. Conditions of learned helplessness are stress-producing; Seligman noted that extreme cases resulted in maladaptive behavior, including the phenomenon of sudden death. Apparently, people die from intense feelings of helplessness, and this seems to result from sudden changes in physiological functioning and increased vulnerability to pathogens or disease-causing organisms that are always present within our environments.

These lines of inquiry emphasize the predictability and the controllability of events from the vantage point of the individual. Attitudes of helplessness and external control are important obstacles to the linkage of values and goals with effective lines of action. Individuals who feel that their social environments are unresponsive to their own needs and interests become victimized by forces that are outside of themselves. They fail to act when action is necessary, and they lack receptiveness to information that has implications for the attainment of goals they would like to pursue.

D. UNDERSTANDING AND ACTION

For the past several decades, a heatedly debated topic in social psychology has been the general relationships between attitudes and behavior. One view attempts to resolve the problem by noting the generally low correlations between attitude measures and overt behavior. Proponents of this view argue that the concept of attitudes is not a meaningful topic for social psychological inquiry (Wicker, 1969; Deutscher, 1966). Others have maintained that attitudes are important forms of social reality in their own right, and there are numerous reasons for arguing that one should not expect attitudes to be highly predictive of behavior (Fishbein, 1967; Ehrlich, 1969). This latter view emphasizes the numerous variables that "intervene" between attitudes and behavior. These include the situational conditions that modify behavioral intentions and thus influence the relationships between attitudes and behavior.

Kenneth L. Stewart (1975) has criticized researchers for their failure to link attitudes and behavior to the symbolic context of social interactions. Meaningful acts are not isolated events, he argues, but outcomes of developing situations in which individuals act and react to one another. From this vantage point attitudes are not so much organized beliefs or behavioral response tendencies as symbolic reactions in which actors define and redefine themselves and social situations. Such a view of attitudes represents a departure from typical treatments by social psychologists and calls attention to the importance of attitudes as symbolic displays in appearances, conversations, and negotiations within the context of everyday interactions.

Most social psychologists do not study attitudes for the meanings that grow out of social interactions, but there is a growing recognition of the importance of situations for the linkage between attitudes and behavior. Lyle Warner and Melvin DeFleur (1969) clarified the research finding of social psychologists by developing the **postulate of contingent consistency.** This postulate holds that the degree of consistency between attitudes and behavior depends on the characteristics of both social actors and social situations. Actors differ in their behavioral intentions (Fishbein, 1967) and in their capacities to carry out planned lines of action (Bradburn, 1969), and situations differ in the kinds of social constraints they impose on individuals. The early idea that a single attitude could be used to predict actual behavior turns out to be an oversimplified view. Social psychologists now direct their research toward specifying the contingencies under which attitudes and behavior are consistent as well as the contingencies under which consistency is least likely to be found.

1. Behavioral Intentions

A great deal of human behavior is routine and habitual, following repetitive patterns that require very little in the way of conscious thought and action. For most people a remarkable degree of consistency in timing is built into such behavior patterns as when we go to bed at night and when we get up in the morning. The sequence of getting ready to go to school or to work often follows a repetitive pattern of showering, brushing teeth, shaving, getting dressed, and eating breakfast, although not necessarily in that order. These repetitive patterns of behavior have been worked out over an extended period of time, and they persist as a means of giving order and stability to one's personal life.

Superimposed on everyday routines, however, we encounter situations in which we must make choices and decisions. These situations are more likely to occur when we are planning to embark on a new line of action, when we encounter pressures from others to make a decision, or in some cases when we rationally formulate a set of goals and consciously seek to implement them. We may think of these planned lines of action as **behavioral intentions.** They include both the immediate and limited goals we wish to pursue, as well as the more long-range plans that will require a great deal of time and effort to attain (Fishbein, 1967).

It is in the planning and decision-making phases of our lives that attitudes play their major part. If we make decisions intentionally and voluntarily, they are likely to be consistent with our basic attitudes. The assessments of social objects and events provide a primary basis for determining which of the alternative goals available to us are the more appropriate ones in terms of our self-identities and our understandings of the social world. When we make concrete plans in selecting a career, in getting married, in deciding where to live, and so forth, a series of attitudes that have built up over an extended period of time is likely to influence our intended line of action.

The attitudes that enter into our decisions may consist of either positive or negative evaluations, of either the desire for the attainment of some goal or the desire for the avoidance of some unpleasant situation. Research on family

BOX 4.5
The Value of Children

Drawing on data from a national survey on the value of children to parents, Lois W. Hoffman and her associates (1978) report several findings on the satisfactions of parenthood for American couples in their childbearing years.

1. The most important set of advantages of children parents perceived as being related to primary group ties and affection. This included an emphasis on love, companionship, and the importance of having a complete family.
2. The second most important set of advantages consisted of seeing children as a source of stimulation and fun. Included here were the perceived rewards of engaging in activities with children and having the pleasure of watching them grow.
3. The third set of advantages related to an expansion of the self. Parents regarded children as a source of self-fulfillment, as giving a sense of purpose to life, and as a re-creation of themselves.
4. Very few couples placed emphasis on other potential advantages of children, such as confirming adult status, providing economic security in old age, having an income-tax deduction, creating a human being, or meeting social expectations.

The study also indicated that there were variations in the perceived advantages of children by educational level, by racial status, and by the career plans of the wife. The variations, however, were of less importance than the overall similarities in the primary emphasis on children as a source of love and affection.

Source: Lois W. Hoffman, Arland Thornton, and Jean D. Manis, "The Value of Children to Parents in the United States," *Journal of Population* 1 (Summer, 1978): 91–131.

formation, for example, has indicated that the desired family size and the positive values assigned to children are highly predictive of the number of children a couple will eventually have. Thus statements about wanting more children correlate highly with subsequent fertility (Freedman, Hermalin, and Chang, 1975).

The research of Alden Speare, Jr. (1974) has indicated that negative evaluations are important considerations in residential mobility. When individuals reach a certain threshhold of residential dissatisfaction, they begin exploring the opportunities for living elsewhere and typically end up making an actual move. A variety of conditions are related to residential dissatisfaction, including an increase in the number of children, the physical deterioration of the neighborhood, a change in job conditions, and the development of stronger social ties elsewhere. But whatever the sources, Speare's research indicates that the level of dissatisfaction is a major variable in the prediction of who moves and who remains in a particular neighborhood.

In making career choices, in the decision to marry, and in deciding on how to spend leisure time, attitudes toward social objects and events become of central relevance. Individuals' conceptions of the desirable and the undesirable are basic to the goals they select, to the means they employ in pursuit of these goals, and to the rewards they anticipate in attaining them. This is not to suggest that there is a one-to-one correspondence between attitudes and behavior, but that generalized attitudes play an important part in the selection of a course of action individuals intend to follow.

2. Efficacious Actions

Individuals differ, however, in the extent to which they are able to act effectively on the basis of their own understanding of the world. This point has been effectively developed by Norman Bradburn (1969) in his discussion of "the structure of psychological well-being."

Personal Troubles
The motorists stuck in a line of traffic on the West Virginia Turnpike are not acting here in a manner consistent with their attitudes, preferences, or intentions.

...Some people seem to have an easy time of it, while others have much greater diffi-culty in accomplishing the things they want to do in life. By difficulties, we mean a whole host of things: they actually fail to get what they want; in the pursuit of their goals, they cause trouble or pain to others; and they suffer from feelings of failure, un-happiness, worry, and even from unpleasant physical symptoms (Bradburn, 1969: 4–5).

Efficacious actions refers to behavior the individual has linked to attitudes in obtaining outcomes he or she desires. This requires that the goals an individual selects be appropriate ones in terms of the basic attitudes he or she holds, that the person employ effective means in the pursuit of these goals, and that the obtained outcomes be desired and intended. In any given case the individual may pursue an inappropriate goal; the means employed may fail to work out; and the consequences that follow may be unforeseen and unwanted.

Changing career plans frequently, experiencing an unwanted pregnancy, and having an automobile accident are each examples of failure in some par-ticular line of action. The effective implementation of an attitude through action, notes Howard Ehrlich (1969), depends on the clarity with which the person holds the attitude, the extent to which the attitude is expressible, and the degree to which the disclosure of the personal attitude is compatible with the attitudes that others reveal.

Attitudes are generalized orientations toward social objects (e.g., religion, public officials, racial minorities), while behavior is oriented toward the pur-suit of specific goals in immediate situations. For example, our beliefs in God and immortality may represent generalized attitudes that do not serve as spe-cific guides for what must be done "here and now." For this reason, many of our religious attitudes do not serve as obstacles to what we wish to do for non-religious reasons, although the person with strong convictions is likely to act out his or her religious attitudes in some manner or another. Allen Liska (1974) notes that in numerous situations, given attitudes are unclear and not expressed in action because they conflict with other attitudes that both ourselves and others hold.

The expression of attitudes in behavior is often inhibited because of the presumed consequences if we disclose our true sentiments (Jourard, 1964). Overt behavior conveys implications for a response on the part of others, while we may hold attitudes with a high degree of impunity if we conceal them in social relationships. In those situations in which interactions occur among those who are unequal in control over desired resources, some level of con-straint is necessarily imposed on the behavior of one party or the other. Thus workers sometimes find it necessary to deceive their employers in order to promote harmonious work relationships, and supervisors sometimes find it necessary to disguise hostile attitudes they hold toward employees. In this respect, social interactions are characterized by political and negotiable com-ponents that are often oriented toward promoting stability in a set of social relationships.

3. Social Constraints

In addition to the variety of personal qualities that reduce our ability to act on the basis of our attitudes, there are also numerous situational variables that prevent consistency between attitudes and behavior. These numerous situational factors may be thought of as the social constraints that our relationships with others impose on us.

We tend to infer motives and attitudes from observing the behavior of those with whom we interact, and they in turn draw inferences from our own words and deeds. As a result we are each subject to the influences of others who are immediately present in social situations. The presence of parents, faculty members, or distinguished visitors to campus may place a damper on the spontaneous expression of personal sentiments among college students. The dormitory is likely to provide a less inhibiting atmosphere than the classroom, and the local tavern lends itself more readily to spontaneous expression than does the courtroom or the formal lecture hall.

If we are interacting with others whom we know to hold attitudes similar to our own, there is likely to be a consistency between our attitudes and our behavior. Attitudes, however, are generally poor predictors of behavior in those situations in which those who are present hold incongruent positions (Frideres, Warner, and Albrecht, 1971). In many cases we do not know the attitudes of those with whom we interact. Under these circumstances the definition of the situation and our orientations toward normal standards of conduct are likely to shape our lines of action.

Ehrlich (1969) noted that some personal attitudes are antisocial in character, and open disclosure may result in unrewarding outcomes. People may avoid expressing such attitudes as racial and ethnic prejudices, for example, in those situations in which such evaluations are contrary to the evaluations made by others. Some sexual attitudes are regarded as being too intimate or too personal to reveal openly in social relationships, and as a result they find their expression primarily in the realm of fantasy. Thus the basic social constraints are those that relate to the imagined expectations of others and to the perceived social consequences of expressing particular attitudes in overt behavior. Most of us are practical enough to recognize that actions incompatible with the expectations of others may have consequences we would prefer to avoid.

E. CHANGING ATTITUDES

The lack of consistency between attitudes and behavior may be understood in part through examining the organization of belief systems and the conditions promoting attitude change. We may readily modify our behavior in given situations in response to social influences, while our basic attitudes are much more resistant to change. This is because our basic attitudes form over long periods of time and become central to our overall belief systems. They serve as stabilizing frames of reference for self-identities and for orientations toward others. To bring about important changes in attitudes requires altering the general frameworks of social meaning and understanding.

Given attitudes vary in the degree to which they are central to our belief systems, in the range of our knowledge and experience on which we base them, and in the intensity with which we hold them. For these reasons, the location and structure of attitudes need to be examined within a general framework of social meaning and action. While attitudes have a social reality in their own right, they do not exist as isolated, free-floating phenomena (Acock and DeFleur, 1972). They tend to shape our receptiveness to new information and they sometimes become obstacles to the attainment of the goals we seek.

1. Centrality

The degree to which a given attitude is susceptible to change depends on the centrality of its location within the general belief system of the individual (Petersen and Dutton, 1975). **Centrality** refers to the fact that some of our attitudes are more important to us than are others. Our more central attitudes are those that are closely related to our self-identities, and we do not take them lightly. We may be more casual about social attitudes that are peripheral to our self-images. But if our religious (or political or sexual) attitudes are central to our self-identities, we are likely to be upset if we encounter others who pose a threat to us by holding views that sharply differ from our own. (See Box 4.6.)

Robert Lauer (1971) observes that the centrality of an attitude is dependent on its location among the numerous beliefs and values that we hold. The greater the connection of a specific attitude with other attitudes, the more central its position within our belief systems. By being interconnected with other beliefs, the more central attitudes are more resistant to change (Rokeach, 1968). They become sources of stability and anchoring points that insulate us against the contradictions and conflicts embedded in social living. Peripheral attitudes, by way of contrast, are less stable and are more amenable to modification as a result of new information and exposure to new kinds of experiences. We are able to change our attitudes more readily in response to changing environmental conditions if the attitudes are located more nearly on the periphery than at the centers of our self-identities.

For example, following the Supreme Court decision in 1973 that liberalized the opportunities for abortion, many people responded by becoming more tolerant of abortion practices, while the opposition to abortion on the part of others became more firmly established (Jones and Westoff, 1978). The differences in response can be understood as stemming from differences in the loca-

---

BOX 4.6
Attitudes Toward Hippies

In a study of attitudes toward hippies among store customers, Steffensmeier and Steffensmeier (1975) conducted a field experiment on shoplifting. Incidents of shoplifting were staged in a natural setting in which half of the shoplifters were "disheveled hippie-appearing" and the other half were "well-groomed straight-appearing." The researchers were interested in finding out how generalized attitudes toward hippies are related to the willingness to report a shoplifting incident to store employees.

Three levels of willingness to report a hippie shoplifter were identified. "A high willingness to report" was assigned to those customers who reported the shoplifting to the first available store employee. "A medium willingness to report" was based on those revealing the incident only after a store employee asked for information on suspected shoplifting. "A low willingness to report" was assigned to those customers who reported the shoplifting only after a second prompting or not at all.

Subsequent interviews with the customers were conducted to determine how attitudes toward hippies were related to the observed willingness to report a shoplifting incident. The results provided support for the research hypothesis. The more negative the general attitudes toward hippies, the greater the likelihood a customer would report a specific shoplifting violation by a hippie-appearing person. By way of contrast, attitudes toward hippies were less predictive of a willingness to report the "straight-appearing" shoplifter. Thus the appearance of the person and generalized attitudes toward the type of person are important variables in the willingness to report a shoplifting offense.

Source: Renee Hoffman Steffensmeier and Darrell J. Steffensmeier, "Attitudes and Behavior Toward Hippies: A Field Experiment Accompanied by Home Interviews," *Sociological Quarterly* 16 (Summer, 1975): 393–400.

---

tion of abortion attitudes within the general belief system of individuals. For some, the abortion issue taps sentiments that are central to self-image, while for others the abortion issue is less closely related to their basic beliefs.

Because of the linkage of abortion attitudes with other beliefs, the opposition to abortion is generally greater among Catholics than among non-Catholics and greater among older age groups than among younger ones (de Boer, 1978). The beliefs linked to abortion include various notions about the creation of human life, the rights of women, the rights of the unborn child, and the will of God. Some look on abortion as murder and would not approve of it under any conditions, while others are fully tolerant of abortion practices.

For most Americans tolerance of abortion is conditional. National sur-

Controversial Attitudes

While sexual attitudes have become more liberal in recent years, a great deal of con-
troversy surfaces from time to time over the issue of pornography. Many of those
opposed to adult movies and bookstores feel that their own standards of morality
should be imposed on others and enforced as community norms. Others feel that the
issue is primarily one of personal morality and that individuals should have the right
to decide for themselves what kinds of movies to see and books to read.

veys show that the vast majority of Americans now approve of abortion if the
mother's health is endangered, if there is a good reason to believe the child
might be deformed, or if the woman has been raped. The abortion issue becomes more controversial if the couple wanting the abortion feel that they
cannot afford another child or if the woman wants an abortion because she is
unmarried. The greatest level of opposition to abortion occurs under those
conditions in which a couple has had an unplanned pregnancy and simply does
not want the child or does not want a child at that particular time (de Boer, 1978).

2. *Information Processing*

The change in attitudes is partly a function of the particular styles of information processing that individuals adopt. For example, following the report of the surgeon general on the health hazards of cigarette smoking, some people made adjustments in attitudes and stopped smoking. Most people did not. Despite the extensive information campaigns on the linkage between cigarette smoking and cancer and the warning labels on cigarette packages, the rates of smoking within the American population remain about the same as they were fifteen years ago. Apparently, many attitudes and behaviors are so deeply ingrained in lifestyles that they are extremely difficult to change (Etzioni, 1972).

The concerns of social psychologists with information processing in part derives from their observation that many folk attitudes are simply in error. For example, many of the attitudes about the biological basis for racial classification and about differences between men and women are based on factually incorrect information. In similar fashion, high levels of religious fundamentalism often occur independently on the level of knowledge about the Bible, and strongly held political convictions may be unrelated to actual knowledge of political affairs (Stipak, 1977).

In viewing attitudes as a form of information processing, there are several major problems that develop for individuals in their relationships with their social environment. One of these consists of a premature closure in attitudes. This is characterized by the individual's failure to be receptive to new information when it is readily available in his or her environment. This style of thought expresses rigidity, fanaticism, or dogmatism (Rokeach, 1960), and we tend to recognize such a manner of thinking when we encounter those who hold views that disagree sharply with our own. The basic problem with rigidly held attitudes is that they are oriented toward stability and permanence at the same time that the social environment may be undergoing extensive changes.

At the other extreme, a high degree of sensitivity to new information and environmental changes also may cause difficulties (Toffler, 1971). If extensive changes are occurring within a relatively short period of time, the individual may develop feelings of uncertainty about the adequacy of his or her basic beliefs. Don Rowney (1976) has described this process as one of **information overload**, and this is a problem that stands in contrast to a style of thought characterized by rigidity and premature closure. Under conditions of information overload, one is highly receptive to environmental changes, but at the same time the new information cannot be integrated adequately into one's total life experiences. As a result, uncertainty develops about what to believe and which course of action to follow. A sense of purpose and planning in life is dependent on a predictable social environment, and if one cannot make predictions with confidence, the process of decision making may become very difficult indeed. (See Box 4.7.)

BOX 4.7
Fear of Decision Making

Walter Kaufmann developed the concept of "decidophobia" to describe the fear of making decisions on crucial life events. Concerns for the consequences of serious life-changing events are often great enough for many people to avoid the making of fateful decisions insofar as this is possible. Among the variety of ways in which people avoid the making of serious life-changing decisions are the following:

Drifting—avoiding decision making by following either of two major courses of action. One consists of accepting the status quo, while the other consists of "dropping out." In either case, the drift occurs through acting only on the impulse of the moment and not knowing in advance what one will be doing next.

Attention to detail—paying attention to such a large number of specific details that one avoids developing an overriding sense of purpose. The performance of small tasks may become all encompassing and serve as a substitute for making crucial life decisions.

An overriding commitment—aligning one's priorities in such a manner that involvement in one particular line of activity serves as a substitute for decision making in other areas. This sometimes occurs with religious conversion, in joining a social movement, or the acceptance of some specific ideology. In these cases, the individual makes "one big decision" that permits avoiding the numerous complexities of social life.

Simplified choices—a style of dichotomous thinking in which the individual views events in categorical terms of right and wrong, good and bad, or true and false. Here, the actor recognizes the need for a choice, but the cards have been stacked in such a manner that the decision practically makes itself.

The making of major life decisions is apparently threatening to many people. The use of the above techniques serves to reduce the complexity of social events. They also permit individuals to avoid the challenges of making crucial choices.

Source: Walter Kaufmann, "Do You Crave a Life Without Choice?" *Psychology Today*, April, 1973, pp. 79–83.

As a result of the perceived complexity of modern social life, many people avoid making serious, life-changing decisions in conjunction with changing environmental circumstances and the emergence of new forms of knowledge (Kaufmann, 1973). Stability in attitudes may develop through a reliance on traditional forms of authority such as organized religion, the political status quo, or the customary patterns of family life. But if the individual rejects the traditional forms of authority, his or her lifestyle may become one of aimlessness and drift, in which the person does not hold attitudes with conviction, and situation pressures, rather than direct and active involvement in the decision-making process, shape life events. If so, the individual's well-being is dependent on chance happenings rather than on the outcome of personally planned events.

SUMMARY

The study of attitudes constitutes one of the major developments in social psychology over the past several decades. The distribution of numerous attitudes within community-wide and national samples is important for a wide variety of reasons. For the social psychologist, the study of attitudes provides an important source of information about social life. The distribution of public attitudes is also important for numerous aspects of social planning. The acceptance or rejection of governmental policies, consumer products, and the content of television programming are often dependent on public sentiments.

An attitude is a set of relatively stable and enduring orientations toward social objects and events. Attitudes vary in their intensity, their generality, and their direction. Intensity refers to the strength of the conviction with which a person takes a position, while generality consists of the range of beliefs and evaluations that are organized into a coherent set of responses. The direction of an attitude relates to whether the evaluations are positive or negative toward the social object in question. Attitudes also differ in the accuracy of the information base on which they depend.

The measurement of attitudes permits the social psychologist to describe, predict, and explain numerous aspects of social behavior. Accurately describing attitudes requires being concerned with the problems of reliability and validity. Reliability refers to the degree to which a set of item-statements follows an internally consistent pattern. Validity, on the other hand, refers to the degree to which an attitude scale actually measures what the investigator claims it measures. Making attitude measurement accurate also depends on selecting subjects for study by means of scientific sampling procedures.

Several conditions are implicated in the formation of specific attitudes. Differences in socioeconomic status, age level, and group membership are among the variables often associated with variations in attitudes. These variables are important because they influence our learning experiences. The kinds of rewards associated with previous experiences determine positive and negative evaluations. In the development of attitudes we generalize about the attributes of objects, persons, and events in the world around us.

Specific behavioral intentions as well as situational constraints affect the linkage of attitudes with specific courses of action. Behavioral intentions are planned lines of action, which include both immediate goals and long-range plans for the future. It is these intentions that give an overall sense of direction to organizing our lives. However, we are frequently not able to act in a manner consistent with our basic attitudes. A main reason for this is that the attainment of goals often requires us to align our own intentions with the intentions of others. Some are routinely able to act effectively on the basis of their own understanding of the world. Others frequently feel helpless in their attempts to exercise personal influence over the course of social events.

The change of attitudes is closely related to the degree of receptiveness to new information and to the organization of belief systems. Attitudes are more amenable to change if they are located on the periphery rather than at the center of a belief system. The centrality of an attitude refers to the fact that some of our attitudes have built up over a lifetime as sources of stability in relationships with others. These are attitudes that are highly resistant to change because of their linkage to basic assumptions about the organization of social life. If individuals are overly receptive to new information from their environment, they may become disoriented because of an inability to achieve an integrated view of events.

BASIC TERMS

Attitude	**Socioeconomic status**
Cognitive component	**Reference groups**
Affectivity component	**Internal versus external**
Behavioral component	**control of reinforcements**
Direction	**Learned helplessness**
Intensity	**Postulate of contingent**
Generality	**consistency**
Reliability	**Behavioral intentions**
Validity	**Efficacious actions**
Stability	**Centrality**
Random sampling	**Information overload**
Pluralism	

REFERENCES

Acock, Alan C. and Melvin L. DeFleur
    1972 "A Configurational Approach to Contingent Consistency in the Attitude-Behavior Relationship," *American Sociological Review* 37 (December): 714–726.
Bonjean, Charles M., Richard J. Hill, and S. Dale McLemore
    1967 *Sociological Measurement: An Inventory of Scales,* San Francisco: Chandler.

Bradburn, Norman M.
1969 *The Structure of Psychological Well-Being*, Chicago: Aldine.
Campbell, Angus
1981 *The Sense of Well-Being in America*, New York: McGraw-Hill.
Daniels, Arlene Kaplan
1967 "The Low Caste Stranger in Social Research," in Gideon Sjoberg (ed.), *Ethics, Politics, and Social Research*, Cambridge, Mass.: Schenkman, pp. 267–296.
de Boer, Connie
1978 "The Polls: Abortion," *Public Opinion Quarterly* 41 (Winter): 553–564.
Derlega, Valerian J. and Alan L. Chaiken
1977 "Privacy and Self-Disclosure in Social Relationships," *Journal of Social Issues* 33, no. 3: 102–115.
Deutscher, Irwin
1973 *What We Say/What We Do: Sentiments and Acts*, Glenview, Ill.: Scott Foresman.
1966 "Words and Deeds: Social Science and Social Policy," *Social Problems* 13 (Winter): 235–254.
Ehrlich, Howard J.
1969 "Attitudes, Behavior, and the Intervening Variables," *American Sociologist* 4 (February): 29–34.
Elder, Glen H., Jr.
1974 *Children of the Great Depression*, Chicago: University of Chicago Press.
Etzioni, Amitai
1972 "Human Beings Are Not Very Easy to Change After All," *Saturday Review* 55: 45–47.
Fishbein, Martin
1967 "Attitude and the Prediction of Behavior," in M. Fishbein (ed.), *Readings in Attitude Theory and Measurement*, New York: John Wiley.
Freedman, Ronald, Albert I. Hermalin and Ming-Cheng Chang
1975 "Do Statements about Desired Family Size Predict Fertility?" *Demography* 12 (August): 407–416.
Frideres, James S., Lyle G. Warner, and Stan L. Albrecht
1971 "The Impact of Social Constraints on the Relationship Between Attitudes and Behavior," *Social Forces* 50 (September): 102–112.
Hoffman, Lois W., Arland Thornton, and Jean D. Manis
1978 "The Value of Children to Parents in the United States," *Journal of Population* 1 (Summer): 91–131.
Jones, Elsie F. and Charles F. Westoff
1978 "How Attitudes Toward Abortion Are Changing," *Journal of Population* 1 (Spring): 5–21.
Jones, Russell A.
1977 *Self-Fulfilling Prophecies*, New York: John Wiley.
Jourard, Sidney M.
1964 *The Transparent Self*, Princeton, N.J.: Van Nostrand.
Kaufmann, Walter
1973 "Do You Crave a Life Without Choice?" *Psychology Today* 7 (April): 79–83.
Kish, Leslie
1965 *Survey Sampling*, New York: John Wiley.

Klinger, Eric
    1977 *Meaning and Void,* Minneapolis: University of Minnesota Press.
Lauer, Robert H.
    1971 "The Problems and Values of Attitude Research," *Sociological Quarterly* 12 (Spring): 247–252.
Liska, Allen E.
    1974 "Emergent Issues in the Attitude-Behavior Consistency Controversy," *American Sociological Review* 39 (April): 261–272.
Miller, Delbert C.
    1977 *Handbook of Research Design and Social Measurement,* 3rd edition, New York: David McKay.
Neal, Arthur G. and H. Theodore Groat
    1974 "Social Class Correlates of Stability and Change in Levels of Alienation: A Longitudinal Study," *Sociological Quarterly* 15 (Autumn): 548–558.
Neal, Arthur G. and Salomon Rettig
    1967 "On the Multidimensionality of Alienation," *American Sociological Review* 32 (February): 54–64.
Neal, Arthur G. and Melvin Seeman
    1964 "Organizations and Powerlessness: A Test of the Mediation Hypothesis," *American Sociological Review* 29 (April): 216–226.
Petersen, Karen Kay and Jeffrey E. Dutton
    1975 "Centrality, Extremity, Intensity: Neglected Variables in Research on Attitude-Behavior Consistency," *Social Forces* 54 (December): 393–414.
Pokorny, Gene
    1979 "Living Dangerously . . . Sometimes," *Public Opinion* 2, no. 3: 10–14.
Robinson, John P. and Phillip R. Shaver
    1973 *Measures of Social Psychological Attitudes,* Ann Arbor: Institute for Social Research, University of Michigan.
Rokeach, Milton
    1968 *Beliefs, Attitudes, and Values,* San Francisco: Jossey-Bass.
    1960 *The Open and Closed Mind,* New York: Basic Books.
Rothman, Robert A.
    1978 *Inequality and Stratification in the United States,* Englewood Cliffs, N.J.: Prentice-Hall.
Rotter, Julian B.
    1966 "Generalized Expectancies for Internal vs. External Control of Reinforcements," *Psychological Monographs* 80, no. 1 (entire issue).
Rowney, Don Karl
    1976 "How History Beats the System: Violence and Disaggregation," in Arthur G. Neal (ed.), *Violence in Animal and Human Societies,* Chicago: Nelson-Hall, pp. 107–140.
Rytina, Joan Huber, William H. Form, and John Pease
    1970 "Income and Stratification Ideology: Beliefs about the American Opportunity Structure," *American Journal of Sociology* 75 (January): 703–716.
Schuman, Howard
    1972 "Two Sources of Antiwar Sentiment in America," *American Journal of Sociology* 78 (November): 513–536.
Seligman, Martin E. P.
    1975 *Helplessness,* San Francisco: W. H. Freeman.

Simon, William and John H. Gagnon
    1976 "The Anomie of Affluence: A Post-Mertonian Conception," *American Journal of Sociology* 82 (September): 356–378.
Speare, Alden, Jr.
    1974 "Residential Satisfaction as an Intervening Variable in Residential Mobility," *Demography* 11 (May): 173–188.
Steffensmeier, Renee Hoffman and Darrell J. Steffensmeier
    1975 "Attitudes and Behavior Toward Hippies: A Field Experiment Accompanied by Home Interviews," *Sociological Quarterly* 16 (Summer): 393–400.
Stewart, Kenneth L.
    1975 "On Socializing Attitudes: A Symbolic Interactionist View," *Sociological Focus* 8 (January): 37–46.
Stipak, Brian
    1977 "Attitudes and Belief Systems Concerning Urban Services," *Public Opinion Quarterly* 41 (Spring): 41–55.
Sudman, Seymour
    1976 "Sample Surveys," *Annual Review of Sociology,* 2: 107–120.
Thomas, Charles W. and Robin J. Cage
    1976 "Correlates of Public Attitudes Toward Legal Sanctions," *International Journal of Criminology and Penology* 4 (August): 239–255.
Toffler, Alvin
    1971 *Future Shock,* New York: Bantam Books.
Ward, Stephen R. (ed.)
    1975 *The War Generation: Veterans of the First World War,* Port Washington, N.Y.: Kennikat Press.
Warner, Lyle G. and Melvin L. DeFleur
    1969 "Attitude as an Interactional Concept: Social Constraint and Social Distance as Intervening Variables Between Attitudes and Action," *American Sociological Review* 34 (April): 153–169.
Wicker, Allan W.
    1969 "Attitudes Versus Action," *Journal of Social Issues* 25 (Autumn): 41–78.

STATUS III
AND IDENTITY

5

What to look for in this chapter:

What is the importance of play and games in the formation of a self?
How does a self-concept develop?
Is there "a real self" behind the many roles we play?
To what extent does the reality of the self resemble the reality of
Santa Claus at Christmas time?

The Social Self

We can apply the concept of the social construction of reality to the self as well as to the external environment. We are not endowed at birth with answers to the questions, Who am I?, What am I doing here?, and Where an I going? We must discover and create answers to these questions. We do so by drawing on the wide variety of clues we receive from others. In the final analysis, who we are and where we belong are notions that emerge from the processes of social interaction and reality construction.

There are numerous variables that may enter into the development of a self. There are the aspects of a self that derive from social classifications, such as age, sex, race, religion, and community. These are the public components of the self, which are typically on display in social relationships, but there are also the inner aspects of a self, which enter into our consciousness during our most solitary moments of fantasy and make-believe. Some features of the self consist of deeply ingrained memories about past events, while other features of the self encompass the hopes and aspirations for the future. The self for some is little more than what others think of it as being, but in other cases there are deeper and less-visible attributes of a self that do not typically show up in social relationships.

Regardless of whatever else may enter into the creation of a self, this much is clear: the meanings that emerge from social relationships to a very large degree shape the formation of a self. We cannot derive a satisfactory answer to the question, Who am I?, from exclusively turning our attention inward. If we look only within ourselves, we are likely to find a great void. Self-discovery emerges from our involvements with other people—with family members, friends, lovers, acquaintances, and people-in-general.

Several classical perspectives in social psychology have emphasized that the images of self and society blend into an inseparable pattern. If our general view of social life is negative in character, we are likely to hold negative attitudes toward ourselves. On the other hand, we are likely to associate positive attitudes toward people-in-general with a sense of well-being and pride in ourselves. In this respect the understandings we develop of society-at-large are closely linked with the self-images we construct.

Images of the self are bounded not only by our experiences in social relationships, but also by our particular locations in time and space. Each of us holds notions about both the best and the worst life possible for us, and at any given time our self-attainment is located somewhere between these two extremes. The meanings we impute to obtaining an education, pursuing a line of work, engaging in a love affair, or embarking on a course of political action tend to link closely with our self-images and our images of the broader society of which we are a part. These images help us sort out the important from the spurious, permit us to assess the opportunities available to us, and enable us to pursue the goals of central interest.

Since the content of the self is a constructed form of reality, the central components included will differ from one individual to another. Some view the self as a unified whole, while others see it as being more situational in character and divide it into several compartments. There are the social self and the private self; there is the self as an object with a location in time and place; and there is the self as a subject that includes the numerous hopes and aspirations expressed in particular lines of action. In view of the multiple and varied meanings that individuals can construct to give coherence to individual existences, we may define the self as an entity individuals postulate as central to their experiences and aspirations. In the formation of a self, individuals establish their identities, develop a sense of purpose in life, and reflect on the qualities of social relationships.

We express our self-identities in many ways through the process of social interaction. We do so not only through talking and listening, but also through facial gestures, qualities of the voice, body postures, forms of clothing, and many other visual displays. The manner of self-disclosure and the style of self-display have important implications for the qualities of social relationships. The sharing of information about the self tends to enhance the development of intimacy, while withholding information frequently promotes suspicion and distrust.

This chapter will consider several aspects of identity in the development, organization, and evaluation of the self. These include the processes by which self-attitudes form, the sources of unity for a self, the manner in which we present the self in everyday life, and the conditions associated with differential self-evaluations. By examining some of the perspectives and research findings on these topics, we should be able to understand more clearly both ourselves and those with whom we interact on an everyday basis.

A. SIGNIFICANT OTHERS

The basic social psychological perspectives on the development of a self derive from the classical works of Charles Horton Cooley (1902) and George Herbert Mead (1934). Cooley and Mead viewed the self as a socially constructed reality

BOX 5.1
Self-Concept and the Voodoo Curse

Accounts of death following a voodoo curse have been noted by numerous anthropologists and travelers in various parts of the world. Walter B. Cannon made an analysis of the mechanisms by which the magical curse may result in the death of an otherwise healthy person. The components of his observations are as follows:

1.   Communal knowledge holds that the sacred curse can kill, so the cursed individual defines the situation as that in which his or her own death will result from the curse that has been put on him or her.
2.   Following the curse, there is a change in the responses of significant others. The voodoo victim falls into the realm of the enchanted, and there is a tendency for friends and relatives to avoid the cursed individual and withdraw social supports.
3.   A second phase of social reactions occurs when the victim encounters the rituals of mourning for the dead. Hearing the mourning of relatives has the effect of attending one's own funeral.
4.   The victim's response is one of extreme fear. This is accompanied by several physiological reactions, including an acceleration of the heart beat, contraction of certain blood vessels, an increased production of adrenaline, and an increased release of sugar into the bloodstream. From the prolonged fear, death results from lack of food and from the physiological effects of a state of shock.

Thus, the voodoo curse sets in motion a set of social and physiological mechanisms that result in death as a self-fulfilling prophecy.

_____

Source: Walter B. Cannon, "Voodoo Death," in William A. Lessa and Evon Z. Vogt (eds.), *Reader in Comparative Religion*, New York: Harper & Row, 1972, pp. 433–439.

and emphasized that the emergent properties of a self derive from social relationships. Once we create images of a self as distinct from others, we may think of selfhood in pretty much the same fashion as we think about persons, objects, and events in the world around us (Blumer, 1969). We create the self as an entity that enters into relationships with others and becomes modified in the process.

The learning that takes place during the years of childhood is important for the development of a conception of self as a social object. As we reflect on the images we receive from significant others, attributes of the self come into focus and take on social meaning. Cooley described this process in terms of "the looking-glass self" and suggested that the responses of others mirror images of the self. These responses provide us with external vantage points for seeing ourselves and for evaluating our social worth. In this respect the self is not an isolated entity but a form of reality construction that emerges from social relationships. (See Box 5.1.)

Refinements in self-awareness are obtained through the process of **role taking**. This means that we can look at ourselves by mentally putting ourselves in the place of outside observers. In taking the role of others, we imagine how we appear to our parents, teachers, peers, or friends. We put ourselves in what we imagine to be their positions and from this vantage point obtain an "independent" assessment of ourselves. Taking the role of the other is a dual process of being ourselves and reflecting on how we appear to others. The self and others then become intertwined in the process of reality construction.

There are, of course, many people who participate in shaping our self-awareness (Rose, 1969). Some are people with whom we are intimately and emotionally involved; some have control over resources that are important to

---

BOX 5.2
Multiple References from Others

Evaluations of self and society are based on the acceptance of information from the social environment. Individuals derive this information from a variety of sources, including acquaintances, friends, lovers, and a variety of others whose opinions matter to them. Webster, Roberts, and Sobieszek (1972) set out to determine the selective process by which individuals receive, interpret, and organize information derived from numerous others.

In their research two variables emerged to account for the acceptance of information received from others. The first consisted of the perceived competence of those giving the information, and the second related to the degree of consistency in the information received from two or more sources. When people receive inconsistent information from different sources, they tend to establish some degree of balance through the use of additive and averaging models. In the additive process, individuals are receptive to all information within a situation, while with averaging process, people attempt to find a midpoint or a middle range in order to arrive at a useful conclusion.

The messages received from others have the greatest influence on self-evaluations under conditions in which those giving the information are perceived as competent and there is consistency in the information received from several sources. The authors conclude that the competency of the sources and the consistency of the messages have a greater impact on self-evaluations than do the positive or the negative implications of the information being received. Their study found no evidence to support the view that the only information accepted is that which supports a positive self-image.

Source: Murray Webster, Jr., Lynne Roberts, and Barbara I. Sobieszek, "Accepting 'Significant Others,'" *American Journal of Sociology* 78 (November, 1972): 576–598.

us; some are casual acquaintances and strangers who reflect our summarized views of society-at-large. Thus many people serve as references for the contents of our thoughts, our actions, and our identities. If you really care about what your parents, your teachers, your friends, or your acquaintances think of you, then they are among your **significant others** and will have a controlling influence on what you think, what you do, and what you are. (See Box 5.2.)

The influence of significant others on individual thought and action is clearly evident in the Wisconsin studies of educational achievements (Sewell, Haller, and Ohlendorf, 1970; Woelfel and Haller, 1971). These studies indicate that variations in educational attainment correlated highly with the expectations of parents, teachers, and peers. The images students hold of themselves and the ways in which their significant others regard them reflect the principle of the self-fulfilling prophecy. Parents, teachers, and peers expect high levels of achievement from certain students, and these expectations serve to shape the subsequent levels of educational attainment. Expecting certain individuals to be failures increases the probability that they will fail, just as expecting other individuals to be achievers increases the probability that they will achieve.

B. CHILDHOOD SOCIALIZATION

John P. Hewitt (1979) has described the acquisition of a self as a human necessity. We do not have a concept of self at birth, and a great deal of social learning must take place before our identities emerge. As a result, an understanding of the attributes of a self requires us to direct some attention toward the process of childhood socialization. The formation of a self depends on such aspects of socialization as learning a language, internalizing social norms, exploring the limits and prospects of the environment, and finding our place within the scheme of human affairs. These forms of learning are practical accomplishments, and they provide the basis on which we elaborate subsequent ideas of self.

The social learning in childhood is of primary importance because early experiences provide the basis on which children clarify and modify subsequent identities. The meanings of a personal name, of sex roles, of sibling birth order, and of age differences are embedded in networks of social relationships. Parents, siblings, playmates, and peers provide the child with reference points for classifying and describing objects and events. In this process caretakers and playmates become important symbols for the child.

In early childhood the world view is ego-centered: the child experiences events from his or her limited vantage point (Piaget, 1962). In the **egocentric world view**, infants and small children perceive themselves as being the center of the universe; they regard objects outside the immediate field of vision as no longer existing; and they experience caretakers as existing only to provide for their needs. The process of acquiring a self requires becoming aware of the existence of other people independently of one's own needs and interests. In effect, the egocentric world view persists until the child becomes capable of expressing sympathy and understanding for others.

With the growth of the child, the world vastly expands as the child re-

Childhood Dependency
Parent-child attachments are important sources of status and identity in our society. The dependency of the child and the care-giving behavior of the parent tend to result in the development of strong social bonds.

fines capacities for imitation and fantasy. In the socialization process a major breakthrough occurs in the use of imagination for taking the role of others. Through role playing the child is able to reflect on his or her behavior from the vantage point of other people. The child creates internal audiences to serve as references for self-evaluations. Once the child is able to make a mental separation between self and others, identities become clear, and the stage is set for subsequent participation in social life.

1. Sources of Identity

Socialization becomes necessary because the human infant depends on others for survival. This dependency extends over a long period of time; nowhere else in the animal kingdom is there a species in which the infant is so poorly equipped to confront the world by drawing directly on its own biological resources. The human child must be cared for by others if he or she is to survive, and this basic fact is of primary importance in the development of a self-identity.

Social norms require parents to provide the attention and care that their offspring needs. Through providing for the basic needs for food, warmth, security, and health maintenance, the care-giving behavior of parents becomes a social act that has meaning from the standpoint of the child. Parents are sources of need fulfillment, and experiences within the family provide the basis on which subsequent social relationships develop (Scott, 1971; Stewart, 1975). (See Box 5.3.)

During the earlier years of life, parents play very important parts in the social development of the child. Through such processes as feeding, bathing, and holding, the infant comes to expect others to be sources of need gratification and pleasure. The child experiences the world as a friendly place and develops feelings of trust if basic needs are warmly and consistently met. But if basic needs are fulfilled only on an erratic or inconsistent basis, the child is likely to feel insecure and mistrustful of others. Such attitudes of trust or mistrust may be the most important form of social learning in the earlier years of child development (Clausen, 1968).

The intimacy of family life confers on the child several aspects of identity. These include the status characteristics that adults and older children clearly recognize and understand. Some of the more important forms of status and identity conferred at birth are family membership, family name, gender (sexual classification), and sibling birth order. Labels are used in the conferral of identities, and the meanings of these labels are established through the drama of family interaction patterns. Siblings and playmates have an important role in shaping identities along age and sex lines, while adults play an important part in the development of attitudes toward authority and social norms.

On moving from the family into the school system, the child becomes aware of a greater variety of people than he or she previously imagined existed.

BOX 5.3
Family Photographs as Memory Aids

The research of Sandra L. Titus (1976) has concentrated on the importance of family photographs for reconstructing reality in later life. She notes that picture taking within families serves the purpose of recording special events and occurrences. An examination of several family albums indicated that photographs tend to have a formal quality about them. The style of dress and the appearances are frequently theatrical in character and are designed to define the situation for those who observe the events in question.

Returning to view family photo albums serves as a memory aid for refining impressions, since the actual occurrences in early life are subjected to reinterpretations in light of subsequent experiences. Photographs are treated as records of actual happenings, whereas memories may be distorted, confused, or simply in error. In capturing an "objective reality" pictures become forms of evidence that give validity to early family experiences.

Titus's analysis of forty-two family albums indicates that the subject matter of photographs places disproportionate emphasis on transitional events. Infant care, early childhood, going to school, and graduation are prominently recorded in pictures in order to create a family archive. The role of parents in early adulthood is clarified through returning to the family of origin. Conceptions of self receive verification through viewing pictures that reflect such themes as family solidarity, personal growth and development, social achievements, and sibling rivalry.

Source: Sandra L. Titus, "Family Photographs and Transition to Parenthood," *Journal of Marriage and the Family* 38 (August, 1976): 525–534.

The increased awareness of how people differ provides the child with a type of looking glass by which to subject a self-image to new forms of reality testing. The child's own family no longer occupies the center of the universe; the child comes to view it as having a more limited place within the broader scheme of social affairs. The child recognizes that classmates come from families that differ from the child's own in numerous ways; personal ideas come into conflict with those of peers (age-mates); and there are new forms of authority (teachers) for enforcing rules and placing emphasis on performance.

Developing an identity requires a great deal of **reality testing.** Children must learn to resolve the contradictions between impulse tendencies and the demands made by others (Robertson and Holzner, 1979). The spontaneous behavior patterns of children are frequently tolerated within the intimacy of family relationships. Parents share the play activity of children and derive pleasure from watching them develop. But as children grow, they must learn to curb their spontaneity. Constraints are imposed by the rights of others, by the organization of activities in some prearranged sequence, and by the penalties imposed for improper conduct. The child must learn that there is a time and place both for talking and for remaining silent.

2. Play and Games

In childhood, involvements in play and games are important for the development of a self (Denzin, 1975). The fantasy in **spontaneous play** activity permits children to take on adult roles. They temporarily become parents, truck drivers, fire fighters, police officers, space heroes, or television celebrities. They achieve all of this through fantasies that permit them to take on the roles of others. In the fun associated with spontaneous play, an important learning is taking place. They are enacting some of the realities they imagine to be associated with adult life. In the process, children learn about adult roles and reflect on the subsequent options available to them.

We may view the play of children as an imitation of adult life that simplifies the complexity of its events (Piaget, 1962). Children duplicate social objects in exaggerated forms; they give free reign to fantasy and to imagination; they derive intrinsic pleasures from exceptional feats and performances. The play world of children is a form of drama based on daydreaming. The child can transpose time, space, and social locations with a minimum of difficulty. The dream world is one of pseudoevents from which notions emerge about the desirable and the possible in adult life.

The importance of play for the acquisition of a self stems from developing a capacity for taking the role of another person. Through play activity the self becomes linked to social roles, and the child is able to draw on language to label social objects and to identify appropriate lines of action. The definition of social roles provides the child with reference points for self-evaluations and for making predictions about sources of personal accomplishment and social approval. The self then becomes expressed in social relationships and becomes something more than just an entity within itself (Charon, 1979).

In comparison to spontaneous play, the **game** is a more highly organized activity. There are rules to specify how the game is to proceed; there are rules to determine winners and losers. The child learns that attempts to win are frequently unsuccessful and that the world does not conform to his or her expectations of it (Denzin, 1975). This requires the development of some degree of control over impulse tendencies. The child cannot have everything at the time he or she wants it. In this regard the learning task is to recognize that the gratification of needs takes place only through acceptable channels.

A game is a participatory type of activity involving one or more players who accept a set of rules as binding on their performances and in which some combination of skill and chance determines who wins and who loses. The skills of the players primarily determine the outcome of some games (e.g., checkers, chess, and basketball), while other games (e.g., dice and cards) place

Fantastic Socialization
The child obviously is aware that the rabbit is not a real rabbit, that rabbits are not larger than people, and that rabbits do not tolerate passengers. Yet make-believe is fun and gives free reign to the imagination. The use of fantasy in the play of children extends the range of the possible.

BOX 5.4
The Games Children Play

From data gathered on 181 fifth-grade children over a one-year period, Janet Lever (1976) analyzed gender differences in the games children play. The data were obtained predominantly from white, middle-class children and consisted of observations on school-yard activities, semistructured interviews, written questionnaires, and diary records of play activity.

Lever's results indicated substantial differences in play activity by gender. As compared to girls, boys play outdoors more often; they play in larger groups; and their play groups are more diversified in age composition. These differences stem from the competitive emphasis in the games boys play and from the requirement of many team sports for a large number of players. Girls frequently play in male games in order to round out the teams, while boys seldom play in predominantly female games. The games girls play tend to be of shorter duration than boy's games, and they tend to have "a ceiling effect" in terms of sustaining interest and developing skills.

Children spend a great deal of time at play, and the manner in which they become involved in games has implications for the refinement of their skills and abilities. The games boys play tend to promote skills in organization, in dealing with rule-bound events, and in adjudicating disputes. By way of contrast, the games girls play contribute to the learning of interpersonal skills that are associated with expressive and nurturance roles. Thus, through the play of children, variations in gender roles are being perpetuated. In adult life, males have numerous advantages in the competitive occupational realm, and many of these advantages have their origins in childhood socialization.

Source: Janet Lever, "Sex Differences in the Games Children Play," *Social Problems* 23 (April, 1976): 478–487.

greater emphasis on chance and a belief in luck. The rules specify the number of players, the conditions under which to play the game, and the procedures for determining winners and losers. The appeal of games lies primarily in their emphasis on engagement in a pleasurable and self-contained activity. (See Box 5.4.)

According to George Herbert Mead (1934), the rule-bound character of games is important for developing notions about the generalized other, for recognizing the limits and prospects of social living, and for locating the boundaries within which one may pursue goals. Successful participation in games requires taking the roles of other players and making adjustments in one's own behavior accordingly. Such participation is a form of training for the challenges in adult life (Snyder and Spreitzer, 1978). The self grows and develops as the child's understanding of society matures (Charon, 1979), as skills develop for social interactions, and as a sense of purpose in life becomes established.

C. ORGANIZATION OF THE SELF

social

The organization of the self is comprised of both objective and subjective aspects. The **objective components of the self** are reflected in answers to such questions as, Who am I?, and Who are you? The person perceives the self and others as social objects defined through the qualities and attributes of role relationships. The language of identity is the language of social classification: the objective self is identified through such vocabularies as those pertaining to sex, age, marital status, religion, race, and occupation. Accordingly, changes in social classifications and definitions are accompanied by changes in the identities of a self.

personal

The role and the person, however, are not necessarily the same because actors frequently define themselves as something more than a composite of all the roles they play. The **subjective components of the self** include all of those feelings and assessments that shape intentions and planned lines of action (Stanage, 1968). The subjective self is the source of creativity and innovation and is reflected in an individual's attitudes toward his or her "real self." Ralph H. Turner (1976: 992) observed that "the real self is revealed when a person does something solely because he wants to—not because it is good or bad or noble or courageous or self-sacrificing, but because he spontaneously wishes to do so." Thus the subjective side of the self reveals itself in impulse tendencies and in the personal evaluations of the roles being performed.

1. Multiple Selves

Manford H. Kuhn and Thomas S. McPartland (1954) conducted a study of college students at a midwestern university to determine the primary components of self-attitudes. Their approach was the direct one of eliciting twenty statements in answer to the question, Who am I? The researchers made no suggestions as to what the self-identities of their subjects might be but left it up to the students simply to list their answers to the question in the order the answers occurred to them. The results of their analysis of "I am _____" statements have been useful in clarifying the components of self-identities.

Analyses of responses to the twenty-statements text revealed a primary emphasis on objective social characteristics, such as "a student," "a girl," "a husband," "Baptist," "from Chicago," "an athlete," "pre-law student," "daughter," "oldest child." To Kuhn and McPartland, these responses reflected consensual categories in the sense that they were based on group memberships and social characteristics readily identifiable by others. The consensual categories were the dominant forms of response, both in terms of the frequency and the order in which students listed them. Their findings, then, indicated that the self as a social object occupies a prominent place in self-attitudes and identities. The

BOX 5.5
Self-Images among Adolescents

Drawing on a sample of 1917 urban school children in grades 3 through 12, Simmons, Rosenberg, and Rosenberg (1973) studied changes in self-images during adolescence. Adolescence is expected to be a stressful phase of the life cycle because during it many changes occur in family ties, in cross-sexual relationships, and in levels of physical and social maturity.

The results indicated that disturbances in self-image appear much greater in the twelve-to-fourteen-age group than among adolescents who are younger or older. These are reflected in higher levels of self-consciousness (sensitivity to the reactions of others), greater instability of self-image, and lower self-esteem. Adolescents in the twelve-to-fourteen-age category were also more likely to think that parents, teachers, and peers viewed them negatively. With increasing age, self-consciousness tends to decline and self-images become more stable, although even in late adolescence self-consciousness and instability manifest themselves to higher degrees than among eight-to-eleven-year-old children.

For any single year, the greatest change in self-images occurs between the ages of 11 and 12. This is reflected in a sharp decline in positive self-evaluations measured in terms of such qualities as being "smart," "good-looking," "truthful," "good at sports," "well-behaved," "helpful," and "good at making jokes." The authors also noted a sharp increase in unhappiness and feelings of depression among twelve year olds. The disturbance in self-image among twelve year olds is influenced to some degree by the shift from elementary school to junior high school.

Source: Roberta G. Simmons, Florence Rosenberg, and Morris Rosenberg, "Disturbance in Self-Image at Adolescence," *American Sociological Review* 38 (October, 1973): 553–568.

emphasis on group memberships and readily identifiable social characteristics shows the importance of social relationships for an anchorage of the self-concept.

The statements that did not relate exclusively to an objective social position were primarily evaluative in character. These included such self-attributes as "happy," "bored," "too heavy," "interesting," "attractive." Many of the evaluation statements were modifiers of particular status characteristics, such as "good wife," "pretty good student," or other status qualifications. The primacy of the objective characteristics over more subjective and evaluative aspects of the self in the twenty-statements test reflects the importance of social labels for defining the situations in which social interactions occur. (See Box 5.5.)

TABLE 5.1
Domains of Status and Identity

Social Classifications	Age
	Sex
	Race
	Family of origin
	Birth order
	Educational attainment
	Marital status
	Place of residence
	Occupation
	Religious identification
Significant Others	Friends
	Parents
	Siblings
	Lovers
	Roommates
	Classmates
	Admired people
Generalized Others	Acquaintances
	Peers
	Neighbors
	Police
	Employers
	Bureaucrats
	Voters
	Advertisers
	Most people
	Americans

The Kuhn and McPartland (1954) approach was based on the assumption that the self is partitioned into multiple components. **Multiple selves** are reflected in the playing of different roles as individuals move from one situation to another. Self-attitudes are oriented toward a diversity of social activities and expressed in the many frames of reference that individuals may bring to bear on any given situation. Special problems emerge from the multiple images of the self in at least two major ways. One consists of the large number of social expectancies others hold toward individuals who occupy some consensual category; the second consists of the competing demands that accompany a person's multiple identities. (See Table 5.1.)

In concentrating on cultural contradictions in sex roles, Mirra Komarovsky (1946) noted the variety of social expectancies of the adult female in our society. For example, the role of the adult female encompasses such diverse components as wife, mother, employee, friend, and domestic. These numerous social definitions are expected of most women, to some degree or another, and as such they often place a heavy set of responsibilities on the individual female. The energies required for splendid performance in all aspects of the female role exceed the capabilities and inclination of most women. As a result, the competing demands and expectancies often lack integration with one another and constitute an important source of stress for the adult female of America in the 1980s.

In similar fashion, the diverse roles of the college professor includes such elements as teacher, researcher, advisor, author, public servant, consultant, and committee member. The adult female and the college professor both face the special risk of becoming overextended to such a degree that they can perform none of these roles well. The problem of self-identity in such cases is one of coming to terms with the competing demands that accompany any particular line of action. Imagine how the problems are compounded for the person who is both an adult female and a college professor! (See Box 5.6.)

BOX 5.6
Multiple Roles in Marriage

Ivan Nye (1974) has identified eight major roles in marriage relationships. Only seven of them have been listed below. Can you guess which one has been left out?

Provider	meeting family financial needs
Companion	serving recreational interests
Housekeeper	maintaining and managing the home
Therapist	listening to problems, serving as "a sounding board," and providing for the release of tension
Child Socializer	training and caring for the child or children
Community Liaison	serving as "a family agent" in community affairs
Family Mediator	getting along with in-laws

How would you rank-order the above roles in terms of their importance for a successful marriage? Are there other important marital roles that are not included in this list?

Source: F. Ivan Nye, "Emerging and Declining Family Roles," *Journal of Marriage and the Family* 36 (May, 1974): 238–245.

The problems of self-identity are further complicated by the variety of social positions that any given individual holds in modern society. Accordingly, the major perspective on any particular set of events may derive from one's work group, from one's marital status, from one's religious affiliation, or from any of several social positions one holds. Such multiple aspects of the self relate to the pluralism and the fragmentation of contemporary social life. With attachments spread across several group memberships, the self becomes less vulnerable to the performance demands from any particular social sector. The checks and balances of numerous group memberships provide the individual with a greater degree of leeway in the organization of his or her own priorities. At the same time, however, the center of an individual's personal existence becomes more difficult to locate.

2. *Unity of the Self*

The multiple aspects of the self in modern society are a reflection of the degree to which separation has occurred within the social realm. Organizationally, the church is separated from the state, careers are separated from family life, and work is separated from play. Among students, love life and play activity often lack integration with the pursuit of academic and career objectives. What takes place inside the classroom is often separated, both intellectually and emotionally, from what takes place outside the classroom. Thus the pluralism of modern society is reflected in the emphasis on the separation of institutions on one hand and on the multiple and overlapping group identities on the other (Presthus, 1978).

Several major analytical concerns emerge in connection with the self-concept. Foremost among these are the questions pertaining to the integration of the self. How does the individual handle the multiple aspects of the self in relation to one other? What is the degree of integration among the multiple aspects of the self? How does the self establish priorities? What is central and what is peripheral to the self-identity in any particular case?

The quest for unity to the self is expressed in many ways. Making a lot of money, working toward success in one's career, joining a religious sect, dedicating oneself to a political cause, and becoming deeply involved in a love affair are among the conditions in which one can achieve a sense of unity within the self through strong and overriding commitments. In such cases, one achieves unity through creating a sense of purpose in life and dedicating oneself to a particular set of goals and values.

Assigning a high degree of importance to some aspect of the self serves the function of setting priorities for the resolution of competing demands and obligations. The dedicated business person may be willing to neglect his or her family if family obligations interfere with career plans; the student in love may be willing to neglect academic assignments if they interfere with the pursuit of romance; the convert to a religious sect may be willing to leave community and friends if such a move is necessary for advancing a sacred cause. The development of commitments and the setting of priorities may result in major achievements. For example, the dedicated scientist may make a major scientific discovery, the small business person may succeed in building a major corporation, or a highly motivated athlete may become an Olympic star.

In many cases, however, extreme involvements do not lead to a major sense of accomplishment but to an intense feeling of failure. While extreme commitments can provide a temporary solution to the problems of the complexity of social life, they also provide special forms of vulnerability. The bases for social supports become highly limited. Cutting oneself off from initial family, from community of origin, from old friends, or from other social attachments in the pursuit of a narrowly circumscribed set of objectives often has the effect of requiring the individual to rely more heavily on his or her own resources in times of trouble.

danger of single priority

Making an extreme commitment risks failing to take into account the consequences, for oneself or for others, of following a single course of action. Disillusionment with a political cause or disenchantment with a religious sect can be a traumatic experience and subsequently require a great deal of effort in building a new set of social relationships. Thus while an extreme commitment provides a clearly identifiable center for a self-identity, it also is a form of risk taking. Dedication to a single goal often requires giving up the numerous social supports that multiple involvements in group memberships may provide.

Very few people in modern society center their identities around dedication to any single cause. A more prevalent pattern is to spread one's identities across a number of groups, such as the family, a limited circle of friends, and the work group. A variety of more limited involvements with acquaintances provides an even broader base for extensions of the self into the broader society. Assigning a greater degree of importance to some identities than to others provides a way of ordering priorities and thus resolving the problem of competing demands without giving up the kinds of reinforcements that multiple group involvements potentially provide. (See Box 5.7.) *VS*

In contrast to those who seek a unified self, some take a situational approach to social relationships and permit the self to assume varied forms according to the cues received from the immediate environment (Lifton, 1970). Such individuals, rather than having a self consisting of stable attributes, are oriented toward becoming what is expected of them according to the circumstances. Varied identities rapidly come into play and become modified as social situations shift. While this approach to social relationships is highly flexible

BOX 5.7
Is There a Quest for Identity?

Over the past two or three decades there has been an extensive literature in the United States dealing with the themes of a search for self-identity, a lack of social attachments, and a sense of being uprooted. To determine the extent to which there is a quest for self-identity, Ralph H. Turner (1975) collected data from a probability sample of more than a thousand adults in Los Angeles County and from another sample of several hundred students at UCLA.

The results of his study indicated that very few adults in the general population admit to ever having been concerned with the question: "Who am I really?" Within the group of those who did express a concern with this question, however, the college educated and young adults predominated. Self-uncertainty decreased with increasing age; Turner found that about eight times as many subjects in the eighteen-to-twenty-nine-age category expressed a concern with problems of identity than did subjects sixty years of age or older. His findings also indicated that college experiences and identity problems tend to go together. In the eighteen-to-twenty-nine-age category, 39 percent of the college educated expressed a concern with self-identity as compared to 13 percent of those with only a grade-school education.

Concentrating on the UCLA sample, Turner found that in contrast to the general population, the majority of students were concerned with the question of identity. In the views of most students the primary routes to self-discovery are through working hard at a difficult and challenging task and being of service to others, rather than through transcending duties, obligations, and normative constraints.

Source: Ralph H. Turner, "Is There a Quest for Identity?," *Sociological Quarterly* 16 (Spring, 1975): 148–161.

and adaptable, it also conveys the risk that one's life will fall into fragments without any identifiable center or primary source of stability. It is a personal lifestyle characterized to some degree as a pattern of aimlessness and drift.

The attributes of self-identity among individuals in modern society, then, are variable in character. The self for some is characterized by a central, overriding identity, while for others the self is much more pluralistic and situational in character. The greater the intensity of involvement in some particular social status, the greater the clarity of purpose and the unity of the self, there is at the same time the lower the degree of adaptability to changing social circumstances. The presence of multiple identities provides a broader basis for group supports, but involves a greater risk that the self will become fragmented into separate and unrelated parts.

D. DISPLAYS OF THE SELF

The social self displays itself through interpersonal communication and becomes meaningful primarily through the bonds established in interactions and relationships. For example, being a teacher has social meaning primarily within the context of students, being a doctor within the context of treating patients, and being a clerk within the context of interactions with customers. Similarly, the notion of being a parent implies the presence of a child, and we cannot adequately take into account the role of wife without also taking into account the role of husband. As a socially constructed form of reality, the self becomes a way of organizing experiences and orienting behavior.

People express their self-identities in interpersonal communication primarily through talking and listening. Conversations frequently result in the disclosure of such aspects of the self as past experiences, social attitudes, personal aspirations, and fears for the future. In some cases, however, individuals make deliberate attempts to disguise or to conceal as much of the self as the situation permits. If individuals freely and openly disclose a great deal of themselves in social relationships, they may be able to elicit high degrees of responsiveness and mutual support. But there is also the possibility that self-disclosure will increase vulnerability through revealing weaknesses and evoking unfriendly reactions.

1. Self-Disclosure

In social relationships, one of the basic decisions is how much of the self to reveal to others (Jourard, 1971). We sometimes conceal aspects of the self out of concerns for safety and protection against unwarranted criticism. In other situations we wish to reveal ourselves in order to sustain or enhance a set of social bonds. The concept of **self-disclosure** is used by social psychologists to describe the degree to which individuals share self-knowledge with others during the course of social interaction.

There are certain aspects of the self that are relatively open and known to others. These are the public aspects of the self, which are closely linked to status characteristics. For example, it is not necessary for an instructor to reveal his or her qualifications for teaching a course in social psychology. These qualifications are established by university officials before teaching assignments are made. Correspondingly, professors know certain attributes of students because of the screening procedures in registering for college courses.

While status characteristics provide broad outlines of an identity, they do not go very far in revealing many of the personal qualities of role occupants. The concealed aspects of the self include all of those personal attributes of an identity that are hidden to others in the course of interaction. Many of an indi-

TABLE 5.2
Identification Displays on T-Shirts

Types of identification display on T-shirts frequently
worn by teenagers and young adults

Membership in a club, organization, or fraternity
Advertisement for beer, rock music group, amusement park, or sport event
Name of college or university (other than the one attended)
Remembering an event:
    I SURVIVED THE BLIZZARD OF '78
    I SURVIVED THE THREE MILE ISLAND ACCIDENT (front)—I THINK (back)
Implied Sexual Attitude:
    I'M NOT PERFECT, BUT PARTS OF ME ARE EXCELLENT
    SWORN TO FUN, LOYAL TO NONE
    SATISFACTION GUARANTEED
    THE BEST LOVERS ARE FROM __(home town)_____
Social Relationships:
    BE KIND TO ME, I'VE HAD A HARD DAY
    INSANITY IS HEREDITARY (front)—YOU GET IT FROM YOUR KIDS (back)
    BABY (arrow pointing to stomach)

Identification displays on T-shirts are similar to the wearing of uniforms in that they announce or advertise an aspect of the self that otherwise may not be known. Such displays serve as attention-getting devices and may be designed to enhance self-esteem or to announce a group connection. They may also serve as conversation openers for interactions with strangers.

vidual's past experiences and social attitudes fall within the private domain and the person may regard them as privileged information. These include personal attitudes, past experiences, and plans for the future. Because of the emotionality associated with certain experiences and commitments, individuals may conceal aspects of the self behind various masks. In anticipation of some desired effect on others, a person may decide to reveal only limited aspects of the self. (See Table 5.2.)

The degree of self-disclosure is linked closely to the level of intimacy in social relationships. The very nature of friendship and love affairs, for example, involves sharing information, expressing personal concerns, revealing past experiences, and reflecting on personal aspirations. These are the conditions that reinforce social bonds and provide for mutual support. The boundaries separating the public and the private domains tend to vanish, and the stress associated with personal troubles tends to lessen. The sharing of problems in intimate relationships can have the effect of reducing the uncertainty associated with loneliness and of having to rely exclusively on one's own resources (Gilbert, 1976).

In allowing private and personal information to surface, men and women show important differences. The evidence in support of this conclusion comes from studies of dating couples, marriage partners, and parent-child relationships. The research findings indicate that women in dating couples generally reveal more of themselves to their boyfriends than their boyfriends reveal in return (Rubin *et al.*, 1980); in marriages, wives tend to reveal more intimate feelings and doubts than do their husbands (Jourard, 1971); and in parent-child relationships, daughters reveal more personal concerns than do sons (Balswick and Balkwell, 1977). The gender differences in self-disclosure appear to be re-

The Individual in the Crowd
One of the major problems the individual confronts is finding a sense of personal meaning and purpose within the context of group living.

lated to role definitions. We expect men to be more unemotional and restrained, while women we expect to be more emotional and expressive. Differential performances in intimate relationships bear out these cultural definitions.

There are consequences that accompany both disclosure and nondisclosure in social relationships. If the people in our lives do not authentically know us, we are likely to be misunderstood. Insufficient information is likely to add uncertainty and mystery to intimate relationships, and these are the ingredients for suspicion and distrust. In contrast, if individuals freely and openly disclose self-attitudes to significant others, the results tend to have bonding effects. The sharing of information tends to draw boundaries that separate insiders from outsiders. But if social relationships begin to deteriorate, knowledge about another person may be used as an offensive weapon. For this reason the conflicts that surface in family squabbles frequently escalate. Each party to the relationship has an awareness of special vulnerabilities of the other person (Bach and Wyden, 1974).

People's decisions to hide rather than to reveal themselves are based frequently on concerns with how others might use this self-knowledge. Yet despite the resistance to self-disclosure, individuals often have a need to talk about themselves and to have others listen. For this reason, having a captive listener on a long-distance bus ride or plane flight sometimes serves a therapeutic function. The individual may reveal to a total stranger many aspects of the self that would be hidden or disguised in ongoing social relationships. If interactions with a stranger are of short duration, there is little risk in disclosing many aspects of past experiences, present concerns, and future plans. In the process of sharing self-knowledge with another person one may obtain some degree of insight into oneself.

In some cases self-disclosure may be inappropriate and inauthentic. For example, a professor may interject into a lecture his or her personal experiences when they clearly have no bearing on the subject matter of the course. The members of a religious cult can be so involved in a set of ideological concerns that they reveal more about themselves than others want to know. And parents may want to talk about their experiences in growing up when their children would prefer not to listen. In such cases self-disclosure has an inauthentic quality since its imposition is out of place. Rather than enhancing a set of social relationships, it may have the opposite effect.

Self-disclosure becomes inauthentic when there is an **overreference** to some aspect of status and identity (Seeman, 1966). The overreference can take many forms. In some cases there may be an undue reference to a physical stigma, to a health problem, to minority status, to being a male or a female, or to the level of success in business. In each of these instances self-disclosure may go beyond acceptable limits. At the other extreme, inauthenticity may take the form of self-denial. This involves a refusal to recognize or discuss serious problems that exist. Avoidance of self-disclosure in this case is a defense mechanism that reflects a fear of confronting the challenges of social living.

2. *The Real Self*

Self-disclosure becomes of concern in interpersonal relationships because of the recognition that there are unique personalities behind the roles being played; that the self is more than a composite of observable characteristics; and that persons have experiences, backgrounds, and aspirations known only to themselves. In some cases there is a close correspondence between the inner self of a person and the person we see; but in other cases appearances may be deceptive, and knowing another person accurately requires probing for the deeper sources of meaning, purpose, and commitment.

According to Robin M. Williams (1970), the belief in the existence of the individual personality is a dominant theme in American social thought. We take for granted the capacities and the rights of individuals to make choices and to engage in the pursuit of personal goals. Williams (1970: 497) notes that "the question as to whether there is actually such an entity as 'the individual,' 'self,' or 'ego' is usually not even thought of, and if raised, is greeted with surprise or shock." In effect, people have real selves because they think of themselves as having real selves. Images of the realities of the self are creations that serve as frameworks for evaluating both ourselves and the people in our lives.

An analysis by Ralph H. Turner (1976) suggests that we experience our real selves through the meanings we give to situations and events. Some of our experiences seem genuine to us, while others we associate with disbelief, fantasy, or misplaced emphasis. Such forms of awareness grow out of the sense of a gap between the way we think of ourselves and what we see as happening in specific situations: we distinguish the genuine from the spurious, important events from unimportant ones, and authentic from inauthentic experiences. Such definitions provide some degree of unity and coherence to the self in the face of the changing demands and requirements of specific situations.

In developing the idea of a real self, Turner makes an important distinction between self-conceptions anchored in institutions and self-conceptions anchored in impulse. For some the true self emerges through the roles played within such institutions as the family, the workplace, religion, or government; for others the experience of a real self surfaces through the pursuit of impulse and spontaneous desire. In the former case the person and the role merge into a common framework of meaning and action; in the latter case, "the true self consists of deep, unsocialized, inner impulses" (Turner, 1976: 992).

Self-conceptions grounded in institutional roles reflect the individual's willingness or the pleasure to do what he or she is expected to do. The person accepts social norms as guidelines to personal conduct. The person creates and

chging ideas of self

achieves the self through the accomplishments in roles that are socially defined and commonly understood. We should not regard such an institutional locus of the self as meaning that the person is a miniature reproduction of society nor that people who play similar roles are carbon copies of one another. Instead, as Turner (1976) observed, the merger of the person with the role implies that the individual can find meaning in life through selecting socially approved goals and working toward their attainment. The conception of self under these circumstances is an ongoing reality created through the acceptance of social challenges.

In contrast to this approach, for some people the experience of a real self may surface through an emphasis on spontaneous desire, inner impulse, or personal freedom. Such individuals make distinctions between role playing and the person and between the individual and society. The self is not created so much through social accomplishments as through a process of discovery and personal experimentation. Turner (1976: 993) observes that "under the impulse locus, the true self is revealed only when inhibitions are lowered or abandoned." The quest for self-realization under such circumstances involves an attempt to bring behavior into alignment with personal desires.

Turner hypothesizes that over the past several decades Americans have shifted emphasis from institutions to impulse as the basis for the real self. Institutional roles obviously are important for the maintenance of orderly social relationships, but young people are increasingly basing their self-conceptions on such impulsive qualities as emotions, feelings, and spontaneous desires, rather than on social roles and status characteristics. The person can find genuine and authentic experiences in pursuing both social roles and personal impulses; but the experiences of a true self appear increasingly to occur within the private rather than the public domains of social life.

E. EVALUATIONS OF THE SELF

In modern society individuals very often confront situations that appear to be devoid of the rewards and meanings necessary for feelings of personal comfort and well-being. The regularity with which such situations occur has implications for the individual's self-evaluation, which may lead to a sense of estrangement from the self. Luther B. Otto and David L. Featherman (1975: 703) have observed,

...The self-estranged life is chronically flat, empty and boring, void of the vitality that the individual feels should somehow be there. He feels deprived of meaning, enslaved by unrewarding activities.

In such cases we may separate the feelings and actions we associate with given situations from what we regard as being important. We tend to take little credit or blame for our sensations and actions in situations in which what is happening to us seems only peripheral to our basic identities. Conformity to the demands of the situation or to the expectations of others we often associate with a sense of estrangement from ourselves.

1. Self-Estrangement

Following Melvin Seeman (1975), we may speak of **self-estrangement** as occurring in those situations in which the individual is unable to derive intrinsic rewards from the activities in which he or she is engaged. Intrinsic rewards are feelings of satisfaction, pleasure, or fulfillment that grow out of involvement in a particular set of activities. The lack of intrinsic rewards arises when a person is unable to act spontaneously on the basis of impulses and has to pursue a course of action that basically is out of harmony with his or her conception of self. Under conditions of self-estrangement the individual has the feeling that "this is not the real me," "I don't believe in what I am doing," "I am not comfortable with myself," or "I dislike what I have to do." Estrangement from the self necessarily implies some degree of discomfort with the activities in which the person engages.

For Seeman, as well as for other investigators, the work sphere has provided the basis for much of the thinking and research on the problems of self-estrangement (Shepard, 1972). In this regard the early writings of Karl Marx have constituted an important source for subsequent analyses of the meanings of work that accompany industrialization.

In Marx's analysis (1844) the self-estrangement of the industrial worker derives from a series of organizational attributes of the factory system. Marx viewed the factory worker as having little to say about the organization of his or her own work activities. Instead, those who manage the industrial system plan the work. Presumably, the lack of participation in the planning process interferes with the individual's sense of meaningful participation in the production enterprise.

Further, Marx noted that factory work becomes monotonous and repetitive, that it affords little opportunity for a sense of craftsmanship in the job. Through the division of labor, so many people are involved in the production of any particular commodity that the individual worker is not able to identify with the completed product or to regard it as an object of his or her own creation. Under these conditions work does not become a basis for self-fulfillment or self-expression but rather an instrumental activity necessary for subsistence. It is a form of drudgery the worker must endure in order to receive a paycheck.

The inability of the industrial worker to derive intrinsic rewards from the job is but a single case of the conditions under which self-estrangement can occur in modern society. Such inability is presumably also the case for the person who is bored with the routine and drudgery of everyday child-care and housework tasks. Problems of self-estrangement emerge for the parent who cooks in order to get the cooking over with, who provides taxi service for the children only out of a sense of duty, or who does the laundry and house cleaning without any feeling of intrinsic reward. Under these conditions there is a lack of unity between overt performances and what the person perceives as the real self.

Apparently, many college students are unable to derive intrinsic rewards from the pursuit of academic objectives (Holian, 1972). The student who is working only for a degree and who is unable to derive a sense of meaning from the academic activities in which he or she is engaged also faces a problem of self-estrangement. In this respect the student's sense of mastery over course requirements and the grading systems may vary independently of the intrinsic rewards derived from the educational process. Reading assignments, taking examinations, and writing term papers may not be regarded as rewarding experiences, but as forms of coerced behavior that the student performs primarily out of a sense of necessity.

Self-estrangement, then, is situational in character and refers to a low degree of correspondence between one's own standards for intrinsically rewarding experiences and the assessments of the course of action that one is currently pursuing. Here we assume that the conceptions of self, like other aspects of social life, are constructed forms of reality. The social psychologist must determine self-estrangement in the spheres of work, home life, and education from the vantage point of the individual and his or her own definition of the situation. Such a vantage point consists of assessing personal desires and rewards as they derive from social relationships and from the activities in which the individual engages.

2. Self-Esteem

In certain situations individuals may be willing to assume the costs of foregoing intrinsic rewards in order to enhance the prospects for attaining other kinds of objectives. Workers may be willing to work at alienating jobs in order to obtain the social approval that accompanies being a good provider for their families. Parents may be willing to tolerate the drudgery of child care and other forms of work around the house in order to reinforce the self-esteem that accompanies a sense of service to others. And students may tolerate the nonrewarding tasks in their educational programs in order to gain entry into the labor force at some desired level of prestige.

Kenneth J. Gergen (1971) points out that the feelings of self-estrangement are not identical with those of low self-esteem. In his view, people will often disguise their true conceptions of self for the purpose of social approval. While the feelings of self-estrangement are specific to the activities in which individuals engage, the concept of **self-esteem** is much broader and relates to the individual's generalized sense of personal and social worth. Being "a good person," "a dependable student," "a competent parent," or "a responsible son or daughter," are examples of the kinds of evaluations that are implied in a sense of self-esteem.

An extremely large volume of research has been conducted by social psychologists on the various problems related to self-esteem. The interests have been directed toward the measurement of self-esteem (Wylie, 1961), the origins of self-esteen from relationships with others (Rosenberg and Simmons, 1972), and the consequences of self-esteem for behavior (Coopersmith and Feldman, 1974).

In a review of the literature on the meaning and measurement of self-esteem, David D. Franks and Joseph Marolla (1976) concluded that the two primary variables consist of inner and outer sources of self-esteem. The outer sources reflect assessments of social worth and the level of approval received from others, while the inner sources of self-esteem consist of the meaning of an individual's actions as he or she perceives them in terms of competency and effectiveness. The authors describe the inner sources of self-esteem as follows:

One's sense of inner self-esteem derives from the experience of self as an active agent— of making things actually happen and realizing one's intents in an impartial world. It involves the general pragmatic notion of that sense of self arising in connection with active striving in the face of obstacles (1976: 326).

There are numerous social implications of this aspect of self-esteem. An important one is that the self-concept serves as a form of the self-fulfilling prophecy. Individuals who think of themselves as competents are likely to think and act in such a manner as to demonstrate that they are competent, while those who think of themselves as incompetents and failures are likely to become incompetents and failures. Success and achievement in numerous areas of social life are likely to be influenced by such a self-fulfilling prophecy. For example, academic achievement, occupational success, and satisfaction with family life are likely to be associated with high levels of self-esteem (Rosenberg, 1979).

The outer sources of self-esteem consist of the kinds and degrees of social support received from significant others. Here the emphasis is on the evidence of self-worth one receives from the external social environment. In this connection the research of Rosenberg (1965) on self-esteem among high school students underscores the importance of parental attitudes toward their children. The parent who expresses a lack of interest in the child's contribution to mealtime conversation, who seems indifferent to the child's friends, or who expresses little concern for the quality of the child's academic performance is very likely to have a child who holds a low estimate of his or her own social

Building Self-Esteem
Success in competitive sport is one of the many ways of building self-esteem. Learning to belong is reflected in team effort and in developing an understanding of the rules of the game. Many people view such activity as an introduction to the games of adult life. Successful performance in competitive sport provides a basis for earning social approval and for demonstrating personal effectiveness.

worth. The low level of self-esteem stemming from the lack of social support has the effect of placing the child in a position of vulnerability with respect to environmental influences and changes (Ziller, 1974).

Stanley Coopersmith (1967) identified some of the major ways in which individuals achieve a validation of their self-evaluations. One way consists of demonstrating effectiveness through exerting influence and control over others; a second derives from receiving acceptance and approval from significant others; and a third consists of adhering to the moral standards by which one thinks of oneself as a "good" person. Thus one validates a positive self-evaluation through perceiving the effectiveness of one's own actions combined with the social approval received from others. The primary variables in a sense of well-being include the view that one's social environment is responsive to personal needs and interests, that social relationships are predictable and dependable, and that one can pursue personal goals with a reasonable degree of confidence. The self becomes problematic under those conditions in which the social order loses its predictability and the social environment becomes unresponsive to personal effort.

SUMMARY

The reality of a social self emerges from the interplay of status and identity. Research on the components of a self-identity indicates that we typically respond to the question, Who am I?, by enumerating and evaluating social locations in such categories as age, sex, race, marital status, religion, occupation, family, and community. The multiple aspects of an identity suggest that in modern society we are exposed to competing social demands. The self for some people is characterized by a central overriding identity, while for others the self is much more pluralistic and situational in character.

Childhood socialization plays an important part in the development of an identity because early experiences provide the basis on which we elaborate subsequent learning. The formation of an identity is possible through the use of imagination, which is enhanced through play, games, and the imitation of others. In both childhood and later life, significant others provide the basic frameworks for assessing who we are, where we are located, and where we are heading.

The self that we display and disclose has important implications for the development of social relationships. For some people the real self is expressed through the pursuit of such institutional roles as jobs, marriage, parenthood, and church attendance; for others the real self emerges from the pursuit of impulse and spontaneous desire. Research over the past several decades suggests that young Americans are placing an increased emphasis on impulsive qualities (emotions, feelings, and spontaneous desires) as a primary basis for self-conceptions and a decreased emphasis on social roles and status characteristics. Thus the composition of what is experienced as a real self varies according to historical circumstances.

Self-evaluations are based on the rewards we obtain from routine activities and role relationships. Estrangement from the self occurs in those situations in which we are unable to derive intrinsic rewards, or a sense of fulfillment, from the activities in which we engage. Involvement in activities with low intrinsic rewards very often occurs in the spheres of work, home life, and the pursuit of educational objectives. The overall sense of self-esteem, however, is much broader in scope and includes our generalized sentiments about personal and social worth. A positive evaluation of self is verified through our own effectiveness in influencing events and through success in obtaining the social approval of others. The levels of self-esteem very often serve as self-fulfilling prophecies by promoting either accomplishments or failures.

BASIC TERMS

Role taking
Significant others
Egocentric world view
Reality testing
Spontaneous play
Game
Objective components of
   the self

Subjective components of
   the self
Multiple selves
Self-disclosure
Overreference
Self-estrangement
Self-esteem

REFERENCES

Bach, George R. and Peter Wyden
    1974 "Why Intimates Must Fight," in Suzanne K. Steinmetz and Murray A. Straus (eds.), *Violence in the Family*, New York: Dodd, Mead, pp. 98–109.
Balswick, Jack O. and James W. Balkwell
    1977 "Self-Disclosure to the Same- and Opposite-Sex Parents," *Sociometry* 40 (September): 282–286.
Blumer, Herbert
    1969 *Symbolic Interactionism*, Englewood Cliffs, N.J.: Prentice-Hall.
Cannon, Walter B.
    1972 "Voodoo Death," in William A. Lessa and Evon Z. Vogt (eds.), *Reader in Comparative Religion*, New York: Harper & Row, pp. 433–439.
Charon, Joel M.
    1979 *Symbolic Interactionism: An Introduction, an Interpretation, and an Integration*, Englewood Cliffs, N.J.: Prentice-Hall.
Clausen, John A.
    1968 *Socialization and Society*, Boston: Little, Brown.
Cooley, Charles Horton
    1902 *Human Nature and the Social Order*, New York: Charles Scribner.
Coopersmith, Stanley
    1967 *The Antecedents of Self-Esteem*, San Francisco: W. H. Freeman.
Coopersmith, Stanley and R. Feldman
    1974 "Fostering a Positive Self-Concept and High Self-Esteem in the Classroom," in Richard H. Coop and Kinnart White (eds.), *Psychological Concepts in the Classroom*, New York: Harper & Row.

Denzin, Norman K.
  1975 "Play, Games, and Interaction: The Context of Childhood Socialization," *Sociological Quarterly* 16 (Autumn): 458–479.
Franks, David D. and Joseph Marolla
  1976 "Efficacious Action and Social Approval as Interacting Dimensions of Self-Esteem," *Sociometry* 39 (December): 324–341.
Gergen, Kenneth J.
  1971 *The Concept of Self,* New York: Holt, Rinehart & Winston.
Gilbert, Shirley J.
  1976 "Self-Disclosure, Intimacy and Communication in Families," *Family Co-ordinator* 25 (July): 221–233.
Hewitt, John P.
  1979 *Self and Society: A Symbolic Interactionist Social Psychology,* Boston: Allyn and Bacon.
Holian, John
  1972 "Alienation and Social Awareness among College Students," *Sociological Quarterly* 13 (Winter): 114–125.
Jourard, Sidney M.
  1971 *The Transparent Self: Self-Disclosure and Well-Being,* New York: Van Nostrand.
Komarovsky, Mirra
  1946 "Cultural Contradictions and Sex Roles," *American Journal of Sociology* 52: 184–189.
Kuhn, Manford H. and Thomas S. McPartland
  1954 "An Empirical Investigation of Self Attitudes," *American Sociological Review* 19: 68–76.
Lever, Janet
  1976 "Sex Differences in the Games Children Play," *Social Problems* 23 (April): 478–487.
Lifton, Robert J.
  1970 *Boundaries: Psychological Man in Revolution,* New York: Random House.
Marx, Karl
  1844 *Economic and Philosophical Manuscripts of 1844,* London: Lawrence and Wishart, 1959.
Mead, George Herbert
  1934 *Mind, Self, and Society,* Chicago: University of Chicago Press.
Nye, F. Ivan
  1974 "Emerging and Declining Family Roles," *Journal of Marriage and the Family* 36 (May): 238–245.
Otto, Luther B. and David L. Featherman
  1975 "Social Structural and Psychological Antecedents of Self-Estrangement and Powerlessness," *American Sociological Review* 40 (December): 701–719.
Piaget, Jean
  1962 *Play, Dream, and Imitation in Childhood,* New York: Norton.
Presthus, Robert
  1978 *The Organizational Society,* New York: St. Martin's Press.
Robertson, Roland and Burkart Holzner
  1979 *Identity and Authority,* New York: St. Martin's Press.

Rose, Jerry D.
1969 "The Role of the Other in Self Evaluation," *Sociological Quarterly* 10 (Fall): 470–479.
Rosenberg, Morris
1979 *Conceiving the Self,* New York: Basic Books.
1965 *Society and Adolescent Self-Image,* Princeton, N.J.: Princeton University Press.
Rosenberg, Morris and Roberta G. Simmons
1972 *Black and White Self-Esteem,* Washington: American Sociological Association.
Rubin, Zick, Charles T. Hill, Letitia A. Peplau, and Christine Dunkel-Schetter
1980 "Self-Disclosure in Dating Couples," *Journal of Marriage and the Family* 42 (May): 305–318.
Scott, John Paul
1971 "The Biological Basis of Social Behavior," in John P. Scott and Sally F. Scott (eds.), *Social Control and Social Change,* Chicago: University of Chicago Press, pp. 9–42.
Seeman, Melvin
1975 "Alienation Studies," *Annual Review of Sociology* 1: 91–124.
1966 "Status and Identity: The Problem of Inauthenticity," *Pacific Sociological Review* 9 (Spring): 67–73.
Sewell, William H., Archibald Haller, and George W. Ohlendorf
1970 "The Educational and Early Occupational Status Attainment Process," *American Sociological Review* 35 (December): 1014–1027.
Shepard, Jon M.
1972 "Alienation as a Process: Work as a Case in Point," *Sociological Quarterly* 13 (Spring): 161–173.
Simmons, Roberta G., Florence Rosenberg and Morris Rosenberg
1973 "Disturbance in Self-Image at Adolescence," *American Sociological Review* 38 (October): 553–568.
Snyder, Eldon E. and Elmer Spreitzer
1978 *Social Aspects of Sport,* Englewood Cliffs, N.J.: Prentice-Hall.
Stanage, Sherman M.
1968 "The Personal World: A Phenomenological Approach," *Pacific Philosophy Forum* 6 (May): 3–46.
Stewart, Kenneth L.
1975 "On Socializing Attitudes: A Symbolic Interactionist View," *Sociological Focus* 8 (January): 37–46.
Titus, Sandra L.
1976 "Family Photographs and Transition to Parenthood," *Journal of Marriage and the Family* 38 (August): 525–534.
Turner, Ralph H.
1976 "The Real Self: From Institution to Impulse," *American Journal of Sociology* 81 (March): 989–1016.
1975 "Is There a Quest for Identity?," *Sociological Quarterly* 16 (Spring): 148–161.
Webster, Murray, Jr., Lynne Roberts, and Barbara I. Sobieszek
1972 "Accepting 'Significant Others,'" *American Journal of Sociology* 78 (November): 576–598.

Williams, Robin M., Jr.
1970 *American Society,* New York: Knopf.
Woelfel, Joseph and Archibald O. Haller
1971 "Significant Others, the Self-Reflexive Act and the Attitude Formation Process," *American Sociological Review* 36 (February): 74–87.
Wylie, Ruth C.
1961 *The Self Concept,* Lincoln: University of Nebraska Press.
Ziller, Robert C.
1974 *The Social Self,* New York: Pergamon Press.

6

What to look for in this chapter:

How do people form social attachments?
Why is adolescence such a turbulent stage of the life cycle?
What are the guiding principles of interpersonal attraction?
Why do high levels of stress accompany the severance of social ties?

Social Attachments

Who we are, how we behave, and what we are to become derive from the variety of social attachments we have formed along the way. These include, for example, the social bonds with the members of one's initial family, the friendship ties that are formed among peers, the attractions of lovers to each other, and the daily interactions among co-workers on the job. While we frequently break old ties and form new ones, they all have their effects on the manner in which we play our parts in the drama of human affairs. Our personal biographies are shaped by the cumulative effects of our social attachments.

You can determine the strength of your present attachments by asking how difficult it would be for you if they were broken. For example, what would be the personal consequences of severing the ties with what is now your favorite member of the opposite sex? Would it be easier for you to break the ties with your friends or with your parents? How easy would it be for you to change your college major or your long-range career plans? Would it really matter if you did not return to your hometown for employment after graduation? How difficult would it be for you to give up your citizenship and go to live permanently in some other country?

The answers you give to these questions are likely to reveal some important aspects of your past experiences and the aspirations you hold for the future. For most people the attainment of the kind of life they want for themselves is dependent on the qualities of their relationships with others. The prospects of fulfilling plans for getting married, having children, developing a career, and enjoying a particular lifestyle are likely to be influenced by the patterns of social attachments that will form along the way.

A process of selectivity operates in the formation of social attachments. We are attracted to some people but are repelled by others; we want some relationships to develop into permanent ones, while the sooner others are terminated the better. The underlying principles that govern the attraction process are important to us, because once we are "hooked" on another person or on a particular line of work, it is much easier to continue with our commitments than to establish new ones. We tend to maintain social attachments because they are dependable and provide stable anchoring points under conditions

BOX 6.1
Advantages of Marriage for Physical Well-Being

Health and mortality data are collected annually on the population of the United States by the National Center for Health Statistics. The results of these surveys routinely show the importance of marital status for physical well-being. At any specific age level, adults who are married are healthier and live longer than adults who are not married. Age-specific rates of incapacitating illnesses and mental health problems show decisive advantages for those who have marital ties.

Understanding these facts requires taking into account a variety of factors. Unhealthy people may be less attractive to members of the opposite sex and for this reason have lower levels of marriageability. Unmarried people are also more likely to have lifestyles characterized by high degrees of risk taking (drinking, smoking, inadequate diet, irregular sleep, and so forth). But more importantly, the unmarried live a more isolated existence and lack the social bonds necessary for a sense of well-being.

Through the realities constructed in marriage, individuals derive a sense of meaning and purpose that tends to inhibit self-destructive impulses. Each party of the relationship shares emerging problems to some degree, and the individual doesn't have to stand alone in confronting the stresses of life. The buildup of joint enterprises in marriage provide forms of therapy that contribute to physical well-being, longevity, and life satisfaction.

Source: Walter R. Gove, "Sex, Marital Status, and Mortality," *American Journal of Sociology* 79 (July, 1973): 45–67.

of uncertainty. We turn to other people to confirm our own understanding of events, and the bonds we forge have important implications for the stability and coherence of our personal lives.

The emotional investments we make in our social attachments tend to promote their continuance and to have consequences for the subsequent opportunities available to us. Yet it is important that we do develop stable and durable attachments in order to prevent our lives from falling into fragments and being without meaning. For example, the evidence is abundantly clear that in adulthood the social psychological advantages clearly favor those people who are continuously married compared to those who are single, divorced, or widowed. Married people tend to live longer, to have better health, to manifest fewer psychosomatic symptoms, and be less likely to commit suicide. (See Box 6.1.)

This is not to suggest that you would be better off to get married right away, but instead, that durable social ties aid the physical and mental well-being of individuals throughout the life course. Social attachments have a powerful impact on the quality of life. The lack of commitments, including the severance of social ties, tends to be associated with intense feelings of loneliness and isolation. An inability to share in the activities of others is likely to result in feelings of the need to rely exclusively on one's own resources, which prevents enjoying the many rewards that membership and belonging may provide.

In this chapter, two major aspects of social attachments have been selected for primary concern. One deals with the process by which social ties form and dissolve during the life cycle, as the individual moves from childhood attachments to such adult commitments as being married, working, becoming a parent, rearing children, aging, and adjusting to the death of a spouse. The second concern is the importance to individuals of weak ties compared to strong commitments. The weak ties are those that may readily be broken, while the stronger ones are those that promote stability and continuity in social relationships. We may note, for example, that cohabitation is generally a weaker social tie than the bonds that form through marriage and becoming a parent. The kinds of attachments that form often have consequences for the role taking and lifestyles that subsequently become available.

A. LEARNING TO BELONG

Binding ties among individuals emerge from the interaction process and the development of shared social meanings. It is during this process that the individual derives a self-identity and selectively assigns reward values to persons, objects, and events. Attachments imply cohesive social relationships, a concern of individuals with the well-being of each other, the desire to help each other out in times of trouble, and a sense of loyalty to group members. For most people the stronger and more enduring social bonds form within small intimate groups; for this reason family relationships become central to the study of social attachments.

Within family relationships there are several attributes of social attachments that are embellished by biological characteristics. These include the bonds of sexuality that cement the husband-wife relationship, the dependency of the human infant on adults for survival, and the initial social placement of individuals by family of origin. These biological factors, however, become meaningful primarily from the symbolism that emerges through the attachments of specific individuals to each other. For example, sexual expressiveness is usually accompanied by emotional involvements that are not likely to be transferrable from one person to another. The dependency needs of children are met through the actions and responses of specific people. And the initial social placement of the child depends on the particular status characteristics of the family of origin.

1. The Family of Origin

In all societies the social attachments deriving from initial kinship ties persist at some level of intensity throughout the entire lifespan of individuals. But more importantly, the initial learning experiences within the family of origin affect the style of affiliation and belonging that individuals subsequently develop. The varied attachments of adult life—at work, at play, in the marketplace, in school, in the temple, and in the general round of community living—are likely to express some of the enduring effects of childhood experiences.

In the United States today the aims of parents in having a child or an additional child tie in closely with the quest to have love and companionship and to avoid a sense of loneliness (Hoffman, Thornton, and Manis, 1978). Having children provides parents with a sense of purpose and the feeling of being needed. Thus the interest in having children and the willingness to assume responsibilities for child care arise from the desire for social attachments. Hugs, smiles, and kisses from the child are among the forms of affectionate repayment parents seek for the costs of having and rearing children.

The social bonds of the parent-child relationship are evident in mutual attraction, in caring for one another, and in expressions of intimacy. The social attachments of children come from their dependency on others for survival. The formation of attachments during dependency are clearly evident when children seek out particular people during times of distress. While help may come from a variety of caretakers, parents and siblings occupy a special place of prominence in the attachments of small children. The nuclear family provides a primary source of security in what otherwise may be experienced as an uncertain environment. From the playing of family roles, a sense of identity and belonging emerges along with the refinement of capacities for learning and problem solving.

Learning to belong requires an awareness of the rules that regulate social relationships. Children engage in a great deal of reality testing as they learn to resolve the contradictions between impulse tendencies and the demands others make. Parents frequently tolerate spontaneous behavior patterns as they share in play activity with their children and derive pleasure from watching them grow and develop. The child must learn, however, that there is a time and a place for both talking and remaining silent. Certain rights of others must be respected; activities are structured in some prearranged sequence; and performances are evaluated and rewarded or punished accordingly. (See Box 6.2.)

As a result of childhood experiences some children come to place emphasis on personal and social achievements, while others develop a strong need for belonging, affiliation, and membership. From a review of several research studies, Richard Boyatzis (1973) concluded that the **need for affiliation** derives from the concerns for security and approval. In his view the major components of the affiliation need are expressed in both approach and avoidance concerns. The approach concern refers to the quest for love, warmth,

---

BOX 6.2
Social Class and Parental Values for Children

The socioeconomic achievements of children when they grow up are highly correlated with the prior achievements of their parents. Children of college-educated parents are likely to obtain a college education. The sons of blue-collar workers are likely to become employed in blue-collar occupations. These are basic social facts that Wright and Wright (1976) sought to explain by replicating previous studies on social class variations in the values that parents transmit to their children.

In their study of consistency in socioeconomic status across generational levels, the Wrights drew on data collected from a national sample in 1973. Their findings provide clear support for the previous research of Melvin Kohn (1969), which indicated that social class was indeed a major variable in the kind of values parents emphasize for their children. The middle class emphasizes "self-direction" and "internal standards for behavior," while the working class concentrates on values associated with "conformity" and "externally imposed rules." The self-direction emphasis in the middle class includes the values of achievement, creativity, and deferred gratification. Working-class parents, by way of contrast, emphasize values that make school performance more difficult and subsequent upward mobility less likely.

These differences in socialization patterns tend to promote consistency in occupational status across generational lines. Working-class parents who emphasize obedience to rules are in effect preparing their children for employment in jobs that are closely supervised. In contrast the emphasis on self-direction in the middle class is more compatible with the responsibilities and decision making that are required in occupations at the higher prestige levels.

Source: James D. Wright and Sonia R. Wright, "Social Class and Parental Values for Children," *American Sociological Review* 41 (June, 1976): 527–537.

---

devotion, and tenderness in social relationships. The avoidance concern refers to exclusion, being left alone, and fear of rejection. Individuals who have a high need for affiliation may be readily influenced by others who provide them with a sense of support and approval (Schachter, 1959).

The task of learning to belong among adolescents is primarily one of resolving the numerous conflicts between family life, the school system, and the peer group. Parents are often annoyed by the music and the friends of their teenage children. Disagreements develop over the time to be in at night, over uses of the family car, over uses of language, and over the scope of family and school responsibilities. The values and moral standards that the family emphasizes are often incompatible with the behavior patterns that one's peers emphasize. Obtaining social approval within the peer group often requires making decisions independently of family influences.

Since feelings of personal effectiveness are subject to frequent change among adolescents, the conditions for acceptance or rejection by the peer group are likely to evoke intensely emotional responses. Peer-group values frequently conflict with the academic objectives of the school system, and teenagers must make some decisions on the relative values of social approval and academic achievement. Those seeking good grades, educational advancement, and occupational attainment are less likely to be concerned with peer-group approval. In this respect high levels of achievement orientation may serve as a buffer against peer group influences.

The choices made in adolescence between social approval and personal achievement are likely to have enduring effects (Dynes, Clarke, and Dinitz, 1962). For example, in later life the emphasis on success goals may take priority over the value placed on social ties to one's family, friends, or community. Some individuals are apparently willing to sacrifice their present social ties in the interest of advancement, while others are not. The resolution of such a conflict depends in part on the level of commitment to success goals on one hand and the reward values derivable from social relationships on the other.

2. Transition into Adulthood

The transition from childhood to adulthood is a complicated process in our society. The transition extends over a long period of time without a clear beginning or end, and it is associated with high levels of stress and tension. The turbulence of adolescence stems from new forms of role playing that develop as previous social ties weaken and young adults seek and form new kinds of attachments. The secure atmosphere of early family life is replaced by increased involvement in unfamiliar and uncertain environments. Confirming sexual identity, confirming social worth, and confirming personal effectiveness are among the struggles adolescents go through as they seek to find their places within the complex web of social relationships. (See Table 6.1.)

In obtaining verification of adult status, individuals must make substantial modifications in the role playing that was appropriate for the childhood years. For example, as adults they are expected to have a healthy attitude toward the potential rewards of sex; as children they were frequently regarded as presexual or asexual. As adults they are expected to be independent; as children they were expected to be dependent. Childhood was looked on as a time for play and spontaneous enjoyment of activities, while adulthood is looked on as a time for deliberate planning and a seriousness of purpose. As adults, dependency on parents must give way to independence in decision making and to demonstrations of personal competency (Foner and Kertzer, 1978).

In the process of growing up, the teenager is exposed to the double-bind of adulthood and childhood. Adults may use adult standards as a basis for criticizing a teenager's performance, while they may invoke childhood status to deny the teenager some desired privilege. Teenagers then become exposed to

TABLE 6.1
Symbols of the Transition to Adulthood

Years of age	Symbolic event
12	Biological maturity
	Bar/Bat Mitzvah
14	Adult movie fare
16	Automobile driver's license
	Part-time job without work permit
18	Graduation from high school
	Eligible to vote
	Eligible for military service and the draft (males only?)
21	Legal drinking age (in some states)
23	Graduation from college
	First full-time employment
?	Marriage
	Parenthood
30	Eligible to serve in the United States Senate

Basic Questions:

When does the boy become a man?	Why does it take so long?
When does the girl become a woman?	What effects does education have?

reality testing and to the problem of having to cope with numerous evaluations from parents, siblings, peers, and others. These assessments frequently suggest that the teenagers are either too old or too young to be doing what they now want to do.

The learning tasks of adolescents include reconciling the expectations from parents, teachers, and peers with their own personal plans for the future. The self-images reflected in the multiple responses of others are frequently inconsistent and contradictory. The adolescent, as well as either or both of the parents, frequently views the age gaps between the generations as being unbridgeable. Teenagers tend to see themselves as being more sensitive than their parents to changes in values, norms, tastes, and preferences. They frequently listen to a different kind of music, speak a different kind of language, and engage in behavior patterns that appear to be mysterious and questionable (Smith, 1970). (See Box 6.3.)

Peer group relationships frequently become important during late adolescence. Confronting similar problems and sharing similar life circumstances tend to produce some degree of solidarity along age and sex lines. Yet the numerous self-evaluations revealed in peer responses are often contradictory and inconsistent. The constructed realities among adolescents reflect the polarized values and norms of the larger society. There are disagreements over the

BOX 6.3
The Generation Gap

During the early years the bonds between parents and their children are very strong since the care-giving behavior of parents is in alignment with the physical and emotional needs of the child. Parents have almost exclusive control over resources that are meaningful to the child. But with increasing maturation parental control over the child's desired rewards diminishes, and children turn increasingly to the peer group for emotional support and approval.

The emergence of a **generation gap** between parents and their children is likely to occur during the years of early adolescence. Dramatic changes occur during adolescence at both the physical and the emotional levels. The attempts of youth to refine an identity and to find their place within the broader scheme of social affairs require to some degree that parents and children go their separate ways. Parents are likely to become confused as their authority weakens and as their children emphasize rewards that they the parents can no longer supply. Adolescents frequently resent the efforts of parents to impose on them the values of an older generation, and they often feel that parents are not "tuned in" to the changes that are occurring in today's world.

Images of a generation gap within families, however, are more often illusory than real. Research studies (e.g., Yankelovich, 1972) have shown that the basic attitudes and values of young adults tend to correlate highly with those held by their parents. Continuities in social life are promoted as the family transmits basic values from one generation to the next. But during adolescence, individuals are still in the process of discovering values, and during this stage of life there is a tendency for both parents and children to overrespond to the points of disagreement among them.

appropriateness of using drugs, over the scope and forms of sexual conduct, over the desirability of military service, over the value of college education, over religious beliefs, and over the adequacy of specific political ideologies. The source of age solidarity primarily results from the inherent uncertainties that are shared to some degree by those who are suspended somewhere between childhood and full-fledged adulthood (Van Gennep, 1960).

Young adults may reduce the complexities of the broader social environment through the formation of social attachments with a small number of people who hold similar interests and values. In this regard the quest for peer-group approval takes the form of developing attachments to specific individuals. Two of the more important social bonds of late adolescence emerge from the development of friendship ties and involvement in heterosexual relationships. These kinds of ties provide important reinforcements for a sense of social worth, security, and identity (Wagner, 1971). However, the social attachments formed during the adolescent years are likely to become fragile because of the high degree of mobility in modern society.

In the early adult years a person must make a large number of consequential decisions about social relationships. Children do not have the option of selecting their parents, nor are they permitted to make decisions about school attendance. These are social relationships imposed on the child. By way of contrast, social horizons often expand vastly in early adult life through the wide range of choices that become available. These include decisions about

Transition into Adulthood: Leaving Home
The freshman who leaves the secure atmosphere of family life and takes up residence in a high-rise dormitory on a college campus will have to make numerous adjustments. While some degree of excitement surrounds attending college for the first time, many experience it as a time of sadness and loneliness. The college student is leaving behind old friends and familiar surroundings and encountering some degree of uncertainty in the new environment. Identities and attachments change as old ties weaken and new ones emerge.

career preparation, heterosexual involvements, uses of leisure, consumer purchases, and place of residence.

With a weakening of initial family ties, individuals in early adulthood increasingly base social relationships on the processes of selection and decision making. Leaving home to attend college, establishing a place of residence separate from one's initial family, and becoming financially independent are events that permit the development of new forms of social relationships. As a result the topic of interpersonal attraction becomes of central concern in the formation of social attachments. Social bonds develop from perceiving others as sources of reward and pleasure.

B. INTERPERSONAL ATTRACTION

Such social bonds as those formed in friendship and in marriage develop from an initial process of interpersonal attraction. The formation of social attachments does not occur on a random basis within society. Instead, attachments develop out of the opportunities for interaction, out of the attractions individuals feel to each other, and out of the emotional investments people have for continuing a set of relationships. Why are we drawn toward certain individuals but repelled by others? Why do we develop a liking for some of our acquaintances but develop a sense of disgust toward others? Why do some love affairs lead to marriage while others do not? Why do some social relationships mature and grow while others decompose?

These concerns are reflected in two alternative approaches to the formation of social attachments. One answers the question of why specific individuals are initially attracted to each other, while the second addresses the question of why individuals become committed to continuing a relationship. Each approach, however, views the attraction process as deriving from the opportunities for social interaction.

Living in the same neighborhood, working for the same firm, enrolling in the same classes at the university, attending the same church, and participating in a common community project are examples of the numerous conditions under which individuals come into contact with and respond to one another. This involves the principle of **propinquity**, which holds that social ties tend to form among those who share a common physical location and who have had the opportunity to interact with each other over an extended period of time.

1. Homophily and Cognitive Consistency

While nearness in physical space is important for the opportunity to develop social attachments, other variables help determine whether individuals are attracted to each other and whether more enduring social bonds do develop.

These other variables include numerous aspects of the principles of **homophily** and shared symbolism. The principle of homophily holds that individuals tend to be attracted to others who resemble them in social and psychological characteristics. Apparently, the attachments among individuals who share several characteristics in common provide support for mutual identities and for shared constructions of reality. We seem to need an independent source of verification for our own understanding of events, and we tend to find it in our associations with those who are in basic agreement with us.

Similarities in status characteristics and cultural experiences are among the important variables that shape the attraction process. The folk wisdom that holds that "birds of a feather flock together" turns out to be essentially correct. Those with like characteristics do tend to be attracted to each other. Numerous studies have confirmed the importance of similarities in education, family background, race, age, and religion as important components in the formation of social attachments (Broderick, 1971). Apparently, commonalities in status characteristics facilitate communication with a minimum of difficulty and provide shared frames of reference for defining social reality. (See Box 6.4.)

Similarities in status characteristics are likely to influence the opportunities for interaction, while the similarities in attitudes and values are likely to be the major determinants of the attraction process. During the past several years a large number of studies have found support for the hypothesis that similarity in attitudes is a major factor in the attraction process (Byrne, 1971; Layton and Insko, 1974). The underlying principle is cognitive consistency. We seek to organize our conceptions of self and others in such a fashion that we experience our lives and environments as harmonious, balanced, and symmetrical. Through being attracted to others who hold similar attitudes, we are provided with support from independent sources that our own constructions of reality are indeed the correct ones, and we are thus able to obtain consistency, stability, and harmony between our personal beliefs and what transpires in our social relationships. The world becomes predictable, and we do not have to defend our views as long as those we care about are in basic agreement with us.

The relationship between attitude similarity and interpersonal attraction, however, is not a self-evident one. We do not know most of the attitudes of those with whom we are acquainted. For this reason, Timothy Curry and Richard Emerson (1970) argue that the imagined similarity in attitudes may be even more important to the attraction process than the actual similarity itself. These researchers maintain that attractions stem from predictions about subsequent involvements in mutually rewarding activities. For example, the individual who enjoys playing tennis, camping, or eating out in high-quality restaurants may be attracted to others whom he or she imagines to share a similar enjoyment of these activities. Such mutual attractions appear to be based on the prospects for joint participation in mutually rewarding activities.

We may describe the progression of social attachments in terms of increasing mutual dependency and emotional involvement. As such, shared symbolic meanings emerge in which the perceived similarities exceed the

BOX 6.4
Status Inequality and Stress in Marriage

While marriage relationships are looked on as self-contained units, the research of Leonard I. Pearlin has suggested that the forces of society often impinge on the family sphere. Pearlin (1975: 345) observed that the study of marital stress "provides an excellent vantage point for observing how arrangements in the larger social order merge within marriage in shaping the inner lives of individuals."

Emphasizing the importance of social class standing, the results of his research indicate that people who place a high degree of importance on status advancement and prestige are likely to experience a high degree of stress in their marriages if their marriages are characterized by **status inequality**—if they marry someone whose status (family of origin) is below that of their own. Basing his study on interviews with 2300 subjects in the Chicago metropolitan area, his findings indicate that people who are status strivers but marry "down" tend to report stress in several crucial areas of family life. These include difficulties in sharing ideas and experiences, in giving and receiving affection, and in arriving at a consensus on family finances and child rearing.

These results indicate that the status differences that divide people within the community also penetrate into the intimate bonds of family relationships. For subjects who attached little or no significance to status advancement, inequalities in the family backgrounds of husbands and wives had little bearing on the qualities of their marital relationships. But if one or both spouses attached a great deal of importance to upward mobility and status values, social inequalities in marriage became a significant source of stress.

Source: Leonard I. Pearlin, "Status Inequality and Stress in Marriage," *American Sociological Review* 40 (June, 1975): 344–357.

actual similarities. Jan Trost (1967) has noted that exaggerations of attitude similarity may be a function of one's tendency to justify continuing a relationship that is viewed as rewarding. The development of social attachments is shaped by the ease of communication, the verification of one's own identity through the responses of the other, and the mutual disclosure of numerous intimate aspects of the personal lives of each. Such attributes tend to enhance the further development of social ties, while the lack of any of the above qualities may produce levels of stress that result in terminating the relationship.

In a study of "steadily attached" couples from two state universities, Levinger, Senn, and Jorgensen (1970) concentrated on a series of variables that contribute to either the continuance or the termination of the relationships. From a study of 330 couples over a period of six months, Levinger and his colleagues concluded that the progression toward permanence is an outgrowth of shared activities rather than initial similarities in attitudes and values.

They concluded that shared values and attitudes are related to "the manner in which two individual partners discover one another," while the progression toward more enduring social ties derives from "the subsequent buildup of a joint enterprise." Over a period of time "pair communality" in property, time investments, and shared activities becomes more important in the continuance of the relationship than "member similarity."

Homophily and Shared Symbolism: Close Friends
The formation of social attachments is based on patterns of both choice and drift. People tend to select friends who resemble themselves in a wide variety of ways. But, the development of friendship ties is also an outgrowth of interaction patterns. Living in the same neighborhood and sharing a large number of activities tend to result in cohesive relationships. Friendship ties weaken if interests develop along different lines and if face-to-face interactions occur less frequently. Such events as going off to college, getting married, or changing jobs often have the effect of severing social ties with an earlier group of friends.

2. Entry into Marriage

Carlfred Broderick (1971) notes that several conditions enter into the decision to marry that have little to do with the qualities of the relationship. This is evident when we concentrate on the timing of marriage rather than on the process of interpersonal attraction. The timing of marriage is often shaped by such considerations as reducing the costs of living separately, filling the vacuum created by graduation from school or the death of a parent, or seeking mechanisms to lesson the effects of previous disillusionment or a sense of loneliness.

There are also social pressures that exert an influence on the decision to marry, and these may be looked on as deriving from socially held notions about the proper timing of entry into first marriage. The vast majority of American men and women enter into their first marriage between the ages of twenty and twenty-five years, have their first child within the first two years of marriage, and complete their childbearing after about seven years of married life (Glick, 1977). Those who depart from the normative timetable are likely to encounter numerous forms of social pressure from relatives, friends, and acquaintances, even though recent historical trends indicate an increased postponement of the first marriage. (See Box 6.5.)

Gudmund Hernes (1972) notes that the social pressures to marry consist of two major sources. The first derives from the age-graded pattern of social interactions; the second derives from the reduced marriageability of the female as she gets older. He notes that as a larger percent of an age group marries, those who remain single will have reduced opportunities to interact with old friends.

...They will be invited less often to parties, dinners or trips, partly because of diverging interests, partly because of the threats to established couples. When singles are invited, hosts often play the role of matchmakers. Thus the psychological experience of the undesirability of celibacy increases as more of the same age group enters into wedlock (Hernes, 1972: 174).

Hernes also notes that the subtle peer-group pressures to marry that increase with age arise from the social definitions that emerge for those who have remained single after most of their age group has married. Males who remain single find their masculinity questioned and are sometimes suspected of homosexuality. In the case of the female the opportunities to marry decrease with increasing age. Reduced marriageability occurs in part because of the effects of aging on personal attractiveness, in part because of the desirability of youthfulness in our society, and in part because of the reduced pool of eligible males due to a general tendency for men to marry younger women.

The social pressures that affect the decision to marry reinforce whatever other qualities are present to promote the development of a social bond. Most couples are unlikely to marry from social pressures alone, but instead enter into family formation with expectations for further refinements of a rewarding relationship. The research of Robert A. Lewis (1973) suggests that we may re-

BOX 6.5
Delay in Marriage for the American Female During the 1970s

From his more than thirty years of experience with the Bureau of the Census, Paul C. Glick (1975) has made a number of observations on the changing patterns of the American family as it has been revealed in the statistics on the total population of the United States.

There is no doubt about it. Young women are now postponing marriage longer than their mothers did in the late 1940's and early 1950's (1975: 17).

In this connection, he has identified a number of variables implicated in the delay in marriage for the average American female. Among them are:

1. The college enrollment rate for women more than doubled between 1960 and 1972. The pursuit of a college education is one of the more important variables in accounting for the delay of entry into marriage.
2. The "marriage squeeze" is another important variable. Because of the baby boom at the end of World War II, during the 1960s there was an excess of women eligible for marriage as compared to men, since women tend to enter their most marriageable age range about two or three years before men who were born in the same year.
3. In recent years there has been a much sharper increase in the employment rate for women than for men, and the increased financial independence for American females is associated with expanding opportunities for women outside of marriage, childbearing, and family life.

While the long-range effects of women delaying marriage are presently unknown, it is clear that the increased educational aspirations of women, the increased employment opportunities for women, and the surplus of marriageable women over marriageable men are important variables in the historical trend toward delayed marriage for the average American female.

Source: Paul C. Glick, "A Demographer Looks at American Families," *Journal of Marriage and the Family* 37 (February, 1975): 15–26.

gard entry into marriage as the outgrowth of a developmental process. From an initial heterosexual attraction, emotional ties develop around shared experiences and mutual interdependency. The relationship develops into a more enduring one with increasing levels of affection and shared symbolism.

Entry into marriage has the effect of formalizing a commitment and eliciting community support for the continuance of a relationship. The more traditional form of the marriage bond is characterized by diffuse obligations. They are diffuse in the sense that the couple has a wide range of both specified and unspecified duties to one another, and the couple regards the relationship as being permanent. In some of the more modern forms of marriage the couple agrees to make the continuance of the relationship conditional in character. They formulate a marriage contract to clearly identify the obligations each assumes toward the other, the rights and privileges they regard as inviolable, and the conditions for terminating the relationship.

The option of specifying the conditions for entering into or continuing a relationship provide the modern couple with opportunities to anticipate problems and to work out solutions in advance. However, J. Gipson Wells (1976) observes that young people contemplating marriage tend to place emphasis on their similarities rather than on their differences. As a result those areas of disagreement that are most likely to emerge as troublesome in a marriage can seldom be anticipated and solved through a personal marriage contract. Through the fact of marriage the nature of the relationship changes, and it is nearly impossible for the never-married person to understand fully what married life involves.

Nevertheless, those couples who seriously undertake the negotiation of a personal marriage contract are entering into the early stages of what Berger

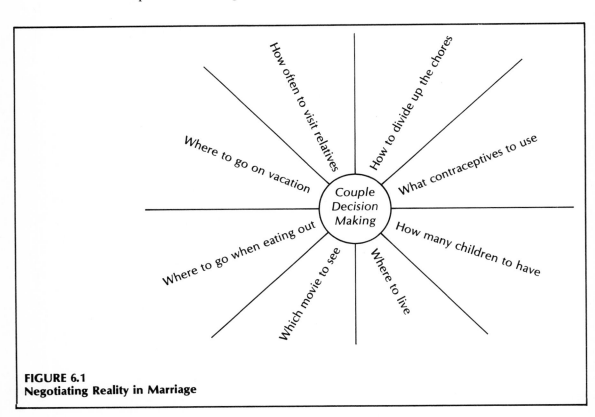

FIGURE 6.1
Negotiating Reality in Marriage

and Kellner (1964) describe as "marriage and the construction of reality." Entry into marriage presents a new reality for the individuals involved and requires that the partners change their definitions of the world and of themselves. In the views of Berger and Kellner, the reconstruction of the world in marriage occurs principally in the course of conversation. This involves, for example, talking through such issues as where to live, what contraceptives to use, how many children to have, and how to use leisure time. The couple must make decisions in order to solve the everyday problems that they confront. Each member of the couple must bring his or her aspirations into alignment with the aspirations of the other, and they must establish the compatibility of their separate definitions of reality. The underlying task is coordinating behavior in solving the problems of family living. (See Figure 6.1.)

3. *Friendship*

The basic social psychological principles in the formation of heterosexual attractions also apply to the development of friendship ties. Attachments form among those who interact with each other over an extended period of time. The initial attractions are based on similarities in life circumstances and world views. We tend to be attracted to people who reinforce our identities and offer prospects for rewarding relationships.

In contrast to marriage, one of the distinguishing characteristics of friendship is that the relationships tend to occur among members of the same sex. Marriages and friendships also differ in many other ways. For example, marriages are more difficult to terminate than friendships because of the greater emotional and financial investments involved. Friendships retain elements of freedom that are lacking in the development of marital ties and family responsibilities. If friendships turn sour, there are no legal entanglements in severing the relationships. We simply make other choices and select new friends who offer more favorable prospects for rewarding relationships.

In our highly mobile society, friendships tend to be situational and temporary. For example, the friendships formed in college tend to last no more than four years, and most last for a much shorter period of time (Murstein, Cerreto, and MacDonald, 1977). Most friendships grow fragile as the graduates go their separate ways, move to different parts of the country, and follow different career patterns. But if specific friendships tend to be temporary, new ones are likely to develop very rapidly. The degree of liking and respect among new acquaintances provide the context out of which new friendship ties develop (Segal, 1979).

The research of Carol Werner and Pat Parmelee (1979) suggests that similarity in activity preferences is one of the stronger motives in friendship choices. In their view, "those who play together stay together." The pleasures derived from interaction tend to increase the cohesiveness of social relationships. The specific content of the activity may be highly varied—for example, playing poker and tennis, going to movies, or becoming engaged in community projects. But whatever the activity it will have special meanings for participants if personal interests receive social supports and if attachments form with others.

When two individuals become close friends, each incurs a set of obligations to provide help to the other in times of trouble. The importance of these obligations may be illustrated from a study of college students by Daniel Bar-Tal *et al.* (1977). They gave their subjects a hypothetical situation in which a student needed and requested help of various others who might or might not have provided it when they had the capacity to do so. The results of this study indicated that the degree of gratitude a person would feel on receiving help and the resentment on not being helped would depend on the closeness of social ties. Females tended to regard their parents as having the greatest obligation to help, while males had greater expectations of help from a close friend. These findings suggest that males are encouraged to be more independent than females and to rely more firmly on peer-group supports.

The research of Bar-Tal and his associates (1977) also indicates that the sense of gratitude on receiving help tends to be greater if the help is provided by a stranger or by a casual acquaintance than by a close friend or a relative. The refusal of parents or a close friend to help is likely to evoke intense feelings of disappointment and resentment, but only mildly hostile attitudes are evoked if a stranger refuses help. Accordingly, attitudes of gratitude and resentment are related to levels of obligation in social relationships.

Because a close friendship tie imposes the obligation of concern for the well-being of another person, many people prefer to avoid deep levels of involvement in interpersonal relationships. For this reason two distinct patterns of friendship are identifiable. One consists of having many friends who are not so close, while the second consists of restricting friendship to only a small number of people. Friendships that are highly restrictive and exclusive tend to be intimate and to involve high levels of self-disclosure. In contrast, if a large number of acquaintances are regarded as friends, the relationships are likely to be casual, and they may be severed with a minimum of difficulty.

Regardless of the intensity of specific involvements, friendships are important for the well-being of the individual throughout the life course. Friendship ties play an important part in the games of children, in the exploratory behavior of adolescents, and in the uses of leisure by adults. Their importance derives not only from the intrinsic rewards they provide but also from the links they establish between the individual and the larger social system. Relationships with fellow workers tend to integrate the employee with the job, and friendship ties among students tend to reduce the impersonality of a large state university.

C. SOCIAL BONDS

The formation of social attachments involves the creation of bonds that have both positive and negative consequences. The bonding aspect of a social attachment implies continuity, unity, cohesion, belonging, and caring. While these are among the more highly valued attributes of social relationships, they also have their negative consequences. For example, while the bonds formed through a marriage offer positive rewards in the development of a relationship, such an attachment may have hemming-in or restrictive effects. Certain opportunities and options that existed previously may no longer be available. With childbearing, women traditionally have had to forego temporarily the development of their careers, and, with the buildup of family obligations, couples frequently are restricted in pursuing recreational interests outside the home.

For most adults in modern society the most important attachments beyond the immediate family group form in the work sphere. Occupational placement is not only a major source of self-identity but also a major source of linkage into the broader social system. Other forms of social attachment, such as attachment to the church or to the political party, are important only on a selective basis. While religious and political involvements constitute intense forms of commitment for some, most people highly limit their degree of participation in these areas. For most adults, marriage and job commitments are usually surrounded by constraints that promote continuance of a line of action. By way of contrast, the limited involvements in religion and politics suggest that organizational disaffiliation in these areas can easily be achieved.

1. Formation of Commitments

In the development of commitments the individual binds to others in an ongoing set of social relationships. This occurs in such diverse activities as forming friendship ties, preparing for a career, taking on a job, joining a social movement, and entering into marriage. Each instance involves a buildup of interaction patterns that have consequences for the well-being of the individual. The formation of commitments derives from an initial process of attraction and the subsequent development of bonds that restrict the range of options available.

The concept of **commitment** has conveyed two distinct meanings in social psychology. One is the sense of a positive commitment, which refers to embracing or dedicating oneself to the pursuit of some particular course of action. This is the aspect of commitment that leads one to prepare for a particular career, to become engaged, or to get married. The positive aspects of commitment relate to the rewards anticipated from the pursuit of an objective or a social relationship. On the other hand there are the negative aspects of a commitment, and these consist of the penalties associated with "backing out," "reneging on a promise," "being undependable" (Stanage, 1970). People are likely to associate the positive aspects of a commitment with the selection of a goal, while the negative aspects of a commitment include the constraints that prevent "being a quitter," "giving up," or "changing one's mind."

Howard Becker (1960) notes that people do not necessarily make commitments at the conscious level but may experience them more nearly as an occurrence or as something that just happens. Continued interactions with the same person over an extended period of time tend to produce consistent lines of behavior; in the formation of a commitment it becomes more expedient to continue than to terminate a relationship. Becker has described the development of a commitment as analogous to "making a side bet." The **side bet** consists of all those considerations that emerge to promote consistency in a line of action and at the same time provide obstacles to the pursuit of other alternatives. For example, in the work sphere the side bets include such practical benefits as seniority, longer vacations, and retirement pay, as well as such emotional benefits as mutual understanding and friendship ties with co-workers.

After an individual has worked at a particular job for a large number of years, he or she is likely to continue working at that job because of the social costs that would accrue from giving it up or pursuing a different line of work. Alutto, Hrebiniak, and Alonso (1973) indicate that the pattern of maintaining commitment to a particular job, in spite of opportunities for another job with better pay, correlates with a number of variables. Among these variables are those of age, experience, and marital status. Consistent with Becker's side bet concept, the research of Alutto and his colleagues indicate that older workers are less willing to change job than are younger ones, those with more years of experience on the job are less willing to change than those with less experience, and those who are married are less willing to move than those who are single.

The unwillingness to change jobs is apparently tied in with the development of routine patterns of behavior that individuals do not wish to give up because of the inconvenience of doing so. Being required to form new social relationships on the job, to learn new work routines, to drive a greater distance to work, or to change residence are among the social costs that enter into the decision to remain at a particular job. Thus the considerations for continuing work are unrelated to the reasons for selecting a particular job in the first place.

Commitments to continuing any course of action, whether work-related or not, are promoted through the development of identities that the individual's significant others know and understand. Through job title and marital status, the individual acquires stable anchorage points in broad networks of social relationships. By knowing where an individual stands, others are able to relate to him or her in a predictable manner. In contrast, if aspects of an individual's identity appear unclear, social supports may be weak for the continuance of a social relationship. Such is apparently the case with the patterns of cohabitation that are emerging as alternatives for some couples to the formal bonds of marriage.

In a comparison of cohabiting and married couples, Michael P. Johnson (1973) found a significant difference in the kinds and degrees of commitment. In his study, cohabitation couples were less likely than married couples to want to stay together for five years or more. Cohabiting couples were characterized by very limited pressures for continuance, and most couples reported that very few people whose opinions they valued would disapprove if the relationship terminated. By way of contrast, numerous constraints and costs among married couples were operating to promote continuity of the relationship.

The social constraints included others' expectancies for consistency, as well as what subjects perceived to be the attitudes of disapproval if the relationship terminates. The personal costs included the undesirable changes that cancelling the marriage would require, such as working out a property settlement and changing aspects of lifestyle like eating, sleeping, and living arrangements. Johnson concluded that the constraints surrounding commitments help to account for much of the consistency of social behavior.

2. The Strength of Weak Ties

The development of social attachments to relatives, friends, neighbors, and co-workers provides the immediate basis for linkage into the broader society, but as Arthur Neal and Melvin Seeman (1964) point out, these more immediate social attachments do not carry a person very far into the social system. The **mediating links** provided by intimate groups are limited, and they often serve to insulate their members from many of the events occurring in the larger society. Intimate groups, because they often lack integration with large-scale associations, fail to represent adequately the interests and concerns of their members.

Intervening levels of social organization serve important functions by providing mediating links between individuals and the broader society. The mediating links include employment, church membership, political party affiliation, and membership in voluntary associations. Compared to an organized collectivity, the single individual is relatively limited in his or her capacity to control events. For this reason, the relationships individuals establish with large-scale organizations become an important consideration in both the pursuit of self-interests and the development of a sense of attachment and belonging within the broader society. (See Table 6.2.)

Within this context, the place of the voluntary association has been prominently emphasized in observations on the linkages of individuals to the totality of modern social life. For example, Robin Williams (1970) regards the proliferation of associations as one of the dominant characteristics of modern social organization. He calls attention to the large variety of voluntary organizations in the United States and sees this development as a response to the historical weakening of the ties to kinship groups and local communities. The loss of a shared sense of community in modern society has been accompanied by an increased emphasis on the formation of the voluntary association as a substitute.

Voluntary organizations have grown because they serve a variety of functions. Many form for such instrumental reasons as to promote economic interests, to protect minority rights, to seek political change, or to perpetuate a social heritage based on national origin. Others are important for their status-

---

TABLE 6.2
A Casual List of Voluntary Associations

Special-interest groups

Society for the Preservation and Encouragement of Barber Shop Quartet Singing in
    America
Horseshoe Pitchers Association of America
People Against Pornography
Society for Voluntary Sterilization
Alcoholics Anonymous
Church of Scientology
Flying Funeral Directors of America
Society for Native Oregon Born (SNOB)
Amputee Shoe and Glove Exchange
Common Cause
American Indian Development Association
The Wilderness Society
League of Women Voters
American Association for Gifted Children
Imperial Order of the Dragon
American Numismatic Society
International Jelly and Preserve Association
Parents Without Partners
Dads of Foreign Service Veterans

Note: While the exact number of formally organized associations in the United States is un-
known, it is clear that numerous new ones are being added each year. The latest edition of the
Encyclopedia of Associations lists more than 14,000 of them, reflecting the proneness among
Americans to organize to enhance special interests.

---

conferral functions, and they appeal to their members as badges of respectability and symbols of prestige. Belonging to such status-conferral groups as the
Daughters of the American Revolution or the First Families of Virginia provides a basis for validating the social worth and the heritage of their members.
    Associations sometimes serve as instruments for vertical mobility. Mem-
berships in country clubs or in civic service organizations often provide opportunities for establishing important personal contacts; they also increase the
sources of information about business and professional opportunities. While
often designed for some other purpose, organizations sometimes have secondary functions of providing mutual support and implementing member interests and aspirations. Mark Granovetter (1973) calls this process the **strength**

The Strength of Weak Ties

The entrances to most small- and medium-sized cities in the United States display a listing of their organizations, giving meeting times and places. Apparently people are proud of their organizations, and the inconspicuous listing of them at the city limits is an implicit way of saying so. Visitors in town may readily draw on the strength of these weak ties. These organizational memberships provide a means of establishing new acquaintances and enhancing business interests. Organizational memberships may also serve as a buffer against the loneliness which often accompanies the role of being a stranger.

of weak ties and emphasizes the importance of social interactions for providing mediating links into broader networks of the social system. Weak ties refer to the range of casual acquaintances available as sources of information to draw on in getting jobs, developing business interests, or solving personal problems.

Some associations are formed primarily for recreational and expressive reasons. Participating in a bridge club, a hobby club, or a bowling league is often intrinsically rewarding and provides a meaningful way of spending time within a congenial atmosphere. These kinds of voluntary associations provide functional substitutes for primary group ties and serve to meet the needs for belonging and social affiliation. In this respect, mediating links into the broader society are provided at a level beyond that of the immediate family or friendship groups, and as weak ties they provide an extended basis for obtaining information and influence in the enhancement of personal interests. (See Box 6.6.)

BOX 6.6
Dominant Status and Voluntary Association Memberships

Numerous studies of voluntary associations have concentrated on the social characteristics of those who participate in voluntary associations compared to those who do not. Lemon, Palisi, and Jacobson (1972) present the theory that differential rates of social participation can be explained in terms of patterns of dominance and control by those who occupy positions of privilege within American society. The results of numerous studies have provided support for the following conclusions:

1. Higher rates of participation are found among those higher in socioeconomic status (education, occupational level, and income) than among those lower in socioeconomic status.
2. Contrary to popular views, males are more likely to be participants in voluntary associations than are females.
3. Married people tend to join and participate in organizations more frequently than single people.
4. Protestants have higher rates of involvement in voluntary associations than do Catholics.
5. Middle-aged persons participate in voluntary organizations more frequently than do either younger or older people.

According to Lemon, Palisi, and Jacobson, these results converge to suggest that dominant status is associated with higher rates of membership and participation. Those who have higher educational, occupational, and income levels tend to dominate those with lower educational, occupational, and income achievements; males tend to dominate females; Protestants are more powerful and influential than Catholics; and those of middle age are in preferential positions of power compared to the young and the aged. Thus the character of involvement in voluntary associations tends to reinforce preferential positions of power and influence within the broader society.

Source: Mona Lemon, Bartolomeo J. Palisi, and Perry E. Jacobson, Jr., "Dominant Statuses and Involvement in Formal Voluntary Associations," *Journal of Voluntary Action Research* 1 (April, 1972): 30–42.

The research on correlates of membership in voluntary associations indicates that socioeconomic status is a major variable in rates of participation. Those higher in education, occupational status, and income tend to be over-represented in voluntary organizational memberships (Hyman and Wright, 1971). These results suggest that those people at the upper socioeconomic levels acquire their influence in part by using organizations to assert control over the outcomes they seek. The capacity of the individual to assert influence and control is limited when he or she is working in isolation from those confronting similar problems or pursuing similar interests. The effectiveness of organization derives from the pooling of resources and the coordination of social efforts.

D. SEVERANCE OF SOCIAL TIES

We cannot adequately understand the development of social attachment without also taking into account the conditions that promote a sense of **social isolation.** If we think of social attachment as involving bonds that reinforce the continuance of social relationships, we may think of social isolation as reflecting its corresponding opposite. Social isolation may be defined as feelings of loneliness, separateness, or apartness from others. Such feelings of isolation may accompany the severance of social attachments (Glaser and Strauss, 1971), and they are associated with a sense of exclusion from the activities of other people.

Georg Simmel (1950), in his classical writings on the stranger, described isolation as manifesting "the unity of nearness and remoteness" in social relationships. The stranger may be physically close to other people but feel that he or she is psychologically far away. The stranger has the vantage point of being "an outsider," yet has to confront the reality of group relationships. The stranger's feelings of isolation include perceiving others as socially distant, unconcerned, and unfriendly, and this has the effect of requiring the individual to rely on his or her own resources. In effect, the isolated individual is like Simmel's stranger in that he or she lacks a firm rootedness in social relationships having permanence and durability.

People tend to experience feelings of isolation more acutely during the transitional phases of the life cycle than during the stages of stability and continuity in social relationships. For example, among teenagers and young adults intense feelings of isolation often accompany the act of leaving home and the relatively long time interval between childhood and the attainment of full-fledged entry into adult life. The feelings of isolation among young adults, however, are usually reduced through marriage and entry into the labor force, although not necessarily in that order.

Marriage and employment are forms of social attachment that serve as stabilizers throughout the middle years and provide basic sources for both self-identity and a sense of contribution to the social system. The development of feelings of isolation in adult life tend to be shaped by such situational factors as those involved in abrupt changes in life conditions (Martin, 1976). These include the sense of loss that accompanies such conditions as divorce or separation (see Box 6.7), death of a spouse or other family member, occupational displacement, and toward the later phases of the life cycle the stress connected with retirement and disengagement from the labor force. **Disengagement** refers to the process by which individuals reduce their levels of involvement and commitment in previous lines of action.

1. Retirement

According to Ruth Cavan (1962), disengagement from work commitments is generally the most acute adjustment older men have to make. While many

---

BOX 6.7
The Emotional Impact of Divorce

The research of Robert S. Weiss indicates that "the disruption of marriage regularly produces emotional distress, almost irrespective of the quality of the marriage or the desire for its dissolution" (1976: 135). While the distress levels of divorce are not as great as those that occur with the death of a spouse, similarities occur in the loss of attachments, and these have serious consequences for one's sense of security and stability. The level of stress tends to be high for the person who initiated the separation as well as for the person who did not.

The social bonds created in marriage tend to persist after a marital separation occurs. Whether the marriage was happy or unhappy, whether the former spouse is respected or detested, a sense of cohesion tends to continue. Many divorced people feel drawn to a former spouse, even if convinced of the undesirability of continuing the relationship. A sense of bonding persists even if the individual has formed substitute attachments and even if the person despised the former spouse.

Shared emotional experiences seem to have enduring effects and become expressed in the numerous responses to the loss of attachments. The divorced person frequently centers attention around images of the lost person. The divorced individual has an urge to establish contact and to be in the presence of the former spouse, and creates fantasies about the return of the separated person. While a sense of euphoria sometimes develops about the prospects for freedom and adventure, separation distress in the forms of anger, fear, and guilt are likely to be recurrent.

Source: Robert S. Weiss, "The Emotional Impact of Marital Separation," *Journal of Social Issues* 32, no. 1 (1976): 135–146.

look forward to retirement as an opportunity to pursue interests that have been neglected, retirement is often stress-producing because of a basic alteration in what had been everyday routines for a large number of years. The stress is greatest in those occupations in which the shift from work to nonwork occurs abruptly, and less so in those occupations in which the performance of work tasks tapers off gradually. Those engaged in agriculture, in small businesses, and in the professions may gradually reduce their engagement in work activity with increasing years. In most industrial and service occupations, on the other hand, abrupt changes occur with retirement in the shift from a full work week to not being employed at all.

The abruptness of retirement in our industrialized society generates a number of problems the retiree must confront. A social vacuum often develops with the loss of an occupational identity. The retired professor is without students to teach, the retired lawyer no longer has a brief to prepare, and the retired carpenter no longer needs tools for building houses. The vacuum created by retirement requires the development of a new self-image, and this is in part forced on the retiree by the responses of others. The looking glass comprised of fellow workers now reflects a changed image. The individual is no longer a productive member of the team but a person who has been "put out to pasture" or "placed on the shelf."

The basic problems associated with retirement are essentially to develop new and meaningful lines of action, along with developing a new identity based on something other than occupational commitments. Like other basic changes in life, retirement has the potential for being a rewarding as well as a disorganizing experience (Bradburn, 1969). Some people find retirement to be a satisfying stage of life, particularly if they view their health and financial resources as adequate. While the loss of work attachments necessarily involves some degree of disruption, particularly for the person who has spent thirty or forty years at a particular job, retirement also offers an opportunity to reorganize life around doing what he or she really wants to do, rather than around what a job required. This may take the form of traveling, pursuing a neglected hobby, or becoming engaged in some sphere of community service.

The degree of success in reorganizing one's life is dependent on the quality of relationships outside the sphere of work. If the marriage stays intact, if friendship ties remain, and if interests continue to expand in the surrounding environment, retirement may simply be another episode that has a proper place within the sequence of life change and development. The research of Bernice Neugarten (1975) indicates that the aging process is characterized by a continuity in personality and lifestyle, that most old people are not neglected by their families, and that most old people report that they are satisfied with their lives since retirement.

The variations in patterns of adjustment to retirement are more impressive than their similarities. While some attain a sense of self-fulfillment in retirement, others face problems of bitterness and despair. Many of the problems of adjustment to retirement are deeply embedded in lifestyles that emerge

Retirement: Pursuing Neglected Interests
_Retirement is a time of expanding interests and the pursuit of neglected hobbies for
some, but a time of hopelessness and despair for others. The responses to retirement
are shaped to a large degree by the attitudes and behavior patterns that develop
throughout the life course._

in the early and middle years. Having few interests outside the sphere of work,
lacking involvement in community organizations, having no friendship ties,
and holding negative attitudes toward the aging process are among the numerous conditions of the earlier years that will eventually have their impact in
later life. Those who are happiest in the later years are those who have brought
their basic life goals into alignment with their capacities for attaining them
(Klinger, 1977).

In the later years of life the most critical adjustment women must make is coping with the severance of marital bonds through the death of a spouse. This adjustment is more likely to be required of women than of men because of two basic facts. The life expectancy is greater for women than for men, and most women marry men who are older than themselves. Thus overall patterns of mate selection and longevity converge to make coping with the death of a spouse a special problem for older women. Census data for the United States in 1970 indicated that the odds were nearly five to one that the surviving spouse would be the wife rather than the husband (Harvey and Bahr, 1974).

We may understand the social isolation produced by widowhood as deriving from numerous sources of meaning and commitment that have built up over a long period of time. The meanings include both the recurrent interactions in the more intimate spheres of family life and the linkage of the couple as a unit to broader networks of social relationships. The interior of family life includes the development of joint enterprises such as coordinating daily schedules, sharing work tasks, planning vacations, making love, and pursuing hobbies. Externally the marital unit tends to become an influential social link, and others come to view the couple in terms of the common front which the two present to the outside world. Through a combination of marital interactions and external social supports, a relatively stable self-identity emerges that is interrelated with that of a spouse.

In a study of more than 300 widows in the Chicago metropolitan area, Helen Lopata (1973) found that the abrupt ending of marriage through the death of a spouse required most women to reformulate their self-identities. Reformulating an identity is a complex process by which widows deal with a sense of incompleteness as a person, with being shunned by others, and with expressions of strain in social relationships. The feelings of inadequacy as a person are often related to being required to do "unfeminine" things, such as handling money problems, maintaining an automobile, and doing a "man's work" around the house. But more importantly, without her husband she cannot reproduce certain interaction patterns, and other people do not treat her as they did before. For example, friends of the widow's husband often avoid her because they are uncomfortable in her presence and do not know how to relate to her. She does not receive invitations to certain events because the events are organized for couples.

From a social psychological standpoint the most intense problems of widowhood are the feelings of loneliness and isolation. Robert Weiss (1976) reports that even in marriages with high levels of conflict, there are usually strong levels of emotional attachment; with the severance of the marital bond numerous disruptions occur that the remaining spouse must confront. The difficulties inherent in coping with these disruptions are reflected in higher suicide rates for the widowed compared to the continuously married; among the widowed the suicide rates are higher for men than for women (Bock and Webber, 1972). Apparently for men the isolating effects that accompany the loss of work attachments intensify with the loss of the marriage bond. The greater difficulties of men compared to women in coping with the death of a spouse suggest that under normal conditions men are more emotionally and socially dependent on their wives than most of them would care to admit.

SUMMARY

Social attachments have their origin in the prolonged dependence of the human infant on others for survival and in the socialization that occurs within the secure atmosphere provided by family life. The commitments formed in adult life emerge from the positive rewards associated with ongoing social relationships and from the numerous social constraints that promote continuance in a given line of action.

Binding ties among individuals derive from the interaction process and from the discovery of shared social meanings. It is within this process that the individual selectively assigns reward value to persons, objects, and events. Individuals who are similar in a large number of social and psychological characteristics tend to be attracted to one another, and from sustained interactions over an extended period of time, they tend to develop systems of shared meaning.

For most adults in our society some of the stronger social bonds are found in family life and in the workplace, while weaker social ties are found in the numerous mediational memberships in the larger society. The mediation hypothesis holds that weak ties are important for the well-being of the individual and that those who lack intervening memberships are likely to experience feelings of social isolation and powerlessness.

The conditions of estrangement from others may occur at various levels of intensity in numerous kinds of social situations. Within the life cycle, feelings of isolation are more likely to occur during the transitional stages, such as moving from childhood to adulthood, changing jobs, and coping with retirement, divorce, or death of a spouse. But feelings of social isolation may also occur on a routine basis if individuals have generalized perceptions that others are unfriendly or unconcerned, if they feel cut-off from meaningful social relationships, and if they are unable to identify with numerous aspects of their own society.

BASIC TERMS

Need for affiliation
Generation gap
Propinquity
Homophily
Status inequality
Commitment

Side bets
Mediating links
Strength of weak ties
Social isolation
Disengagement

REFERENCES

Alutto, Joseph A., Lawrence G. Hrebiniak, and Ramon C. Alonso
    1973 "On Operationalizing the Concept of Commitment," *Social Forces* 51 (June): 448-454.
Bar-Tal, Daniel, Yaakov Bar-Zohar, Margarete Hermon, and Martin S. Greenberg
    1977 "Reciprocity Behavior in the Relationship Between Donor and Recipient and Between Harm-Doer and Victim," *Sociometry* 40 (September): 293-298.
Becker, Howard S.
    1960 "Notes on the Concept of Commitment," *American Journal of Sociology* 66 (July): 32-40.
Berger, Peter and Hansfried Kellner
    1964 "Marriage and the Construction of Reality," *Diogenes* 46 (Summer): 1-24.
Bock, E. Wilber and Irving L. Webber
    1972 "Suicide among the Elderly," *Journal of Marriage and the Family* 34 (February): 24-31.
Boyatzis, Richard E.
    1973 "Affiliation Motivation," in David C. McClelland and Robert S. Steele (eds.), *Human Motivation*, Morristown, N.J.: General Learning Press, pp. 252-278.
Bradburn, Norman M.
    1969 *The Structure of Psychological Well-Being*, Chicago: Aldine.
Broderick, Carlfred B.
    1971 "Beyond the Five Conceptual Frameworks: A Decade of Development in Family Theory," *Journal of Marriage and the Family* 33 (February): 139-159.
Byrne, Donn
    1971 *The Attraction Paradigm*, New York: Academic Press.
Cavan, Ruth S.
    1962 "Self and Role in Adjustment During Old Age," in Arnold M. Rose (ed.), *Human Behavior and Social Processes*, Boston: Houghton Mifflin, pp. 526-536.
Curry, Timothy J. and Richard M. Emerson
    1970 "Balance Theory: A Theory of Interpersonal Attraction," *Sociometry* 33 (June): 216-238.
Dynes, Russell R., Alfred C. Clarke, and Simon Dinitz
    1962 "Levels of Occupational Aspiration: Some Aspects of Family Experience as a Variable," in Bartlett H. Stoodley (ed.), *Society and Self*, New York: The Free Press of Glencoe, pp. 495-501.
Foner, Anne and David Kertzer
    1978 "Transitions over the Life Course," *American Journal of Sociology* 83 (March): 1081-1104.
Glaser, Barney G. and Anselm L. Strauss
    1971 *Status Passage*, Chicago: Aldine-Atherton.
Glick, Paul C.
    1977 "Updating the Life Cycle of the Family," *Journal of Marriage and the Family* 39 (February): 5-14.
    1975 "A Demographer Looks at American Families," *Journal of Marriage and the Family* 37 (February): 15-26.
Gove, Walter R.
    1973 "Sex, Marital Status, and Mortality," *American Journal of Sociology* 79 (July): 45-67.

Granovetter, Mark S.
      1973 "The Strength of Weak Ties," *American Journal of Sociology* 78 (May):
            1360–1380.
Harvey, Carol D. and Howard M. Bahr
      1974 "Widowhood, Morale, and Affiliation," *Journal of Marriage and the Family*
            36 (February): 97–106.
Hearn, H. L. and Patricia Stoll
      1975 "Continuance Commitment in Low-Status Occupations: The Cocktail
            Waitress," *Sociological Quarterly* 16 (Winter): 105–114.
Hernes, Gudmund
      1972 "The Process of Entry into First Marriage," *American Sociological Review*
            37 (April): 173–182.
Hoffman, Lois L., Arland Thornton, and Jean D. Manis
      1978 "The Value of Children to Parents in the United States," *Journal of Popula-
            tion* 1 (Summer): 91–131.
Hyman, Herbert H. and Charles R. Wright
      1971 "Trends in Voluntary Association Memberships of American Adults,"
            American Sociological Review 36 (April): 191–206.
Johnson, Michael P.
      1973 "Commitment: A Conceptual Structure and Empirical Application," *Socio-
            logical Quarterly* 14 (Summer): 395–406.
Klinger, Eric
      1977 *Meaning and Void,* Minneapolis: University of Minnesota Press.
Kohn, Melvin
      1969 *Class and Conformity,* Homewood, Ill.: Dorsey Press.
Layton, Bruce D. and Chester A. Insko
      1974 "Anticipated Interaction and the Similarity-Attraction Effect," *Sociometry*
            37 (June): 149–162.
Lemon, Mona, Bartolomeo J. Palisi, and Perry E. Jacobson, Jr.
      1972 "Dominant Statuses and Involvement in Formal Voluntary Associations,"
            Journal of Voluntary Action Research 1 (April): 30–42.
Levinger, George, David J. Senn, and Bruce W. Jorgensen
      1970 "Progress Toward Permanence in Courtship," *Sociometry* 33 (December):
            427–443.
Lewis, Robert A.
      1973 "A Longitudinal Test of a Developmental Framework for Premarital Dyadic
            Formation," *Journal of Marriage and the Family* 35 (February): 16–25.
Lopata, Helen Znaniecki
      1973 "Self-Identity in Marriage and Widowhood," *Sociological Quarterly* 14
            (Summer): 407–418.
Martin, Walter T.
      1976 "Status Integration, Social Stress, and Mental Illness," *Journal of Health and
            Social Behavior* 17 (September): 280–294.
Murstein, Bernard I., Mary Cerreto, and Marcia G. MacDonald
      1977 "A Theory and Investigation of the Effect of Exchange-Orientation on Mar-
            riage and Friendship," *Journal of Marriage and the Family* 39 (August): 543–
            548.

Neal, Arthur G. and Melvin Seeman
    1964 "Organizations and Powerlessness: A Test of the Mediation Hypothesis,"
        American Sociological Review 29 (April): 216–226.
Neugarten, Bernice L.
    1975 "Grow Old Along with Me! The Best Is Yet to Be," in Saul D. Feldman and
        Gerald W. Thielbar (eds.), *Life Styles: Diversity in American Society*, Boston:
        Little, Brown, pp. 321–328.
Pearlin, Leonard I.
    1975 "Status Inequality and Stress in Marriage," *American Sociological Review*
        40 (June): 344–357.
Schachter, Stanley
    1959 *The Psychology of Affiliation,* Stanford: Stanford University Press.
Segal, Mady Wechsler
    1979 "Varieties of Interpersonal Attraction and Their Inter-Relationships in
        Natural Groups," *Social Psychology Quarterly* 42 (September): 253–261.
Simmel, Georg
    1950 *The Sociology of Georg Simmel* (ed. and trans. by Kurt Wolff), Glencoe, Ill.:
        The Free Press.
Smith, David M.
    1970 "Adolescence: A Study of Stereotyping," *Sociological Review* 18: 197–211.
Stanage, Sherman M.
    1970 "A Phenomenological Model of Commitment," *Sociological Focus* 3 (Spring):
        33–42.
Trost, Jan
    1967 "Some Data on Mate-Selection: Homogamy and Perceived Homogamy,"
        Journal of Marriage and the Family 29 (November): 739–755.
Van Gennep, Arnold
    1960 *The Rites of Passage,* Chicago: University of Chicago Press.
Wagner, W.
    1971 "The Increasing Importance of the Peer Group During Adolescence," *Adoles-
        cence* 6:53–58.
Weiss, Robert S.
    1976 "The Emotional Impact of Marital Separation," *Journal of Social Issues* 32,
        no. 1: 135–146.
Wells, J. Gipson
    1976 "A Critical Look at Personal Marriage Contracts," *Family Coordinator* 25
        (January): 33–38.
Werner, Carol and Pat Parmelee
    1979 "Similarity of Friends' Activity Preference," *Social Psychology Quarterly* 42
        (March): 62–65.
Williams, Robin M., Jr.
    1970 *American Society,* New York: Knopf.
Wright, James D. and Sonia R. Wright
    1976 "Social Class and Parental Values for Children," *American Sociological
        Review* 41 (June): 527–537.
Yankelovich, Daniel
    1972 *The Changing Values on Campus,* New York: Simon & Schuster.

7

Work and Leisure

Some of the more important social attachments are those that form through work activities and the uses of leisure. The routines associated with keeping work schedules, completing assigned tasks, and meeting family financial needs are important sources of personal stability and order. Through attachments to jobs and career the personal interests of individuals align with the needs of the social system. Having a paid job serves to verify social worth and to establish a self-identity. But perhaps more importantly, having a paid job enables individuals to gain access to desired resources for use in the pursuit of valued activities in the nonwork sphere.

Because of the multiple meanings that are given to work and leisure in modern society, the relationships between these two spheres of activity are of concern to social psychologists. For many people, work has lost its potentially creative appeal and has become associated with drudgery, duty, obligation—"something you have to do." These are primarily negative images of work and reflect the limited place of jobs and careers among the intrinsic rewards of modern society. Those who do not regard their work activity as a central life interest seek compensations by searching for meaning in the nonwork sphere—in family life, in hobbies and crafts, in spectator sports, in outdoor recreation, and in mass entertainment.

The view of work as a form of drudgery and as a set of obligations does not apply to many skilled artisans who take pride in their jobs, nor does it apply to many professionals who derive intrinsic satisfactions from their involvements in the occupational sphere. Thus it is not the objective activity itself that makes something work or play, because an activity that some regard as play constitutes the work of others. For example, professional athletes may work at playing golf or football, and some of their six-digit incomes suggest how well they may be paid for this kind of play. Thus in some cases the dividing line between work and play is very thin, and there are no clear boundaries to indicate where the job stops and leisure begins.

These images of work and leisure contain a number of contradictions that are difficult for researchers to resolve as they attempt to separate the spheres of work and leisure. Using the criterion "getting paid" would exclude from work the chores performed around the house (cooking, cleaning, washing, mending, and so forth). Yet the qualities of family life and economic well-being are very much dependent on the performance of these tasks. On the other hand the social significance of work in recent years has increasingly centered around what Daniel Yankelovich (1978) has described as "the symbolism of the paid job." Getting paid verifies the value of one's work, and there can be little doubt about its utility at least to someone.

Not only is it difficult to specify the boundaries of work; there are problems of a similar magnitude in deriving an adequate definition of the sphere of leisure. Numerous sociologists reject the view that leisure consists of the time remaining after the obligations of the workday have been completed. The demands on the individual's time and energies for taking care of such chores as making repairs around the house, shopping, and visiting relatives may reflect a

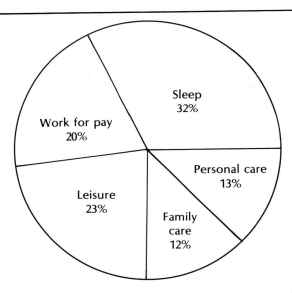

Note: The figures given are averages based on a sample of adults residing in urban areas (Robinson, 1976). Variations in the overall pattern occur when comparing men to women, single to married people, and employed to nonemployed people.

Source: Data from U.S. Department of Commerce, *Social Indicators 1976*, Washington, D.C.: Government Printing Office, 1977.

John P. Robinson, "Changes in America's Use of Time, 1965–1975," *Report of the Communication Research Center*, Cleveland State University, 1976.

FIGURE 7.1
Time Allocation among Americans

set of obligations that are commensurate with the obligations incurred in the workplace. The data in Figure 7.1 show the overall pattern of time allocation among Americans.

Because of the variety of subjective meanings that surround the spheres of work and leisure, clear objective definitions are not easily derivable. For this reason a more adequate approach to the study of work and leisure may consist of looking at these two spheres of life activity from the vantage point of the individuals involved. The meaning of work or leisure in any given case is a social construction of reality. Such meanings shape the character of the linkages between self-interests and the interests of others in the broader community. The variety of these linkages interests social psychologists more than do attempts to specify the essential character of either work or leisure.

Having said this we may also note that there are general observations social psychologists make about the importance of work and leisure in the life-worlds of men and women. The processes of becoming involved in a given occupation and in specific patterns of leisure are shaped by the choices and decisions people make in view of the options available to them. These decisions become consequential because they set limits within which a great deal of adult activity takes place. The conditions of work and leisure become more important ingredients that enter into assessments about social worth, the stability of one's personal life, and the degree of self-fulfillment.

Attitudes toward work and leisure are two major indicators of how people evaluate the qualities of their lives in general. Those who feel good about the kind of work that they do tend to be satisfied with the overall qualities of their lives. In similar fashion the levels of happiness and life satisfaction are closely related to the levels of enjoyment people derive from their uses of leisure time. Those who enjoy their work and their leisure are satisfied with the overall qualities of their lives, while those who are dissatisfied in either of these areas are likely to feel that life is something less than it could or ought to be.

A. THE MEANING OF WORK

The total resources available in modern society are adequate to free permanently some segments of the population from the drudgery of work altogether. Yet most people would not want to have a complete life of leisure even if this option were made available to them. The desire to work at a paid job is nearly universal among adults in modern society. This is evident in the concerns of young people for gaining initial entry into the labor force, in the increasing numbers of married women who seek employment, and in the pressures coming from older workers to change the rules that mandate retirement at some specific age.

The meanings that are given to the world of work are numerous and varied. Obviously people work for money and what money will buy, but there are numerous other connotative meanings that surround the sphere of employment. These additional meanings include a number of variables that are important components of a sense of psychological well-being (Bradburn, 1969). A paid job provides an external referent for validating some degree of social worth, for providing a sense of engagement in a productive enterprise, for giving predictability and coherence to one's life through the performance of tasks at regularly scheduled times and places. In brief, the symbolism of the paid job permits one to achieve a sense of stability in one's personal life as well as in one's relationships with others (Yankelovich, 1978).

1. Extrinsic Rewards

The avowed justification for work primarily centers around getting paid for the performance of a task. People work in order to get the money they need for meeting financial obligations and for supporting the kind of lifestyle they desire. However, we may look on work—to the extent that its involvements are motivated primarily by money concerns—as being extrinsic in character. This suggests that people do not regard work as a rewarding activity in its own right, but as a way of gaining access to desired rewards in the nonwork sphere.

Extrinsic rewards include all of those benefits and advantages of gainful employment that are external to the work itself. These include the numerous evaluations and assessments of the utility of the paid job within the broader context of social life. For example, the extrinsic rewards of work are manifested in evaluations individuals make about whether their jobs are adequate for meeting the financial needs of the family and for supporting their lifestyle. Also included in the extrinsic rewards are the status and prestige advantages that a job title affords in social relationships; the numerous fringe benefits one receives in the way of insurance, sick leaves, paid vacations, and retirement pensions; and a sense of fairness about the adequacy of the pay received for the work performed.

From the results of national surveys conducted in several of the more highly industrialized countries of the world, Connie deBoer (1978) observes that the vast majority of workers report being satisfied with their jobs. The gratifications from paid job apparently derive from an evaluation of the extrinsic rewards of employment. The majority say that the primary reason for working is to earn money, rather than to find self-fulfillment or to do one's duty as a member of society.

As deBoer notes, there is little surprise in the finding that most people say they are satisfied with their work, "since dissatisfaction would indicate that they are dissatisfied with their entire life, their position, and their role in society" (1978: 415). Yet she also observes that there are variations in the degrees of satisfaction, and those variations are in part related to the economic situation of the individual and in part to the job opportunities of the broader society. For example, changing jobs is more likely to be a feasible option under conditions in which there is a high demand for labor; while during times of high unemployment, workers are likely to be satisfied that they have any job at all.

By probing further, we find that the major purpose reported for being in the labor force is to meet the financial needs of the family (deBoer, 1978). These needs, however, are highly variable among families, and what is regarded as a living wage in one case may be regarded as inadequate in another. The emphasis on the adequacy of paid work for meeting family needs suggests that the overall lifestyles play an important part in satisfaction with a specific job. Paid work, family concerns, and the uses of leisure become interrelated in the life designs of specific individuals.

From a study of job satisfaction in four countries, William Form (1973) concludes that where poverty is widespread workers are likely to be concerned with survival and job security. People with a standard of living near the subsistence level are more likely to define work as a necessary part of living, and the idea that a job may be intrinsically rewarding or a source of self-fulfillment is not likely to occur. People in the more highly industrialized countries, however, are more likely to be concerned with the intrinsic rewards of work. The notions that work should be creative, challenging, interesting, and psychologically fulfilling are more likely to emerge in societies characterized by a relatively high standard of living.

2. Intrinsic Rewards

The distinction between the extrinsic and the intrinsic rewards of work is central to the concerns of social psychologists. As already mentioned, the extrinsic rewards of work include the numerous resources of the paid job that have meaning within the nonwork sphere. By way of contrast, the **intrinsic rewards** of a job are satisfactions that derive from the performance of the work activity itself. The intrinsic rewards are greater if one derives a sense of creativity from the use of specialized skills (Seeman, 1967), if the work performed relates to one's central life interests (Dubin, 1956), and if the job lends itself to the use of personal initiative and the acceptance of responsibility (Tudor, 1972). These are among the conditions promoting an overall sense of self-fulfillment through the tasks performed in the labor market. (See Box 7.1.)

To remove the economic element from the meaning of work, Nancy Morse and Robert Weiss (1955) designed a question that presented a hypothetical situation to a sample of 400 workers: "If by some chance you inherited enough money to live comfortably without working, do you think you would work anyway or not?" Approximately 80 percent indicated that they would prefer to continue working. Subsequent uses of a similar question in national surveys of work attitudes consistently support the conclusion that a substantial majority of workers would prefer to continue at work, even if the money were no longer needed (deBoer, 1978).

The research of Morse and Weiss (1955) also indicated that the commit-

The Intrinsic Rewards of Work
Many skilled craftspeople derive intrinsic rewards from the visual appeal of making something, from the social value of the objects of their creation, and from a sense of personal control in solving work-related problems.

ment to continue working was stronger than the attachment to any specific job. Many of their subjects indicated they would attempt to change jobs if they could, but very few would stop working altogether. The reasons for continuing work, in the absence of financial need, included the views that life without work would be less purposeful, less stimulating, less exciting, and less active. In effect, the reasons for wanting to continue to work suggested the variety of intrinsic rewards that may be found in the workplace.

While individuals may derive numerous satisfactions from involvement in the workplace, there are several research studies suggesting that intrinsic rewards on the job are more likely to occur among skilled crafts people and among professionals than among other major segments of the labor force. In the more highly skilled crafts (carpenters, master printers, tool and die makers, and so forth) the sense of creativeness comes from making something that is both visible and useful and which may be regarded as the product of one's own skills and efforts. Research studies by Robert Blauner (1964) and William Faunce (1968) suggests that craftsmanship is associated with personal freedom in the organization of materials and resources, a feeling of pride in one's work, and a sense of identity with the objects of one's own creation.

BOX 7.1
Dirty-Work Designations

Everett Hughes (1971) used the term **dirty work** to designate certain kinds of tasks found in all occupations. Dirty work does not stem from the nature of the task itself, but from the conditions under which individuals are required to do certain jobs that go against their better judgments. Tasks designated as dirty work include those that are viewed as "messy," "disgusting," "deplorable," or "morally degrading."

In a study of a community mental health team over an extended period of time, Emerson and Pollner (1976) made several observations on the kinds of tasks that were labeled by psychiatric social workers as "shit work." These included situations that required the use of coercion for implementing policies that were not in the best interests of their clients. The preferred work of the psychiatric emergency team was that of helping people who were confronting some immediate crisis. In many cases the treatment available was effective in producing therapeutic results, while in other cases the required action was not helpful to their clients.

Many of the emergency calls dealt with individuals who could not be helped. The dirty-work designation was applied to those cases in which the intervention team was prevented from doing anything for the betterment of their clients. This included the uses of deception, coercion, and constraint against subjects who wished to be left alone. When the emergency team designated as dirty work such acts as using force to hospitalize a hostile client involuntarily, they were able to justify the general character of their work as helping people rather than as doing something bad to them. The use of forceful restraint was a necessary, but not valued, part of their general sense of providing a socially useful service.

Source: Robert M. Emerson and Melvin Pollner, "Dirty Work Designations: Their Features and Consequences in a Psychiatric Setting," *Social Problems* 23 (February, 1976): 243–254.

The more highly skilled crafts people constitute the aristocracy of the working class, not only in terms of the intrinsic rewards their work affords, but also in terms of the esteem with which they are held in the broader society. Professionals are also a privileged category of the labor force because the type of work they do is associated with job dedication, personal autonomy, and achievement. The intrinsic rewards that accompany the work of professionals (doctors, lawyers, college professors, and so on) are associated with highly specialized skills and knowledge, an ethic of public service, and a high degree of work autonomy. The long period of training that is necessary for entry into professional status tends to generate high levels of work commitment as a central life interest. The emphasis on service is accompanied by expert knowledge that enables the professional to have a high degree of autonomy in the performance of work tasks (Hughes, 1963).

3. Work Alienation

By probing beyond the surface meanings of work, we may find abundant evidence for numerous forms of work alienation, even though the majority of workers report that they are satisfied with their jobs. Most people do not work as crafts people or as professionals, and many working conditions prevent the working individual from having a sense of personal accomplishment or self-fulfillment. The conditions that generate feelings of work alienation are those in which the motives for working are primarily extrinsic in character. Studies have concentrated on several aspects of the problem of alienation among industrial and lower-status, white-collar workers.

One of the major recurrent themes is the worker's lack of personal control and mastery over the work process itself. This stems from the closeness with which the individual worker is supervised in carrying out the plans and the work schedules established by higher levels of management. Through being excluded from the planning process, the worker encounters a system that requires an emphasis on discipline, and this discipline is often directed toward the performance of routine and monotonous tasks. The repetitive character of factory work very often leaves little leeway for the exercise of personal initiative or innovative skills.

The research of Blauner (1964) indicates that in assembly-line (automobile) and machine-tending (textile) industries, the repetitive aspects of the work and the close ties of the workers to their machines tend to generate a low sense of self-control and self-fulfillment while on the job. In assembly-line work, the pace of the job is determined by the conveyor-belt technology rather than by the workers themselves. The layout of the factory, the rhythm of the work tasks, and the degree of routinization are conditions contributing to feelings of alienation in the workplace. Because of the close attention that workers must give to the detailed and repetitive work, they have few opportunities for social interaction with fellow workers on the job.

The monotonous and routine character of work is often the result of the fragmentation of work tasks that accompanies industrial development. Through the division of labor the system of production is divided into small units of repetitive work that permits a high degree of efficiency and standardization of output. The division of labor is highly rational from an organizational standpoint, but from the experiences of the worker it may not produce enough of a challenge to make the work seem stimulating or interesting (Seeman, 1967; Faunce, 1968). The worker may contribute such a small part to the completion of a product (e.g., an automobile or TV set) that he or she is not able to identify with the finished product or to regard it as an object of his or her own creation. The fragmentation of work tasks also makes it difficult for the individual to develop an appreciation of how his or her own work tasks are making a contribution to the total productive enterprise.

While the research on problems of worker alienation has primarily con-

BOX 7.2
The Proletarianization of Clerical Work

At the turn of the century, the staff in most offices was comprised of a small number of clerical workers. These workers handled a wide variety of tasks, including numerous responsibilities that today would be regarded as managerial in character. Their status was clearly middle class, their identities were closely linked with higher levels of management, and their work placed emphasis on mental rather than manual abilities.

With the growth of large organizations, there was a substantial increase in the hiring of clerical workers, and machines were increasingly used to achieve greater office efficiency. These changes significantly altered the conditions of work along lines which Glenn and Feldberg (1977) characterized as the proletarianization of clerical work.

Proletarianization refers to the process by which middle-class occupations take on characteristics similar to the factory jobs of industrial workers. The research of Glenn and Feldberg indicates that the modern office is characterized by an increased emphasis on performing highly limited and specialized tasks. The work is shaped by the requirements of the machines that are used, leaving very little room for personal autonomy or discretionary decision making. The job has become more monotonous and repetitive and subject to evaluation in terms of the number of pages typed, the number of forms processed, or the number of cards punched.

Increases in the alienative character of clerical work derives from the growing similarities between office work and factory work. In contrast to the past, most clerical workers today are closely supervised by office managers, and interactions with higher level officials are unlikely to occur. The tasks performed are repetitive, the worker has little to say in the planning of his or her own work, and the intrinsic rewards of the job are limited.

Source: Evelyn Nakano Glenn and Roslyn L. Feldberg, "Degraded and Deskilled: The Proletarianization of Clerical Work," *Social Problems* 25 (October, 1977): 52–64.

centrated on factory workers (Shepard, 1977), there are several studies suggesting that the organization of work in many of the middle-class occupations (e.g., clerical work and nursing) tends to produce various forms of alienation. For example, Leonard Pearlin's (1963) study of alienation among nurses indicated that the authority of doctors and hospital administrators was utilized to emphasize obedience and following orders, and nurses had limited opportunities for using their specialized abilities and training. In similar fashion, the research of Evelyn Glenn and Roslyn Feldberg (1977) suggests that the experiences of clerical workers in large bureaucratic organizations often resembles the experiences of factory workers. (See Box 7.2.)

BOX 7.3
The Concept of Burnout

After an individual has worked at a particular job for several years, feelings of disillusionment and disenchantment sometimes set in. This is the condition that has become labeled **burnout**, and it refers to the buildup of emotional and physical fatigue from job-related causes. Exposure to stress on a regular basis may result in a sense of emptiness or in a lack of personal control over one's work. Under conditions of burnout, the individual feels drained, unresponsive, and ineffective. Career development has not turned out as expected, the job has "turned sour," and one becomes fatigued from confronting recurrent problems.

While burnout may occur in any line of work, the problem is more likely to surface in those occupations that require dealing with numerous clients on an everyday basis. This is particularly the case with public school teachers (McGuire, 1979) and social workers (Maslach, 1978). The causes include the recurrent stresses of dealing with problems that have no apparent solutions. Inadequate resources, poor staff relationships, and problematic clients are among the numerous conditions that have serious emotional consequences over a long period of time.

Social workers sometimes come to feel that they are ineffective in helping their clients, and teachers sometimes feel that the numerous problems in schools make teaching extremely difficult. According to Maslach (1978), clients play an important part in staff burnout because clients are often hostile and fail to follow the staff's professional advice and guidance. Indications of burnout include poor job performance, low morale, poor health, and changing jobs.

Drawing on a national sample of workers, the research of Bill Tudor (1972) indicates that feelings of powerlessness are more often found among unskilled, service, semiskilled, sales, and clerical workers than among those employed in professional, managerial, and skilled occupations. The results of this study suggest that job complexity and the level of education and training required are important variables for differentiating the intrinsic rewards and meanings that are derivable from the world of work. The use of highly developed skills in confronting complex challenges is a condition associated with a sense of self-fulfillment in the workplace. (See Box 7.3.)

B. RELATIONSHIPS BETWEEN WORK AND LEISURE

There are several alternative views among social psychologists on the part that work plays in the overall life plans of individuals. Some look on the social and psychological impact of work as being so great that it influences all other major aspects of life. This view holds that humans have a tendency to develop consistent attitudes and behavior patterns, and as a result what happens on the job is likely to have "spillover effects" on the uses of leisure and on the qualities of family relationships. Accordingly, the impact of alienating work over an extended period of time takes a toll on the choices that people make in the nonwork sphere. Creative and self-fulfilling uses of leisure are more likely to derive from a sense of purpose in the workplace, while nonrewarding uses of leisure are more likely to be shaped by the routine performance of dull and uninteresting work.

Others are inclined to put work in its "proper place" by pointing out that the workday has a beginning and an end, and the uses of leisure involve decisions that have little bearing on what transpires on the job. According to this view, modern society is a "segmented society" (Wiebe, 1975), in which each segment develops its own peculiar set of qualities independently of the other spheres of activity. Thus workers who do not regard their work as intrinsically rewarding may successfully find self-expression in family life or in the pursuit of leisure. Considerable variations do exist in the meanings and uses of leisure within given socioeconomic levels; this is because the attributes of leisure permit greater freedom of choice than the work sphere often does. In effect, this perspective emphasizes the **compartmentalization** in the work and leisure relationship, while the first view concentrates on the "spillover effects" of work experiences into the uses of nonwork time.

1. Compartmentalization

In a study of industrial workers, Robert Dubin (1956) concluded that most of his subjects did not regard their work as intrinsically rewarding. Instead, factory workers based their job commitments mainly on instrumental concerns for obtaining the resources necessary to meet family financial needs. Because of the nature of the tasks performed, the workers generally did not obtain intrinsic rewards and a sense of self-fulfillment from the work activity itself. About three out of every four industrial workers in Dubin's sample did not regard their work activity or the workplace as a central life interest. Instead, work was compartmentalized from other aspects of life, and they gave only a low reward value to social experiences within the workplace.

The basis for job attachments among industrial workers depends on their perception that work is necessary for the realization of other life interests and on the routinization of work-related behavior. Workers develop a sense of obligation to arrive at the place of work at some specified time, to carry out the work indicated by their supervisors, to perform certain tasks with machines and equipment under controlled conditions, and to have their time and performance measured as a basis for pay.

Dubin observed that adequate levels of performance are exhibited when

The End of the Workday: Compartmentalization
The parking lot symbolizes the compartmentalization of the work and nonwork spheres for many people. The workday begins and ends at specified times; the place of residence is physically separated from the place of work; and social relationships on the job differ in many respects from those in the nonwork spheres (photo by Tom Shaffer).

workers view the work as obligatory even though they do not value it. The commitment to a job involves a sense of obligation to continue in a particular line of activity, and if the job is not meaningful it then becomes necessary to pursue valued activities in some other social sphere—such as spending time with the family, with nonwork friends, with hobbies, and with the entertainment provided by the mass media.

In Dubin's view, social experiences are necessarily segmented within an industrialized society, where people live out each segment somewhat independently of the others. Work and leisure occur under conditions that are separable and unrelated to each other. If work does not provide a primary source of meaning, then workers may seek a sense of self-fulfillment in the nonwork sphere. From this vantage point, workers simply come to terms with the conditions of their existence, viewing work as necessary but not as very rewarding in itself. The big task of the worker is not to convert the job into a major source of satisfaction, but to manage his or her life in such a fashion as to obtain satisfaction from the pursuit of spontaneous, creative, and rewarding experiences in the uses of leisure.

In contrast to Dubin, other social psychologists maintain that individuals cannot easily separate the spheres of work and leisure in their life-worlds. Basic social attitudes are shaped in the workplace over an extended period of time, and there is a carryover of these attitudes into the nonwork spheres. From this view the choices people make in the uses of leisure (e.g., engrossment in television viewing or taking an extended trip in a private automobile) are shaped by the character of the work that people do. Clement Greenburg (1958: 38) observed, "Leisure—even for those who do not work—is at bottom a function of work, flows from work, and changes as work changes."

The generalization hypothesis holds that the work involvement is a crucial determinant of total life circumstances, and there are spillover effects from the conditions of work into other areas of social life. If individuals work at boring and unrewarding tasks over an extended period of time, this will lower their sense of satisfaction in other institutional areas. Here the assumption is that uses of time away from the job may be no more intrinsically rewarding nor self-fulfilling than the time spent on the job itself. David Riesman (1958), for example, is pessimistic about the possibility of obtaining self-fulfillment in the uses of leisure unless work activity is also regarded as a meaningful and creative process. Riesman states,

I believe that we cannot take advantage of what remains of our pre-industrial heritage to make leisure more creative, individually and socially, if work is not creative too (1958: 371).

The thesis of **generalization** emphasizes the unity of social life and places work in a central position for shaping basic attitudes and values. This view does not assume that work experiences operate in a direct and rational fashion to define orientations toward the nonwork spheres, but only that the time and energies most adults devote to the labor force do have cumulative effects in shaping numerous aspects of the lifestyles they develop. Worklife absorbs a major part of the day and provides a basic form of linkage into the broader social system. Occupational placement affects the ways in which individuals think about themselves and the ways in which they interact with others.

The research of Melvin Kohn and Carmi Schooler (1969) suggests that the exercise of self-direction in work (the use of initiative, independent thought, and personal judgment) is conducive to seeing possibilities for self-direction in other areas of life as well. Drawing on a national sample representing all occupational levels, Kohn and Schooler found that self-direction in the work sphere was more prominent in the higher status jobs, while an emphasis on conformity was more nearly evident in lower status occupations. These differences were also reflected in generalized perceptions of personal competence and of the responsiveness of the larger society. Those with low levels of self-direction in the work sphere more often viewed themselves as "less competent members of an essentially indifferent or threatening society" (1969: 676). Thus the results of this study suggest that work experiences have profound effects on both conceptions of self and the broader society. These are effects that go beyond the work sphere itself.

3. *Complementarity*

Rather than emphasizing the effects of work on the nonwork spheres, the theme of **complementarity** focuses on the support relationships between leisure and work. This theme emphasizes leisure as "re-creation," and is reflected in the popular saying that "all work and no play makes Jack a dull boy." The complementary approach emphasizes that the uses of leisure fulfill important needs for personal relaxation and through enhancing overall life satisfaction are likely to improve the quality of the on-the-job performance. Here the emphasis is on recreation as a form of revitalization, which may offer a buffer against the drudgery of "keeping one's nose to the grindstone," or becoming a workaholic.

In viewing the uses of leisure as serving important functions in their own right, John Neulinger (1974: 120) observes,

It is not necessary that we downgrade work in order to raise the value of leisure. Leisure is not non-work; leisure is not time left over from work. Leisure is a state of mind; it is a way of being, of being at peace with oneself and what one is doing.

From this perspective, nonwork time should not be equated with leisure, since many of the activities off the job are not, in and of themselves, intrinsically rewarding. Those who are highly committed to the work ethic sometimes find it difficult to enjoy their recreational activities. Certainly, the historical emphasis on the "gospel" of work has been accompanied by negative judgments about the uses of leisure. The old adage that "idle hands are the devil's workshop" reflects the ethical embellishment of work at the expense of leisure in the life commitments of individuals. (See Box 7.4.)

The complementary view of work and leisure emphasizes that these two spheres of activity represent separable but equally important forms of reality in the life-world of individuals. The popular notions about "letting off steam," "getting away from it all," "resting from fatiguing work," and "becoming rejuvenated" are all views that emphasize the recreational aspects of leisure as independent sources of meaning and self-fulfillment. The uses of leisure as important sources of purpose and identity become especially important as means of relief from the numerous forms of stress that emerge from the demands of work (Kando and Summers, 1971).

BOX 7.4
Emerging Attitudes Toward Work and Leisure

Drawing on the results of several national surveys, the research of Yankelovich (1978) clearly indicates that American attitudes toward work and leisure are changing. The earlier positive attitudes toward dedication and hard work are being replaced by an increased emphasis on leisure in the life designs of individuals. Americans increasingly separate work, leisure and family life, recognizing the manner in which these areas differ as major sources of life satisfaction.

Yankelovich notes that millions of people hold jobs so unappealing that there is little incentive to work hard or to be dedicated. As workers experience less emotional support on the job, they often compensate by increasing pressure for better pay and looking for greater rewards in the nonwork sphere. When work and leisure are compared as sources of satisfaction, national surveys indicate that only about one out of five people report their work to have more meaning to them than their uses of leisure.

With the increased employment of women, several attitudes have emerged to help clarify the symbolism of the paid job. The traditional roles of mother and homemaker have become downgraded and considered less important as bases for self-esteem and social status. Through being employed, regardless of the job, women are no longer totally dependent on their husbands for financial support. The paid job has become the key to greater personal autonomy and independence. These changes suggest that women are increasingly adopting the work-oriented values that were male-dominated in the past.

While the symbolism of the paid job is important for both men and women, major life satisfactions are regarded as deriving from one's private life instead of work. Job titles are becoming less important as a basis for self-esteem, and emphasis is placed on the person behind the job rather than on the nature of the work itself.

Source: Daniel Yankelovich, "The New Psychological Contracts at Work," *Psychology Today* 11 (May, 1978): 46–50.

Apparently there are many individuals who are unable to derive satisfaction from vacations or from other uses of leisure. This is the case with those who become so totally committed to their work that they relegate all other sources of meaning in life to unimportant positions. The terms *workaholic, work addict,* and *compulsive plodder* have crept into the modern vocabularies to describe those individuals who become so deeply engrossed in their work that they give much more time and effort to a job than is required or even desirable from the standpoint of the accomplishments obtained. (See Box 7.5.)

Such deep involvements in the world of work may be sources of enjoyment and peace of mind if they do indeed result in major accomplishments

BOX 7.5
The Workaholic

In recent years, the term **workaholic** has emerged to describe the person who becomes excessively committed to work activity. The individual becomes addicted to work in pretty much the same fashion that others become addicted to smoking, drinking, eating, or taking drugs. Compulsive work attitudes emerge when individuals become incessantly involved in work activity to the exclusion of other values and interests. The symptoms include putting in an excessive number of hours on the job and persisting in the work activity even when it is unproductive or unnecessary.

Such individuals are not able to enjoy themselves on vacations, and they often refrain from taking vacations altogether. The workaholic develops anxieties in the nonwork sphere, and life appears to be without purpose or meaning apart from the self-imposed requirements of the job itself. The workaholic who is married is likely to view relationships with his or her spouse or children as having few intrinsic rewards. The workaholic also lacks interest in hobbies or in the pursuit of leisure-time activities.

One should distinguish compulsive work attitudes from enjoying one's work and from being effective on the job. Producing results may vary independently of the amount of time spent in work activity. The realities constructed by the workaholic tend to have hemming-in effects, and interpersonal relationships are likely to suffer, since fellow workers are unlikely to hold similar attitudes. Workaholism reduces the complexities of the world through compulsive work habits, but the social costs are often very great indeed.

Source: Paul Martin, "Hooked on Work," *Science Digest* 80 (December, 1976): 72–77.

(in science, in business, in government, and so forth) and the attainment of personal ambitions. In many cases, however, such compulsive attitudes toward work are unproductive, and may result in the deterioration of family relationships, in stress-induced illnesses, or in attitudes of resentment from co-workers. The complementary view emphasizes the importance of maintaining a balance between the quest for achievement on the job and the search for pleasures in family life, relaxation, and entertainment (Yankelovich, 1978).

4. Integration

A fourth perspective on the work and leisure relationship emphasizes the theme of **integration.** In this view, leisure and work activities may become so closely linked that the boundaries separating the two spheres become inseparable. In this type of situation, work and leisure are highly coordinated, the individual feels that he or she enjoys doing what the job demands, and the pursuit of leisure closely resembles the activities at work (Kelly, 1975). Such a coordination of work and leisure is primarily found among professionals who are satisfied with the work they are doing and feel that they have a high degree of personal autonomy both on and off the job.

For example, much of the reading that professionals do for pleasure has some bearing on their work. Travel to conventions is work-related, but at the same time it has numerous recreational components. The three-martini lunch may be irritating to the tax specialist, but to business people it is often viewed as a necessary and work-related expense. Among highly dedicated professionals and business people, we are less likely to find a need "to get away from it all." Escape from the drudgery and routine of work is not necessary if the work itself is regarded as pleasurable. For such people, working time often permeates the rest of life, and even such voluntary pursuits as memberships in organizational and country clubs become inseparable from the pursuit of occupational objectives.

The opportunity for integrating work and leisure appears to be greater for those who hold higher occupational positions, but John R. Kelly (1975) offers a caution against thinking about the work and leisure relationships in deterministic and stereotypic terms. After all, the pursuit of leisure does involve a voluntary element, and the same lines of involvement for one individual may be unrewarding to another. Kelly particularly cautions against the stereotype of the blue-collar worker with a can of beer in front of the TV set and the view of the salesperson playing golf more as a business venture than as a game. These stereotypes fail to recognize the adaptability of men and women to the conditions of their existence and the varieties of meaning they may give to any specific activity.

Studies of occupational choice and recruitment emphasize that there may be a higher degree of integration of lifestyles in the working class than the compartmentalization view would suggest. The integration view assumes that in occupational choices, individuals tend to gravitate toward the kinds of work that are compatible with their own needs and interests (Carisse, 1975). During the socialization process children are prepared for later jobs that are compatible with the values of their families and social class. Working-class families, for example, emphasize conformity to rules, which is compatible with the discipline and close supervision of factory jobs. By way of contrast, middle-class families tend to emphasize self-determination, which tends to orient their children toward subsequent work that requires dealing with nonroutine tasks, making independent decisions, and coping with complexity (Kohn, 1969). In this respect, the effects of the worker on the job and the job on the worker follow a general pattern of reciprocal influence and coordination (Kohn and Schooler, 1973).

C. LEISURE STYLES

A vast literature suggests that the uses of leisure are important for freeing the individual from the conventionality and routines that our technologically-oriented society generates (Orthner, 1975). In the nonwork sphere, opportunities are available for exploring alternative modes of interaction with others and becoming engaged in activities that are of personal interest. Individuals vary, however, in the degree to which they are able to take advantage of opportunities for self-expression. Some people obtain a high degree of meaning and self-fulfillment in uses of leisure, while others experience carryover of behavior patterns that resemble the routines of work.

Dennis K. Orthner (1975) notes that in several ways Americans work at play. This occurs, for example, in planning family vacations down to the minutest detail and in measuring the success of a vacation by the number of miles traveled, the number of pictures taken, and by the number of sites visited. The weekends for many Americans become organized around an endless list of things to be done. The emphasis on achievement in the occupational sphere extends over into the recreational aspects of team sports. This is evident in the pressures placed on children to perform in Little League competition; and among adults the refinement of skills in participatory sports often takes priority over the intrinsic pleasure of the activity itself. According to Lionel S. Lewis and Dennis Brisset (1967), even having sex is frequently viewed in terms of schedules, techniques, and exceptional levels of performance.

From their investigation of leisure, B. G. Gunter and Nancy C. Gunter (1980: 361) observe that "both the granting and the realization of leisure have become complex problems for many people in our times." The complexity relates to the abundance of leisure for some and a shortage of leisure for others. The complexity also relates to the problem of misplaced emphasis. Just as work attitudes may intrude inappropriately into the leisure sphere, the sharp separation of work and leisure also may be unwarranted. In the Gunters' view, there may be some degree of leisure in virtually any human activity, and as a result we should think of leisure as a continuous rather than a discrete activity. (See Figure 7.2.)

In developing their theory of leisure, the Gunters (1980) emphasized two primary variables. One consisted of the level of **involvement** in an activity and the second related to the **time-choice dimension.** As you may note in Figure 7.2, involvement constitutes a continuum in which there is a high degree of engagement and pleasure at one extreme and disengagement and apathy at the other. The time-choice dimension relates to the degrees of freedom and constraint in the allocation of time, energies, and resources. At the free end of the continuum the activity results from the personal preferences of the individual and represents what he or she actually wants to do. Constraint, on the other hand, occurs in those situations in which some level of force and coercion is present.

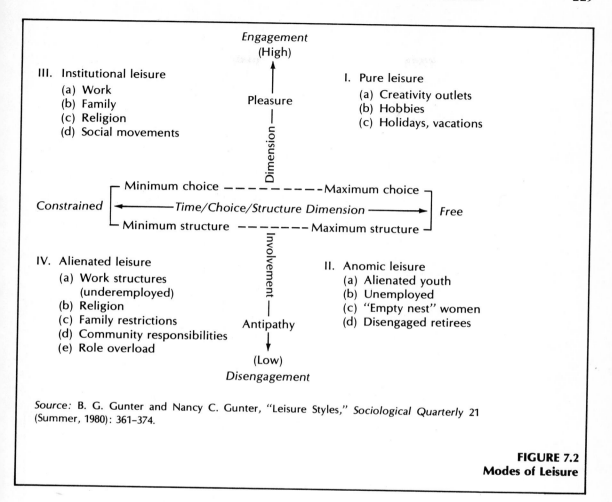

III. Institutional leisure
  (a) Work
  (b) Family
  (c) Religion
  (d) Social movements

I. Pure leisure
  (a) Creativity outlets
  (b) Hobbies
  (c) Holidays, vacations

Engagement (High)

Pleasure

Dimension

Minimum choice — — — — — — — *Maximum choice*

Constrained ◄— — — *Time/Choice/Structure Dimension* —► *Free*

Minimum structure — — — — — — *Maximum structure*

Involvement

IV. Alienated leisure
  (a) Work structures
      (underemployed)
  (b) Religion
  (c) Family restrictions
  (d) Community responsibilities
  (e) Role overload

II. Anomic leisure
  (a) Alienated youth
  (b) Unemployed
  (c) "Empty nest" women
  (d) Disengaged retirees

Antipathy

(Low)
Disengagement

Source: B. G. Gunter and Nancy C. Gunter, "Leisure Styles," *Sociological Quarterly* 21 (Summer, 1980): 361–374.

FIGURE 7.2
Modes of Leisure

By combining the variables of involvement and time-choice, the Gunters identified four styles of leisure. The first style consists of **pure leisure**: one has freedom of choice to participate in an intrinsically rewarding activity. Engagement in pure leisure frequently occurs with involvement in hobbies, with planning for and taking vacations, and with the celebration of holidays. The range of choices that may provide excitement and a creative outlet is very broad. Some find pure leisure in collecting old cars; others find it in amateur photography; for still others the creative outlet may take the form of learning to play a musical instrument or making furniture.

The second style of leisure in the Gunters' typology consists of **anomic leisure**. This form of leisure occurs under those circumstances in which there is an abundance of free time but a lack of purpose or meaning. Freedom from work and other obligations does not necessarily lead to the good life. Instead, having only marginal ties to work and other institutions may be associated with strong feelings of despair, disenchantment, hopelessness, and uselessness. Such sentiments are frequently found among unemployed youth, among displaced homemakers, and among disengaged retirees. They may hold negative attitudes toward their life circumstances despite the availability of free time and the lack of obligations.

Drawing on the theme that degrees of leisure are involved in virtually any human activity, the Gunters labeled the third style **institutional leisure**. This form of leisure occurs with high levels of involvement in the workplace, in family life, in religious worship, and in social movements. Commitments in these spheres of activity tend to have constraints associated with them, and the range of options may be limited by time demands and socially imposed obligations. The activities are leisure-like in character insofar as the participant regards them as pleasurable and as sources of dedication and purpose. For some people, strong commitments are the ingredients of self-satisfaction and personal growth, even if individual freedom is at a minimum.

The fourth style of leisure, **alienated leisure**, is the polar opposite of pure leisure. Alienated leisure occurs in those situations fraught with responsibilities and obligations that carry a low reward value for the individual. Roles are performed out of necessity and social pressures rather than out of personal choices and preferences. For example, resentments may accompany the performance of family chores and duties to the church. Attitudes of bitterness may develop for the individual who feels that he or she is being consumed by the job, by the family, or by community responsibilities. In many respects these conditions are those of nonleisure. The Gunters included them in the typology of leisure as reference points for clarifying the lack of pleasure and freedom that may be associated with socially approved undertakings.

One conclusion to derive from this discussion of leisure types is that the same activity may have widely different meanings for individuals. The social constraints imposed by institutional commitments may become sources of pleasure and freedom for some but a lack of identification and purpose for others. The pure forms of leisure account for only a small proportion of the time allocations for most people, and having large amounts of time available is not necessarily accompanied by a sense of opportunity and self-fulfillment.

D. USES OF LEISURE

In focusing on the pleasure aspects of leisure, Joffre Dumazedier (1967) noted that the primary rewards consist of entertainment, relaxation, and personal development. Relaxation permits recovery from fatigue; entertainment offers a buffer against boredom; and personal development enables one to enhance a

TABLE 7.1
Uses of Leisure among Recent College Graduates

Reporting frequent involvement in leisure activity	Total (N=837)	Females (N=462)	Males (N=373)
Listen to musical records or tapes	73%	75%	71%
Listen to the radio	73	74	72
Watch television	68	68	67
Hobbies and crafts	66	74	55
Entertain friends in your home	63	68	57
Read a book or novel	60	68	50
Travel	58	58	57
Visit relatives	55	64	45
Play games such as cards or chess	38	40	36
Attend sport events	36	32	40
Church activities	35	39	30
Play competitive sports	33	23	47
Go to the movies	31	32	31
Attend stage plays	17	20	13
Attend musical concerts or operas	17	17	16

Note: The sample consisted of graduates of a midwestern university between 1965 and 1975.

Source: Data from David W. Chilson, H. Theodore Groat, and Arthur G. Neal, *Some Differential Consequences of Higher Education,* mimeographed report, Bowling Green, Ohio: College of Arts and Sciences, Bowling Green State University, 1978.

sense of self through involvement in physical and emotional activities that are separate from the utilitarian concerns of life. We can explore these themes by examining such prominent uses of leisure as television viewing, travel and tourism, family vacations, and competitive sports. (See Table 7.1.)

1. Television Viewing

After the amount of time spent sleeping, eating, working, and doing household chores has been subtracted from daily or weekly schedules, the majority of Americans spend most of their remaining time watching television. Ownership of at least one TV set is now nearly universal within American families, and the amount of time spent watching television programs is very great indeed. Rolf Meyersohn (1968) has noted that those who have a great deal of time for leisure are likely to become engaged in a variety of leisure activities. However, from the standpoint of time allocation, watching television has clearly emerged as one of the more prevalent forms of leisure use for most Americans.

The leisure functions of the mass media are to provide entertainment for large viewing audiences, and the manner of achieving this often consists of providing light, superficial, trivial, and sometimes vulgar programming content. The research of Gerhart Wiebe (1970) suggests that the viewing of programs that provide "light entertainment" predominate in the actual uses of leisure. While surveys indicate that people tend to express an interest in having available more informative and quality education programming, their actual behavior indicates given a choice they would select the lighter and more entertaining forms of programs. Programs designed to educate rather than to entertain have been less successful in generating large viewing audiences.

A national survey conducted in 1974 indicated that 46 percent of the adult population of the United States reported watching television as their favorite leisure activity (U.S. Department of Commerce, 1977). While television is the favorite pastime of all major segments of the general population, there are variations measured by several social characteristics, in the number of hours spent each week in actually watching television programs. Older people (those over fifty) tend to watch more programs than do those who are younger. Individuals at the poverty level of income tend to spend more hours each week watching television than do those at the higher income levels. Those with less than a high school education tend to watch television more often than those who are college graduates. Among married women those who are not in the labor force spend more time watching television than do their counterparts who are employed.

Kathy Calkins (1970) suggests that television viewing may be a way of "marking time," of doing something to fill in the gaps between committed lines of action. Those who spend the largest amount of time watching television are those least committed to their work activity as a central life interest, and they are overrepresented among those who are less likely to become involved in voluntary associations or in community-betterment programs. While all segments of the population enjoy the entertainment provided by television, the variations in viewing patterns suggest that the amount of time allocated to watching television is a function of the amount of uncommitted time available and of the limited opportunities for active participation in the broader society.

The interest in watching television primarily derives from its relaxing qualities: it provides the viewers with forms of escape and fantasy under safe conditions, requiring a low expenditure of personal effort. It also extends viewers' awareness of the broader society beyond their immediate and limited sphere of direct experience. As a result of television exposure, attitudes and opinions are held by more people on a wider variety of issues than was possible in any previous generation (Krugman and Hartley, 1970). Becoming aware of broader social events through television viewing occurs under conditions unrelated to immediate needs and circumstances. The images which are developed of events in the broader society emerge as forms of "passive learning," since the viewers give no overt resistance to what they are learning, and there is no necessary commitment to any particular line of action.

2. Tourism

The interest in being entertained through extending one's awareness of broader social events has also contributed to the emergence of travel and tourism as an important form of leisure for a large number of people. This is evident in the emergence of tourism as a major industry in numerous regions of the United States and in several other countries. Tourism has become a prominent form of leisure due to increases in the efficiency of transportation, the wealth and affluence of the masses, and the general interest in having experiences unavailable in one's usual locale.

Tourism refers to using personal resources and available time to travel to places offering attractions not available in one's native habitat. The quest is for adventures that will extend one's direct awareness of places and events. In this respect, the tourist differs from the television viewer because the tourist, by actually traveling to places, has direct and personal experiences, in contrast to the more vicarious and indirect experiences the viewer derives through the communications media. As an observer, the tourist seeks first-hand knowledge of objects and events publicized as noteworthy attractions. The tourist seeks the experiences, however, as an outsider who comes to observe but not to be involved in creating or shaping the places or events of interest. (See Box 7.6.)

Daniel Boorstin (1961) observes that prior to the twentieth century travel was "uncomfortable, difficult, and expensive." Because of the time requirements and the expense, tourism up until the last part of the nineteenth century was primarily a leisure activity of the very rich. Boorstin (1961: 79) describes the recency of travel for pleasure as follows:

After allowing for the increase in population, there is about five times as much foreign travel by Americans nowadays as there was a hundred years ago. As a nation we are probably the most traveled people of our time, or any time. What is remarkable, on reflection, is not that our foreign travel has increased so much. But rather that all this travel has made so little difference in our thinking and feeling.

The actual linkage between the tourist and the attraction is less important than the authentic and collective images that tourism generates. For example, many tourists travel several hundred miles to reach Mt. Rushmore, South Dakota, but many spend no more than fifteen or twenty minutes at that

BOX 7.6
On the Varieties of Tourists

Erik Cohen has proposed a typology of four tourist roles in international travel. These are as follows:

1. *The organized mass tourist* describes the traveler who subscribes to a guided tour that provides for a fixed itinerary prepared in advance. The tour may consist of visiting as many as eight countries in fifteen days, with activities organized to provide only a superficial exposure to cultural differences. The tour is processed to provide the tourists with the illusion of novel experiences while retaining all the creature comforts of home.

2. *The individual mass tourist* is one who makes arrangements for the trip though a tourist agency without being bound by a fixed schedule or by travel with a group. Excursions into unfamiliar areas, however, are limited, and the traveler restricts his or her activities to low-risk and familiar situations. This type of tourist seeks greater novelty than is obtainable through the guided tour, but also wants the security and safety that accompanies movement within well-charted territory.

3. *The explorer* is one who arranges his or her own trip and seeks to "get off the beaten path" as much as possible but wants comfortable accommodations and reliable means of transportation. The explorer is willing to venture out into novel situations as an observer, while being prepared to rush back to a familiar environment if "the going gets rough."

4. *The drifter* is an adventurous type of traveler who has no fixed schedule or well-defined set of plans. He or she regards the usual tourist activities as superficial and avoids tourist agencies. The drifter tries to live the way of life of the people of the country visited, working at odd jobs, sharing in local foods, and participating in local customs. This type of tourist is a risk taker and seeks to maximize the novelty of his or her travel experiences.

Cohen observes that with the emergence of the tourist industry as big business most tourists fall into one of the first three types. As a result, limited changes in attitudes and values occur as a consequence of the travel experiences. Mass tourism is organized around visiting attractions, and these become designed to separate the tourist from the everyday life of the host society.

Source: Erik Cohen, "Toward a Sociology of International Tourism," *Social Research* 39 (Spring, 1972): 164–182.

mountain from the time they pull into the parking lot until they are on the road again. They spend only enough time to look at the stone faces, to take a few pictures as proof that they were there, and to feel good about having seen one of the major symbolic attractions of our society.

The research of Dean MacCannell (1976) suggests that the quest for authentic experiences is a major variable in the appeal of tourist activity. The value of an attraction is in part measured by the amount of time and distance the tourist travels in order to reach it. Being there and seeing objects and events firsthand emphasizes the authentic character of experiences and verifies the correctness of one's knowledge and awareness of remote events.

MacCannell views the quest for a broader scope of social meaning through travel experiences as a function of the limited vision of the individual in modern society in view of the complexity of the totality of social life. Local areas are not self-contained units but instead are influenced by decisions and events occurring in the world at large. Being a part of the modern world requires that the individual direct his or her attention beyond the limited confines of the daily workplace and community of residence. Through using leisure time to

Tourism and Authenticity
Several hundred thousand tourists each year verify the authentic existence of Niagara Falls.

visit exotic places and to have experiences with remote attractions, the individual seeks firmer linkage with the totality of modern social life.

3. Family Vacation Travel

The extension of social awareness in conjunction with the emphasis on recreation and family solidarity is evident from research on vacation travel. Paul Rosenblatt and Martha Russell (1975) suggest that the family vacation trip has become a widespread pattern for the American middle class. The general expectation is "that people will return from a family vacation excursion refreshed, relaxed, healthier, and with greater family togetherness" (1975: 209).

Their research, however, suggests that during vacation travel there are numerous sources of change in family relationships that increase the potential for stress and conflict. These include the restrictions on personal space and an increase in interactions among family members who in everyday activities tend to go their separate ways. Rosenblatt and Russell (1975: 210) observe:

Disputes may arise over who can sit where, who has the right to control the family radio, who can use what furniture or space in a motel room, and so on. The territorial problems may be worked out over time, but new ones may arise as families enter new territories.

Despite the tensions and difficulties (car trouble, bad weather, family arguments, illness, and so forth) that emerge in connection with family vacation travel, most people do report that their experiences were positive and rewarding ones. According to Rosenblatt and Russell, this is the operation of a self-fulfilling prophecy. People expect to enjoy their vacation, and the pleasure of being away from work, school, and other responsibilities may more than offset the difficulties.

The research of K. Peter Etzkorn (1964) on the family camping trip tends to bear out this observation. His data indicate that "getting away from it all" was the most frequent answer to the question, "What do you most like about camping?" This suggests that camping as a form of outdoor recreation is motivated by "escape" and an emphasis on "the return to nature." However, other aspects of his findings fail to confirm these explanations. His results indicate that the majority of campers generally do not fit the stereotype of urban dwellers seeking forest recreation to escape the congestion and stress of living in a large city.

Etzkorn (1964) also found that the major planned activities of the stay in camp also failed to reflect the vacationers' expressed interest in getting away from it all. The major activities of interest included swimming, reading, listening to the radio, and playing with the children. These are activities just as readily accessible to the campers at home. The majority of campers did not emphasize such activities as hiking, bird watching, or nature study as being important. Thus the enjoying of activities uniquely available in outdoor recreational areas was not as important as continuing routine recreational patterns that were available within the home environment.

The desire for consistency between vacation activities and everyday routines was also observed by William Burch (1965) in his research on outdoor recreation. He found that the usual sexual division of labor continued (women did the cooking and tending to the children, while the men went hunting or fishing), and notions about how to improve recreational areas included an emphasis on facilities to enhance creature comforts, such as having better and cleaner toilets, having piped-in water, and installing electrical hookups. The concern for access to the technological efficiencies of everyday life suggested that the "pioneering spirit," which provides a partial justification for outdoor recreation, is highly qualified. People seek forest areas as places of relaxation and communion with nature as long as there is access to the technological conveniences of modern civilization. These results suggest that the uses of leisure generally bear a close affinity to the organization of everyday life, and while people seek novelty, they do so within the limits of activities that are familiar and commonplace.

4. Competitive Sports

In contrast to the spectator activities of television watching and tourism, competitive sports require a much greater degree of personal involvement. Games and sports are participatory types of activity that involve the process of social interaction and the acceptance of some predetermined set of rules that are binding on the players. The participants must adhere to the rules if a game is to proceed in an orderly fashion; perhaps for this reason engagement in athletic contests is an important part of recreational patterns in nearly all of the known cultures of the world (Herron and Sutton-Smith, 1971).

Drawing on the research of Eldon Snyder and Elmer Spreitzer (1978), we may define sport as a rule-bound activity that places a special emphasis on demonstrating physical skills. The rule-bound character of sport is shared with the playing of games. Rules provide the framework within which to express skills; rules define the beginning and the end of the contest; they specify the conditions for achievement; and they establish the norms for the evaluation of performance. Because competition in sport is regarded as a microcosm symbolic of life in general, training for athletic contests is primarily an activity promoted among children and young adults. Older people are overrepresented among those who become involved as spectators, deriving vicarious pleasures from observing the splendid performance and from the festival-like character of sport events.

The construction of social reality in competitive sports resembles the process of constructing reality in everyday life. For this reason, the uses of lei-

Competitive Sports
The losers in competitive sports are sometimes expected to display sportsmanship by congratulating the winners.

sure enable people to learn how to play their parts within the broader society (Parker, 1971). Eldon Snyder (1972) noted the socialization aspect of sport in his analysis of the slogans placed in dressing rooms by high school coaches. His research indicates an emphasis on reinforcing such qualities as aggressiveness, competitiveness, mental alertness, physical fitness, perseverance, self-discipline, and being a member of the team. The emphases on these slogans in competitive sports reflect several of the dominant values of the broader society.

The research of Snyder and Spreitzer (1978) indicates that involvement in sports is positively correlated with an overall sense of psychological well-being. They see this relationship as stemming from the intrinsic pleasure of engagement in competitive sports and games. Their view is that sports generate levels of tension and excitement that contrast with the mundane and routinized aspects of everyday living. Sports function to increase tensions of a kind that contribute to a sense of mental and physical well-being. The release of tensions through engaging in the pleasurable activities of games and sports tends to be associated with avowed personal happiness as well as with a positive sense of being a member in society.

Both children and adults in play are enacting social roles testing attributes of their self-identities, and reinforcing social relationships. Games often provide the players with a sense of self not readily attainable in everyday life (Goffman, 1961). The player may demonstrate a proficiency in the use of winning strategies as well as a capacity for taking chances and beating the odds. Such demonstrations of self-worth occur under conditions of low personal risk, since in playing games the emphasis on supportive social relationships usually takes priority over any real-life consequences of winning or losing.

SUMMARY

Both extrinsic and intrinsic meanings are implicated in the attachments of workers to their jobs. The extrinsic meanings of work refer to the rewards derivable from employment that have utility in the nonwork sphere, while the intrinsic rewards consist of the satisfactions derivable from the work activity itself. Although most people report that their primary reason for working is "for the money," the majority also indicate that they would want to continue working even if they did not need the money. The symbolism of having a paid job is important to most people, and the routines of work schedules provide stability and coherence to the organization of daily life.

Social psychologists hold several perspectives on the overall relationship between work and leisure. Some look on modern society as being segmented; meanings derived from the sphere of work are separate from the meanings obtained in the uses of leisure time. Others hold a more unified view of social life, maintaining that there are numerous spillover effects from the job into family relationships and other nonwork spheres. Some people succeed in integrating work activities with uses of leisure to the point that the two spheres become indistinguishable, while others are more likely to look for personal meaning in the uses of leisure to compensate for the performance of alienating work.

The availability of mass entertainment, tourism, family vacations, and the playing of competitive games provides a variety of choices for entertainment, diversion, and personal development. For most Americans, watching television is the most frequent and preferred use of leisure. Involvement with television is motivated primarily by an interest in being entertained and in developing an awareness of many more social events the viewer could experience directly. Travel for entertainment (tourism) is another popular use of leisure that serves the function of increasing social awareness and of providing verification for the authenticity of remote events. The recreational choices people make have important consequences for a personal sense of well-being, and the rewards derivable from work and leisure are major ingredients in overall life satisfaction.

BASIC TERMS

Extrinsic rewards
Intrinsic rewards
Dirty work
Proletarianization
Burnout
Compartmentalization
Generalization
Complementarity
Workaholic

Integration
Involvement
Time-choice dimension
Pure leisure
Anomic leisure
Institutional leisure
Alienated leisure
Tourism

REFERENCES

Blauner, Robert
1964 *Alienation and Freedom: The Factory Worker and His Industry*, Chicago: University of Chicago Press.

Boorstin, Daniel J.
1961 *The Image: A Guide to Pseudo-Events in America*, New York: Harper Colophon Books.

Bradburn, Norman M.
1969 *The Structure of Psychological Well-Being*, Chicago: Aldine.

Burch, William R., Jr.
1965 "The Play World of Camping: Research into the Social Meaning of Outdoor Recreation," *American Journal of Sociology* 70 (March): 604–612.

Calkins, Kathy
1970 "Time: Perspectives, Marking and Styles of Usage," *Social Problems* 17 (Spring): 487–501.

Carisse, Colette B.
1975 "Family and Leisure: A Set of Contradictions," *The Family Coordinator* 24 (1975): 191–197.

Chilson, David W., H. Theodore Groat, and Arthur G. Neal
1978 *Some Differential Consequences of Higher Education*, mimeographed report, Bowling Green, O.: College of Arts and Sciences, Bowling Green State University.

Cohen, Erik
1972 "Toward a Sociology of International Tourism," *Social Research* 39 (Spring): 164–182.

deBoer, Connie
1978 "The Polls: Attitudes Toward Work," *Public Opinion Quarterly* 42 (Fall): 414–423.

Dubin, Robert
1956 "Industrial Workers' Worlds: A Study of the Central Life Interest of Industrial Workers," *Social Problems* 3 (Fall): 131–142.

Dumazedier, Joffre
1967 *Toward a Society of Leisure,* London: Collier-MacMillan.
Emerson, Robert M. and Melvin Pollner
1976 "Dirty Work Designations: Their Features and Consequences in a Psychiatric Setting," *Social Problems* 23 (February): 243–254.
Etzkorn, K. Peter
1964 "Leisure and Camping: The Social Meaning of a Form of Public Recreation," *Sociology and Social Research* 49 (October): 76–89.
Faunce, William A.
1968 *Problems of an Industrial Society,* New York: McGraw-Hill.
Form, William H.
1973 "Auto Workers and Their Machines: A Study of Work, Factory, and Job Satisfaction in Four Countries," *Social Forces* 52 (September): 1–15.
Glenn, Evelyn Nakano and Roslyn L. Feldberg
1977 "Degraded and Deskilled: The Proletarianization of Clerical Work," *Social Problems* 25 (October): 52–64.
Goffman, Erving
1961 *Encounters,* Indianapolis: Bobbs-Merrill.
Greenburg, Clement
1958 "Work and Leisure under Industrialism," in Eric Larabee and Rolf Meyersohn (eds.), *Mass Leisure,* Glencoe, Ill.: The Free Press, pp. 38–42.
Gunter, B. G. and Nancy C. Gunter
1980 "Leisure Styles," *Sociological Quarterly* 21 (Summer): 361–374.
Herron, Robert E. and Brian Sutton-Smith
1971 *Child's Play,* New York: John Wiley.
Hughes, Everett C.
1971 *The Sociological Eye: Selected Papers,* Chicago: Aldine.
1963 "Profession," *Daedalus* 92 (Fall): 655–668.
Kando, Thomas M. and W. C. Summers
1971 "The Impact of Work on Leisure," *Pacific Sociological Review* 14 (Summer): 360–371.
Kelly, John R.
1975 "Life Styles and Leisure Choices," *The Family Coordinator* 24: 185–190.
Kohn, Melvin
1969 *Class and Conformity,* Homewood, Ill.: Dorsey Press.
Kohn, Melvin L. and Carmi Schooler
1973 "Occupational Experience and Psychological Functioning," *American Sociological Review* 38: 97–118.
1969 "Class, Occupation, and Orientation," *American Sociological Review* 34: 659–678.
Krugman, Herbert E. and Eugene L. Hartley
1970 "Passive Learning from Television," *Public Opinion Quarterly* 34 (Summer): 184–190.
Lewis, Lionel S. and Dennis Brisset
1967 "Sex as Work: A Study of Avocational Counseling," *Social Problems* 15 (Summer): 8–18.
MacCannell, Dean
1976 *The Tourist: A New Theory of the Leisure Class,* New York: Schocken Books.

McGuire, Willard H.
1979 "Teacher Burnout," *Today's Education* 68, no. 4: 5.

Martin, Paul
1976 "Hooked on Work," *Science Digest* 80 (December): 72–77.

Maslach, Christina
1978 "The Client Role in Staff Burnout," *Journal of Social Issues* 34, no. 4: 111–124.

Meyersohn, Rolf
1968 "Television and the Rest of Leisure," *Public Opinion Quarterly* 32 (Spring): 102–112.

Morse, Nancy C. and Robert S. Weiss
1955 "Function and Meaning of Work," *American Sociological Review* 20 (April): 191–198.

Neulinger, John
1974 "On Leisure," *Behavior Today*, April 29: 120.

Parker, Stanley
1971 *The Future of Work and Leisure*, New York: Praeger.

Pearlin, Leonard
1963 "Alienation from Work: A Study of Nursing Personnel," *American Sociological Review* 27 (June): 314–325.

Orthner, Dennis K.
1975 "Familia Ludens: Reinforcing the Leisure Component in Family Life," *Family Coordinator* 24 (April): 175–184.

Riesman, David
1958 "Leisure and Work in Post-Industrial Society," in Eric Larabee and Rolf Meyersohn (eds.), *Mass Leisure*, Glencoe, Ill.: The Free Press, pp. 363–388.

Robinson, John P.
1976 "Changes in America's Use of Time, 1965–1975," *Report of the Communication Research Center*, Cleveland State University.

Rosenblatt, Paul C. and Martha G. Russell
1975 "The Social Psychology of Potential Problems in Family Vacation Travel," *Family Coordinator* 24 (April): 209–216.

Seeman, Melvin
1967 "On the Personal Consequences of Alienation in Work," *American Sociological Review* 32 (April): 273–285.

Shepard, Jon M.
1977 "Technology, Alienation, and Job Satisfaction," *Annual Review of Sociology* 3: 1–21.

Snyder, Eldon E.
1972 "Athletic Dressingroom Slogans as Folklore: A Means of Socialization," *International Review of Sport Sociology* 7: 89–102.

Snyder, Eldon E. and Elmer Spreitzer
1978 *Social Aspects of Sport*, Englewood Cliffs, N.J.: Prentice-Hall.

Tudor, Bill
1972 "A Specification of Relationships Between Job Complexity and Powerlessness," *American Sociological Review* 37 (October): 596–604.

U.S. Department of Commerce
1977 *Social Indicators 1976*, Washington, D.C.: Government Printing Office.

Wiebe, Gerhart D.
    1970 "Two Psychological Factors in Media Audience Behavior," *Public Opinion Quarterly* 33 (Winter): 523–536.
Wiebe, Robert H.
    1975 *The Segmented Society,* New York: Oxford University Press.
Yankelovich, Daniel
    1978 "The New Psychological Contracts at Work," *Psychology Today* 11 (May): 46–50.

GROUP **IV**
PROCESSES

8

Role Relationships

We may look on the formation of social attachments and the development of self-attitudes as emergent outcomes of role relationships. Over time the enactment of gender roles, marital roles, and work roles generally results in stable identities and predictable patterns of social behavior. The recurrent character of role-related behavior has led several social psychologists to note the resemblance between behavior in everyday life and the staged performances of theatrical actors. Through the enactment of social roles the self becomes linked with others, and attitudes emerge as shared constructions of reality.

The drama of social living is expressed in the self-images people attempt to project in their relationships with each other. In some cases the role performance is closely linked with a person's identity, while in other cases the enactment of a social role bears little relationship to the more central and stable aspects of the self (Turner, 1978). Erving Goffman (1959; 1961; 1963; 1967; 1969) has emphasized the separation of the public from the private aspects of the self in his distinction between being "on-stage" and being "off-stage." From the individual's standpoint the problem is to distinguish between one's normal relaxed self and the performances one deliberately stages because they are required, expected, or designed to have some calculated effect on others.

This distinction is not between what is real or unreal in an objective sense, since both the normal, relaxed self and the social performances are socially constructed forms of reality. Instead the problem is that of recognizing that there are circumstances in everyday life in which a discrepancy occurs between what one thinks of as a real self and the performance that projects a self at variance with one's identity (Turner, 1976).

Social roles are not enacted in a vacuum. They always involve social interaction; they are always embedded in social relationships; and they are always reciprocal. The role of parent has no meaning without children, nor the role of doctor without patients, nor the role of teacher without students, nor the role of clerk without customers, nor the role of taxi driver without passengers. The understanding, intentions, and actions of one person must move into alignment with the understanding, intentions, and actions of others if people are to play roles with competence and if social relationships are to develop in an orderly manner. Role relationships are not always cooperative in character, but for them to occur at all individuals must be responsive to one another.

When we interact with each other, we usually do so on the basis of some role-related aspect of our identities, which involves a set of prewritten social scripts as well as a set of individualized performances. The social scripts provide us with general knowledge of how roles are typically performed, thus permitting us to make predictions with a reasonable degree of accuracy. We expect the skills, identities, and performances of a police officer to differ from those of a minister, those of a college professor to differ from those of a truck driver, and those of a classmate to differ from those of our parents.

While role behavior involves the enactment of social scripts, there are also nuances of style that reflect the particular talents and inclinations of actors who engage in their own forms of script writing as they go along. For this reason, the meanings given to role relationships are often problematic and are always in process. The construction of meaning is contingent on one's own

---

BOX 8.1
Elements of Social Life as Theater

Social life as theater is a form of drama in which interacting individuals engage in various kinds of performances in order to construct satisfactory versions of reality for themselves and for others. Patterns of interaction occur among specific individuals who are responding to the identities of each other and who engage in various kinds of action in order to produce desired outcomes. The components of social life as theater include the following:

1. The setting—attributes of the situation as the interacting individuals define them. These include the time and the place, the people who are present, and the reasons for the interactions.
2. Actors—the social identities of those who are responding to one another (e.g., lovers, friends, peers, clients, acquaintances, strangers, and so on).
3. Social scripts—the enactments of behavior expected of those who occupy some particular social position (e.g., cab drivers, police officers, Catholics, women, teachers, and so on forth).
4. Performances—actions oriented toward producing some intended effect on others who are present. Successful performances are those in which observers accept as valid the realities that an actor constructs.
5. Roles—combination of expectancies and performances on the part of those who are interacting with each other.
6. Outcomes—realization of the advantages and disadvantages from the interaction, including the reasons for continuing or ending a specific social relationship.

action in conjunction with the reaction of others (Stokes and Hewitt, 1976). The process is one in which actors justify and refine their respective identities through responsiveness to each other.

The components of role analysis include the social situation, the awareness context, the actors in the situation, the performances of the actors, and the responses of observers. In combination these components of everyday life have their analogs in the theater, including the stage setting, the script, the performances, and the viewing audience. Studies of role relationships point to the inescapable conclusion that humans are mutually interdependent as they engage in the pursuit of their own self-interests. (See Box 8.1.)

In dealing with role playing in everyday life, we will direct our attention to the problem of meaning for the individual actor as he or she moves outside the more intimate forms of attachment into the spheres of action within the broader society. The study of role relationships should enable us to develop a fuller appreciation of the place of appearances and illusions in human affairs, of the importance of face saving, of reality definitions as a negotiated process, and of the merger between persons and roles. These are central aspects of social living; they should be easier for us to understand as a result of social psychological inquiry. In interviewing for a job, in making purchases, in obtaining medical services, and in dating other people, the roles we play are likely to have an important bearing on our degree of success or failure.

A. SOCIAL INTERACTION

The process of **social interaction** refers to an encounter in which two or more individuals come into contact with each other and grant mutual rights for communication and response. Any gathering may be analyzed as an encounter as long as the participants maintain continuous engagement in an activity and are aware that in achieving their own aims and goals the expectations and responses of others must be taken into account. Interactions take place within social settings and involve role playing as participants reciprocally take each other into account, modifying their behavior accordingly.

Erving Goffman (1961) used the term *focused gathering* to describe the social encounters that occur in everyday life. Interactions are focused in the sense that participants draw boundaries around their activities, and this has the effect of temporarily sealing them off from alternative sources of meaning and action. There is an underlying purpose or source of unity to the interactions that bind the participants through their mutual responsiveness to each other. For example, the overriding purposes of the class, the football game, the celebration of a holiday, or the shopping trip are known and understood by those who are engaging in the interaction process. The focuses of interactions are guided by social definitions and norms that define and redefine what is of relevance or significance.

1. Social Expectancies

Role relationships are guided by both social expectancies and by the performances of actors in given situations. A **social expectancy** is the subjective prediction a social actor makes that an event will occur under some specified set of circumstances. As such, expectancies consist of mutually understood rules of appropriate and probable conduct. For example, students are expected to attend the classes in which they have enrolled and to prepare themselves for taking examinations. Students are also expected to write their own term papers, to give proper credit to the academic sources of the ideas developed, and to turn them in when due. Most students assume these obligations and student performances become orderly and predictable through doing so.

Professors can predict with a reasonable degree of accuracy that students will attend the classes for which the professors have prepared lectures and that most of the students attending class on any given day will remain until the lecture is completed. Such forms of predictability derive from an awareness of the scripts that accompany social roles. Teachers are expected to teach; scientists are expected to do research; lawyers are expected to defend their clients; and auto mechanics are expected to make repairs on cars. These commonly understood performances are socially defined roles for those who hold particular social positions.

The specialization of roles provides some assurance for meeting the needs of a particular group of people. Splendid performance in a social role tends to enhance the level of respect for a role occupant, while repeated negligence of duties and responsibilities becomes a source of irritation. Students are likely to be annoyed by the professor who routinely fails to prepare for his or her lectures, who shows disdain for interacting with students, or who remains so aloof as to be inaccessible. On the other hand, professors are likely to be disappointed with students who fail to attend class, who are unprepared for exams, or who are routinely late in completing their assigned work.

The predictability of performances is based on knowledge of specific role relationships and awareness that only selected attributes of those interacting with each other are known or considered to be of relevance. Numerous aspects of the personal lives of professors have no bearing on what takes place within the classroom, just as the personal lives of students are extraneous to the standards for evaluating classroom performances.

In the more intimate social relationships, such as those occurring among friends and family members, the social experiences take on a qualitatively different form. These types of relationships more nearly direct concerns toward the total well-being of the individuals involved. Many aspects of the life-world of one individual overlap with those of another; through sharing a wide variety of experiences, individuals become interdependent and mutually supportive. One's well-being becomes related to the well-being of one's closest friend, one's lover, or one's favorite relative. One derives rewards from relationships with other persons, and obtains verification for one's own self-identity.

Role Expectations: Students Attending Class
The increase in pedestrian traffic on campus during the change of classes indicates that students are complying with role expectations. Would we be correct in assuming that regular class attendance means students have a genuine interest in learning what their professors have to teach?

In intimate groups as well as in the more impersonal relationships, however, a correspondence between expectancies, performances, and self-identities often becomes problematic for both the social actor and the observer. In many types of situations individuals may perceive the social pressures they feel as misplaced or as incongruent with their personal identities. While compliance with the expectancies of others is an important basis for orderly social relationships, such role playing requires confronting the stresses and conflicts derived from the contradictory demands placed on individuals.

2. Negotiating Reality

It is the shared understanding of how rules operate that makes social life possible; but this understanding frequently is inaccurate, and a great deal of uncertainty is implicit in all social relationships. The problem of uncertainty stems from the fact that roles are not played by human robots. Instead roles are played by people who differ from one another in many ways, and ongoing social relationships require a great deal of reflection on the qualities and attributes of the other people in one's life.

The basic problem of social interaction is that of lining up the performances of one individual with the understanding and responses of another. The process by which expectancies and performances are brought into alignment is called **role taking**. Role taking results when one uses the imagination to put oneself in the place of another in order to make predictions about the lines of action that appear reasonable and appropriate to the other person (Turner, 1962; Blumer, 1969). Parents make judgments about what would be pleasing to their children; the police make judgments about the conduct of suspicious characters; and partners in marriage make assessments of the respective attributes of each other as their marriages develop (Stryker, 1967). Through taking the role of another person we can shape our own behavior and anticipate likely responses.

Some degree of predictability is present in most social interactions because of the known scripts of the social actors and the focus of the activity. In any given case, however, the predictions are tentative, and some degree of uncertainty is likely to grow out of the novel performances and unknown qualities of co-participants. As social relationships unfold and develop, actions are initiated, adjusted, and created. The underlying process is called **role making**: participants improvise social scripts, discover limitations and possibilities, make decisions, redirect the focus of the activity, and redefine situations. Role making thus entails the performances of individuals as they enact social scripts and do some script writing of their own. Alignments occur between the performances of actors who are engaged in reciprocal roles.

Because we are limited in our capacities actually to know whether our own definitions of reality are shared by those with whom we interact, we are often confronted with what Thomas J. Scheff (1968) described as the problem of "negotiating reality." The **negotiation of reality** is a process by which individuals with opposing views establish a mutually agreeable definition of the situation. This does not necessarily imply that they obtain a consensus, but only that they establish a workable relationship. Since individuals interact on the basis of reciprocal influences, they determine the outcomes in terms of costs and benefits through negotiation and compromise (Blumstein, 1974). We may look on the reciprocal influences as a dialectical process that cannot be fully reduced to the ordinary routines of everyday life. Instead, the influences entail a give-and-take sequence of differential offers and payoffs for the actors involved.

The need for negotiation of reality stems from conditions of uncertainty, and the essential problems are those of establishing shared frames of reference. It is necessary to reach some level of agreement on the course of action compatible with the aspirations and intentions of the parties involved (Day and Day, 1977). Very often the negotiations of reality do not occur among peers but rather among those who have unequal capacities for determining the outcomes. The observations made by Scheff (1968) emphasize the importance of authority in negotiating reality, especially in the diagnosis of illness and the processing of criminal cases.

Bargaining between the prosecutor, the defense attorney, and the accused often leads to negotiating a plea of guilty to a lesser offense. For example, a defendant initially arrested on an armed-robbery charge may agree to plead guilty to a charge of unarmed robbery. The bargain results in an easy conviction for the prosecutor and in leniency for the accused. Some observers of our criminal justice system have noted that the majority of convictions are obtained through the process of plea bargaining. Such procedures in our court system reflect a contradiction between the actual practice of compromise on the one hand and the moral expectation concerning universal standards of justice on the other. The negotiations stem from the problems inherent in establishing guilt in specific cases and from the risks for the defendant of being prosecuted for a more serious offense if he or she fails to cooperate.

In the plea-bargaining process the parties involved are concerned not so much with determining the facts of the case as with constructing a form of reality that will be satisfactory under the circumstances to all involved. The courts face the general problem of obtaining convictions, which will certify the effectiveness of the criminal justice system, and with the specific problem of processing a particular case. Obtaining a conviction through a plea of guilt to a lesser offense provides a basis for "closing the books" in any given case. In achieving this, court hearings are structured in such a fashion as to deny the transaction that actually occurred. When pleading guilty to a lesser offense, the accused is required to testify that he or she is making the plea voluntarily and is actually guilty of having committed the offense for which prosecution is being sought. All parties are explicitly aware that official realities are being negotiated during plea bargaining. (See Box 8.2.)

In medical diagnoses, by way of contrast, the interacting parties are less explicitly aware of the process of negotiating reality. In a large percentage of the instances in which the services of a physician are sought, there is no readily identifiable organic disorder. Apparently many people become ill as a result of their inability to cope adequately with the stresses of everyday life. Under these circumstances, establishing a definition of the patient's illness becomes a bargaining process between the doctor and the patient.

The transaction is one in which the patient proposes various illnesses that the physician may reject, and the diagnosis continues until an illness has been identified that is mutually acceptable to both the doctor and the patient. In some cases the physician may influence the outcome of the medical diagno-

BOX 8.2
Lawyer-Client Negotiations of Reality

Negotiations of reality are oriented toward constructions of meaning that are acceptable to the parties involved. Each may hold definitions of the situation that the other does not share as a result of differences in the roles being played. But the goal of the relationships is to derive a plausible plan of action. Clients utilize the services of professionals (doctors, lawyers, and so on) because they need help in solving personal problems. Professional helpers, by way of contrast, have their own set of concerns, and they draw on their expertise to exercise control over the inter-action process.

From a study of lawyer-client relationships in a federally funded legal services clinic for the poor, Hosticka (1979) observed several techniques employed in the negotiation of reality. A secretary initially screened the clients and decided if they were eligible to see a lawyer. At the time of the appointment clients were not per-mitted to give their own accounts of their problems (e.g., receiving an eviction notice from a landlord). Instead, lawyers exercised control over the topics of con-versation by requesting the client to fill out forms, by asking leading questions (to which the lawyers already knew the answers), and by interrupting clients if they started to give their own personalized accounts.

The lawyers permitted only the information that would enable them to de-termine "the facts of the case." This permitted control over definitions of "what happened," "what is happening now," and "what is going to happen." At no time were clients "given the floor" to express their own sentiments about the attributes of their personal troubles. The lawyers exercised control in order to secure out-comes that they regarded as being legally desirable.

Source: Carl J. Hosticka, "We Don't Care about What Happened, We Only Care about What Is Going to Happen: Lawyer-Client Negotiations of Reality," *Social Problems* 26 (June, 1979): 599–610.

sis independently of the patient's actual condition; according to Scheff (1968), this may stem from the doctor's notions about the kind of illness that is proper for a patient to have. Once a label has been established for characterizing an illness, the patient very often feels relief in being freed from the uncertainty of not knowing how to describe his or her condition.

In the process of negotiating reality there is often a lack of balance be-tween the power or the authority of those interacting with each other. In the cases cited by Scheff (1968) the authority of the physician exceeds that of the pa-tient in negotiating the appropriate label for an illness; the prosecutor also is in a greater position of power than is the accused in the plea-bargaining process, having the final say on whether the plea of guilt to a lesser offense will be per-mitted. The outcomes of such negotiations are in large measure shaped by variations in the rights and privileges of those involved in role relationships.

Individuals differ in their needs and in their control over desired resources; as a result, dependency on experts and specialists is a prominent feature of modern social life.

B. IDENTITY AND DECEPTION

Social behavior in given situations is shaped by the interplays of awareness and understanding of the interacting parties. In any specific case the actor is clearly aware of a personal identity and of the intentions which lie in back of his or her performance. It is the awareness on the part of those responding to the performance that becomes problematic. The task of sorting the known from the unknown aspects of each other's identities is present to some degree in all social interactions (Guiot, 1977). People deliberately reveal certain aspects of their self-identities while intentionally withholding other forms of knowledge of relevance to the situation. Deception occurs when one or more of the social actors deliberately disguise aspects of a self-identity or deliberately withhold relevant information about the other person.

1. The Awareness Context

The model of social life as theater becomes of special relevance under those circumstances in which the true identities of those interacting with each other are not mutually known. Barney Glaser and Anselm Strauss (1964) have characterized this problem in terms of the awareness context, which involves the dual concern of accurately perceiving the identity of others and having one's own identity correctly perceived by the relevant others. The effects of having only partial awareness are evident in numerous client-oriented relationships that involve obtaining services from those employed in technical and professional occupations. In receiving medical services, for example, there is typically a backstage that is "off limits" to clients; as a result patients are often processed without their having direct access to information of central relevance to their sense of physical well-being.

According to Glaser and Strauss (1964), the basic source of variation in the awareness context derives from the degree to which available information is shared. In the **open-awareness context** the actors are aware of the true identities of each other, and they share information that is of relevance to the transaction. By way of contrast, in the **closed-awareness context** those involved in the relationship do not know each other's true identities, and they withhold crucial forms of information from each another. Under conditions of closed or suspicious awareness people make guesses about the identities of others and about some of the aspects of the situation that lack verification and open disclosure.

BOX 8.3
Closed Awareness and Hospital Organization

Glaser and Strauss observed that the following attributes of hospital organization promote a closed-awareness context for patients:

1. Medical diagnosis is reported in a specialized vocabulary that most patients cannot understand even if it were made available to them.
2. Medical records are kept at places within hospitals that are inaccessible to patients.
3. As a result of training, the medical staff develops skills for withholding information from patients and for using a demeanor around patients that will not reveal medical secrets.
4. The patient seldom has social ties with employees of the hospital who can help uncover medical secrets.
5. In the case of terminally ill patients, family members will often collude with the medical staff to withhold information from the patient.

Thus patients in hospitals do not typically have access to the "backstage" of the performances of medical personnel.

Source: Barney G. Glaser and Anselm L. Strauss, "Awareness Context and Social Interaction," *American Sociological Review* 29 (October, 1964): 669–679.

In their study of the processing of clients in hospital settings, Glaser and Strauss (1965) illustrated the importance of the awareness context by concentrating on the management of impressions in staff relationships with terminally ill patients. The awareness context in hospitals is typically one in which patients do not have open access to their medical records, and as a result the medical staff often has knowledge about the health problems of a patient that is not available to the patient. (See Box 8.3.)

In the case of terminally ill patients the closed awareness context is inherently unstable. With the passing of time, or perhaps with repeated trips to the hospital, the patient either constructs a true awareness of the situation from exposure to the cues from the environment, or develops an attitude of suspicion and distrust toward others. Under conditions of suspicious awareness, the patient no longer takes verbal statements at face value but "with a grain of salt"; the patient tends to look behind them for a hidden motive. Glaser and Strauss (1965: 64) observe that

When patient and staff both know that the patient is dying but pretend otherwise— when both agree to act as if he were going to live—then a context of mutual pretense exists. Either party can initiate his share of the context; it ends when one side cannot, or will not, sustain the pretense any longer....

Thus successive interactions tend to transform the awareness context and the receptive definitions of the situation.

Mutual pretense in social relationships generally occurs in those situations in which there is a shared interest in disguising knowledge of some uncomfortable fact. Thus people avoid conditions of potential embarrassment and construct as an alternative what they generally regard as a more satisfying reality. While Glaser and Strauss concentrated their study on the mutual pretense in a set of client-oriented relationships, similar principles operate in more intimate groups, such as in the sustained relationships within marriage.

Among married couples, conditions of mutual awareness and pretense are determined in large degree by the communication patterns between husband and wife. Their pretense of agreeing on specific attributes of family life may be a way of promoting harmonious relationships. As a result many couples are not aware of the levels of disagreement they have with each other over such issues as where to live, what furniture to buy, how many children to have, and what contraceptives to use. The lack of mutual awareness among couples may in part stem from one member or the other of the marital couple routinely concealing or disguising personal sentiments and values as a way of promoting the stability of the relationship (Neal and Groat, 1976).

2. Nonverbal Communication

There are visible cues to certain aspects of the identities of individuals in most interactions. These cues consist of such biological characteristics as sex, race, and age, as well as such social characteristics as styles of clothing, speech patterns, and physical appearances. Deborah Schiffrin (1977) has observed that "identification displays" are socially meaningful in separating those who are available for interactions from those who are unavailable. The wearing of uniforms (as in the case of military personnel, bus drivers, police officers, and nurses) is a way of announcing an identity and thus becoming available for certain kinds of social interaction. In the absence of uniforms or other visible emblems of an identity, interactions are frequently oriented toward reducing the unknown qualities of those in close physical proximity.

The process by which we know and think about the people in our lives depends on much more than talking and listening. A good deal of human communication is nonverbal in character. We respond not only to what a person has to say, but also to how the person says it, to voice tone and inflection, to facial expression, and to many other nonverbal signals and displays. In social relationships, roles are conveyed nonverbally in smiles and frowns, in eye contact and eye avoidance, in touching and withdrawing, and in negotiations for the use of physical space.

Nonverbal communication incorporates the full gamut of body cues and signals by which information is conveyed about self-identities. The nonverbal cues include facial gestures, qualities of voice, body postures, forms

The Wearing of Uniforms
The person who wears a uniform in public places announces an identity and increases his or her accessibility to interaction with strangers.

of clothing, manner of deportment, and all other signs that display an identity. In nonverbal communication the message sender and the message receiver may not agree fully on the meaning of the behavior involved. The key element is mutual responsiveness rather than an exchange of clearly understood information. Nonverbal cues frequently convey only general ideas about the kinds of interactions people seek or desire. Attempts to verbalize the meanings of postures, facial expressions, or gestures are likely to make the nonverbal behavior appear more deliberate than the person actually intended it to be (Cassell, 1974).

The self presented to others is necessarily ambiguous and incomplete. As a result we tend to read too much or too little into the messages we receive. For the people of concern to us we are likely to go beyond the direct visual cues to fill in the information gaps. In doing so we are drawing on an implicit personality theory. This is a set of ideas about personal traits and attributes that tend to be associated with each other. The traits that are known become clues

---

BOX 8.4
Beautification and Adornment

The attempts to produce more satisfactory realities for observers through creating appearances and illusions are evident on a widespread basis in modern society. The concerns with beautification and personal adornment are major expressions of this emphasis. Beautification refers to the process of attempting to improve physical appearance. In the United States the numerous uses of beauty products and services constitute a multibillion dollar industry. More than $4 billion are spent annually in beauty salons and barber shops alone, and there are several cosmetic companies that have annual sales exceeding $100 million.

Attempts to adorn and alter body appearances for the enhancement of self-images take a wide variety of forms. These include undergoing hair transplants, seeking solutions to the problems of baldness, attempting to reduce or eliminate the wrinkles associated with aging, and exercising or dieting to produce desired body builds and shapes. These efforts at embellishment of the body are efforts to create and sustain self-images through some calculated effect on others.

The social value of physical beauty reaches its peak in the imagery surrounding the media creations of celebrities. The celebrities of stage, screen, and the music world become symbolic of the hopes and aspirations of their fans and admirers. Through imitations of hairstyles, clothing styles, and lifestyles, individuals seek to increase their own social desirability, to provide emblematic displays of social status and worth, to increase attractiveness in relationships, and to convey such selective images as youthfulness, athletic prowess, and sophistication.

---

to the missing parts. Thus we tend to generalize from a limited number of signs, displays, and signals (Rosenberg and Jones, 1972).

If there is some known set of traits about a person that we happen to like, we tend to assume the presence of other likeable traits that are not visible to us. This is "the halo effect," and it plays an important part in our perceptions of people. For example, we might assume that rich people are also intelligent, that the physically attractive are socially desirable, and that the well-dressed are self-confident. These assumptions may be unwarranted in any given case, but we draw on them as a way of smoothing out the gaps in personal knowledge (Newcomb, 1961).

Alfred Schutz and Thomas Luckmann (1973) used the term **typification** to describe perceptions of the usual ways in which the qualities and attributes of people are linked in the performance of social roles. The usual ways of thinking about types of people and making typical predictions may be illustrated by drawing on the importance of physical beauty. All social groups have notions about what makes a person beautiful, and given individuals may be evaluated by locating them on a scale from beautiful to ugly. The halo effect and the perceptions of social types are likely to operate especially as first impressions and in situations in which only a very limited amount of information is available. These were the conditions studied by Alan E. Gross and Christine Crofton (1977). Their research on college students indicated that perceptions of physical attractiveness, personal abilities, and probabilities for success are highly intercorrelated. The underlying thesis suggests that the good and the beautiful tend to become intertwined in the perceptions of people in everyday life.

Because physical appearance is such an important part of the social display of the self, a good deal of time and effort goes into devising conduct and appearances that are intended to evoke the desired typifications by others (Hewitt, 1979). Apparently the self as a meaningful social object requires some degree of embellishment. Body building, clothing, and cosmetics are among the means employed by many people for the enhancement of public images (Goffman, 1979). Such accoutrements in the public display of the self provide the individual with some degree of control over the impressions given situations evoke. Presenting oneself in a favorable light aims at eliciting desired responses from others. (See Box 8.4.)

C. SOCIAL LIFE AS THEATER

The display of the self provides not only a basis for linking known to unknown qualities but also a means for defining situations and relationships. The demeanor and deference individuals accord to each other is expressed largely through visual cues and nonverbal symbols. According to Erving Goffman (1967: 77), **demeanor** is "that element of the individual's ceremonial behavior typically conveyed through deportment, dress, and bearing." Demeanor becomes important as a way of packaging the self to reinforce social relationships and to promote harmonious interactions. On the other hand, deference is a symbolic way of conveying to others the prestige and appreciation to which they are entitled. In combination, demeanor and deference serve as emblems of group membership and demonstrate an interest in maintaining proper role relationships (Cassell, 1974). Public displays and role relationships thus establish linkages between the individual and society.

Individuals frequently confront the problems of linkage in interactions with each other in a heterogeneous and mass-like society. The complexity of modern social life is expressed through the extensive division of labor and specialization of roles, as well as through the recurrence of episodic relationships among those who lack a set of ongoing social ties. The ephemeral and episodic interactions that occur in public places seldom bear a permanent relationship to either the structure of the self or to the broader organization of the social system. Under these circumstances, people use communication to manage impressions, and the presentations of their identities are in large measure staged performances (Goffman, 1963).

1. Management of Impressions

On a daily basis we typically interact with many people who are strangers to us, and except for those who are wearing uniforms we generally lack an awareness of the social identities of those we encounter. Such ambiguities in social status are in part a reflection of the high degree of mobility and urbanization in our society. Social relations under these circumstances provide only a small degree of overlap in the life-worlds of those who are in physical proximity to each other. Social relationships among strangers especially lend themselves to the management of impressions and to role performances characterized by some degree of pretense (Goffman, 1969).

Performances in public places become theatrical in character because they are designed for producing an intended effect on others rather than for revealing what the social actors perceive as their true selves. An individual may design personal demeanor in the lobby of a hotel or in a bus station, for

Management of Impressions
The man with the stovepipe hat is not really President William Henry Harrison. The occasion is primarily ceremonial, and the residents of Perrysburg, Ohio, enjoy the pretense. Such performances give concrete referents to historical memories. Community pride is enhanced through remembering that important historical events occurred in their town.

BOX 8.5
The Taxi Driver and the Passenger

Taxi drivers in large metropolitan areas lack a steady clientele, and the typical work-day consists of sequential encounters with passengers who are strangers. Since the tip makes the difference between subsistence and a living wage, taxi drivers use various strategies to reduce the uncertainty connected with the size of the tip.

One strategy consists of constructing a typology of passengers that permits the driver to quickly reduce the uncertainties about the passenger's identity. Passengers range from those who regard the driver as a "nonperson" to those who evoke emblems of being "the sport," "the blowhard," "the business person," "the lady shopper," and "the live one." The taxi driver tailors his or her driving behavior and the control of conversation to fit the hypothesized attributes of the passenger.

The various strategies for increasing the tip include fumbling for change, producing "the hard-luck story," and adding fictitious charges for the obviously inexperienced cab user. Darting in and out of traffic and jerky starts at traffic lights are techniques the driver uses to impress the passenger (and reassure the driver) that driving a cab requires specialized skills and talents. Despite these performances, tipping remains a situation characterized by inherent uncertainty and variability primarily beyond the control of the driver.

Source: Fred Davis, "The Cabdriver and His Fare: Facets of a Fleeting Relationship," *American Journal of Sociology* 65 (September, 1959): 158–165.

example, in such a fashion to communicate his or her accessibility or inaccessibility for interaction with others (Schiffrin, 1977). A person may communicate in subtle ways disrespect for those present within a situation. For instance, the newcomer to an elevator may deliberately and without comment punch the elevator button for the second time, thereby reflecting a judgment on the intelligence of those waiting there.

The regulation of normal behavior in public places is primarily facilitated by commonly held expectations of those whose role identities are readily apparent (Turner and Shosid, 1976). Thus the uniform that identifies police officers or bus drivers is emblematic of their accessibility for certain kinds of social interactions of short duration. In public places social relationships tend to be role-specific, limited to the task at hand, and to be client-oriented. Taking a cab, making a purchase, and receiving medical services are examples of public contexts that promote the staging of appearances and the management of impressions. The theatrical type of performance is most clearly evident in client-oriented relationships in which those interacting with each other have no ongoing social ties. A convincing role performance by one or the other defines the social reality for both. (See Box 8.5.)

Social performances by service workers and their clients become evident in the practice of tipping. While tipping is expected but not required of patrons, it conveys much more than a token of appreciation for outstanding service. Wages are reduced by employers to make an allowance for tipping, and in occupations such as driving a cab or waiting on tables, approximately 40 to 60 percent of the worker's income comes from the tips received from clients. Tipping then serves as an important wage supplement for service workers and in part as a means of verifying the social status of a client. Obtaining "a living wage" is often dependent on the degree of success in concealing personal sentiments while delivering prompt and courteous service. The pretense in back of

BOX 8.6
Frontstage and Backstage Regions

Erving Goffman has clarified the process of managing impressions by distinguishing the settings in which social interactions occur. The frontstage region is the setting in which some prearranged performance is enacted for a viewing audience; the backstage region is an "off-limits" area where the background work is performed. The backstage areas are designated a private sphere not only to get the necessary work done without interference but also to keep the activities taking place there from discrediting the impressions made in a frontstage area.

In an analysis of funeral directing, Turner and Edgley (1976) demonstrate the importance of backstage settings for the theatrics surrounding the death crisis in our society. From their description of the backstage setting in which the corpse is prepared for viewing, it becomes evident that most of us would prefer to be excluded from such areas or activities.

Here the corpse is washed, shaved, sprayed with disinfectant, sliced, pierced, creamed, powdered, waxed, stitched, painted, manicured, dressed, and positioned in a casket. Embalming involves the draining of blood *via* the major arteries while simultaneously refilling them through an injection point in the neck or armpit with fluid. Through the use of other chemicals the flesh is softened, stretched, shrunk, restored, colored, and even replaced (Turner and Edgley, 1976: 381).

Observing such procedures are likely to have a shocking effect on the friends and relatives of the deceased. The frontstage area, by way of contrast, is characterized by a widely different set of performances and definitions. People speak softly to one another; they attempt to control their expressions of grief; and they make references to "the loved one" as looking "natural" or as appearing to be in "a deep and tranquil sleep." Such images are supported only by shielding observers from the activities connected with preparing the corpse for viewing in the backstage.

Source: Ronney E. Turner and Charles Edgley, "Death as Theater," *Sociology and Social Research* 60 (July, 1976): 377–392.

the demeanor and deference of service workers reflects both the expectations of them and the manipulations of the marketplace.

Dean MacCannell (1973) has noted that the calculated efforts that go into creating and sustaining an illusion are evident in many aspects of modern social life. Politicians design their speeches to give their listeners what the listeners would like to hear; food handlers inject hams with chemical nitrates in order to make them appear more appetizing and ham-like; and the mortician treats a corpse to make it appear life-like. Each of these examples consists of productions that occur in a back-stage area in order to facilitate the enactment of the desired illusion or appearance "up front." (See Box 8.6.)

2. Routinized Techniques

In the theater as well as in everyday life actors and the viewing audience may become so caught up with a splendid performance that illusions and realities blend into an inseparable pattern. In the course of watching a play the members of an audience may become so carried away with the performance that they lose sight of the prewritten script, the rehearsals, and the persons inside the costumes. The fall of the curtain announces to the audience that the play is over, and the return of the players for applause not only serves to reinforce the egos of the performers, but also to bring the audience "back to reality." This promotes a transition from an emotional experience to one that engenders a reflective, intellectual attitude toward the sequence of events. In everyday life there are seldom such sharply drawn boundaries between the realm of make-believe and the realm of reality. On an everyday basis an actor's successful performance is one that produces and sustains an illusion for the observer.

The illusions produced for the observer are in part an outgrowth of the specialization that has occurred in modern society. Social relationships in public places typically take place among individuals with highly specific role identities. In given situations they confine their attention to immediate goals and consider all else to be off limits. As Brenda Danet and Michael Gurevitch (1972) pointed out, individuals in specific role relationships bring into interaction only those segments of their selves that are directly relevant to the particular problem at hand. Through limiting the scope of concerns, those who work at jobs involving the processing of clients may rehearse and refine their techniques for obtaining the desired outcomes in relationships with strangers and transients. (See Box 8.7.)

In our consumer-oriented society the customer-clerk relationship is one of the more recurrent forms of a specific role relationship. In large department stores the salesclerk is generally known not as a person but as what C. Wright Mills called "a commercial mask"; this is reflected in the anonymity and insincerity of the clerk's greeting and in expressions of appreciation for patronage. The salesperson uses his or her appearance and personality to manipulate

BOX 8.7
The Concept of Altercasting

Weinstein and Deutschberger (1963) developed the concept of altercasting to describe several creative aspects of role relationships. The concept of **altercasting** refers to the process of eliciting an audience response congruent with an actor's goals and interests. The actor's interpersonal task is to create a role for others that will permit him or her to be the kind of character he or she wishes to portray. The attainment of personal goals requires limiting the lines of action that others may select in any given encounter.

Individuals frequently employ several techniques in casting the roles to be played between ego and alter (self and others). The use of such terms as *we* or *us* tends to structure the relationship into one of interdependency. Flattery, deference, or demeanor are sometimes used to reduce status differences and to establish the relative placement of identities in an encounter. Revealing personal feelings, needs, and concerns frequently lays the groundwork for the degree of intimacy the social actor will permit. Offering assistance and support establishes superiority, and making a request for help creates an obligation for a response. The person may use techniques to create a common bond by calling attention to a correspondence of interests or the presence of a shared problem.

In developing the concept of altercasting, Weinstein and Deutschberger assume that social interactions cannot be understood adequately in terms of normatively written scripts (socially expected behavior). Instead, human behavior is goal-oriented, and the attainment of personal goals requires eliciting the desired response from others. The techniques of altercasting limit the possible lines of action to those that suit the purposes of the individual.

Source: Eugene A. Weinstein and Paul Deutschberger, "Some Dimensions of Altercasting," *Sociometry* 26 (December, 1963): 454–466.

the potential buyer. One of the role-taking tasks for the salesclerk is to routinize techniques for creating an acceptable illusion that repeated interactions will sustain.

In a study conducted by Mills (1951), planted observers were placed in a large department store in New York City. Here is an observation about the performance of one of the sales women:

I have been watching her for three days now. She wears a fixed smile on her made-up face, and it never varies, no matter to whom she speaks. I have never heard her laugh spontaneously or naturally. Either she is frowning or her face is devoid of any expression. When a customer approaches, she immediately assumes her hard, forced smile. It amazes me because, although I know that the smiles of most salesgirls are unreal, I've never seen such calculation given to the timing of a smile (Mills, 1951: 184).

TABLE 8.1
Emphasis on Technique in Book Titles

How to Win Friends and Influence People
How to Be Loved
How to Survive the Loss of a Love
How Am I Supposed to Love Myself?
How to Be Your Own Best Friend
How to Make Things Go Your Way
How to Become Rich
Practical Ways to Build a Fortune in the Stock Market
How to Live with Your Investments
How to Enjoy Your Life and Your Job
How to Stop Worrying and Start Living
How to Raise Good Kids
How to Get Through Your Struggles
How to Be Happy Though Married
How to Get Control of Your Time and Your Life
How I Found Freedom in an Unfree World
How to Get Whatever You Want Out of Life

From the above it is clear that writers are applying the modern concerns with technique to virtually all aspects of social relationships. The titles suggest that readers will derive practical benefits from personal mastery over specific problem-solving techniques.

Some department stores send their new employees to a "charm school" to develop mastery over the skills and techniques for manipulating customers. Mills observed that the friendly smile behind the counter becomes a type of commercial lure, and both management and the customers expect the salesperson to be helpful, tactful, and courteous at all times. This requires the salesperson to develop techniques for separating his or her personal reactions to customers from overt appearances. The individual conceals negative sentiments toward customers through staged performances.

The emphasis on routine techniques to be employed by sales personnel in customer relationships is but a single case of a more generalized emphasis in our society on elaborating standardized approaches to social relationships. Jacques Ellul (1964) has maintained that the emphasis on technique in nearly all aspects of social life has become one of the more prominent attributes of modern society. This "how to" theme is evident in scanning book titles in any modern bookstore. Numerous book titles are suggestive of the underlying notion that identifiable problems can be turned into technical problems and that standardized solutions are available for producing the desired outcomes. (See Table 8.1.)

The concept of a technique, as developed by Ellul (1964), refers to the elaboration of a standardized means for achieving some predetermined result. Social behavior aims in a deliberate and rationalized direction rather than flowing from emergent and spontaneous responses. To achieve desired outcomes, people have attempted to reduce love making, marital relationships, and mental health to a standardized set of techniques in much the same fashion that business and government develop standardized procedures in their concern with efficient operations.

The elaboration of standardized operating procedures is essential for numerous aspects of modern social life. This is especially evident in situations that involve the processing of a large number of people within a relatively short period of time, as in the spheres of public transportation and mass entertainment. We can imagine the difficulties in air travel, for example, if it were not for the system of reservations, luggage checks, seat assignments, and prearranged schedules. Similarly, the processing of a large number of people at sport events or celebrity performances proceeds smoothly only because of the prior development of routinized procedures. Variations from prearranged schedules and procedures very often result in chaotic and unpredictable outcomes.

D. THE ROLE AND THE PERSON

The preceding discussion of the dramaturgical model should not lead to the conclusion that Erving Goffman and other social psychologists view social life as simply "one big con game after another." Sincerity, honesty, and other positive qualities are as much a part of the drama of social living as are the deliberate uses of impression management and manipulation techniques. Social actors frequently regard their performances as authentic and genuine. Role playing requires the alignment of conduct, and illusions and realities frequently blend into inseparable patterns.

In some cases there is a closer merger between the role and the person (Turner, 1978), while in other cases the person makes a separation between role playing and his or her conception of a true self. The distinction between the role and the person is not a distinction between what is real or unreal in an objective sense, but rather a question of the degree to which individuals are satisfied or comfortable with the roles they are playing. The manner in which roles are played varies according to social circumstances and personal commitments. Role merger occurs under those conditions in which the actor regards his or her performances as expressions of an authentic self, while role distance surfaces in those instances in which a gap develops between overt behavior and self-attitudes.

1. *Role Distance*

Goffman (1961) developed the concept of **role distance** to take into account those situations in which individuals engage in performing what is expected of them, while at the same time they hold private views of a different order. A discrepancy exists between appearances and convictions, and the actor's definition of the situation is at variance with the social demands placed on him or her. Here the problem is essentially that of protecting a conception of self while at the same time complying with the requirements of situational pressures. (See Figure 8.1.)

Under these conditions it becomes apparent that the congruence between self-identity and overt behavior is not evident in social relationships. The individual's self-concept, the display of behavior, and the responses of others often combine to produce some degree of conflict for the actor in given situations. The conflict is at a minimum if personal qualities combine with social expectancies in such a fashion that the role incumbent may readily sustain a self-image and at the same time provide support for the image held by other people.

Role distance is expressed in those situations in which the actor holds

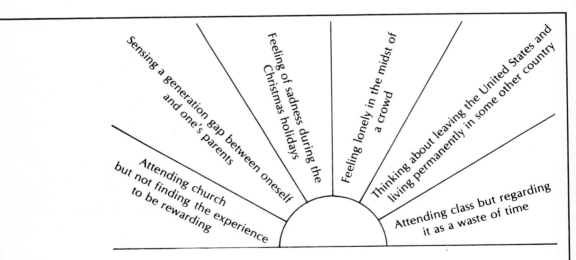

These experiences suggest that individuals may be involved in sets of role relationships without being able to identify with them or to regard them as important sources of rewards.

FIGURE 8.1
The Concept of Role Distance

some degree of disdain, disaffection, or resistance to the role the actor is performing. The display of disdain for what one is doing is a way of circumventing embarrassment or a loss of face (Ho, 1976). It is a plea that others not regard one's performance as a reflection of one's inner self. Goffman directed attention in his studies toward the various techniques by which observers became aware of the gap between an actor's self-identity and the role he or she currently is playing.

Goffman (1961) used the example of the performance of the older child on the merry-go-round to illustrate the concept. The older child uses clowning behavior to indicate that this form of play activity is not being taken seriously. While the ten-year-old boy may be riding the merry-go-round to please a grandmother, he needs to communicate to others that he knows that he is too mature to engage in such an activity, and hence he communicates through his behavior that observers should not associate his self-identity with his current activity. He achieves this through such techniques as making facial expressions of boredom and in response to the music, treating the wooden horse as though it were a racing one, and vigorously reining in the horse when the ride is completed.

Thus role distance sometimes involves an inauthentic performance on the part of a social actor. Such cases frequently involve a type of melodrama in which roles are overplayed and performances are accompanied by a tongue-in-cheek attitude. The actor shapes his or her performances to circumvent the intentions of those who are writing the social script. Observers become aware that the actor holds a personal set of inner meanings and designs that are being disguised in the dramatic performance. Role distance usually occurs under conditions of coercion in which the actor follows the path of least resistance by outwardly conforming to situational pressure while inwardly rejecting the meanings attached to his or her behavior by those observers in positions of power (Neal, 1976).

While role distance frequently occurs in everyday life, the dramaturgical aspects of social behavior become more clearly evident in extreme situations. These are conditions of coercion in which actors encounter hostile forces that they cannot resist without suffering dire consequences. Examples are captive populations such as prison inmates, prisoners of war, and those living in an occupied country. Individuals under these circumstances are confronted with an overwhelming power structure that requires some form of role adaptation for circumventing the punishments that accompany noncompliance while at the same time preserving their perceptions of self-esteem and self-respect.

Drawing on his own experiences and those of others, Czeslaw Milosz (1955) observed the adaptations among artists and intellectuals in occupied Poland following World War II. He noted a variety of techniques they employed for making an outward display of compliance with a repressive regime, while at the same time preserving a more personalized set of values and identities.

Since there was no reasonable basis for expecting a return to the traditional society that intellectuals had known prior to the war, they had no options available other than those of making some form of accommodation to the changing political realities.

Once they recognized that there were no reasonable alternatives to compliance, they used deception to demonstrate to themselves their own superiority over those in positions of power, and this was a source of psychological pleasure. Milosz (1955) noted that in public places Polish intellectuals who were actually unsympathetic to the political regime would carry with them a communist newspaper or magazine and give the appearance of being spontaneous in the whistling of Russian tunes. The successful use of deception is a resource available to those lacking the capacity to engage in organized resistance.

In extreme situations role distance offers a buffer against giving up in the face of overwhelming odds, and in more ordinary circumstances it may be looked on as a manifestation of the need to cope with changing life events. Some degree of role distance is likely to occur for the graduate student who walks into the classroom as an instructor for the first time, for the adolescent who buys his or her first drink in a public bar, for the army recruit who is being inducted into basic training, and for the husband and wife who take on the role of parents at the birth of their first child. In these cases role distance is temporary; it reduces as self-identities and performances blend into a congruent pattern (Thornton and Nardi, 1975).

Role distance also surfaces under conditions in which people are deeply involved and committed to their roles. For example, the television series *MASH* makes use of a crucial activity to develop a comedy situation. Members of the medical staff in the Korean War were clearly aware of the importance of providing medical services for the wounded; but they also were aware of the dangers that accompany war, and if they had a choice they would choose to be someplace else. Role distance is reflected in joking relationships, in playing pranks, and in witty remarks. In treating the wounded (even in the performance of surgery), joking and other exchanges of humor became a means of reducing stress and tension. Such displays of role distance do not indicate that the medical staff was unconcerned about the wounded, but that there was a need to reduce the personal insecurity that would have accompanied full involvement in the roles being played.

2. Role Merger

In contrast to role distance, **role merger** occurs to the degree that individual actors sees themselves primarily through the roles they are playing and are similarly defined by others in the communication process. According to Ralph Turner,

Role Merger (Wearing of Costumes)
The costumes worn in parades and on other ceremonial occasions do not communicate the true identities of the people involved. Under such circumstances role merger is unlikely to occur for either the performers or the observers.

some roles are put on and taken off like clothing without lasting personal effect. Other roles are difficult to put aside when a situation is changed and continue to color the way in which many of the individual roles are performed. The question is not whether the role is played well or poorly or whether it is played with zest or quite casually.... The question is whether the attitudes and behavior developed as an expression of one role carry over into other situations. To the extent that they do, we shall speak of a merger of role and person (Turner, 1978: 1).

Turner identifies several criteria of role merger by drawing on the social actor as the unit for analysis. Merger has occurred to the extent that a role continues to be played in situations where the role does not apply. Instances of such merger occur with the business person who continues to act like one in relationships with his or her family; with the entertainer who carries staged performances into offstage settings; and with the worker who continues at a particular job when a better job is readily available. In such cases the person has become the role that he or she is playing. Self-attitudes become linked with the attitudes, values, and skills that are appropriate for performances in a particular social role.

Merger of the person with the role can occur in any major sphere of social action. It is not limited to work or family roles, but may also be found in pursuit of a hobby, in involvement in a game, or in playing a competitive sport. Clifford Geertz (1972) has noted that strong commitments to a set of activities may result in conditions of "deep play." Deep play occurs when an individual becomes so engrossed in a role that he or she is willing to take unusual and consequential risks that "no reasonable person" would be willing to take: potential costs are high relative to the benefits that can be gained. Such a high degree of engagement in role playing can be illustrated in the following quote from Norbert Elias on the uncontrolled violence in the sports arena of ancient Greece.

... The competitors fought with every part of their body, with their hands, feet, elbows, their knees, their necks and their heads; in Sparta they even used their feet. The pancratiants were allowed to gouge one another's eyes out.... they were also allowed to trip their opponents; lay hold of their feet, noses, and ears; dislocate their fingers and arms; and apply strangleholds. If one man succeeded in throwing the other, he was entitled to sit on him and beat him about the head, face and ears; he could also kick and trample him. ... the contestants quite literally fought tooth and nail and bit and tore one another's eyes out (cited in Sutton-Smith, 1971: 76).

The games of the city-state of ancient Greece were played with such extreme seriousness that far more than fun and enjoyment were involved. Roles and persons merged to such a degree that athletic contests were regarded as serious encounters among the players. In modern societies games usually are less violent, although there are occasions in which a great deal of violence does occur. The research of Michael D. Smith (1979) suggests that violence frequently erupts in connection with such games as hockey and soccer. Players and fans sometimes become "fanatics" as their commitments to winning take priority over the rules of sportsmanship. Similarly, the games played outside the sports arena, such as the war game, the con game, or playing the stock market, may be undertaken with such a degree of seriousness that role performances become closely linked with perceptions of oneself as a successful or as an unsuccessful person.

Mergers of the role and the person, however, are not always dependent on the level of involvement in an activity. The reason for this is that mergers occur not only in self-perceptions but also in perceptions of other people. We are likely to see a congruence between the persons and the roles under those circumstances in which we do not actually know very much about the people who enter our lives for short periods of time. Simply regarding the person and the role as being the same for all practical purposes shows an economy of effort (Gerhardt, 1980). We need not reflect on whether there are persons in back of the roles of salesclerk, automobile mechanic, medical doctor, or police officer. Instead, we are likely to regard the role and the person as being one and the same.

Assumptions of merger usually are adequate as long as we do not see the person playing many different roles or observe qualities of the role occupant that violate our scheme of social classification (Turner, 1978). For example, we are likely to separate the person from the role if our typification scheme fails to be upheld. Being waited on by a male nurse in a hospital setting, being arrested by a female police officer, or observing a physically handicapped person working at a physically demanding job are cases that at the present still fall outside our usual predictive frameworks about people and social roles. Under these circumstances the observer in thought and response is likely to separate the person from the role. Shock, disbelief, and the perception of an extraordinary development are among the conditions that lead to separations of roles from persons in the course of everyday life.

In conclusion, the degree of merger between the role and the person depends on the situation in which roles are enacted and is reflected in perceptions of self and others. In self-attitudes role merger is likely to grow out of deep involvement in a particular line of activity, while in perceptions of other people role merger is likely to stem from the opposite circumstances. We link our self-attitudes with roles to which we are strongly committed, but we merge the role with the other person in social interactions when we are unconcerned with the difference between the two or when we actually know very little about the other person in any other type of role activity.

SUMMARY

There are dynamic qualities to role relationships that are unique and innovative as well as responsive to the problems of order in social living. The scripts of daily life are partially predetermined and partially written by the actors themselves as they relate with one another. Social interaction involves both role taking and role making as the actors establish their respective identities and respond to the stimuli provided by their co-participants in the immediate environment. Situations are defined and redefined as individuals pursue the goals of interest, respond to one another, and bring their actions into alignment.

Role playing includes both the commonly held expectancies of those who occupy some identifiable social position and the nuances of the performances of actors in given situations. The drama of role relationships requires communication among the participants and some degree of consensus on the basis for social interaction. Aspects of the identities of co-participants are revealed, and activities become focused, refined, and modified as relationships develop. The primary interactional task is to negotiate relationships and outcomes that are compatible with the identities and interests of the co-participants.

Through the process of typification, we place individuals into such categories as age level, gender, race, and occupational status. These typifications are comprised of assumptions about the qualities and attributes of individuals as members of social categories, and they play an important part in nonverbal communication. Deference and demeanor, management of impressions, and implicit personality theory are among the ingredients of role playing that both clarify and confuse social relationships.

The dramaturgical model of Erving Goffman draws on the theater as an analog to social life in general. Viewing social life as theater focuses attention on social settings, actors in specific situations, social scripts, performances, and audience responses. The theatrical analogy may be applied to virtually any aspect of social life, including occupational performances, the transactions of the marketplace, interactions among strangers, or the dynamics of intimate marital relationships. Theatrics are expressed particularly in the management of impressions and in the use of routinized techniques for producing intended outcomes in social relationships.

In some situations the person and the role merge, while in other situations the role and the person are separated. Role distance is expressed under those conditions in which a social actor displays a lack of full involvement in an activity. Visual cues and verbal statements communicate to observers that the person is not fully committed to the performance. In contrast, role merger occurs when there is a close linkage between the person and the role. Some degree of merger occurs both in the identity of the actor with the role as well as in the definition of the person and the role by observers. Such linkages are important for self-attitudes and for the qualities of social relationships.

BASIC TERMS

Social interaction	**Nonverbal communication**
Social expectancy	**Typification**
Role taking	**Demeanor**
Role making	**Altercasting**
Negotiation of reality	**Role distance**
Open-awareness context	**Role merger**
Closed-awareness context	

REFERENCES

Blumer, Herbert
1969 *Symbolic Interactionism*, Englewood Cliffs, N.J.: Prentice-Hall.

Blumstein, Philip W.
    1974 "The Honoring of Accounts," *American Sociological Review* 39 (August): 551–566.
Cassell, Joan
    1974 "Externalities of Change: Deference and Demeanor in Contemporary Feminism," *Human Organization* 33 (Spring): 85–94.
Danet, Brenda and Michael Gurevitch
    1972 "Presentation of Self in Appeals to Bureaucracy: An Empirical Study of Role Specificity," *American Journal of Sociology* 77 (May): 1165–1190.
Davis, Fred
    1959 "The Cabdriver and His Fare: Facets of a Fleeting Relationship," *American Journal of Sociology* 65 (September): 158–165.
Day, Robert A. and JoAnne V. Day
    1977 "A Review of the Current State of Negotiated Order Theory," *Sociological Quarterly* 18 (Winter): 126–142.
Ellul, Jacques
    1964 *The Technological Society,* New York: Vintage Books.
Geertz, Clifford
    1972 "Deep Play: Notes on the Balanese Cockfight," *Daedalus* 101 (Winter): 1–23.
Gerhardt, Uta
    1980 "Toward a Critical Analysis of Role," *Social Problems* 27 (June): 556–569.
Glaser, Barney G. and Anselm L. Strauss
    1965 *Awareness of Dying,* Chicago: Aldine.
    1964 "Awareness Context and Social Interaction," *American Sociological Review* 29 (October): 669–679.
Goffman, Erving
    1979 *Gender Advertisements,* New York: Harper Colophon Books.
    1969 *Strategic Interactions,* Philadelphia: University of Pennsylvania Press.
    1967 *Interaction Ritual,* Garden City, N.Y.: Anchor Books.
    1963 *Behavior in Public Places,* New York: The Free Press.
    1961 *Encounters,* Indianapolis: Bobbs-Merrill.
    1959 *The Presentation of Self in Everyday Life,* Garden City, N.Y.: Anchor Books.
Gross, Alan E. and Christine Crofton
    1977 "What Is Good Is Beautiful," *Sociometry* 40 (March): 85–89.
Guiot, Jean M.
    1977 "Attribution and Identity Construction," *American Sociological Review* 42 (October): 692–703.
Hewitt, John P.
    1979 *Self and Society,* Boston: Allyn and Bacon.
Ho, David Yau-fai
    1976 "On the Concept of Face," *American Journal of Sociology* 81 (January): 867–884.
Hosticka, Carl J.
    1979 "We Don't Care about What Happened, We Only Care about What Is Going to Happen: Lawyer-Client Negotiations of Reality," *Social Problems* 26 (June): 599–610.
MacCannell, Dean

1973 "Staged Authenticity: Arrangements of Social Space in Tourist Settings," *American Journal of Sociology* 79 (November): 589–603.

Mills, C. Wright
1951 "The Great Salesroom," in *White Collar*, New York: Oxford University Press, pp. 161–188.

Milosz, Czeslaw
1955 *The Captive Mind*, New York: Vintage Books.

Neal, Arthur G.
1976 "Compliance Without Commitment," in Arthur G. Neal (ed.), *Violence in Animal and Human Societies*, Chicago: Nelson-Hall, pp. 87–94.

Neal, Arthur G. and H. Theodore Groat
1976 "Consensus in the Marital Dyad," *Sociological Focus* 9 (October): 317–329.

Newcomb, Theodore M.
1961 *The Acquaintance Process*, New York: Holt, Rinehart & Winston.

Rosenberg, Seymour and Russell A. Jones
1972 "A Method for Investigating and Representing a Person's Implicit Theory of Personality," *Journal of Personality and Social Psychology* 22 (June): 372–386.

Scheff, Thomas J.
1968 "Negotiating Reality: Notes on Power in the Assessment of Responsibility," *Social Problems* 16 (Summer):3–17.

Schiffrin, Deborah
1977 "Opening Encounters," *American Sociological Review* 42 (October): 679–691.

Schutz, Alfred and Thomas Luckmann
1973 *The Structures of the Life-World*, Evanston, Ill.: Northwestern University Press.

Smith, Michael D.
1979 "Hockey Violence," *Social Problems* 27 (December): 235–247.

Stokes, Randall and John P. Hewitt
1976 "Aligning Actions," *American Sociological Review* 41 (October): 838–849.

Stryker, Sheldon
1967 "Role Taking Accuracy and Adjustment," in Jerome G. Manis and Bernard N. Meltzer (eds.), *Symbolic Interaction*, Boston: Allyn and Bacon, pp. 481–492.

Sutton-Smith, Brian
1971 "Play, Games, and Control," in John Paul Scott and Sarah F. Scott (eds.), *Social Control and Social Change*, Chicago: University of Chicago Press.

Thornton, Russell and Peter M. Nardi
1975 "The Dynamics of Role Acquisition," *American Journal of Sociology* 80 (January): 870–885.

Turner, Ralph
1978 "The Role and the Person," *American Journal of Sociology* 84 (July): 1–23.
1976 "The Real Self: From Institution to Impulse," *American Journal of Sociology* 81 (March): 989–1016.
1962 "Role Taking: Process Versus Conformity," in Arnold M. Rose (ed.), *Human Behavior and Social Processes*, Boston: Houghton Mifflin, pp. 20–40.

Turner, Ralph H. and Norma Shosid
1976 "Ambiguity and Interchangeability in Role Attribution," *American Sociological Review* 41 (December): 993–1005.

Turner, Ronnie E. and Charles Edgley
    1976 "Death as Theater," *Sociology and Social Research* 60 (July): 377–392.
Weinstein, Eugene A. and Paul Deutschberger
    1963 "Some Dimensions of Altercasting," *Sociometry* 26 (December): 454–466.

9

Exchange Relationships

While role analysis concentrates on the expectations and performances of social actors, the study of exchange relationships places emphasis on the pay-offs for the parties involved. How do we as individuals gain access to socially desired resources? What is to keep the strong and the powerful from simply taking what they want? How important is the justice motive in social relationships? What are some of the basic principles in the distribution of social rewards? How do we go about obtaining the objects and services we desire when they are under the control of someone else? The study of exchange relationships should permit us to clarify our answers to some of these basic questions.

The components in a social exchange include the parties to the transactions, the differences in control over resources, the bargaining process, and the transfer of valuables. Other people have control over resources we desire, and to gain access to them we must have something to offer in return. In the study of exchange relationships social psychologists emphasize the process by which individuals make decisions on the allocation of social valuables (money, prestige, love, approval, and so on). Studying this process should enable us to see more clearly the numerous costs and benefits that are implicit in social relationships.

The essential condition for an exchange relationship is that a set of actors in a given situation transfer goods and/or services. In the economic sphere, exchange transactions are clearly evident when customers make purchases at a store and creditors extend loans at a bank, when patrons trade at a public auction, and when employees work for a fixed wage or salary. In social psychology, the interest in exchange relationships is reflected not only in purely economic behavior, but also in such social behavior as extending a greeting, expressing approval or disapproval of another person, and sending gifts to relatives on their birthdays. (See Table 9.1.)

For an exchange to take place there must be a willingness to give up control over some resources in order to gain access to others. For example, in obtaining a college education there are numerous costs in terms of money, effort, and deferred gratification. But on the other hand the potential rewards for the graduate are also great in terms of subsequent earnings and lifestyles. Thus

TABLE 9.1
The Vocabulary of Exchange

Having resources	Engaging in transactions	Deriving rewards
Beauty	Bartering	Approval
Strength	Coercing	Respect
Skills	Serving	Prestige
Expertness	Providing	Payment
Power	Forcing	Domination
Authority	Supervising	Accomplishment
Money	Buying	Consumption
Property	Investing	Wealth
Status	Bargaining	Esteem
Gifts	Giving	Obligation

the value of what is given up relative to what is being received is a key concern in the study of exchange relationships. For an exchange to be mutually beneficial, each party to the transaction must receive rewards that exceed the costs incurred. The university receives financial support from students for its various operations, and students in turn receive learning experiences and diplomas that increase their options for participating in the broader society.

Social psychologists concentrate their concerns on the social rules for regulating the distribution of costs and rewards in exchange relationships. The rules of exchange are important for the orderliness of social relationships because they impose limits on the extent to which any given individual may seek to maximize his or her gains at the expense of others (Black, Weinstein, and Tanur, 1974). Notions of fair play and the rules of the game require that the interacting parties arrive at an agreement on the relative worth of the valuables exchanged. People try to get out of an exchange what they feel that they deserve (Cook, 1975), and this reflects ideas about fairness and justice.

The process of social exchange is facilitated by individuals making selections among the opportunities available. In any given case, for example, a person's decision may consist of whether to continue his or her formal education or to terminate it, whether to marry or to remain single, whether to become a parent or to remain childless. Since time, energies, and resources are always limited, we must necessarily choose and make decisions (Heath, 1976), and we usually do so in terms of what we perceive as being in our own best interest. For this reason the assessments that enter into exchange transactions consist of weighing the potential costs and benefits of the options available to us.

The study of exchange relationships should enable us to clarify for ourselves an overall view of human nature. Are people in general rational or irrational, selfish or socially considerate, pleasure-seeking or self-sacrificing? These

Subjective Values
Spinning wheels, oaken buckets, and wooden cages have little value as everyday objects in the modern world; yet the price tags placed on them in antique shows indicate that they have considerable value to collectors and to those who wish to remember the past.

are, of course, fundamental questions that we cannot fully resolve through scientific investigation because of the high degree of variability in the conditions and the content of social action (Abrahamsson, 1970). Yet the conclusions we reach on these issues do have important implications for us in terms of our orientations toward people in general and toward individuals with whom we interact on a daily basis.

A. DECISION MAKING

Peter Singelmann (1972) observes that studies of exchange relationships are oriented toward general explanations of why individuals behave as they do in given social situations. These studies assume that individuals tend to act rationally, and regard social interactions as offering mutually rewarding outcomes for the parties involved. Individual behavior is directed toward making decisions and selecting lines of action that the actor regards as offering profitable outcomes or rewards. Selecting friends, preparing for a given career, and getting married are each instances of choices that involve making current investments in anticipation of some future payoff.

The primary limitations to the assumption of human rationality are found in the constraints and competing demands that are placed on us in given situations. We are often not able to act rationally in terms of our own self-interests because of the incompleteness of our knowledge about the options available. We sometimes have difficulties in making decisions, or we fail to make decisions altogether, because of our feeling of uncertainty. In such instances we experience the course of social life as following a pattern of drift, in which we deliberately and intentionally do not make decisions. Rather, we view social outcomes as happenings, chance occurrences, or as the workings of fate.

1. Rational Choice

Many of the basic assumptions in the study of exchange relationships have been clarified in the writings of George Homans (1961; 1974), Peter Blau (1964), and John Thibaut and Harold Kelley (1967). These assumptions derive from a utilitarian style of thought and reflect variations on the basic themes of egoism, hedonism, and rationality. Exchange theorists generally regard some variation on these three interrelated themes as the basis on which social actors evaluate alternatives and make decisions.

The conception of **egoism** holds that individual actions are shaped by self-interests as these interests are perceived by the interacting individual. In its purest form the notion of self-interest holds that individuals tend to make decisions in anticipation of receiving benefits of greater utility than the costs they will incur in attaining those benefits (Michener, Cohen, and Sorensen, 1977). This means that the selection of a particular line of action is based on a favorable assessment of the potential rewards relative to the perceived costs. The selection of goals, and of the means used in their pursuit, exchange theorists look on as being motivated by the pursuit of self-interests.

This assumption is reflected in the following observation by Gerhard Lenski (1966: 30) on the likely outcome of any given choice between promoting private interests and those of one's community.

...When men are confronted with important decisions where they are obligated to choose between their own or their group's interests and the interests of others, they nearly always choose the former.

Hence the egoistic assumption asserts that a great deal of human behavior can be explained by the simple idea that individuals act on the basis of what they perceive as their own self-interests. Altruism (helping behavior) is more likely to occur when the need of those being helped is great and the cost to the donor is very little (Black, Weinstein, and Tanur, 1974). Even with altruism the generosity may bring a personal payoff to the donor in terms of increased prestige and self-esteem.

The related conception of **hedonism** emphasizes the importance of

---

TABLE 9.2
The Relative Value of Children

Advantages of children are:

Having a real family life.
Having a source of affection and love.
Adding something exciting to my life.
Gaining a sense of personal accomplishment.
Establishing myself as a mature person.
Having someone to carry on a part of me.

Disadvantages of children are:

Having children requires a drastic change in lifestyle.
The responsibilities of child care take up too much time.
Children cause too much disorder in the household.
Having children contributes to the population problem.
Children cause too much worry and tension.

Are children more important than:

Having extra money to spend, save, or invest?
Having extra time for leisure activities?
Freedom from child-care responsibilities?
Coming and going as I wish?
The wife's opportunity to work full-time?
Having a neat and orderly household?
Being alone with my spouse?

These perceptions of the advantages, disadvantages, and relative value of children are taken into account by many couples in arriving at decisions on the desired family size. Are the above considerations important in shaping your own attitudes toward the desirability or undesirability of becoming a parent? What has been left out of this list?

Source: Arthur G. Neal, H. Theodore Groat, and Jerry W. Wicks, *Family Formation and Fertility Control in the Early Years of Marriage,* Bethesda, Md.: Center for Population Research, 1981.

rewards, benefits, or pleasures as the major considerations in the pursuit of goals. The quest for any specific set of benefits, however, is limited by the anticipated costs, sacrifices, displeasures, or stresses likely to accompany its attainment (Abrahamsson, 1970). According to Homans (1974), the vigor with which an individual pursues a course of action is based on the magnitude of the potential reward relative to the anticipated cost. Again, exchange theorists look on the ratio of benefits to costs as the key explanatory variable in back of the individual's decision making in any given case. Further, the hedonistic view holds that humans have an insatiable desire for goods and services, and the more they have the more they want. As a consequence exchange theorists view the level of human aspiration as always soaring above what is actually attainable at any given time.

The third primary conception of general theories of exchange is that of **rationality**. If humans are motivated by self-interests and by the pleasure principle, then rational decision making is the process by which these underlying concerns are linked with a specific course of action. When we speak of rationality, three sets of issues are implicated. These include the selection of a goal, the development of means for implementing a goal, and a concern for the consequences that are likely to follow from the pursuit of a goal. Rationality in goal selection requires that the individual evaluate the alternative courses of action and that the specific decision be the most appropriate one for the individual in terms of his or her values and circumstances. The means employed in social action are rational insofar as they are efficient in producing the desired results. Rationality in assessing the consequences of a course of action requires anticipating not only the desired outcomes but also any potential side effects that may be implicit in goal attainment. (See Table 9.2.)

The assumptions about human rationality are generally useful ones for thinking about a great deal of behavior, but such assumptions also need qualification. People do make serious mistakes; they blunder into choices that are not in their best interests. Decisions that seem rational to a social actor may appear nonrational to an outside observer. Plans frequently do not work out as expected, and often there is a failure to act when action is necessary. Because of the complications of human choices, many social psychologists are concerned with the conditions that interfere with human rationality.

2. Obstacles to Rationality

Among social psychologists, the emphasis on social choices and decision making often results in some degree of ambivalence about the overall prospects for the human condition. On the one hand the possibility for making choices implies conditions of human freedom (Hillery, Dudley, and Morrow, 1977) and suggests that people shape their personal destinies through the kinds of decisions they make (Glidewell, 1970). On the other hand there are numerous unintended consequences that often result from the lines of action people follow. We may think of the difficulties in decision making and the unplanned consequences of human action as constituting a series of obstacles to rationality.

One of the primary obstacles to rationality derives from the **incompleteness of knowledge** about the options available in any given situation (Heath, 1976). Humans are encapsulated in the sense that their development of conceptions of self and society provides them with an identity as to who

Environmental Pollution
Few people deliberately intend to deface the natural environment, but the improper disposal of trash frequently has that effect. The solution of one problem (in this case, getting rid of one's own garbage) may result in the creation of additional problems of an even greater magnitude.

they are, where they are located, and what options are available to them. Such forms of social learning provide the individual with the only world he or she knows at any given time, and often this does not correspond very well with the objective environment as others know and understand it.

A second obstacle to rationality derives from the **inherent uncertainty** built in to the human condition. Rational action is always limited to the information that is available, and what we often thought of as a rational course of action may more nearly consist of "backing into" the future because of the side effects of what we do. For example, collectively we have recognized the advantages of industrial development, and the benefits we have received in the way of goods and services have been very great indeed. Habermas (1971) observes that prior to the industrialization of the past 300 years, no known society of the entire world ever achieved a standard of living equivalent to a per capita income of $200 per year. But the developments that provided an overall increase in the standards of living were also accompanied by increased pollution of the environment and by a rapid depletion of fossil energy resources.

What is happening in the way of unintended byproducts of group behavior in industrialized societies we may look on as being analogous to the decision-making process at the individual level. Such crucial life decisions as continuing one's education, getting married, having a particular career, or becoming a parent are often made on the basis of inadequate information and on the basis of chance occurrences (Groat and Neal, 1975). As a consequence, individuals often select and pursue goals with a relatively low level of confidence that they are appropriate or that the outcomes can be clearly envisioned at the outset. Thus a process of social drift is operative to some degree in the life plans of individuals; we may regard this as deriving from environmental changes that the individual neither intended nor anticipated.

More importantly, we need to temper the pursuit of our self-interests by recognizing that attaining our more important goals is dependent on the quality of our relationships with others. This basic fact of the human condition places primary emphasis on the negotiable aspects of the goals we pursue and on the means we employ in their attainment. While we may have mastery over our own aspirations and intentions, our actual goal attainment is often dependent on our relationships with those who have control over the resources we desire.

Our pursuit of self-interests in any specific exchange relationship is conditioned by our conceptions of how social life is usually organized. These assumptions about the organization of social life permit us as individuals to have some leeway in deciding on the relative worth of the goals being pursued. These assumptions also provide guidelines for determining the steps necessary for attaining the goals and for assessing the consequences likely to follow from embarking on one course of action compared to another (Meeker, 1971). In effect, the perceptions of our social environment include a set of attitudes about the limitations and prospects that are available in given kinds of situations.

While the assumptions of everyday life constitute the social backgrounds for entering into exchange relationships, the transactions themselves deal with emerging forms of social reality. Our own assumptions and interests are not fully congruent with those that others hold (Blumstein, 1975). As a result, exchange situations are shaped by role taking and by alignment of the self and others for constructing a shared reality. In an exchange relationship each individual has control over resources, services, or events that have some degree of value to others. Transactions proceed by negotiating realities in the allocation of resources and services and in the transfer of valuables (Michener, Cohen, and Sorensen, 1977).

B. RULES OF SOCIAL EXCHANGE

One of the major rules of exchange relations relates to the equivalent values of the resources and services being traded. This is particularly the case with non-

---

BOX 9.1
Money as a Social Construction of Reality

In his classical writings, Georg Simmel emphasized the importance of money for exchange relationships. Money does not have an "intrinsic" value of its own. As a matter of fact, if it weren't for its value in exchange relationships, money would verge on being worthless for most of us. Yet as a socially constructed form of reality, money frequently becomes very important to most of us because we work to get it, and once we have it we may exchange it for a wide variety of goods and services.

Imagine the difficulties in getting stereos, television sets, radios, refrigerators, automobiles, and telephones if we had to obtain them without the use of money. Without money as a common denominator of value, exchange relationships would be based necessarily on a system of barter. A great deal of time and effort would be necessary to establish the equivalency between the goods and services offered and those received. Having money as a common denominator of value facilitates exchange relationships among strangers and symbolizes many of the qualities of interactions in urban areas. These qualities include social interactions of short duration, impersonality, and a rational calculation of self-interests.

Agreement on the use of money as a medium of exchange permits reducing objects and services that are qualitatively different to a common quantitative basis. The question How much does it cost? can be applied to such unrelated activities as attending a rock concert, enrolling in college, buying a car, raising a child, or taking a trip to Las Vegas. The availability and use of money thus permits rational calculations of the potential costs and benefits we can derive from social relationships.

Source: Georg Simmel, *The Philosophy of Money* (trans. by Tom Bottomore and David Frisby), Boston: Routledge & Kegan Paul, 1978.

exploitative relationships that are expected to continue over an extended period of time. The problem is essentially to establish some degree of balance among the benefits one bestows on another and the rewards one gets in return (Meeker, 1971). Since qualitatively different resources are available for exchange in most social relationships, the problem of equivalency cannot be settled by reducing all benefits to a common standard of value.

In purely economic relationships money serves as the common medium of exchange, and all qualitatively different values may be assessed through the pricing mechanism of buying and selling. Among the primary questions for the buyer in the marketplace are, What is the use to me of that which is being sold? and, How much does it cost? But in most social relationships, especially those that are intimate in character, such a monetary basis for evaluating the benefits given and received is not available. As a consequence the interaction process is essentially one of negotiating the relative merits of what is available for exchange. (See Box 9.1.)

1. The Norm of Reciprocity

Alvin Gouldner (1960) clarified the notion of equivalency in exchange relationships by developing the concept of the **norm of reciprocity**. It involves two basic moral principles: first, that people incur an obligation to help those who have previously helped them, and secondly, that an individual becomes morally bound not to harm a person who has previously bestowed a favor on him or her.

The manner and timing of the repayment of a favor varies from one society to another. In some cultures the fulfillment of all obligations to another person may be regarded as an insult; it is often taken to mean that the individual who does this to another person wishes to terminate the relationship. Instead of establishing direct equivalency in such intimate relationships as friendship or a love affair, the benefits bestowed on another are regarded as an investment that may have payoffs at some future time. Gouldner (1960) illustrated this principle by drawing on the *compadre* system of the Philippines in which ritual kinship bonds form among close friends. The bonds of the *compadre* relationship require giving and receiving help from one's friend when it is needed. For example, if a man pays for the doctor bill of his friend who is having financial troubles, his friend may later be obligated to return the favor by assisting the former's son in getting a job in the government. Thus the benefits exchanged may be qualitatively different, but should be roughly equivalent in value to those who are engaged in social interaction.

Following the norm of reciprocity, we can see that the obligations incurred in a social relationship are commensurate with the level of benefits previously received. The value of the benefits is in part dependent on the conditions under which they were received. One of these conditions is the status of the donor relative to that of the recipient (Komorita and Brinberg, 1977). The subjective value of the benefit, and hence the amount of the debt incurred, are in part a function of the needs of the recipient at the time the benefit was received, and in part a function of the abundance of the resources of the donor. Being helped by a friend in time of need, giving more than one can afford, or voluntarily bestowing a favor on another when it is not required are instances of the conditions of exchange relationships that intensify obligations beyond the actual value of the goods or services being exchanged.

As a corollary to the principle of equivalency, the second component of the norm of reciprocity holds that one who has received a favor from another person is obligated not to cause harm or injury to that other person. In our society this particular norm often comes to be associated with a conflict of interests. We may note, for example, that in the case of the police officer the informal norm of reciprocity may conflict with the formal requirements of the job. If an officer observes a close friend violating a traffic regulation, he or she may be undecided about what to do under the circumstances. If the officer gives the friend a ticket in pretty much the same fashion as he or she would give a ticket to anyone else, this would violate the norm of reciprocity which is binding in their relationship. If the police officer does not give a ticket, however, he or she has violated the oath of office to enforce the law in an impartial manner.

The emphasis in our society on a universal system of justice, which in theory applies equally to everyone, produces more in the way of conflict for office holders than is the case in many of the more traditional societies in which favoritism is accepted as the normal course of governmental operations. But according to Gouldner the norm of reciprocity is universal: it is implicit in all social relationships and hence a basic principle of help giving and morality in all social systems.

The obligation to return a favor for previous benefits received has two basic consequences for social relationships. First, the norm of reciprocity has a stabilizing function since it tends to promote mutual support through the favors one bestows on others and through the rewards one receives in return. Second, the norm of reciprocity serves as a buffer against sheer exploitation and the pursuit of self-interests in its extreme form (Johnson and Allen, 1972). The quest for the enhancement of self-interests at the expense of others either promotes a hovering cloud of indebtedness that requires future repayment or it has an inhibiting effect on the subsequent social supports one may receive from others. (See Box 9.2.)

The binding properties of the norm of reciprocity are clearly evident in trade relationships, where buying and selling or borrowing and repaying are used on establishing an acceptable equivalence of the objects or services exchanged. For example, in obtaining a loan from a bank, one enters into a contract that clearly specifies how and when to repay the borrowed money and at what rate of interest. There are no obligations to the lending institution other

BOX 9.2
Refusal of the Elderly to Accept Help

Why do many of the elderly fail to take advantage of programs and services designed to help them? To obtain answers to this question Elizabeth Moen conducted a series of interviews with both potential clients and service personnel. Her findings indicate that the elderly have their own definitions of personal need and the acceptability of social services.

Many of the elderly in her study denied the existence of needs that were apparent to service workers. These elderly refused to take advantage of available services because of their emphasis on remaining independent and self-sufficient. Some were not knowledgeable about services for the aged and did not want to become involved in the bureaucratic hassles necessary for obtaining what they perceived as meager benefits.

Many of those reluctant to accept services were living below the poverty level but refused to accept an official designation of having "poverty status." They found services to be acceptable if made available on the basis of age, rather than poverty status. Moen's findings (1978: 296) suggest that many of the elderly are "super proud," "do not want to admit that they are poor, do not want to be thought of as poor, and do not want to be associated with poverty programs." Many refused to accept services because they had negative images of "unworthy chislers." They had a strong disdain for those who take advantage of welfare by cheating to gain access to benefits that were undeserved and not actually needed. They generally regarded Social Security as being acceptable, since it is based on benefits earned through previous payments into the system. Unearned benefits, however, they regarded as being unacceptable.

Source: Elizabeth Moen, "The Reluctance of the Elderly to Accept Help," *Social Problems* 25 (February, 1978): 293–303.

than those formally stated in the contract, and there is no presumption of a continuing relationship beyond the terms of the transaction itself. Both parties enter into the agreement voluntarily and there is mutual understanding on the equity of the payoffs from the transaction.

2. Prosocial Behavior

The obligations incurred in a social exchange, by way of contrast, differ in several important respects from those that are purely economic in character. The nature of the indebtedness in receiving a favor from a parent or a friend remains ambiguous since the action has no basis for determining value directly equivalent to money. Expressions of approval, respect, and emotional support cannot be calculated precisely in monetary terms, but may be no less valuable to the individual than the goods and services that have a specified price in the marketplace.

The term **prosocial behavior** is used to encompass the positive forms of social behavior and is applied to helping or donating under circumstances in which the individual gives up more than he or she can reasonably expect to receive in return. The norm of reciprocity is not expected to operate through a direct equivalency of tradeable objects and services. Instead, "the milk of human kindness" prevails, and more is voluntarily given than is expected in return. Prosocial behavior is altruistic in the sense that the concern is with helping others, with reducing levels of human misery, and with being of service to those in need (Wispe, 1972). Helping behavior is sufficiently frequent that the view of human nature as selfish needs serious qualification.

The research of Carol B. Stack (1974) on an urban, black neighborhood indicates the importance of social attachments and kinship networks as systems of mutual aid. Under conditions in which economic resources are greatly limited or undependable, help is needed from many sources. The kinship networks established with parents, siblings, in-laws, and former in-laws provide a large number of people to draw on during times of trouble. When people lose jobs, when their marriages break up, or when they need care for their children, there are many people available for help. The grandmother frequently takes care of the children while the mother works; parents who are having money problems may receive help from a daughter on welfare; or women may call on former husbands for help when it is seriously needed.

The social exchanges within urban, black neighborhoods are based on strong social attachments, some of which are stable and some of which are not. The initial bonds with parents and siblings tend to be enduring, and these ties are reinforced through the positive values that are placed on having and caring for children. The attachments to lovers, both in and out of marriage, frequently fail to endure. The economic basis for stable relationships frequently is lacking. The welfare check (Aid for Dependent Children) is often more dependable than the husband's earnings. The maternal grandmother is particularly important as a source of stability and social support. Both males and females retain strong attachments to maternally based households, and having children greatly increases the number of households from which help can be obtained.

In the neighborhood that Stack (1974) studied, the giving of help to those in need was promoted by the norm of social responsibility. The **norm of social responsibility** refers to the obligation to provide sympathy and aid to those in need without regard for reciprocity or some equivalent benefit in return. Ervin Staub (1972: 140) suggests, however, that the norm of responsibility has its origins in "the extension of a reciprocal exchange network to all members of the social group." By providing help to persons too old, too sick, or too young to help themselves, the individual can expect to be helped by others if the need arises. If so, social networks are important as systems of mutual aid, and through helping others one's own sense of security is increased.

In effect, helping others is an investment in human capital and provides assurance that help for oneself would be forthcoming "if the chips were down."

3. Gift Giving

The norms of both reciprocity and social responsibility operate directly in the transactions involved in gift giving. In most societies the gift is looked on as a voluntary transfer of property rights without the giver receiving compensation in return. The rewards in gift giving are based primarily on the donor's intrinsic satisfaction of eliciting approval and respect, and in anticipating the gratifications the gift will provide for the recipient. In our society the giving of gifts is regarded as an irrevocable transfer of ownership, and there are no legal requirements of reciprocity. Thus the basis for gift giving must be examined as deriving from motives and functions other than those involving purely economic interests.

While gift giving may be an unsound procedure on economic grounds, the functions it serves for reinforcing social relationships are very important. Gift giving is symbolic of mutual interdependency; the transfer of ownership is a token of social unity and solidarity. This is evident in what Marcel Mauss (1954) described as the obligation to give, the obligation to receive, and the obligation to repay. In accepting a dinner invitation from a friend, for example, we are necessarily incurring an obligation to reciprocate in some way or other, but the manner of repayment is not open for negotiation. We would look on it

TABLE 9.3
Social Psychological Aspects of Gift Giving

Reinforcing social relationships:	Showing that you care Keeping in touch Expressing gratitude Enhancing intimacy Promoting continuity
Producing an obligation:	Seeking a later payoff Building up social capital Investing in future relationships Asserting control over others Obtaining social security
Redistributing the wealth:	Displaying generosity Helping those in need Contributing to the common good Gaining prestige Demonstrating social worth

as strange behavior indeed if we attempted to negotiate with a friend on the kind of favor expected in return for the dinner invitation. But the individual who repeatedly fails to reciprocate with generosity of some form or another will eventually find himself or herself without either a dinner invitation or a friend (Blau, 1964).

Benefits that are freely offered to others produce an obligation to accept or to receive. If a gift is refused, the refusal may very well constitute an insult. The gift is a way the donor has of implicitly saying, "You are an important person to me," and "I value the relationship I have with you." The refusal of a gift under these circumstances becomes a delicate issue and may provide the basis for producing serious stress in a social relationship. (See Table 9.3.)

The occasions on which gifts are given in our society are primarily ceremonial in character, such as commemorating a birthday, a graduation, a marriage, the birth of a child; assuming an office; or celebrating a holiday. The motives for gift giving on these occasions are oriented not so much toward redistributing the wealth as toward reinforcing social relationships. There are numerous ceremonial occasions that are designed for reasserting social ties, but the celebrations of Mother's Day and Father's Day stand out as special reflections of this function.

Mother's Day and Father's Day have come to be institutionalized as occasions for adults to interrupt their usual activities and to reflect on the many unfulfilled obligations to their parents. In our highly mobile society those people who have become geographically and socially separate from their initial family unit feel some degree of guilt toward their parents. Earlier in American history the obligations of adult children were repaid through providing financial and emotional support for their aged parents. With the high degree of mobility in modern society, the elderly have become increasingly isolated and lacking in attachments to continuous kin relationships (Gordon, 1976). As a result many adult children endure to some degree a sense of guilt about unpaid social and financial debts to their parents.

While the giving of a gift may be motivated by the reward of self-gratification for the giver, the gift may also be effectively used as a means of social control and to manipulate others. Despite the lack of legal support the norm of reciprocity is one of the major components of gift giving as a process. The person who accepts a gift from another becomes bound to the relationship through the obligation to reciprocate and through the implied agreement to refrain from causing harm to the giver. Such attributes of the gift as generosity in giving, the expression of gratitude in receiving, and the creation of a social debt tend to promote solidarity and a sense of continuity in social relationships.

Although gift giving generally serves to strengthen social ties, it may under certain circumstances serve to clarify the differentials in the status of the parties involved. The potlatch ceremony among the Kwakiutl Indians of the American Pacific Northwest clearly illustrates the importance of socioeconomic concerns in the gift-giving process. The **potlatch** was a formal ceremony in which a ritual display of wealth was demonstrated through its

BOX 9.3
The Christmas Potlatch

Christmas is celebrated in our society as both "a holy day" and "a holiday." For some Christmas is primarily a sacred occasion; for others it is a vacation, time off from work, or relief from the performance of everyday tasks; for still others it represents a major opportunity for commercial ventures and profit making. The prevailing images, however, are those related to gift exchanges and the renewals of social ties. The scope and intensity of gift exchanges led Gregory J. Moschetti to describe the celebration of Christmas as a "gigantic potlatch."

The potlatch character of Christmas is reflected in the inequalities that occur in the exchange of gifts. Moschetti described several forms of exchange as "asymmetrical," in that the value of what is given is disproportionate to what is received in return. Such inequalities of gift exchanges grow out of everyday interactions among those who differ in status, power, and control over desired resources. For example, employers give employees gifts of greater value than those they receive in return, and parents give gifts to their children that are more expensive than those children give their parents. Service workers, such as those who perform secretarial services or those who deliver newspapers or the mail, receive gifts without being expected to give gifts in return.

In these cases the giving of gifts conveys symbolic messages that go beyond the reinforcement of social ties and the expression of gratitude. It also gives symbolic expression and meaning to status differentials. Donors display power, wealth, and prestige, while recipients are relegated to a subordinate and dependent status. In this light, we may understand Christmas as a ceremonial occasion for demonstrating superior social status, for confirming everyday patterns of deference, and for eliciting expressions of gratitude and respect.

Source: Gregory J. Moschetti, "The Christmas Potlatch," *Sociological Focus* 12 (January, 1979): 1–7.

destruction and through generously bestowing gifts on rivals to gain status. By giving more valued objects than the recipient could give in return was a way of shaming the recipient into a subordinate status and at the same time verifying the superiority of the giver. The giving of gifts that cannot possibly be repaid serves to relegate the recipient to a position of indebtedness in terms of deference, respect, and gratitude (Blau, 1964). (See Box 9.3.)

C. COERCION AND CONTROL

Generosity in the display of wealth may very well serve as a means of forcing others into submission. In the potlatch, as well as in many other exchanges, the dividing line between social behavior and exploitation becomes very thin.

Sociability often constitutes an outward facade for concealing serious conflicts that may be implicit in a relationship. The appearance of being friendly
or of expressing concern for the well-being of another person may be an outward disguise for a hidden interest in manipulation (Christie and Geis, 1970).
We are somewhat prone to recognize the insincerity of the friendliness of a
salesperson, while the more subtle persuasions in the relationships with an
employer, a teacher, a parent, or a spouse are not so clearly evident. Yet in the
latter cases the potential for the manipulative attitude is always present. While
we may ignore the salesperson, individuals in a dependency position recognize
the potential costs of failing to comply with what is minimally expected by
those who have the advantage in control over desired resources.

1. Power Dependency

The dependency of one individual on another is shaped by the degree to which
one person seeks access to goals that are controlled by another. Richard Emerson (1962) has described **power dependency** as an outgrowth of the ties
of mutual dependence among parties in an exchange relationship. The degree of
control is greatest when access to the desired goal is not available from any
other source and when the desire for attaining the goal is strong. For example, a
high level of dependency occurs in a dyadic (two person) relationship in which
one person desires a reward under the control of the other one and the desired
reward cannot be obtained outside the relationship with that specific person.
This may occur in an intense love affair in which the desired rewards are presumed not to be available from any other source. As a result the person who is
less committed to the relationship may have a great deal of control over the
behavior of the person who has the strongest attachment.

From a social psychological standpoint, the major attribute of power is a
sense of mastery over the events in which one engages. This involves having
control over desired resources and access to the variety of means regarded as
necessary in attaining valued goals (Rogers, 1974). But an individual's personal
experience with the exercise of power is likely to be accompanied by someone
else's responses to being controlled. The essential test of power is to see whose
will prevails under conditions of resistance. If a person is dependent on another
for friendship and respect, for example, he or she may be influenced by the
other person to engage in a criminal act which under ordinary circumstances
he or she would resist. If college students are dependent on their parents for
financial support, then parents have a basis for continuing to assert some control over the conduct of their sons and daughters. Thus dependency provides
the grounds for having a person's behavior be controlled by others (Emerson,
1962). (See Figure 9.1.)

As a consequence of the occupational specialization that has developed
in modern society, one of the more prominent forms of dependency is of the

individual on the services provided by the expert. The power of the expert resides in the ability to provide clients with rewards of a type that would be prohibitively expensive if the client had to derive them exclusively from his or her own resources. Most of us could not in the course of a lifetime develop competency in very many of the specialized forms of knowledge that are important for our own senses of well-being. As a result an important part of the background learning for involvement in exchange relationships is grasping the basic rules for drawing on and utilizing the services of experts (Bacharach and Lawler, 1976). (See Box 9.4.)

Dependency on the specialized resources of the expert places the client in a somewhat vulnerable position, in part because such relationships are based on an implied contract which may not be honored and in part because there is a lack of social ties beyond the specific transaction (Piven and Cloward, 1971). In negotiating for the services of a repair person, an automobile mechanic, a lawyer, or a physician, we necessarily assume that the expert is indeed competent and specialized in the task to be performed (Richardson *et al.*, 1973) and that the cost of the service will be reasonable. Dependency on the expert is based on the need for the services to be performed and on the extent to which

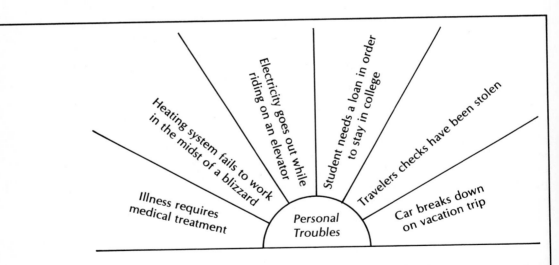

Power dependency becomes evident when we are faced with an emergency that requires obtaining help from others. The above are examples of situations that have the potential for developing into serious crises, especially if those people having control over desired resources are unable or unwilling to make them available to us.

FIGURE 9.1
Situations of Power Dependency

BOX 9.4
Waiting Time and Expert Power

According to Schwartz (1974), power entails among other things the capacity to require waiting time of those who desire to receive a scarce resource. Those with expert power possess skills that are in short supply, and clients who are in need of them are in a dependency relationship. Clients usually show their deference to the power holding by expressing a willingness to wait, not only in getting an appointment but also during the time scheduled for the appointment itself. Many physicians, for example, will sometimes schedule more than one appointment at the same time, or several appointments in close succession, in order to have an assurance that no idle time will result from the failure of a patient to show. The expert may enhance his or her own status by deliberately causing those who are dependent on him or her to wait in obtaining services.

The discomfort of being required to wait not only stems from a nonproductive use of time and energies, but also from the implication that the waiting person's own time is of less value than that of the person who requires the waiting. The waiting time reflects the waiter's subordination, and the delay reminds the waiter of his or her own insignificance as compared to the person for whom he or she waits. On the other hand, Schwartz notes that those who confront obstacles to obtaining services tend to place a greater value on them once they have received those services. Thus requiring clients to wait verifies the superiority of the expert and increases the subjective worth of the service received.

Source: Barry Schwartz, "Waiting, Exchange, and Power: The Distribution of Time in Social Systems," *American Journal of Sociology* 79 (January, 1974): 841–870.

---

alternatives to these specific services are available. We depend on the specialist because the perceived benefits exceed the perceived costs, and this is contingent on attitudes of mutual trust and the effectiveness of social norms in limiting the degree of exploitation.

2. Exploitation

In their social interactions, individuals who expect to continue their relationship over an extended period of time tend to place emphasis not so much on maximizing personal gain as on receiving benefits regarded as fair and just. Meeker (1971: 487) noted that "people try to get out of an exchange what they think they deserve on the basis of what they have put into it." The observation by Meeker expresses the idea of **distributive justice**, formulated by Homans (1961) and Blau (1964) as the principle that rewards in exchange relationships be allocated proportionate to the costs and investments of the inter-

BOX 9.5
Who Believes in a Just World?

In developing a scale for measuring belief in "a just world," Rubin and Peplau (1975) have clarified some of the contradictions in folk beliefs about social justice. One position holds that the world is essentially a just place in which people get what they deserve out of life. Such a notion of social justice is reflected in the views that students deserve the grades they get in school, people who do their jobs well will rise up to the top, and men who exercise will reduce their chances of suffering a heart attack. In similar fashion, the belief in a just world also holds that people bring misfortunes on themselves, that the punishment children get is almost always for good reason, and that it is rare for the innocent to be wrongly sent to jail.

By way of contrast, others are inclined to see high levels of social injustice in human affairs. From this vantage point many people suffer through no fault of their own, careful drivers are as likely as anyone else to get hurt in traffic accidents, honest political candidates rarely get elected, and the guilty frequently get off free in American courts. The beliefs in a just or unjust world represent overall views of social life, and frequently lead to making judgments on the basis of incomplete information.

Research on college students suggest that belief in a just world is associated with negative attitudes toward underprivileged groups, a tendency to derogate victims even when there is no evidence that the victim was responsible, and admiration for political leaders and social institutions. On the other hand, those who reject the view of a just world tend to be more suspicious and distrustful in their relationships with others, particularly with those in positions of authority.

Source: Zick Rubin and Letitia Anne Peplau, "Who Believes in a Just World?," *Journal of Social Issues* 31, no. 3 (1975): 65–89.

acting parties. Thus those who have invested the most in terms of talent and energies should receive a larger share of the benefits that are distributed (Parcel and Cook, 1977.) (See Box 9.5.)

Exploitation occurs in situations in which the demands made by those in positions of power exceed what is generally regarded as fair and just. Those in power may successfully make relatively heavy demands of others if they offer adequate compensations in return. Subordinates experience the relationship as exploitation only if the subordinates feel they are being forced to perform services for others without the prospects of receiving just or equitable payoffs. In exploitation the norm of reciprocity fails to operate, and the individual defines the situation as one in which he or she is required to give substantially more than he or she is receiving in return.

In terms of exchange theory, a part of the youthful resistance to the war in Vietnam may be understood as resentment of young people required to make a potentially extreme sacrifice for a cause they perceived as being unjust. Many viewed the demands for compliance as having insufficient payoffs for the costs that might be involved. In analyzing industrial capitalism, Marx regarded the exploitation of workers as stemming from their failure to receive a fair and equitable share of the benefits derived from their labor. Thus compliance with the demands made by an employer or by a government may be regarded as a form of exploitation if the individual perceives these demands as being unreasonable or as lacking in sufficient benefits to cover the personal costs incurred.

Even under conditions of exploitation, the voluntary element is usually present in some degree as it is in other forms of exchange relationships, since

---

BOX 9.6
Is Client Alienation Inevitable?

Frank Tripi takes issue with the notions that client alienation is an inevitable outcome of bureaucratic structures, such as welfare, medical, police, and prison bureaucracies. Concentrating on the welfare bureaucracy of a metropolitan area on the West Coast, Tripi found that clients who became organized were effective in exercising control in dealing with welfare officials. Tripi noted more favorable treatment of those who were members of a welfare rights' organization compared to those who weren't. His study indicated that less than 1 percent of welfare clients were members, but those who were had a stronger sense of personal mastery and destiny control.

Unaffiliated clients are passive and often unsuccessful in gaining their ends, and have almost no power in their encounter with local officials. Differently, affiliated clients are often successful in gaining their ends and have considerable power in their dealings with local officials (1974: 437–438).

Sources of destiny control by the organized were derived from their knowledge of welfare rules and regulations and from gaining access to higher officials when they could not solve their problems at a lower level. Their political approach permitted them to manipulate and reform welfare officials. The organized clients were less likely to be required to sit in waiting rooms for long periods of time, and because of their potential aggressiveness officials found it easier to give in to them than to go through a hassle. Thus the organization of clients is a major solution to the problems of client alienation (powerlessness). The unorganized, by way of contrast, often view officials as superiors who can either bestow or withhold benefits in an arbitrary manner.

Source: Frank Tripi, "The Inevitability of Client Alienation: A Counter Argument," *Sociological Quarterly* 15 (Summer, 1974): 432–441.

the employee could quit his or her job, the individual could emigrate to another country, the student could drop a course that a particular professor is offering, or the wife could sue her husband for a divorce. The capacity of one individual to assert control over another is always limited as long as the other is able to disaffiliate, or withdraw, from a particular relationship. In many cases, however, a person may not perceive disaffiliation as a feasible option if the minimal needs being fulfilled in the relationship are not regarded as being available from any other source. Changes in jobs, spouses, and citizenship are difficult for most people to make; as a result they make numerous other kinds of adaptations to exploitive relationships. (See Box 9.6.)

In industry the supervisor who makes excessive demands of the workers is very likely to encounter numerous forms of retaliation. While such a supervisor may get from workers a high level of performance in his or her presence, the level of productivity is likely to drop precipitously when the supervisor is away from the shop. If the supervisor encounters a special set of problems with higher levels of management, he or she may not be able to count on the cooperation of those he or she supervises for help. But more importantly, workers who feel exploited on the job may deliberately sabotage the work process. In the automobile industry, for example, workers on the assembly line have been known to seal a coke bottle, or a fellow worker's lunch, in the door of a new car. Such an undetected form of sabotage is one way of retaliating, a symbolic means of getting even, a form of justice for what is regarded as an unjust set of demands.

Blau (1964) observed that in many cases retaliation against oppressors may be more satisfying then continuing to secure meager rewards. The research on race relations during the late 1960s and early 1970s indicated that there was much more retaliation and resistance in the American system of slavery than had previously been reported (Graham and Gurr, 1969; Hofstadter and Wallace, 1970). The numerous instances of slave rebellions had not been emphasized as a major topic of concern prior to the racial disorders that erupted in American cities during the 1970s. The formation of pockets of resistance and the development of organizations for retaliation are potential responses of people who are exposed to what they perceive as conditions of exploitation.

Because of the capacities of subordinates to withhold their services and to retaliate in some form or another, the norm of reciprocity is usually operative in social relationships. The excessive use of force becomes a risky procedure for the holders of power, and it is generally one of the less efficient ways of obtaining assistance from others (Scott, 1976). Compliance by means of social approval and through the disbursement of rewards, if it can be achieved, becomes a much more efficient strategy because subordinates may more willingly supply the assistance desired. The excessive use of force tends to generate and solidify the opposition and to result in the formation of coalitions through which the exploited ban together to counteract the forcefulness of the power holder (Coleman, 1973).

On Strike
Organizing a strike may be regarded as necessary by workers who feel that they are treated unfairly by their employers (photo by Tom Shaffer).

D. DISTRIBUTIVE JUSTICE

The drama of social conflict frequently is enacted within the framework of social inequality in exchange transactions. Some people feel that they are entitled to more than they get. Others seem to want more no matter how much they have. In some situations people become indignant because their standards of justice fail to operate in the sharing of resources and in the exchange of tradeable valuables. Emotions such as anger, fear, and hostility sometimes surface as individuals interact in the pursuit of desired resources that are in short supply. The goals pursued by some often conflict with the goals pursued by others; in some cases the individual may maximize his or her own gains only at the expense of someone else.

1. Fairness Judgments

According to Gerhard Lenski (1966), the basic forms of social conflict stem from the uses of power and privilege in the allocation of scarce resources within a social system. Whatever the abundance of resources in a society, there is never enough to gratify all human needs and desires. As a result, conflict grows out of the process of determining who gets what, when, and how. Any society has a basic concern with the survival of its members; but after the survival needs have been met, the problem emerges of how to distribute the surplus resources. The resolution of this problem, according to Lenski, is determined by the outcome of power relationships. If humans are basically selfish and oriented toward promoting their own self-interests, then social surpluses are likely to go to those who are more influential and powerful.

The uneven distribution of wealth, income, privilege, and other valuables may be viewed as just if people feel that they are getting what they deserve on the basis of their efforts and contributions. A sense of injustice surfaces when the rewards received fall below the range of what the recipient expected. William Philliber and William Fox (1977: 375) have noted that the sense of discomfort with the allocation of rewards is in part dependent on the perceived total amount of the rewards available. They noted, for example, that "a union may make stronger demands for higher wages in years when a company's profits are up." Such demands are made on the assumption that the workers are entitled to a proportionate share of the returns derived from their labor.

Feelings of **relative deprivation** emerge when individuals think that they are not getting a fair share of the total resources available. These feelings may be based on the view that others who are less deserving are getting more. Thus people tend to judge their own circumstances by comparing their rewards with what they imagine to be the rewards and accomplishments of others. A sense of relative deprivation may not be based on objective facts, since people who are well-off in terms of meeting their basic needs for income, housing, food, and medical care may feel deprived if they think they are not sharing proportionately in the rewards available. The feelings of relative deprivation, therefore, reflect a gap between what people believe they should have and what they actually get. (See Box 9.7.)

Drawing on a sample of subjects from a major metropolitan area, Philliber and Fox (1977) found that the perception of available resources in American society is significantly related to socioeconomic status. Subjects with low family incomes tended to perceive high levels of affluence within the general population. For example, low-income subjects overestimated the percentage of people in the general population who could afford a luxury car, a built-in swimming pool, an expensive house, a major trip at least once a year, and membership in a country club. In comparison, subjects with higher levels of income tended to perceive significantly lower levels of affluence among Americans in general. The exaggeration of affluence by the poor constituted a denial that scarcity exists within the society at large. Such a judgment reflected their separation from the mainstream of social life, their own feelings of economic deprivation, and their perceived lack of opportunities for achieving major life goals through their own efforts.

BOX 9.7
Equity with the World

Equity with the world refers to the assessments made by individuals of the overall fairness of the rewards obtained from numerous social relationships within a given period of time. In some situations individuals may receive less than their fair share of the available benefits, while in other cases the rewards may be excessive. Equity with the world is achieved through seeking a balance between shortages and surpluses of rewards from the totality of one's social relationships.

Austin and Walster (1975) conducted research experiments to determine how people subsequently react to being treated unfairly in a situation. Unjust treatment may consist of either receiving more than one's share or receiving less. Austin and Walster's experiments were designed to determine how subjects who received unjust treatment in one situation responded to reward distributions in subsequent situations. In general the results indicate that people attempt to obtain or to restore equity with the world over time and across a series of social relationships.

Subjects who received excessive benefits (unjust rewards) in one situation attempted to establish equity with the world through a display of generosity to others in subsequent situations. Underrewarded subjects in the first experiment tended to take more than their fair share of the rewards in the next experiment. Thus individuals do not treat their various social relationships as isolated from each other but tend to seek a correction of previous inequities in subsequent encounters. Satisfaction with social relationships is greatest for those who perceive a correspondence between what they feel they deserve and what they actually get.

Source: William Austin and Elaine Walster, "Equity with the World," *Sociometry* 38 (December, 1975): 474–496.

Joan Rytina, William Form, and John Pease (1970) describe the major justifications for inequality as a set of beliefs about the personal qualities of individuals and the opportunities that are available within the social system. In American society the views of wealth as earned and deserved are based on the notion that a combination of hard work, ability, and initiative will be rewarded. It follows that the rich deserve to be rich because of their special qualities and the values of their contributions to society. From this view it also follows that the poor deserve to be poor because they are "lazy and shiftless," and because they "lack motivation." Although these ideas provide justifications for inequality, there is widespread disagreement about the extent to which differences in such attributes as income, prestige, and influence are in reality based on fairness and justice.

Several research studies have shown that the degree of fairness associated with social inequality varies with the position of the individual within the stratification system. The rich are more likely to believe that the existing

Fairness of Wealth and Poverty
Differences in wealth and poverty are reflected in residential patterns and in the qualities of housing. Private swimming pools, expensive houses, and luxury automobiles are among the symbols of high social status. Such symbols provide the basis for judgments about the American opportunity structure and the degree to which distributive justice prevails.

inequalities in the distribution of wealth are just, while the poor tend to view the rich as getting more than they deserve. Members of the middle class are in a pivotal position, and they are divided in their opinions about both the special privileges of the rich and the attributes of the poor.

Rytina, Form, and Pease (1970) conducted a survey in Muskegon, Michigan, and found substantial differences by income levels in beliefs about America as a land of opportunity. The rich were strong in their convictions that "there's plenty of opportunity," and "anyone who works hard can go as far as he or she wants," that "a college education is available for all young people of high ability," and that "the poor have as much of an opportunity as the rich to influence the governmental process." The rich also viewed those on relief as being unwilling to work and as lacking an interest in "getting ahead."

In a replication of the Muskegon study, Steve Stack (1978) discovered that substantial changes occurred in the beliefs about distributive justice between 1967 and 1977. During the ten-year period, community-wide beliefs about opportunity had moved in the direction of the views previously held by the poor. The majority of subjects rejected the view that the rich and the poor have equal opportunities for getting ahead. Both low-income and middle-income respondents were convinced that distributive justice does not prevail and that the rich are more likely to get ahead through scheming and shady deals than through hard work. The majority also rejected the traditional views that the impoverished are lazy and work less hard than the affluent. Members of labor unions held views similar to those of the poor about a gap between what is and what ought to be in the distribution of income and wealth.

Furthermore, the study gave no evidence to indicate support for giving increased benefits to the impoverished, although Stack found that members of the white middle-class majority increasingly shared the views of the poor about the immorality of the rich. Stack's findings suggest that the middle class frequently feels caught between two "parasitic" groups. They view the rich as getting more than they deserve, but they also feel that the government has done too much for the poor. In describing the position of the middle class, Stack presents a dual-enemy thesis. This thesis holds that during times of economic hardship, the middle class tends to develop negative attitudes toward the privileges of the rich as well as toward the welfare benefits of the poor. Members of the middle class who view the allocation of available resources on some basis other than merit thus experience a sense of relative deprivation.

2. Social Equality

The system of justice that prevails at any given time and place represents a major variable in the study of social conflict. The reason is that justice in the regulation of conflict is a problem that must be solved in social relationships at all levels of organization. In the family, the marketplace, the street corner gang, the political campaign, and in all social groups orderly social life is possible only because of the constraints that develop to prevent completely unregulated conflict from occurring. The basic control mechanisms in all social relationships are the shared conceptions of justice and fair play, which include the many aspects of what is understood as the operative codes and rules of conduct (Lerner, 1975).

For social justice to prevail, the shared rules of conduct must be applied impartially to all social groups. The notion of impartiality embraces the principles that equals are to be treated equally and that like cases are to be treated in a like manner. Using these universal principles, we may define **social justice** as the degree to which the general rules for regulating conduct are applied in a coherent and consistent manner to all social groups (Deutsch, 1975).

In the more highly industrialized societies of the West, the overriding rule for specifying equivalency is based on the concept of citizenship. Here the system of justice emphasizes that certain rights and privileges are to be applied universally to those accorded the status of citizen (Groat, 1976). Equivalency in the rights of citizenship is based on the notion that individual differences by sex, religion, property, and national origin are irrelevant for determining the rights of access to various parts of the social system (Williams, 1970).

Nearly all segments of the population accept the principle that equal opportunity is desirable, but there have been substantial disagreements as to whether or not such equality does in fact exist (Rytina, Form, and Pease, 1970). There is often a disparity between abstract principles and the decisions made in specific situations. As noted by Ginsberg (1965), the principle that equals are to be treated equally does not in and of itself supply the basis for determining who is to be regarded as equal, nor does it supply the means by which to treat equals equally within a social group.

One may readily note inequalities among individuals in a wide variety of ways. People do differ in terms of such variables as wealth, income, power, physical beauty, or athletic ability, and such differences do have a bearing on the judgments about social desirability and worth (Rothman, 1978). However, some forms of inequality are more troublesome than others. In modern society, inequalities based on certain biological categories have engendered intense hostilities and resentments. These include the conflicts resulting from classifications along the lines of race, sex, and age.

All societies differentiate their members by placing individuals into categories. These categories are accompanied by social definitions of the attributes of the members, and these definitions have implications for social relationships. Many of these classifications are ascribed to individuals at birth. Among them are sex, race, and family of origin. Such placements are based on folk definitions of how boys differ from girls, how blacks differ from whites, how the rich differ from the poor, and how men differ from women. Notions about these differences surface in arguments about social justice and the qualifications of individuals for treatment as equals.

The patterns of dominance and subordination, which are implied in definitions of inequality, express the basic social fact that within social groups some members become subjected to coercion by others, and desired rewards are allocated on some basis other than merit (Burgess and Neilsen, 1974). The subordinate status of women derives from the assumption that women are inherently unequal to men in many ways. Yet the cultural elaborations on how men differ from women often bear little relationship to purely biological characteristics (Kriesberg, 1973). The male dominance of certain occupations, for example, is often based on notions that exaggerate the physical and temperamental differences of men and women.

Like the folk notions about sexual differences, ideas about racial differences are drawn on as a basis for denying equal access to socially desired rewards. Those who hold positions of power and privilege are often unwilling to give up voluntarily their special advantages, and this reluctance constitutes a source of conflict in social relationships (Duke, 1976). Bus boycotts, sit-in demonstrations, adversary court proceedings, urban looting, and other forms of social protest may be understood as a quest for justice on the part of those who feel that they are being treated unfairly (Dynes and Quarantelli, 1968).

The tests for clarity, consistency, and coherence in the application of the general rules of justice are not self-evident, nor do they emerge on an automatic basis. Instead, there is a political and negotiable dimension to the process of justice that requires establishing the rules that will be applied in any given case and the evidence that will be admissible. The political concerns include the questions of how decisions are to be made and who has the right to decide. Answering these questions often involves controversy, but is crucial nevertheless for the resolution of conflict and the attainment of social justice (Deutsch, 1975).

SUMMARY

Studies of exchange relationships proceed from the assumptions that social transactions are based on the pursuit of self-interests, that humans are pleasure-oriented in seeking to maximize their benefits and to reduce their costs, and that behavior may be looked on as reflecting rationality as the individual actor defines it. These assumptions are potentially useful for applying to a wide range of social behavior, but they need to be qualified by the many social constraints that are placed on individuals. Obstacles to rationality include the incomplete knowledge about the options available and the inherent uncertainties that are built in to the human condition. The pursuit of self-interests is tempered through recognizing that the attainment of important goals is dependent on the qualities of social relationships.

One of the universal rules of social exchange pertains to establishing the equivalency in value of the objects and benefits being traded. The norm of reciprocity holds that in an ongoing social relationship the receiving of a benefit from another produces an obligation to return some equivalent benefit at some time in the future. From this it then follows that gift giving is a way of both reinforcing social relationships and producing an obligation on the part of the recipient. Under the conditions of exploitation, by way of contrast, one or more of the parties to a transaction believe that the norm of reciprocity fails to operate. Under these conditions they develop a variety of techniques for coping with what they perceive as unjust costs and demands.

The concept of prosocial behavior encompasses the positive forms of social behavior. It refers to helping or donating under circumstances in which the individual gives more than he or she can reasonably expect to receive in return. The guiding rule is the norm of social responsibility, which holds that the members of a social group are obligated to provide help to those in need, especially to those who are too old, too young, or too sick to help themselves. Social attachments and kinship networks are important as systems of mutual aid, providing a large number of people for the individual to draw on in times of trouble. The scope of helping behavior is sufficiently great that the views of human nature as being egoistic or selfish need serious qualification.

Engagement in exchange relationships is necessary where there is unequal distribution of resources. Those who have control over desired resources have "the upper hand" and are in a privileged position in the bargaining process. Conditions of power dependency frequently exist in relationships between experts and clients, between parents and children, and between employers and employees. The degree of dependency is greatest when access to the desired goal is not available from any other source and when the desire for attaining the goal is strong.

Issues pertaining to distributive justice are some of the major sources of conflict in modern society. Some feel that they are entitled to more than they get, while others want more regardless of how much they have. Feelings of relative deprivation surface when individuals feel that they are not getting their fair share of the total resources available. The rich are more likely than the poor to hold beliefs in the fairness of social inequality, suggesting the importance of one's socioeconomic position for determining the nature of judgments about distributive justice. Intense conflicts have developed in American society over issues of social justice, and the major concerns are with patterns of discrimination on the basis of such ascribed characteristics as race and gender.

BASIC TERMS

Egoism
Hedonism
Rationality
Incompleteness of
 knowledge
Inherent uncertainty
Norm of reciprocity
Prosocial behavior

Norm of social
 responsibility
Potlatch
Power dependency
Distributive justice
Exploitation
Relative deprivation
Social justice

REFERENCES

Abrahamsson, Bengt
 1970 "Homans on Exchange: Hedonism Revived," *American Journal of Sociology* 76 (September): 273–285.
Austin, William and Elaine Walster
 1975 "Equity with the World," *Sociometry* 38 (December): 474–496.

Bacharach, Samuel B. and Edward J. Lawler
    1976 "The Perception of Power," *Social Forces* 55 (September): 123–134.
Berger, Joseph, Bernard P. Cohen, and Morris Zelditch, Jr.
    1972 "Status Conceptions and Social Interaction," *American Sociological Review* 37 (June): 241–255.
Black, Charlene R., Eugene A. Weinstein, and Judith M. Tanur
    1974 "Self-Interest and Expectations of Altruism in Exchange Situations," *Sociological Quarterly* 15 (Spring): 242–252.
Blau, Peter M.
    1964 *Exchange and Power in Social Life*, New York: John Wiley.
Blumstein, Phillip W.
    1975 "Identity Bargaining and Self-Conception," *Social Forces* 53 (March): 476–485.
Burgess, Robert L. and Joyce McCarl Neilsen
    1974 "An Experimental Analysis of Some Structural Determinants of Equitable and Inequitable Exchange Relations," *American Sociological Review* 39 (June): 427–443.
Christie, Richard and Florence L. Geis
    1970 *Studies in Machiavellianism*, New York: Academic Press.
Coleman, James S.
    1973 "Loss of Power," *American Sociological Review* 38 (February): 1–17.
Cook, Karen S.
    1975 "Expectations, Evaluations and Equity," *American Sociological Review* 40 (June): 372–388.
Deutsch, Morton
    1975 "Equity, Equality, and Need," *Journal of Social Issues* 31 (Summer): 137–150.
Duke, James T.
    1976 *Conflict and Power in Social Life*, Provo, Utah: Brigham Young University Press.
Dynes, Russell and Quarantelli, E. L.
    1968 "What Looting in Civil Disturbances Really Means," *Transaction* 5 (May): 9–14.
Emerson, Richard
    1962 "Power-Dependence Relations," *American Sociological Review* 22 (February): 31–41.
Ginsberg, Morris
    1965 *On Justice in Society*, Ithaca, N.Y.: Cornell University Press.
Glidewell, John C.
    1970 *Choice Points*, Cambridge, Mass.: MIT Press.
Gordon, Suzanne
    1976 *Lonely in America*, New York: Simon & Shuster.
Gouldner, Alvin W.
    1960 "The Norm of Reciprocity," *American Sociological Review* 25 (April): 161–178.
Graham, Hugh Davis and Ted Robert Gurr
    1969 *Violence in America*, New York: Signet Books.
Groat, H. Theodore
    1976 "Community and Conflict in Mass Society," in Arthur G. Neal (ed.), *Violence in Animal and Human Societies*, Chicago: Nelson-Hall, pp. 49–78.

Groat, H. Theodore and Arthur G. Neal
    1975 "Alienation Antecedents of Unwanted Fertility," *Social Biology* 22 (Spring): 60–74.
Habermas, Jurgen
    1971 *Toward a Rational Society,* Boston: Beacon Press.
Heath, Anthony
    1976 *Rational Choice and Social Exchange,* London: Cambridge University Press.
Hillery, George A., Jr., Charles J. Dudley, and Paula C. Morrow
    1977 "Toward a Sociology of Freedom," *Social Forces* 55 (March): 685–700.
Hofstadter, Richard and Michael Wallace
    1970 *American Violence: A Documentary History,* New York: Vintage Books.
Homans, George C.
    1974 *Social Behavior: Its Elementary Forms,* revised edition, New York: Harcourt, Brace and World.
    1961 *Social Behavior: Its Elementary Forms,* New York: Harcourt, Brace and World.
Johnson, David W. and Stephen Allen
    1972 "Equity vs. Self-Interest Theory," *Sociological Quarterly* 13 (Spring): 174–182.
Komorita, Samuel S. and David Brinberg
    1977 "The Effects of Equity Norms in Coalition Formation," *Sociometry* 40 (December): 351–360.
Kriesberg, Louis
    1973 *The Sociology of Social Conflicts,* Englewood Cliffs, N.J.: Prentice-Hall.
Lenski, Gerhard E.
    1966 *Power and Privilege,* New York: McGraw-Hill.
Lerner, Melvin J.
    1975 "The Justice Motive in Social Behavior," *Journal of Social Issues* 31 (Summer): 1–20.
Mauss, Marcel
    1954 *The Gift,* Glencoe, Ill.: The Free Press.
Meeker, B. F.
    1971 "Decisions and Exchange," *American Sociological Review* 26 (June): 485–495.
Michener, H. Andrew, Eugene D. Cohen, and Aage B. Sorensen
    1977 "Social Exchange," *American Sociological Review* 42 (June): 522–535.
Moen, Elizabeth
    1978 "The Reluctance of the Elderly to Accept Help," *Social Problems* 25 (February): 293–303.
Moschetti, Gregory J.
    1979 "The Christmas Potlatch," *Sociological Focus* 12 (January): 1–7.
Neal, Arthur G., H. Theodore Groat, and Jerry W. Wicks
    1981 *Family Formation and Fertility Control in the Early Years of Marriage,* Bethesda, Md.: Center for Population Research.
Parcel, Toby Lee and Karen S. Cook
    1977 "Status Characteristics, Reward Allocation, and Equity," *Sociometry* 40 (December): 311–324.
Philliber, William W. and William S. Fox
    1977 "Race, Class, and Perceptions of Affluence," *Sociological Focus* 10 (October): 375–382.
Piven, Frances Fox and Richard A. Cloward
    1971 *Regulating the Poor,* New York: Vintage Books.

Richardson, James T., John R. Dugan, Louis N. Gray, and Bruce H. Mayhew, Jr.
   1973 "Expert Power: A Behavioral Interpretation," *Sociometry* 36 (September):
      302–324.
Rogers, Mary F.
   1974 "Instrumental and Infra-Resources: The Bases of Power," *American Journal
      of Sociology* 79 (May): 1418–1433.
Rothman, Robert A.
   1978 *Inequality and Stratification in the United States*, Englewood Cliffs, N.J.:
      Prentice-Hall.
Rubin, Zick and Letitia Anne Peplau
   1975 "Who Believes in a Just World?," *Journal of Social Issues* 31, no. 3: 65–90.
Rytina, Joan Huber, William H. Form, and John Pease
   1970 "Income and Stratification Ideology: Beliefs about the American Oppor-
      tunity Structure," *American Journal of Sociology* 75 (January): 703–716.
Scott, John Paul
   1976 "The Control of Violence," in Arthur G. Neal (ed.), *Violence in Animal and
      Human Societies*, Chicago: Nelson-Hall, pp. 13–34.
Schwartz, Barry
   1974 "Waiting, Exchange, and Power: The Distribution of Time in Social Sys-
      tems," *American Journal of Sociology* 79 (January): 841–870.
Simmel, Georg
   1978 *The Philosophy of Money* (trans. by Tom Bottomore and David Frisby),
      Boston: Routledge & Kegan Paul.
Singelmann, Peter
   1972 "Exchange as Symbolic Interaction: Convergences Between Two Theoreti-
      cal Perspectives," *American Sociological Review* 37 (August): 414–424.
Stack, Carol B.
   1974 *All Our Kin: Strategies for Survival in a Black Community*, New York: Harper
      & Row.
Stack, Steven
   1978 "Ideological Beliefs on the American Distribution of Opportunity, Power,
      and Rewards," *Sociological Focus* 11 (August): 221–234.
Staub, Ervin
   1972 "Instigation to Goodness: The Role of Social Norms and Interpersonal Influ-
      ence," *Journal of Social Issues* 28, no. 3: 131–150.
Thibaut, John W. and Harold H. Kelley
   1967 *The Social Psychology of Groups*, New York: John Wiley.
Tripi, Frank
   1974 "The Inevitability of Client Alienation: A Counter Argument," *Sociological
      Quarterly* 15 (Summer): 432–441.
Williams, Robin, M., Jr.
   1970 *American Society*, New York: Knopf.
Wispe, Lauren G.
   1972 "Positive Forms of Social Behavior," *Journal of Social Issues* 28, no. 3: 1–20.

10

Authority Relationships

Authority is a part of social reality that we must take into account as one of the basic facts of life. In the workplace, in the family, in the state, and in the church, the authority dimension is important for social relationships. We become keenly aware of the existence of authority when we are coerced into doing something we would prefer not to do. This is evident in paying taxes when we would prefer to keep the money for ourselves, in going to work when we would prefer to stay home, in keeping within the speed limit when we would like to drive faster, in complying with rules and regulations when it is inconvenient to do so, in writing a term paper when we would prefer to go to a movie, and in studying for an exam when we would prefer to be playing at the recreation center.

We experience authority as a social force that resides outside of ourselves and as a set of legitimate claims on our conduct. Other people have control over the resources and services we desire, and to get what we want out of life we must learn how to cope with dependency relationships. It is by means of authority that rules are established, interpreted, and enforced. It is by means of authority that binding decisions are made and moral jurisdictions are imposed on conduct. Authority is legitimate power; this implies that the orders, commands, directives, and requests that are issued by others become binding on our own conduct.

One of the major ways for identifying the presence of authority in any given situation is by raising a series of questions about the decision-making process. How are decisions to be made? Who has the right to decide? Under what circumstances are decisions binding on conduct? How are the available resources to be allocated? If decisions are made, can we count on them to be backed up by an official line of action? These questions are answerable in any given case through an awareness of the social drama embedded in authoritative acts.

If we cannot answer these questions with confidence, the social world becomes chaotic and lacking in coherence. Systems of authority contribute to stable and predictable social relationships. Only certain individuals are permitted to do certain things, and this has the effect of fixing responsibilities.

The predictability of events and a person's sense of mastery and control are closely related to judgments about how to cope effectively with authority. We incur duties and obligations in the pursuit of desired goals, and the costs of noncompliance may be very great indeed. Compliance with "the system," "working within the system," and "beating the system" are popular expressions that reflect the necessity of coming to terms with the conditions of authority.

Authority involves more than issuing commands and insisting on obedience. It also involves the rights of specific individuals to engage in certain kinds of performances. Parents have the right to speak on behalf of the family in community affairs, to establish "house rules" for family residents, to decide on the proper use of the family car, and to allocate family resources in making consumer purchases. As with all authority relationships the rights of parents are grounded in cultural traditions and social norms. Children also have their rights and privileges (Takanishi, 1978), and their responses may impose certain limits on the manner in which parents exercise their authority.

If certain individuals are granted the authority to issue requests, directives, or mandates, others are authorized to make fairness judgments and assessments of leadership effectiveness. For example, students have the right to expect professors to be competent in their areas of specialization and to be fair in their grading practices. For these reasons the authority of the professor is controlled to some degree by the responses of students, by academic standards, and by a professional code of ethics. Authority is limited to the

---

TABLE 10.1
The Vocabulary of Authority

Agents	Actions	Meanings
Boss	Ordering	Strong—Weak
Employer	Commanding	Soft—Hard
Supervisor	Forcing	Warm—Cold
Director	Deciding	Right—Wrong
President	Assigning	Moral—Immoral
Executive	Establishing	Just—Unjust
Presiding officer	Arbitrating	Valid—Invalid
Chair	Enforcing	Rational—Irrational
Expert	Permitting	Sincere—Insincere
Consultant	Recommending	Effective—Ineffective
Ruler	Enacting	Benevolent—Malevolent
Judge	Allowing	Clear—Unclear
Warden	Demanding	Sharp—Dull
Police officer	Enforcing	Fast—Slow
Guardian	Exempting	Greedy—Generous

legitimate exercise of power, and the test for legitimacy is the compatibility of decisions with group values and norms. Consequently, authority relationships are properties of social groups and are encompassed within normative boundaries and limits. (See Table 10.1.)

Since social interactions proceed on the basis of the respective identities of those involved, authority and status become closely linked. For this reason an adequate understanding of authority relationships requires being concerned with status conferral, the process of legitimation, and the trustee functions of leadership positions. These concerns relate to the processes of attaining legitimate power, of justifying authoritative acts, and of being accountable for group effectiveness.

The character of authority relationships constitutes one of the basic sources of conflict within modern society (Dahrendorf, 1959). Authority relationships often emphasize rational values at the expense of tradition, enhance selfish interests at the expense of the common good, and draw on claims to legitimacy as a basis for manipulation and control. The accountability of authority figures frequently places a heavy set of demands on them, while subordinates often feel coerced into serving interests other than their own. Such conditions lend themselves to a great deal of controversy and debate, and the outcomes of social relationships are often based on negotiations and compromises.

A. STATUS CONFERRAL

Within social groups, authority is primarily expressed through the division of labor. Certain individuals are given such responsibilities as making binding decisions on behalf of the group, supervising the work activities of members, and enhancing group effectiveness. The conferral of status on certain individuals fixes responsibilities on them for the doing of certain things. It authorizes bosses to issue orders and to insist on compliance from subordinates. Teachers have the authority to give examinations, to evaluate performances, and to assign grades. And police officers are permitted to direct traffic, to deter criminals, and to make arrests.

The connection between authority and status is a major part of everyday understanding about the organization of social life. In our patterns of interaction we necessarily make assumptions about the attributes of those who have had a particular status conferred on them. These attributes are an outgrowth of notions about the manner by which individuals are recruited for filling social positions. Such assumptions about status and authority are necessary for maintaining stable social relationships, for making norms binding on conduct, and for predicting future events. By growing up in a particular society, the individual learns to accept numerous aspects of authority as being the normal, natural, and preferred state of affairs.

Symbol of Authority
The privileges that accompany positions of authority are also accompanied by responsibilities. Those who hold higher positions of authority become involved in such complex responsibilities as issuing directives, setting priorities, allocating resources, supervising subordinates, resolving internal group conflict, and making binding decisions. While some seek power and authority, others prefer to avoid positions of management and responsibility. (Credit: Sharon A. Bazarian)

1. Appointment

Status conferral at the higher echelons of authority involves the designation of certain individuals as experts. They become experts on the basis of their credentials, and their appointments to positions of responsibility confirm their qualifications. The central forms of authority in modern industrialized societies reside within large-scale associations (Dahrendorf, 1959), such as business corporations, universities, hospitals, and governmental bureaucracies. As Weber (1947) pointed out in his classical statement on bureaucracy, authority in large-scale associations is not an attribute of the individual office holder but a property of the group itself.

Responsibility is exercised on behalf of the organization, and the completion of assigned tasks is oriented toward the attainment of group goals. Rights and duties are formally specified, and the type and scope of authority is always limited. Specific individuals are authorized to do only certain things, and they are potentially accountable to others both up and down through the chain of command. The reason for fixing responsibility is to make the system predictable. This means that the group's organizers create the specialized parts in a manner they believe to be rational for carrying out some designated mission. Claims for rationality contribute to the emergence of two separable types of experts in large-scale organizations. One consists of professionals, while the other consists of administrators.

The professional is an expert in a substantive area, such as medicine, science, law, and engineering. Here the expert authority rests on claims for superior knowledge, experience, and competency in the performance of highly

---

BOX 10.1
The Revolt of the Client

Authority relationships in modern society reflect increasing sophistication in reality construction and in the utilization of expert knowledge. Lopata (1976) has noted that the emergence of such labels as consultant, interpreter, policy designer, professional, technologist, and technician reflects the emphasis on seeing certain individuals as possessing a body of knowledge and skills that may be applied to the solution of clients' problems. Upgrading the status of specific occupations is reflected in the trend that has been described as "the expertization of everyone."

Along with the trend toward designating all employed people as experts in one thing or another, there has also been a trend among the population at large toward attaining higher levels of education and social awareness. Those who receive expert services, such as clients, customers, trainees, students, and patients, are generally knowledgeable men and women who are prone to questioning the competency of those who present themselves as experts. While clients voluntarily seek the services of experts, they are increasingly revolting against the finality and wisdom of expert decisions (Haug, 1975).

The unwillingness of clients to submit to the decisions of expert authority is likely to occur under a variety of conditions. Greater freedom occurs for the client if the needed services are available from a variety of sources. The client may obtain second opinions about the need for a given service or about the format in which the service is to be performed. If the individual is knowledgeable concerning the services available, he or she is less dependent on the possible shoddy performance of any specific person designated as a professional or as an expert. In some cases individuals may seek to perform the services for themselves (e.g., auto repair) or learn to live without the services altogether.

specialized tasks. The knowledge of the professional is esoteric in the sense that it is based on the use of terminology that those outside the area of expertise normally do not understand (Hughes, 1963). Research scientists, psychiatrists, brain surgeons, and nuclear engineers are examples of those whose authority rests on professional knowledge and experience. (See Box 10.1.)

Administrators—the second kind of expert—are those highly qualified as supervisors, coordinators, and managers. The authority conferred on them is based on the assumption of expertise in the mobilization of personnel and resources in goal attainment. They are presumed to be skilled in making decisions and issuing directives on behalf of an organization. The administrative experts do not have to have superior knowledge in the substantive sense, but they must know how to draw on and utilize the knowledge of others in the management of organizational affairs (Blau, 1968).

The appointments of substantive experts to positions of authority are based on their training and certification. Because of their superior knowledge and talent, they become objects of respect both up and down through the chain of command. They must have some degree of autonomy in order to effectively carry out the unique tasks for which they are especially qualified (Wilensky, 1964). For example, deans and college presidents do not have the qualifications for closely supervising the research activities of the scientist in the laboratory. Corporation executives frequently lack the necessary knowledge for direct involvement in the solution of technical problems. And hospital administrators typically do not have the credentials for supervising the surgery that takes place in the operating room.

Conflicts frequently occur between managers and professionals because of differences in personal concerns and in the sources of authority. Professionals frequently perceive a lack of support for their favorite projects, and they tend to resent the control by administrators over organizational resources and the conditions of work. They sometimes feel that managers are requesting them to perform inappropriate tasks, and that there is not enough freedom to conduct their professional activities. On the other hand, administrators are frequently disappointed with the time required for the solution of certain problems, with what they see as the lack of practical results, and with the gap between abstract principles and the immediate problems that require solutions.

Substantive experts are frequently appointed to administrative positions on the basis of their achievements in some specialized area. For example, an outstanding research scientist may be selected for the position of dean, a skilled surgeon appointed as hospital administrator, or an inspiring teacher chosen as school principal. Such decisions are often based on the assumption that expertness in one line of endeavor may be generalized to expertness in another.

This process reflects the operation of "a halo effect." The principle of the halo effect operates in observing splendid performance in one area of competence and expecting splendid performance in some unrelated area. If a vacancy occurs in some department or agency, it seems reasonable to fill the vacancy by promoting an individual who has been doing a good job at a lower echelon in the chain of command. In reality such an assumption often turns out to be invalid. The values and commitments that promote success in a specialized area may not be compatible with the performance requirements in some more generalized position of authority. The frequency with which this occurs led to the formation of the Peter Principle which holds that employees tend to advance in large-scale organizations until they reach their own level of incompetence (Peter and Hull, 1969). They then become frozen in jobs for which they have only limited qualifications. This explanation appears reasonable as a basis for observing the levels of incompetence of many who occupy positions of authority.

2. Ascription

The creation of authority relationships, like other aspects of group living, is expressed in the social construction of reality. As social groups and organizations become larger in size, two major variables tend to shape the reality construction process. These include the perceived needs of the organization and the perceived qualifications of personnel. Ideas about organizational needs result in the creation of offices, while notions about the qualifications of applicants serve as guidelines for making appointments and conferring status.

While appointments are presumably based on assessments of talent, the top positions of authority within the United States are held disproportionately by middle-aged, white males. Women, blacks, and ethnic minorities tend to be excluded from major positions of authority. These forms of exclusion rest on a series of assumptions about the qualifications and attributes of those who are characterized by certain types of ascribed status.

Some of the advanced indicators of the status attainment process are already operating at the time of birth. The social scripts set in motion by social placement at birth are important correlates of the levels of authority that individuals will subsequently attain. Males have an advantage over females, whites have an advantage over blacks, and those with college-educated parents have an advantage over those with parents who have had only a high school education or less. For these reasons those who have a strong desire for status attainment should begin by "choosing" their parents wisely. The enduring effects of ascribed status are operative in the motivations of individuals, in the styles of social interaction, and in the perceptions of opportunities and restrictions.

An **ascribed status** is conferred on the basis of a set of assumptions about the biological differences of individuals. These presumed differences provide justifications for assigning certain privileges and responsibilities on the basis of membership in a social category (Marwell, 1975). For example, the subordinate status of women is based on a series of assumptions about the ways in which women naturally differ from men. These include ideas about what makes women the happiest, what they are best qualified to do, and how they best serve the needs of the family and the larger social system.

BOX 10.2
The Preference for Men as Professionals

"Would you prefer a man or a woman when choosing a _____ (dentist, accountant, lawyer, physician, realtor, or veterinarian)?" The research of Ferber, Huber, and Spitze (1979) indicates that most people respond to this question by showing a preference for a man rather than a woman when selecting a professional. The choices apparently are based on definitions of women as being less suited than men for positions of leadership and authority.

The underrepresentation of women in professional and managerial positions is in part due to the preference of employees for men as bosses. Personal characteristics of authority figures that have nothing to do with competence or job performance often enter into the willingness of customers, clients, or workers to accept supervision or to make use of expert knowledge. The exclusion of women from job authority is based on beliefs held by managers and subordinates alike that women are temperamentally unsuited for management roles.

The study by Ferber, Huber, and Spitze found that the acceptability of women as authority figures varies by the social characteristics of respondents. Women find women to be more nearly acceptable as bosses than do men. College-educated people find women more acceptable in leadership roles than do those with only a high school education or less, and younger people hold a higher regard for professional women than do older people. These findings suggest that those who readily accept women as authority figures are more likely to have been personally acquainted with a female professional.

Source: Marianne Ferber, Joan Huber, and Glenna Spitze, "Preference for Men as Bosses and Professionals," *Social Forces* 58 (December, 1979): 466–476.

Despite the widespread beliefs about equality of opportunity in the workplace, the research of Wendy Wolf and Neil Fligstein (1979) indicates that women are generally restricted from positions of authority. Having a position of authority in the work setting means being "higher up," engaging in the management of resources, and having the right to control the work activities of others. While the exclusion of women from positions as managers and supervisors may in part be due to differences in qualifications and experiences (Grimm and Stern, 1974), there are also numerous other variables involved. These include the attitudes of those who do the hiring and firing, as well as the attitudes of the women themselves.

The employment opportunities for women are greatest in those jobs that have limited promotion possibilities (nurses, librarians, secretaries, and so on). However, even when women do have the experiences and qualifications required for supervisory positions, promotions are often denied to them. Wolf and Fligstein (1979) noted that this happens because of attitudes about the general attributes of women. Many employers feel that women are too emotional and therefore unfit to be put in a position of authority. Strong beliefs also exist that women should not supervise male or mixed groups. Since men are believed to resent having a woman for a boss, employers do not promote women in order to avoid potential trouble. Thus being a member of a gender category may be a basis for exclusion from higher positions of authority, regardless of other qualifications. (See Box 10.2.)

The traditional views of female roles are reflected in women's attitudes toward their own capabilities. A large number of women have doubts about their own qualifications for positions of authority and do not desire to be placed in supervisory roles. The socialization of women does not typically involve preparation for leadership, and as a result they do not regard themselves as

---

BOX 10.3
Racial Exclusion from Job Authority

While recent studies have shown an improvement in the educational and occupational status of black Americans, racial exclusion from job authority still persists. Job authority means to hold positions that give the right to supervise the work of others and to manage organizational resources. Kluegel (1978) has identified several of the variables frequently involved in the underrepresentation of blacks in jobs as managers, foremen, and supervisors.

One of the basic reasons for the exclusion of blacks from higher positions of authority derives from the vagueness of the criteria for making promotions. Educational requirements are clearly visible and open to scrutiny. However, numerous other considerations are taken into account by those who do the hiring and promoting. These include judgments about loyalty, good character, and leadership potential. Such subjective components are reflected in decisions about the general characteristics of blacks and how blacks are likely to perform in supervisory positions.

The politics of race surfaces in the assumption that because of social and cultural differences, blacks cannot be effective in interacting with whites at the higher levels of authority. From this belief it then follows that the appointment of blacks to positions of authority should be limited to jobs that involve interaction with a black clientele or the supervision of black workers. Among both blacks and whites there is a prevailing belief that blacks should be overqualified before being placed in positions of authority. This reflects a desire to be certain that if blacks are promoted they will succeed. Such obstacles to job authority place blacks at a disadvantage in status attainment and partially account for the persistence of racial difference in income levels.

Source: James R. Kluegel, "The Causes and Cost of Racial Exclusion from Job Authority," *American Sociological Review* 43 (June, 1978): 285–301.

capable of assuming managerial responsibilities. Because of potential interruptions of employment, for a wide variety of reasons (family need, childcare, husband's mobility, and so forth), many women are unwilling to make the kind of long-term commitments that higher positions of authority frequently require. Consequently, a type of self-fulfilling prophecy operates to perpetuate the subordinate status of women both within the family and within the workplace.

The exclusion of women and blacks from higher positions of authority is then based on a set of justifications related to organizational needs and the qualifications of personnel. (See Box 10.3.) These kinds of justifications constitute the legitimating myths believed by those who hold positions of authority. Their actions become endowed with constructions of reality for validating the decisions that they make (Habermas, 1973). For these reasons, the process of legitimation becomes central to the authoritative acts involved in making appointments, issuing directives, and allocating resources.

B. LEGITIMATION

The legitimacy of the actions by those who hold positions of power is not automatic nor self-evident. For this reason an important distinction needs to be made between legal authority and legitimacy. **Legal authority** refers to the right to make decisions, issue commands, or formulate policy on the basis of appropriate procedures. Legislators have the legal authority to enact laws, police have the legal authority to make arrests, and judges have the legal authority to issue penalties. Authority within large-scale organizations also rests on a legalistic basis. Professors have the authority to make classroom assignments, bosses have the authority to supervise work activities, and consultants are granted the authority to make recommendations.

Legitimation refers to the process by which claims for authoritative acts are accepted as valid ones. This includes not only the justifications presented by those in authority, but also the responses of those engaged in the authority relationship (Kantner, 1966). Legitimacy claims become essential under conditions in which conflicts emerge over the appropriateness of decisions, policies, and the allocation of resources. Claims and counterclaims, arguments and debates, negotiations and compromises are among the major attributes that surround social relationships when "a crisis of legitimacy" emerges (Habermas, 1973).

The leaders of large-scale organizations seek to win routine support for their policies through public validation of their claims for legitimacy. Such support is often essential since most organizations and institutions are dependent on community environments favorable to the pursuit of their interests. To illustrate this process, let us examine research that has focused on the legitimating myths of colleges and universities within the United States. Their primary source of authority resides in the right to certify certain individuals as college graduates.

1. Legitimating Myths of Higher Education

The research of David Kamens (1977) suggests that the legitimating myths of higher education play an important part in designating certain individuals as having a special set of qualifications. Independent of any specific learning that may have taken place, conferring the status of college graduate on certain individuals accords them the right to certain kinds of jobs and other social meanings for use in the larger society.

If the legitimating myths about the quality of educational experiences are to be accepted by employers and other agencies in society, colleges and universities must present some evidence to substantiate the claim that schooling makes a difference. In addition to giving students formal certification and conducting rituals of status change for them, Kamens notes, colleges achieve this difference through the development of a differentiated curriculum. The courses listed in college bulletins constitute a symbolic index of the kinds of social learning that have occurred. Through selective mastery of this subject matter at some minimum level of proficiency, graduates present evidence that they are changed persons and entitled to special status rights.

The primary legitimating myths of Ivy League and certain other private schools center around the selection and training of individuals for elite status. The organizational supports for these claims rest on keeping enrollments small, screening applicants, setting up residency requirements, recruiting a highly qualified staff, and maintaining a high faculty-to-student ratio. The exclusion of the less-qualified from attendance confers an elite status on those who are admitted. The residency requirement removes students physically from other kinds of influences and subjects them to identity-changing experiences. The qualifications of the faculty serve as evidence for the special competence of graduates. The general acceptance of these status-conferral features gives the graduates of private schools an advantage in subsequent placement, independent of any specific learning experiences that may have taken place through attendance.

The legitimating claims of colleges and universities are generally accepted within highly industrialized societies. Organization and political complexities require personnel with a wide range of experiences and competencies for performing specialized tasks and for adapting to social change. The primary services performed by schools are those of providing an initial screening of individuals and selecting out for subsequent appointment those who have developed the requisite skills for making it within the system. The disadvantaged in this contest disproportionately consist of those with poverty backgrounds and minority status (Hauser and Featherman, 1976). Poor people and those of minority status are less likely to attend college, and if they do they are less likely to remain for graduation.

The actual validity of the numerous claims about college graduates may not be nearly so important as the implications of the label for subsequent occupational placement (Yankelovich, 1979). There is a series of assumptions

Avenue to Status Attainment
*Graduation from college is one of the major avenues to attaining status in our society.
Certain opportunities for job placement and job advancement become available to
the college graduate that are denied to those with only a high school education or less.*

people frequently make when they know that an individual is a college graduate. These include implicit judgments about his or her social worth, moral character, levels of knowledge, and motivations. The assumptions about college graduates also include a variety of notions about skills and proficiencies. College graduates are expected to be skilled in verbal communication, in critical thinking, in writing ability, and in interpersonal relationships. The assumptions about how individuals acquire certain attributes may very well constitute the basis for the differential occupational placement of college-educated people.

2. Big Business Ideology

The process of legitimation is essentially gaining acceptance for decisions and actions by showing their compatibility with cultural values and group norms.

David Rothstein (1972) has noted that cultural values may be thought of as systems of shared knowledge and meaning for the construction of social reality. These include widely held assumptions about the natural environment, about human motivations, and about the orderliness of social relationships. As a set of shared perceptions, these assumptions may be drawn on by individuals as the basis for justifying social action.

Problematic situations may develop in authority relationships from a wide variety of sources. Authority figures are often confronted with an image problem. They may be looked on as being "too aloof," "heavy-handed," "insincere," or "too soft." These images are important ones since they have a bearing on the willingness of individuals to lend their support to organizational goals and priorities. For example, business corporations are faced with a series of image problems that potentially affect their client relationships. These include the views of business corporations as greedy, as willing to do anything "to make a buck," as concealing their power, as deceiving the public, and as making excessive profits. As a result of their concerns with image polishing, many business corporations have a special public relations department and sometimes seek the services of professionals in attempts to change their public identities.

According to the principles of legitimate power, gaining control over desired resources requires justifying that control in terms of cultural values and social norms. The need for this is evident in view of the size and complexity of American business corporations. The volume of sales for some of America's largest business corporations exceeds the total value of all the goods and services produced in the majority of the countries of the world. Because of the vast resources under the control of corporations, justification to the public for business practices becomes necessary. Otherwise consumers might avoid the products of a given company, or pressures might develop for more effective governmental regulations.

The justifications for economic practices have been described by Maynard S. Seider (1974) as "American big business ideology." This ideology consists of a series of beliefs about the numerous ways in which business practices serve the needs and interests of workers and consumers. The legitimating claims also include an emphasis on the compatibility of business practices and concerns with the continuing vitality of the country as a whole. (See Figure 10.1.)

Seider (1974) made an analysis of public addresses delivered by top-ranking corporation executives and published in the periodical *Vital Speeches* between 1954 and 1970. His results indicate that several themes were prominently emphasized. These include the claim that profit making was necessary for a healthy economy and for national well-being. The view of the economy as self-regulating was presented as a way of showing the lack of a need for governmental rules and agencies. The theme of social responsibility was also a recurrent one. The business corporation was presented as being concerned with solving social problems, improving the quality of community life, and directing its resources toward areas not directly related to profit making.

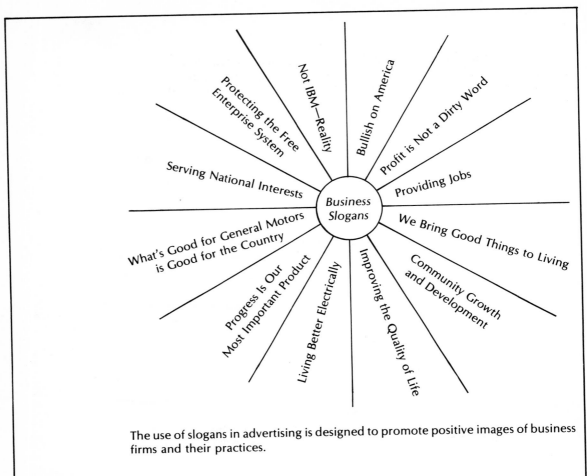

The use of slogans in advertising is designed to promote positive images of business firms and their practices.

FIGURE 10.1
The Ethical Embellishment of Business Interests

While these justifications were directed toward an ethical embellishment of business interests in general, Seider's results indicated that specific themes varied by type of industry. Executives from industries heavily involved in military contracts (i.e., aerospace) tended to emphasize the needs of the nation for a strong defense system. Spokespersons from industries heavily involved in overseas markets tended to emphasize nationalistic themes and the need for a strong nation to protect American interests.

By way of contrast, different sets of themes were more prominent in speeches from executives in the more consumer-oriented (retailing and service) industries. These executives spoke the language of social responsibility and concern for the quality of life. Representatives from monopolistic industries (e.g., the electric utilities) waxed most eloquently about the advantages of the free enterprise system and the negative aspects of governmental rules and agencies. Thus the business spokespersons tended to draw on the values of nationalism, social responsibility, and the free-enterprise system. But the selective emphasis on these themes reflected an enhancement of their own special interests. (See Box 10.4.)

The problem of legitimation derives from the imperative of making choices among available alternatives and developing justification that will be socially accepted as valid and appropriate. This process adds a political dimension to social relationships, since both groups and individuals seek to validate their own interests by obtaining social support. Certain kinds of actions are commonly understood as being socially appropriate, and these are drawn on to justify goal selection and the means for goal attainment. The legitimations of authoritative acts often rest on arguments about the responsibilities incurred in serving trustee and custodial functions.

BOX 10.4
Cover-Up and Collective Integrity

Out of a concern for their public images, organizations tend to cover up the deviance that occurs among their members. The cover-up is possible because of the sharp separation of the authority within organizations and the external authority of the broader society. According to Katz (1977), there is a natural antagonism between these two sources of authority. Organizations seek to promote public images of effective internal control in order to prevent such external authorities as the police, courts, and regulatory agencies from becoming involved in their internal affairs.

The basic form of organizational cover-up consists of **shielding** members from external forces. For example, if an embezzlement occurs, or if there is a misuse of company funds, the offender may be given an opportunity to "voluntarily" resign as an alternative to being fired or prosecuted. Managers are concerned with maintaining positive images among stockholders and customers in order to avoid bad publicity or court proceedings.

If external agents penetrate into the internal affairs of an organization, the outcome is still likely to consist of some form of cover-up. For instance, in the public schools a school principal is likely to appear sympathetic to an outraged parent, but in the final analysis will defend and protect the teacher. The shielding of subordinates is necessary for the respect and authority accorded to higher officials. The protection of members and the nonenforcement of norms are techniques employed by organizations to circumvent interference from external agents of authority.

Source: Jack Katz, "Cover-up and Collective Integrity on the Natural Antagonism of Authority Internal and External to Organizations," *Social Problems* 25 (October, 1977): 3–17.

C. TRUSTEESHIP

Authority figures derive their legitimate power from the social groups whose interests they represent. The conferral of authority involves presumptions about both qualifications and trustworthiness. Being granted the right to make decisions on behalf of a social group and serving as a spokesperson for the group in the external environment incurs a set of trustee responsibilities. **Trusteeship** refers to the obligations for the conduct of group affairs and for the effective management of group resources. Through this process authority figures serve as symbols of group effectiveness and become accountable to members for group effectiveness.

1. Collective-Good Decisions

Anne McMahon and Santo Camilleri (1975) have described certain authoritative acts as **collective-good decisions.** These are decisions that are shaped by those in positions of authority, and the concern of the decision makers is with eliciting voluntary support and participation from their constituencies. McMahon and Camilleri describe a collective-good decision as follows:

The defining characteristics of a collective-good decision is that its outcome accrues to everyone in the organization by virtue of the simple fact of membership. For any member to receive the rewards associated with the outcome of such a decision, it is necessary only that decision be made, *not* that he participate in making it (1975: 616).

Authority figures at all levels of organization—national, state, and local—tend to legitimate their decisions on the basis of arguments for the best interests of their constituencies. While these arguments are necessary for effective social action, such claims also tend to reinforce leadership positions of power and influence. The degree to which officials actually believe what they say may not be nearly so important as their actions. Officials may draw on group sentiments as motivational sources of action and use them in a practical and expedient matter to justify the exercise of power.

Bernard Beck (1978) observed that those in powerful and authoritative circles speak "in the name of society" as a way of imposing mutual responsibility on the part of all group members. The use of this procedure permits an extension of the scope of governmental authority into areas previously regarded as the private domain. For example, the range of public concerns has been extended to include environmental quality, the uses of energy, the adequacy of housing, the purity of food, the rights of children, the availability of credit, and the employment of women. Beck noted that the politics of speaking in the name of society has now become so pervasive that virtually no aspect of life is excluded from the realm of the common good. The underlying assumption is that anyone's actions can have an effect on the well-being of others, and as a result we all become mutually accountable.

Collective-Good Decisions
Collective-good decisions are reflected in the creation of public parks and plazas. Most of the people who benefit from such decisions did not participate in making them.

The emphasis on mutual accountability has contributed to the numerous concerns for raising the quality of life above some minimum level for all segments of the population. Several organizations have emerged to serve this purpose, and they are oriented toward changing people who are presumed to be in need of help. These include schools, hospitals, mental health facilities, and correctional institutions. Such organizations and agencies face the dual problems of demonstrating that the pool of potential clients is a fairly large one and that the services they offer will be beneficial to both society and the individuals involved.

Yeheskel Hasenfeld (1972) noted, by way of contrast, that several organizations have also emerged for processing, rather than changing, people. **People-processing organizations** are designed for conferring a public status on certain individuals whose attributes may otherwise be in doubt. The conferral of status may consist of the authority to certify certain individuals as being "below the poverty level," "minority persons," "senior citizens," "unemployed," "disabled workers," or "welfare clients," or as having "good-credit ratings." Individuals are designated as possessing characteristics presumed to be of relevance in the larger environment. The conferral of a public status is an assessment that determines what lines of official action are appropriate. This may constitute an eligibility for certain kinds of rights and benefits, or it may consist of the need for referral to some treatment agency.

2. *Priority Designations*

In numerous aspects of social life, legitimate claims to public resources tend to exceed the availability of those resources. For example, police departments are not able to investigate all of the crimes that are reported, mental health clinics would not be able to provide therapy if all those in need applied for treatment, and welfare agencies are often not able to validate all of the claims legitimately made on their resources. Since resources are always limited and numerous options are usually available, agencies must make decisions about the relative importance of performing some tasks compared to others.

The validity claims for authority within social groups may be evaluated in terms of the priorities established for goal attainment. To illustrate the process of priority designation, we may draw on the research of Thomas Drabek and Judith Chapman (1973) on the operative codes of police departments. Limited resources and personnel do not permit a thorough investigation of all crimes reported to the police. As a result, they designate some offenses as having high priority, while giving very little attention to other reported crimes. For instance, if someone stole your bike while you were in class today, the police would probably give a very low priority to a thorough investigation of the crime. But if a bank robbery were reported, they would probably dispatch police cruisers to the scene of the crime almost immediately.

Agents of authority are required to make decisions, and the priority designations are likely to be based on notions about how best to achieve effective performance in the light of competing goals and demands. Surely it must be easy for you to understand why the police cannot investigate the theft of your bike or locate the person who backed into the door of your car in an unattended parking lot. Low-priority designations that affect you may not make you very happy about law enforcement, but they may be required by the social constraints placed on the system. (See Box 10.5.)

Priority designations refer to decisions by those in positions of authority on how to allocate available resources for the attainment of group goals. The task frequently becomes a challenge because of the complexity of the alternatives available in many types of situations. Most large-scale organizations—even small groups, for that matter—tend to be characterized by a set of shared beliefs about an overriding purpose, aim, goal, or objective (Price, 1971). Such beliefs provide for a sense of unity and for the division of responsibilities. Certainly it is clear that the purpose of schools is to educate, the

---

BOX 10.5
The Triage Proposal

Paddock and Paddock (1967), in their discussion of the French medical staff during World War I, reported an interesting case of priority designation. There were occasions in which the casualty rates from the trench warfare were very high. Since the available personnel and resources were limited, effective medical treatment could not be provided for all soldiers receiving wounds in battle. Under such circumstances the staff had to make decisions and establish priorities for the allocation of medical resources.

Priorities were designated by drawing on a threefold classification of wounded soldiers. First, there were "the walking wounded," who would benefit from medical aid but would probably recover if nothing were done immediately. The second category consisted of soldiers so seriously injured that they were likely to die regardless of treatment administered by the medical staff. The third category was made up of those who would benefit the most from available medical resources. These were the soldiers who were likely to die if they did not receive immediate treatment from medical personnel.

Decisions on priorities resulted in "the **triage proposal** (three categories of priority)," which held that available resources should be allocated to the tasks likely to produce the most effective results. Accordingly, the highest priority was designated for the treatment of soldiers who would likely die if they did not receive immediate medical help.

Source: William Paddock and Paul Paddock, *Famine 1975!*, Boston: Little, Brown, 1967. 1967.

---

purpose of the military is to defend the country, the purpose of a business corporation is to make a profit, and the purpose of a police department is to enforce the law.

While most organizations are characterized by some overriding, explicitly defined set of goals, there are also competing demands for the use of available resources. For example, while the explicit purpose of universities is to create and communicate knowledge, such a generally stated objective does not contain any direct specification of how to achieve this. Educators differ among themselves on the best ways to teach, and students differ from their instructors on what students ought to know. As a consequence, numerous conflicts emerge within universities over the allocation of resources to one program or department compared to another. Student interests are not fully compatible with those of either the faculty or the administration. Because of the conflicting notions about what the specific goals of a university should be, some form of authority becomes necessary as a basis for making decisions and establishing priorities.

BOX 10.6
Conflict for the Front-Line Supervisor

Front-line supervisors are agents of authority who are required to carry out the decisions and policies made by officials at higher levels. Front-line supervisors are at the lower echelons of the chain of command, and the performance of their duties requires implementing organizational goals at the grassroots level. The platoon leader in combat does not shape the overall policies for the conduct of a war but is required to carry out the decisions that have been made by the higher command. The foreman in industry does not make the major decisions about production but is expected to represent the interests of management in supervising the work activities of employees. In similar fashion, nurses are required to implement hospital policies in relationships with patients, and teachers are expected to comply with the rules of school administrators in working with students.

The numerous conflicts that frequently emerge for front-line supervisors derive from the "double-bind" situation. The supervisors are not included in the making of major policy decisions, but they are required to carry them out. If they place their allegiance with higher authorities, they become subjected to resistance and hostility from subordinates. Front-line supervisors are exposed to potential antagonisms from those they supervise simply because they are bosses and have the authority to enforce behavior of subordinates. Supervisors who fully identify with subordinates are likely to find their effectiveness impaired when working with those above them in the chain of command. Supervisors are then on the firing line, so to speak, since they must absorb the shocks of clashing and opposing forces.

The establishment of priorities represents a specification of the relative importance of alternative goals and the tasks toward which to allocate the available resources. This process is often cumbersome, and once a decision has been made, the task is to obtain the necessary support for its implementation. The effectiveness of a group in attaining some specified objective may conflict with the competing goal of providing for the personal security and satisfaction of its members. Effective leaders may not be very benevolent, just as benevolent leaders may not be very effective.

In some situations the concern for member satisfaction may be compatible with group effectiveness. If so, the position of the leader may be very rewarding and comfortable. But in other types of situations the two sets of objectives may be clearly incompatible. For example, the platoon leader in combat may be in a situation in which he or she must decide between carrying out the assigned mission or being concerned with the welfare of the platoon's soldiers. The leader may not be able to do both. Ordering a charge against an enemy-held position is not compatible with a concern for the personal safety and security of platoon members. (See Box 10.6.)

In similar fashion, the foreman in industry may be concerned with meeting the production quotas set by higher levels of management, but in achieving these objectives the foreman may have to forego the privilege of being liked by his or her subordinates. The professor may make heavy demands on students to achieve learning objectives, but this may require some sacrifice in student ratings on the professor's teaching effectiveness. Thus agents of authority must sometimes choose between promoting member satisfaction or being effective in the completion of some designated task (Simmons, 1968).

D. ACCOUNTABILITY

Authority roles involve several aspects of **accountability.** These include being held responsible for one's qualifications, for one's deeds and performances, and for all of the other things one should do in supervising the actions of others. These attributes or responsibilities become the bases for admiration and respect in cases of splendid role performances. They also constitute the grounds for charges of role failure, incompetence, and neglect of duty. For example, the authority of the expert becomes unreliable when he or she fails to produce the expected results. Professors become undependable when they routinely deliver lectures without being adequately prepared. Governmental programs are regarded as untrustworthy when they are introduced without adequate research and planning.

1. Two Types of Responsibility

The accountability of authority imposes responsibilities in two major ways (Hamilton, 1978). One is responsibility in the causal sense of being effective, making things happen, producing results, and exercising control. **Causal responsibility** is often based on the assumption that the occurrences and happenings are intended by those in positions of authority. However, we do not have direct knowledge about many of the happenings that concern us. As a result we tend to impute causality as a way of making sense out of events (Hewitt and Hall, 1973). One example of this is the numerous public responses to the gasoline shortages and price increases of 1979. Notions about the causal agents included "a conspiracy on the part of oil companies," "greed on the part of oil producing countries," "a do-nothing congress," and "the president of the United States."

The imputation of responsibility in the causal sense may occur independently of the facts of the case. For example, the president of the United States may not actually be responsible for such events as inflation, energy shortages, air pollution, or unemployment. But at the same time the president may be held accountable by the voters the next time there is an election. His accountability may be based on the people's observation that these events occurred while the president was in office, and it was the president's responsibility to do something about them.

Authority figures incur a responsibility for the outcome of events, whether they made the events happen through their own actions, or whether they allowed them to happen through the actions of others. This suggests the importance of normal expectations as a second major source of responsibility. **Normative responsibility** relates to what should be done or ought to be done under a given set of circumstances. An authority figure may violate normal expectations through an overreaction to a superficial episode or through a failure to act when action is necessary. For example, the default on responsibilities may result in the execution of a military officer. General Yamashita of Japan was hanged for war crimes after World War II, not because of any order he had given but because of the actions of soldiers under his command (Hamilton, 1978).

In similar fashion the forced resignation of President Nixon may not have been due to his direct responsibility for the Watergate affair. Apparently he did not "order" or "supervise" the Watergate break-in, but he did allow certain events to occur. Through having knowledge of the illegal conduct of his subordinates and failing to take appropriate presidential action, he became accountable for the episode and was forced to resign. Thus accountability requires agents of authority to be responsible for what takes place under their jurisdiction in both the causal and the normative sense.

While authorities may be held accountable for their actions, they also have a great deal of leeway in decision making and in role performances. They may withhold information from subordinates, they may work on refining their public images as a substitute for substance, and they may control group resources in a manner that enhances their own self-interests. They also tend to have control over the more effective means of communication, and they may use collective resources to win support to their own particular causes. Thus the accountability of authority does not operate automatically, but it does constitute a set of background considerations that may be invoked when problematic situations arise. Under conditions of crisis, authority figures become subjected to close scrutiny and may be blamed for happenings that were not directly under their control.

2. Obedience

If some individuals have the authority to make decisions and to issue commands, others have the duty to carry them out. If some have the experience *of* power, others have experiences *with* power. If some are giving orders, others are receiving orders. Because of the selective vantage points of authority figures and subordinates, a given set of social events are likely to have widely divergent meanings. Presumably, those who are in positions to coordination actions are able to see how the various parts of an organization fit together into a coherent whole. In contrast, those whose activities are closely supervised by others may not be able to see the interrelatedness of events, nor the manner in which their own activities serve a broader purpose (Seeman, 1975).

Subordinates tend to internalize a sense of discipline and to emphasize their willingness to follow orders (Kohn, 1969). Enforcement of these values is important because certain individuals excluded from the making of plans are required to perform the necessary tasks for carrying them out. Among subordinates in large-scale organizations, **obedience** refers to receiving commands, following instructions, and completing the assigned tasks. If subordinates conform to the requirements of the system, their positions become secure and they become entitled to the benefits that accompany dutiful service. The control over rewards that are meaningful to subordinates enables authorities to obtain the expected degree of conformity (Garnier, 1973).

Obedience to authority reflects an authentic response from subordinates when they perform tasks voluntarily and view the tasks as being consistent with their own perception of norms and values (Etzioni, 1968). Here there is a correspondence between the subordinates' performance and their underlying beliefs about its usefulness and appropriateness. By way of contrast, obedience involves an inauthentic response when a subordinate presents a symbolic front of conformity to serve as a cover for underlying feelings of resentment

Obedience to Authority
The spontaneous behavior of children frequently represents a challenge to the authority of supervisors; but to the extent that the children are learning to play by the rules, they are being socialized for obedience to authority in later life.

and hostility. The subordinate appears to comply while at the same time feeling a sense of exclusion and social distance (Archibald, 1976). Because obedience to authority often stems from coercion, we should not assume that compliant behavior is consistent with underlying values and attitudes.

According to Stanley Milgram (1969: xii), "the essence of obedience consists in the fact that a person comes to view himself as the instrument for carrying out another person's wishes, and he therefore no longer regards himself as responsible for his actions." From this perspective, obedience involves submission to an authority agent. The authority figure may be an official of the church, a boss at work, a teacher in the classroom, or a governmental agent. Authorities have control over group resources, set group priorities, and impose obligations on subordinates under their command. Milgram clarified the character of obedience in a series of experiments on the willingness of individuals to comply with the wishes of malevolent authorities.

The Milgram experiments confirmed the willingness of individuals to engage in acts of aggression toward others on the basis of nothing more than a set of instructions from an authority figure. In these experiments the researcher was the authority figure and the subordinates were volunteers participating in the study. The experiment was presented as a study of the effects of punishment on learning. Subjects were instructed to take the role of a "teacher" and to administer electric shocks to a "learner" who gave incorrect answers to a series of questions. The volunteer was to increase the magnitude of the shock with each incorrect answer by pulling switches ranging from 15 volts to 450 volts.

The interest in the experiments was not with the learner, but with how far the subject was willing to go in administering punishment to another person on the basis of nothing more than the experimenter's instructions. Many subjects obeyed the experimenter by continuing to administer shocks up to the full 450 volts, despite the pleading and the apparent agony on the part of the victim. The experiments were conducted under a variety of settings and indicated that almost two-thirds of the volunteers (people from working, managerial, and professional classes, as well as students) were obedient subjects who followed the experimenter's instructions.

A great deal of subsequent controversy has surrounded the Milgram experiments over the uses of human subjects in research, and especially with the deception involved on the part of researchers. The learners in the experiments did not actually receive electric shocks, but they sat in chairs that appeared to be wired and their arms were strapped to prevent excessive movements. The subjects participating in the experiments did not know that the learners were aides of the researchers and were only acting their parts. The subjects also did not know that the researchers were really interested in obedience to authority, rather than in the effects of punishment on learning.

While such studies would now be regarded as unethical in their use of human subjects, their findings did have important implications for an understanding of the conditions under which individuals voluntarily submit to orders received from malevolent authorities. Milgram's findings do suggest

---

BOX 10.7
Public Responses to the Trial of Lt. Calley

What should combat soldiers do if they receive an order to shoot all inhabitants of a village, including old men, women, and children? Should they comply, or should they refuse to follow a military directive of this type? Shortly after the trial and conviction of Lt. William Calley for the My Lai incident in the Vietnam War, a national study conducted by Kelman and Lawrence (1972) found that the majority of Americans agreed that the soldier should "follow orders and shoot."

The defense in Lt. Calley's trial did not deny that the order was given and that he was causally responsible for the killings that took place. Instead, it was argued that Calley was doing what any good soldier would do—namely, follow the commands received from higher officers, even if this included killing defenseless civilians who may or may not have aided the enemy. In this view the trial was regarded as unfair because it held an individual accountable for the performance of military duty in a combat situation.

While most Americans agreed with Calley's defense, a substantial number of people believed that the individual soldier must be accountable for personal actions in the conduct of war. If an improper order is given, there is a moral obligation to disobey. The individual soldier obviously is not responsible for the overall conduct of the war, but is accountable for his or her own personal actions. Such a condemnation of Calley tended to occur among the college educated, while the rightness of following orders was emphasized by those with a high school education or less.

Source: Herbert C. Kelman and Lee H. Lawrence, "Assessment of Responsibility in the Case of Lt. Calley," *Journal of Social Issues* 28, no. 1 (1972): 177–212.

---

that the willingness of ordinary people to inflict injuries on others may stem from little more than a sense of duty to follow the orders received from an authority figure.

While the gap is enormous between the Milgram experiments and the atrocities of organized war, the basic social psychological principles appear to be similar. Subordinates may set aside moral scruples when acting out of a sense of duty and simply following orders. Brutality toward an enemy during times of war may stem not so much from attitudes of hatred or malice as from the sense of duty on the part of subordinates who are complying with orders and directives. Personality attributes or social background characteristics tend to be less important than the social pressures that are inherent in the structure of authority relationships. (See Box 10.7.)

The willingness to follow orders stems from the tendency to divest oneself from a sense of personal responsibility. Subordinates attribute the primary responsibilities for malevolent acts to authority agents in both the causal and the normative senses. But in many cases, compliance becomes much more of a moral dilemma for those who are receiving orders. If they comply with the wishes of malevolent authorities, subordinates may be held accountable by other agencies of authority within the broader society. If subordinates fail to follow orders, they default on their duties and may become exposed to the penalties of insubordination.

Although authorities emphasize the importance of following orders, subordinates are obligated to evaluate the rightness or the wrongness of the orders they receive. The decisions that individuals make under these circumstances reflect numerous assessments of the costs and benefits that given situations offer. Some people are routinely willing to submit to authority for opportunistic reasons. Others are more nearly oriented toward presenting an exterior mask of compliance while holding private attitudes of a different order. These patterns of response to authority reflect the manner by which individuals come to link their own personal interests and concerns with a broader series of events in the larger society.

SUMMARY

Authority refers to the exercise of legitimate power. It is expressed through the division of labor and reflects the rights and duties of certain individuals to make decisions that are binding on others. Authority relationships are expressed through interactions among those who are unequal in status characteristics. If some have the authority to issue directives and to supervise, others are obligated to comply and to obey.

Positions of authority are attained primarily through the process of status conferral. In modern societies people attain the more important forms of authority in public life by means of appointment. The recruitment of administrators and experts rests on a series of assumptions about organizational needs and the qualifications of personnel. Exclusions of sexual, racial, and ethnic minorities from top positions of authority depend primarily on a set of notions about the manner in which qualifications relate to ascribed status characteristics.

Those who hold positions of authority are entrusted with a set of trustee functions. Trusteeship refers to obligations for the conduct of group affairs and for the effective management of group resources. Those in positions of authority become accountable for group effectiveness. Decisions and authoritative acts require justification, especially if decisions become problematic or if they require group support for their implementation. Justification usually takes the form of arguments for the collective good and for the importance of designating priorities, since available resources are always limited.

Authority figures are held accountable through potential accusations of role failure, incompetence, and neglect of duties. When such issues arise, two forms of responsibility are likely to be of concern. These are responsibilities in both the causal and the normative senses. Causal responsibility refers to the outcome of events directly under the supervision of an authority figure, while normative responsibility refers to occurrences that are permitted to happen in spite of an obligation to prevent them. Authority figures may be held accountable, therefore, through invoking either the causal or the normative forms of responsibility.

Because of the selective vantage points of authority figures and subordinates, a given set of social events is likely to have divergent meanings. If some individuals have the authority to issue orders, others are confronted with the obligation to carry out the orders. In most cases, subordinates are willing to follow orders out of a sense of duty, especially if the orders are properly given. In cases of malevolent authority, however, subordinates are confronted with a serious dilemma. Compliance with authority may require participating in what the subordinate perceives as an immoral act, while the refusal to obey may subject the individual to the penalties of insubordination. But for most people, compliance with authority is usually voluntary, perceived as useful, and consistent with personally held norms and values.

BASIC TERMS

Ascribed status
Legal authority
Legitimation
Shielding
Trusteeship
Collective-good decisions
People-processing
  organizations

Triage proposal
Priority designations
Accountability
Causal responsibility
Normative responsibility
Obedience

REFERENCES

Archibald, W. Peter
  1976 "Face-to-Face: The Alienating Effects of Class, Status, and Power Divisions," *American Sociological Review* 41 (October): 819–837.
Beck, Bernard
  1978 "The Politics of Speaking in the Name of Society," *Social Problems* 25 (April): 353–360.
Blau, Peter
  1968 "The Hierarchy of Authority in Organizations," *American Journal of Sociology* 73 (January): 453–467.
Dahrendorf, Ralf
  1959 *Class and Class Conflict in Industrial Society*, Stanford, Calif.: Stanford University Press.
Drabek, Thomas E. and Judith B. Chapman

1973 "On Assessing Organizational Priorities," *Sociological Quarterly* 14 (Summer): 359–375.

Etzioni, Amitai
1968 "Basic Human Needs, Alienation, and Inauthenticity," *American Sociological Review* 33 (December): 870–885.

Ferber, Marianne, Joan Huber, and Glenna Spitze
1979 "Preference for Men as Bosses and Professionals," *Social Forces* 58 (December): 466–476.

Garnier, Maurice A.
1973 "Power and Ideological Conformity," *American Journal of Sociology* 79 (September): 343–363.

Grimm, James W. and Robert N. Stern
1974 "Sex Roles and Internal Labor Market Structures: The 'Female' Semi-Profession," *Social Problems* 21 (June): 690–705.

Habermas, Jurgen
1973 *Legitimation Crisis,* Boston: Beacon Press.

Hamilton, V. Lee
1978 "Who Is Responsible? Toward a Social Psychology of Attribution," *Social Psychology* 41 (December): 316–327.

Hasenfeld, Yeheskel
1972 "People Processing Organizations," *American Sociological Review* 37 (June): 256–263.

Haug, Marie R.
1975 "The Deprofessionalization of Everyone?," *Sociological Focus* 8 (August): 197–213.

Hauser, Robert M. and David L. Featherman
1976 "Equality of Schooling: Trends and Prospects," *Sociology of Education* 49 (April): 99–120.

Hewitt, John P. and Peter M. Hall
1973 "Social Problems, Problematic Situations, and Quasi-Theories," *American Sociological Review* 38 (June): 367–374.

Hughes, Everett C.
1963 "Profession," *Daedalus* 92 (Fall): 655–668.

Kamens, David H.
1977 "Legitimating Myths and Educational Organization," *American Sociological Review* 42 (April): 208–219.

Kantner, Stuart
1966 "An Examination of Legitimate Power," *Ohio Valley Sociologist* 31 (June): 1–13.

Katz, Jack
1977 "Cover-up and Collective Integrity: On the Natural Antagonism of Authority Internal and External to Organizations," *Social Problems* 25 (October): 3–17.

Kelman, Herbert C. and Lee H. Lawrence
1972 "Assessment of Responsibility in the Case of Lt. Calley," *Journal of Social Issues* 28, no. 1: 177–212.

Kluegel, James R.
1978 "The Causes and Cost of Racial Exclusion from Job Authority," *American Sociological Review* 43 (June): 285–301.

Kohn, Melvin
   1969 *Class and Conformity*, Homewood, Ill.: Dorsey Press.
Lopata, Helena Z.
   1976 "Expertization of Everyone and the Revolt of the Client," *Sociological Quarterly* 17 (Autumn): 435–446.
McMahon, Anne M. and Santo F. Camilleri
   1975 "Organizational Structure and Voluntary Participation in Collective-Good Decisions," *American Sociological Review* 40 (October): 616–644.
Marwell, Gerald
   1975 "Why Ascription," *American Sociological Review* 40 (August): 417–427.
Milgram, Stanley
   1969 *Obedience to Authority*, New York: Harper & Row.
Moen, Elizabeth
   1978 "The Reluctance of the Elderly to Accept Help," *Social Problems* 25 (February): 293–303.
Paddock, William and Paul Paddock
   1967 *Famine 1975!*, New York: Little, Brown.
Peter, Laurence F. and Raymond Hull
   1969 *The Peter Principle*, New York: Morrow.
Price, James L.
   1971 "Organizational Effectiveness," *Sociological Quarterly* 13 (Winter): 3–15.
Rothstein, David
   1972 "Culture-Creation and Social Reconstruction," *American Sociological Review* 37 (December): 671–678.
Seeman, Melvin
   1975 "Alienation Studies," *Annual Review of Sociology* 1: 91–123.
Seider, Maynard S.
   1974 "American Big Business Ideology: A Content Analysis of Executive Speeches," *American Sociological Review* 39 (December): 802–815.
Simmons, Roberta G.
   1968 "The Role Conflict of the First-Line Supervisor," *American Journal of Sociology* 73 (January): 482–495.
Takanishi, Ruby
   1978 "Childhood as a Social Issue: Historical Roots of Contemporary Child Advocacy Movements," *Journal of Social Issues* 34, no. 2: 8–28.
Weber, Max
   1947 *The Theory of Social and Economic Organization* (trans. and ed. by A. M. Henderson and Talcott Parsons), New York: The Free Press.
Wilensky, Harold L.
   1964 "The Professionalization of Everyone?," *American Journal of Sociology* 70 (September): 137–158.
Wolf, Wendy C. and Neil D. Fligstein
   1979 "Sex and Authority in the Workplace: The Causes of Sexual Inequality," *American Sociological Review* 44 (April): 235–252.
Yankelovich, Daniel
   1979 "Who Gets Ahead in America," *Psychology Today* 13 (July): 29–34f.

11

What to look for in this chapter:

What is social conflict?
Why is ethnicity becoming more important in our society?
What conditions promote the emergence of collective violence?
How and why do people differ in their responses to social protest?

Social Conflict

Authority relationships do not always proceed in a friendly, harmonious manner. Under certain conditions the legitimacy of authoritative acts is called into question. For example, subordinates sometimes express doubts about the competency of their superiors and become unwilling to follow their commands; or sometimes those in authority attempt to impose their own views and decisions on those beneath them. There are many situations such as these in which concerns emerge over the operative codes of a social system. Some members of that system then feel that justice does not prevail and that the use of defiance and rebellion are necessary for righting social wrongs. (See Figure 11.1.)

Conflicts in social relationships frequently reflect the emergence of a crisis of authority. Such a crisis occurs when those who are authorized to make binding decisions come to be perceived as untrustworthy or arbitrary in their decision making by those who are affected. The latter come to view the authoritative acts from on high as invalid, irrational, or reflecting incompetence (Habermas, 1973). There may be several different explanations for such judgments. It may mean that uncertainties have emerged about the adequacy of existing social norms, that those in authority are applying social norms inappropriately, or that they are being unresponsive to the needs of their constituencies (Dahrendorf, 1959).

Social psychologists broadly define social conflict to include the numerous forms and conditions of antagonistic social relationships. At the group level, social conflict is expressed in war, mass uprisings, parliamentary debates, organized protest, and legal entanglements. These expressions of conflict consist of power struggles in which one party attempts to gain access to scarce resources at the expense of others. In this competitive struggle both sides express antagonisms in "getting to know the enemy" and in directing energies and resources toward neutralizing, injuring, or eliminating the objects of hostility. In the escalation of conflict one opponent may focus attention so intensely on weakening the position of the other that the initial struggle for scarce resources recedes into the background.

Antagonistic interactions frequently reflect the collision of incompatible definitions of social reality. For example, traditional values conflict with

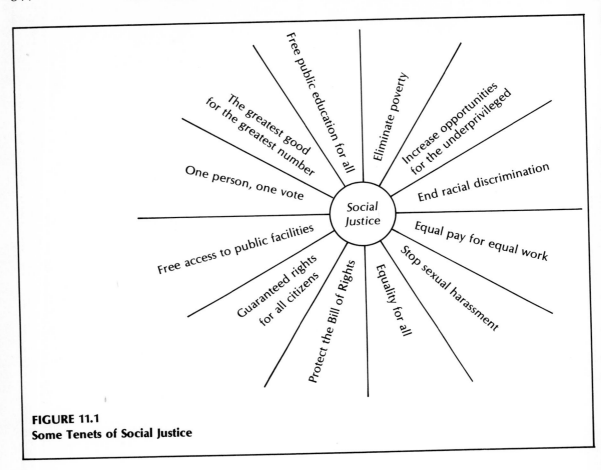

FIGURE 11.1
Some Tenets of Social Justice

the newer forms of morality; racial attitudes clash with emerging conceptions of social justice; sexist ideologies collide with changing definitions of the proper role of women. An awareness develops that ignoring certain kinds of problems in role relationships has degrees of cost for some members of a social system. The topic of race becomes of increasing concern under conditions of racial disorders; the topic of sex discrimination is thrust into consciousness when segments of the population are seeking to end discriminatory practices in employment; and the problems of social change become important in a society in which youthful lifestyles run counter to the basic beliefs and commitments of many older people. (See Table 11.1)

Most of the conflicts that erupt within a social system are amenable to resolution through negotiation and compromise. These are the forms of conflict that derive from self-interests and from a concern for promoting inequality

	TABLE 11.1 **The Vocabulary of Conflict**
Parties involved:	Enemies Foes Adversaries Opponents Oppressors Exploiters Contenders Antagonists Contestants Competitors
Emotions and sentiments:	Anger Hostility Hatred Rage Indignation Resentment Antipathy Distress Misery Adversity
Overt actions:	Attacking Injuring Abusing Limiting Demanding Defending Degrading Negotiating Compromising Litigating Isolating

in one's own favor. But other forms of conflict involve not so much a concern with utilitarian interests as with inflicting injury on an adversary. Making nonnegotiable demands and advocating the use of violence often appear as nonrational, since the objectives are oriented not so much toward attaining self-interests as toward expressing moral indignation over the lack of justice within the social system. The nonrationality of such commitments derives from the sense of obligation to act on the basis of some inner set of convictions without regarding the consequences for oneself or for others.

The overt expression of conflict within modern society is in part related to the process identified by C. Wright Mills (1959) as one in which personal troubles are turned into public issues. For example, during times of economic recession and relatively high levels of unemployment, some individuals blame themselves for economic hardships while others blame the social system. Those who blame themselves often experience vague and relatively undefined feelings of stress and anxiety; those who blame the system more often experience such emotions as anger, hostility, and resentment.

Since the prospect of openly expressing conflict is always associated with some degree of uncertainty and stress, people develop coping mechanisms for minimizing their overt expressions of hostility. Some may pretend that conflicts do not exist; others may recognize that conflicts exist but avoid facing up to them. People frequently keep as much social distance as possible between themselves and those they resent and deliberately avoid situations in which they are likely to confront conflicts. Such patterns of behavior prevent the constructive results that may arise from recognizing that certain problems do exist that they have hitherto not confronted and that consequently need attention. In recognizing the existence of a problem, individuals can strengthen their social relationships by working toward the attainment of mutually beneficial solutions.

This chapter will primarily examine the topics of racism and sexism. These themes in American society reflect overriding concerns with social injustice, with conflicting definitions of social reality, and with contested struggles. The ways in which a person copes with conflict are important for that person's sense of well-being; it is important for us to understand these coping mechanisms so we can see how personal identities are linked with broader patterns of group relationships. Although conflicts may appear to be disruptive and stressful, they frequently have the long-range effect of contributing positively to the enrichment of social life.

A. CONFLICTING REALITIES

To understand social conflict, it is important to recognize that we do not live in a world of objective reality but in a world of symbolic meanings. These meanings are expressed in views on how people differ by such social characteristics as race, sex, age, and national origin; in judgments about differential rights and privileges; in concerns about social justice and fairness; and in perceived differences in wealth and opportunity. Many differences exist in views on the fairness of an existing social order. Some feel deprived and make claims for remedial action, while others defend existing social arrangements.

Conflicts intensify when the older and more stable patterns of social interaction become unsatisfactory or intolerable to one or more parties. Under these conditions groups develop new definitions, update previous assump-

Traditional Versus Modern Values
The family portrait typically reflects a collection of people that is heterogeneous in terms of age, sex, marital status, and dependency relationships. Within such a heterogeneous group, underlying conflicts between traditional and modern values often come to the surface. In many cases, the younger generation is more receptive to changing norms and values, while the older generation is more firmly committed to customary norms and traditions.

tions, and make adjustments to changing social conditions. The clashes between traditional and modern values have been dramatically expressed in American race relations and in the changing definitions of the proper roles for women. **Traditionalism** refers to the acceptance of customary beliefs and practices as valid ones. In this view, definitions of reality are grounded in the social heritage and are thought to reflect the accumulated wisdom of past generations. By way of contrast, **modernism** is oriented toward inventing the future and creating a new system of values. The modernists emphasize the need to organize social relationships in a more rational and beneficial manner, and such an emphasis frequently comes into conflict with established norms and values.

The conflicts between traditional and modern constructions of reality are expressed in several ways. For example, they may occur in the clash between a traditional social norm and the emergence of a new morality; they may be found in the refusal of some to offer the deference expected by others; they show up in the gaps between traditional family forms and modern experiments with group living and cohabitation. But among the conflicts expressed in recent social changes, few match the intensity and soul searching that have accompanied various folk beliefs about the nature of race and the proper roles of women.

1. Racial Conflict

Racial conflicts within a social system spring from the process of differentiating among the social attributes of group members. The emergence of race as a special form of social classification has a modern historical origin and was based on the notion that identifiable biological differences in appearance are associated with differential capacities for cultural development and social participation (Rose, 1968). Early biologists and anthropologists worked out elaborate schemes of racial classification based on hair texture, size and shape of the nose, skin pigmentation, body build, and geographical location. The scientific attempts were directed toward identifying meaningful biological categories for subdividing the human species. It soon became apparent that these efforts were futile because the scientists could develop no consensus on the number of races nor on the defining characteristics. Furthermore, they found racial differences to be unrelated to innate abilities or to capacities for cultural development. In the absence of an empirical basis for racial classification, the scientific community concluded that race is an arbitrary construction that bears little relationship to objective reality. Ashley Montagu (1963) concluded from his review of the scientific literature that race is "man's most dangerous myth" and is based on "cultural fictions."

As the scientific community was recognizing the futility of racial classifications, ideas about race were intensifying in popular thinking. The notion developed that an individual should be classified as "a Negro" if he or she had "a single drop of Negro blood" or a single trace of African ancestry. Such views are absurd from a scientific standpoint. Anthropologists generally agree that human evolution very likely occurred on the plains of Africa about four or five million years ago, and so we all have a trace of African ancestry. The inadequacy of a biological basis for racial classification is recognized by the Bureau of the Census, and as a result its race statistics are based on self-reports, or on what individuals think of themselves as being.

The social construction of race we may view as a special case of the more general process of stereotyping used in the development and refinement of social categories. To clarify the concept of **stereotype** for scientific analysis, Walter Lippmann (1961: 79) made this observation:

Each of us lives and works on a small part of the earth's surface, moves in a small circle, and of those acquaintances knows only a few intimately. Of any public event that has wide effects we see at best only a phase and an aspect.... Inevitably our opinions cover a bigger space, a longer reach of time, a greater number of things than we can directly observe. They have, therefore, to be pieced together out of what others have reported and what we can imagine.

Following Lippmann's observation, we can say that stereotypes refer to notions about the attributes of a social group that are based on only partial or incomplete information. Stereotypes are errors in social thinking that derive from exaggeration and overgeneralization. Stereotypical thinking presumes similar characteristics to prevail among those who make up a social category, while underemphasizing individual differences and variations. Racial stereotypes include many folk beliefs about the biological differences between blacks and whites, such as differences in intelligence, temperament, sexuality, and other attributes that shape qualifications for participating in several aspects of social life (Mackie, 1973).

Racial contacts tend to modify stereotypes *if* the social interactions occur among those of similar socioeconomic status and *if* those individuals who interact share goals. Cooperative experiences may occur, for example, among racially mixed athletic teams and among integrated military units during times of war. In each of these cases, social relationships are characterized by the pursuit of shared goals and by an emphasis on mutual support and teamwork. These conditions promote group solidarity and cohesion, and racial stereotypes recede into the background.

The meanings that are given to racial classifications serve as self-fulfilling prophecies in a variety of ways. People tend to act on the basis of their stereotypes, and in race relations this tendency has been associated with patterns of discrimination and avoidance. Many people who would grant minorities their rights to employment and political participation prefer to exclude them from the more intimate circles of social relationships such as friendships, social clubs, and marriage. Moreover, there tends to be a high degree of generality in stereotypes. Those who would not admit blacks to their neighborhood or have them as friends also tend to reject other minorities defined according to national origin, religion, or deviant lifestyles (Ehrlich, 1973).

Self-fulfilling prophecies begin with definitions of how blacks differ from whites. These initial definitions may then serve as justifications for limiting the opportunities of blacks from involvement in numerous activities (professional schools, labor unions, social clubs, and so forth). Because of such restricted opportunities, blacks in turn become limited in their levels of achievement. Such lack of accomplishments is then taken as evidence that blacks are less qualified for several aspects of social participation. At this point the self-fulfilling prophecy has come full circle. The consequences resulting from false beliefs provide "evidence" that the initial assessments were correct.

Stereotypes often serve as self-fulfilling prophecies in race relations, not only through the patterns of avoidance and exclusion but also through the destructive effects that hostile imagery has on the self-identities of racial minorities. Members of racial minorities not only confront the common problems that everyone else faces in the development of a self-identity, but also the unique problem of coming to terms with racial stereotypes. Racial stereotypes serve as self-fulfilling prophecies under those circumstances in which the members of a minority group accept the folk beliefs and apply these negative images to themselves (Grier and Cobbs, 1969).

The factors that enter into the development of racial identities become reflected in life chances and opportunities. For example, one line of research indicates that the darker the skin among females, the greater the disadvantage in terms of status attainment through marriage (Udry, Bauman, and Chase, 1971). Other studies show that among males, gaining entry into the more prestigeful occupations occurs more frequently among light-skinned than among

---

BOX 11.1
Skin Color and Mate Selection

Drawing on a sample of 350 black couples in Washington, D.C., Udry, Bauman, and Chase (1971) analyzed the relationships between skin color, status attainment, and mate selection. Their concern was with determining the extent to which skin color had declined in significance as a social characteristic in the areas of employment and marriage.

The results of their analysis provide qualifications to the idea that in recent years skin color has become a less-important social feature within the black community. Among younger subjects the males with darker skins have fared better in the area of occupational attainment than those with lighter skins. However, a closer examination of the higher occupational attainment of dark-skinned males reveals important differences in mobility values. In comparison to their lighter-skinned counterparts, the darker males are more mobility-oriented and are willing to make greater personal sacrifices in order to advance in the occupational realm. These results appear to stem from the increased racial pride of younger males in recent years.

The findings for females show an entirely different pattern from that of males. Although there has been a trend toward fewer educational disadvantages for the darker-skinned females, the disadvantages in status attainment through marriage remain unchanged by age level. The more successful dark-skinned males tend to overselect light-skinned females as their marriage partners. These results suggest that the shifts in the status value of dark skin tend to favor men but not women. The status advantage of light-skinned women in preferential marriages has not been changed in recent years.

Source: J. Richard Udry, Karl E. Bauman, and Charles Chase, "Skin Color, Status, and Mate Selection," *American Journal of Sociology* 76 (January, 1971): 722–733.

BOX 11.2
Assimilation Versus Ethnicity

One prominent view during the 1940s and 1950s was that racial minorities would eventually become fully assimilated within American society. Assimilation is the pattern in which immigrant groups give up their separate identities by becoming Americanized and blending in with the general population. With the reduction of racial prejudice and discrimination, race was expected to decline in importance as a basis for social classification.

The conflict perspectives that emerged during the 1960s and 1970s viewed the topic of race in a different light. The conflict theorists viewed racism as an integral part of American life with numerous advantages for those who make up the white majority. Consequently, the stresses derived from race relations persist, and overt conflict continues to emerge on a sporadic basis. Obtaining full integration into American life is not a realistic option for most blacks, since the white majority will not voluntarily give up their special privileges. As a result, it is important for blacks to develop a separate ethnic heritage and to view race relations as a contested struggle for desired resources.

These perspectives point to different, but equally real, aspects of a complex and persisting problem. The assimilationists place emphasis on social justice and view racism as a carry-over from the past that will eventually disappear. In contrast, conflict theorists reject the notion of cultural unity and maintain that the incompatible interests of black and white America will endure. Consequently, advantages may very well accrue to the black Americans who develop pride in their ethnic heritage and recognize the pluralism of modern social life.

Source: L. Paul Metzger, "American Sociology and Black Assimilation: Conflicting Perspectives," *American Journal of Sociology* 76 (January, 1971): 627–647.

dark-skinned blacks (Ransford, 1970). These findings tap the subtle ways in which stereotypes are applied in such diverse domains as marriage and employment. Blackness has stood for inferiority in popular thinking, and such a belief shows up in differential life chances for minority persons. (See Box 11.1.)

The relationship between skin color and status attainment may be due to the combined effects of two sets of variables operating in social interactions. One consists of the discrimination that occurs in the subtle judgments the white majority makes in the application of racial stereotypes. The second consists of the lower degree of self-confidence in darker-skinned blacks, who also accept and apply in subtle ways the racial stereotypes of the larger society.

There are two separable problems these variables impose in adjustments to minority status: first, that of developing an authentic self-awareness apart from the negative connotations in folk beliefs, and second, that of evolving a sense of confidence and mastery in attaining desired goals within the broader social system. These two problems became evident during the 1960s in two major social movements that emerged among American blacks. One consisted of an emphasis on black nationalism, or black pride, as reflected in the slogan "black is beautiful," while the second consisted of an emphasis on "black power," with the concern directed toward the use of organization and pressure tactics for the attainment of desired ends. (See Box 11.2.)

2. Emergent Ethnicity

Ethnicity refers to the shared historical experiences, cultural values, and lifestyles that characterize a subgroup within a larger population. The emergence of an emphasis on black culture among Afro-Americans derived from the view among blacks that they would lose a great deal if they aimed toward full assimilation into American life. The widespread appeal of Alex Haley's search for his own roots in the conditions of slavery and in the social heritage of Africa springs from the recognition that a sense of history is important for developing self-awareness. In this respect, an identity stems not only from present locations within a social system but also from a social heritage and shared group experiences. The growing interest in black culture and history constituted a basis for the development of self-pride, which stood in opposition to the racial stereotypes deeply embedded in folk beliefs and history (Wilson, 1970).

With the emergence of Afro-American associations during the late 1960s and early 1970s came an emphasis on black experiences and black culture. Becoming aware of the historical distinctiveness of black experiences and creating an authentic black subculture became important concerns. Black historians gave explicit recognition to heroic struggles with conditions of slavery and oppression and to the many contributions blacks have made to American life. Such positive elements in black culture form the basis for the emergence of ethnic consciousness among blacks and provide an alternative to the racial stereotypes historically reflected in the folk beliefs of the white majority (Maykovich, 1972).

In a synthesis of recent studies on black identity and self-esteem, Porter and Washington (1979: 57) drew the following conclusion:

The literature on black adolescents and adults most clearly demonstrates the effect of the black consciousness movement on racial self-esteem, showing greater positive associations with the color black in recent than in earlier times.

However, the development of black consciousness has had an impact on self-esteem that differs in degree according to age level and socioeconomic status. Levels of racial pride and self-esteem tend to be higher among younger than among older subjects, and higher among the college-educated than among those with only a high school education or less. These differences appear to stem from the greater receptiveness of the young and the better educated to modern constructions of reality. Members of these groups are more likely to empha-

BOX 11.3
Urban Black Attitudes Toward Separatism

In studying the perspectives held by urban blacks on intergroup tensions, Turner and Wilson (1976) were concerned with the attributes and correlates of a separatist ideology. Separatism refers to sentiments favoring exclusive control by blacks over institutions serving black populations. For example, the separatist view is expressed in the attitude that public schools in the black community should be run solely by black educators and black committee members. Further, the separatist view encourages the withdrawal of blacks from participation in social activities dominated by whites.

While a sense of black solidarity has increased in recent years, the research of Turner and Wilson suggests that the majority of blacks do not embrace a separatist point of view. Their study of 1000 households in urban areas indicates that the degree of acceptance of separatist views is related to age, sex, and regional location. Support for separatism is significantly greater for those under thirty years of age than for those thirty or older. Males are more likely to favor separatism than females, and separatist sentiments are stronger in the North than in the South.

Blacks who favor the creation of separate institutions for blacks are more likely to be fearful of the consequences of interracial cooperation. They are more likely to feel alienated from the surrounding society, and they are more likely to endorse the use of violence to achieve black aims and objectives. Thus separatism is associated with black militancy and opposition to policies promoting racial integration.

Source: Castellano B. Turner and William J. Wilson, "Dimensions of Racial Ideology: A Study of Urban Black Attitudes," *Journal of Social Issues* 32, no. 2 (1976): 139–152.

size black pride, to blame the system rather than themselves, and to discern structural barriers to opportunity for racial and ethnic minorities (Gurin and Epps, 1975).

While recognizing that ethnicity emphasizes the positive aspects of a subculture, Wilson (1970) noted that the parallel emergence of the black-power movement constituted a more direct response to developments in the surrounding society. Black-power militants of the late 1960s advocated the use of force and coercion in dealing with whites and the existing power structure. They assumed that the full assimilation of blacks into the mainstream of American life was not likely to occur and that it was not desirable anyway. They rejected the idea of cultural unity, and they maintained that the incompatible interests of black and white Americans would endure. Black-power militants viewed it as necessary for blacks to organize and to pursue their own self-interests within the framework of a multigroup society (Barbour, 1968). (See Box 11.3.)

This is an example of emphasizing **cultural pluralism**; proponents are concerned with elaborating separate institutions and action programs along racial and ethnic lines. Here the emphasis is on exclusiveness, a sharp separation between insiders from outsiders, and the development of a strong sense of in-group cohesion and solidarity. Action programs are designed to enhance the uniqueness of an ethnic heritage and culture. These developments reflect an interest in stressing the positive aspects of racial classification while at the same time directing efforts toward practical lines of action (Elder, 1971). Race relations then become **contested struggles**, and the disadvantaged persons in this contest must pool their resources for personal protection and for the enhancement of group interests.

B. CONTESTED STRUGGLES

John Horton (1966) observed that the conflict perspective views society as being made up of groups with opposing aims and values. Under these conditions social relationships become contested struggles, which are enacted in historically specific situations. Social justice does not prevail, some segments

The Myth of National Unity
The American myth of national unity is symbolized by the flags and crosses employed in Memorial Day celebrations. In commemorating the military dead, the themes of "national unity" and "personal sacrifices for the common good" are emphasized. Such themes temporarily shift attention away from the heterogeneous character of the subgroups and life circumstances that divide the nation.

BOX 11.4
The Declining Significance of Race

William Julius Wilson maintains that American race relations have undergone fundamental changes in recent years. The life chances of individual blacks now are linked more closely with economic class than with racial category. Wilson's thesis holds that such variables as education, family income, and occupational status are becoming increasingly important in shaping the life-worlds of individual blacks, while racial classifications are declining in significance.

Throughout the nineteenth century and the first half of the twentieth century, the efforts of whites to construct racial barriers had profound effects on the lives of black Americans. According to Wilson (1978: 1),

Racial oppression was deliberate, overt, and is easily documented, ranging from slavery to segregation, from endeavors of the white economic elite to exploit black labor to the actions of the white masses to eliminate or neutralize black competition, particularly economic competition. As the nation has entered the latter half of the twentieth century, however, many of the traditional barriers have crumbled under the weight of the political, social, and economic changes of the civil rights era.

The traditional forms of racial segregation and discrimination persist in social clubs and in residential patterns. In the political and economic spheres, however, social class has become more important than race in social opportunities. Many talented and educated blacks are achieving positions of prestige and power comparable to those of whites with equivalent qualifications. The large proportion of blacks at the lower socioeconomic levels, in contrast, are falling further behind the rest of society in achieving "the good life."

Source: William Julius Wilson, *The Declining Significance of Race*, Chicago: University of Chicago Press, 1978.

of the population are exploited for the benefit of others, and the uses of force and coercion shape the outcome of events. The conflict perspective looks on the authority of the state as being oppressive, serving primarily the interests of those in power. These are the conditions that promote the development of strong and cohesive organizations for the protection of minority rights.

In the view of conflict as a contested struggle, minorities become significant primarily because of their disproportionate location at the lower echelons of the socioeconomic system. This view also deemphasizes the importance of race because it is based on a cultural fallacy (Banton, 1974). The blockage of opportunities for social participation and the restrictions on freedom of movement are among the class-related aspects of minority status (Snyder and Hudis, 1976). Contested struggles emerge in the quest for social justice and in the attempt to validate new definitions of role relationships. (See Box 11.4.)

Like race, sexual status is a characteristic ascribed at birth. This status has implications for patterns of interaction that are independent of subsequent education, income, or other forms of personal and social accomplishment. Some people presume women to be biologically and temperamentally different from men in ways that justify their subordinate status. These are cultural elaborations on observable biological differences that are utilized in giving men the upper hand in privileges and opportunities. As with folk definitions of racial differences, the folk definitions of sexual differences are drawn on as a basis for denying equal access to socially desired rewards within the social system. Since men are unwilling to give up voluntarily their special positions of power and privilege, inequality and discriminatory practices constitute sources of conflict in gender relationships.

In discussing the position of women in social stratification, Acker (1973) observed that men and women lack equality in social status both within the family and within the larger society. Acker noted that numerous criteria may be drawn on to delineate sexual inequality, including the variables of prestige in the community, lifestyle, privilege, opportunities, group memberships, income, education, and power. Within the broader American society, social status is often based on having full-time employment and on the direct financial rewards bestowed on those engaged in the labor force. Wives who provide important support for the development of their husbands' careers do not share equally in the social and psychological rewards that accompany the socioeconomic position of the family as a social unit. Accordingly, we can look on adult females in our society as individuals who have identities and life chances that vary independently from those of the significant males in their lives (Huber, 1976).

1. Gender Stereotypes

The existence of social inequality, whether in race or in sex roles, is accompanied by a set of justifications designed to account for how and why inequalities in social relationships are essentially proper and fair. The justifications are often biologically based stereotypes, which emphasize differences in inherent abilities and in capacities to participate in numerous facets of social life. The character of these accounts became of major concern with the emergence of the women's movement in the 1970s and with a series of studies that concentrated on the mechanisms by which patterns of sexual discrimination have developed (Broverman et al., 1972). Several research studies indicate that from a very early and impressionable age females are socialized into roles that serve as self-fulfilling prophecies of their subsequent subordination to males.

In a study of sex-role stereotypes, Weitzman and her associates (1972) concentrated on the themes emphasized in prize-winning books for preschool children. The results of their analysis indicated that boys were overrepresented by a ratio of about three to one in the pictures, titles, and central role activities of the books. The lower visibility of girls in the stories tended to give the im-

BOX 11.5
Images of "The Nice Girl"

"What's a nice girl like you doing in a place like this?" To voice such a question conveys a series of images about what the proper role of women should be, as well as judgments about the moral worth of women who fail to comply with social norms. Drawing on data from various cultures, Greer Fox (1977) concentrated on images of "the nice girl" as social control mechanisms used to restrict the participation of women in public affairs.

Many traditional societies draw on nice-girl images to confine the activities of women to the family unit. In these situations women tend to be restricted to the boundaries of the home, and interactions within the broader social world become highly limited. In other cases women are permitted to venture beyond the confines of the home but only under the protective custody of an escort. In the emphasis on confinement and protection, the culture's major concern is maintaining the social control of women by restricting their freedom of movement and providing for surveillance of their behavior.

In modern societies, by way of contrast, women are permitted to be in most public places, but there are numerous normative restrictions associated with nice-girl images and lady-like behavior. Under conditions of modernism women are not subjected to external control so much as to controls by an internalized set of norms and values. Being "a good girl" or being "lady-like" are not attributes that can be confirmed with any degree of finality. Such an achieved status always remains in jeopardy and is subject to verification in each instance of social interaction. Efforts toward becoming a lady are directed toward attaining what is essentially an unattainable status.

Source: Greer Litton Fox, "Nice Girl: Social Control of Women Through a Value Construct," *Signs* 2 (1977): 805–817.

pression that "girls are not very important because no one has bothered to write stories about them" (1129). This study also noted that boys were presented in more-exciting and adventurous roles and were engaged in more varied activities that expressed greater independence. On the other hand, girls were portrayed as being more passive and emotional and engaging in less-exciting activities. The girls in the stories were less achievement-oriented and expressed the image of being successful by "looking pretty" and "serving others." The authors concluded that the stereotypes of these stories encouraged the development of greater self-confidence among boys and more vacuous identities and passive orientations among girls. (See Box 11.5.)

Research studies have shown that parents have an overwhelming preference for a boy as the first child and a girl as the second child in the two-child family. Thus the subordinate position of the female occurs early in the development process. From birth, parents tend to respond differently to sons and daughters. They teach little girls to please and to strive for love and approval. Conversely, they teach little boys to be more active, to show more task involvement, and to become more independent than little girls (Hoffman, 1972). The need for social approval places the female in a much more vulnerable position in her relationships with others. Her sense of well-being is dependent on forces that are beyond her control, on responses that are made by her significant others (Fox, 1977). In contrast, the achievement-orientations of male role models encourage the male to be more dependent on his own self-generated levels of motivation and effort.

2. Changing Sex Roles

Although the women's movement has been one of the more vocal sources of concern with sex roles, the changes that have occurred in recent years correlate with the demographic trends of the family within American society. Of particular note is the emphasis on greater freedom and role alternatives for women.

Recent trends in the American family indicate that more women are postponing marriage until a later age and are having smaller families. The modal preference is for two children, and the average American woman has had her last child by the age of twenty-seven (Glick, 1977). More women are now voluntarily remaining childless, and abortion is becoming more readily acceptable as an alternative to having an unwanted child. These developments within society express the profound changes that are occurring in the status of women.

The trend toward smaller families is accompanied by increased participation of women in the labor force. At the present time about half of the women of working age are employed, and in recent years an increasing proportion of all workers have been women (U.S. Department of Commerce, 1977). However, despite increased participation in the labor force, most women are employed within a narrow range of occupations. Women are overrepresented in nursing, social work, librarianship, school teaching, and clerical work (Grimm and Stern, 1974), and underrepresented in the higher-paid and more prestigious professions (Featherman and Hauser, 1976). These demographic attributes of the status of women reflect contradictory ideas about sexual differences, about the kinds of opportunities that should be available for women, and about the ways in which the chores of family living should be allocated between husbands and wives.

From interviews with single males who were seniors at an Ivy League college, Mirra Komarovsky (1973) found that the majority agreed with the modern view that it is appropriate for the mother of preschool children to take a full-time job. But in responding to this questionnaire item, many of the respondents added qualifications to their approval. These included stipulations that "the home is run smoothly," that "the children do not suffer," or that "the wife's employment does not interfere with her husband's career." About one-fourth of the subjects were traditionalists and stated outright that they intended to marry women who would find sufficient fulfillment in domestic, civic, and cultural pursuits without seeking outside employment. About half of the respondents took a modified traditionalist approach, favoring a sequential pattern in which wives work prior to the birth of a first child, withdraw from the labor force during the years of more intensive child-care responsibilities, and eventually return to work as the children become more independent. Only 7 percent of the then-unmarried subjects indicated a willingness to modify their own career plans in order to facilitate career development for their future wives.

The research evidence is abundantly clear that traditional sex attitudes have weakened, but that at the same time they are far from being relinquished. Komarovsky (1973) observed that her subjects had contradictory values and sentiments. Males who held traditional values concerning the importance of the domestic roles of wife and mother also held negative attitudes toward the role of housewife. Thus a contradiction occurs in the low status accorded to housewives along with the conviction that there are no adequate substitutes for the mother's care of young children. Further inconsistencies may be noted in the view that women should have equal rights to pursue a career, but that the typical male would not like being married to an intellectually superior woman whose success in career development exceeded his own.

The contradictory sentiments expressed in the attitudes of males become even more problematic for the female, whose self-identity requires confronting and resolving the conflicts between traditional and modern values. Most women do place a high degree of value on marriage, children, and gainful employment (Parelius, 1975). Although men emphasize these same values, women experience greater conflicts because of the competing demands of developing a career and meeting the obligations deeply embedded in social attitudes toward the appropriate role of the adult female (Coser and Rokoff, 1971).

Traditionalism persists in social attitudes toward the adult female role (Mason and Bumpass, 1975). The traditionalist view emphasizes beliefs about the appropriateness of the subordinate position of women relative to that of men. Folk attitudes include the notion that "a woman's place is in the home," that "a woman's most important task in life should be taking care of her husband and children," and "the husband should be the major provider for the family," and that "it goes against nature to put women in positions of authority over men." Such traditional attitudes tend to segregate the roles of men and women within society and within the family. Women are expected to do the chores around the house and to take care of the children, while the husband is expected to be the major wage earner. Women are also expected to perform secretarial services in the home and on the job. They are the ones who make the coffee and who run the errands.

In contrast to views on the traditional roles of women, attitudes of egalitarianism and modernism are receiving increased emphasis (Scanzoni, 1975). The egalitarian, modernist view holds that with the increase of women in the labor force and the trend toward smaller family size, we should place greater emphasis on sharing chores within the family, on increasing the involvement of fathers in child care and child rearing, on equal employment opportunities for women, and on fairness in pay for men and women who do the same work. The modern values are far from being uniformly held; as a result the conflicts between traditional and emerging values frequently generate stress in relationships between husbands and wives, as well as between parents and their children.

C. VIOLENCE IN PUBLIC PLACES

New images of society and social relationships are created as social conflicts escalate. Various groups make claims that injustices prevail, that those in positions of authority are unresponsive to the needs of their constituents, and that extreme measures are necessary for producing the desired changes. Under these circumstances people hold mass demonstrations, seek remedial actions, and sometimes participate in sporadic violence. Some make attempts to coerce public officials into doing something about the problems that have been neglected.

The occurrence of violence in public places derives from the perception that force is necessity in social relationships and that one cannot meet personal needs and interests by going through legitimate channels. The underprivileged, the oppressed, and the disenchanted see authorities as rigid, inflexible, and unresponsive to the needs of the people and view the norms of everyday life as impediments to the attainment of desired goals. As a result, they use coercive techniques to force those in positions of authority to take note of existing problems. They are no longer willing to endure an unjust system. Through engaging in violent acts they can no longer be ignored by those in positions of authority.

1. Unresponsive Environments

The **unresponsive environment** is a social setting in which a sense of entrapment develops for individuals. Their perceptions of justice and fair play are out of alignment with the way they view the social system as operating. They see membership in a social group, a community, or a society as imposing obligations and responsibilities without producing a shared sense of identity or a common sense of purpose. Such individuals feel estranged: the kind of life they desire for themselves or for their significant others cannot be attained by working within the existing social order.

Living in an unresponsive environment involves making judgments about authority relationships and the location of power. Individuals may be coerced into paying taxes they perceive as being unjust, conscripted into military service when they would prefer to be doing something else, or forced into working at a job devoid of intrinsic meaning. Such developments suggest that such individuals perceive authority as it operates within a social unit as lacking in legitimacy. Their personal concerns and interests are not incorporated into the collective-good decisions. Instead, they perceive authority structure as being hostile and unresponsive.

Perceptions of an environment as unresponsive do not stem exclusively from the objective attributes of a social system. One may have a comfortable standard of living and still be highly dissatisfied with the conditions of one's existence. The kinds of discontent that lie in back of civil violence and protest derive from both relative deprivation and rising expectations. Revolutionary actions are not likely to occur under conditions of extreme deprivation or struggle for survival. Instead, the employment of collective violence as an instrument of social change becomes a more likely choice by those who have escalating hopes and aspirations for the future.

As developed by James Davies (1972), the theory of **rising expectations** holds that civil violence is more likely to occur if there is an economic downturn following a period of sustained growth. From this perspective people's hopes and aspirations tend to soar above levels of attainment possible at any given point in time. If social advances are being made, there is a tendency to expect the gains to continue. But if an advance comes to a halt or a reversal occurs, a sense of discontent emerges, and the gap between aspirations and realities becomes intolerable. Individuals are prevented from realizing their goals, and their previous gains appear to be threatened.

Relative deprivation refers to the gap between what people feel they deserve and what they actually receive (Gurr, 1972). Changes in the reward distributions within a society lead to a situation where people are winners and losers in terms of their relative standings. Those who are deserving do not always get what they feel they are entitled to, just as some are able to manipulate the system in order to maximize their own gains. Under conditions of relative deprivation, individuals feel that a system of distributive justice does not prevail, that sacrifices are made unevenly, and that some people are obtaining undeserved benefits. If such individuals compare themselves with the more privileged members of society, the conclusion may be inescapable that the good things in life are being distributed unevenly and unjustly. The blocks to opportunity may be seen as deriving from numerous sources, including racial discrimination, greediness on the part of the rich, or role failure on the part of authority agents. Rising expectations and relative deprivation may have been at the core of the racial unrest that occurred in American society during the 1960s (Geschwender, 1968). While numerous gains had been made through the civil rights movement, blacks perceived their opportunities to participate in the mainstream of American life as being held in check due to continuing discrimination.

Blacks and other minorities had not shared proportionately in the prosperity of the post–World War II years. Although blacks generally were better off than were their grandparents, the relative gap between "the haves" and "the have nots" had possibly widened. The hopes of many blacks had been raised by the political promises of the 1960s and by the introduction of Great Society programs. From the failure of the system to deliver on these promises, hopes and aspirations turned to anger, and the resulting discontent took a violent form (Killian, 1968).

Widespread feelings of exploitation, deprivation, and discontent do not necessarily lead to collective violence. Men and women may endure conditions of injustice for long periods of time and regard them as basic realities of

---

BOX 11.6
Targets of Violence

Richard A. Berk and Howard E. Aldrich (1972) examined patterns of vandalism during urban riots by concentrating on social relationships between inner-city residents and local business people. They based their study on interviews with owners and managers of small businesses located in inner-city neighborhoods. One set of interviews was conducted prior to the riots of 1968 and another set of interviews was conducted after the disturbances had occurred, permitting a comparison of those stores that had been vandalized with those that had not.

Berk and Aldrich noted that riot-related damage was not randomly distributed; nor did it support such images of the crowd that emphasize emotional contagion, irrationality, and mindless destruction. Their findings indicated that stores with the more attractive (and expensive) merchandise were more likely to be vandalized. Further, the looting of a store tends to be a localized event. Prior knowledge of the store's characteristics (familiarity) and the location of the store in a riot area (exposure) were additional variables associated with the risk for vandalism. These variables suggest that the selection of targets during civil disorders is based on rational choice by at least some of the rioters.

Other variables related to the selection of targets reflected the theme of retaliation. Negative attitudes of store owners toward black customers and their aspirations increased the vulnerability to attack. Overcharging, distasteful demeanor, and selling inferior goods were among the many business practices that generated resentments. Finally, there was only limited evidence that violent behavior was directed toward stores as symbols of white society. Businesses owned by whites had only a slightly higher probability of attack than those owned by blacks.

Source: Richard A. Berk and Howard E. Aldrich, "Patterns of Vandalism During Civil Disorders as an Indicator of Selection of Targets," *American Sociological Review* 37 (October, 1972): 533–547.

social living. Instead of taking an active approach toward bringing about basic changes, attitudes of resignation and passivity may develop. Fear of repression and punishment is often strong enough to inhibit any tendency toward open rebellion. People may perceive the social control mechanisms as so overwhelming that they regard protest or opposition as unworkable and futile (Bruce, 1979). The use of violence is likely to occur only after some individuals feel so strongly about their discontent that they are no longer willing to endure an unjust world.

Violent reactions to an unresponsive environment are likely to occur only in conjunction with the development of justifications for the use of physical force. For example, the research of Russell Dynes and E. L. Quarantelli (1968) indicated that urban rioting and looting in the United States during the 1960s were accompanied by the emergence of social norms that condoned violent acts. The looting in urban riots was not so much the taking of property for utilitarian reasons as it was a symbolic expression of discontent. This was notable particularly in the selectivity of the objects of destruction (Berk and Aldrich, 1972), in the sharing of loot with total strangers, and in the encouragement of bystanders to participate. Civil disturbances may be regarded as messages from the deprived sector of the population that its members will resort to violence in attempts to bring about desired changes. (See Box 11.6.)

2. Collective Violence

Collective violence refers to conditions of insurgency in which the orderliness of social life is disrupted through unauthorized uses of force and coercion. Insurgents display a lack of respect for authority, give inflammatory speeches, threaten acts of sabotage, and make what they call nonnegotiable demands. The disruptions take the form of social protest, express the willingness of participants to take chances, and frequently result in physical injuries and property damage. While collective violence finds one of its most frequent expressions in urban riots, it also includes the more highly organized forms of disobedience that occur, such as terrorism, sabotage, political assassinations, and preparations for civil war.

The emergence of collective violence is dependent on some precipitating event for mobilizing the resources of the disenchanted. The precipitating event is only the immediate cause for the occurrence of disruptions, and when it does occur it builds on the resentments that have accumulated over an extended period of time. For example, numerous riots broke out in American cities following the assassination of Martin Luther King. On college campuses numerous demonstrations and riots followed the announcement that the Vietnam War had been extended to include bombing raids in Cambodia. The disruptions on college campuses escalated following the killing of students at Kent State University by the National Guard.

The precipitating events are not in and of themselves the primary causes of the vast disruptions that can occur with collective violence. Instead, the responses to news items provide the grounds for acting out several concerns about social reality. The disruptions produced by mass demonstrations, rioting and looting, and acts of sabotage become crisis events in the sense that they represent threatening departures from the routine patterns of everyday life. The facades of harmony and tranquility in the social realm have broken down, and one can no longer regard the future as an extension of the present. Forces are at work that one can neither fully understand nor control. Such conditions dramatize the conflicts inherent within a social system and thus bring to the surface a wide variety of resentments and moral judgments.

The very existence of an internal crisis is symbolic of role failure on the part of those whose job it is to manage and maintain a social order. Public officials and law enforcement personnel are unable to remain neutral during times of civil disorder, and often must act in response to the urgency of the situation. The unscheduled character of the unfolding events prevents the possibility of relying exclusively on administrative routines. Instead, social relationships become negotiable in character, since the usual moderating controls of social norms have lost their hold over individual conduct. Patterns of obedience are no longer operative, and people place pressures on public officials to take decisive stands in the restoration of order (Neal, 1976).

The police sometimes find themselves at the center of social justice controversies. Highly coercive and punitive measures generated through police

Symbols of Oppressive Authority
Police cars and their occupants may become primary symbols of oppressive authority and social injustice during times of civil disorder.

efforts to cope with mass-murder cults, with violent activists, and with terrorists can become a form of violence. Unusual and excessive use of force in the name of law and order can intensify, rather than resolve, the problems of social conflict. For example, the public debates continued for many years over the actions of the Ohio National Guard at Kent State University, over the manner in which the Chicago police force handled the demonstrations at the Democratic National Convention in 1968, and over the killings that occurred in suppressing the Attica prison riot of 1971. Social norms require that only as much force as is necessary should be employed in law enforcement and that the rights of the innocent should be protected.

D. SOCIETAL REACTIONS TO VIOLENCE

The role of the police in collective violence is unclear because of the ambiguity over the boundaries separating legitimate social protest from criminal acts. Collective violence is embellished with a moral cause and with a plea to correct social injustice, while criminal violence is viewed as resulting from uncontrollable passions and self-interests. Although acts of criminal violence such as armed robbery and muggings are clearly forms of deviant behavior, acts of social violence are not so clear. A great deal of uncertainty surrounds public thinking about collective violence, and as a result the societal reaction to violence has become of concern to social psychologists.

The participants in urban riots, campus demonstrations, and organized protest cannot alone solve the problems of social injustice. They must win sympathy and support for their causes through an appeal to either those in positions of authority or to those who are observers of the events in question. The participants in collective violence are risk takers in the sense that they may be labeled as deviants, criminals, or troublemakers. But they may also gain self-respect and pride by becoming champions of a greater cause and by making personal sacrifices for the improvement of social conditions. The extent to which violent acts are regarded as legitimate social protest or as criminal conduct depends on how numerous others respond and on what meanings they give to these acts. Success or failure in the uses of collective violence lies outside the hands of the participants themselves. The final outcomes reside with public opinion and with the responses of social control agencies.

1. The Credibility of Protest

Some forms of collective violence do not relate to any identifiable concern for corrective social action; sometimes they occur in conjunction with victory celebrations. Gary Marx (1972) refers to these disruptions as **issueless riots**. For example, following the surrender of Japan at the end of World War II, the celebration in San Francisco got out of control. The police stood by helplessly as the crowds broke store windows, attacked streetcars, overturned automobiles, and destroyed posters that reminded them of war. Similar acts of destruction sometimes accompany rock concerts and the celebration of athletic victories. Defeating a bitter rival in an athletic contest, winning a conference championship, going to the Rose Bowl, or winning the Super Bowl may produce levels of excitement that spill over into acts of destruction.

Because of the linkage between celebration and destruction, acting crowds are frequently characterized by a carnival atmosphere, by elements of fun and games, by expressive behavior, and by the quest for additional excitement. However, issueless riots differ qualitatively from those that develop out of the frustrations of a long and heroic struggle. The urban riots of the 1960s followed the epic struggles of the civil rights movement and contained elements of both social protest and criminal conduct. Similarly, the disturbances on college campuses in the spring of 1970 followed the frustrations over national involvement in a protracted war that many believed to be unnecessary and unjust.

Ralph Turner (1969) has identified the conditions promoting a definition of collective violence as social protest. The **credibility of protest** is dependent on the conviction that social injustices (e.g., unfair treatment, historical oppression, or police brutality) have occurred, and that the people involved cannot correct the situation through their own actions alone. So the people must make appeals to levels of morality higher than those involved in the operative codes of a social system. Further, the people must draw attention to a set of grievances, and must seek ameliorative actions. The designation of collective violence as social protest requires some balance between appeals and threats in their efforts to win sympathy for a cause. (See Figure 11.2.)

Vincent Jeffries, Ralph Turner, and Richard Morris (1971: 448) make the following observation on the balance between appeals and threats in establishing the credibility of social protest:

A public fails to identify a disturbance as a protest when the appeal—the identification of grievances and the call for help—is too soft to be heard, or when the threat to the hearer is so loud that it drowns out the appeal.

The uses of moral appeals alone are usually ineffective as attention-getting devices. They take on a greater degree of urgency if they are accompanied by threats and if some degree of fear can be generated. On the other hand, if threats become so intense that negotiated settlements do not appear feasible, those in positions of authority may suppress disturbances through the coercive powers of the state without giving any official recognition to the moral appeals.

Research on the responses of whites to the 1965 Watts riot in Los Angeles indicated that definitions of the disturbance as social protest depended on several conditions (Jeffries, Turner, and Morris, 1971). Viewing the riot as social protest required the beliefs that there was a great deal of racial discrimination in Los Angeles, that the civil rights movement in general rested on a just cause,

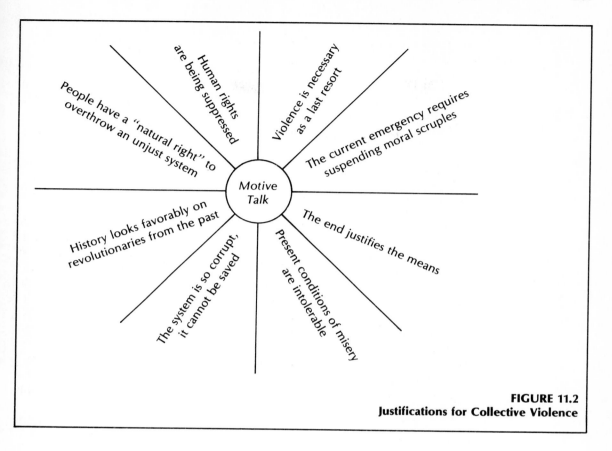

FIGURE 11.2
Justifications for Collective Violence

that a large number of people had participated in the riot, and that the demonstrators represented the basic sentiments of the black community.

In contrast, viewing the riot as deviant and criminal conduct was related to concerns about law and order, personal fears about the consequences of collective violence, opposition to the civil rights movement, and the belief that the demonstrators had only limited support within the black community. Thus previous attitudes about justice and order have a great deal of influence on defining a given disturbance as social protest or as criminal action. In general, college-educated people were more likely to view the riot as based on justified grievances, while those with a high school education or less tended to see the event as a manifestation of deviancy. (See Box 11.7.)

The appointment of prestigious people to commissions investigating the conditions surrounding public disturbances (such as the Kennedy assassination, urban riots, criminal violence, and the disruption of the Democratic National Convention) serves multiple purposes. Making such appointments

BOX 11.7
Blue-Collar Anger

Two forms of protest were covered extensively by the news media in the late 1960s and early 1970s, and this generated strong emotional reactions among many Americans. A series of race riots broke out in American cities, and blacks made several demands for historically based reparations and for the preferential hiring of blacks in industry. On college campuses, student demonstrations were directed toward protesting the war in Vietnam, taking over buildings, and making demands for the rights of students to participate in university governance.

H. Edward Ransford (1972) made a study of public attitudes toward student and black protest by concentrating on the anger expressed by members of the working class. Drawing on a sample of 477 Caucasian adults from the Los Angeles metropolitan area, Ransford's research indicates that those employed in manual occupations were disproportionately among those who expressed punitive attitudes toward student demonstrators and among those who believed that blacks were pushing too hard for undeserved privileges.

Several variables were found to influence the anger toward student and black protest. The disrespect for authority clashed with the working-class values of discipline, obedience, and conformity. The working class regarded education as an avenue of upward mobility for their sons and daughters, and expressed resentments toward middle-class youth for assaults on educational institutions. Working-class hostility over black protest related to feelings of political powerlessness, to the belief that the government was doing too much for minorities, and to the view that the basic concerns of the working class were being neglected. They regarded blacks as gaining undeserved privileges at the expense of the working class and viewed students as undermining basic American values.

Source: H. Edward Ransford, "Blue Collar Anger: Reactions to Student and Black Protest," *American Sociological Review* 37 (June, 1972): 333–346.

gives recognition to the complexity of the issues involved and begins the process of seeking authoritative solutions. However, appointing a commission to investigate collective violence also becomes a way of buying time and taking the pressure off public officials for some immediate line of action (Lipsky and Olson, 1969).

2. Police Violence

One of the recurrent findings from the commissions that investigate the causes, conditions, and consequences of violence in American life is that law-enforcement agencies play an important role in the escalation of violence once a disruption occurs. The drama of collective violence does not occur within a vacuum. Instead, it involves interactions between those who are engaged in protest activities and those who have the responsibility for maintaining social order. The drama is reflected in how opposing forces respond to each other. Attempts to use repressive measures and to demonstrate what happens to those who engage "in criminal conduct" frequently have a boomerang effect: the efforts at law enforcement increase rather than reduce the incidence of civil disorder. Apparently this happened in the attempts of the Ohio National Guard to suppress the antiwar demonstrations on the campus of Kent State University. In the confrontation that occurred four students were killed and nine others were wounded. Following this episode, demonstrations against the war became

Bridge over Troubled Water
The sculpture entitled "Bridge over Troubled Water" was designed as a memorial to the students slain at Jackson State and Kent State Universities in the spring of 1970.

intensified at many colleges and universities throughout the United States. Students disrupted classes and made speeches against the war and against militaristic institutions; universities came under attack; and business-as-usual came to a halt.

About a year after the shooting of the students, Raymond J. Adamek and Jerry M. Lewis (1973) conducted interviews with 233 undergraduates at Kent State University to determine how experiences with the episode of 1970 influenced their attitudes toward violence and activism. The results of the survey indicated that the self-reports of students revealed feelings of greater proneness toward using violence, rather than less. If social control force is perceived as excessive, the responses become those of anger and indignation. These feelings tend to increase the readiness of people to become violent, rather than to make them more peaceful.

BOX 11.8
Sensitivity Training for the Police

The work of the police often is located somewhere on a scale between a set of military operations for maintaining social control at one end and a set of service functions for meeting the needs of local residents and neighborhoods at the other. Members of the police force in large metropolitan areas frequently are not prepared to deal adequately with the complex tasks they confront. Some officers respond to their own sense of anger and frustration by resorting to the use of excessive force in attempts to resolve social conflict.

The New York City Police Department uses several procedures for the retraining of violent law-enforcement officers. An early-warning system monitors the performance of each officer: records are kept on the number of times firearms are discharged, on civilian complaints of police brutality, and on the type and extent of force used in making arrests. These screening procedures permit identifying those officers who are prone to the use of violence in the course of their work.

Drawing on the assumption that human behavior is learned in a social context, the police department designed training programs to help officers understand role demands and expectations and to help them develop ways for coping with aggressive impulses. Group sessions were designed to reflect situations involving police confrontations. By interacting with officers facing similar problems, the police refined their skills for dealing with role ambiguity and developed new norms of personal conduct. Through the use of group principles and role playing, they gained insights into the problems common to police work, and the proneness to an excessive use of force was brought under control.

Source: Harvey Schlossberg, "Treating the Violent Law Enforcement Officer," In Irwin L. Kutash, Samuel B. Kutash, and Louis B. Schlesinger (eds.), *Violence: Perspectives on Murder and Aggression*, San Francisco: Jossey-Bass, 1978, pp. 413–437.

The role of the police in civil disturbances is an important one, not only because the job of the police calls for law enforcement, but also because they become important symbols of the established social order. The badge and the uniform as emblems of authority in everyday life frequently become symbols of oppression and injustice to the disenchanted. While beliefs about police brutality are sometimes valid, they often become magnified in the realities constructed by those involved in acts of confrontation. The police themselves sometimes become objects of abuse and have to deal with their own inner feelings of fear in the face of open resentment and hostility. (See Box 11.8.)

The conflicts for large urban police forces frequently become unresolvable when they are thrust into large-scale confrontations over human rights and political conflicts (Schlossberg, 1978). A lack of guidelines on police procedures frequently exists as novel situations develop, and officers become objects of a great deal of antagonism and distrust as disruptions occur. The police create their own system of criminal justice through the process of law enforcement and sometimes regard the suppression and resolution of conflict as the products of their own accomplishments. In this process police violence often results from attempts to assert authority and to enforce personal notions about legitimate conduct.

3. Hostile Environments

The societal reactions to the problems of violence reflect the differential linkages of individuals to the social system. The actual causes of violence may not be nearly so important as the attitudes people hold about the causes and solutions to the problems of violence. From the vantage of some individuals, all forms of violence should be treated as criminal conduct, and violations of the law should be severely punished.

The problems of criminal violence are of special concern to two major segments of the population. One of these consists of the law-enforcement personnel whose job requires that as agents of authority they confront and cope with the problems of violent conduct. The second major category consists of those who worry about the crime problem and see themselves as potential victims of violent acts. The public attitudes toward criminal violence may be regarded as socially constructed realities that serve as guidelines to behavior in public places. The degrees of comfort and of threat that an individual feels in the numerous interactions among strangers are conditioned by the person's judgments about personal vulnerability and the prospects for victimization.

A **hostile environment** is one in which the individual views his or her safety as being in jeopardy. Threats to personal safety engender a sense of fear, and the person cannot take for granted the security of his or her property and valuables. The images of a hostile environment imply that social relationships are undependable, that the individual must rely heavily on his or her own resources, and that strangers are to be viewed with suspicion and distrust.

The fear of criminal violence is of sufficient magnitude that many people see themselves as living in a highly threatening and hostile environment. The fear is greater among those who live in large cities than among those who live in small towns or rural areas. Concerns about becoming a victim of criminal violence are more intense among blacks than among whites, among women than among men, and among the elderly than among young people (Silberman, 1978). Thus variations in the fearfulness of criminal violence are related to the status characteristics and life circumstances of individuals.

The fear response may be adaptive if it occurs over a relatively short period of time. Fear is an early warning system for alerting an individual to impending danger, and physiological resources are mobilized for either flight or an attack (Scott, 1976). Unusual feats of physical strength or mental clarity can occur under conditions of fear. But if the attitudes of fear extend over a long period of time, their effects tend to become pathological. Sleeplessness, loss of appetite, and a sense of impairment in freedom of movement are among the consequences that frequently follow.

The fears of criminal violence are often based on the distrust of strangers and on the judgments made about environments thought to be threatening. Most people living in urban areas characterized by high crime rates are less fearful if they remain within their neighborhoods than if they are required to travel to a strange part of the city. Familiarity tends to produce a sense of security, while the novelty of strange places is more likely to engender suspicion and distrust (Silberman, 1978). This perhaps accounts for the greater fear of street crimes than of violence within the family, despite the fact that the official statistics would suggest that these fears should be reversed.

Some of the more intense fears of criminal violence are held by those who are least likely to be victimized by it. For example, elderly women who live alone are likely to fear criminal violence more than any other major segment of the American population, yet the elderly are less likely to be victimized than are younger people. This is not to suggest, however, that the fears of the elderly are unrealistic and irrational. Instead, perceptions of a hostile environment derive from conditions of vulnerability that may vary independently of actual victimization rates.

The research of Steven Balkin (1979) indicates that the elderly manifest fears of crime because they are less able to protect themselves against victimization. Fear tends to deter exposure to crime, and this is reflected in the caution exercised by the elderly when they go out at night. They restrict their activities by avoiding the kinds of situations in which they may be attacked, robbed, or molested. They are also more likely to use security locks for protecting their homes at night.

While the fear of crime may engender a sense of despair, it is also likely to reduce the degree of personal exposure. The success of the elderly in taking these precautions may account for their lower rates of actual victimization.

This does not mean that the elderly are irrational about the crime issue, but that they take reasonable precautions for protecting themselves in what they see as a potentially hostile environment.

Young adults, by way of contrast, are less fearful of criminal violence but more likely to be victimized by it. Balkin's (1979) analysis suggests that these facts derive from the greater exposure of young people to situations in which violence is likely to occur. Going out at night, having a sense of confidence about defending oneself, and believing that victimization is something that happens only to other people are youthful lifestyles and beliefs that increase youths' vulnerability to criminal violence. When victimization does occur, it is more likely to be accompanied by shock, disbelief, and an enduring sense of uncertainty.

The emotional impact of assault by a stranger is likely to have effects that go far beyond the event itself. The problem becomes that of making sense out of one's social environment. Victims of criminal violence tend to develop a continuing sense of vulnerability. They frequently expect a similar event to happen again, and they tend to lose confidence in their ability to respond correctly to the cues provided by others (Silberman, 1978). They are less likely to define familiar surroundings as safe and secure, and their social world loses a great deal of its predictability.

SUMMARY

Antagonistic interactions frequently reflect the collision of incompatible definitions of social reality. Traditional values conflict with the newer forms of morality; racial attitudes clash with emerging conceptions of social justice; and sexist ideologies collide with changing definitions of the proper role of women. Under conditions of conflict an awareness develops that certain kinds of problems in role relationships have hitherto been ignored at some degree of cost for certain members of a social system. The study of conflict encompasses the many forms of hostile and antagonistic social relationships.

Social conflicts are expressed in contested struggles and in appeals for remedial action. Some of the more serious forms of social conflict in American society have resulted from the process of social differentiation by which individuals are placed into racial, sexual, and age categories. Such classifications are constructed forms of reality that are endowed with stereotyped imagery. Both racial conflicts and the stresses associated with sex roles rest on false beliefs about biological differences, which are presumed to have a bearing on capacities to participate in several aspects of social life. Stereotypes become problematic for the minority group member in the development of a self-concept and in the restrictions they impose on the individual's freedom of movement.

Demonstrations, riots, terrorism, and sabotage are collective forms of violence that originate in concerns over social justice. The underprivileged, the oppressed, and the disenchanted turn to acts of violence when they are no longer willing to endure what they perceive as an unjust system. The outbreak of collective violence is dependent on some precipitating event, and crises frequently are produced for the police and for others entrusted with the maintenance of social order. Excessive uses of force by law-enforcement agencies may within itself constitute a form of violence, especially if the punitive measures go beyond the acceptable boundaries of police procedures.

Societal responses to violence play an important part in the manner of conflict resolution. Some segments of the population may define public disturbances as legitimate social protest, while others may define it simply as criminal violence. The resolution of the conflicts underlying collective violence is often dependent on public opinion. In contrast to violence involving social protest, such forms of criminal violence as robbery and muggings are clearly out of alignment with the normative order. The fear of criminal violence is prominent in environmental perceptions among the elderly and seems to derive from their sense of vulnerability and their lack of resources for self-defense.

BASIC TERMS

Traditionalism	**Unresponsive environment**
Modernism	**Rising expectations**
Stereotype	**Relative deprivation**
Assimilation	**Collective violence**
Ethnicity	**Issueless riots**
Cultural pluralism	**Credibility of protest**
Contested struggles	**Hostile environment**

REFERENCES

Acker, Joan
   1973 "Women and Social Stratification," *American Journal of Sociology* 78 (January): 936–945.
Adamek, Raymond J. and Jerry M. Lewis
   1973 "Social Control Violence and Radicalization: The Kent State Case," *Social Forces* 51 (March): 342–347.
Balkin, Steven
   1979 "Victimization Rates, Safety and Fear of Crime," *Social Problems* 26 (February): 343–358.
Banton, Michael
   1974 "1960: A Turning Point in the Study of Race Relations," *Daedalus* 103 (Spring): 31–44.

Barbour, Floyd B.
1968 *The Black Power Revolt*, Boston: Porter Sargent.
Berk, Richard A. and Howard E. Aldrich
1972 "Patterns of Vandalism During Civil Disorders as an Indicator of Selection of Targets," *American Sociological Review* 37 (October): 533–547.
Broverman, Inge K., Susan R. Voget, Donald M. Broverman, Frank E. Clarkson, and Paul S. Rosenkrantz
1972 "Sex Role Stereotypes: A Current Appraisal," *Journal of Social Issues* 28, no. 2: 59–78.
Bruce, Dickson D., Jr.
1979 *Violence and Culture in the Antebellum South*, Austin: University of Texas Press.
Coser, Rose L. and Gerald Rokoff
1971 "Women in the Occupational World: Social Disruption and Conflict," *Social Problems* 18 (Spring): 535–553.
Dahrendorf, Ralf
1959 *Class and Class Conflict in Industrial Society*, Stanford: Stanford University Press.
Davies, James C.
1972 "Toward a Theory of Revolution," in Ivo K. Feierabend, Rosalind L. Feierabend, and Ted R. Gurr (eds.), *Anger, Violence, and Politics*, Englewood Cliffs, N.J.: Prentice-Hall, pp. 67–84.
Dynes, Russell and E. L. Quarantelli
1968 "What Looting in Civil Disturbances Really Means," *Transaction* 5 (May): 9–14.
Ehrlich, Howard J.
1973 *The Social Psychology of Prejudice*, New York: John Wiley.
Elder, Glen H., Jr.
1971 "Intergroup Attitudes and Social Ascent among Negro Boys," *American Journal of Sociology* 76 (January): 673–697.
Featherman, David L. and Robert M. Hauser
1976 "Sexual Inequalities and Socio-Economic Achievement in the United States," *American Sociological Review* 41 (June): 462–483.
Fox, Greer Litton
1977 "Nice Girl: Social Control of Women Through a Value Construct," *Signs* 2: 805–817.
Geschwender, James A.
1968 "Explorations in the Theory of Social Movements and Revolutions," *Social Forces* 47 (December): 127–135.
Glick, Paul C.
1977 "Updating the Life Cycle of the Family," *Journal of Marriage and the Family* 39 (February): 5–14.
Grier, William H. and Price M. Cobbs
1969 *Black Rage*, New York: Bantam Books.
Grimm, James W. and Robert N. Stern
1974 "Sex Roles and Internal Labor Market Structures," *Social Problems* 21 (June): 690–705.
Gurin, P. and E. Epps
1975 *Black Consciousness: Identity and Achievement*, New York: John Wiley.

Gurr, Ted Robert
    1972 "Psychological Factors in Civil Violence," in Ivo K. Feierabend, Rosalind L. Feierabend, and Ted R. Gurr (eds.), *Anger, Violence, and Politics,* Englewood Cliffs, N.J.: Prentice-Hall, pp. 31–57.

Habermas, Jurgen
    1973 *Legitimation Crisis,* Boston: Beacon Press.

Hoffman, Lois Wladis
    1972 "Early Childhood Experiences and Women's Achievement Motives," *Journal of Social Issues* 28, no. 2: 129–156.

Horton, John
    1966 "Order and Conflict Theories of Social Problems as Competing Ideologies," *American Journal of Sociology* 71 (May): 701–713.

Huber, Joan
    1976 "Studies in Sex Stratification," *Social Science Quarterly* 56 (March): 547–552.

Jeffries, Vincent, Ralph H. Turner, and Richard T. Morris
    1971 "The Public Perception of the Watts Riot as Social Protest," *American Sociological Review* 36 (June): 443–451.

Killian, Lewis M.
    1968 *The Impossible Revolution,* New York: Random House.

Komarovsky, Mirra
    1973 "Cultural Contradictions and Sex Roles: The Masculine Case," *American Journal of Sociology* 78 (January): 873–884.

Lippmann, Walter
    1961 *Public Opinion,* New York: Macmillan (original edition published in 1922).

Lipsky, Michael and David J. Olson
    1969 "Riot Commission Politics," *Transaction* 6 (July/August): 8–21.

Mackie, Marlene
    1973 "Arriving at 'Truth' by Definition: The Case of Stereotype Inaccuracy," *Social Problems* 20 (Spring): 431–447.

Marx, Gary
    1972 "Issueless Riots," in James F. Short, Jr. and Marrin E. Wolfgang (eds.), *Collective Violence,* Chicago: Aldine, pp. 47–59.

Mason, Karen Oppenheim and Larry L. Bumpass
    1975 "U.S. Women's Sex-Role Ideology, 1970," *American Journal of Sociology* 80 (March): 1212–1219.

Maykovich, Minako Kurokawa
    1972 "Reciprocity in Racial Stereotypes," *American Journal of Sociology* 77 (March): 876–897.

Metzger, L. Paul
    1971 "American Sociology and Black Assimilation: Conflicting Perspectives," *American Journal of Sociology* 76 (January): 627–647.

Mills, C. Wright
    1959 *The Sociological Imagination,* New York: Oxford University Press.

Montagu, Ashley
    1963 "The Concept of Race," in *Anthropology and Human Nature,* New York: McGraw-Hill, pp. 70–102.

Neal, Arthur G.
    1976 "Crisis, Commitment, and the Legitimation of Violence," in Arthur G. Neal (ed.), *Violence in Animal and Human Societies,* Chicago: Nelson-Hall, pp. 79–106.

Parelius, Ann P.
1975 "Change and Stability in College Women's Orientations Toward Education, Family, and Work," *Social Problems* 22 (February): 420–431.

Porter, Judith R. and Robert E. Washington
1979 "Black Identity and Self-Esteem: A Review of Studies of Black Self-Concept, 1968–1978," *Annual Review of Sociology* 5: 53–74.

Ransford, Edward
1972 "Blue Collar Anger: Reactions to Student and Black Protest," *American Sociological Review* 37 (June): 333–346.
1970 "Skin Color, Life Chances, and Anti-White Attitudes," *Social Problems* 18 (Fall): 164–179.

Rose, Peter I.
1968 *The Subject Is Race*, New York: Oxford University Press.

Scanzoni, John
1975 *Sex Roles, Life Styles, and Childbearing: Changing Patterns in Marriage and the Family*, New York: The Free Press.

Schlossberg, Harvey
1978 "Treating the Violent Law Enforcement Officer," in Irwin L. Kutash, Samuel B. Kutash, and Louis B. Schlesinger (eds.), *Violence: Perspectives on Murder and Aggression*, San Francisco: Jossey-Bass, pp. 413–437.

Scott, John Paul
1976 "The Control of Violence: Human and Nonhuman Societies Compared," in Arthur G. Neal (ed.), *Violence in Animal and Human Societies*, Chicago: Nelson-Hall, pp. 13–34.

Silberman, Charles E.
1978 *Criminal Violence, Criminal Justice*, New York: Random House.

Snyder, David and Paula M. Hudis
1976 "Occupational Income and the Effects of Minority Competition and Segregation," *American Journal of Sociology* 41 (April): 209–234.

Turner, Castellano B. and William J. Wilson
1976 "Dimensions of Racial Ideology: A Study of Urban Black Attitudes," *Journal of Social Issues* 32, no. 2: 139–152.

Turner, Ralph H.
1969 "The Public Perception of Protest," *American Sociological Review* 34 (December): 815–830.

Udry, J. Richard, Karl E. Bauman, and Charles Chase
1971 "Skin Color, Status and Mate Selection," *American Journal of Sociology* 76 (January): 722–733.

U.S. Department of Commerce
1977 *Social Indicators 1976*, Washington: Government Printing Office.

Weitzman, Lenore J., Deborah Eifler, Elizabeth Hokada, and Catherine Ross
1972 "Sex-Role Socialization in Picture Books for Preschool Children," *American Journal of Sociology* 77 (May): 1125–1150.

Wilson, William Julius
1978 *The Declining Significance of Race*, Chicago: University of Chicago Press.
1970 "Revolutionary Nationalism Versus Cultural Nationalism," *Sociological Focus* 3 (Spring): 43–52.

12

Family Violence

Attempts to resolve social conflict sometimes result in acts of violence. People tend to become angry and hostile toward those who disagree with them, and occasionally use force and threats in attempts to coerce others into submission. Through violent acts individuals are abused, beaten, stabbed, shot, brutalized, or in some other way maltreated. The objects of hostility can be innocent people, public officials, or close friends, as well as adversaries, enemies, or oppressors.

Violence is only one of several possible outcomes of antagonistic interactions. Some people may engage in a rational discussion of issues in order to resolve conflicts in a mutually satisfactory manner. Others may engage in verbal abuse as a means of venting hostility. Some turn to violence as a means of inflicting physical injury on an adversary. The injuries that result from acts of violence run counter to social norms and may consist of either bodily harm or property damages.

Violence has an explosive quality about it because extensive and radical changes occur within a relatively short interval of time (Gotesky, 1974). People lose their tempers, go into fits of rage, and sometimes do things they regret later. However the violence is expressed, it involves a violation of the rights of others (Stanage, 1974). The norms for regulating conduct have lost their hold over individual conduct; the constraints associated with orderly social life have broken down, leaving individuals to suffer the indignities that accompany an exercise of brute force. Nevertheless violent acts occur within the framework of social interactions, and use of physical force is often accompanied by moral justification. The perpetrator of violence may feel that he or she was only standing up for basic rights, that the victim deserved to be injured, or that an unwarranted act by another provoked the violent response. Perpetrators of violence include jealous wives, angry husbands, and abusive parents, as well as muggers, kidnappers, and terrorists. (See Table 12.1.)

The objects of violence can include a variety of others, and the situations in which violent acts can occur are as varied as the major forms of human interaction. Such violent acts as hijackings, kidnappings, assassinations, and terrorism frequently occur in public places, whereas the battering of a spouse or

TABLE 12.1
The Vocabulary of Violence

Conditions	Agents	Violative acts
"Up against the wall"	Criminals	Abusing
"The cornered rat syndrome"	Murderers	Degrading
"Uncontrollable anger"	Muggers	Brutalizing
"A fit of passion"	Kidnappers	Raping
"In the trenches"	Terrorists	Killing
"Surviving in a jungle"	Vigilantes	Fighting
"Being provoked"	Revolutionaries	Beating
"Defending one's honor"	Avengers	Injuring
"Deserving to be killed"	Rapists	Kidnapping
"Getting even"	Deviants	Terrorizing
"Vendetta"	Irate husbands	Wounding
"An eye for an eye"	Angry wives	Torturing
"Protecting one's property"	Abusive parents	Humiliating
"Defending one's rights"	Disenchanted lovers	Maltreating
"An act of desperation"	Assassins	Damaging

Source: The above list was partially derived from Stephen T. Margulis, "Conceptions of Privacy," *Journal of Social Issues* 33 (1977): 5–21.

the abusing of a child usually takes place within the private and intimate confines of family life. The diversity of objects and places of violence suggests that the emotions of anger, fear, and hostility are potential outcomes of any major form of social interaction.

The study of violence has a special relevance to an understanding of our time and place. During the course of the twentieth century, the number of people that have died violently is greater than for any previous century (Elliot, 1972). In the first half of this century, social life was shattered by two major world wars. For example, there were more than 40 million civilian and military casualties in World War II alone; an additional 6 million people were annihilated in the holocaust of Nazi Germany, and a comparable number of killings resulted from purges in the Soviet Union. Single bombing raids during World War II resulted in as many as 100,000 civilian fatalities. Dropping the atom bomb on the Japanese cities of Hiroshima and Nagasaki dramatized the potentials of warfare and increased human awareness of dangers inherent in the unrestrained conflicts among technologically advanced nations.

Violent acts are distinguishable, however, from other forms of physical injury that can be understood within the framework of orderly and predictable social relationships. For example, external war is qualitatively different from the forms of violence with which social psychologists are concerned, since

Militarism and Violence
The markers at Arlington Cemetery suggest one serious consequence of modern warfare.

inflicting injury on an enemy in times of war is associated with bravery and meritorious conduct and receives social approval. Furthermore, the physical punishment a child receives from his or her parents is not violence unless it becomes excessive, abusive, and constitutes a form of maltreatment.

The question of what constitutes excessive physical force is at the center of several social controversies. Some people look on capital punishment (the death penalty for committing crimes) as necessary for "law and order," while others regard the death penalty as immoral, inhuman, and unjustified under any circumstances. Some people regard physical punishment of children as necessary for training the child and building character, while others view any use of physical punishment as unnecessary in childrearing. Some people look on war, or the preparation for war, as the example *par excellence* of violent behavior, while others define the military emphasis as necessary for national security and the building of national character. The designation of specific acts

BOX 12.1
Predicting Violent Behavior

Mental health professionals (psychiatrists and clinical psychologists) frequently are requested to give expert opinion about the need to institutionalize potentially dangerous individuals. Social control agencies seek expert evaluations as relevant information in making custodial decisions and dispositions of criminal cases.

John Monahan has examined several practical, moral, and scientific issues involved in presenting expert opinion on an individual's potential for being dangerous. The requests for evaluation are incompatible with the therapeutic and ethical concerns of mental health practitioners. Psychiatrists and clinical psychologists are oriented toward helping people rather than doing things "to" them. Confinement to a mental institution or to a prison is seldom in the best interest of the person involved. But more importantly, there are serious doubts about the accuracy of predictions in specific cases. Statistical predictions can be made by drawing on a large number of cases, but there are many errors connected with predicting what a specific individual will do at some time in the future.

In his analysis of clinical predictions, Monahan noted several common errors. Mental health professionals are often unclear about what they are asked to predict (murder, rape, assault, and so forth). Acts of violence are specific and occur within particular social settings. In the absence of a clear basis for making predictions, the most frequent assumption is that, because an individual has engaged in criminal violence in the past, he or she is likely to become violent again at some time in the future. The statistical data, however, show that a single instance of violence cannot be used as an accurate basis for predicting future violent acts. Doubts about the accuracy of clinical predictions raise serious questions about the appropriateness of mental health professionals becoming involved at all in the prediction process.

Source: John Monahan, *Predicting Violent Behavior*, Beverly Hills, Calif.: Sage, 1981.

as violent or nonviolent has a great deal of bearing on the proneness of individuals to use physical force for the resolution of social conflict. (See Box 12.1.)

The problems of violence are not foremost among the concerns of everyday life. Yet when violence does occur, its impact is unmistakable, not only on the people directly involved but also on those who are responding to the event. Acts of violence generate a crisis within the social realm; routine activities temporarily come to a halt; and individuals are required to reflect on the qualities of their social relationships and on the overall organization of social life.

A. THE DISCOVERY OF FAMILY VIOLENCE

The 1960s was a turbulent decade in American history. The assassinations of President John F. Kennedy and Reverend Martin Luther King had an intense emotional impact on the nation and led to the examination of several aspects of American life. Ghetto uprisings, protest against American involvement in Vietnam, and demonstrations on college campuses were among the disturbing episodes of a turbulent decade. Uneasiness in the social realm resulted in the appointment of several presidential commissions to examine the causes, conditions, and consequences of violence in American life. The conclusions of these commissions pointed toward the "discovery" of social facts that had long been recognized by criminologists: namely, that if we are to adequately understand the full scope of violence in American life, we must direct attention toward the family and toward the forms of physical abuse that grow out of intimate social relationships.

The official statistics on murders, stabbings, and beatings clearly show that intimate groups are potentially dangerous. For example, very few murders are committed by total strangers, yet images of strangers are central to the fears of many people about the risks of victimization. The statistical probability of being killed by a friend or a relative is substantially greater than the statistical probability of being killed by a stranger or a casual acquaintance. The baseline data from the *Uniform Crime Reports* (Statistics from the Department of Justice) indicate that about one-fourth of all the homicides each year in the United States are committed within the family. And of the murders within the family, about half involve spouse killing spouse, with about equal proportions of the wife or husband as the victim (Wolfgang, 1978).

Prior to the 1960s very little had been published on physical abuse within the family, except for specialized reports in criminology and social work journals. During the 1960s, however, family violence became a major concern of several physicians, sociologists, psychologists, and others with an interest in the qualities of family life. These concerns were prompted by a recognition that several aspects of the maltreatment of family members had previously been ignored. For example, the new uses of X-ray technology permitted physicians to notice old healed fractures in children that could have been caused by repeated physical blows from their caretakers. The phrase *battered-child syndrome* entered the vocabulary of the medical profession, and by 1968 all fifty states had enacted laws requiring medical personnel to report cases of suspected child abuse (Straus, Gelles, and Steinmetz, 1980). In 1974 the National Center on Child Abuse and Neglect was established to increase knowledge about child abuse and the maltreatment of children.

There is no evidence that the scope and intensity of violence within the family increased during this period. Instead, a fundamental change occurred in images of family life. During the 1950s and the early 1960s, the family became idealized as a social institution. It was viewed as providing "a place to retreat from the world," "a peaceful place," "a nonviolent setting," a place where people "care about one another." From such idyllic perspectives, family violence was viewed as pathological, as stemming from mental instability or immaturity, or as due to drugs and alcohol abuse. Subsequent research on the scope and severity of violence within the family provided a new set of definitions. The uses of verbal aggression, physical punishment, and violence became recognized as strategies widely employed in attempts to resolve family conflicts. From their several years of research on family violence, Richard Gelles and Murray Straus (1979: 15) concluded:

With the exception of the police and the military, the family is perhaps the most violent social group, and the home the most violent setting in our society. A person is more likely to be hit or killed in his or her home by another family member than anywhere else or by anyone else.

The 1960s was also a decade in which concerns were directed toward many aspects of human rights and the qualities of social life. Childhood and adolescence had become established as status categories clearly separable from adulthood. In contrast to the images of a previous century, children and adolescents were no longer viewed as being miniature adults, but as having rights, roles, and responsibilities that differed from those of adults. At the same time the women's movement was gaining momentum, directing special attention toward power and status relationships within the family. Consciousness-raising sessions indicated that the exploitations of women within the family were neither isolated events nor socially justified (Gelles and Straus, 1979). Within the context of growing concerns for human rights, we may view this examination of the problems of family violence as a quest for improvements in the qualities of life both within the public and the private spheres.

B. INTIMACY AND CONFLICT

The significance of the family for the social, physical, and emotional well-being of the individual is clearly evident. Nearly all young people look forward to getting married eventually, and the vast majority of divorced people subsequently remarry. Further, the stress levels that accompany separation, divorce, or the death of a spouse confirm the emotional importance of attachments within the family. However, the same conditions that promote meaning, purpose, and stability for individuals also make them highly vulnerable to acts of aggression and hostility.

Social psychologists who study family violence are interested in the interaction patterns that culminate in physical injuries. Researchers are concerned with the manner in which families cope with the inevitable conflicts that emerge from interactions over an extended period of time. While love, respect, admiration, and sympathy are important underpinnings of family relationships, these positive sentiments do not always prevail. All social relationships rest to some degree on the use of force or the potential threat of force (Goode, 1974). Some degree of conflict is unavoidable, and for this reason all couples must develop means of coping with the disagreements and incompatible goals that surface in marriage relationships.

As Georg Simmel (1950) pointed out in his classical essay on the stranger, all human relationships are characterized by some combination of "nearness" and "remoteness." The closeness of the relationship derives from the shared experiences that bind individuals together and the common values and attitudes of parties to the relationship. But as closeness develops in a relationship, intimate aspects of each individual are revealed. Couples become aware of their points of disagreement, some measure of conflict becomes unavoidable, and interactions take a variety of antagonistic forms (Sprey, 1974).

1. Emotion Rules

The vulnerability of intimate relationships to violent acts in part stems from the emotionality of the relationships. Diverse emotions such as love, sympathy, jealousy, fear, and anger are likely to surface in intimate relationships because of the range of activities that require coordinated efforts. For example, fights and disagreements can arise over family finances, consumer purchases, the circumstances for having sex, plans for vacations, responsibilities for child care, and the performance of household chores. The realities negotiated in marriage involve harmonizing the plans of the wife and the husband, establishing priorities, and allocating family resources. Since family activities take such a variety of forms, the potentials are great for the emergence of conflict. Most couples cannot readily cope with all of the hopes and aspirations one or the other brings to the relationship.

The interplay of sentiments is central to intimate relationships, yet there is a lack of clarity in normative rules for the control and management of emotional expression. For example, the rule of irrelevance, which applies to social interactions in public places (Goffman, 1963), is not applicable to the intimate bonds of family relationships. In public places, only those concerns that are related to the specific rules of the interacting individuals (customer and clerk, doctor and patient, and so forth) are of relevance. There are curbs on the expression of emotions individuals may feel toward each other. By way of contrast, the exchanges of family life have few such rules of irrelevance for the display of emotions. The agenda for husband-wife interactions is relatively open, and either spouse may require the other to direct attention toward the topic of special concern.

The arousal of such emotions as anger, jealousy, and fear entails physiological changes. Increases in heart rate, blood pressure, lung capacity, and production of adrenelin are among the bodily processes triggered by the emotional state of the individual. But as Susan Shott (1979) points out, the behavior of the individual is not shaped by physiological conditions alone. There are cognitive aspects of emotional arousal, and individuals face the problem of defining and managing their emotions within given situations. For example, whether individuals are prone to vent their anger through calm discussion, verbal abuse, or physical assaults depends on their definitions of the situation. Is the situation one in which it is appropriate to express emotions, or is it one that requires inhibiting and concealing emotions? What constitutes appropriate lines of action for the emotions that the individual is experiencing? How should the person manage unwanted emotional states? The answers to these questions are the **emotion rules** that the individual has internalized to serve as guidelines to action.

Some emotion rules are clearly established through widely understood social norms, while others remain unclear and ambiguous. For example, in our society it is appropriate to feel sad at funerals and to feel happy at weddings. But such feeling states do not come automatically, nor are they inherent or natural outcomes of the human condition. The meaning of an emotional state is a constructed reality. According to Arlie Russell Hochschild (1979), everyone is required to do a certain amount of "emotion work" in order to arouse the feelings they believe they should have or to establish the appropriateness of an

Family Heterogeneity
Families are intimate social groups, but they also are characterized by heterogeneity. At a family cookout one can notice how family members differ by generational level, gender, personal interests, and interaction patterns.

emotional feeling state. The emotion work in family life requires dealing not only with such positive feelings as love and affection but also with such negative feelings as anger, hostility, and resentment. The very conditions that promote the attractiveness of family life also contain the potential for emotional expressions to get out of hand.

2. Behind Closed Doors

Married couples spend a great deal of time with each other, and most of their interactions occur in what Goffman called an off-stage area (see Chapter 8). The appearances and performances in public places lose their facades within the intimate bonds of family relationships. In the relaxed atmosphere of family life many aspects of the self are disclosed, and in this process the qualities of relationships change (Gilbert, 1976). Disclosure frequently has an impact on the relative worth of each and on what may subsequently happen in the relationship. Revealed weaknesses, flaws, and limitations become sources of vulnerability in the later development of conflict situations. As hostilities emerge, spouses are frequently well-equipped with knowledge of each other's weaknesses and use this to inflict damage.

The conflicts within the family unit are generated in part by the heterogeneity of its membership. The family includes persons of both sexes and individuals from different generation levels. As a result "the battle of the sexes" is enacted within the family setting, and the controversies that develop along generational lines show up as a generation gap within the intimate confines of family life. These differences in values, interests, and basic concerns are of sufficient magnitude that Suzanne K. Steinmetz (1977b) described the family as a battleground for assertive, aggressive, and abusive interactions.

In the course of the twentieth century the American family has become smaller as a social unit and more fully isolated from other social relationships. We now define the **nuclear family**, which is limited to the married couple and their dependent children, as the basic living unit. A great deal of interaction takes place among a small number of people, and there tends to be an overreaction to the conflicts that emerge. Social norms call for the exclusion of outsiders from family squabbles; the importance of this rule may be noted in the fact that 22 percent of the incidents in which police are killed in the line of duty occur in connection with the investigation of family quarrels (Evans, 1979).

The police dislike the task of investigating family squabbles and recognize that intrusion into a private domain is a risky type of undertaking (Straus, Gelles, and Steinmetz, 1980). The norms creating and maintaining the boundaries of privacy around family life are viewed as promoting an important set of values and as providing protection from uninvited intrusion. Both the police and the courts tend to view domestic violence as a private matter that should

The Private Family Dwelling
The family dwelling is defined by social norms as one of the more important spheres of privacy in our society. As a result the family tends to become an isolated unit, and social supports are often lacking when interpersonal conflicts develop among family members.

be worked out between the husband and wife without intervention from social control agencies. In some cases the police use what they call "the stitch rule": they will arrest an abusing husband only if he injures the wife seriously enough that she requires surgical sutures. And the courts frequently face the frustration of cases in which the spouse presses charges, only to later request that they be dropped.

The married couple having control over a private dwelling that only they and their dependent children occupy is an important image of American family life. Cultural norms reinforce living arrangements and place special emphasis on the rights to privacy in the family domain. The home is defined as a place for the refinement of intimate relationships as well as a place where individuals can be protected from environmental intrusions. The rules of privacy promote the exclusion of outsiders, the rights to build a joint family enterprise,

TABLE 12.2
Meanings of Privacy in Popular Thinking

Privacy as Control over Information:
  "Behind closed doors"
  "Intimate knowledge"
  "Skeletons in the closet"
  "Keeping secrets"
  "Protection from public disclosure"
  "Personal control over personal information"
  "Personal affairs"
  "Controlled access"
  "Confidential"

Privacy as Control over Space (Territoriality):
  "A retreat from the world"
  "An exclusive place"
  "For members only"
  "Off limits"
  "No trespassing"
  "Admission by invitation only"
  "Secluded"

Privacy as Individualism and Isolation:
  "Freedom to do what you want to do"
  "Personal autonomy"
  "Being left alone"
  "Not being bothered"
  "Being able to work without distraction"
  "Solitude"
  "Away from public view"

Source: Partially derived from Stephen T. Margulis, "Conceptions of Privacy," *Journal of Social Issues* 33, no. 3 (1977): 5–21.

and the opportunities to seek self-fulfillment through family interactions. (See Table 12.2.)

Control over information about oneself and about the internal dynamics of one's family life is at the core of the rights to privacy within American society (Laufer and Wolfe, 1977). Accordingly, the disclosure of information about family life is regarded as a private decision, since family members may be concerned with the images of their intimate lives that such disclosure presents to the rest of the world. Concern for the opinions held by members of a kin network, by neighbors and acquaintances, tends to promote a cover-up of the many conflicts that develop out of family interactions.

3. Escalation of Conflict

George Bach and Peter Wyden (1974) observed that violent families may not experience any greater degree of conflict than nonviolent families. Instead, the differences in level of physical abuse relate to variations in the coping strategies family members employ and in their degree of success in managing family conflict. According to Bach and Wyden, (page 98) "couples who fight together are couples who stay together—provided they know how to fight properly." They are referring in this comment not to fighting in the physical sense but to the manner in which couples confront their points of disagreement and negotiate settlements.

From his studies of the **conflict tactics** employed within families, Murray Straus (1979) notes that violence is only one of several means employed in the settlement of differences. Another set of tactics consists of emphasizing reasoning and rational discussion. Couples who take this approach attempt to discuss an issue calmly and to seek a solution without disrupting the positive qualities of their relationship. Violence is less likely to occur if couples openly talk about their disagreements and keep the conflict on an intellectual level. If they cannot resolve their disagreements this way, they may make efforts to manage the conflict in such a manner as to minimize its potentially disruptive impact.

Some couples are prone to respond to conflict by engaging in verbal aggression and abuse rather than rational discussion. Such tactics include yelling at each other, launching insults, derogating the other person, sulking, or walking out of the room. While these tactics may be symptomatic of a deteriorating relationship, they are sometimes applied recurrently within marriages that endure. But if verbal hostility frequently occurs in a marriage relationship, physical abuse is likely to follow. From a study of 385 couples, Straus (1974) found that verbal aggression correlates positively with attempts at physical injury. Couples who routinely scream at each other are likely to eventually engage in violent acts.

The willingness to use destructive forms of conflict arises from an intolerance of uncertainty and from a commitment of one or both parties to winning a clear victory in the contested struggle (Deutsch, 1975). The destructive forms of conflict sometime become a **zero-sum game**, in which one party in the struggle can achieve benefits only at the expense of another. Defining conflict as win-or-lose situations often results in the use of strategies of coercion and deception and the blockage of effective communication between the contending parties (Coser, 1967). The quest for a clear victory of one party over another frequently results in a further escalation of the conflict. In such cases the two parties are not likely to confront the underlying causes of their conflict, and social relationships become power-oriented, coercive, and threatening in character.

Thomas Milburn (1977) notes that the nature of the **threat** consists of making demands that are accompanied by a promise of danger if the demands are not carried out. Threats are usually designed to reduce the options available to an adversary, but for a variety of reasons they are seldom effective in producing the desired results. One of the more important reasons has to do with the variations in the perceptions of the threat sender and the threat receiver. The threat sender focuses attention on the demands he or she is making and on the desired outcomes. In contrast, the threat receiver is likely to evaluate the nature of the threat in terms of the intentions of the threat sender. The threat receiver's concern is whether or not the demands can be reasonably met and what the prospects are that the threat will be carried out. Problems in saving face and in the loss of credibility are likely to follow if the threat sender lacks the capability of carrying out the threat.

William Goode (1974) maintains that the family is a power system and, like all other social units, rests to some degree on force or threat of force. Force is a resource in exchange relationships and it is useful in getting things done. The resources for persuading, influencing, and manipulating others are numerous: physical strength, authority, social norms, and money are examples. The threat of withdrawing affection and approval can also be used as a resource in persuasive situations. Goode (1972: 511) maintains that "it is not overt force that defines a situation of coercion, but our desire not to obey the command, and our perception that the cost of resistance is too high, whether it is physical punishment, loss of esteem, money, or affection." In recognizing that force is a generic social process, one should not infer that compliance under pressure is devoid of rewards for the individual. To the contrary, the pursuit of self-interests, whether in the family or elsewhere, requires the development of skills both in being manipulated and in manipulating others.

Threats of punishment and the uses of physical abuse are not among the most effective uses of resources. No social group can endure for long by drawing exclusively on physical force as a means of eliciting assistance from one another. Instead, physical force is frequently thought of as a **last resort**, as a resource to employ as a final solution after all other attempts at persuasion have failed. Last resorts are extreme measures, and within the family they may consist of inflicting physical abuse, seeking a divorce, or running away from home. People justify these procedures as last resorts on the grounds that all other reasonable attempts to deal with family troubles have failed to work or turned out to be inadequate.

Last-resort arguments frequently are invoked in court cases in which the accused present justification for acts of violence against a family member. For example, a wife may claim that she murdered her husband only after having endured years of abuse and maltreatment, that the act was in self-defense or in defense of her children, or that there was no avenue of escape from an unendurable situation. Robert Emerson (1981) notes that the acceptability of such claims rests on the credibility of the evidence that the defendant tried normal remedies or typical solutions to family problems but they failed to work; that "doing nothing" was not a feasible option; that there was "no avenue of retreat"; and that the extreme measure was the only course of action that remained. In effect, last-resort procedures are justified on the grounds that all previous attempts to solve the problem resulted in failure, there was no decision to make, and there was nothing else that could be done.

C. VICTIMS OF FAMILY VIOLENCE

Violence within a family reflects the attempt of one individual to impose his or her definition of reality on another. Situations develop in which opposing

---

BOX 12.2
Family Violence as a Form of Communication

Emanuel Marx maintains that aggressive behavior is purposeful and that violence is frequently employed as a form of communication. In developing his thesis on violence, Marx makes a distinction between **coercive violence** and **appealing violence**. Coercive violence is an attempt to force others to serve one's interests, while appealing violence is a plea to be helped through the sharing of problems.

Appealing violence stems from personal troubles that defy solutions by ordinary means. For example, a man may fully accept the responsibilities of being a good provider for his family but perceive a sense of failure through difficulties in obtaining a regular job, satisfactory housing, or adequate welfare payments. A woman may feel trapped through the vast amount of work associated with the wife and mother roles or she may feel unappreciated for trying to balance a career and home life. Under such circumstances, the physical abuse of family members communicates a sense of despair and constitutes a plea for others to recognize and share the problems being confronted.

If the violent appeal is to be successful as a form of communication it must be confined within strict limits. Slapping or hitting a person is certainly a way of getting the person to take notice and pay attention. However, the use of violence must not convey such a high level of threat that the person initiating violence doesn't lose the sympathies and supports of the person receiving it. The messages sent through violent acts are ambiguous and thus require the receiver to reflect on their underlying meaning and significance. The troubles faced by the aggressor tend to be evaluated by the family unit and solutions frequently are sought by all parties involved. There are risks connected with the use of violence as a form of communication, but the aggressor may perceive these risks as necessary under conditions of stress and desperation.

Source: Emanuel Marx, *The Social Context of Violent Behavior*, London: Routledge and Kegan Paul, 1976.

BOX 12.3
Locations in the Household for Family Violence

In a study of family criminal violence, Marvin Wolfgang (1978) examined 588 homicides in Philadelphia to determine the circumstances surrounding the lethal acts. Approximately two-thirds of the husband-wife homicides were precipitated by domestic quarrels, and almost a fourth were due to jealousy. Wolfgang's findings indicated that 85 percent of the slayings of a spouse occurred at home, with the proportions about the same for wives and husbands.

Within the home, the murder of a spouse is more likely to occur in the bedroom than in any other place, but this generalization needs to be qualified by gender of the person killed. The bedroom is a more lethal place for wives than for husbands. Wolfgang's data indicated that 45 percent of the wives were killed in the bedroom, while only 23 percent of the husbands were killed there. A reverse pattern was found for the kitchen. Husbands were twice as likely as wives to be killed in the kitchen. Stabbing was the method most frequently used by wives, and the butcher knife or the paring knife was used more often than any other weapon. Husbands were more varied in the methods of murder. Shootings, stabbings, and beating to death were employed in about equal proportions.

Wolfgang's analysis of court dispositions indicated that more lenient treatment was given to women than to men following the killing of a spouse. Husbands were more often convicted of murder, while wives were usually charged with manslaughter. Husbands were more frequently found guilty, while wives were more often acquitted. His findings also indicated that husbands were much more likely than their wives to commit suicide following the slaying of a spouse.

Source: Marvin Wolfgang, "Violence in the Family," in Irwin L. Kutash, Samuel B. Kutash, and Louis B. Schlesinger (eds.), *Violence: Perspectives on Murder and Aggression,* San Francisco: Jossey-Bass, 1978, pp. 238–253.

forces are at work, and negotiations break down as one individual proceeds to inflict physical injury on another. Intimate relationships may change into hostile, coercive relationships as the right to exert an influence gets out of hand. In acts of violence, the aggressor is expressing resentments toward the intended victim, making efforts to degrade the other person, and trying to coerce the opposition into submission.

All members of family units are potential victims of physical abuse and maltreatment. Adult children may beat their aged parents; angry wives may kill their husbands; jealous husbands may abuse their wives; parents may torture or molest their children; and siblings may injure or brutalize one another. Acts of violence may stem from such varied conditions as "an uncontrollable fit of passion," "an act of desperation," "getting even," "protecting one's rights," or "defending one's honor." (See Box 12.2.)

Much of the violence that occurs within families goes undetected because it is successfully concealed from public view. The abuse is usually serious before it is brought to the attention of social service agencies, medical personnel, or the police (Gelles, 1976b). The cover-up is primarily due to the nature of family squabbles and the norms that preclude meddling by outsiders into the intimate sphere of family life. Outside help is usually sought only when one party to the conflict is no longer willing to endure abusive behavior, or when the physical injuries are serious enough to require medical attention.

1. The Battered Spouse

The battered spouse is one who is physically abused. The violations include beating, stabbing, molesting, raping, and other forms of physical injury. Although the full scope of physical abuse is not known, the available data have led to conservative estimates that during any given year at least 500,000 wives are beaten by their husbands, and about 250,000 husbands are physically abused by their wives. Further, of the men who are killed by women each year about 57 percent are killed by their wives, suggesting that the safety of the husband within the family is not to be taken for granted (Evans, 1979). (See Box 12.3.)

The situational character of spouse abuse is reflected in the variations in family violence that occur in the time of day, the day of the week, and the time of the year (Gelles, 1972). Physical combat is more likely during the evening hours (between dinner and bedtime) than at other times of the day; during Saturdays and Sundays than during all other days of the week combined; and during Christmas and anniversaries than at any other times of the year. These temporal variations in family violence suggest that physical abuse is more likely to occur on those occasions in which a couple spends more time together and in which the opportunities are greatest for reflecting on the qualities of family relationships. The routines associated with work activities, for example, impose structure and predictability to behavior patterns, which are missing during the nonwork of the evenings, weekends, and holidays. The times for fighting are the same times that are socially defined as the times for leisure, relaxation, and self-fulfillment.

The conflicts that precipitate violent acts may be picky, everyday, annoying things, as well as large-scale and serious issues (Steinmetz, 1977b). In everyday life irritating personality differences are tolerated, but occasions develop in which individuals, no longer able to handle these differences, explode into acts of violence. Leaving the toothpaste tube uncapped, using annoying eating habits, throwing dirty clothes on the floor, or putting cold water in the refrigerator in wintertime are among the irritating personal habits that have triggered explosive violence in couple relationships. The more serious sources of controversy, however, relate to such matters as disciplining the children, managing household finances, and handling suspicions of extramarital affairs. The attempts of one spouse to reshape or reform the other sometimes leads to aggressive outcomes that were neither intended nor expected.

Outbreaks of violence in couple relationships are not due exclusively to the qualities of either the wife or the husband, but to the negotiations growing out of interactions with each other. Wives who remain with their husbands after being physically abused offer several justifications for violence. Interviews with abused wives (Gelles, 1972) indicate that victims of slappings and beatings frequently believe that they deserved to be hit. In such cases the victim justifies an attack on the grounds that she precipitated it: "I asked for it"; "it was my own fault"; "I was nagging my husband"; "I wouldn't stop until he hit me." Such justifications may be viewed as attempts of victims to reestablish normal family relationships and repair the damage that has been done by blaming themselves. The offender may respond to his abusive act by feeling guilty and by promising that he will not do it again, that he will change his ways, or that he will make it up to her. Investments in the joint enterprise of

---

BOX 12.4
Abused Wives: Why Do They Stay?

The research of Richard J. Gelles (1976a) addressed the question of why a woman who has been physically abused by her husband would remain with him, rather than seek outside intervention or a dissolution of the marriage. In obtaining answers to this question, Gelles conducted in-depth interviews with forty-one spouses who had been abused by their husbands. Some of the wives had called the police about incidents of abuse, others had sought help from a social service agency, some had obtained a divorce, but more than a fourth had suffered beatings or stabbings without so much as calling a neighbor.

Several variables were related to the wives' responses. In cases where the violence was less severe and less frequent, the wife was more likely to remain with her husband. Further, the wife was likely to remain with an abusive spouse if she had been struck as a child by her parents. Some women regarded violence between spouses as normal and expressed the view that it was acceptable for a husband to beat his wife "every once and a while." Apparently, victimization as a child increases the tolerance for violence in married life.

Other variables consisted of the complex meanings associated with commitments to a relationship. These meanings were shaped significantly by the educational and occupational characteristics of the wife. Endurance of an abusive husband was likely to occur among those who were unemployed, among those with limited work experiences, and among those with only a high school education or less. Women who were college-educated or employed were more likely to respond to physical maltreatment by leaving their husbands or seeking outside help. The wives who stayed were characterized by a sense of entrapment and by a perceived lack of suitable alternatives.

Source: Richard J. Gelles, "Abused Wives: Why Do They Stay?," *Journal of Marriage and the Family* 38 (November, 1976): 659–668.

family life tend to promote a desire for continuity even after acts of violence have occurred.

Many couples attempt to maintain the privacy of the family sphere and to neutralize the social stigma of physical abuse, rather than to seek help from social service agencies or to report acts of family violence to the police. Some believe that occasionally hitting or slapping a spouse is socially acceptable and that some degree of physical violence in family relationships should be permitted and tolerated. Rather than viewing violence as a last resort, some look on physical force as a normal remedial action for misconduct. In some cases the abused spouse will seek a divorce; frequently, however, the spouse decides to stay and endure an undesirable relationship. The research of Gelles (1976a) indicates that the tendency of a spouse to remain in an abusive relationship derives from conditions of commitment and entrapment. (See Box 12.4.)

Several forces develop to promote continuance of a relationship when a couple has been married for several years. The couple becomes defined as a social unit by friends, relatives, and acquaintances. The desire to promote the myth of peaceful family life generates a tendency to cover-up internal conflicts and to keep them within the private sphere. Calling the police or seeking outside help would constitute a public announcement of failure. Some men and women would prefer to endure a deteriorating relationship than to make such a public announcement.

More importantly, however, a sense of entrapment develops in many marriage relationships. The buildup of a joint enterprise produces a dependency of the husband and wife on one another (Nye, 1976). The very conditions that promote dependency also reduce the prospects of being able to stand alone. The wife or the husband may be frightened at the prospect of having to build a new personal life. The spouses may perceive the external environment as hostile, unfriendly, and unreceptive to personal needs and interests without the social anchorage of family life. Such perceptions imply entrapment and a lack of suitable alternatives to enduring an undesirable relationship.

2. The Abused Child

While physical abuse between husband and wife is serious, it is not the most prominent form of violence within families. Children are much more vulnerable to violent acts than are adults, and the opportunities for their abuse are much greater. The child may be abused by other siblings (brothers and sisters) as well as by parents. Further, the social norms pertaining to punishment are more tolerant of the use of force and coercion in parent-child interactions than in interactions between adults.

The physical punishment of children does not in and of itself constitute abuse and violence. The punishment becomes abusive under conditions of maltreatment in which serious physical injury is inflicted on the child. The problem with the rights of parents to employ physical punishment is that the use of force may get out of hand. The caretaking function may recede into the background as children become the objects of anger and hostility. In cases of abuse the social learning of the child becomes of less concern than the acting out of an emotional state by the parent (Dailey, 1979).

The vulnerability of children within the family results from their potential use as "shock absorbers" for adult frustrations. The sources of trouble within families are varied and tend to have cumulative effects over time. Although the physical abuse is usually triggered by some form of misconduct on the part of the child, maltreatment by a hostile parent results from a combination of high stress levels and an underlying sense of incompetence in the role as caretaker (Garbarino, 1977). Any normal individual becomes a potential abuser if the level of emotional stress is high, if there is a generally poor understanding of child management, and if interactions with the child are especially difficult. (See Box 12.5.)

BOX 12.5
Demythologizing Child Abuse

In order to enhance a more accurate understanding of child abuse, Richard Gelles (1976b) has identified some of the prominent myths to surface in recent years. The main myth is that there has been a dramatic increase in child abuse. Other myths relate to beliefs about the scope, causes, and prevention of child abuse.

During the past two decades there has been an increase in public and professional attention directed toward child abuse and neglect. Because of the lack of concern with child abuse prior to 1960, many people came to the conclusion that the recent focus on the maltreatment of children has been a direct response to an actual increase in the rate of abuse. Many definitions of child abuse have arisen, and discussions included reference to neglect, abandonment, malnutrition, and a failure to meet the psychological needs of the child. According to Gelles, one of the myths is that the use of the term *child abuse* refers to a uniform set of behaviors. If the concept of abuse is limited to instances of physical violence, there is no empirical evidence that the extent of child abuse has increased in recent years.

Drawing on theories of deviance, Gelles observes that designating specific cases as child abuse may more nearly reflect a labeling process than the actual extent of abuse within a society. Official statistics can be misleading because they are likely to reflect unusual cases and to include only those individuals who are detected and labeled as abusers. A reasonable conclusion is that an awareness of the child-abuse problem, rather than an actual increase in the amount of violence toward children, is what has increased in recent years. Another myth is that the child abuser is a mentally deranged person. There is no evidence that any specific personality disorder of the abuser is a major cause of violence toward children.

Source: Richard J. Gelles, "Demythologizing Child Abuse," *Family Coordinator* 25 (April, 1976): 135–142.

The abused child is likely to have been an unwanted child (Gelles, 1975). The occurrence of an unwanted pregnancy is symptomatic of the difficulties many couples have in exercising control over crucial family events. Obstacles to mastery and control in part stem from the failure of couples to effectively communicate with each other. Difficulties arise from the unwillingness of one or both spouses to sit down and calmly discuss plans and aspirations for the future. As a result of the failure to engage in long-range planning of family events, the lifestyles of many couples follow a pattern of aimlessness and drift (Neal and Groat, 1980).

Becoming an abusive parent is associated with having to cope with numerous changes in life circumstances and with an ensuing sense of frustration and helplessness (Garbarino, 1977). The addition of an unwanted or unplanned child tends to magnify other family problems. Troubles at work, financial difficulties, poor health, and dissatisfaction with one's sex life are among the changing life circumstances that intensify levels of family stress. Such events may impose additional obligations or responsibilities on an individual, and a sense of entrapment may follow. Many couples are able to cope successfully with stress without becoming violent, although the probability for child abuse increases with higher stress levels.

Since the child is defenseless and unable to retaliate, he or she becomes a ready-made victim for acts of violence. Whether parents abuse their children depends in large measure on the extent to which they themselves were victims of maltreatment during childhood (Conger, Burgess, and Barrett, 1979). Violence begets violence. Having been victimized in childhood increases the probability of later becoming an abusive parent. Parents who abuse their children frequently believe that it is appropriate to beat children for disobedience, or that it is alright to hit someone for doing something wrong. Parental treatment of children is based, then, on the role models provided in their own interaction experiences as children.

Drawing on a representative sample of 2143 American families, Gelles and Straus (1979: 23) concluded that "the extreme forms of parental violence are not likely to be one shot events." If violence occurs at all, it is likely to follow a recurrent pattern. Children are unlikely to experience parental violence as a once in a lifetime event. Further, the generality of violent acts within families is reflected in the use of physical aggression among multiple combinations of family relationships. The abused child is likely to also live in a family in which numerous hostilities surface between parents and in which a great deal of fighting takes place among siblings (Steinmetz, 1977a).

In summary, the abused child is likely to be a member of a family that frequently employs violence as a means of resolving conflict. The use of physical force is a learned behavior in which parents simply draw on their earlier experiences as a basis for treating their own children. The abused child is likely to be an unwanted child and to be troublesome to his or her parents. Maltreatment and victimization occur in situations in which numerous stresses build up to the point of an explosion within family relationships.

3. Siblings

The aggressors in abuse of children are not limited to the caretakers. The most frequent form of physical abuse in our society is generally recognized as occurring among siblings. We look on fighting among children as normal and necessary for growth and development: "boys will be boys," we say, and being tough we value frequently as a desired characteristic (Henry, 1974). We sometimes view skills in fighting as useful in dealing with friends, schoolmates, and peers. Squabbles among brothers and sisters we tend to take for granted and to view as a type of basic training for assertive and aggressive behavior in later life (Steinmetz, 1977b). Because of the emphasis on competitive values in our society, we generally regard fighting in sibling relationships as inevitable, socially desirable, and important for contributing to the socialization of the child.

The perceived importance of sibling socialization is reflected in the negative stereotypes Americans hold toward the person who has grown up as an only child. The research of Toni Falbo (1976) indicates several aspects of the negative imagery of only children in popular thinking. The only child is viewed as selfish, self-centered, lonely, maladjusted, unable to share, and unprepared to deal with conflict. While these images are widely held and can be seen in the planning of family size, Falbo's research fails to confirm these popular beliefs. There appear to be no major disadvantages in later life to having grown up as an only child. Yet the stereotypes persist, and in the United States today more couples prefer to remain childless than to have an only child (Groat, Wicks, and Neal, 1980). The disdain for the only child appears to stem from the negative consequences parents pressume will accrue to the child not socialized by siblings.

The character of fighting among siblings varies by age level: fighting occurs more frequently and over different things among younger compared to older children (Steinmetz, 1977b). Small children frequently fight over possessions, especially over toys or over having some object at the same time. Fighting in early adolescence often centers around invasions of privacy and personal space: touching and pinching; making faces and looking funny; name calling and excessive teasing. During the middle and late teens the frequency of violence reduces, but the violence that does occur tends to be more serious. The reduced violence among teenagers stems from increased sophistication in dealing with conflict as well as from the reduced frequency of interaction as siblings go their separate ways.

A good deal of the fighting among siblings can be understood as an outgrowth of justice concerns, the learning of social norms, or the playing of social roles. Fights and disagreements are frequently associated with such virtues as defending one's honor, standing up for one's rights, proving one's masculinity, and taking care of oneself. The quest for justice frequently lies behind the uses of aggression and coercive power (Tedeschi, Gaes, and Rivera, 1977). Revenge, self-defense, or getting even are recurrent justifications as siblings proceed to punch one another. Siblings frequently regard their self-esteem and social worth as being at stake, and in the contested struggle one gains an advantage only at the expense of another. Aggressive acts often require retaliation because a reluctance to fight may be regarded as evidence of weakness.

Overall rates of violence within families vary according to family size and to the sexual composition of siblings. The larger the family size, the greater the probability of living in a violence-prone home. For example, the research of David Gil (1971) indicates that families with four or more children experience more physical abuse than families with only two or three children. The violence in larger families appears to stem from higher levels of stress, from a wider combination of possible antagonistic relationships, and from greater competition among family members for scarce resources. Further, the rates of violence are greater in families comprised of all male siblings than in families comprised of all girls or a mixture of the sexes (Straus, Gelles, and Steinmetz, 1980). The emphasis on competitive values and assertive roles for males result in higher levels of aggression in male-dominated households.

Parents play an important role in sibling violence. In many cases parents tend to ignore aggressive acts in the hope that siblings will be able to work out their differences among themselves. But as the conflict escalates, noninvolvement is no longer feasible, patience wears thin, and parents attempt to suppress sibling conflict through some form of punishment. Parents frequently employ physical punishment in their efforts to produce nonaggressive and peaceful children. As Albert Bandura (1973) points out, however, using physical punishment to suppress aggressive impulses is counterproductive. The parent is providing the child with an **aggressive role model**; physical force used to punish children tends to promote rather than to reduce their aggressive tendencies. While the child's immediate aggressive acts may be suppressed, the long-range effects may be a further induction of violence. Fighting among siblings is likely to be recurrent in families in which parents use a great deal of physical punishment to resolve conflicts among siblings.

D. COPING WITH CONFLICT

The conflict perspective in social psychology holds that conditions of stress, antagonism, and opposing interests are pervasive in social relationships and that they can never be completely eliminated (Horton, 1966). To the extent that this is the case, it becomes important for individuals to develop mechanisms for coping with conflicts that emerge in their social relationships. It is particularly important to recognize that it is normal for opposing interests and antagonisms to develop in intimate social relationships as well as in relationships that are more impersonal in character. The recognition of conflict provides an opportunity for confronting issues, clarifying goals, and working toward the development of creative solutions to the problems of group living. On the other hand, the denial of conflict takes its toll: generalized feelings of anxiety and latent hostilities persist that cannot be dealt with because they are not recognized (Bach and Wyden, 1970).

Special problems arise when individuals respond to the overt expressions of conflict and fail to confront its underlying sources and causes. For this reason one should recognize the distinction between manifest and latent conflict. **Manifest conflict** is a direct expression of hostility and antagonism that is both intended and recognized in a given situation. It may take the form of a verbal attack or a physical assault, and it is clearly recognized by one or more of the parties as a hostile act. **Latent conflict**, on the other hand, is not clearly recognized by the individuals involved. It has a variety of causal factors that lie beneath the stresses and antagonisms in given situations. Thus manifest conflict is a surface phenomenon, while latent conflict encompasses a greater proportion of the total situation and includes the many complexities underlying antagonistic interactions (Rummel, 1976).

1. Social Awareness

Conflict is inherent in the differential meanings that interacting individuals give to social events. Since on an everyday basis there is often a limited awareness of the opposing attitudes, individuals seldom bring incompatibilities out into the open. When confrontations do emerge in the form of demands and threats, the responses are likely to be those of discomfort and uncertainty for one or more of the parties in the relationship. Awareness is the catalyst by which individuals are able to develop mechanisms for coping with social conflict. A full awareness of conflict involves a recognition not only of one's own interests but also of the opposing interests of others. Such awareness also includes the development of an understanding of the conditions generating the conflict and the potential consequences in costs and benefits both for oneself and for others.

Mechanisms of coping with stress are required for reducing the potentially harmful effects of social living. **Coping** is a cognitive process of making adaptations in those situations in which conflicts cannot be directly confronted or eliminated. The individual perceives that he or she is vulnerable, psychological damage can occur, and problems exist that he or she cannot solve through any practical line of action. Under these circumstances the coping mechanisms can be understood as the subjective meanings the individual gives to events in the mobilization of social and psychological resources (Pearlin *et al.*, 1981).

Drawing on a sample of 2300 subjects in Chicago, Leonard Pearlin and

Carmi Schooler (1978) studied the manner in which individuals cope with the conflicts that surface in everyday life. Their study concentrated on the conflicts that emerge in marriage and parenthood as well as on those that emerge in the workplace and in the management of finances. They identified several coping responses; the ones that were used most frequently involved neutralizing threats by controlling the meanings given to conflict situations. These methods included making positive comparisons, using selective inattention, and reordering priorities.

Making **positive comparisons** consisted of evaluating one's own situation favorably relative to that of others: "count your blessings"; "we're all in the same boat"; "conditions could be worse." The time dimension of family life provides reference points for making positive comparisons. One may regard current hardships as less severe than hardships experienced at some time in the past or may view present difficulties as only "a forerunner," "a stepping-stone," or "a hurdle in the way" to a better life in the future. One can achieve an appreciation of one's own family life by knowing how bad conditions can get in other families. One can regard the troubles in one's own family as mild in comparison to the troubles friends or relatives have had or in comparison to the miserable family life portrayed on television and in the movies. Pearlin and Schooler (1978) observe that the frequency of making such comparisons suggests that "misery truly loves company."

There are good times and bad times in family life, and the bad times can be endured if one "thinks positively" and "avoids negative thoughts." **Selective inattention** is a coping strategy that emphasizes the importance of rewarding family experiences and plays down the sources of conflict. The individual makes efforts to contain the conflicts as much as possible, to put them in perspective, and to look for the "silver lining." Pearlin and Schooler (1978) note that selective inattention is typically achieved by searching for some positive attribute of a troublesome situation. Noxious circumstances can be trivialized by magnifying the importance of what is worthwhile and gratifying. Such a style of coping tends to equate problem solving with the avoidance of worry and tension. The underlying aims are to avoid confrontation, to relax so that difficulties become less important, and to permit problems to disappear with the passing of time.

Reordering priorities is a technique for confining stress to those areas that are only of secondary importance: "a job is just a job"; "money isn't everything"; "other things in life are more important." In this form of coping, one downgrades specific priorities in family life in order to control the meaning of a problematic situation and to minimize its potential threat. An idyllic view of family life may be tempered with a recognition that compromises are necessary and that hopes and aspirations cannot always be achieved. In demeaning the importance of some specific goal for oneself, one's children, or one's family life, one seeks protection from the stressful consequences of troubles and problems.

Although these and other coping responses do not eliminate the sources of conflict, they do permit individuals to protect themselves from harmful emotional consequences. Altered states of awareness are techniques for asserting symbolic control over stressful situations; they involve forms of denial, avoidance, and defensiveness. Such coping strategies are only some of the many possible responses to conditions of conflict. Some couples do work out problems by taking a direct approach and seeking uncomplicated solutions. The success of couples in confronting and resolving conflicts in a mutually satisfactory manner depends to a very large degree on what social supports are available and on what uses they make of family and other resources.

2. Conflict Resolution

Over long periods of time, conflict tends to be an inherently unstable form of social relationship. Either the conflict escalates through the mutual responsiveness of the parties involved, or the relationship comes to be redefined in a manner that encourages cooperation and tolerance. Louis Kriesberg (1973) observes that the resolution of social conflict nearly always involves some degree of compromise on the part of the parties involved. The compromise may take the form of a negotiated settlement in which both parties decide how to split the differences or use bargaining so that each party gives something to the other and receives something in return (Rubin and Brown, 1975).

Joann Horai (1977) maintains that the outcomes of conflict are shaped by an attributional process in which each of the interacting parties attempts to manage and control the causal explanations of events. Assigning blame, expressing indignation, and attempting to force the other party to accept one's own point of view are among the strategies that tend to intensify rather than lessen the conflicts involved. The conflicting explanations often cannot be reconciled by the contenders, and as a result, the outcomes of social conflict are often dependent on the assessments made by impartial observers. The processing of legal cases, for example, frequently involves the resolution of conflicting claims about the responsibility for the events in question. The job of the jury consists of deciding between the alternative causal explanations offered by the defense and the prosecution. Causal explanations serve the function of fixing responsibility and often become crucial considerations in the settlement of any given case. (See Box 12.6.)

Third parties play an important part in conflict resolution, particularly in cases of conflict that involve the rights of those who are at a disadvantage within the power structure. Government agencies are the primary third parties that have the authority to resolve conflicts in a social system, and the kinds of decisions they make have important implications for the system of justice and for the qualities of group relationships. Emphasis on the rights of women, the rights of children, and the legal recognition of marital rape are among the political solutions to the problems of family conflict. The recognition of oppos-

Conflict Resolution
The county courthouse provides an official setting for resolving the conflicts that people are not able to resolve among themselves. Courts are designed for judges and juries to hear the evidence, to weigh contending claims, and to arrive at just and binding decisions. In the proceedings of the court, laws are enforced, penalties are imposed, and social norms are clarified.

BOX 12.6
Legal Contests and the Rule of Irrelevance

George Simmel, in his classical writings, emphasized legal contests as expressions of conflict in its purest form. The purity of conflict in legal proceedings stems from adherence to the rule of irrelevance, which states that only those facts that have an objective bearing on the case are admissible as evidence. All other considerations are considered out-of-order and extraneous to the issue at hand. The purity of conflict is achieved through authoritative decisions on what is central and what is peripheral to adversary proceedings.

Reality constructions in the legal process are designed to reduce the complexities of actual social situations. Antagonistic interactions in everyday life often grow out of complex sets of misunderstandings and hostilities. Individuals frequently talk "past" one another, fail to listen, and read unintended meanings into the actions of others. Thus social relationships can come to resemble competitive sports in that they require referees and negotiators to maintain orderly proceedings. Individuals are frequently unable to resolve their differences because of their emotional responses to conflict events. As a result third-party interventions become necessary to prevent contested struggles from transforming into violent acts.

Invoking the rule of irrelevance permits placing emphasis on the conflict itself rather than on the personal sentiments of the antagonists. Social conflict is amenable to resolution primarily because of the willingness of each party to abide by the decisions of authority agents. All parties are equally bound to legal norms: the individuals involved are obliged to recognize that the procedures of the contest are irrevocably valid and that the final decision gives meaning and certainty to their subsequent acts.

Source: Georg Simmel, *Conflict and the Web of Group Affiliations,* New York: The Free Press, 1955.

---

ing forces may be necessary for social relationships to develop in a productive, creative, and rewarding manner. Refusals to recognize conflicts or attempts to solve conflicts through simplistic solutions are likely to have consequences that are undesirable for both the parties involved and the overall quality of group life.

The social supports provided by friends, acquaintances, and relatives are also important for coping with adversity and stress (Turner, 1981). Having someone to turn to in times of trouble is useful for a cognitive appraisal of conflict situations. The other person may provide assistance not only for controlling emotional responses but also for working toward practical solutions. Talking about problems can lead to the individual's recognition that the problem is actually trivial, that the individual is overresponding to an inconsequential matter, that the problem is not unique, or that the individual should refrain from doing something that he or she will regret later. On the other hand, talking about troubles may convince the individual that the problem is more serious than previously recognized and that he or she must do something about it.

A basic decision in dealing with family conflicts is whether to continue or to terminate a marriage relationship. The research of J. Richard Udry (1981) indicates that the individual's perceptions of social support networks are important for the kinds of decisions he or she makes. Udry's findings indicate that control over personal and social resources outside the family increases the scope of **marital alternatives**. The marital alternatives may consist of actually having someone else in mind as a more desirable partner or simply deciding that there would be major advantages to not being married at all. The perceived ability to replace a present spouse with another partner of equal or greater value enters into the decision to dissolve rather than to endure an undesirable relationship. Such a decision rests on having negotiable resources for entering new exchange relationships, on perceiving oneself as a valued social object, and on being confident that one can achieve what one wants out of life.

SUMMARY

Family violence has been recognized as a serious problem by social workers, psychiatrists, and criminologists for a long time, but it was not until the 1960s that physical aggression within the family was widely defined as a public issue. The emergence of concerns with violence during the 1960s and 1970s provided new images of family life and the potential qualities of intimate relationships. The views of the family as an institution built on love, affection, and caring for one another was called into question and seriously qualified. It became widely recognized that the escalation of conflict in intimate groups has the potential for developing into violent relationships.

The vulnerability of the modern family to violent acts stems from several aspects of the relationship between intimacy and conflict. Multiple roles are played in family life and it is difficult for any one individual to play all of the roles successfully; emotion plays an important part in intimate relationships, yet rules for the management of emotions in intimate groups are not clearly defined. The isolated, nuclear family frequently is separated from broader networks of social supports, and the privacy of family life promotes the cover-up of many forms of conflict and violence. The severity of physical abuse within families grows out of the strategies various members use for conflict management.

A good deal of family violence goes undetected because the family conceals it from public view. The family seeks outside help usually only when one party to the conflict is no longer willing to endure an abusive relationship or when the physical injuries are serious enough to require medical attention.

Several variables are associated with a person's decision to endure an abusive relationship rather than to seek a divorce or call the police. A sense of entrapment develops out of dependency relationships and from the fear of not being able to stand alone.

The rights of the child are violated more often than the rights of any other family member. The child frequently becomes a shock absorber for adult frustrations because the child is weaker and less able to fight back. The abused child is likely to have been an unwanted child and an especially difficult child for a parent lacking in child-management skills. Social norms permit parents to use physical punishment in the training of children, but the use of physical force often gets out of hand. Parents frequently view fighting among siblings as normal, natural, and inevitable in their children's socialization. The scope of fighting among siblings, however, is shaped by the adult role models within the family. Parents who do a lot of fighting are likely to produce aggressive and violence-prone children.

BASIC TERMS

Emotion rules	**Aggressive role model**
Nuclear family	**Manifest conflict**
Conflict tactics	**Latent conflict**
Coercive violence	**Coping**
Appealing violence	**Positive comparisons**
Zero-sum game	**Selective inattention**
Threat	**Reordering priorities**
Last resort	**Marital alternatives**

REFERENCES

Bach, George R. and Peter Wyden
    1974 "Why Intimates Must Fight," in Suzanne K. Steinmetz and Murray A. Straus (eds.), *Violence in the Family*, New York: Dodd, Mead, pp. 98–109.
    1970 *The Intimate Enemy*, New York: Avon Books.
Bandura, Albert
    1973 *Aggression: A Social Learning Analysis*, Englewood Cliffs, N.J.: Prentice-Hall.
Conger, Rand D., Robert L. Burgess and Carol Barrett
    1979 "Child Abuse Related to Life Change and Perceptions of Illness," *Family Coordinator* 28 (January): 73–78.
Coser, Lewis A.
    1967 *Continuities in the Study of Social Conflict*, New York: The Free Press.

Dailey, Timothy B.
    1979 "Parental Power Breeds Violence," *Sociological Focus* 12 (October): 311–322.
Deutsch, Morton
    1975 "Equity, Equality, and Need," *Journal of Social Issues* 31 (Summer): 137–150.
Elliot, Gil
    1972 *The 20th Century Book of the Dead,* New York: Ballantine.
Emerson, Robert M.
    1981 "On Last Resorts," *American Journal of Sociology* 87 (July): 1–22.
Evans, Thomas R.
    1979 "Domestic Violence," *Newsletter* (vol. 4, no. 2, Fall), Cleveland: The Begun
        Institute.
Falbo, Toni
    1976 "Does the Only Child Grow Up Miserable?," *Psychology Today* 9 (May):
        60–65.
Garbarino, James
    1977 "The Human Ecology of Child Maltreatment," *Journal of Marriage and the
        Family* 39 (November): 721–736.
Gelles, Richard J.
    1976a "Abused Wives: Why Do They Stay?," *Journal of Marriage and the Family* 38
        (November): 659–668.
    1976b "Demythologizing Child Abuse," *Family Coordinator* 25 (April): 135–142.
    1975 "Violence and Pregnancy," *Family Coordinator* 24 (January): 81–86.
    1972 *The Violent Home,* Beverly Hills, Calif.: Sage.
Gelles, Richard J. and Murray A. Straus
    1979 "Violence in the American Family," *Journal of Social Issues* 35, no. 2: 15–39.
Gil, David G.
    1971 "Violence Against Children," *Journal of Marriage and the Family* 33 (No-
        vember): 637–657.
Gilbert, Shirley J.
    1976 "Self Disclosure, Intimacy and Communication in Families," *Family Coor-
        dinator* 25 (July): 221–233.
Goffman, Erving
    1963 *Behavior in Public Places,* New York: The Free Press.
Goode, William J.
    1974 "Force and Violence in the Family," in Suzanne K. Steinmetz and Murray A.
        Straus (eds.), *Violence in the Family,* New York: Dodd, Mead, pp. 25–44.
    1972 "The Place of Force in Human Society," *American Sociological Review* 37
        (October): 507–519.
Gotesky, Rubin
    1974 "Social Force, Social Power, and Social Violence," in Sherman M. Stanage
        (ed.), *Reason and Revolution,* Totowa, N.J.: Littlefield, Adams, pp. 183–206.
Groat, H. Theodore, Jerry W. Wicks, and Arthur G. Neal
    1980 *Differential Consequences of Having Been an Only Versus a Sibling Child,*
        Bethesda, Md.: Center for Population Research.
Henry, Jules
    1974 "Making Pete Tough," in Suzanne K. Steinmetz and Murray A. Straus (eds.),
        Violence in the Family, New York: Dodd, Mead, pp. 238–240.
Hochschild, Arlie Russell

1979 "Emotion Work, Feeling Rules, and Social Structure," *American Journal of Sociology* 85 (November): 551–575.

Horai, Joann
1977 "Attributional Conflict," *Journal of Social Issues* 33, no. 1: 88–100.

Horton, John
1966 "Order and Conflict Theories of Social Problems as Competing Ideologies," *American Journal of Sociology* 71 (May): 701–713.

Kriesberg, Louis
1973 *The Sociology of Social Conflicts*, Englewood Cliffs, N.J.: Prentice-Hall.

Laufer, Robert S. and Maxine Wolfe
1977 "Privacy as a Concept and a Social Issue," *Journal of Social Issues* 33, no. 3: 22–42.

Margulis, Stephen T.
1977 "Conceptions of Privacy," *Journal of Social Issues* 33, no. 3: 5–21.

Marx, Emanuel
1976 *The Social Context of Violent Behavior*, London: Routledge and Kegan Paul.

Milburn, Thomas W.
1977 "The Nature of Threat," *Journal of Social Issues*, 33, no. 1: 126–139.

Monahan, John
1981 *Predicting Violent Behavior*, Beverly Hills, Calif.: Sage.

Neal, Arthur G. and H. Theodore Groat
1980 "Fertility Decision Making, Unintended Births, and the Social Drift Hypothesis," *Population and Environment* 3 (Winter): 221–236.

Nye, F. Ivan
1976 "Ambivalence in the Family: Rewards and Costs in Group Membership," *Family Coordinator* 25 (January): 21–32.

Pearlin, Leonard I., Morton A. Lieberman, Elizabeth G. Menaghan, and Joseph T. Mullan
1981 "The Stress Process," *Journal of Health and Social Behavior* 22 (December): 337–356.

Pearlin, Leonard I. and Carmi Schooler
1978 "The Structure of Coping," *Journal of Health and Social Behavior* 19 (March): 2–21.

Rubin, Jeffrey Z. and Bert R. Brown
1975 *The Social Psychology of Bargaining and Negotiation*, New York: Academic Press.

Rummel, R. J.
1976 *Understanding Conflict and War: The Conflict Helix*, New York: John Wiley.

Shott, Susan
1979 "Emotion and Social Life: A Symbolic Interactionist Analysis," *American Journal of Sociology* 84 (May): 1317–1334.

Simmel, Georg
1955 *Conflict and the Web of Group-Affiliations*, New York: The Free Press.
1950 *The Sociology of Georg Simmel* (ed. and trans. by Kurt Wolff), Glencoe, Ill.: The Free Press.

Sprey, Jetse
1974 "On the Management of Conflict in Families," in Suzanne K. Steinmetz and Murray A. Straus (eds.), *Violence in the Family*, New York: Dodd, Mead, pp. 110–119.

Stanage, Sherman M.
    1974 *Reason and Violence*, Totowa, N.J.: Littlefield, Adams.
Steinmetz, Suzanne K.
    1977a"The Use of Force for Resolving Family Conflict," *Family Coordinator* 26
        (January): 19–26.
    1977b*The Cycle of Violence*, New York: Praeger.
Steinmetz, Suzanne K. and Murray A. Straus
    1974 *Violence in the Family*, New York: Dodd, Mead.
Straus, Murray A.
    1979 "Measuring Intrafamily Conflict and Violence," *Journal of Marriage and the
        Family* 41 (February): 75–88.
    1974 "Leveling, Civility, and Violence in the Family," *Journal of Marriage and the
        Family* 36 (February): 13–30.
Straus, Murray A., Richard J. Gelles, and Suzanne K. Steinmetz
    1980 *Behind Closed Doors*, Garden City, N.J.: Anchor Books.
Tedeschi, James T., Gerald G. Gaes, and Alba N. Rivera
    1977 "Aggression and the Use of Coercive Power," *Journal of Social Issues* 33,
        no. 1: 101–125.
Turner, Jay R.
    1981 "Social Support as a Contingency in Psychological Well-Being," *Journal of
        Health and Social Behavior* 22 (December): 357–367.
Udry, J. Richard
    1981 "Marital Alternatives and Marital Disruption," *Journal of Marriage and the
        Family* 43 (November): 889–898.
Wolfgang, Marvin
    1978 "Violence in the Family," in Irwin L. Kutash, Samuel B. Kutash, and Louis B.
        Schlesinger (eds.), *Violence: Perspectives on Murder and Aggression*, San
        Francisco: Jossey-Bass, pp. 238–253.

V

PSYCHOLOGICAL MODERNITY

13

Social Movements

Social movements have their origins in whatever is defined as the troubles and problems of a social system (Mauss, 1975). The designation of troubles is a selective process by which groups and associations recognize that something is wrong and that remedial action is necessary (Emerson and Messinger, 1977). The group defines some state of affairs as unpleasant, irritating, dangerous, or intolerable. Further, it makes the claim that something can and should be done about it. The group makes attempts to establish new rules of conduct, to correct perceived injustices, and to usher in what it believes to be a more desirable social order. Thus movements are grounded in the definitions of social problems, in the claims that social life is something less than it ought to be, and in the remedial lines of action that are employed (Blumer, 1971).

The malfunctioning of a social system and the existence of human misery do not directly give rise to social movements. People may live under deplorable conditions for long periods of time without giving a great deal of public attention to them. For example, urban environments at the turn of the twentieth century were polluted by horses and stables, by wood- and coal-burning stoves, and by the methods of trash disposal. But these conditions were not defined as serious public issues. It was not until recent years that environmental concerns have been thrust to the forefront of public attention. Several concerns about the inequalities of women are of recent vintage, although sex discrimination by purely objective criteria was of much greater scope a hundred years ago. Similarly, racial discrimination was more rampant in the 1920s than it was at the peak of the civil rights movement in the 1960s. Such examples show that a significant gap often exists between objective conditions and subjective responses to them. Problems do not exist unless they are recognized as problems and designated as conditions that are undesirable, dangerous, or harmful (Blumer, 1971).

The claims of a social movement provide new perspectives for looking at social life and the resolution of social problems. If the claims of a social movement are accepted as valid and legitimate ones, many people are likely to be drawn into the movement and the movement will seek remedial action (Spector and Kituse, 1973). The claims include a diagnosis of what is wrong with a contemporary situation, a set of recommended procedures for correcting current problems, and ideas about how the world will become a better place if the movement is successful. The claims of a social movement become important as shared symbols and meanings for binding people together and justifying sacrifice, risk taking, and dedication to a cause.

Specific claims and remedial actions vary widely from movement to movement. Some regard religion as the major means for improving social life; others see direct political or economic action as necessary. Many religious movements seek guidance from spiritual and supernatural sources, value conversion experiences (being "born again"), and seek compensations at the supernatural level for injustices experienced in the world of here and now. Some religious movements prepare for a "second coming," wait for the rapture, and expect divine intervention to achieve justice. Other religious movements deemphasize the importance of the supernatural, believe that God has lost interest in humanity, and maintain that humans must create their own sacred and spiritual values. Thus movements that fall within the religious sphere differ widely among themselves. Some are characterized by other-worldliness, while others concentrate on the perfection of institutions in the present world.

In contrast, political and economic movements are always oriented toward the secular sphere, attempting to achieve practical benefits and outcomes in human affairs. Organization of labor unions, enactment of gun-control legislation, environmental protection, conservation of scarce and nonrenewable resources, protection of endangered species, consumer rights, and elimination of nuclear power plants are among the claims for remedial action in the political sphere. While movements frequently aim toward practical politics, they also draw on sacred values and religious sentiments in efforts to win public support. Labor unions in the United States during the nineteenth century frequently sang hymns and religious songs in their meetings (Kornbluh, 1965); the civil rights movement was regarded as a crusade, blending Christianity with practical politics; and the Radical Right movement in the United States during the late fifties and early sixties was characterized by a mixture of Christianity and patriotism in their militant responses to the perceived threats of hidden communists. In actuality, regardless of whether the focus is mainly on religious or political values, there usually is a blending of the sacred and the secular in social movements.

Through news coverage and mass media exposure, social movements can have a high degree of visibility in modern society. If the activities of a social movement are reported on the nightly news, millions of television viewers are provided with new images and reference points for reflecting on social life and the prospects for its improvement. The degree of public sympathy for a particular cause may eventually determine the success or failure of a social movement. Favorable public opinion frequently results in initiation of the proposed changes in some form or another, while unfriendly attitudes are likely to result in the failure of the movement. The launching of a social movement depends on society accepting its claims as valid and legitimate concerns.

Social movements are characterized by the use of persuasive appeals in seeking to win support for a set of claims. Such appeals reduce the complexities of social life by telescoping highly specific problems and issues. The appeals identify an overriding cause, leadership emerges to promote the goals of a movement, and the group directs efforts toward creating a sense of moral community among a movement's followers (Traugott, 1978). The movement emphasizes the prospects for success through the pooling of resources. The persuasive appeals also draw on the specific grievances that the disenchanted have with the established order. The objective of these appeals is to produce commitments among followers in their quest for a better life.

The study of social movements should enable us to see more clearly the importance of the reality construction process in modern social life. The idealism in social movements reflects the importance of hope and wishful thinking as men and women dedicate themselves to repairing what they see as the defects of a social system. The realities constructed by social movements vary in content and extend the range of choices and options available on a collec-

Persuasive Appeals
The persuasive appeals of the evangelist on campus are usually met with some degree of student resistance.

tive basis. An awareness of the dynamics of social movements should lead to a fuller appreciation of the manner in which people attempt social changes through the use of collective efforts.

A. CRISIS OF AUTHORITY

Step 1.

Mark Traugott (1978) observes that social movements coalesce around social conflicts and have an **antiinstitutional orientation**. They are anti-institutional in that they stand outside the constraining framework of existing institutions and practices. For example, religious movements frequently assign a greater allegiance to the will of God than to the laws of the state. People raise objections over banning prayers in public schools, over a curriculum that includes sex education, and over teaching the theory of organic evolution rather than creationism as set forth in the Book of Genesis. Movements thus recommend that some aspect of the routines of everyday life be suspended or modified and that institutional practices be changed or transformed. If a social movement is successful in advancing its claims, some form of confrontation

2.

necessarily occurs between it and the existing social order.

The emergence of a social movement implies to some degree that those entrusted with the management of social institutions have failed to provide adequate leadership and initiatives. Some segments of the population view authority decisions as being initiated by uninformed people, as reflecting misplaced priorities, and as failing to meet the needs of the social system. Under these conditions authority loses its validity and groups extend challenges, and recommend changes. Those pressing for changes encounter resistance from those who wish to maintain existing arrangements.

Type I no flexibility to social chg (unresponsive)

One form of crisis emerges when the authority structure becomes overly rigid and tends to perpetuate social norms and procedures that have outlived their usefulness. Such a crisis of authority reflects the inability of those in positions of power to respond adequately to the forces of social change (Rowney, 1976). The management style becomes one of benign neglect: those in power govern by ignoring problems that need attention (Heilbroner, 1970). The members of a social movement view the social system as being in a state of disarray and as in need of repair.

In their attempts to maintain the existing order, authority agents may draw on coercive power to impose their own versions of social reality on others. In doing so others come to view them as inflexible and unresponsive to the needs of the social system. Under such conditions compliance to authority is likely to become coercive and problematic. The challenges of a social movement represent a plea either for recognition of changing conditions, sentiments, and interests or for going back to some previous arrangement.

Type II too many probs/too little time (overloaded)

A crisis of authority may also develop if such a large number of problems are identified that they cannot be solved adequately within a reasonable amount of time. The crisis of authority in this type of situation grows out of an overloaded system rather than an unresponsive one. For example, in the United States during the 1960s, a large number of social problems were recognized as legitimate concerns in need of official responses. Public attention and legislative action focused on such domestic problems as poverty and social inequality, racial discrimination, environmental degradation, and the rights of women, as well as on such international problems as the spread of world communism, the war in Vietnam, and the specter of world hunger. The resources available are always limited, and a social system can become subjected to considerable stress if the group recognizes a large number of problems as legitimate concerns. A sense of impatience may develop over the slowness of the process by which problems are being solved. Such conditions promote a great deal of social movement activity over the reallocation of resources and the realignment of priorities.

Verification of Claims Making
The decisions of those who vote in elections sometimes result in verifying the claims made earlier by social movements.

1. Modernity

While men and women sometimes desire permanence and stability, they experience the inevitable realities of change and alteration. Tradition and custom lose their holds over conduct as people seek new solutions for old problems, make new choices and decisions, and develop numerous fears and anxieties from thinking about the future. Social movements build on and dramatize the strains and contradictions built into modern social living (Smelser, 1962).

The notion of **modernity** refers to the perceived realities of contemporary social life. Being modern implies being up-to-date in one's thinking, making judgments about how the present differs from the past, and recognizing that changes and trends are occurring in the social realm. In some cases modern ideas stand in opposition to tradition and offer challenges to customary practices and existing institutions (Berger, Berger, and Kellner, 1974). The women's liberation movement is a prime example of such a social movement. The liberation theme suggests that its proponents regard new freedoms, new opportunities, and new forms of social experimentation as both necessary and desirable.

The rapid rates of changes in modern society are accompanied by differential consequences for subgroups of the population. For example, in the economic sphere, some occupations become increasingly important, while others decline in significance. Wealth and income levels increase for some individuals, while ownership and purchasing power decline significantly for others. In the competitive struggle for scarce resources, there are winners and losers; and some people come to feel that the norms of distributive justice fail to operate. Some individuals feel that they are giving disproportionately in comparison to what they are receiving in return, while others feel that their basic human needs are not being met. The development of labor unions in the United States, for example, grew out of the concerns of workers for distributive justice. Big businesses were viewed as greedy, and unions were geared toward obtaining for the workers a fair share of the rewards of modern industry. Movements directed toward civil rights grew out of indignation over discriminatory practices and the lack of opportunities for the deprived and the oppressed. Under such conditions, collective efforts are directed toward finetuning the system in the quest for fairness and justice.

In other cases the concerns are not so much related to distributive justice as to perceived trends toward moral decay and the degeneration of social life. Here cherished beliefs and values are being challenged by new lifestyles and new moralities. Some movements develop as moral "crusades," strongly insisting that their own conceptions of right and wrong be accepted by and applied to the rest of society (Gusfield, 1963). Crusades against the evils of alcoholism, pornography, and abortion are oppositional movements that view the authority structure as being too lenient and permissive. Crusades direct efforts toward upholding moral mandates, restoring traditional values that are being eroded, and restraining the forces of evil. (See Box 13.1.)

> **BOX 13.1**
> **Antipornography as a Symbolic Crusade**
>
> Social movements are not limited to the oppressed, the underprivileged, and the exploited sectors of a population. Movements sometimes emerge among those who occupy positions of power, wealth, and privilege, especially when certain changes in society challenge a cherished lifestyle.
>
> The process of pooling resources to revive and perpetuate a lifestyle regarded as traditional and proper has been described by Joseph Gusfield (1963) as a **symbolic crusade**. A symbolic crusade is a social movement that grows up around a specific symbol selected to indicate the degenerative character of modern social life. Earlier in American history the Prohibition movement focused on alcohol as the master symbol of moral decay. More recent symbolic crusades have concentrated on "the evils of Communism" in American life, the fluoridation of water supplies as a Communist conspiracy, the banning of prayers in the public schools, and the legal tolerance of abortion.
>
> Louis A. Zurcher and his associates (1971) found the antipornography campaigns they studied to have several characteristics of a symbolic crusade. Participants in the campaigns were concerned about the erosion of several traditional values, such as the growing disrespect for authority, the loss of patriotic sentiment, the decline of religious values, and the weakening of the work ethic. However, the participants selected pornography as the key issue and as the master symbol of moral decay. Smut peddlers, public nudity, explicit sex, adult bookstores, and X-rated movies became the objects of attack. The people involved in these campaigns were seeking legislation to ban pornography not so much to actually change sexual behavior as confirm that certain moral values of decency were the official morality of the society.
>
> *Source:* Louis A. Zurcher, Jr., R. George Kirkpatrick, Robert G. Cushing, and Charles K. Bowman, "The Anti-Pornography Campaign: A Symbolic Crusade," *Social Problems* 19 (Fall, 1971): 217–237.

In contrast to reviving and perpetuating sacred values, some social movements become utopian. Many of these movements draw on rational and secular values in their efforts to perfect human relationships and social institutions. Utopian movements are oriented toward inventing the future through social experiments that set up models for others to emulate. Some experiments in group living have been based on the teachings of Karl Marx and the communal ownership of property (Mills, 1962), while others have been based on psychological theories or some combination of psychological and philosophical principles (Skinner, 1972). But whatever the specific guiding principles, utopian movements see themselves as agencies of social change, regard contemporary social life as amenable to substantial improvement, and seek through their own efforts to create a more desirable future.

Utopian Movement

2. *Remedial Action*

Social movements often fail to develop because the claims for the existence of a social problem are not recognized as valid and legitimate (Spector and Kituse, 1973). For example, a report submitted to President Truman more than thirty years ago called attention to the depletion of nonrenewable energy resources and emphasized the need for a national energy policy. Only a few people recognized the seriousness of energy problems prior to the 1970s, and it was only after the oil embargo of 1974 curtailed travel that the country recognized a

---

BOX 13.2
Remedial Action of the Environmental Movement

The emergence of the environmental movement in the 1960s was based on growing concerns about the degradation of the physical world. The movement focused attention on the problems of trash disposal, pollution of air and water, the environmental effects of strip mining, the disappearance of wilderness areas, and an increase in the number of endangered species. The movement claimed that the human damages to the physical world were having negative effects on the quality of life.

Robert A. Stallings (1973) found in researching environmental activists that they agreed on the existence of a crisis in the relationship between humans and their physical environment, but were in disagreement on the causes of the problem. Some saw the American consumer as the responsible agent; some fixed responsibility with business corporations and their emphasis on the profit motive; others placed blame on the failure of governmental regulatory agencies; and still others emphasized the high standards of living for more than 200 million people. The perceived causes of the problem were related to the perceived defects of the social system.

Stallings also found disagreements among environmental activists on the appropriate forms of remedial action. Some saw the cure as residing with greater control over business corporations, while others focused on consumer behavior; some emphasized governmental action, while others were distrustful of government; some argued for instituting new norms and rules of conduct, while others sought basic changes in values and lifestyles. Members of a social movement often conceal such disagreements from public view in efforts to win support and mobilize constituencies. However, from Stallings's research it is clear that the popular view of social movements as being comprised of like-minded individuals needs serious qualifications.

Source: Robert A. Stallings, "Patterns of Belief in Social Movements," *Sociological Quarterly* 14 (Autumn, 1973): 465–480.

potential energy crisis. Visions of possible troubles have little social impact unless claims are recognized as legitimate grounds for remedial action.

The recognition of some condition as undesirable or deplorable is not a sufficient basis for developing a social movement. Deplorable conditions may be endured as "inevitable," "as the workings of fate," or as "unshakable social facts." It is only through a call to remedial action that social movements flourish and develop. **Remedial actions** refer to actions based on the assumption that something can be done about the problem of concern. The movement designs action programs to bring about modifications in social life and directs persuasive appeals toward the discontented. The movement offers hope for a better world as an alternative to despair and fatalistic resignation. Rather than giving up in the face of overwhelming odds, the movement offers to those

---

TABLE 13.1
Voluntary Associations as Social Movements

The following is a casual list of voluntary associations that are oriented toward improving the social system through remedial action:

> National Abortion Rights Action League
> Americans Against Union Control of Government
> National Tax Limitation Committee
> Klanwatch: The Southern Poverty Law Center
> National Council to Control Handguns
> Women's Equity Action League
> National Organization of Women
> Congress of Racial Equality
> Southern Christian Leadership Conference
> National Association for the Advancement of Colored People
> Anti-Defamation League
> American Civil Liberties Union
> Gay Liberation Front
> Society for the Prevention of Cruelty to Animals
> Women's Christian Temperance Union
> National Peace Academy Campaign
> Amnesty International
> Socialist Workers Party
> People for the American Way
> The Conservative Caucus, Inc.
> The Christian Anti-Communism Crusade
> Liberty Lobby

From the above list it is clear that the ideological content, the remedial actions, and the goals of social movements are highly varied.

[margin note: STALLINGS — people win movement NOT like-minded]

who lend support to its activities better prospects for improving social living conditions.

The research of Robert Stallings (1973) indicates that it is a mistake to think of a social movement as comprised of like-minded individuals. His study of environmental activists found participants in agreement on the seriousness of environmental problems, but in substantial disagreement over the specific remedial actions that should be taken. (See Box 13.2.) In focusing on a general problem, the participants in social movements assemble relevant information, explore feasible solutions, and evaluate alternative lines of action (Swanson, 1970). In this process, the participants direct their concerns toward maintaining a movement's internal solidarity, toward mobilizing a constituency, and toward making inroads into the broader social system. (See Table 13.1.)

3. Emergent Norms

The formation of a social movement is accompanied by the creation of social norms that stand in opposition to prevailing social practices. **Emergent norms** are rules of conduct that grow out of social interactions and attempts at problem solving (Turner and Killian, 1972). They provide a new agenda for conduct and serve to regulate the activities and interactions among a movement's members. Normative controls clarify ambiguous situations and give coherence and purpose to the plans for action.

[margin note: Emergent norms not widely adopted]

In the civil rights movement of the 1960s, for example, a variety of social norms emerged in specific situations to give focus and purpose to group activities. Civil disobedience in the form of bus boycotts and lunch-counter sit-ins came to be normatively approved by movement participants. The emergent norms served to give direction to available energies in the quest for ending racial discrimination in public places. Similarly, the emergence of demonstrations and organized protest on college campuses gave a focus to the resentments against American involvement in the Vietnam war. The norms arose out of widespread discussion and deliberation over the questions of what should be done, how, and why. We may view the results as a type of rational decision making on the limitations and prospects inherent in a given situation (Berk, 1974).

[margin note: Use of E. Norms — 1) framework for decision/action 2) grp support for members 3) disturb non-members]

Norms and values may be created to discredit those in positions of power and authority, to improve the conditions under which men and women live, and to offer alternatives to attitudes of despair (Wallace, 1972; Barber, 1972). The immediate effects of emergent norms are to provide frameworks for decisions and actions, to offer group supports for a movement's members, and to produce some level of disturbance in the lives of those who are being challenged. As movements develop, its members refine and elaborate strategies in efforts directed toward mobilizing support for a cause.

B. MOBILIZATION

The drama of a social movement is enacted through the mobilization of a constituency. **Mobilization** refers to the procedures employed by the leaders of a social movement to win support for a cause. The procedures include the use of ideology, the creation of charismatic leadership, the use of persuasive appeals, and the development of commitments among those sympathetic to the cause. Through mobilization, the leaders of a social movement frequently provide their followers with alternatives to hopelessness and despair. In offering hope for a better world, the leaders draw on collective resources in attempts to bring about the desired social changes.

Mobilization is achieved through the development and use of an overriding ideology. The **ideology** is a generalized set of beliefs that provide a framework for reality assessment (Smelser, 1962). These realities include not only a diagnosis of the present state of affairs but also a set of notions about the manner by which social conditions can be improved. The creation of an ideology gives a sense of direction and purpose to the collective actions of the participants. Thus ideologies are designed to provide a basis for understanding and action. They reduce the complexity of the world and give focus to particular lines of action.

Social movements grow and develop by implementing generalized beliefs through social interactions. Movements draw on ideologies to create a new sense of purpose, to justify an intended plan of action, to persuade potential converts to join, and to produce a sense of solidarity among members. The growth of a movement is shaped by the persuasiveness of its appeals and the extent to which members are willing to make personal sacrifices for enhancing the goals of the movement.

1. Ideology and Charisma

Social movements do not develop automatically out of conditions of hardship and deprivation. Human misery may be endured for long periods of time without a call for any particular line of social action (Graham, 1976). Programs for social change are dependent on the construction of realities that provide alternatives to endurance, apathy, and resignation (Kituse and Spector, 1973). The ideology of a social movement builds on discontent and gives a sense of clarity to social troubles. It defines some set of existing conditions as undesirable, unjust, or deplorable. Further, the ideology asserts that solutions are available, but that these solutions will require concerted efforts from those who have valid knowledge and understanding (Oberschall, 1973).

The core members of a social movement frequently regard their ideological beliefs as being infallibly correct. Such strong convictions provide justifi-

BOX 13.3
When Prophecy Fails

Messianic movements are religious groups that predict the occurrence of "an apocalypse," "the end of the world," "the second coming," or some other supernatural event that will radically transform social life as it is presently known and understood. Whatever the predicted event, the righteous are believed to constitute a select group that will be saved; all others will suffer or be destroyed. The acceptance of knowledge revealed from biblical scriptures or from supernatural contacts has led several messianic groups to set specific dates for the destruction of the world.

Leon Festinger and his associates (1956) made a study of one such group to determine how they cope when a prophecy fails to be fulfilled. The group had set a specific date for the end of the world, and the members had made extensive preparations for the special occasion. An outside observer might think that the failure of such a prophecy would have unequivocally refuted the accuracy of such a belief. Surely such a specific prediction as the world ending on a particular day had been subjected to a clear, definitive, and crucial test.

Festinger's research indicated that rather than initial beliefs being rejected because of the failure of prophecy, convictions became even stronger than before. The group's members now felt the world had been saved by their devotion and commitment. For a short period of time following the "disconfirmation," the movement increased in fervor and directed efforts toward winning additional converts. Thus strongly held beliefs depend on social supports for confirmation, rather than on objective, verifiable evidence.

Source: Leon Festinger, Henry W. Riecken, Jr., and Stanley Schachter, *When Prophecy Fails*, Minneapolis: University of Minnesota Press, 1956.

cations for extensive personal sacrifices and risk taking. Members verify the correctness of their beliefs through selective perceptions and by the mutual supports they obtain through interaction with each other. Ideologies arouse strong emotional sentiments, and their validity is not dependent on objective or scientific evidence. For example, the Flat Earth Society still insists that the earth is flat, despite the pictures of a round earth taken from outer space and despite the consensus in the scientific community on the geometric shape of our planet. Ideological beliefs frequently are accepted as intuitively valid, and contradictory information is ignored or discounted (Festinger, Riecken, and Schachter, 1956). (See Box 13.3.)

In social movements the emergence of charismatic leadership frequently provides the validation of an ideology. The authority of a charismatic leader does not derive from an existing legal order, nor does it rest on tradition or custom (Weber, 1947). It comes from extraordinary personal qualities and experiences. For example, the authority of the religious prophet is based on a supernatural experience, such as receiving a message from God, having a visitation, or receiving "a gift of grace." Such experiences are not to be taken lightly. They are accompanied by a mandate, and the leader feels compelled to act on the basis of the knowledge received.

Charismatic authority, however, is not automatically conferred on an individual because of extraordinary knowledge and experiences. It must be verified in the social interactions with a group of followers. Because the claim to authority resides outside of the existing normative order, any specific individual may be labeled "a false prophet," "strange," "weird," or as "mentally deranged." The creation of charismatic authority is then dependent on the social relationships between leaders and followers.

Charisma refers to the extraordinary qualifications a group of followers attributes to a leader. The charismatic qualities include an emphasis on the personal power, the forcefulness, and the morality of the leader. He or she has valid knowledge, is capable of producing desired results, and serves as a symbol of group cohesion and unity. Charisma is created as a valued social resource by the members of a movement and does not refer to any particular set of qualities or attributes determined by purely objective criteria. Napoleon Bonaparte, Adolf Hitler, Reverend Jimmy Jones, and Jesus Christ were all charismatic leaders, but they had very few personality characteristics in common. The charisma of the leader is a reality constructed to symbolize the hopes and aspirations of a constituency.

The effectiveness of a movement frequently relates to the skills of a charismatic leader in making appeals to spectators, neutral observers, and potential converts. The persuasiveness of the appeals is determined by the acceptability of a leader's claims to those who are responding to a social movement. The followers accept some claims as valid, while dismissing or ignoring others (Spector and Kituse, 1973). Whatever the case, all movements require leadership, whether the focus of the activity is religious salvation, the creation of a commune, the formation of a political opposition party, or the quest for economic reform.

2. Persuasive Appeals

The specific ideologies promoted by social movements vary widely. The focus of attention, for example, may consist of concerns for the protection of the environment, the promotion of equal rights for women, or the increase in the number of converts to a religious movement. The varied content of social movements also may be noted in the formation of constituencies to protest pornography, abortion, legalized drinking, an unpopular war, or taxation. In any case, the movement makes attempts to establish partisan definitions of reality as the prevailing realities for the total society.

While the contents of ideologies vary, similarities recur in the persuasive appeals drawn on in attempts to win support. The persuasive appeals argue for

Social Protest
A great deal of social movement activity in recent years has been directed toward the concern with human rights.

persuasive appeal

the necessity, the desirability, and the feasibility of the proposed changes. The language of persuasive appeals emphasizes the effectiveness of collective action in producing desired results, the importance of cohesion and solidarity among those who are enlightened about the need for change, and the importance of dedication and commitment as a means of giving purpose and meaning to one's personal life.

Ideological appeals are based on a doctrine of hope in conjunction with an emphasis on collective mastery and control. Men and women do not embark on a major social campaign unless there is a conviction that the prospects are favorable for eventual success. The appeals argue that the attainment of desired outcomes depends on the pooling of collective resources. The appeal provides an alternative to attitudes of resignation and helplessness. Through making use of their energies and resources, people themselves can make a difference in the way the world is run (Jenkins and Perrow, 1977).

While social movements aim at bringing about changes in society, their persuasive appeals also draw on the emotional and affiliative needs of individuals (Marx and Holzner, 1975). Persuasive appeals relating to personal and collective identities promote group solidarity. The movement directs mobilization toward binding individuals together and providing them with a shared symbol system of beliefs and ideas. Movements direct efforts toward building social and psychological bonds as a basis for self-pride, social consciousness, and concerted lines of action. In some cases, movements focus attention so intensely on promoting member satisfaction that their prior concerns with changing society recedes into the background.

The promotion of group solidarity and organized action is accompanied by persuasive appeals related to a sense of purpose and meaning, arguing that people need not accept the chaos and drift in modern social life as inevitable (Toch, 1965). An individual may attain a personal sense of purpose, mastery, and belonging by endorsing a movement's ideology. People's acceptance of persuasive appeals is perhaps evident in the conversion experiences that some-

---

BOX 13.4
The Religious Conversion Experience

Religious adherents interpret the sudden conversion experience in terms of "charisma," "possession by the Holy Ghost," "the gift of grace," or some other supernatural explanation. Both the convert and those in contact with the convert view him or her as a changed person and regard the changes as stemming from a sudden and dramatic transformation of self-identity. This conception of conversion as a radical transformation of the self is incompatible with social psychological explanations of how a self forms over an extended period of time. To investigate the difference in religious and social psychological perspectives on the self, James V. Downton (1980) made a study of converts to the Divine Light Mission.

The conclusion of Downton's study indicated that identity transformations were an outgrowth of evolutionary developments rather than the results of sudden changes in personality. The developments included growing feelings of personal inadequacy and disillusionment with the prevailing lifestyles of modern society; increased faith in spiritual solutions to personal and social problems; more frequent interactions with "spiritual people"; futile attempts to attain spiritual fulfillment through personal efforts; and increased involvement in the activities of a religious community. The eventual conversion involved surrendering to spiritual authorities and accepting the problem-solving perspectives of the religious movement.

However, the conversion experience may be understood as a sudden change in levels of awareness and reality perception. The willingness to make personal sacrifices for a cause intensifies and the individual makes a sharper separation between "insiders" and "outsiders." Rather than a radical transformation of a self-identity, the conversion symbolizes individual integration into a religious movement and the culmination of a gradual development.

Source: James V. Downton, Jr., "An Evolutionary Theory of Spiritual Conversion and Commitment: The Case of Divine Light Mission," *Journal for the Scientific Study of Religion* 19 (December, 1980): 381–396.

times accompany the joining of religious movements. The conversion experience provides the individual with a new identity, changes the person, and creates for the person a new vantage point for relating to others. (See Box 13.4.)

The process of mobilization is political in character, since it is oriented toward building a power base for implementing an ideology. The success of persuasive appeals in winning converts serves to verify the correctness of a movement's ideology and the effectiveness of its symbolic leadership. The movement's purpose is to tap a potential constituency by developing dedication and commitment to a social cause.

3. Developing Commitments

Through persuasive appeals, social movements attract an assortment of constituents. Some people are sympathetic to a cause but are unwilling to participate actively. Among those who do participate, there are variations in the kinds and degrees of social and psychological involvements. The level of commitment is limited for some, while for others dedication to a cause becomes a preoccupation and a central life interest.

Commitment to a cause may provide an overall sense of purpose in life; if this occurs, the individual may become highly dedicated, willing to make extensive personal sacrifices. The various parts of the person's life become integrated in a positive, coherent, and understandable way. Becoming committed involves accepting the persuasive appeals of the movement as valid ones. The individual accepts the movement's ideology, leadership, and goals as realities that can be depended on as a basis for understanding and action.

While many social movements do not require high levels of dedication from their members, there are some that do. One example of extreme cases of commitment is the large number of the mass suicides that occurred among the members of the People's Temple of Guyana. In the fall of 1978 the world was shocked to hear that Reverend Jim Jones and more than 900 of his followers had committed suicide in conjunction with the investigation by Congressman Leo Ryan and his staff. The People's Temple was a religious cult that required high levels of dedication, loyalty, and sacrifice from its members. Rehearsals for mass suicide and demonstrations of a willingness to die for the cause had been a part of the cult's internal planning. They had expected outside interference and so implemented their advanced plans for mass suicide during Congressman Ryan's investigation.

The techniques for producing common commitments among the members of the People's Temple were similar to those identified by Kanter (1972) in a study of nineteenth-century religious communes in the United States. In Kanter's (1972) study, the utopian communities that endured for an extended period of time were those that succeeded in producing strong "we" feelings and sentiments. These communities achieved solidarity by requiring sacrifices and investments from members. The investments included the time and efforts put into the activities of the movement as well as requirements for financial donations and the assignment of the recruit's property to the community. There were no refunds available for defectors. Furthermore, sacrifices were required in terms of individual lifestyles. These included giving up such things as tobacco, alcohol, sex, personal adornment, and personal property. All activities became centered around the community, which involved renouncing outside friends and family ties. At the same time, internal cohesion was promoted through songs, group singing, confessions, and other ceremonies, which tended to separate members from outsiders.

The techniques for producing commitments in utopian communities are found to some degree in all social movements. Producing the commitments of members is achieved through a combination of procedures relating to social control and social cohesion. Some degree of entrapment frequently occurs because of the numerous costs associated with dropping out. Becoming "hooked" on a social movement sometimes has the effect of reducing the range of options and alternatives subsequently available. For example, political movements are frequently characterized by a type of religious fervor. The ideology and persuasive appeals become accepted as realities that are binding on the conduct of members. Self-fulfillment and actualization become linked to the goals and successes of the movement. In becoming committed, the individual accepts the symbolic goals of the movement as personal goals, and social bonds develop among those with similar interests (Wilson and Orum, 1976).

C. STRATEGIES OF CHANGE

When people are disenchanted with some aspects of a society, several choices, decisions, and options become available at the action level. Some movements attempt to withdraw from the broader society and to seek perfection through the creation of religious communes. Others seek direct political action by attempting to initiate desired changes by working within the system. Some may seek to produce a revolution or to engage in sustained acts of terrorism and violence. These are among the many strategies that may be undertaken by those engaged in social movements. They range from peaceful, nonviolent, and passive responses at one extreme to acts of militancy, hostility, and coercion at the other.

range of actions

All social movements face a dual set of problems that they must solve if they are to survive. One consists of promoting member satisfaction and commitment, while the other consists of working out a program for producing the desired changes in society. In solving these problems, the movement must take some stand on the question of how to implement beliefs and ideologies through developing a concrete plan of action. The plans for action include negotiating to maintaining the internal solidarity of the movement and sending messages to opposing groups and authorities.

2 aspects of Soc. Mvmt.

The strategies of a social movement refer to how it uses available resources

TABLE 13.2
Black Civil Rights Organizations by Strategy and Tactics

Black civil rights organizations (year formed)	Strategies	Tactics of protest
National Association for the Advancement of Colored People (1909)	Legalistic	Negotiation, voting, educational training
National Urban League (1910)	Educational	Education, negotiation, community organization, persuasive activities, consulting
Congress of Racial Equality (1942)	Activism (ranging from revolutionary to reformist)	Sit-ins, stand-ins, wade-ins, nonviolent direct action, freedom rides, voter registration
Southern Regional Council (1944)	Educational	Persuasion, use of mass media, circulation of journal, research
Southern Christian Leadership Conference (1957)	Activism	Direct action, voter registration, leadership training, citizenship education, direct personal confrontation
Student Non-Violent Coordinating Committee (1960)	Activism (militant)	Sit-ins, voter-education work, communication (negotiation), nonviolent direct action, direct personal confrontation

Source: Doris Yvonne Wilkinson, "Tactics of Protest as Media: The Case of the Black Revolution," *Sociological Focus* 3 (Spring, 1970): 17.

in seeking to attain goals and objectives (Wilkinson, 1970). If the demands for social justice are massive in scope and if many collective resources are available, several competing organizations are likely to emerge that advocate and employ a variety of strategies (Killian, 1968). For example, the history of the civil rights movement encompasses many organizations working for the elimination of racism in American society. Some groups advocated the use of such nonviolent means as moral appeals, passive resistance, and educational programs. Others became militant and advocated the use of revolutionary violence. (See Table 13.2.)

1. Nonviolence

Movements that advocate nonviolent strategies seek to achieve their goals without bloodshed. This requires working within a normative framework and using such resources as moral appeals, political campaigns, the courts, the legislative process, and the education of the uninformed. The realities constructed out of nonviolent tactics seldom involve creating something entirely new. Instead, the movement attempts to enhance the qualities of social life through applying existing norms and values more effectively. Drawing on such widely held values as those relating to participatory democracy, human rights, and distributive justice permits the disenchanted to mobilize resources for challenging the existing authority structure. These strategies are designed to call attention to the issues of concern in the hope that corrective actions will be taken (Mauss, 1975).

Social movements frequently modify their ideologies and strategies in response to changing social conditions. The viability of one set of techniques as compared to another in part depends on the levels of resistance that develop among opposing and competing groups. The opposition stems not only from the antagonisms generated by segments of the broader population, but also from the conflicts within the movement over the appropriateness of one set of strategies compared to another. For example, in the development of the labor movement within the United States, some groups formed around an emphasis on revolutionary violence and an overthrow of the system (Renshaw, 1968), while others were primarily concerned with such practical benefits as higher wages and better working conditions. The success of a social movement often does not reside within the movement itself but with societal and authoritative responses to its initiatives. The factions of the labor movement that were successful were the ones that took a moderate approach. The country as a whole came to recognize the rights of workers to unionize and negotiate contracts as legitimate, while the public, as well as the workers themselves, rejected the use of revolutionary violence.

An important turning point in the civil rights movement occurred with the elaboration of the techniques of **nonviolent resistance** under the charismatic leadership of Martin Luther King (Killian, 1968). The use of nonviolent resistance added a moral dimension to practical politics. The movement extended challenges to authority agents by drawing on the prevailing standards of morality and justice. The system, in effect, was turned upon itself. By deliberately violating laws and norms, the civil rights movement intended to produce arrests and to demonstrate the injustices of the system. Through an appeal to a higher level of morality, the movement underscored and highlighted the underlying defects of the system.

The techniques of nonviolent resistance were employed in the bus boycott in Birmingham, Alabama, in order to end discriminatory seating practices. In the use of the consumer boycott (refusal of clients to use existing services or products), moral appeals were combined with economic pressures to bring about social change. Subsequently, lunch counter sit-ins, swimming pool wade-ins, freedom rides, and voter-registration campaigns were initiated to bring an end to discriminatory practices in numerous areas of public life (Wilkinson, 1970). These procedures were attention-getting devices for arousing public concern about the events in question. Reflective attitudes were generated, and the holders of power were required to examine their own moral consciences.

While the demonstrators in the civil rights movement were advocates of nonviolence, the responses of hostile groups and law-enforcement officials were often of a violent character. The use of water hoses, police dogs, and physical abuse were among the repressive measures directed toward those engaged in the movement. However, use of abusive measures has its limits since the spiritual, religious, and moral convictions of oppressors tend to generate sym-

---

BOX 13.5
The Role of Extremists in Social Movements

Extremism in social movements is associated with fanaticism and the willingness of specific individuals to use socially unapproved means to attain a movement's goals. The extremists are those who are willing to back up their convictions with overt action; who advocate the use of coercive force and violence; who antagonize those in positions of power and authority; and who evoke repressive measures from social control agencies. In effect, the extremists become impatient with the slow pace of events and insist on taking a more direct and active approach to bringing about social change.

The research of Lewis M. Killian (1972) suggests that extremists play an important, but indirect, role in the success of a social movement. The language and action of extremists serve an attention-getting function. The mass media give coverage to the rhetoric and activities of extremists, and in this process, public images form, issues polarize, and bystanders reflect on the movement's concerns and objectives. Repressive measures of social control sometimes result in the creation of martyrs, and sympathizers of the movement come to admire the extremists. Because of the concern of authorities for curbing the radicalism of a social movement, the presence of extremists frequently enhances the bargaining position of moderate leaders. Authorities are willing to negotiate with moderates because they appear to be reasonable men and women.

Extremists are seldom effective in bringing about changes through the means they advocate; but they do play an important role in social movements because of the responses they evoke from observers and from social control agencies. Defined as criminals by some and as heroes by others, extremists symbolize the contradictions inherent in the concerns for social justice.

Source: Lewis M. Killian, "The Significance of Extremism in the Black Revolution," *Social Problems* 20 (Summer, 1972): 41–49.

pathy for the oppressed and to restrict the use of violence toward those who are unable or unwilling to fight back.

The use of strategies such as boycotts, strikes, and public demonstrations are often effective in producing the desired results through nonviolent means. The passive resistance employed by Ghandi in India did result in the toppling of the British regime. The massive demonstrations and general strikes in France during the spring of 1968 were followed by the resignation of Charles De Gaulle as the president of the French Republic. And within a year after the demonstration of more than 250,000 people on the Washington, D.C. mall, Congress enacted the civil rights act affirming the constitutional rights of black and other minority Americans (Wilson and Orum, 1976).

Widespread social movements frequently lack unity in leadership and become characterized by internal debates over competing programs of action. There may be agreement on general beliefs and goals but sharp disagreements over the manner by which the goals may be attained. In the civil rights movement those who saw the use of nonviolent strategies as producing only meager results became impatient. Alternative strategies came to be proposed by the extremists who advocated separation and revolutionary violence (Barbour, 1968). (See Box 13.5.)

2. Violence

Radical violence is likely to manifest a widening of the gap between the ideology of a social movement and the prevailing values of the dominant society (Beach, 1977). The ideology appears extremist to observers as those who speak on behalf of a social movement advocate the use of violence for attaining desired ends. The means they advocate or employ become increasingly unacceptable. The movement becomes increasingly at odds with the legitimate social order, and the level of conflict intensifies.

Radicals in social movements may become so angry at the opposition or so intensely committed to the correctness of their own moral position that they consider compromises or negotiations out of the question. In this sense the frustrations and idealism of radicals take the form of fanaticism. Their own convictions become moral imperatives; they feel compelled to act on the basis of their own understanding and assessments without regard for the consequences. They may prefer to die for their cause rather than to compromise moral principles.

While radical extremism involves a moralistic stand, it also refers to the willingness to use violence to bring about the desired social changes. Extremists advocate violence as a necessary strategy for producing results, and if they come to dominate a social movement, preparations are made for civil war and paramilitary operations. As a strategy, social movements are likely to employ violence on a sporadic basis. Sustained military operations are usually not a feasible option, since the technologies for waging open warfare are under the monopoly control of the state.

Terrorism as a strategic practice, however, does not require a great deal in the way of resources. The aims of terrorists are to disrupt the orderly patterns of everyday life, to challenge the authority of the state, and to instill attitudes of fear in some segments of the population. Placing a bomb in a building, hijacking an airplane, carrying out a political assassination, or taking hostages may be achieved by a lone individual or by a very small group of people. Disruptions of a social system require only a limited amount of resources on the part of those who rationally plan and organize for acts of terror (Thornton, 1964).

The military objectives of terrorists are negligible in comparison to the symbolic character of the results that they seek. Through the use of disruptions and agitation, terrorists are announcing their withdrawal of support from the existing normative order. In demonstrating their willingness to use violence, terrorists seek to win support for their cause and at the same time to baffle authorities who are attempting to maintain the social order.

According to E. J. Hobsbawm (1959), terrorists may be regarded as "primitive rebels" who frequently become folk heroes and legendary figures. State authorities often define primitive rebels as criminals and offer rewards for their capture. In contrast, people who see themselves as deprived and oppressed may regard them as super-heroes. As symbolic persons, terrorists may be offered protection and security by sympathizers and shielded from arrest by authorities. In such cases they more nearly become collective symbols than real persons, and some regard their acts of violence as "a cry for vengence on the rich and the oppressors, a vague dream of some curb upon them, a righting of individual wrongs" (Hobsbawn, 1959: 5). Accordingly, the aims of terrorism are not those of revolution but are a reflection of hopes for a traditional world in which justice prevails and people receive their fair share of the available resources. As criminals to some and as heroes to others, terrorists symbolize the stresses and contradictions that are inherent in the concerns about social justice.

D. ORGANIZED INSECURITY

Social movements are inherently insecure forms of organization. Their inherent instability stems from the internal characteristics of the movement as well as from the pressures derived from the external environment (Zald and Ash, 1966). Internally, movements are frequently faced with disagreements and arguments over specific goals and strategies for achieving the desired changes. The aims and purposes of the movement become subject to varied interpretations with the passing of time. Competing leadership arises, coalitions form within the movement, and oppositional groups frequently arise. Under some conditions, movements decay and disappear because of an inability to resolve the numerous problems of internal conflict.

Through building on discontent and perceived injustice, movements stand in opposition to the existing authority structure of a society. As such, they become subject to the reactions of social control agencies and to the ebb

---

BOX 13.6
Seeking the Support of Neutrals

The changes sought by a social movement frequently are not attainable through the efforts of the members alone. The success of a movement is dependent to a very large degree on the level of support it receives from neutral observers. The neutrals are those who play an important role in social movements as third-party observers of the processes in which two adversaries attempt conflict resolution.

Martin E. Spencer (1971) observed that social conflict is frequently understood to mean the clash of two opposing forces, such as occurs between the oppressors and the oppressed, the exploiters and the exploited, the rich and the poor, the rulers and the ruled. The prevailing images emphasize conflict as a dialectical process, as an antagonistic form of social interaction, as a power struggle. According to Spencer, however, the most common form of conflict transpires between at least three parties rather than two. The hostilities between opposing parties cannot be understood adequately without taking into account the important roles played by observers and bystanders. The neutrals have no direct vested interest in the conflict, but they do have an interest in the broader concerns with social justice and with conflict resolution.

In modern society two of the major types of third-party neutrals include the roles played by public opinion and by the government. For example, legislatures set the limits within which social movement activities are tolerated, the courts enforce the rules by which conflict may be expressed, and the police impose limits on the use of a private militia. Public opinion also plays an important part, not only because of its affect on government, but also through its direct influence on adversary relationships. The decisions and actions of private citizens frequently enhance or weaken the position a social movement takes.

Source: Martin E. Spencer, "Conflict and the Neutrals," *Sociological Quarterly* 12 (Spring, 1971): 219–231.

---

and flow of public opinion. For example, religious cults in the United States came under close scrutiny as a result of the public disclosure of ritualistic murders by the Manson gang (Perry and Pugh, 1978). Further evaluations and critiques of religious movements occurred following the mass suicides at Jonestown, Guyana. The emergence of friendly or hostile environments frequently depend on forces that reside outside of the movements themselves. The judgments made by neutral observers frequently determine whether the public will condone or condemn the movements (Spencer, 1971). (See Box 13.6.)

1. Repression and Cooptation

Whether they win or lose, social movements do not endure for long periods of time. They frequently undergo rapid rates of growth, become stalemated, and decay. The process of development is one of clashing and opposing forces responding and reacting to each other. Some movements win sympathizers and supporters, while others evoke intense hostilities and resentments. The claims of some movements are recognized as legitimate, while the claims of others are rejected as inappropriate. Thus the outcome of a social movement depends on the interplay between the movement's participants, agencies of social control, and public opinion.

The strategies advocated and the responses to them sometimes promote the repression of a social movement. **Repression** occurs under those circumstances in which authority agents refuse to recognize claims as legitimate and respond with harsh and punitive measures (Wilson, 1977). The authority of the state may be brought to bear on groups defined as deviant, disloyal, unpatriotic, or dangerous. The heavy hand of social control agencies is usually supported by public opinion favoring the use of force for the resolution of confict.

If public opinion turns against a movement and social control agencies undertake harsh repressive measures, a social movement may be suppressed. This was the fate of the IWW (International Workers of the World) during World War I. The IWW was a union movement that advocated revolutionary control of industry by the workers. The Wobblies, as they were called, refused to register for the draft because they saw the war as requiring the members of the working class in one country to kill members of the working class in another. They viewed the life circumstances and social bonds of the workers as transcending national boundaries.

Because of the strong patriotic sentiment in the country during the first World War, the IWW became a hated organization. A large percentage of the Wobblies were arrested, and the movement in effect was suppressed. The convergence of public opinion and repressive forms of social control produced a hostile environment in which the IWW could no longer endure as a social movement (Kornbluh, 1965). Under such circumstances movements sometimes go underground and continue as secret organizations. But in the case of the IWW, many of the members shifted their allegiance to the American Communist Party, while others joined the ranks of labor unions that were more moderate in their goals and demands.

The aims of social movements are to transform society, institutions, and individuals, rather than to provide a regular set of services (Zald and Ash, 1966). Yet the pursuit of these objectives frequently results in unexpected and unanticipated consequences. Upton Sinclair, in his book *The Jungle*, hoped to win sympathy for the working class and to demonstrate the need for socialism. The readers of his book, however, responded to his descriptions of the food-processing industry by becoming concerned about the purity and safety of food. Rather than identifying with the workers and seeing the advantages of socialism, the public clamored for governmental regulation and control in the food industry. They responded to the Chicago stockyard rats that had fallen into lard vats, rather than to the deplorable conditions of the workers employed in the food industry.

The ideas that originate in social movements frequently are discovered and implemented by other agencies within society. For example, more than a hundred years ago, the manifesto of the Communist Party advocated such radical changes as free public education, a graduated income tax, and a social security system. Today these recommendations have become accepted facts and are no longer regarded as radical or outrageous proposals.

While social innovations frequently have their origins in social movements, the movements themselves often do not receive accolades for their accomplishments. Several former radicals came to feel that what should have been the epitaph for Norman Thomas (leader of the Socialist Party) was being written across the tombstone of Franklin D. Roosevelt. Roosevelt's New Deal legislation of the 1930s adopted many of the programs that had been advocated by left-wing movements for a long time. Thus, if social movements are not repressed and if they do not decay from their own inertia, they frequently become coopted by existing institutions. Social welfare legislation legitimated the claims that had been made by the Socialist Party, but the remedial action was initiated under the banner of a mainline political party. Such is often the fate of political third parties in the United States. If ideas initiated by a social movement win popular support, the credit frequently goes to those who initiate the changes within the existing authority structure.

Cooptation refers to the process by which the programs or the leadership of a social movement becomes integrated into the regular administrative and institutional structure of a society. The energy may be taken out of a social movement by draining off its leadership into an institutional channel. After a Julian Bond gets elected to the legislature, or an Andrew Young becomes appointed as the United States Ambassador to the United Nations, they are no longer participants in a social movement but have come to take their places within the established social order. While such cooptation partially reflected the success of the civil rights movement, it was also symbolic of the demise of the movement itself. Success in the attainment of its goals tends to destroy the movement-like character of an organization.

If social movements are successful in gaining a large following, they usually do so by bringing their ideologies and programs into alignment with the prevailing sentiments of a society. When this occurs, they tend to lose their radicalism and show a greater willingness to compromise on social issues. A major shift develops in leadership concerns. Leaders direct their efforts toward managing the organization rather than toward initiating vast changes in the social system. The religious sect becomes an established church, and the radical political movement becomes a more conservative political party.

2. Islands of Resistance

While most social movements exist for only short periods of time, some remain as enduring islands of resistance. Such extraordinary groups as the Dukhobors,

Traditional Churches
Many of the traditional churches of today originated as social protest movements.

the Mennonites, and the Amish have endured for several hundred years. They have done so by withdrawing from the surrounding secular society, creating an internal sense of moral community, and insulating their members from outside influences.

Social movements become **islands of resistance** through withdrawing allegiance from the broader society and seeking to perfect social institutions and social relationships on a substantially reduced scale. They resist modernization and its emphasis on rational, secular values. The movement defines dominant social changes in negative terms and focuses on the prospects of creating a more satisfying lifestyle for its members. It directs attention toward the development of a moral community in which social ties are based on sacred values. Its ideology reduces the complexity of the world and draws hard boundaries between members and nonmembers.

The collective efforts toward the creation of utopian communities, however, take a variety of forms. The multiple realities are evident in the normative regulation of members' conduct. Kephart (1976) noted in his study of religious communities that the Hutterites emphasized economic communism, while the Mormons believed just as strongly in the free-enterprise system. The Oneida community advocated free love, while the Shakers insisted on celibacy. The Old Order Amish are farmers who live in rural areas, while the Father Devine Movement was urban both in location and orientation. Such patterns of diversity suggest that the content of ideological supports for moral communities are highly varied and diverse.

While the resistance of religious communities is often a gentle form of rebellion, the communities frequently encounter a great deal of hostility from the surrounding society. Recurrent difficulties with the state emerge over the failure to pay taxes, the refusal to serve in the army, opposition to modern medicine, and the unwillingness to comply with the requirements for compulsory school attendance. Each of these examples of conflict derives from the incompatibilities between collective-good decisions of the state and the specific moral principles of religious communities. The community's troubles with the state are often compounded by hostile public attitudes of people who are intolerant of what they perceive as deviant lifestyles.

In given historical situations the hostility toward religious communities may become sufficiently intense that the survival of the movement is at stake. If a social environment becomes increasingly hostile or if public sentiment becomes increasingly unsympathetic, a social movement may seek to sustain its goals and programs through migration. Moving to a more permissive region of a particular country and moving to a new country altogether have been frequent historical responses of religious movements to conditions of repression.

Migration under these circumstances is associated with an ideology of hope and the perception of chances for new beginnings and for new opportunities. In the United States the Mormons migrated from the American Midwest to the Territory of Utah. In Canada the Dukhabors followed the movement of the frontier westward to their present location in British Columbia. And more recently the movement of the People's Temple from San Francisco to Guyana reflected efforts to find a more friendly environment for conducting a social experiment in group living.

Over a period of time social movements undergo numerous changes. Some changes occur internally through the reinterpretations of the movement's traditions and through the adjustments made to changing environmental conditions. In other cases social movements take on a new set of relationships with the surrounding society. For example, Lancaster, Pennsylvania, has now become a major tourist attraction for the thousands of people who visit the Amish community each year. A highly commercial dimension has intruded into the Amish lifestyle. Those promoting the tourist trade demonstrate traditional arts and crafts, sell souvenirs, enact social drama, and construct fast food franchises and motels (Kephart, 1976). Over long periods of time, the inroads of tourism and commercial interests are likely to alter the social character of a religious community.

SUMMARY

Social movements are grounded in the definitions of social problems, in the claims that social life is something less than it ought to be, and in the remedial lines of action that they employ. If the claims of a movement's leaders are accepted as valid and legitimate, many people are likely to be drawn into the collective quest for social change. Movements coalesce around conditions of conflict and challenges to existing institutions. Emergent norms develop to provide a new agenda for social conduct and to serve as a focus for the energies and activities of a large number of people.

The leaders of social movements seek to attain their goals through the mobilization of a constituency. The mobilization efforts include the development and use of ideology, the creation of charismatic leaders, and the use of persuasive appeals. The ideology is a generalized set of beliefs about the existing state of affairs and what needs to be done. The charismatic leader symbolizes the hopes and aspirations of followers and becomes endowed with extraordinary qualities of powerfulness, moral virtue, and benevolence. In seeking to win converts to a cause, the language of persuasive appeals includes the themes of a moral community among adherents, public power through the pooling of collective resources, and the infallible correctness of the movement's doctrine. The winning of converts is followed by an emphasis on producing commitments. Dynamic social movements seek to produce dedication to a cause and a willingness to make extensive personal sacrifices on behalf of group goals.

The scope and substance of social movements are reflected through the range of strategies and tactics they employ. Widespread concerns with social justice frequently result in the emergence of competing organizations with alternative strategies of social change. In the American civil rights movement some groups advocated the use of such nonviolent methods as moral appeals, passive resistance, legislative reform, and judicial action; other groups became more militant and advocated the use of revolutionary violence. Since social movements are experimental groups, ideologies and strategies frequently are modified in response to changing social conditions. The scripts of social movements are written through the dynamic interplay between members, competing organizations, sympathizers, spectators, and authority figures.

All social movements are engaged in efforts to initiate new forms of social relationships; some are successful in achieving their objectives, while others are not. Social movements tend to be unstable because of disagreements over specific goals and strategies, because of internal struggles for leadership control, and because of the formation of competing movements. Under some conditions social movements are destroyed if they are unable to resolve internal conflict. Some movements are repressed due to hostile authority figures and the lack of support in public opinion. Movements that are successful are also characterized by instability. The cause advocated by a social movement may be adopted as official policy, or the leadership of a movement may be coopted through the appointment of leaders to positions of authority within established institutions. In some cases, however, social movements may endure for long periods of time as islands of resistance within the rest of society. Thus the outcomes of social movements are varied and reflect many facets of reality construction in their attempts to reorganize social life.

BASIC TERMS

Antiinstitutional
  orientation
Modernity
Symbolic crusade
Remedial actions
Emergent norms
Mobilization

Ideology
Charisma
Nonviolent resistance
Repression
Cooptation
Islands of resistance

REFERENCES

Barber, Bernard
  1972 "Acculturation and Messianic Movements," in William A. Lessa and Evon Z. Vogt (eds.), *Reader in Comparative Religion*, New York: Harper & Row, pp. 512–515.
Barbour, Floyd D. (ed.)
  1968 *The Black Power Revolt*, Boston: Porter Sargent.
Beach, Stephen W.
  1977 "Social Movement Radicalization," *Sociological Quarterly* 18 (Summer): 305–318.
Berger, Peter, Brigitte Berger, and Hansfried Kellner
  1974 *The Homeless Mind*, New York: Vintage Books.
Berk, Richard A.
  1974 *Collective Behavior*, Dubuque, Iowa: Wm. C. Brown.
Blumer, Herbert
  1971 "Social Problems as Collective Behavior," *Social Problems* 18 (Winter): 298–305.
Downton, James V.
  1980 "An Evolutionary Theory of Spiritual Conversion and Commitment: The Case of Divine Light Mission," *Journal for the Scientific Study of Religion* 19 (December): 381–396.
Emerson, Robert M. and Sheldon L. Messinger
  1977 "The Micro-Politics of Trouble," *Social Problems* 25 (December): 121–134.
Festinger, Leon, Henry W. Riecken, Jr., and Stanley Schachter
  1956 *When Prophecy Fails*, Minneapolis: University of Minnesota Press.
Graham, James Q.

1976 "Historical Analyses of Violence," in Arthur G. Neal (ed.), *Violence in Animal and Human Societies*, Chicago: Nelson-Hall, pp. 141–170.

Gusfield, Joseph R.
1963 *Symbolic Crusade*, Urbana: University of Illinois Press.

Harris, Irving D.
1978 ""Assassins," in Irwin L. Kutash, Samuel B. Kutash, Louis B. Schlesinger, and Associates (eds.), *Violence: Perspectives on Murder and Aggression*, San Francisco: Jossey-Bass, pp. 198–218.

Heilbroner, Robert L.
1970 "Benign Neglect in the United States," *Transaction* 7 (October): 15–22.

Hobsbawn, E. J.
1959 *Primitive Rebels*, New York: Norton.

Jenkins, J. Craig and Charles Perrow
1977 "Insurgency of the Powerless," *American Sociological Review* 42 (April): 249–267.

Kanter, Rosabeth Moss
1972 *Commitment and Community: Communes and Utopias in Sociological Perspective*, Cambridge, Mass.: Harvard University Press.

Kephart, William M.
1976 *Extraordinary Groups*, New York: St. Martin's Press.

Killian, Lewis M.
1972 "The Significance of Extremism in the Black Revolution," *Social Problems* 20 (Summer): 41–49.
1968 *The Impossible Revolution*, New York: Random House.

Kituse, John I. and Malcolm Spector
1973 "Toward a Sociology of Social Problems," *Social Problems* 20 (Spring): 407–418.

Kornbluh, Joyce L.
1965 *Rebel Voices*, Ann Arbor: University of Michigan Press.

Marx, John H. and Burkhart Holzner
1975 "Ideological Primary Groups in Contemporary Cultural Movements," *Sociological Focus* 8 (October): 311–342.

Mauss, Armand L.
1975 *Social Problems as Social Movements*, Philadelphia: J. B. Lipincott.

Mills, C. Wright
1962 *The Marxists*, New York: Dell.

Oberschall, Anthony
1973 *Social Conflict and Social Movements*, Englewood Cliffs, N.J.: Prentice-Hall.

Perry, Joseph B., Jr. and M. D. Pugh
1978 *Collective Behavior*, St. Paul, Minn.: West Publishing Company.

Renshaw, Patrick
1968 *The Wobblies*, Garden City, N.Y.: Anchor Books.

Rowney, Don Karl
1976 "How History Beats the System: Violence and Disaggregation," in Arthur G. Neal (ed.), *Violence in Animal and Human Society*, Chicago: Nelson-Hall, pp. 107–140.

Skinner, B. F.

1972 *Beyond Freedom and Dignity*, New York: Vintage Books.
Smelser, Neil J.
1962 *Theory of Collective Behavior*, New York: The Free Press.
Spector, Malcolm and John I. Kituse
1973 "Social Problems: A Re-Formulation," *Social Problems* 21 (Fall): 145–158.
Spencer, Martin E.
1971 "Conflict and the Neutrals," *Sociological Quarterly* 12 (Spring): 219–231.
Stallings, Robert A.
1973 "Patterns of Belief in Social Movements," *Sociological Quarterly* 14 (Autumn): 465–480.
Swanson, Guy E.
1970 "Toward Corporate Action: A Reconstruction of Elementary Collective Processes," in Tamotso Shibutani (ed.), *Human Nature and Collective Behavior*, Englewood Cliffs, N.J.: Prentice-Hall, pp. 124–144.
Thornton, Thomas Perry
1964 "Terror as a Weapon of Political Agitation," in Harry Eckstein (ed.), *Internal War*, New York: The Free Press, pp. 71–99.
Toch, Hans
1965 *The Social Psychology of Social Movements*, Indianapolis: Bobbs-Merrill.
Traugott, Mark
1978 "Reconceiving Social Movements," *Social Problems* 26 (October): 38–49.
Turner, Ralph and Lewis M. Killian (eds.)
1972 *Collective Behavior*, Englewood Cliffs, N.J.: Prentice-Hall.
Wallace, Anthony C.
1972 "Revitalization Movements," in William A. Lessa and Evon Z. Vogt (eds.), *Reader in Comparative Religion*, New York: Harper & Row, pp. 503–511.
Weber, Max
1947 *The Theory of Social and Economic Organization* (ed. and trans. by A. M. Henderson and Talcott Parsons), New York: The Free Press of Glencoe.
Wilkinson, Doris Yvonne
1970 "Tactics of Protest as Media: The Case of the Black Revolution," *Sociological Focus* 3 (Spring): 13–22.
Wilson, John
1977 "Social Protest and Social Control," *Social Problems* 24 (April): 469–481.
Wilson, Kenneth and Tony Orum
1976 "Mobilizing People for Collective Political Action," *Journal of Political and Military Sociology* 4 (Fall): 187–202.
Zald, Mayer N. and Roberta Ash
1966 "Social Movement Organizations: Growth, Decay, and Change," *Social Forces* 44 (March): 327–340.
Zurcher, Louis A., Jr., P. George Kirkpatrick, Robert G. Cushing, and Charles K. Bowman
1971 "The Anti-Pornography Campaign: A Symbolic Crusade," *Social Problems* 19 (Fall): 217–237.

14

Mass Society

We may summarize the nature of our time and place as a mass society. This is a kind of society in which millions of people are organized along lines that differ in several important respects from any previous society in human history. Whether we live in an urban area or elsewhere, our modern consciousness includes an awareness of the presence of many people and a recognition that vast geographical areas have become politically, economically, and culturally linked as interdependent units. This linkage is evident in the involvement of the masses in spheres of social life once reserved for the top echelons of the stratification system.

The designation of modern society as a mass society is in part an objective description of our time and place. Education is geared toward the masses; automobiles and refrigerators are produced for mass consumption; and entertainment is oriented toward sizable viewing audiences. In these examples, the term *mass* obviously implies a large number of people—as clients, as customers, as voters, and as decision makers. Those who hold positions of authority in our major institutional areas must take into account the sentiments, attitudes, and predispositions of the masses.

The conditions under which people live in the latter part of the twentieth century differ in several important respects from those of any previous century in history. The private automobile has permitted an increase in the freedom of movement, enabling large numbers of people to travel over long distances for work and pleasure. The availability of higher education has increased the overall levels of knowledge and social awareness for many people. And with the introduction of the radio, movies, and television, large viewing audiences have become increasingly aware of much more than they could experience directly. Under these conditions, access to information, entertainment, and materialistic lifestyles have promoted the entry and integration of several million people into forms of social living that were not possible previously.

Happenings in faraway places affect the daily lives of individuals, providing multiple reference points for evaluations of social life. The conditions promoting the impingement of remote events into the homes and lives of millions of people have been described by Marshall McLuhan (1965) as those lead-

ing to the transformation of society into "a global village." The development of
sophisticated systems of technology have altered the conditions under which
men and women live. Modern technologies in transportation, communication,
and electronic data processing have extended human capacities; as a consequence, daily consciousness includes an awareness of events that are world-
wide in scope.

We may agree by purely "objective" criteria that modern society is unique
and different in several ways from society in the past. The number of people
has increased significantly, transportation is more efficient, news travels faster,
and crowdedness is more likely to occur. From a social psychological standpoint, however, ideas about a mass society are constructions of reality. For
example, we tend to think of our modes of communication as being highly
significant and different from a hundred years ago; but the perception that
news travels fast is a relative judgment. The people of ancient Greece thought
that news traveled fast on foot with the marathon runners; and Americans in
the late 1800s perceived news as traveling fast with the pony express, while
many Americans complain today about the slowness of the postal service.
Perceptions of society are then realities constructed by individuals in their
attempts to finding meaning and social purpose within the context of modern
social life. (See Table 14.1.)

Those who perceive modern society to be unique tend to show disdain
for the study of history, since they suppose history to deal with the past and
have little bearing on contemporary social life. The declining enrollments in

---

TABLE 14.1
Descriptive Labels for Modern Society

Because of the complexity of modern social life we do not have an officially designated title for the kind of society in which we live. Several descriptive labels have
been employed in book titles and popular literature. The following list of labels
attempts to capture in summary form the unique character of our time and place.

Urban society	Multigroup society
Technological society	Segmented society
Capitalist society	Stalled society
Industrial society	Open society
Postindustrial society	Democratic society
Consumer-oriented society	Permissive society
Pluralist society	Polarized society
Organizational society	

The mass-society model draws on many of the images conveyed through these
descriptive labels.

history classes in American universities during the 1970s suggests that many students apparently feel that social life lacks continuity and that the modern world differs qualitatively from the past. Certainly telephones, automobiles, television sets, computers, and space travel are products of the twentieth century; and they have altered the conditions of social life. People now listen to new types of music, are entertained through new media of communication, create new standards of conduct, and make new adaptations to a changing environment. But if they perceive a lack of continuity, their social relationships become altered. Tradition is no longer an adequate guide to conduct; generation gaps are likely to develop within families; people are likely to regard the elderly as obsolete persons; and students are likely to avoid history courses within universities if possible.

lack of history = lack of continuity

A. SYMBOLS OF MASS SOCIETY

The meaning of mass society for the average individual tends to surface around several potent symbols of our time and place. These symbols often include perceptions of crowdedness, images of sophisticated technology, and a sense of dependency on others. We create the symbols of a mass society to explain ourselves to ourselves and not simply to describe modern society literally.

1. Crowdedness

Crowdedness is not so much a literal description as an image of the density resulting from occupied space. In our modern experiences crowdedness is evident in the heavy traffic on the highways, in the congestion associated with Christmas shopping, and in the multitudes who occupy public beaches on a warm Summer day. Yet crowdedness is a perception rather than an objective reality. Cities have always been crowded as even small towns and villages can be. With our emphasis on population growth and size we have created a vocabulary for describing crowdedness and congestion.

The symbols of crowdedness draw on the underlying trends in population growth and the increased size of American cities. At the time of the American Revolution people regarded Philadelphia as a large city by the standards of its day. In 1776 Philadelphia was the second largest English-speaking city in the world, and it had a population of about 25,000 people. Today most of us think of a community of 25,000 as a small town. There are currently many metropolitan areas with more than a million people, suggesting that vast changes have occurred over the past 200 years.

The growth of cities involves the concentration of large groups of people within a limited amount of physical space. On a typical workday in downtown Manhattan more than 24 million people occupy a ten-mile radius area. This is more than six times the total population of the United States in 1790, as indicated by the first decennial census. The increase in the magnitude of population groupings have also been accompanied by increases in perceptions of the complexity, confusion, and chaos of modern social living (Hauser, 1969).

The complexity and confusion of modern society are mainly perceptions of the heterogeneity and diversity of the people who occupy the same geographic area or life space (Hauser, 1969). Differences in culture, language, ethnicity, social class, attitudes, values, and behavior suggest that those in close physical proximity do not hold the same underlying assumptions about everyday life. Individuals are involved in the pursuit of their own personal goals, and in this pursuit the need arises to calibrate their own behavior with that of others. Competition emerges for the occupancy of physical space and for the utilization of available resources.

BOX 14.1
Perceptions of Crowding

The essential feature of crowding is not the actual number of people in a limited amount of space, but the perception of congestion on the part of those involved. Some people might define a given situation as exciting and rewarding while others in the same objective situation might emphasize its lack of privacy, developing from it feelings of stress.

In an experimental setting, Cohen, Sladen, and Bennett (1975) investigated the effects of several situational variables on judgments about crowding. Their research indicates that perceptions of crowding are more likely to occur in relationships among strangers than in relationships among acquaintances. Close physical proximity is less stress-producing among people who know each other than among people who have no previous social ties. The perception of crowding is also related to the focus of activities. Judgments of crowding are more likely to emerge if people are pursuing independent lines of action than if they are engaged in a joint enterprise. Further, the domain of social action also relates to perceptions of crowding. If the focus of the activity is recreational, people will tolerate a higher density without having perceptions of crowding than if the activity is work-related. More elbow room apparently is required for a sense of personal comfort at work than in the pursuit of pleasure or the use of leisure.

These findings document the importance of cognitive variables in human experiences with crowding. The amount of physical space required for a sense of personal comfort depends on the qualities of social relationships and the organization of activities. The meanings of population density are realities that grow out of social interactions, and these meanings vary independently of sheer increases in the number of people.

Source: Jerry L. Cohen, Bernard Sladen, and Barbara Bennett, "The Effects of Situational Variables on Judgments of Crowding," *Sociometry* 38 (June, 1975): 273–281.

Early research on people and space concentrated only on density, and did not include subjective judgments and perceptions. Today researchers recognize the importance of making a distinction between density and crowding (Cohen, Sladen, and Bennett, 1975). **Density** refers to the number of people who occupy some given area, while **crowding** refers to the stress-related responses that accompany perceptions of high population density. In the normal flow of human traffic, perceptions of crowdedness are expressed in the experience of being hemmed in, of having one's personal space invaded, and of lacking personal freedom. In effect, crowdedness occurs when the presence of people results in discomfort and interferes with doing something one wishes to do. Three or four people can be experienced as a crowd if they live in the same room of a college dormitory, while a larger number of people can result in positive experiences in other types of settings. Population density at a football game can add to the excitement of the event, while the congestion of work traffic or in long lines at a check-out counter can be stress-producing rather than exciting. (See Box 14.1.)

In a mass society much of the daily interactions take place among those who are strangers to each other and who lack any ongoing set of social relationships. Goffman (1963) described many forms of behavior in public places as unfocused interactions. They are unfocused in the sense that individuals act in awareness of the physical presence of others, negotiate to occupy space, but fail to communicate in an open and direct fashion. In situations that do not call for verbal communications, people communicate in other ways. The style of dress, facial decorations, and emotional expressions become forms of public display, but they do not in and of themselves provide the grounds for interpersonal involvement.

The social distance among those in public places becomes symbolic of the problem described by William Kornhauser (1959) as the atomization of the masses. **Atomization** refers to the separation, detachment, and discreteness of individuals as they go their separate ways. Under these circumstances, individuals lack a common sense of group identity, belonging, or community. They are bound together by the common authority of the state, and their life circumstances are such that their personal autonomy is threatened by forces outside of themselves. In Kornhauser's view memberships in primary groups such as families or friendship circles do not go very far in protecting and insulating the individual from social forces and events.

2. Interdependency

The mass-like character of modern society is reflected in much more than a sheer increase in population density. It is also the result of changing patterns of organization and new forms of social integration. For example, the development of technology for travel and communication provides linkages among

Sophisticated Technology
The radar disc used in conjunction with communication satellites is one of the evident symbols of a technologically advanced society.

large groups of people that were not possible prior to the twentieth century. Air travel now permits rapid movement from one part of the country to another. In less than two hundred years travel time from New York to San Francisco has been reduced from several months to only a few hours. Such developments provide new options and choices as large geographical areas become accessible for business and pleasure. In the area of mass communications, the development of radio and television permits messages originating in a central location to be distributed almost instantaneously to all parts of the country. These developments have greatly altered the conditions under which men and women live, work, and play.

The technology that permits rapid communication to millions of people also produces new forms of dependency on activities that originate in remote places. Electricity for New York City is supplied by a power plant located at

Niagara Falls, cars driven in Florida were produced in Detroit, and the entertainment provided by a local theater very likely originated in California. Such developments suggest that individuals have become highly dependent on others for goods and services they are not able to provide for themselves.

Routinely, food is available from grocery stores, medical service is available in a doctor's office, and electricity is there when we want to turn on a light. These self-evident aspects of modern social life require very little in the way of reflection. However, when a major system fails, we tend to become acutely aware of the extent to which our everyday lives depend on forces outside of ourselves.

Such an episode of system failure occurred with the electrical blackout of the northeastern United States in November of 1965. In New York City an estimated 800,000 people were trapped in subways, many people were stuck in elevators, the street lights went out, and massive traffic jams developed when traffic lights failed to work. A small malfunction in the power transmission system at Niagara Falls had temporarily crippled a vast population area and dramatized the interdependent character of modern life (Burke, 1978).

Increases in the size of the population have been accompanied by increases in the scope and complexity of the division of labor. As a result of the trend toward specialization, we have become highly dependent on others for the production and distribution of our goods and services. Most of our personal needs are fulfilled through social interactions that are focused on highly specific role relationships. For example, in the interactions between a customer and a clerk, the only relevant concerns are those that relate to the exchange of the desired objects. The clerk may be no more knowledgeable than the customer about the qualities and attributes of the tradeable objects. Their safety, dependability, and the manner in which they were produced are usually unknown to those who distribute or utilize them. (See Box 14.2.)

The masses of consumers who utilize the objects of modern industry do so on the basis of attitudes of trust and assumptions about dependability. They become dependent on specialists and experts who are unknown and invisible. The perceived complexity of this interdependency became evident in public responses to "the nuclear accident" at Three Mile Island near Harrisburg, Pennsylvania, in March of 1979. A leak of radioactive steam from a nuclear generator set off an intense national controversy over the risks and benefits of nuclear power plants. The emerging controversy over the use of nuclear power tapped not only concerns about the technical problems in generating electricity, but also strengthened general attitudes toward the dangers and hazards created by modern industry and technology.

In a survey conducted in 1978 (prior to the Three Mile Island episode), two-thirds of those questioned reported believing that environmental dangers to the average person's health and safety had increased in recent years. Only one in five thought the dangers were receding, and they cited advances in medicine, pollution control, and safety regulations as evidence for their views.

BOX 14.2
Two Types of Rationality

We frequently have to stand in lines without knowing why such lines are necessary; we encounter people in positions of power who appear to be incompetent; we see a great deal of waste and inefficiency in business and government; we are often bound by rules that do not make sense to us. Such perceptions frequently stem from our having incomplete information or inadequate understanding of the total situation. Because of differences in level of information, the decisions that some would regard as rational are defined as irrational by others.

Karl Mannheim (1960), in his classical writings, made an important distinction between functional and substantive types of rationality. Functional rationality occurs in organizations and rests on the use of standardized procedures for coordinating the activities of many people. Rationality and efficiency are the guiding principles in centralized planning and in solving organizational problems. Substantive rationality, by way of contrast, refers to the capacity of an individual to understand the interrelatedness of the social events in which he or she is engaged.

Mannheim maintained that functional rationality has increased historically, while substantive rationality has declined. Organizations have increased in size and complexity through the division of labor, through the need for coordinating the activities of many people, and through the mobilization of vast resources to achieve specific goals. Planners, experts, consultants, and administrators are presumably in positions for seeing how events interrelate, while most people as subordinates, employees, customers, or clients are prevented from the possibility of developing an adequate grasp of the totality of events. As a result those who have only incomplete information frequently define the "rationality" of those in positions of power as arbitrary and irrational.

Source: Karl Mannheim, "Types of Rationality and Organized Insecurity," in C. Wright Mills (ed.), *Images of Man*, New York: George Braziller, 1960, pp. 508–528.

Among those concerned with environmental dangers, opinions were divided on whether the responsibility for reducing the risk should reside primarily with the government or with the individual (Pokorny, 1979).

The incident at Three Mile Island brought to the surface a variety of latent concerns about governmental regulations, everyday dependence on the decisions of specialists and experts, and the degree of environmental safety. In many parts of the country people registered their concerns in public demonstrations, and a hastily organized rally in Washington, D.C., drew a crowd of more than 60,000. The controversy over nuclear power tapped attitudes toward the possibility of a risk-free environment, as well as views on the costs and benefits of modern technology and industry (Nisbet, 1979).

3. Focused Events

The episode at Three Mile Island is an example of what we may regard as a focused event. A **focused event** is one that becomes the object of attention among a large number of people during a relatively short period of time. The media coverage of the Three Mile Island accident was dramatic, and for an extended period of time the episode remained the lead item on the evening news. Anxieties were raised about the potential hazards of increased radio-activity in the surrounding area, about the prospects for a nuclear explosion, and about the safety of similar nuclear power plants located elsewhere. To alleviate anxieties, President Carter visited the damaged power plant, and officials reported that his exposure to radiation was less than that which occurs any day of the year in Denver, Colorado, or at jet-flight altitudes (Nisbet, 1979).

Another example of a focused event was the visit of Pope John Paul II to the United States in the fall of 1979. Several large crowds formed to see and hear the distinguished visitor. More than 400,000 people crowded onto Boston Common, and it was estimated that more than a million people crowded the parade route in Lower Manhattan. Some disappointment was expressed by organizers that only 175,000 people showed up at the Washington Mall to hear the Pope's address.

The focused event may center around some particular crisis, such as the Buffalo Creek flood in West Virginia (Erikson, 1976) or an earthquake in California. The attention of many people may be directed toward a sports event, such as the World Series, the Super Bowl, or the Boston marathon. The activity may also consist of a political convention, an urban riot, mass murders, or any other event regarded by the news media and the viewing audience as worthy of attention. Focused events become of special significance within a mass society because of the huge number of people involved and because of the opportunities they provide for the examination of selected aspects of social life. The interactions consist of the interplay between the event itself, and media coverage, and the responses of the viewing audience.

Focused events shape our constructions of reality through the reflective attitudes they evoke. Such events as an emerging energy crisis, a nuclear accident, or the holding of hostages become intrusions into everyday life that require us to think about how our society is organized, what changes are necessary, and how our personal lives are affected. We temporarily question our assumptions and make adjustments to changing circumstances.

We are inclined to think of our awareness of remote events as a distinctly modern phenomenon; but in other times and places remote events were also of major concern, even if news did not travel as fast as it does today. For example, during the Crusades of the twelfth century, Europeans focused attention on the Holy Wars and the events in Jerusalem. Faraway places were almost mythic places that most people could never see, but the verbal and graphic images used to portray the Holy Land may not have differed that much from the literal pictures we see on television today. Barbara Tuchman (1978) suggests that the realities we construct to describe modern society tend to emphasize our historical uniqueness at the expense of a concern for understanding the lives of other people at other times and places. Rather than limiting our attention to modern problems, she maintains that we can draw on the calamitous events of the fourteenth century for an understanding of the modern world.

B. MASS COMMUNICATION

In modern society it is through television, radio, and other news media that a society becomes informed about itself (Gans, 1979). Newsworthy events become focused accounts of what people regard as major happenings. The millions of people who watch the evening news and read a daily newspaper are seeking information that is consequential for social thought and action. In this process, news events serve as a stimulus for reflection on social norms and deviancy, on public attitudes and behavior, and on social trends and unusual developments. Awareness of societal happenings serves to validate the individual's everyday assumptions and to determine the need for modification and refinement of his or her own understanding.

Mass communication refers to the process by which the members of a society seek to become informed about themselves. The process includes centralized news-gathering agencies, one-way communication, and dispersed audiences. The messages created and disseminated represent what those in the news media regard as newsworthy and important for people to know. Access to information becomes an important basis for personal thought and action, and the recipients of news refine and elaborate the messages they receive. Receptiveness to news provides a basis for fine tuning the assumptions that are essential for the orderliness of everyday life.

Two processes are thus involved in mass communication. One is the process by which news is gathered, processed, and distributed, while the second relates to the manner by which individuals receive news and incorporate it into their understanding of events. In each case an imperative of selection operates. Only certain aspects of events can be known and reported; time and space serve to limit the scope of coverage; and the recipients of news cannot give serious attention to very many of the events reported in a daily newspaper or television broadcast. People ignore most news events completely or give them only slight notice in passing.

1. News Media

A mass society uses several media for transmitting the news. The media used for information on societal events include radio, television, newspapers, and

---

BOX 14.3
Uses of Media for Important Things

People differ in what they define as important in life, and these differences show up in the uses of mass media. The research of Katz, Gurevitch, and Haas (1973) concentrated on a sample of 1500 subjects in Israel to determine how newspapers, books, television, radio, and cinema differ in their use and effectiveness for meeting social and psychological needs.

Respondents generally regarded newspapers as the most effective media for supplying information about the sociopolitical system and the social environment. Understanding relationships between the individual and the larger Israeli society was more frequently derived from newspapers than from any other source. Israelis used books more frequently than other media for strengthening knowledge and understanding of the self, enhancing cultural traditions, and developing personal skills. The movies, on the other hand, led all other media in meeting the needs for relaxation and entertainment. Television and radio were widely used media, but the uses to which they were put tended to be less clearly related to specific social and psychological needs than were newspapers, books, and the cinema.

Rather than viewing media as instruments of social control by the ruling class, Katz and his associates suggest that people "bend" the media to fit their own needs, social roles, and psychological predispositions. For example, the print media (newspapers and books) increase in importance as educational level increases, while the electronic media (radio and television) assume greater importance among those with lower levels of education. Respondents reported using movies to reinforce friendship ties, while television was reported as promoting family-centered activities. Thus the uses of media vary by social roles and by the importance individuals assigned to specific social and psychological needs.

Source: Elihu Katz, Michael Gurevitch, and Hadassah Haas, "On the Use of Mass Media for Important Things," *American Sociological Review* 38 (April, 1973): 164–181.

news magazines. The majority of people prefer to use television for obtaining a general understanding of societal happenings, while consulting daily newspapers and news magazines for more precise details and a broader scope of coverage. The popularity of television news grows out of the limited effort required of viewers and television's selective emphasis on the consequential happenings of the day. (See Box 14.3.)

Herbert Gans (1979) concludes from a content analysis of television news that it tends to emphasize dramatic events, unusual happenings, and moral disorders. The activities of ordinary people are seldom reported unless they are engaging in social protest or acting in opposition to some established institution. Rather, the activities of government officials are disproportionately reported because their actions and decisions symbolically represent the policies of the nation. The problems of the underprivileged also receive a great deal of coverage, especially under those conditions in which they pose a threat to the existing social order. The reporting of the news is then a symbolic account of the personalities and events presumed to be of importance to the nation at any given time.

The content of the evening television news is shaped by the imperative of selection. The initial choice is between what to include and what to exclude in the news coverage. Newscasters ignore some events, and select others for detailed elaboration. A half-hour news broadcast devotes only about 23 minutes to news (Gans, 1979), and this time restriction places limits on the scope of events that can be reported. In deciding what is news, newscasters make judgments about the relative importance of the many happenings in any given day: which aspects of the events deserve attention and how is the viewing audience likely to respond? The major news networks compete with each other for the largest share of the viewing audience. In seeking to enhance audience appeal, they intend the presentations to be informative as well as entertaining.

An assortment of themes recur in the process of informing a society about itself. Reports on political blunders reflect the incompetence of government officials; reports on crime stories reflect the problems of evil; reports on natural disasters reflect the vulnerability of humans to environmental forces. Specific events are simplified and personalized in order to make them understandable, while the vast array of activities covered confirms the complexity of modern social living. In informing people about their society, news journalists confront limitations and constraints as they attempt to construct credible accounts of the events that they cover (Frank, 1973).

The constraints on news journalists stem from their involvement in relationships with multiple sets of powerful others. If news accounts are highly critical of public officials, there is always the possibility of governmental sanctions in the forms of censorship, withholding information, or increased regulation and control. Powerful business interests must also be appeased, or the loss of advertising revenues will reduce the profitability of the news-gathering enterprise (Cirino, 1974). The consumers of news must also be pleased with the product, or they will seek information from some other source. In addition, the news journalist is also bound by a professional code of ethics that emphasizes neutrality and objectivity (Sigelman, 1973). Thus news journalists must serve several constituencies in their efforts to meet schedules, to be relevant, to be accurate, to be informative, and to entertain.

2. Audience Responses

The distinguishing feature of the audience in a mass society is that the activities of a small number of people are observed selectively by millions of spectators. Messages originate at some centralized location and are disseminated over a large geographical area. However, the messages sent and the messages received are not the same. Readers, viewers, and listeners impose their own realities and definitions on the situation. For example, the flight of the space shuttle Columbia in November of 1981 was a source of national pride for many Americans. Some viewed the journey into outer space, the return to orbit, and the landing of the craft as spectacular accomplishments. Others were less impressed and associated the feat with an overemphasis on military technology. Still others viewed the episode with misgivings and regarded the rebuilding of American cities, the development of mass transit, or increased social welfare benefits as better investments of national resources. Thus the meanings extracted from newsworthy events vary, and they reflect attempts to clarify relationships between personal and collective identities (Klapp, 1969).

Audience responses to the mass media are shaped by the symbolic mes-

---

BOX 14.4
Attitudes and Knowledge in Survey Research

In the early days of survey research (1940s and 1950s) researchers discovered that people who had strong prejudices against known groups (Orientals, blacks, and Jews) also had strong negative attitudes toward unknown and nonexistent groups ("Danireans" and "Wallonians"). In tapping attitudes toward public issues of the day, researchers also found that people would express attitudes toward such nonexistent issues as "the Metallic Metals Act" or other issues contrived by the researchers.

In the early studies investigators "deceived" their subjects by eliciting attitudes toward nonexistent groups and issues. To avoid the ethical question of deception, Schuman and Presser (1980) included questionnaire items in a national survey for tapping attitudes toward two legislative acts (the Agricultural Trade Act of 1978 and the Monetary Control Bill) so obscure that they felt safe in assuming the ignorance of the general public to be nearly complete. Their results indicated that about a third of a national sample expressed an opinion on each of the issues when "don't know" was omitted from the response form. Subjects, in effect, expressed attitudes toward public issues about which they knew nothing.

Some subjects apparently preferred expressing an opinion to admitting ignorance, but more importantly Schuman and Presser found that subjects used generalized attitudes in making uninformed judgments about specific issues. Those distrustful of the government or of the government's management of the economy were opposed to the legislation, while those expressing confidence in the government tended to favor the two measures. Thus people's overall attitudes toward government tend to shape their judgments on specific political issues about which they actually know very little.

Source: Howard Schuman and Stanley Presser, "Public Opinion and Public Ignorance: The Fine Line Between Attitudes and Nonattitudes," *American Journal of Sociology* 85 (March, 1980): 1214–1225.

sages that the audience receives. These include not only the basic facts being transmitted, but also the connotative meanings that people give to events. Such happenings as a presidential resignation, a nuclear accident, an oil embargo, or a sharp increase in the cost of living may be generally understood as noteworthy events. However, the specific meaning of these events are shaped by differences in the life circumstances of individuals. The millions who comprise a television or a movie audience face different kinds of personal problems and concerns; they differ in their social characteristics; and they differ in their hopes and aspirations for the future.

In any given case, the understanding of events is likely to be sketchy and incomplete. The individual readily fills the gaps in information in order to provide a general understanding of events. The concern is not so much with precise and detailed knowledge of "what actually happened," as with the implications of the event for personal thought and action. For example, news about moral disorders in government can readily confirm prior beliefs about political corruption and the dishonesty of public officials. The crimes reported in the daily newspaper can provide support for notions about sin and evil and how people go about making blunders and mistakes. (See Box 14.4.)

The specific meanings and social consequences of news events tend to vary in systematic patterns among subgroups of the population. For example, increases in fuel costs have special implications for the elderly who live on fixed incomes. The closing of an automobile assembly plant frequently has serious consequences for the local economy and for the families of those facing impending unemployment. When the government requires registration for the draft, it taps many latent sentiments, including pride in one's country for some and intense hostility toward the military for others.

The effects of the mass media on viewing audiences are shaped to some degree by the more immediate patterns of social interaction. News events are daily topics of conversation, and through the discussions that take place in intimate groups, people refine and elaborate their understandings and explanations. The messages that flow from the media are interpreted and passed on through informal social relationships (DeFleur and Ball-Rokeach, 1975). The importance of social relationships for the meanings they give to news events suggests that individuals do not respond to mass communications as "atomized masses," but as members of small and intimate groups.

To describe this process, Paul Lazarsfeld, Bernard Berelson, and Helen Gaudet (1944) developed the idea of the **two-step flow of communication**. The first step involves the initial receptiveness to news events and messages from the communications media. Small and intimate groups tend to have certain members who are attentive to mass communication, and these individuals become opinion leaders in family units and friendship circles. The second step in the communications process involves the spread and elaboration on the messages people receive from the media. The symbols of mass society take on significance through the exchanges and interpersonal communication that occur in small groups.

Two-Step Flow of Communication
In some cases people ignore messages originating from a central source, while in other cases they refine and interpret the messages through interpersonal communication.

The adoption of ideas tends to result in concerted lines of action from the two-step flow of communication. Families tend to vote as a unit in political elections, and best friends tend to engage in similar forms of consumer behavior. The research of Everett M. Rogers (1962) suggested that the adoption of agricultural innovations follows a similar process in the two-step flow of communication. Opinion leaders in a farm community may recognize the advantages of new forms of farm technology, and through their influences their neighbors accept the innovations. Thus the impact of mass communication frequently is tempered by the reality constructions of small and intimate groups.

C. MASS PERSUASION

The mass-like character of modern society provides individuals with opportunities for making many choices and decisions. Choices are involved in selecting a career, deciding where to live, making a purchase of clothing, endorsing a political candidate, and buying a car. Sources of meaning and reality construction among individuals occur within the context of large groups of people. As a result the technology that permits rapid communication with millions of people also provides opportunities for mass persuasion. The nearly universal availability of radio and television now makes available extremely large numbers of people for manipulation and control.

The term **mass persuasion** means the sending of messages to large numbers of people in order to influence opinions and actions. The audiences of concern may consist of thousands or millions of people and be dispersed over a vast geographical area. The intent of persuasion efforts is to influence public sentiments and behaviors in order to serve partisan interests. The partisan interests are reality constructions favorable to some special group, such as a business corporation, a governmental agency, or a social movement. Through drawing on mass media (radio, television, and newspapers), a special-interest group can rapidly distribute throughout the population the ideas originating from some central location.

1. Centralized Decision Making

From the perspective of C. Wright Mills (1956), a mass society exists when elites have control over the effective means of mass communication. The elites consist of those who hold the top positions of power and authority in business, in government, and in the military. According to Mills, the importance of elites stems from their capacity to make decisions that have serious consequences for a large number of people. These involve decisions about war and peace, about jobs and prices, and about the introduction of new governmental programs. Insofar as elites are in control, their decisions may be imposed on a society without adequate debate and argumentation in public forums.

In Mills's analysis, control over the means of effective communication has resulted in the transformation of publics into masses. A **public** is a collection of people who confront an issue, engage in debate over the issue, and seek to arrive at a solution to the issue. One example of a public in this sense is the town meeting in which citizens get together to discuss the topics of concern to them. People participate in the decision-making process at the grassroots level, and there are nearly as many people giving opinions as receiving them. In contrast to the participatory democracy of a town meeting, the masslike character of modern society is reflected in the control and management of information sources. Awareness of remote events is facilitated by the mass media. Large numbers of individuals are receiving information and opinions without adequate opportunities for being well-informed, for speaking back, or for expressing a personal point of view. In Mills's terms, the masses are readily accessible for manipulation and control, and an understanding of this fact "is one of the keys to the social and psychological meaning of modern life in America" (Mills, 1956: 300).

The defining characteristic of a mass society according to William Kornhauser (1959) is to be found in the interplay between elites and the masses. On the one hand, the elites of power and influence, as previously mentioned, have access to the mass media, and as a result the masses are available for manipulation and control. At the same time, Kornhauser maintains, the elites themselves are not immune to mass sentiments and to persuasive appeals from organized groups. The formation of policies and programs that lack support in mass sentiments are likely to result in failure. In the political sphere, officials who advocate unpopular causes are likely to be removed from office. Television programming that lacks viewer appeal is likely to be removed from

---

BOX 14.5
Alternative Models of Mass Society

What is the ultimate source of power and control within modern society? Do the effective forms of control reside with a power elite or with the masses? The answers given to these questions reflect important images of modern social life and how it is organized. In an inventory of the major models of mass society, William Kornhauser (1959) observed that the models provide several answers to these questions. Each type of answer is built on value judgments and critiques of modern social life.

The **aristocratic critique** claims that the uniqueness of modern society lies with the encroachment of the masses into virtually all aspects of social life. The masses are seen as gaining access to higher education, controlling politics and government, dominating the production of culture, and shaping industrial production along the lines of consumer tastes and preferences. The effective centers of power do not reside with an elite of culture, refinement, and sensibility but with the millions of people who dominate society through the principles of popular democracy. The aristocratic critique holds that since the time of the French Revolution, elites and elite values have no longer been insulated from the vulgarity of mass influences and preferences.

The **democratic critique**, by way of contrast, holds that the effective centers of control do not reside with the masses but with a ruling class or a power elite. Those holding top positions in business, government, and the military dominate the society because of the central places these institutions have come to hold in modern times. The masses in the United States are looked upon as resembling the masses of Nazi Germany in that they are manipulated and controlled by a power elite. The democratic critique views the masses as following the wishes of those in positions of power, even though it is not in their own best interests to do so.

Source: William Kornhauser, *The Politics of Mass Society*, New York: The Free Press of Glencoe, 1959.

the air. And the design and production of automobiles that are incongruent with consumer preferences are likely to result in substantial corporate losses. In a mass society, then, elites and masses respond to one another; each attempts to persuade and influence the other. (See Box 14.5.)

From this discussion it is clear that a mass society is one in which persuasive appeals may originate from a variety of sources (Halebsky, 1976). Powerful elites attempt to win public support for their decisions; highly organized groups, such as labor unions and professional associations, attempt to influence public policies; and social movements emerge to call attention to social problems that are being neglected. These observations suggest that, on balance, the power structure of a mass society is a highly permissive one. As a result the important questions to raise about power and influence are those related to the perceived realities of power and the ways in which subjective definitions of power shape social thought and behavior.

2. Perceptions of Power

1) power elite
2) specialists
3) masses

Because of the size and complexity of modern society, social scientists are not able to agree on the major sources of power and control. Some share Mills's view that social control resides with a power elite (Domhoff, 1967), while others maintain that control is in the hands of experts and specialists who selectively influence events within their own specific spheres of competence (Keller, 1963). Yet another prominent view holds that social control in the final analysis resides with the masses and the level of consensus that emerges out of public opinion (Nisbet, 1970). Still others insist that the dominant forms of power reside with large-scale organizations, such as business corporations, labor unions, and professional associations (Presthus, 1978). The process of reality construction by the students of power resembles the assessments of events by people-in-general. People draw on their own personal experiences and selective observations in developing ideas about the manner in which power and control operate in the social realm.

In a community study of Muskegon, Michigan, William Form and Joan Rytina (1969) concentrated their research on the ideological beliefs about the distribution of power in the United States. The results of their study indicate that perceptions of power closely correlated with socioeconomic status. Those at the upper- and middle-income levels were more likely to see the power structure as pluralistic and spread across a series of organized interest groups. Poor people and blacks, by way of contrast, tended to see the control of society as being in the hands of a power elite. Perceptions of political influence also related to class. Low-income groups tended to see big business as having a dominant influence on government, while those at the higher income levels tended to emphasize the power of labor unions.

The perceptions of power among college students apparently resemble the views of minorities and the poor rather than those of rich people. Drawing on male students at a state university as subjects, Stanley Eitzen and his colleagues (1976) found that the majority subscribed to the power-elite model rather than to the pluralistic model. A serious gap existed between their preferences and what they saw as the realities of power. Subjects preferred the pluralistic model, but saw the actual exercise of power as reflecting the existence of elite control.

The beliefs of most people about power are lacking in sophistication, are only partially clear, and are not at all free from contradictions. Beliefs about the primary sources of control and influence include competing ideas about where power resides, how it works, and how it may be used. In view of the uncertainties about power, we may regard public beliefs as explanations and justifications. Perceptions of the locus of power may be used in given situations for making sense out of societal events (new taxes, new governmental programs, or new citizen responsibilities) that promote or interfere with some set of personal interests.

3. Attributions of Causality

The perceptions of power are important because they relate to the manner by which men and women define the primary sources of causal responsibility in their community or society. Beliefs about power and influence reflect attempts to give coherence to major societal happenings, to explain how and why things happen as they do, and to impute blame and responsibility. In everyday life the average person is unlikely to reflect on the issues of social control and influence. The individual directs attention toward the immediate concerns of the moment. But when the orderliness of everyday life becomes disrupted, the person is likely to reflect on issues of responsibility and causality.

W. Russell Neuman (1981) has observed that there are few opportunities among the mass citizenry to act directly on the basis of their political perceptions, but that there are ample opportunities for symbolic activity. The attribution of causality is one of the major ways for engaging in symbolic control over the social world. Causal attributions promote an understanding of the social world, even if erroneous, and they reinforce a sense of management both in the social realm and in one's personal life (Forsyth, 1980). The two themes of group interests and the nature of our times are causal explanations that express the concern with management in the political and economic realms.

The attribution of causality is prominent among the responses to emerging problems that are having an impact on personal lifestyles. This may be illustrated through the varied judgments that have been made in the late 1970s and early 1980s about the major causes of inflation. A sharp rise in the cost of living had an effect of eroding the purchasing power of American wage earners, and individuals responded by citing what they regarded as the major forms of

TABLE 14.2
Perceived Causes of Inflation

The following is a casual list of causal attributions in everyday conversations about the increasing costs of living:

Blaming the Government:
  The government is printing too much paper money without having anything to back it up with.
  The government is spending too much money, and the national debt is getting too large.
  Too much money is wasted on social welfare programs.

Blaming Big Business:
  Business corporations are power-hungry and greedy.
  Business people try to squeeze as much profit as possible out of every dollar they get.
  Big business contrived the energy crisis to increase its profit level.

Blaming Labor Unions:
  Workers continuously make demands for higher wages.
  Worker productivity is dropping, while labor costs are increasing.
  The "work ethic" is gone.
  People want more but are not willing to work for it.

Blaming Consumers:
  People overuse their credit cards.
  People don't put enough money into savings.
  There is too much overspending.
  Affluent lifestyles are depleting the world's resources.

injustice and responsibility. Those who reflected on the growing difficulties in making ends meet offered highly specific explanations. Editorials in newspapers and explanations in everyday conversations contained contrasting ideas about the effects of governmental spending, the power of labor unions, the control by business corporations, and the scarcity of resources growing world-wide.

As the severity of a problem increases, there tends to be an increase in the variety of explanations offered. Table 14.2 provides only a partial list of the explanations one could glean from newspapers and magazines on why the costs of living have increased so rapidly during the late 1970s and early 1980s. The causal explanations provide an opportunity for the expression of latent hostilities and resentments. The readiness to believe one explanation over another is closely related to the perceived defects of the social system and to the underlying views about human nature.

These views on inflation draw heavily on the themes of alienation and the sense of exclusion from avenues of effective participation in the decision-making process. The attribution of causality to the federal government, to labor unions, and to big business relies on perceived concentrations of power and responsibility. The inability to identify with one's government or with large-scale organizations places the individual in a position of vulnerability. The person views control over events as residing with external forces that are beyond his or her capacities for effective social action and self-determination.

In the context of mass persuasion, power involves getting one's own way and getting others to serve one's own interests (Parenti, 1978). From this viewpoint, power involves a set of relationships in which some individuals cause things to happen, while others have to cope with events that go against their own desires and interests. In this sense, life is a competitive struggle, and there are winners and losers. Those who have the lowest degree of control over desired resources (students, the poor, and minorities) are among those likely to view the agencies of control as hostile and alien. They are also among those who are in a weak position for having a persuasive influence on others. Under these circumstances the attributions of causal responsibility reflect judgments about those who do have control and about the manner in which certain groups utilize resources to enhance their special interests.

D. MASS ENTERTAINMENT

The political stability of a mass society is not fully dependent on the use of coercive methods of social control. Harmony within the social realm is promoted through enlargement of the public sphere, through winning support for public policies, and through increasing the availability of public recreational facilities (Gitlin, 1979). Leisure as a social institution has become enlarged and elaborated in modern times. Both participatory and spectator activities have been extended; when people are being entertained, they are less likely to engage in social protest and more likely to accept as valid the ideology of the ruling class (Gramsci, 1971).

Enlargement of the public sphere is especially evident in the increased availability of recreational facilities. The development of parks, museums, highways, and outdoor recreational facilities has made available a vast number of options for the use of leisure time. Public recreational areas are used extensively for such activities as fishing, hunting, camping, boating, and hiking. According to the Bureau of Outdoor Recreation, more than 160 million Americans participate each year in picnicking and swimming (U.S. Department of Commerce, 1977). The degree to which public recreational facilities are utilized reflects the increased importance of leisure activities in modern society.

The preferred form of entertainment for most Americans, however, consists of watching television. Nearly all Americans have access to television

Outdoor Recreation
Many people in our society highly value opportunities to visit public parks and to sense a closeness with nature.

sets, and the productions designed for mass audiences are available on a daily basis. From analyses of time allocations from 1965 to 1975, Robinson (1979) concluded that the amount of time spent watching television increased faster than time spent in any other single activity. The appeal of television reflects the success of centralized productions in tapping the predispositions of the viewing audiences. To a large degree this success results from the vicarious experiences that are readily available with only a limited expenditure of personal effort.

1. Symbolic Events

The large pool of potential movie goers and television watchers serves as a type of judiciary on the entertainment value of cultural productions. The decisions made by millions of people, acting as individuals and out of self-interest, have decisive effects on the kinds of entertainment made available. A veto over television productions may be exercised by many people simply switching to another channel or by deciding not to watch television at all (Gitlin, 1979).

As a result of the interplay between producers and audiences, mass entertainment is oriented toward revealing several aspects of the joys and conflicts implicit in social living. Mass entertainment thus portrays **symbolic events**, in the sense that they dramatize personal troubles, historical events, and social conflicts. Through symbolizing events, television entertainment becomes a type of collective mirror that reflects the individual's self-image and the image of society (Klapp, 1969). From the mirroring of multiple aspects of social life, we may conclude that we live in a hazardous environment, that people sin and suffer from it, that heroic undertakings have successful outcomes for some people, and that our own personal problems are small compared to those confronted by others.

Gaye Tuchman (1978: 3) observed that "Americans learn basic lessons about social life from the mass media, much as hundreds of years ago illiterate peasants studied the carvings around the apse or the stained glass windows of medieval cathedrals." Tuchman maintains that like any other society our society must pass on its heritage from one generation to the next and prepare people for the challenges of changing conditions. The transmission of American culture is evident in television programming, and the messages created frequently draw on and elaborate stereotyped images. For example, a study by Judith Lemon (1978) concentrated on the portrayal of power and dominance in situation comedies and crime stories on prime time television. Her results indicate that the program she studied captured folk notions about the importance of social class in the exercise of power and reinforced popular views on the general dominance of men over women. The images of relations between men and women, between the rich and the poor, and between blacks and whites confirmed the typifications prevailing in the thoughts of the viewers. Thus television maintains societal stereotypes in its portrayal of power and dominance relationships.

The uses of television for mass entertainment may be described as a form of gamesmanship on the part of sponsors and producers. The primary contestants are the networks, and the viewing audiences determine the winners and losers. The game itself consists of the productions and performances that are designed to tap a responsive chord among the masses. Concern with the responsiveness of viewers is evident not only in television commercials that clearly are designed to persuade (Schuetz and Sprafkin, 1978), but also in the content of the programming. There is always some degree of risk taking in television productions because of the inherent uncertainty of audience responses.

The intent of mass-produced entertainment is not to get a message across, as communication is usually understood, but to strike a **responsive chord** in the viewing audience (Schwartz, 1973). In a successful production the viewers are drawn into the performance as they mentally take on the roles of the characters portrayed and identify with the situations created. In this process the realities of the technology by which television is produced is of little concern or interest to most of the viewers. The script writing, the rehearsals, the stage props, the photography, and the moving dots of light on an electronic screen

Television Sets
The wide scope of television ownership in our society stems from the popularity of programming content. The viewer almost always focuses attention on something other than the movement of dots on an electronic screen.

recede into the background as viewers become engrossed in the symbolic events being portrayed. The self-attitudes, emotions, and predispositions of the viewers shape and refine the content and the entertainment value of television productions.

While our language separates time dimensions into past, present, and future, our experiences tend to unify them as we reflect on the character of symbolic events. The realities of the past take on special meanings through our current perceptions of them, and the future becomes a mixture of present fears and aspirations. From audience experiences with media entertainment, the time dimension may be described as "everywhen." There were certain events that happened in the past that could also happen now and are likely to happen again in the future (Stanner, 1965). The time dimension becomes a form of eternal dream time in which individuals travel psychologically to remote places and respond to the activities of people who represent both the living and the dead.

BOX 14.6
Authentic Sources and Media Entertainment

The research of Virginia Platt (1978) suggests that in commercial television entertainment value tends to take priority over historical accuracy. The popularity of historical drama is revealed in the sizable viewing audience that became engrossed in the television production of Alex Haley's *Roots*. Haley's efforts to reconstruct his family's history and the concerns of television producers with winning a large viewing audience reflect the gap between the concerns of historians with authentic sources and the process of reality construction in mass entertainment.

In the absence of written documents, Alex Haley relied on an oral tradition in his efforts to reconstruct his family's history. He supplemented tales told to him by a maternal grandmother with research into the history of American slavery and with travel to Gambia for additional information transmitted through folk memory. Haley described his book *Roots* as a mixture of fact and fiction, since his imagination was used to develop plausible explanations in the absence of direct information. Historians question the accuracy of Haley's research, but even more so they question the accuracy of the TV show that elaborated on his book. The television series tended to emphasize dramatic and violent events rather than the routine events of everyday life, and stereotypes prevailed in the depiction of social roles.

The prevailing modes of communication and the sources of information have an important bearing on the images any given group of people hold of their historical past. Platt maintains that written documents are the preferred media for historical accuracy but that the electronic media are used increasingly for developing images of the historical past. Entertainment is currently being maximized at the expense of historical accuracy.

Source: Virginia B. Platt, "Authentic Sources and the Media," in James Monaco (ed.), *Media Culture*, New York: Delta Books, 1978, pp. 270–278.

In the realm of mass entertainment the past becomes a form of selective memory, since the factual details of what actually happened in the Old West, in the American Revolution, or in the Korean War often are neither known nor knowable. Historical events are treated as symbolic events that are used for reflections about the problems and challenges of contemporary living. Under these circumstances history becomes a form of remembering in which the mixture of fact and fiction is of less concern than the entertainment value of the production (Platt, 1978). For example, the importance of history as a form of remembering was evident in the mass appeal of the television production of Alex Haley's *Roots*. The size of the viewing audience reached record levels, and the program tapped a responsive chord in the collective search for identity. (See Box 14.6.)

The drama of mass entertainment involves interactions between producers, performers, and audiences in the development of symbolic events. The process is reciprocal as each takes the other into account and modifies behavior accordingly. The performances and productions are oriented toward generating excitement and entertainment by providing audiences with what they would like to see and hear. Mass entertainment elaborates pseudo events as real-life situations, and creates celebrities for winning audience identification with splendid displays and performances.

2. Celebrities

Celebrities are well-known and famous individuals who are admired by a large number of people. Celebrities have little in common with each other except for their glorified personalities. In some cases celebrity status is based on splendid performances, as with the superstars of television and the movies, the colorful leaders in the political realm, or the famous in competitive sports (Monaco, 1978). However, celebrations of the famous may not be limited to a person's performances. They may also be based on what audiences presume to be the personal qualities or attributes of the person. The notoriety of a beauty queen, a poster queen, or a sex symbol may rest on qualities imputed to certain individuals because of the images they present, and the forms of lust and desire they evoke.

We may view the appeal of celebrities as a quest for compensation at a symbolic level for what is missing in daily experiences. People frequently work at jobs that lack a sense of fulfillment. The pay may be good enough, but the material rewards are not accompanied by adequate psychological payoffs. Under these circumstances the mirrored reflections in media productions provide new ways for people to see themselves in relationship to the perceived totality of social life. The search for identity in collective symbols is an emotional gesture designed to overcome feelings of being short-changed, cheated, or unfulfilled in the practical activities of everyday life (Klapp, 1969). Identification with the celebrities of the mass media serves to divert attention from the stresses and tensions of the immediate environment. (See Box 14.7.)

The scope of events and the range of personalities which can become the objects of public attention are substantially greater than they used to be (Klapp, 1964). Remote places and happenings intrude into consciousness with increasing frequency, and accordingly the activities of everyday life become refocused and extended. The actual social distance between celebrities and their admirers is so great that there is no sanctioning power of one over the other (McEvoy and Erickson, 1981). In the absence of direct interactions, celebrities become identification models that enable individuals to vicariously reflect on their own hopes and aspirations. The imagery is a form of daydreaming in which human emotions intensify and gain concrete focus. Such daydreaming humanizes impersonal events and allows the individual through the use of imagination to project the self into someone's else's world of meaning, understanding,

BOX 14.7
Television Viewing and Conflict Avoidance

By the time of graduation from high school, the average young adult in the United States today has spent more time watching television than being in the classroom. Yet both children and adults differ in the amount of time they watch television, and it is these differences that were of concern to Paul Rosenblatt and Michael Cunningham (1976) in their study of households in Minneapolis. They also were interested in the connection between television watching and family tensions. Their research provides support for the hypothesis that the more time a television set is on in a dwelling, the higher the level of tension in family relationships. Households reporting the largest amounts of time watching television also more frequently reported family members as being "too critical," as having "temper outbursts," or as being "moody." In effect, their findings showed that the amount of time watching television correlated positively with the level of unhappiness with family life.

Rosenblatt and Cunningham interpret their results to mean that television is used to escape family problems. Becoming engrossed in television reduces the amount of talking, avoids tense family interactions, and keeps potential combatants separated. The relationship between tension levels and television viewing was pronounced in households characterized by large family sizes and by crowdedness. The lack of opportunities for privacy increased the importance of television as a means of avoiding conflict and confrontation. Thus television viewing appears to serve as an alternative to verbal abuse and physical aggression under conditions of crowdedness and within the intimate confines of family living.

Source: Paul C. Rosenblatt and Michael R. Cunningham, "Television Watching and Family Tensions," *Journal of Marriage and the Family* 38 (February, 1976): 105–114.

and action (Fraser, 1974). In this process, entertainment and information, fact and fiction, realities and facades, and time and place blend with the response of those comprising mass audiences. The public performances and the personal lives of celebrities serve as models of what to do, how to live, and what is possible.

The manipulations in the creation of celebrities are not designed to produce models worthy of emulation. To the contrary the concern is simply to get attention, which may be achieved by whatever is necessary for eliciting momentary recognition and social responses in the viewing audience. As creations of the mass media, modern celebrities typically are not the men and women of heroic accomplishments, such as characterized the symbolic leaders of the past. Instead they are often antiheroic, openly opposed to conventional morality, and lacking in a sense of social responsibility (Boorstin, 1961). Heroic accomplishments are lost in the bombardment of the senses with pseudo events. The trivial and the incredible tend to be dramatized, and the "collective search for identity," as Orrin Klapp (1969) calls it, continues as a never-ending quest.

SUMMARY

The idea of a mass society centers around the historical uniqueness of modern social conditions. The theme of uniqueness is reflected in descriptions and conceptualizations of mass society in literal and objective ways. By objective criteria, a mass society is characterized (1) by sophisticated technology that extends human capabilities and binds people together in ways not possible only a hundred years ago; (2) by a large population base accompanied by increased urbanization and increased complexity in social relationships; (3) by the centralization of political power over vast geographical areas and over millions of people; and (4) by economic integration that promotes a great deal of economic activity and extensive specialization in the division of labor. These characteristics suggest that the masses are now drawn into spheres of public life once reserved for the upper classes or the aristocracy. Mass education, mass entertainment, mass production, mass communication, and mass persuasion are among the distinguishing attributes of our time and place.

While the notion of a mass society is an objective theory of society, it is also a concept or an idea about the nature of our times. The mass-like character of modern society is a symbolic construction for organizing experiences and for understanding the social order. An obvious symbol is the crowdedness that occurs in traffic congestion, during Christmas shopping, and at amusement parks. Images of population density add to the complexity, confusion, and chaos of modern social living. Interdependency is another evident symbol of mass society. On an everyday basis we take for granted the availability of supermarkets, telephones, and electricity; but when systems fail, as with the blackout of New York City, we become aware of our dependency on the goods and services produced by unknown and faceless people. Finally, the focused event is another way that dramatizes the mass-like character of modern society. Millions of people temporarily focus their attention on events such as a volcano in the Pacific northwest, Iran's taking and holding Americans hostage, or an attempt to assassinate the President. Focused events are significant because of the many people involved and because of the opportunities they provide for an examination of selected aspects of social life.

Mass communication refers to the process by which a society seeks to become informed about itself. The news media (television, radio, and newspapers) select events from the many activities of any given day in efforts to inform and to entertain. The technology that facilitates mass communication also can be drawn on for mass persuasion. Those who hold centralized positions of power may use the media to promote special interests and partisan causes. However, viewing audiences refine and elaborate the meanings they have extracted from the media through discussions in small and intimate groups. People are not persuaded directly by the media, but by opinion leaders and social interaction patterns at the grass-roots level.

The primary purpose of mass entertainment is to tap a responsive chord through dramatizing societal events. The entertainment provided by television, the movies, and news journals is oriented toward producing an emotional response. The television networks compete with each other for the largest viewing audience, and this competition gives the viewer a great deal of control over programming content. From the interplay between producers and audiences, mass entertainment is oriented toward dramatizing the conflicts and contradictions implicit in modern social living. From the collective mirror provided by television entertainment, we can conclude that we live in a hazardous environment, that people sin and suffer from it, that heroic undertakings sometime have successful outcomes, and that personal problems are small compared to those confronted by others. The symbolic events portrayed in mass entertainment provide opportunities for verification or refinement of assumptions about the organization of everyday life.

BASIC TERMS

Density
Crowding
Atomization
Focused event
Mass communication
Two-step flow of
    communication

Mass persuasion
Public
Aristocratic critique
Democratic critique
Symbolic events
Responsive chord
Celebrities

REFERENCES

Boorstin, Daniel J.
    1961 *The Image: A Guide to Pseudo-Events in America,* New York: Harper Colophon Books.
Burke, James
    1978 *Connections,* Boston: Little, Brown.
Cirino, Robert
    1974 *Power to Persuade: Mass Media and the News,* New York: Bantam Books.
Cohen, Jerry L., Bernard Sladen, and Barbara Bennett
    1975 "The Effects of Situational Variables on Judgments of Crowding," *Sociometry* 38 (June): 273–281.
DeFleur, Melvin L. and Sandra Ball-Rokeach
    1975 *Theories of Mass Communication,* New York: David McKay.
Domhoff, G. William
    1967 *Who Rules America?,* Englewood Cliffs, N.J.: Prentice-Hall.
Eitzen, D. Stanley, Curtis J. Cole, Linda Baer, Charles Duprey, and Norman J. Thompson
    1976 "The Perception of Societal Models of Power Distribution by Recent Male College Graduates," *Sociological Focus* 9 (October): 361–366.

Erikson, Kai T.
    1976 *Everything in Its Path*, New York: Simon & Schuster.
Form, William H. and Joan Rytina
    1969 "Ideological Beliefs on the Distribution of Power in the United States,"
        American Sociological Review 34 (February): 19–30.
Forsyth, Donelson R.
    1980 "The Functions of Attributions," *Social Psychological Quarterly* 43 (June):
        184–189.
Frank, Robert S.
    1973 *Message Dimensions of Television News*, Toronto: Lexington Books.
Fraser, John
    1974 *Violence in the Arts*, London: Cambridge University Press.
Gans, Herbert J.
    1979 *Deciding What's News*, New York: Pantheon Books.
Gitlin, Todd
    1979 "Prime Time Ideology," *Social Problems* 26 (February) 251–266.
Goffman, Erving
    1963 *Behavior in Public Places*, New York: The Free Press.
Gramsci, Antonio
    1971 *Selections from the Prison Notebooks* (ed. by Quintin Hoare and Geoffrey
        Nowell Smith), New York: International Publishers.
Halebsky, Sandor
    1976 *Mass Society and Political Conflict*, London: Cambridge University Press.
Hauser, Philip M.
    1969 "The Chaotic Society," *American Sociological Review* 34 (February): 1–18.
Katz, Elihu, Michael Gurevitch, and Hadassah Haas
    1973 "On the Use of Media for Important Things," *American Sociological Review*
        38 (April): 164–181.
Keller, Suzanne
    1963 *Beyond the Ruling Class*, New York: Random House.
Klapp, Orrin E.
    1969 *Collective Search for Identity*, New York: Holt, Rinehart & Winston.
    1964 *Symbolic Leaders*, Chicago: Aldine.
Kornhauser, William
    1959 *The Politics of Mass Society*, New York: The Free Press of Glencoe.
Lazarsfeld, Paul F., Bernard Berelson, and Helen Gaudet
    1944 *The People's Choice*, New York: Duell, Sloan, and Pearce.
Lemon, Judith
    1978 "Dominant or Dominated? Women on Prime-Time Television," in Gaye
        Tuchman, Arlene K. Daniels, and James Benet (eds.), *Hearth and Home:
        Images of Women in the Mass Media*, New York: Oxford University Press,
        pp. 51–68.
McEvoy, Alan and Edsel L. Erickson
    1981 "Heroes and Villians," *Sociological Focus* 14 (April): 111–122.
McLuhan, Marshall
    1965 *Understanding Media*, New York: McGraw-Hill.
Mannheim, Karl
    1960 "Types of Rationality and Organized Insecurity," in C. Wright Mills (ed.),
        Images of Man, New York: George Braziller, pp. 508–528.

Mills, C. Wright
    1956 *The Power Elite*, New York: Oxford University Press.
Monaco, James
    1978 *Celebrity*, New York: Dell.
Neuman, W. Russell
    1981 "Differentiation and Integration: Two Dimensions of Political Thinking," *American Journal of Sociology* 86 (May): 1236–1268.
Nisbet, Robert
    1979 "The Rape of Progress," *Public Opinion* 2, no. 3: 2–6.
    1970 "The Context of Democracy," in Marvin E. Olsen (ed.), *Power in Society*, New York: Macmillan, pp. 196–208.
Parenti, Michael
    1978 *Power and the Powerless*, New York: St. Martin's Press.
Platt, Virginia B.
    1978 "Authentic Sources and the Media," in James Monaco (ed.), *Media Culture*, New York: Delta Books, pp. 270–278.
Pokorny, Gene
    1979 "Living Dangerously... Sometimes," *Public Opinion* 2, no. 3: 10–14.
Presthus, Robert
    1978 *The Organizational Society*, New York: St. Martin's Press.
Robinson, John P.
    1979 "Toward a Post Industrial Society," *Public Opinion* 2, no. 4: 41–46.
Rogers, Everett M.
    1962 *The Diffusion of Innovations*, New York: The Free Press of Glencoe.
Rosenblatt, Paul C. and Michael R. Cunningham
    1976 "Television Watching and Family Tensions," *Journal of Marriage and the Family* 38 (February): 105–114.
Schuetz, Stephen and Joyce N. Sprafkin
    1978 "Spot Messages Appearing Within Saturday Morning Television Programs," in G. Tuchman, A. K. Daniels, and J. Benet (eds.), *Hearth and Home: Images of Women in the Mass Media*, New York: Oxford University Press, pp. 69–77.
Schuman, Howard and Stanley Presser
    1980 "Public Opinion and Public Ignorance: The Fine Line Between Attitudes and Nonattitudes," *American Journal of Sociology* 85 (March): 1214–1225.
Schwartz, Tony
    1973 *The Responsive Chord*, New York: Anchor Press.
Sigelman, Lee
    1973 "Reporting the News," *American Journal of Sociology* 79 (July): 132–151.
Stanner, W. E. H.
    1965 "The Dreaming," in William A. Lessa and Evon Z. Vogt (eds.), *Reader in Comparative Religion*, New York: Harper & Row, pp. 269–277.
Tuchman, Barbara W.
    1978 *A Distant Mirror*, New York: Knopf.
Tuchman, Gaye
    1978 "The Symbolic Annihilation of Women by the Mass Media," in Gaye Tuchman, A. K. Daniels, and J. Benet (eds.), *Hearth and Home: Images of Women in the Mass Media*, New York: Oxford University Press, pp. 3–38.
U.S. Department of Commerce
    1977 *Social Indicators 1976*, Washington, D.C.: Government Printing Office.

15

The Quality of Life

Perceptions of the quality of life vary widely among human beings, often bearing little relationship to objective circumstances or past accomplishments. Obtaining a college degree is no guarantee of an easy life, and achieving sudden wealth may complicate one's life in unforeseen ways. People in good physical health are sometimes bored with the monotonous routines of everyday life, and people who work at well-paying jobs are often dissatisfied with other aspects of their lives. The gap between the objective circumstances of life and subjective responses to them represents the departure point for social psychological studies of avowed happiness and reports on life satisfaction.

The notion of quality implies evaluations and judgments about what is desirable. Quality is an attribute of one's personal thinking rather than an inherent characteristic of persons, objects, or events. For example, by purely objective standards those living at the poverty level in modern industrialized societies of the West have standards of living that exceed those of the nobility in fourteenth-century Europe. The quality of food, the quality of housing, and the quality of health care, for example, have improved for nearly everyone. But there is no evidence to indicate that these advances have been accompanied by corresponding increases in human happiness.

The multiple facets of human life preclude taking any single one of them as the key to happiness or contentment. Your level of life satisfaction may not increase as much as you might think if you were suddenly to become wealthy by winning the state lottery or inheriting a considerable amount of property. Surely you would not have to worry as much about paying the bills, but the level of stress in other areas of life might increase considerably. Neither money, health, marriage, nor any other single activity provides an exclusive basis for a sense of well-being. All of these items just listed are certainly involved in many people's evaluations and assessments, but the sources of human meaning and purpose are richly varied.

Individuals may be satisfied with some domains of their lives while being dissatisfied with others. College students, for example, may be pleased with their educational accomplishments but feel that other important things are missing from their lives. Students may feel that they do not have enough money to do many of the things they would like to do; they may regret having to postpone marriage to a later age; they may resent not having the status that goes along with a paid job; they may feel that they are simply "marking time" and that they do not live in "the real world." Such conditions do not make for a very high level of satisfaction with present life circumstances, but students are making investments for future payoffs. For those who do not attend college, one prominent form of dissatisfaction in later life is level of educational attainment (Campbell, 1981).

Evaluations of life circumstances involve both retrospective judgments and hopes and aspirations for the future. If you are a typical college student, you are likely to feel that you have a better life now than you had five years ago. The turbulence of adolescence is past, and you are beginning to enjoy the pleasures of adult status. But it is also a good bet that you expect your personal circumstances to improve substantially five years from now. Hopes and aspirations play an important part in human affairs, and, except for such special categories as the very old or the recently divorced, people approach personal futures with optimism. The present becomes tolerable if the future is expected to be better.

This chapter will examine the sense of **well-being** by taking into account the findings from national surveys over the past several years. The research shows that the vast majority of people have little difficulty in responding to the question, "How do you feel about your life as a whole?" Frank Andrews and Stephen Withey (1976) report that less than 1 percent of subjects in national surveys respond by saying, "Never thought of it." Issues related to the qualities of life apparently are a part of daily consciousness. The sense that life is worthwhile or that life circumstances can be improved is a basic supporting idea for daily activities and for plans for the future.

In making evaluations of the quality of life, people make sharp separations between personal circumstances and the conditions that prevail in society. People can be both optimistic about personal futures and at the same time pessimistic about the future of their country. We will explore the theme of alienation to possibly account for the gaps between evaluations at the individual and societal levels. Just as improvements in social conditions by objective standards may not be accompanied by increased happiness, optimism about one's personal future may vary independently of optimism about the future of one's society. Attitudes of apathy and views that societal events are beyond the control of individuals and that public officials cannot be trusted are among the states of mind that promote an emphasis on the private sphere. Most people seem to feel that they will be able to beat the system and improve their personal lives more than conditions can be improved in their country.

A. THE SENSE OF WELL-BEING

Much more is involved in the concept of well-being than such objective conditions as earning a high income, having good physical health, owning a large

Optimism of Youth
Young people in the United States today tend to be more optimistic about their personal futures than about the future of their country.

and expensive automobile, and living in a socially desirable neighborhood. Physical comfort and access to the good life are certainly among the ingredients of well-being for many people, but these ingredients in and of themselves are not enough. The sense of well-being is a state of mind, an appraisal of the meaningfulness of life, and a feeling of comfort with one's life circumstances. Such subjective evaluations frequently are at variance with objective social conditions. People who are highly respected and admired within their communities sometimes confront serious mental health problems that require the services of psychiatrists; others who live under wretched conditions from the standpoint of an outside observer make healthy and effective adjustments to their life circumstances. Thus the sense of well-being depends on the quality of one's personal experiences and on feelings of being happy or contented (Campbell, 1981). The individual may know such states of mind directly, but social psychologists may study them through examining verbal responses to questionnaire items.

Several research strategies have been employed by social psychologists in studies of life satisfaction and avowed happiness. The more productive of these strategies have consisted of asking people directly how they feel about their life circumstances, what they worry about most, what their hopes and aspirations are for the future, and what level of comfort they have with the separate spheres of their lives. The sense of well-being includes not only an overall evaluation of life circumstances but also the level of satisfaction with such separate domains as finances, physical health, and family life. The responses to questionnaires permit inquiry into the conditions that lead some to find their lives to be gratifying and others to look on life as a struggle with unrewarding experiences (Andrews and Withey, 1976).

1. Self-Anchorage

Hadley Cantril's (1965) **self-anchorage** scale is one of the most widely used measures of the sense of well-being. The measure uses a ladder to represent a ten-point scale. A score of 10 represents the best life possible as the individual conceives it, while a score of 1 represents the worst possible life. The top anchoring point reflects the standing of the individual with respect to hopes, aspirations, and personal definitions of the good life; the bottom anchoring point represents the standing of the individual with respect to fears, anxieties, and negative experiences. In deriving self-anchorage scores, researchers ask subjects to rate their present standings on the ladder of life, where they stood five years ago, and where they expect to stand five years from now. The responses permit the researchers to assess the self-anchorage of individuals within a time dimension and according to the individuals' own values and aspirations. (See Box 15.1.)

As a way of relating self-anchorage to collective definitions of the quality of life, Cantril collected data from thirteen countries of the world in various stages of economic development. By summing the aggregate responses in the various countries, he derived several conclusions about the hopes and aspirations of a large percentage of the world's population.

Most people in most of the countries he studied perceived their self-anchorage to be at a higher level of attainment than five years before. Reflecting the importance of hope, most people expected their locations to be at a higher level five years in the future. Respondents generally expressed similar aspirations and expectations in their assessments of past, present, and future attainments for the respective countries. Thus individuals tended to perceive the course of change as facilitating their own attainment of a better life, and this was accompanied by perceptions of a general improvement in conditions within their own countries.

In discussing the pattern of his results, Cantril (1965) observes that a personal sense of psychological security derives from an interest in protecting the gains that have been made and in using them to launch further advances. The trend on a world-wide basis would seem to reflect a generalized sense of

---

BOX 15.1
The Self-Anchorage Scale

All of us want certain things out of life, and we have some idea of the kind of life that would make us happiest. We also have some ideas of the kind of life that would make us most miserable. Below is a picture of a ladder. Let us assume that the top of the ladder (step 10) represents the best possible life for you and that the bottom (step 1) represents the worst possible life for you.

---

1. Where on the ladder do you feel that you personally stand at the *present* time?
   Step number _____
2. Where on the ladder would you say you stood *five years ago?*
   Step number _____
3. Where do you think you will be on the ladder *five years from now?*
   Step number _____

Ladder of Life

Best Possible

| 10 |
| 9 |
| 8 |
| 7 |
| 6 |
| 5 |
| 4 |
| 3 |
| 2 |
| 1 |

Worst Possible

If you are typical of college students, your present score is higher than it would have been five years ago and you expect to make additional gains in the next five years.

Source: "Self-Anchoring Scale," from *The Pattern of Human Concerns* by Hadley Cantril. Copyright © 1965 by Rutgers, The State University.

---

rising expectations, regardless of the current level of economic development. The more affluent countries, such as the United States and West Germany, were characterized by subjects who sought an enrichment of the intrinsic qualities of their lives, while subjects from the developing countries of Africa and Asia were more likely to aspire to the types of economic gains that have been made in the more highly industrialized countries.

The Cantril study emphasized the importance of being confident that one's social environment will be orderly and predictable and that one's society will provide the conditions to permit the fulfillment of personal aspirations. These are assumptions that may or may not be warranted in any given case. The consequence of unexpected disruptions in the broader environment is often the impairment in individual effectiveness. The subjects' major aspirations for the future were to preserve conditions that permit enhancing the qualities of family life, while the major sources of worry and concern related to health and physical well-being.

The theme of striving emerges from the results of studies on the quality of life. People seek to hold on to the gains that they have already made and to take advantage of the opportunities available in their immediate environments. Striving for the attainment of a better life, however, is accompanied by qualified optimism. Most people recognize that certain kinds of societal disruptions would interfere with the realization of hopes and aspirations for the future. The major national fears in Cantril's study were the awesome possibility of a major war, the potential impact of further economic instability, and the consequences of a breakdown in law and order. Personal striving under these circumstances occurs in conjunction with the desire for an orderly and predictable social system.

A series of studies over the past several years has concentrated on measuring changes in the quality of life as perceived by most Americans. The basic change reflected in national surveys between the early 1960s and the early 1980s is that Americans have become increasingly pessimistic about the future of their country while remaining optimistic about the prospects for improving the qualities of their personal lives. Drawing on national surveys in the early 1980s, William Watts (1981: 38) notes that "when asked to compare the nation's current life with that of the recent past, Americans tended to give the present lower marks, indicating a sense of national decline." In contrast to the optimism of the 1960s, Americans in the 1980s do not expect social conditions to improve in the near future, and they tend to have lower levels of aspiration for their children.

Historical circumstances are clearly implicated in evaluations of American life. For example, the fear of communism, the threat of war, the concern about moral decay, and the emphasis on family life declined in overall significance between 1964 and 1981; economic issues, on the other hand, became more important (Watts, 1981). Concerns about the prospects for a lower standard of living, for higher rates of inflation, and for higher rates of unemployment were among the emerging anxieties of the early 1980s. Political issues were replaced by issues that were primarily economic in character. Thus changes in the content of worries within a nation reflect shifting definitions of the problems that are likely to have an impact on the future course of societal events.

While surveys on the quality of life permit indexing overall trends, they also permit examining variations in perceptions of the past and future among subgroups of the population. For example, the analysis by Watts (1981) indicates that the decline in national confidence was greater among blacks than among whites. The prospect for ending discrimination had become increasingly elusive to many black Americans, and this is reflected in their growing pessimism about the future of the country. In contrast, the optimism of blacks about their personal futures has increased at a higher rate than for whites in recent years.

Variations in self-anchorage and perceptions of national trends also occur by age levels. Young adults (those between eighteen and twenty-nine years of age) tend to look much more negatively on America's recent past than do older Americans, and they rate their present lives well below the national norm. Young adults simply view their nation as having made little progress in recent years, and they give themselves relatively low scores on the self-anchorage scale. However, a distinguishing characteristic of American youth is their optimism about their personal futures: they expect their personal lives to improve much more over the next five years than do Americans in general. In contrast, the present looks much better to older Americans (those over fifty), and they evaluate the recent past in more positive terms. Older people perceive greater advances both for themselves and for their country in recent years; but personal futures they view with lessening optimism, especially those over sixty-five years of age.

2. Domains of Life Satisfaction

The types of activities that provide primary sources of meaning vary among individuals and among subgroups of the population. Some look for a sense of social purpose in their work activities, while others find the primary sources of meaning in leisure-time pursuits. The quest for peace of mind is important for some, while others value seeking stress-producing activities. The **domains of life satisfaction** are the many spheres of activities (family life, religion, entertainment, physical fitness, community involvement, and so on) that people pursue in efforts to enhance the qualities of their personal lives.

Within the diverse range of activities that serve as sources of meaning and purpose, most people share some major regions or domains of life. Family life and friendship are two basic regions within the sphere of intimate relationships; each confers identity and provides intrinsic rewards. While the proportion of unmarried people has increased in recent years, the vast majority of Americans (about 90 percent) do marry at some time or another. Financial situations, the qualities of housing, the places of residence, the states of physical health, and the uses of leisure are among the additional domains that command a great deal of attention. While there is no common pattern of concern to all Americans, these domains provide the settings for a great deal of human activity. They also provide major reference points for social psychological studies of the components that enter into an overall sense of well-being. (See Figure 15.1.)

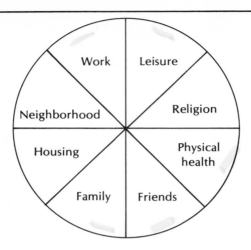

Individuals differ in the level of satisfaction derived from the various domains of their lives. How would you presently rate the above areas for their contributions to your overall sense of well-being? How do you expect these ratings to change over the next ten years?

FIGURE 15.1
Domains of Life Satisfaction

Research on the sense of psychological well-being indicates that Americans in general obtain greater satisfaction from family life than from any other social domain. Among married couples the overwhelming majority (about 75 percent) report being "completely satisfied" or "very satisfied" with their marriages. No other domain of social life evokes such a positive response, suggesting that married couples find greater sources of reward and meaning within marriage than in any other area (Campbell, 1981). The high levels of satisfaction with family life are perhaps due to the importance of the emotional supports that highly intimate relationships provide. Along these lines Angus Campbell (1981: 75) makes the following observation:

Marriage, of all human experiences, appears to have unrivaled potential for joy and torment, fulfillment and frustration. For most people the positives outweigh the negatives, and their feeling of the quality of their marriage contributes crucially to their perception of the quality of their lives.

In contrast to the high levels of satisfaction with intimate social relationships, the more impersonal domains of social life receive lower scores. Much lower satisfaction scores are reported for economic status, educational attainment, and place of residence. The low scores in these domains provide some important cues for an understanding of how individuals reach decisions on a sense of well-being. Standards of measurement are readily available for evaluating one's own position relative to that of others in areas of low satisfac-

---

BOX 15.2
Some Grounds for Determining Life Satisfaction

Outside observers may make inferences about the qualities of life for a given group of people that are at odds with the way the people think about themselves. Drawing on studies of social class and self-esteem, Morris Rosenberg and Leonard Pearlin (1978) note several principles used in making subjective evaluations. These include social comparison, reflected appraisals, self-perception theory, and psychological centrality.

Social comparison refers to making evaluations of our own circumstances by drawing on the attributes and qualities of others. For example, moderate-income families may think of themselves as being well off if they compare their own situation with that of the poor; but if they make comparisons with rich people, they may feel impoverished and deprived.

Reflected appraisals are our responses to ourselves as individuals from the standpoint of other people. Appraisals in this sense are based on a type of self-fulfilling prophecy: we tend to assess our own circumstances by drawing on the perceptions of others. We use our imaginations to take the perspectives of others and in this process we evaluate ourselves.

Self-perception theory is the set of insights into personal attributes derived from observation of our own behavior. We evaluate ourselves and our life circumstances in pretty much the same way that others form judgments of us—namely through observing our own behavior and interpreting its outcomes. Success or failure in the pursuit of goals provides a practical basis for determining the overall qualities of our lives.

Psychological centrality refers to assigning a greater degree of importance to some aspects of self, behavior, and life circumstances than to others. The individual constructs a scale of values to sort out his or her priorities. For some people money is most important for making evaluations; for others physical health receives top priority; while for still others friendship or family ties are at the top of the scale of values.

The many principles individuals use in evaluating the qualities of their lives suggest that multiple realities are involved in making judgments about life satisfaction. Interpersonal relationships, group comparisons, and self-concepts are among the many variables that enter into indivduals' experiences with their social environments.

Source: Morris Rosenberg and Leonard I. Pearlin, ''Social Class and Self-Esteem among Children and Adults,'' *American Journal of Sociology* 84 (July, 1978): 53–77.

tion. Regardless of current income levels, most people are well aware of others who are earning more. Similarly, the number of years of formal schooling provide a common referent for self-evaluations, and most Americans are not college graduates. In the areas of family life and friendship there are no such consensual measures for social comparisons. As a result, people may focus attention on the positive rewards that they obtain from intimate relationships without a clear understanding of how the quality of their own situations compare with those of others. (See Box 15.2.)

The domains of life that contribute most to overall life satisfaction vary by social circumstances and by cultural values, yet general patterns have emerged from several decades of research on American samples. Satisfaction with family life, marriage, friends, and work accounts for a great deal of what is known about the conditions promoting a sense of well-being. These are the areas of life that generate intrinsic rewards for many people. The domains relating to the external environment exert less influence in making overall evaluations of the level of happiness. The community, the neighborhood, housing, and the nation at large are certainly important in the thoughts and actions of individuals, but these domains contribute less to general life satisfaction than do the more intimate spheres of social relationships.

B. SOCIAL INDICATORS

Folk images of the good life are often directed toward objective social conditions and readily identifiable symbols. These include the notions that it is better to be rich than to be poor; that it is better to be college-educated than to be a high school dropout; that it is better to be in good physical condition than to be overweight; that it is better to live in a small town than to live in a big city; and that it is better to be married than to be divorced, widowed, or single. There is divided opinion, to be sure, on the circumstances promoting the good life. But there is little doubt that most people have given a great deal of thought to the sources of human happiness and to the conditions that would improve their own sense of well-being.

Social scientists have also given a great deal of attention to the conditions shaping the quality of life. Many government-sponsored studies have concentrated on "objective" indicators of the quality of life over the past fifty years. The concerns of the studies have been with changes in the overall qualities of social life and with variations in the quality of life among subgroups of the population. For example, indicators of the quality of life in given geographical areas have included the average level of education, life expectancy, infant mortality rate, median family income, extent of home ownership, suicide rate, crime rate, and frequency of civil disorder. While social psychologists recognize the importance of these objective criteria for determining the quality of life, they also view such studies as being incomplete unless the studies also

Sources of Human Happiness
A personal sense of well-being is shaped by evaluating both positive and negative experiences.

take into account the perceptions and subjective feelings of the people involved. A personal sense of well-being is often at odds with the objective conditions of social existence.

Social psychologists draw on **social indicators** to determine the level of correspondence between objective social conditions and subjective responses to them. In effect, a social indicator is a correlation. Social researchers are concerned with the ways in which differences in such specific indicators as income, education, physical health, and age level correlate with differences in the sense of well-being. The use of social indicators does not imply an assumption of causality. We can seldom say that a person's sense of well-being is caused by some identifiable condition. Instead, researchers are interested in the confidence of making better-than-chance predictions that people living under certain kinds of circumstances are more likely to be satisfied with their lives than are people living under other circumstances.

Several social indicators have been investigated in connection with the quality of life. These have included religion (Hadaway, 1978), participation in competitive sports (Snyder and Spreitzer, 1978), involvement in voluntary organizations (Palmore and Luikart, 1972), place of residence (Fischer, 1981), and gender (Gove, 1972). Each of these variables has been found to make a modest contribution to our understanding of the quality of life. However, the variables that have most consistently correlated with a sense of well-being have included the socioeconomic variables of education and income, conditions of physical health, and stages of the life cycle. Both positive and negative experiences accompany the activities in which people are engaged, and some circumstances offer more privileges and opportunities than do others.

1. Socioeconomic Status

The results of survey research over the past several decades have consistently indicated the overall advantage of education and income for the level of life satisfaction. People who have higher socioeconomic status are accorded prestige and respect in their communities; they have greater control over desired resources; they have more leeway in making choices and decisions; and they enjoy lifestyles that others envy and seek to emulate. Such advantages become reflected in a greater sense of psychological well-being for the rich compared to the poor and for the college-educated compared to those with only a high school education or less.

While the number of years of formal schooling has little effect on self-esteem among children, it is a significant correlate of life satisfaction among adults. The research of Morris Rosenberg and Leonard I. Pearlin (1978) suggests several reasons for the importance of education in adult life. A college degree confers a valued status on the individual, providing an advantage in terms of social comparison with those who have completed fewer years of formal schooling. Appraisals of self-worth are validated through the responses of others, and our society regards educational attainment as one of the major life accomplishments. A college diploma is achieved through personal efforts and provides proof of an individual's effectiveness in achieving desired goals.

The college diploma, however, provides no guarantee of an easy life. The results of survey research over the past several years indicate that the college degree fails to provide a buffer against negative feelings. In a summary review of these findings, Angus Campbell (1981: 61) observes that the "years of education do not appear to protect a person from seeing life as hard, feeling tied down, being frightened or worried, although they do reduce one's concerns about meeting household bills." The advantages of education are more evident in reports on positive experiences in the recent past. People with college degrees are more likely to remember being excited, pleased, proud, or happy than are those with lower levels of education.

The research of Ronald Kessler and Paul Cleary (1980) indicates that exposure to stressful life experiences varies very little by social class level. The importance of socioeconomic status lies primarily in differential capacities for coping with psychological distress. Such occurrences as illness in the family, trouble on the job, traffic tickets, or difficulties in one's sex life produce some level of psychological distress for everyone; but the emotional impact of these events and the coping capacities of individuals tend to vary by social class level. People with limited educational attainment tend to respond more intensely to the crises of life; and they have fewer resources for dealing with problematic situations. In contrast, the more highly educated have a greater range of psychological resources for coping with the stresses growing out of social living; they have a greater sense of personal effectiveness; and they have a higher level of tolerance for uncertainty and complexity.

The importance of social status for the quality of life stems from control over resources as well as from competence in problem solving. Although education is associated with the capacity for dealing with complexity (Kohn, 1977), income is a more direct reflection of control over resources. People with high incomes tend to report high levels of life satisfaction, regardless of educational level. Among those with high incomes, college graduates have no more advantages than those with less formal schooling; the level of life satisfaction is about the same. For those people below average in income, however, education does make an important difference. College graduates earning low incomes generally have a more positive sense of well-being than less-educated groups with low incomes (Campbell, 1981). Apparently, income has a different meaning for the college-educated than for other people. The educational experience possibly broadens the range of interests and concerns beyond those that are materialistic in character.

National surveys on life satisfaction in the United States over the past several decades have indicated, nevertheless, that the percentage of "happy" or "very happy" people increases with increasing levels of income (Campbell, 1981). Having "all the happiness a person can reasonably expect out of life" is closely associated with several materialistic values emphasized by most Americans. Ownership of a home on one's own land, ownership of a private automobile, long-distance vacation travel, financial security, creature comforts, and a wide range of consumer choices are among the advantages of wealth and income in our society. Insofar as materialistic values play an important part in the lifestyle aspirations of many Americans, it is not surprising that people with high incomes report high degrees of life satisfaction. (See Box 15.3.)

The relationship between income and life satisfaction, however, requires several qualifications. Having a relatively high income is not the same as being satisfied with one's income or with one's style of living. Many people with only modest incomes report being satisfied with their financial situations, while several of the affluent fail to reflect a generalized sense of well-being. The celebrated case of Howard Hughes and the lives of the Ewings on the television series *Dallas* clearly reflect the lack of a correspondence between wealth

BOX 15.3
Does Money Buy Happiness?

Richard Easterlin (1973) examined the paradox that what is true at the individual level may not necessarily be true for society as a whole. Increases in income may increase individual life satisfactions without increasing the overall sense of well-being within a nation. For example, in the United States between the late 1940s and 1970, the purchasing power of the American family had increased by about 60 percent. There is no evidence to indicate, however, that Americans were any happier in 1970 than they were in the late 1940s.

Easterlin noted that for many Americans the pursuit of happiness is equated with the pursuit of money and that materialistic values play an important part in definitions of the good life. The results of national surveys do indicate a modest correlation between level of income and reported level of life satisfaction; yet increases in the overall standard of living within the population have not contributed to corresponding increases in levels of happiness.

The basic reason for the gap between happiness and material well-being, according to Easterlin, lies in the vast changes that have occurred in the scale by which material well-being is judged. What concerns people the most are matters of everyday experiences rather than long-range, historical advances. Standards for evaluation have moved upward, and living conditions defined positively in our grandparent's day would be regarded by many as unacceptable today. People now think they need more, and such thinking is encouraged both by peer pressure and commercial advertising. The result is that perceived needs at the individual level have grown, and this upward shift has offset the effects of income growth on the sense of well-being for people in general.

Source: Richard A. Easterlin, "Does Money Buy Happiness?," *The Public Interest* 30 (Winter, 1973): 3–10.

and happiness. Thus while survey research has consistently found a relationship between income and life satisfaction, the correlations obtained are modest at best. Several variables other than income are important correlates of a sense of well-being.

2. Physical Health

People who have problems of physical impairment or disability do not find their lives to be as satisfying as those who are healthy. Physical health is an important fact of life, and disabilities frequently prevent individuals from doing many of the things they want to do. Several studies have found physical health to be a major determinant of life satisfaction, exceeding in importance either income or education for a sense of well-being (Palmore and Luikart, 1972; Clemente and Sauer, 1976). Apparently being healthy increases the prospects for leading an active life, for being a socially valued person, and for pursuing goals with a reasonable degree of confidence.

The overall relationship between physical health and life satisfaction is clear and definite, but several facets of this relationship need to be clarified. The general state of health for the American population has improved substantially over the course of the twentieth century, but improvements at the community and national levels have not been accompanied by perceptions of physical well-being at the individual level. Collectively we may be "doing better but feeling worse," as researchers in the field of health have frequently noted. A significant gap exists between the objective facts about health and the subjective responses of individuals.

Improvements in the health of the general population have been impressive. Several diseases such as smallpox, polio, and tuberculosis have been brought under control through the results of medical research; and improvements in nutrition and sanitation have contributed to the health of the nation. The life expectancy at birth has increased enormously from 1900 to 1980: more than twenty-five years have been added to the average life expectancy

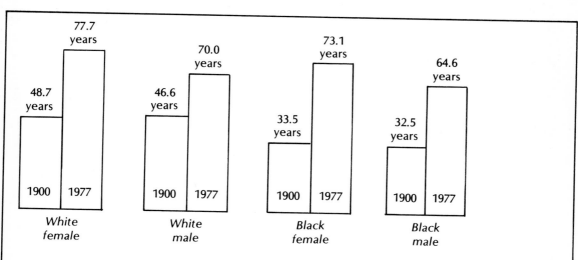

Source: Data from René Dubos, "Health as Ability to Function," in Norman Cousins (ed.), Reflections of America: Commemorating the Statistical Abstract Centennial, Washington, D.C.: Bureau of the Census, 1980, page 107.

FIGURE 15.2
Life Expectancy at Birth for the United States in 1900 and 1977 by Race and Sex

of the white population, and the changes are even more dramatic among blacks. The average life expectancy for blacks more than doubled, increasing from 33.5 to 73.1 years for black females and from 32.5 and 64.6 years for black males (Dubos, 1980). Thus if we concentrate only on the objective indicators of the quality of life, we would be likely to conclude that substantial gains have been made in recent years. (See Figure 15.2.)

Such a conclusion, however, would not be fully warranted. Improvements in health by objective criteria have occurred along with increasing demand for medical services and new forms of anxiety about health-related problems (Dubos, 1980). The lack of exercise, the consequences of cigarette smoking, the increase in air and water pollution, and the use of chemical food preservatives are among the recent health-related concerns of Americans. Exercise, jogging, vitamin supplement, and weight-watching programs are among the

Physical Fitness
Some people regard physical fitness as being very important for an overall sense of well-being. Those who participate in a "fun run" may be motivated less by expectations of winning than by a concern with proving their capacity to complete the 10,000 meter race.

activities that reflect efforts to improve health and correct deficiencies in lifestyles.

The results of a national survey by Erdman Palmore and Clark Luikart (1972) indicates that self-rated health is a more important correlate of life satisfaction than are the health ratings given by physicians. Many people who face physical impairments as measured by objective criteria do not typically define their lives as being miserably unhappy. Some who have health problems see themselves as happy and serene individuals, while others approach their life circumstances with despair. The variations in response are in part due to definitions of pain and what people expect out of life. Infirmities and disorders that people accepted as inevitable in the past are less tolerable by modern standards. (See Box 15.4.)

BOX 15.4
Cultural Definitions of Pain

The meanings given to the human experience of pain vary by social situations and cultural definitions. The pain experienced in childbirth has meanings that differ from the pain associated with injuries in sports or warfare. Self-inflicted pain (body mutilations) is defined differently than the spontaneous pain engendered by illness or accidental injury. These variations in the social definitions of pain suggest that humans give meanings to pain that go far beyond physiological experiences alone.

Mark Zborowski (1975) observed responses to pain among hospital patients in New York City and concluded that the definition and management of pain varied among ethnic subgroups. Confirming the impressions of the medical staff, Zborowski's findings indicate that patients with Italian or Jewish backgrounds tended to reflect a more emotional response and a greater sensitivity to pain than did other subgroups such as those of Irish descent or those from "older American" stock.

Zborowski's analysis indicates, however, that similar emotional displays may be associated with important differences in the definition and the meaning of pain. Patients of Italian background were oriented toward the immediacy of pain, toward the management of discomfort, and toward seeking relief through the use of medication. They had a high degree of confidence in doctors, and relief from the symptoms of pain usually had a calming effect. Patients of Jewish background, by way of contrast, continued to manifest anxiety after the pain had been relieved. They were concerned with the habit-forming potential of medication, with the distinction between temporary relief and a cure, and with the incompetence of doctors. They viewed pain as a long-term threat to health and employment, and their emotional responses were designed to win sympathy from family members.

Source: Mark Zborowski, "Cultural Components in Responses to Pain," in Saul D. Feldman and Gerald W. Thielbar (eds.), *Life Styles: Diversity in American Society,* Boston: Little, Brown, 1975, pp. 368–382.

The annual surveys conducted by the National Center for Health Statistics indicate that about 20 percent of the adult population face some significant disabling condition. The results also show that young adults are the healthiest age category of the American population and that the seriousness of disabilities increases with increasing age (Campbell, 1981). The effectiveness of control over many diseases has resulted in changes in the primary causes of death among young adults at specific age levels. For example, in the 1980s suicide will be the most likely cause of death for the thirty-year-old white female, and murder will be the most likely cause of death for the twenty-year-old black male. Suicide is second only to accidents as the leading cause of death among college students (Dubos, 1980).

If physical health were the primary ingredient of a sense of well-being, young adults would score much higher on life satisfaction than those who are older. The research findings from the 1970s and 1980s fail to confirm this view. National surveys conducted in the early 1960s did indicate higher levels of life satisfaction for younger Americans (Bradburn, 1969). By the 1970s, however, the advantages of youth vanished. Surveys conducted during the 1970s and the early 1980s clearly indicate that middle-aged and older Americans were more highly satisfied with their lives than were younger people. With the exception of satisfaction with physical health, which does favor the young, increasing age is conducive to higher levels of satisfaction with all other major domains of life—with financial situation, with family life, with place of residence, and with uses of leisure. The greater satisfactions among middle-aged and older people may stem from the higher levels of stability in their personal lives and from the payoffs provided by a lifetime of accomplishments. The greater sense of stress among young people possibly stems from the many crucial life decisions that remain to be made and from the hemming-in effects of child-care responsibilities during the early years of family formation.

C. URBAN ALIENATION

The quality of life in the United States as measured by several objective indicators would seem to suggest that social conditions are improving. The purchasing power of the American family has increased substantially over the past several decades; a larger percentage of the population is living to an older age; fewer people are required to work at physically demanding jobs; and the time available for leisure pursuits has become more abundant. Although such positive features of the twentieth century are among the basic social facts, no evidence indicates that people are happier or that the overall sense of psychological well-being has increased.

To the contrary, the results of survey research conducted over the past several decades indicate that levels of alienation increased during a time period in which the overall standards of living were going up. The increases were

especially evident within the political sphere. The distrust of public officials
and the sense of political helplessness increased among Americans between
1952 and the early 1970s (House and Mason, 1975). But the increasing sense of

---

BOX 15.5
On the Meaning of Alienation

Melvin Seeman noted that the themes of alienation have come to occupy a prominent place in reflections on modern social life. Within this context, Seeman observed that the concept of alienation is being defined in several different ways.
From his inventory of definitions Seeman concluded that six major meanings of the
alienation concept are in current use in social psychological inquiry. A brief summary of them is presented here.

Powerlessness—feelings of helplessness on the part of the individual; a low expectancy for control through personal efforts over the events in which one is
engaged; a sense of being manipulated and controlled by social forces external to oneself; perceptions of being trapped.

Meaninglessness—the feeling that predictions cannot be made with confidence,
that one's understanding of events is inadequate, or that social life is incoherent and chaotic; the lack of a sense of purpose; an inability to define a
clear set of goals for onself; seeing social events as overwhelmingly complex.

Normlessness—the expectancy that socially unapproved behavior is necessary in
goal attainment; the perception that social norms are ineffective in regulating
conduct; attitudes of suspicion in social relationships; distrust of experts,
repairpersons, public officials, or strangers; fear of criminal victimization.

Isolation—a sense of loneliness or a feeling of apartness from others; emphasis on
the impersonality and anonymity of modern social life; the perception that
others are unfriendly or disinterested; the perception of social relationships as
undependable; having to rely on one's own resources in times of trouble; the
lack of a sense of community or belonging.

Cultural Estrangement—a sense of disdain or rejection of the lifestyles that prevail
in one's society; assigning a low reward value to mass entertainment, competitive sports, vacation travel, or other activities regarded as meaningful and
rewarding by most people; a rejection of materialistic values; a personal
preference for living at some other time or place; seeing oneself as a stranger
in the modern world.

Self-Estrangement—an inability to derive intrinsic rewards from the activities in
which one is engaged; the lack of a sense of creativity or fulfillment in the
work sphere, in family life, or in the pursuit of academic assignments; the
feeling that one's personal life is fragmented; an inability to identify with the
roles being played.

Source: Melvin Seeman, "Alienation Studies," *Annual Review of Sociology* 1 (1975):
91–124.

despair was not limited to the political sphere. There was also an increased distrust of basic institutions, an increased fear of criminal victimization (Erskine, 1974), and an increased sense of complexity and chaos in the social realm (Zeller, Neal, and Groat, 1980).

The negative feelings that accompany relatively high standards of living can be summed up under the idea of urban alienation (Seeman, 1971). The use of urbanism as the descriptive reference for alienation is based on the importance of the city and the lifestyle it represents for individual assessments of modern society. These assessments include the perception of norms too weak to effectively regulate conduct, the sense of loneliness in the midst of strangers, the inability to understand adequately the interrelatedness of events, and the feeling of powerlessness in an unresponsive environment.

The urban way of life symbolizes modern society in several respects (Wirth, 1980). With the increasing centralization of services, more and more people have come to live and carry out their major life activities within areas of high population diversity and density. The central cities and their satellite suburbs have become central places for trade and commerce, for shopping and banking, for work and play. To be sure, the city does not represent the totality of American life, but it does reflect the forms of social organization and the diversity of lifestyles associated with modern social living. Wherever one resides, in a rural area or elsewhere, the impact of the urban way of life is unmistakable. The individual's sense of comfort or despair with contemporary social life is likely to require coming to terms, in some way or another, with the circumstances of urban life.

We may characterize the major forms of urban alienation as styles of cognitive mapping, definitions of social situations, or personal understandings of the events in which one is engaged. The central meanings of alienation in the literature of social psychology have been summarized by Melvin Seeman (1972) as powerlessness, meaninglessness, normlessness, isolation, cultural estrangement, and self-estrangement. Seeman regarded these varieties of alienation as reactions to modern forms of social organization, as well as determinants of several specific forms of social behavior. The concepts of alienation have potential relevance for understanding the problems of stimulus overload, suspicion and distrust in social relationships, and feelings of loneliness and isolation. (See Box 15.5.)

1. Information Overload

In a psychological analysis of the urban experience, Stanley Milgram (1980) emphasizes the theme of overloaded cognitive capacities. Milgram borrowed the concept of overload from systems analysis, where it refers to the inability of a system to function effectively because of too many inputs or because the inputs are coming so rapidly that the system is not able to cope with them.

Information Overload
Neon signs in urban settings sometimes bombard the senses with more information than the individual is capable of processing. Blocking out or selectively ignoring environmental stimuli is a necessary adaptation for urban dwellers.

For example, an electrical system can become overloaded from the increased use of air conditioners on a hot summer day; a transportation system can fail to function effectively if a great deal of vacation travel is added to work traffic; and a telephone system can become overloaded if an unusually large number of personal calls are made during the business day. When applied to the urban experiences of individuals, **information overload** refers to a state of being overstimulated, to a bombardment of the senses by a wide range of stimulants, and to the occurrence of social encounters in rapid succession.

In a classical essay entitled "The Metropolis and Mental Life," Georg Simmel (1950) called attention to several adaptive responses to the urban environment. The individual relates to the city as a total entity only in a highly selective sense. Not noticing, not caring, and not helping are adaptive responses to the size and complexity of urban areas. Simmel described these responses as reflecting "a blasé attitude," and it is manifested in disregarding the street people, in ignoring appeals for help from those in trouble, and in failing to notice the blatant neon signs that advertise goods and services. The individual comes to direct attention only toward those activities of his or her immediate concern.

According to Simmel, a basic psychological characteristic of urban residents is their sophisticated ability to select from an enormous range of environmental stimuli. City dwellers draw tight boundaries around the objects of their concern, around social relationships, and around focused events. They minimize the problem of overload by getting to the point in social transactions. The storytelling and exchanges of personal experiences that have typified rural and small-town life have diminished in frequency with the spread of urban culture. Social relationships have come to be characterized by a greater degree of impersonality and anonymity.

According to Alan Berger (1978), urban residents respond to their environments with their heads rather than with their hearts. Using one's head is a reflection of being on guard and having the capacity to give quick and adequate response to very limited environmental cues. These are the qualities that give the appearance of sophistication and intellectuality to urban dwellers. The intellectuality of city life grows out of the need for a system of classification that permits a decisive response to very limited information about persons, objects, and events. The decisive response is necessary for preserving a coherent sense of self under conditions of uncertainty and for aligning personal behavior with the activities of many people.

Ignace Feuerlicht (1980) observes that the heightened stimulation from external inputs results in the **fragmentation** of the self in urban environments. The life-world of the individual becomes internally divided in response to relentless environmental demands. Having too many interests to pursue all of them, having many desires and wants that remain unfulfilled, and being pulled in too many directions at the same time are among the ingredients of stress and overload that require setting priorities. Time and energies are limited, and the sense of being spread too thin precludes feelings of comfort with one's life circumstances. It becomes necessary to neglect some goals in order to pursue others with greater enthusiasm.

The sensory stimulation to which Simmel referred can be contained through developing attitudes of selective indifference to one's surroundings. In any given case the individual can reduce the external inputs into his or her life-world by turning off the television set, by refusing to read daily newspapers, and by withdrawing from the public spheres of social life. Retreat into the secure atmosphere of a privately created world permits avoiding the complexities of urban environments, but such a simplification is achieved at a considerable cost to oneself and to one's community.

A large number of people tend to relegate concerns for the affairs of their community to positions of low priority. Richard Sennett (1976) has described

THE QUALITY OF LIFE   499

this process as "the fall of public man," here referring to the psychological emphasis on the private sphere in the modern world. The conditions of indifference toward public affairs is reflected in several ways. For example, in the
autumn of 1980 several million more Americans watched the television episode that revealed who shot the character J.R. than voted for all of the candidates combined in the presidential election. While political events have important consequences for the nation, individuals frequently assign them low
priority in their immediate concerns. The failure to be informed about political events, the failure to contribute to political campaigns, and the failure to
vote in elections are among the many expressions of the apathetic view toward
the public spheres. In its extreme form, political apathy is expressed in the total
lack of concern for the affairs and governance of one's community (Dean, 1960;
Finifter, 1972). (See Box 15.6.)

BOX 15.6
Privacy and Secrecy: A Conceptual Comparison

Some measure of suspicion and distrust in social relationships is promoted by the
principles of **secrecy** in human affairs. Carol Warren and Barbara Laslett (1977) observed that secrecy involves concealing qualities, attributes, or information that
would be negatively evaluated if it were disclosed. Social relationships among
strangers are shaped by uncertainty over the scope of the secrets that might prevail.
In the absence of adequate information about other people, one's response is frequently to avoid them, out of a concern with personal safety and a desire to avoid
complicating one's personal life.

Warren and Laslett make an important distinction between secrecy and privacy. The private sphere is a social creation in which the uninvited are excluded,
and individuals are granted by others the right to pursue interests and activities
apart from public view. The domains of privacy and secrecy are separate in our
society and this separation may be noted in the contrasting social definitions of
homosexuality and sexual intercourse in marriage. Homosexuals frequently surround themselves with secrecy as a means of avoiding social stigma and the sanctions that might be imposed by those who define this form of sexuality as deviant,
abnormal, or bizarre. Heterosexuality, by way of contrast, is defined as normal as
long as sexual intercourse is performed in private between consenting adults.

The major difference between privacy and secrecy lies in the perceived moral
content of the activities concealed. Privacy involves a legal right to pursue personal
interests after public obligations have been fulfilled. By way of contrast, there are no
legal rights to secrecy. Secrecy is an extreme form of concealment in that the very
existence of secrets is withheld from others.

Source: Carol Warren and Barbara Laslett, "Privacy and Secrecy: A Conceptual Comparison," *Journal of Social Issues* 33, no. 3 (1977): 43–51.

Social psychologists see a correlation between the causes of political apathy and the causes of urban alienations (Dean, 1960). Political issues may appear to be incoherent if individuals are exposed to counterarguments from several different sources. If the individual's minimal standards for clarity in decision making are not met, the individual may choose to avoid politics altogether rather than to struggle with complex social issues. Further, those people who are distrustful of government may not take official statements at face value but direct attention toward hidden motives, toward political corruption and deception, and toward uses of public power for private ends (Gamson, 1968; Finifter, 1972).

2. Suspicion and Distrust

The attitudes of suspicion and distrust are additional expressions of urban alienation. The individual looks on control over events as residing outside of his or her own hands and regards the normative order as being ineffective in regulating conduct. Suspicion and distrust are states of mind that grow out of the heterogeneity of people who make up an urban environment (Wirth, 1980). The city is a mixture of people who differ in national origins, in racial classifications, and in social class. The diversity of underlying values, attitudes, and norms prevent the individual from assuming that others also share his or her own understanding of events.

The impersonality and anonymity in social relationships permits freedom of movement and provides a great deal of latitude for social experimentation. Alternative lifestyles are tolerated to a much greater degree in the city than in traditional communities (Berger, 1978). The permissiveness of urban environments makes them attractive to many types of people, including those who have a social blemish, those oriented toward a life of crime, and those involved in the creative arts. The confusion stemming from the diversity of people and the rapid pace of living results in the acceptance of insecurity and instability as routine aspects of everyday life.

The suspicion and distrust represents a lack of unity and coherence in the urban environment. The size of the metropolis and the diversity of its population tend to have overwhelming consequences for the lone individual. The lack of a shared sense of moral community requires the individual to rely heavily on personal resources in the course of everyday life. Systems of social support may not be available when needed; as a consequence the individual develops a cautious attitude toward the many unknown people in the surrounding environment.

Attitudes of suspicion and distrust tend to be reflected in social relationships among strangers. As Alfred Schutz (1960) noted, strangeness and familiarity are categories in our own interpretations of the world. The stranger is an individual whose social background is neither known nor understood, and as a result his or her loyalties and commitments remain in doubt. The doubtful loyalty of the stranger is prompted not only by awareness of such external symbols as speaking a different language or wearing a different style of clothing, but also by the suspicion that the stranger may not share our own set of values, norms, and understandings. Hostility toward Cuban refugees, an unwillingness to admit the Boat People, opposition to interracial marriages, and resistance to open housing we can understand as an outgrowth of the distrust of strangers. Diversities in cultural backgrounds may be valued on a college campus, where a shared interest in the learning process has a unifying effect. But the presence of strangers (migrants, transients, and immigrants) in an urban environment is likely to engender fears and anxieties for many people. Familiarity creates a sense of comfort and security, while exposure to persons and events out of the ordinary tends to raise the levels of anxiety. The distrust of strangers reflects an attempt to hold on to traditional assumptions about everyday life under circumstances in which changes are occurring.

Being cautious in dealing with people, being on guard against being taken in, avoiding unfamiliar neighborhoods, and not going out alone at night are among the responses to fears and doubts about strangers. The research of Claude Fischer (1973) suggests that the psychological world of urban dwellers is organized around immediate networks of social relationships rather than around the totality of city life. Neighborhood identification (Guterbock, 1980), membership in voluntary associations, the bonds of kinship, and the formation of friendship ties (Tomeh, 1964) are among the networks that reduce the impersonality of urban life. While these forms of organization provide systems of mutual support and integrative experiences for individuals, they do not go very far in producing a coherent sense of community or a sense of comfort with the totality of social life. Instead, those people comfortably entrenched within their own networks of social relationships may hold attitudes of distrust for "most people."

The movement outward from the central city to the suburbs represents a selective attempt to minimize the heterogeneity and complexity of urban living. Upward mobility for urban residents has been disproportionately associated with movement to the suburbs in the quest for better housing and a more desirable lifestyle. Over the past several decades the suburbs have had a special appeal to young people in the early years of family formation. A major attraction of the suburbs is their perceived safety and desirability as neighborhoods for the rearing of children. The socialization of children may occur without exposure to the corrupting influences of urban life.

While housing developments and building codes have contributed to the appearance of uniformity and standardization in suburbs, residential patterns do not go far in reducing the problems of alienation. The appearance of homogeneity in suburbia masks the many different problems and interests of those who reside there. Research studies have shown that suburban residents do not differ significantly in their attitudes and values from central city residents of the same social class standing and age level (Berger, 1978). The influences of urbanism cannot be erased by establishing residence within a more homogeneous neighborhood. The influences growing out of a mass society preclude the development of self-contained communities as exclusive sources of meaning and integration. Whether one resides in a suburb, a small town, a rural area, or elsewhere, decisive events of the larger society intrude into daily lives and exert an impact upon one's sense of well-being.

3. Bystander Apathy

The complexity of modern society tends to produce many more spectators than active participants in social events. Observing rather than acting requires less effort, involves less of a threat, and eliminates the likelihood of being held accountable for personal conduct. Doing nothing reduces the risk of making a mistake. In many cases the failure to act stems from generalized feelings of helplessness. Such states of mind have been examined extensively by social psychologists following dramatic reports in the news of bystanders failing to provide help for people in trouble. In cases where it was clearly within the capacities of bystanders to provide aid for those in trouble, none came forward to do so.

The Kitty Genovese case has become the most widely discussed instance of **bystander apathy**. There have been many other cases, but the circumstances surrounding this particular murder case have been drawn on for examining the moral conscience of the city as well as for clarifying certain aspects of human behavior. On the night of March 13, 1964, Kitty Genovese was attacked by a stranger on the street of a respectable neighborhood in New York City as she was returning home from work. Over a thirty-five-minute period she screamed many times for help while being stabbed repeatedly. During this time interval, thirty-eight of her neighbors witnessed the incident, but not one intervened in any way. The first call to the police was made only after Kitty Genovese was dead.

Although the death of Kitty Genovese occurred many years ago, the incident continues to evoke a great deal of interest and concern among social psychologists. Two decades of research have provided several insights into the conditions surrounding this and other examples of bystander apathy. The research has been instructive, not only for a clarification of human nature and for an understanding of how cities may differ from other places, but more importantly for a demonstration of the situational character of social behavior. Intervention or nonintervention does not stem so much from altruism, selfishness, or other personal qualities as from the context in which the need for help arises.

From many studies in both experimental and natural settings, several situational factors have been identified that promote or inhibit helping behavior. These include the ambiguity of the situation, the cues taken from observing the nonintervention of others, the diffusion of responsibility, and the fear of making a mistake (Latane and Darley, 1970).

The ambiguity of the situation is one of the initial factors in responses to emergencies. Before intervention can occur, people must notice an event and must identify a need for help. Smoke pouring from a building may indicate a fire or it may be an unusual visual effect from the heating system; an epileptic seizure may be misinterpreted as drunkenness; an attack by an assailant may be dismissed as a lover's quarrel; or a plea for help may be defined as part of a con game. In such ambiguous situations, there is a tendency to take cues from others who are present. Social influences tend to operate. If others are responding calmly to an event, or if they seem to be unconcerned, the individual is likely to dismiss the need for any overt line of action on his or her part (Mynatt and Sherman, 1975).

The diffusion of responsibility is an additional variable in bystander apathy (Latane and Darley, 1970). From a commonsense view it would appear that the larger the number of people present in a situation the greater the probability the person or persons in trouble would receive help from at least someone. Research studies indicate that this is not the case. The plight of a victim receives a more sympathetic response if there is only a single observer. If only one person is present, he or she cannot shift responsibility to someone else, and is more likely to provide assistance. But as the number of observers increases, the sense of responsibility is reduced for any particular individual. The notion that there is safety in numbers may hold in many cases, but those urgently in need of help are more likely to receive it if only a small number of people are present.

Audiences tend to have an inhibiting effect in emergency situations. Intervention by any particular bystander is less likely to occur because others would witness the involvement. There is always the possibility of making a mistake or of defining the situation inappropriately. A person may sense that he or she lacks the skills for providing effective help, that intervention would only make the situation worse, or that he or she would be held accountable for inappropriate conduct. To avoid the possibility of embarrassment, people in large groups suspend the usual norm of social responsibility (Berkowitz, 1978). The obligation to help those in need is superseded by the social pressures against being noticed, standing out, or doing the wrong thing in a crowd situation.

The studies of bystander apathy should not be interpreted as reflecting dimensions of human cruelty and selfishness, but as indicating that people impose their own forms of rationality on ambiguous situations. Some people do provide help to strangers when it is needed, and considerable evidence could also be assembled to reflect aspects of altruistic behavior. Public requests for blood donors usually receive a favorable response, and sizable contributions are made to many charities each year on a purely voluntary basis. The retreat into the private sphere, and the pursuit of self-interests, would seem to reflect reasonable responses to increases in the scope, complexity, and rapid pace of modern social living.

In an address to the nation in the summer of 1979, President Carter made reference to America's sense of malaise, or "the crisis of national spirit." He noted the results of survey research that showed growing concerns about the nation's future, about social drift, and about the prospects for mastery and control in the political realm. Such concerns reflect the difficulties of individuals in developing an adequate grasp of the totality of modern social life. Feelings of helplessness, the lack of a clear sense of social purpose, and the absence of community are among the states of mind that enter into collective evaluations of the qualify of life. Chapter 16 will turn to these concerns by examining the nature of relationships between the individual and society.

SUMMARY

Social psychologists study the quality of life by concentrating on how individuals perceive and evaluate their life circumstances. Researchers have concluded that neither money, health, marriage, nor any other single activity provides an exclusive basis for a sense of well-being. A gap frequently exists between such objective indicators as money, health, or education and such subjective indicators as perceived happiness or the sense of well-being. Increases in the standard of living over the course of the twentieth century have not been accompanied by corresponding increases in human happiness.

Research on self-anchorage indicates that people tend to see themselves as moving closer to the best life possible over the past five years; further, most expect to make additional advances over the next five years. These results show the importance of hope in an individual's sense of well-being. While most people are optimistic about their personal futures, they are also pessimistic about the future of their country; this suggests that individuals tend to perceive their personal circumstances as separate from broader societal events.

The sense of well-being includes not only an overall evaluation of life circumstances but also the level of satisfaction with such separate domains as finances, physical health, and uses of leisure. Research studies indicate that Americans generally obtain greater satisfaction from family life than from any other social domain. Income, occupation, and education are important correlates of life satisfaction, but their contribution to an overall sense of well-being are less important than such intimate relationships as friendship and marriage.

Perceptions of the quality of life include both positive and negative evaluations. The term urban alienations is used by social psychologists to describe the forms of estrangement growing out of modern social organization. Such estrangement includes the problems of information overload, suspicion and distrust in social relationships, and feelings of loneliness and isolation. The use of urbanism as the descriptive referent for alienation is based on the importance of the city and the lifestyle it represents in modern society.

The research of social psychologists on bystander apathy indicates that the failure of bystanders to provide help for people in trouble stems from the ambiguity of the situation, the diffusion of responsibility, and the inhibiting effects of an audience. People retreat into the private sphere and the pursuit of self-interests as a response to the complexities of modern social living.

BASIC TERMS

Well-being	**Psychological centrality**
Self-anchorage	**Social indicators**
Domains of life satisfaction	**Information overload**
Social comparison	**Fragmentation**
Reflected appraisal	**Secrecy**
Self-perception theory	**Bystander apathy**

REFERENCES

Andrews, Frank M. and Stephen B. Withey
    1976 *Social Indicators of Well-Being,* New York: Plenum Press.
Berger, Alan S.
    1978 *The City,* Dubuque, Iowa: Wm. C. Brown.
Berkowitz, Leonard
    1978 "Decreased Helpfulness with Increased Group Size Through Lessening the Needy Individual's Dependency," *Journal of Personality* 46 (June): 299–310.
Bradburn, Norman M.
    1969 *The Structure of Psychological Well-Being,* Chicago: Aldine.
Campbell, Angus
    1981 *The Sense of Well-Being in America,* New York: McGraw-Hill.
Cantril, Hadley
    1965 *The Pattern of Human Concerns,* New Brunswick, N.J.: Rutgers University Press.
Clemente, Frank and William J. Sauer
    1976 "Life Satisfaction in the United States," *Social Forces* 54 (March): 621–631.
Dean, Dwight G.
    1960 "Alienation and Political Apathy," *Social Forces* 38 (March): 185–189.
Dubos, Rene
    1980 "Health as Ability to Function," in Norman Cousins (ed.), *Reflections of America: Commemorating the Statistical Abstract Centennial,* Washington, D.C.: Bureau of the Census, pp. 105–112.
Easterlin, Richard A.
    1973 "Does Money Buy Happiness?," *The Public Interest* 30 (Winter): 3–10.
Erskine, Hazel

1974 "The Polls: Corruption in Government," *Public Opinion Quarterly* 37 (Winter): 628–644.

Feuerlicht, Ignace
1980 *Alienation: From the Past to the Future,* Westport, Conn.: Greenwood Press.

Finifter, Ada W.
1972 *Alienation and the Social System,* New York: John Wiley.

Fischer, Claude S.
1981 "The Public and Private Worlds of City Life," *American Sociological Review* 46 (June): 306–316.
1973 "On Urban Alienations and Anomie," *American Sociological Review* 38 (June): 311–326.

Gamson, William A.
1968 *Power and Discontent,* Homewood, Ill.: Dorsey Press.

Gove, Walter R.
1972 "The Relationship Between Sex Roles, Marital Status, and Mental Illness," *Social Forces* 51: 34–44.

Guterbock, Thomas
1980 *Machine Politics in Transition,* Chicago: University of Chicago Press.

Hadaway, Christopher Kirk
1978 "Life Satisfaction and Religion," *Social Forces* 57 (December): 636–643.

House, James S. and William M. Mason
1975 "Political Alienation in America, 1952–1968," *American Sociological Review* 40 (April): 123–147.

Kessler, Ronald C. and Paul D. Cleary
1980 "Social Class and Psychological Distress," *American Sociological Review* 45 (June): 463–468.

Kohn, Melvin L.
1977 *Class and Conformity,* Chicago: University of Chicago Press.

Latane, Bibb and John M. Darley
1970 *The Unresponsive Bystander: Why Doesn't He Help?,* New York: Appleton-Century-Crofts.

Milgram, Stanley
1980 "The Urban Experience: A Psychological Analysis," in George Gmelch and Walter P. Zenner (eds.), *Urban Life,* New York: St. Martin's Press, pp. 48–57.

Mynatt, Clifford and Steven J. Sherman
1975 "Responsibility Attribution in Groups and Individuals: A Direct Test of the Diffusion of Responsibility Hypothesis," *Journal of Personality and Social Psychology* 32 (December): 1111–1118.

Palmore, Erdman and Clark Luikart
1972 "Health and Social Factors Related to Life Satisfaction," *Journal of Health and Social Behavior* 13 (March): 68–79.

Rosenberg, Morris, and Leonard I. Pearlin
1978 "Social Class and Self-Esteem among Children and Adults," *American Journal of Sociology* 84 (July): 53–77.

Schutz, Alfred
1960 "The Stranger," in Maurice R. Stein, Arthur J. Vidich, and David M. White (eds.), *Identity and Anxiety,* Glencoe, Ill.: The Free Press, 98–109.

Seeman, Melvin
1975 "Alienation Studies," *Annual Review of Sociology* 1 (1975): 91–124.

1972 "Alienation and Engagement," in Angus Campbell and Philip E. Converse (eds.), *The Human Meaning of Social Change*, New York: Russell Sage.
1971 "The Urban Alienations: Some Dubious Theses from Marx to Marcuse," *Journal of Personality and Social Psychology* 19 (August): 135–143.
Sennett, Richard
1976 *The Fall of Public Man*, New York: Vintage Books.
Simmel, Georg
1950 *The Sociology of Georg Simmel* (trans. and ed. by Kurt Wolff), New York: The Free Press.
Snyder, Eldon E. and Elmer Spreitzer
1978 *Social Aspects of Sport*, Englewood Cliffs, N.J.: Prentice-Hall.
Suttles, Gerald D.
1968 *The Social Order of the Slum*, Chicago: University of Chicago Press.
Tomeh, Aida K.
1964 "Informal Group Participation and Residential Patterns," *American Journal of Sociology* 70 (July): 28–35.
Warren, Carol and Barbara Laslett
1977 "Privacy and Secrecy: A Conceptual Comparison," *Journal of Social Issues* 33, no. 3: 43–51.
Watts, William
1981 "Americans' Hopes and Fears: The Future Can Fend for Itself," *Psychology Today* 15 (September): 36–48.
Wirth, Louis
1980 "Urbanism as a Way of Life," in George Gmelch and Walter P. Zenner (eds.), *Urban Life*, New York: St. Martin's Press, pp. 9–25.
Zborowski, Mark
1975 "Cultural Components in Responses to Pain," in Saul D. Feldman and Gerald W. Theilbar (eds.), *Life Styles: Diversity in American Society*, Boston: Little, Brown, pp. 368–382.
Zeller, Richard A., Arthur G. Neal, and H. Theodore Groat
1980 "On the Reliability and Stability of Alienation Measures," *Social Forces* 58 (June): 1195–1204.

16

What to look for in this chapter:

What are the primary uses of social psychology?
Why is the social construction of reality necessary?
What are some of the basic human concerns?
What are the major types of freedom?

The Promise of Social Psychology

The completion of a course in social psychology should provide an occasion to reflect on the journey traveled and on what lies ahead. Students sometimes study a particular subject to meet a requirement, to complete a course, and then to be done with it. If you are able to put aside the subject matter of social psychology, once the final exams are taken and the course is over, then this undertaking has been a failure. Its primary purpose has been to introduce you to the richly varied subject matter of social psychology and to provide you with a new set of perspectives on the human condition. This textbook has raised many questions and given some answers. If it has been successful, you will continue to ponder the topics that have been discussed and draw on them in later life as special situations or occasions develop.

The central theme of the course has been reality construction in its many phases and aspects. We do not live in a world of solid facts or objective reality but in a symbolic world that we create individually and collectively. Definitions of the situation, placebos, stereotypes, management of impressions, power dependency, justifications, and excuses are among the realities of everyday life. We all face the problems of separating the genuine from the spurious, the valid from the invalid, the authentic from the inauthentic. The resolutions we make of these problems shape the qualities of our lives, determine our confidence levels in making decisions and pursuing goals, and reflect our degrees of comfort with living in modern society.

The basic message of the course has been that humans are characterized by consciousness and awareness and that they selectively give meaning to the objects and events in the world around them. The aim has not been to tell you how to live your life, how to be happy and well adjusted, nor how to apply social psychology in business or pleasure. However, social psychology does have such practical applications, and an understanding of social psychology is one of the more practical forms of learning in our society. But to specify what these applications should be depends on your own system of values and the values held by the significant people in your lives.

The research findings of social psychology become a part of communal knowledge and they are available on a free, open, and democratic basis for use by anyone for whatever purpose. Research findings may be used in business to manipulate customers for commercial purposes, in industry to increase the productivity of workers, and in government to form public policy and manage discontent. The vast majority of social psychologists do not advocate such uses of their findings. The underlying assumption of most social psychologists is that the free access and availability of knowledge will in the long-run lead to a betterment of the human condition; that human subjects will benefit, rather than be harmed, from permitting social psychologists to enter into their life-worlds for research purposes. At the same time we should recognize the possibility that social psychology can be used by business corporations for commercial purposes or by governmental agencies for the purpose of manipulation and social control.

It is true that employment for social psychologists is provided primarily by the government, either through the teaching jobs supplied by state-assisted universities and colleges or through the research projects funded by governmental agencies. To some extent the old adage may be true that whoever pays the piper calls the tune. There is some evidence to indicate that this may be the case in social psychology as in most other areas of academic life. The availability of funds for the sponsorship of research is increasingly contingent on seeking solutions to clearly identifiable problems of concern to some governmental agency. The growing emphasis on applied research leaves much to be desired from the vantage point of those who have committed themselves to academic careers. Ideas in the early stages of development may wither through the lack of social support and research sponsorship. The promise of social psychology is to provide general perspectives and explanations of human behavior, rather than to find specific solutions to the problems selected by someone else.

A. THE CONSTRUCTIONIST VIEW OF SOCIAL LIFE

The overall conclusions to draw from the past several decades of research in social psychology are those related to the importance of cognitive processes and to reality constructions at both the individual and the collective levels. Images of the self and society grow out of social interactions in specific situations. We create images of the self and society in order to give some degree of order and stability to our experiences; but in the final analysis, such images at best become working hypotheses. Creating and maintaining images of the self and society require a great deal of mental effort because of the changes occurring within ourselves and within our environments.

We cannot say with full honesty that all aspects of human life are exclusively a matter of reality construction. Exclusive claims are exaggerated claims, and they are likely to take their place at some future date among the many simplistic explanations from the past that have been proposed, considered, and rejected. The present claim in the emphasis on the social construction of reality is primarily that this theme is useful and that it provides us with new images of ourselves in environmental settings and in our relationships with each other. The promise of social psychology has been to offer explanations of human behavior on the basis of the best available research evidence. The social construction of reality is the prevailing theme in social psychology today. It is not an exclusive claim; it cannot explain all aspects of human behavior. But it does offer a great deal of promise for explaining many aspects of both everyday behavior and responses to crisis situations.

BOX 16.1
The Witch Craze of Western Europe

An interesting example of reality construction occurred with the witch craze of Western Europe between the fourteenth and seventeenth centuries. Nachman Ben-Yehuda (1980) estimates that during this time period more than 200,000 people were executed as witches. As witchcraft beliefs spread through Europe, women were disproportionately selected for execution, a demonic supernatural order was created, and the moral boundaries of social conduct were redrawn.

During the fourteenth and fifteenth centuries, church officials wrote several books about witchcraft and elaborated theories about the existence of a demonic order. The Church maintained that humans can and do enter into the worship of Satan, engage in sex orgies with demonic beings, and gain magical powers through a pact with the devil. The creation of a demonic order established a battleground between the epic forces of good and evil. The witch hunts, vigorously pursued by public officials, attempted to stamp out "the hidden enemies."

The witch craze grew out of the efforts of church officials to create new moral boundaries for regulating conduct. The authority of the church was eroding, new moralities were developing, and fear of impending doom was growing. The execution of women as witches developed from the increased involvement of women in roles other than those of wife and mother. For example, a growing percentage of adult women were without family attachments; the practice of birth control became widespread; and prostitution increased with the growth of cities. Society defined women as sinful creatures with insatiable sexual desires. The witch hunts, cruel tortures, and executions may be understood as a form of scapegoating directed toward reasserting the authority of the church.

Source: Nachman Ben-Yehuda, "The European Witch Craze of the 14th to 17th Centuries: A Sociologist's Perspective," *American Journal of Sociology* 86 (July, 1980): 1–31.

The reality construction theme is in some respects an optimistic view of the human condition; in other respects it is a pessimistic view. The optimism lies in the prospects it offers for human mastery and control over the events of concern. This perspective conveys a sense of human responsibility, the prospects for decision making on the basis of the information available, and the opportunities for self-determination through social action. Individuals are not just passive recipients of environmental information; instead, they are oriented toward shaping events through the lines of action that they follow. These observations constitute the "good news," but there is "bad news" as well.

We may turn to history for a few dramatic examples of the atrocities resulting from the social constructions of reality. Examples of symbolic constructions in the past are the witch craze of Western Europe between the fourteenth and seventeenth centuries that resulted in the execution of more than 100,000 people as witches (Ben-Yehuda, 1980) (see Box 16.1); the Aztec sacrifice of thousands of human beings to a blood-thirsty god; the genocide committed by Nazi Germany; and the political purges in the Soviet Union. Our own history includes the systematic annihilation of American Indians by settlers bent on confiscating tribal lands; the brutality directed toward captives transported from Africa for the American institution of slavery; and the vigilante activity of the Ku Klux Klan. This list could go on and on, but the point is that such happenings grew out of the realities constructed in the past and that such types of events still occur and will continue to occur in the future. The spectres of overpopulation, world hunger, environmental contamination, depletion of energy resources, and nuclear annihilation are among the possibilities we imagine in our more solitary moments. If any of these do occur, the explanations must necessarily lie with the joint enterprises resulting from the ideologies, decisions, and actions of a very large number of people.

1. Environmental Perceptions

The study of social psychology provides an action-oriented view of the world. The emphasis on reality construction suggests that the human problem is not just one of maintaining and adjusting to a natural environment. The perspective emphasizes that natural environments change in fundamental ways as people give new definitions and new images to them. The world we live in is not a literal world of unshakable facts, but a world in which a great deal is possible and in which the potential range of realities is very broad indeed.

We may draw on historical examples to illustrate the creation of new images of the physical world and of human environments. The evident or direct realities of the physical world as people perceived them in the past have now been replaced by new images and by what we now believe to be a valid set of solid facts. Only a few hundred years ago the objectivist view primarily maintained that the world was comprised of a flat surface surrounded by water

The Physical World
The sciences elaborated in the twentieth century have provided us with new images of the physical world. We are aware that we know neither the boundaries of outer space nor the capabilities and limits of our planet.

and located at the center of the universe. We now have a different set of notions about the earth. The pictures from outer space have confirmed the hypothesis that the earth is round; we have lost our location as the center of the universe; we now see our planet as a relatively small "spaceship" in orbit around a star located somewhere in the Milky Way. Rather than regarding the physical environment as an evident reality to be taken for granted, we now have new images to describe the environment in much more fragile terms. Harrison Brown (1954: 3), for example, described the human environment as a biosphere, or the "thin film of life covering the earth's surface." In the immense space of the universe, our human environment is seen as being between the earth's crust and its surrounding atmosphere.

Social psychologists seldom pay attention to the biosphere, but they are concerned with the specific environmental settings in which the human drama is enacted. Harry Heft (1981) notes that the literature of social psychology is characterized by two opposing sets of assumptions about the relationships between people and their environments. These two approaches are the **constructionist perspective** and the **objectivist perspective** in environmental social psychology. The constructionists place emphasis on cognitive processes and information processing, rather than on the qualities and attributes of the environment. By way of contrast, the objectivists postulate ecological systems or environmental layouts that have direct and unmediated effects on human organisms. The constructionists concentrate on the symbolic meanings of environmental settings, while the objectivists focus on the environmental determinants of human behavior.

The objectivist view of the environment emphasizes its physical and materialistic basis, including land, air, water, and other vital resources for life-support systems. Objectivists regard land, air, and water as direct realities—environmental inputs or stimulus objects that have a direct bearing on the qualities of human life. Constructionists also view noise levels, odors, and crowdedness as objective features of environments that evoke direct human responses. These are indeed the elements most of us would include in descriptions of an objective environment, but the implications one can infer from such a view can also be misleading. Humans are not merely passive recipients of environmental inputs; instead, they actively engage in creating and shaping the environments in which they live (Humphrey and Buttel, 1982).

According to the constructionist view, the responses humans make to their environments are joint enterprises through which they create and elaborate symbolic meanings as guidelines to action. The environment is not something that is just "there." Only a few of the many objects in the environment are of concern; most are not even noticed, or if noticed are ignored. Humans select objects for emphasis and give attention to only some aspects of the objects they select. Neither our attention span nor our mental capabilities permit a photographic reproduction of our environments. We are limited to selecting and exaggerating the objects of our concern. In doing so we superimpose a symbolic environment on the physical world.

These observations are not to be understood as claiming that the physical world does not exist, but only that the human understanding and responses to the physical world require a great deal of repair work on an ongoing basis. For example, at the turn of the century people defined smokestacks in urban areas in positive terms, seeing them as representing industrial development, jobs, and progress. Today we have a quite different view of smokestacks, which have come to be associated with air pollution, breathing difficulties, and mortality rates. Heavy industry and electric power plants are still important to us, but we want the benefits they have to offer without the air pollution they bring. Smokestacks are still okay, but only if they are equipped with pollution-control devices.

Environmental perceptions are ways of giving human meaning to the physical world. In many primitive societies, for example, environments are endowed with spirit beings, animistic beliefs, and human-like characteristics that mandate living harmoniously with the physical world (Tedlock and Ted-

Man-Made Environments
The creation and maintenance of physical environments is increasingly a human enterprise.

lock, 1975). Industrialized societies, by way of contrast, tend to regard environmental resources as impersonal objects to be used, molded, and manipulated by those who have access to them. Housing complexes, super highways, railroads, airports, factories, and other human creations increasingly define the environments in which people live and find meaning. We set aside "natural areas" for recreational purposes and for permitting us to have "authentic experiences" with the physical world; but as noted in Chapter 7 (Work and Leisure), the availability of natural areas does not result in the "direct reality" experiences for which they were designed. The behavior patterns in national parks and camping areas bear a close resemblance to the behavior patterns of everyday life. Such modern technologies as radios, Coleman stoves, campers, and athletic equipment usually accompany the quest for "communion with nature."

We are inclined to view our own assumptions and definitions as literal and valid ones, but we are not isolated units of meaning. We are required to bring our own understanding into alignment with the understanding of others.

For this reason our own definition of reality is necessarily tentative, a type of working hypothesis, a plausible set of assumptions. The ongoing character of social life requires modification, fine tuning, and sometimes rejection of reality definitions. Such adjustments are required for coping with the people in our lives and for responding to the changes that are occurring both within ourselves and within our external environments.

2. The Technological World View

The shape and meaning of a personal life is confirmed through social relationships in particular environmental settings. If we humans were only capable of responding directly to our environments, we would not have elaborate systems of technology, nor would we occupy our position of dominance within the animal kingdom. We would not be able to communicate by telephone or letter writing; we would not be able to build bridges or war machines; we would not be able to watch television or drive automobiles. In fact, if we were stripped of our propensity for using symbols, and if we were conditioned to respond only to direct environmental stimuli, society as we presently know it could not exist. Technological environments increasingly define the boundaries within which we live modern social life, and these environments are created through human efforts.

The **technological world view** is a major distinguishing characteristic of modern social life according to Jacques Ellul (1964). From Ellul's vantage point we overlook the importance of technology if we associate it only with machines and gadgetry. Technology is much more than automobiles, refrigerators, television sets, and computers. It is a state of mind, an approach to problem solving, and an emphasis on standardized techniques as standardized solutions. The technological world view holds that identifiable problems are solvable; proceeding with this assumption has contributed to the many technological innovations of the twentieth century.

In some respects the technological world view within itself constitutes a reality construction perspective. For example, it assumes that problems can be solved long before any actual solutions are developed. Landing a man on the moon, inventing an airplane, developing a vaccine for polio, eliminating smallpox, and building an atom bomb are among the spectacular achievements of the twentieth century, for better or worse, that have resulted from technological approaches to identifiable problems. Recognizing that these possibilities prevailed in human imaginations for long periods of time before they were actually accomplished conveys an important message for social psychology: human behavior involves much more than responding to environmental stimuli. Humans actively create their worlds through the lines of action they follow, and these lines of action are shaped by intentions and grow out of decision-making processes.

The message, however, requires several qualifications for a clearer understanding of the human condition. The technological world view also conveys overtones of arrogance in its assumption that all identifiable problems are solvable through mobilizing materials, technical personnel, and financial resources. The War on Poverty did not succeed in eliminating poverty; the appropriation of huge sums of money for cancer research have not resulted in finding a cure for cancer; and the research of alchemists did not result in turning base metals into gold. While technological approaches to the world prevail in our society, there are also many ambivalent sentiments about the possibilities of technology and about what the technological approach can actually do. Science and technology may be able to discover or invent new sources of energy that are cheap, abundant, and efficient; but it is also possible that satisfactory solutions to current energy problems cannot be found. The depletion of nonrenewable energy resources may eventually weaken the fabric on which highly industrialized societies depend. (See Figure 16.1.)

A sense of personal mastery in the lives of individual men and women frequently is not linked with the spectacular achievements of the larger society. Instead, more and more people come to feel that their destinies are dependent on sources of control that are external to themselves (Gurin, Gurin,

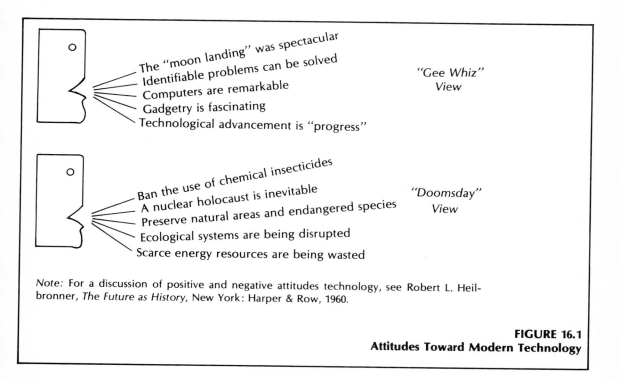

The "moon landing" was spectacular
Identifiable problems can be solved
Computers are remarkable
Gadgetry is fascinating
Technological advancement is "progress"

"Gee Whiz" View

Ban the use of chemical insecticides
A nuclear holocaust is inevitable
Preserve natural areas and endangered species
Ecological systems are being disrupted
Scarce energy resources are being wasted

"Doomsday" View

Note: For a discussion of positive and negative attitudes technology, see Robert L. Heilbronner, *The Future as History*, New York: Harper & Row, 1960.

FIGURE 16.1
Attitudes Toward Modern Technology

and Morrison, 1978; Shepard, 1977). Such sentiments were captured in the comment by Robert Nisbet (1962: 22) that

it is impossible to escape the melancholy conclusion that man's belief in himself has become weakest in the very age in which his control of environment is greatest. This is the irony of ironies.

Landing a man on the moon, traveling beyond the speed of sound, splitting the atom, and launching communication satellites apparently have had little bearing on the sense of control individuals feel over their personal destinies. The irony to which Nisbet referred is that the individual's sense of mastery over personal fate varies independently of collective accomplishments in solving specific problems. People typically regard the technological achievements of the modern world as the works of specialists or experts, occurring within frameworks far removed from the spheres of meaning and action for most people.

3. The Micro Politics of Everyday Life

A conceptual separation between individual and society has occurred in the modern world, and this separation is having profound effects on the conditions of social life. As noted in Chapter 15, recent research indicates that Americans make a clear separation between their personal circumstances and the conditions of their society when evaluating the qualities of life; most people are more optimistic about their personal futures than about the future of their country. The quest for a sense of purpose in life, the quest for social identity, and the quest for personal mastery and control are distinctly modern forms of consciousness that stem from the weakness of social ties, from the fragmentation of social life, and from the responsibilities placed on individuals for control over their own destinies.

The duality of society and the individual is evident in the group's emphasis on an orderly and predictable social life and through the actor's concern with control over his or her environment (Dawe, 1970). Social order is sustained through shared conceptions of the normal state of affairs, through the rules that serve as the regulators of conduct, and through the shared understanding that gives form and coherence to the activities of everyday life. The actor's control over his or her environment is facilitated by definitions of the situation, by selection of goals from among the alternatives available, and by knowledge of what must be done to attain the goals of interest.

The construction of reality by individuals is built on several layers of social organization. People confirm the shape and meaning of their personal lives through social action, through the messages they receive from significant others, and through the attitudes they develop toward what exists and what is possible. Conceptions of society represent the outer layers of social reality and constitute the individual's definition of the types of people and the rules of conduct that prevail in his or her historical time period. The more immediate realities are situational; they constitute the meanings people give to social acts as they respond to one another. The realities negotiated in everyday life we may understand as involving micropolitics. The process is political in the sense that the social interactions of everyday life are practical accomplishments, involve negotiations and exchanges, and have important social and psychological payoffs for the parties involved.

Several theoretical perspectives in social psychology emphasize the dynamic qualities of social life by emphasizing social interaction as the basic social process. The theatrical model, as presented in Chapter 8, provides one set of answers to the question of how individuals construct their realities and shape their conduct. The theatrical model emphasizes the importance of social behavior in specific social settings as individuals enact social roles. From this perspective human behavior is shaped both by established social scripts and by innovative script writing on the part of social actors. Appearances and illusions play an important part in human affairs as actors engage in performances designed to have calculated effects on observers. Because of differences in perception, personal goals and intentions must necessarily be coordinated with the goals and intentions of others if social life is to be workable.

In contrast to the emphasis on roles and performances as the key to social behavior, exchange theory emphasizes the importance of decision making, the payoffs in social transactions, and the concerns with distributive justice. The assumption of rationality is the starting point for examining the process by which people trade valued resources. A great deal of human behavior can be looked on as involving the exchange of valued resources as individuals engage in the pursuit of their self-interests. Exchange theory emphasizes the transfer of resources as a central feature of orderly social life. Accordingly, perceptions of opportunity and fairness in social relationships become of primary importance in levels of satisfaction with group living.

The subjective definitions of everyday life are the starting points for several theoretical perspectives in social psychology. But whatever the differences among them, these viewpoints see the meanings given to everyday behavior as rational creations and practical accomplishments. To describe "the people's method" of making sense out of social life, Harold Garfinkel (1967) coined the term **ethnomethodology**. His emphasis is on the ways in which individuals organize their life-worlds into sets of meaning and orient them toward practical lines of action. Decisions, plans, and intentions are shaped within a social context and represent an outgrowth of the limits and prospects of everyday life.

The concern with the normality of everyday life, according to Andrew Weigert (1981), is a distinctly modern type of problem. Traditional societies take everyday life for granted and reflect on normality only during times of crisis. But in the modern world, everyday life is problematic on a routine and recurrent basis. The assumptions about the continuity of social life are shattered by social and environmental disruptions, as well as by the potential threats (environmental pollution, energy crisis, runaway inflation, nuclear war, terrorism, and so on) to existing lifestyles. The concerns with normality become particularly important times of crisis; it is perhaps for this reason that the attributes of everyday life become of interest to social psychologists as well as to people in general.

B. BASIC HUMAN CONCERNS

The content of human concerns is highly varied and often involves such concrete matters as health, the well-being of family members, success or failure on the job, salvation of one's soul, payment of bills, and sexual expressiveness. In any given case the problems that receive the highest priority in the attentions of individuals may not correspond very well to what any particular observer may think these concerns should be. People who are in good physical condition worry about their health, and people who are financially secure worry about economic problems. Humans direct a good deal of worry toward problems that turn out to be inconsequential, and frequently ignore important matters. Yet it is the ideas people carry around in their heads that shape the lines of action they follow.

Men and women live in immediate acts of experience, and their behavior is oriented toward objects and events that have the highest priority of the moment. The concerns of the moment, however, tend to have cumulative effects that are expressed in attitudes and values persisting through time and across a variety of situations. These are the relatively enduring frameworks of understanding that make up one's overall images of the self and society.

The primary human concerns are those that derive from the problems of identity and conflict in social relationships. These concerns involve blending feelings of mastery and control in some situations with helplessness in others, a sense of understanding with perceptions of complexity and chaos, and feelings of membership and belonging with those of personal loneliness and social isolation. These themes of alienation and integration have commanded the attention of social psychologists for more than two decades. What are the conditions promoting feelings of helplessness and hopelessness? What are the conditions that promote a sense of personal effectiveness in the pursuit of social goals? What are some of the implications of social attachments for a sense of comfort with one's society? These are among the implicit themes of social psychology, and to develop an understanding of how they operate in the lives of individuals should be of central relevance to an awareness of what is happening to oneself and to others within the context of modern social life. (See Table 16.1.)

	Integration	Alienation
		TABLE 16.1 **The Vocabulary of Basic Human Concerns**
Membership and Belonging:	Attachment	Loneliness
	Affiliation	Isolation
	Cohesion	Avoidance
	Solidarity	Atomization
	Commitment	Dropping-out
	Community	Estrangement
	Involvement	Disengagement
	Association	Anonymity
	Togetherness	Apartness
Purpose and Prediction:	Making plans	Sense of drifting
	Establishing goals	Surprising developments
	Seeking objectives	Unintended happenings
	Having intentions	Accidental consequences
	Explaining events	Encountering complexity
	Holding probabilities	Chaotic experiences
	Being certain	Confused thinking
	Having confidence	Shocking experiences
Mastery and Control:	Being effective	Helplessness
	Making things happen	Powerlessness
	Producing results	Resignation
	Shaping events	Fatalism
	Manipulating	Restrained
	Organizing	Blocked
	Managing	Thwarted
	Supervising	Stalled
	Forcing	Encapsulated
	Persuading	Imprisoned

1. Purpose and Prediction

According to Viktor Frankl (1965), the search for meaning is the primary sustaining force in human affairs. Finding a purpose for living and sorting out those things that are important from those that are not are basic human concerns. The components of the quest for meaning include discovering the options available, setting personal priorities, and striving to attain goals that the individual regards as being worthwhile. In Frankl's view, there is futility in the search for an overriding sense of unity and coherence to either one's personal life or the events in one's surroundings. The basic human problem is to find a more limited sense of purpose by striving for specific goals that the individual perceives as attainable.

The problem of finding an overriding sense of purpose in life is confounded by the multiple roles people play and the many ways in which given social actors become involved in social life. In discussing some of the effects of the division of labor, Charles Dudley (1978: 101) observed that social life is fragmented.

People are parents, children, workers, and members of civic, social and political clubs; they spend part of their time in leisure activity; and they spend much time in groups where they obtain needed resources (food, housing, clothing, etc.). In short, each actor in the society fits into numerous places in the division of labor, and as the society becomes more differentiated, the actor's participation in it grows more extensive, involving the actor in a greater variety of group activities.

Only a small portion of the life of the typical individual is carried out within any specific set of social relationships. Work is separated from family life; the religious sphere is separated from the political sphere; and attitudes are separated from behavior. As the domains of social life have become more highly specialized and separated by time and place, the social actor finds it increasingly difficult to achieve a sense of unity and coherence among the diverse roles and social positions he or she occupies.

Modern society has extensively elaborated multiple roles, and the activities of concern to individuals occur in many different places and involve many different kinds of social relationships. The social environment becomes comprised of increasingly specialized activities as groups form to provide specialized services and products. Social actors respond in turn by increasing the scope of involvements in social relationships. Self-sufficiency becomes more and more elusive, and individuals must develop skills for adequately dealing with the many strangers who enter into their life-worlds on a momentary basis. The range of multiple and overlapping social relationships increasingly shapes the linkages between the individual and society (Ogilvy, 1979).

The pursuit of meaning is complicated by conditions of uncertainty. Perceptions of social life as chaotic and unpredictable are evident in the lack of confidence to select and pursue social goals. Joachim Israel (1971) observes that the condition of meaninglessness is the most serious form of alienation in modern social life. In this form of alienation, the individual feels that his or her minimal standards for clarity in decision making are not being met (Seeman, 1975). Conditions of uncertainty are promoted by the increasing complexity of social life, by the rapid pace of social change, and by the perception of an unpredictable future.

From an actor's standpoint the pursuit of goals with a reasonable degree of confidence requires an adequate understanding of the events in which he or she engages. An adequate understanding implies a grasp of how social life is organized and how to go about attaining the goals of interest. Attitudes about the predictability of social events are of special relevance to making personal plans for the future. If one feels that the course of social events lacks predictability, then planning does not appear to be feasible and one's personal life takes on a pattern of aimlessness and drift. Making plans for the future may proceed with confidence only if one feels that the goals selected are appropriate and attainable.

A primary characteristic of our society is that young adults must make such a large number of decisions under conditions of uncertainty. Deciding to continue or to terminate one's formal education, deciding to marry or to remain single, deciding which line of career development to follow, and deciding how to spend one's leisure time are among the many choices one must make. The ways in which these decisions are made do have important consequences, since they have a bearing on the directions of committed lines of action in later life. The stress connected with making major life decisions frequently stems from their irreversible character. As noted in Chapter 6, investments of time, energy, and resources in committed lines of action make it difficult for individuals to back out or to pursue a different set of alternatives. Yet if decisions are not deliberately and intentionally made, the pattern of life may become one of drift in which one responds only to the pressures of the moment. Under such conditions, one is likely to view life in general as something less than it could or ought to be.

2. Mastery and Control

An additional set of human concerns relates to the problems of mastery and control. Individuals may feel that their understanding of events is adequate but that the prospects for control over these events is highly limited. Death and taxes are frequently viewed as certainties of life; defined as unshakable social facts, they fall outside the realm of personal control and mastery. Beliefs about the consequences for society of energy shortages, environmental pollution, and runaway inflation may appear clear and definite at the same time that they seem uncontrollable. In the personal realm, individuals may be clear about their hopes and aspirations for the future, while feeling that the prospects for attaining their dreams are growing dim.

A sense of mastery and control refers to our individual expectation that we can attain desired outcomes in our environments through the use of personal efforts (Seeman, 1972). Being effective, being able to produce desired results, and being confident in the successful completion of tasks are among the ingredients of a sense of personal mastery and control. If we define our environment as one that is responsive to our needs and interests, we then feel some degree of comfort with the social system of which we are a part. Under these circumstances, we view success or failure in goal attainment as being related to the level of personal effort we put forth, and we have internalized a sense of personal mastery over the events in which we engage (Rotter, 1966).

Some cultures place emphases on humans living harmoniously within the natural environment; others emphasize a passive acceptance of the world as it exists. Contemporary cultures orient their value systems toward activity (Etzioni, 1968) and the assertion of mastery over the surroundings. In his research on American society, Robin Williams (1970) noted that personal mastery becomes of special concern in those societies that emphasize the responsibility of individuals for their own destinies. If the consequential events in the lives of individuals are regarded as the outcomes of their own behavior, then "blaming the victims" tends to take priority over "blaming the system" in accounting for human misery (Ryan, 1976). Accordingly, social accomplishments are likely to be looked on as the accomplishments of individuals rather than as advances promoted by an entire society.

Feelings of powerlessness and helplessness are more likely to occur for some population subgroups than for others. For example, survey research has found consistent support for the hypothesis that socioeconomic status correlates positively with a sense of mastery and control over events. Poverty status, low levels of education, and employment in low-status occupations are among the major variables associated with feelings of powerlessness and helplessness (Lystad, 1972). The lack of status attainment in our society is associated with a lack of personal mastery and control. In contrast, achieving a college education, a relatively high-status job, and a comfortable income level apparently provide psychological and social resources to draw on for asserting control within social environments. The status attainment process provides experiences with mastery and control, and these experiences generalize to other areas of life. Those individuals with a sense of personal mastery tend to be receptive to control-relevant information in their environments and to draw on this information to attain their goals (Bullough, 1969; Neal, 1971; Seeman, 1972). (See Box 16.2.)

The relationships between socioeconomic status and attitudes of personal mastery, however, need qualification. There are several aspects of modern society that have pervasive effects on the capacities of individuals to control the consequential events in their lives. The scarcity of jobs, the shortage of cheap energy, the threats of war, and the rising costs of food and housing are among the many happenings that have ripple effects on the lives of individuals somewhat independently of their own efforts and strivings. About thirty years ago, C. Wright Mills (1953: xii) made the following observation on the American middle class:

BOX 16.2
The Poverty Cycle

During the 1960s social scientists directed a great deal of attention toward the persistence of poverty in a society characterized by overall improvements in the standards of living. Why does poverty persist in the midst of affluence? Why is poverty transmitted from one generation to another? What are some of the major social psychological obstacles confronted by the poor?

Daniel P. Moynihan (1969) suggested that some of the answers to these questions lie in examining the vicious cycle in which poverty breeds poverty. Conditions of poverty tend to generate attitudes of helplessness and despair. Individuals feel that they are not able to actively control their own destinies through their own efforts. By holding these assumptions, the poor fail to take advantage of the opportunities others see as being available in their environments. Seeking education and being persistent in submitting job applications are in part dependent on a sense of confidence that these efforts will pay off at some time in the future. These are assumptions that many of the poor do not hold, and as a result the cycle of poverty is perpetuated as a type of self-fulfilling prophecy.

The "war on poverty" failed in part because of its failure to take into account the social psychological and environmental conditions affecting the lives of the poor. Poverty programs were initiated and operated by privileged members of the middle and upper classes, rather than by poor people and minorities. The resources allocated to poverty programs, according to Moynihan, were disproportionate "to our knowledge of the subject." Inadequate knowledge and understanding were among the conditions resulting in a failure to reduce the scope of poverty in American life.

Source: Daniel P. Moynihan, *On Understanding Poverty,* New York: Basic Books, 1969, pp. 3–35.

...The white-collar man... is more often pitiful than tragic, as he is seen collectively, fighting impersonal inflation, living out in slow misery his yearning for the quick American climb. He is pushed by forces beyond his control, pulled into movements he does not understand; he gets into situations in which his is the most helpless position. The white-collar man is the hero as victim, the small creature who is acted upon but who does not act, who works along unnoticed in somebody's office or store, never talking loud, never talking back, never taking a stand.

Mills was commenting on the linkage between personal troubles and public issues. Mills did not regard the problems of alienation as being limited to minorities and the poor but as concerns of most people in contemporary social life. While individuals do make a distinction between the controllability of personal and societal events (Gurin *et al.*, 1969), from the standpoint of an outside observer the distinction breaks down in several respects. Individuals are not self-contained units and, in the pursuit of self-interests, they necessarily form linkages with broader social units. The speed with which societal events impinge on the life-worlds of individuals prevents them from having a sense of effective control over most of the happenings in society. The basic problem for individuals is that there are no organizational frameworks for self-protection, for speaking back, or for having their interests taken into account.

3. Belonging and Membership

Another of the basic human concerns relates to the kinds and degrees of involvement in social relationships. Belonging and membership reflect the qualities of family bonds, friendship ties, love affairs, career commitments, and other cohesive relationships that offer support for one's identity. If these relationships are rewarding, then one may proceed with a high degree of confidence in developing personal goals and plans for the future. But if one views significant people as being indifferent and unsupportive, experiences of loneliness are likely to follow and the feeling develops that one must rely exclusively on one's own resources in times of trouble.

The lack of rewards in social relationships, the sense of apartness from others, and the loss of social attachments frequently are serious problems in modern society. These problems surface for the worker who feels trapped in an unrewarding job, for the professor who senses being out of touch with students, for the person who finds church attendance to be unrewarding, for the couple whose marriage has turned sour, or for the parent who feels lonely as the youngest child leaves home for college or the army. Humans are indeed social animals, but the qualities of their social attachments are highly variable. Most people at some time or another are likely to feel a sense of apartness from others, just as under other circumstances they are likely to experience a strong sense of belonging and membership. The degree of comfort with one's society relates closely to the overall qualities of social relationships. These are shaped through engagement in events and activities with others.

The sense of loneliness is a more intense problem for the very young and for the very old than for other segments of the population. The feelings of isolation among young adults in general and students in particular frequently stem from the lack of social commitments (Keniston, 1965). Most students are single rather than married, and they are preparing for careers rather than being directly involved in employment. Exclusion from the labor force and the lack of involvement in family obligations tend to promote a sense of freedom among ·college students. But as Erich Fromm (1941) noted, the freedom that stems from a lack of social commitments is also likely to be accompanied by feelings of loneliness and isolation. The sense of being excluded from many aspects of

Loneliness
The sense of loneliness may reach a high level of intensity under those conditions in which the individual feels that personal problems cannot be shared with others.

social life does not stem so much from the lack of opportunities as from the fear of making the wrong kind of choices.

While students feel excluded from many aspects of social life, they also are optimistic about their personal futures. As noted in Chapter 15, college students expect the quality of their lives to improve substantially within the five years following graduation. The results of national surveys, however, indicate that life satisfaction is unlikely to increase as much as expected (Campbell, Converse, and Rogers, 1976). Building a career, establishing a place of residence, managing family finances, and rearing children are all activities that interfere with a sense of stability in the personal lives of individuals. The extensive responsibilities that accompany the early years of family formation often have hemming-in effects and reduce the opportunities for building social attachments outside the home (Neal, Ivoska, and Groat, 1976).

The sense of comfort with modern social life tends to be greater among middle-aged and older Americans than among those who are in their twenties and thirties. Social attachments become more firmly established as people grow older. Those in their forties and fifties are overrepresented in voluntary organizations; they tend to be secure both financially and in the development of their careers; they are generally more satisfied with their friends; and they have the resources regarded as necessary for pursuing central life interests. The surveys during the 1970s and 1980s found the highest levels of life satisfaction among people in their sixties (Campbell, 1981). Apparently it is during this stage of life that past accomplishments have their greatest payoff.

The negative stereotypes of the aged fail to be supported by survey research. The appearances and social definitions of the elderly are often more

---

BOX 16.3
Friendship Ties and Life Satisfaction among the Aged

Vivian Wood and Joan Robertson (1978) investigated the effects of differential social involvements on the level of life satisfaction among grandparents. Involvements were measured by the number and frequency of activities the subjects engaged in with grandchildren, friends, and organizations. Wood and Robertson's comparative analysis of social attachments shows that friendship plays a more important part than either grandchildren or organizations in maintaining life satisfactions among the elderly.

Many of the needs of the aged are not met effectively through interactions with grandchildren. The interactions of grandparents with grandchildren frequently consist of babysitting, taking children to the zoo or to a movie, playing with them, or reading them stories. Grandparents usually remember birthdays and give gifts to children at Christmas, but interactions with grandchildren tend to be sporadic and limited to special occasions. Only a few grandparents reported telling grandchildren about family history or teaching them special skills such as sewing or fishing. Important gaps existed between the major life interests of grandparents and their grandchildren.

While subjects attributed a great deal of significance to grandparenthood, their involvements with grandchildren were not nearly so important as friendship in overall levels of life satisfaction. The importance of friendship seems to rest on the freedom of choice the individual has in developing attachments and on building joint enterprises from common experiences and interests. Apparently, such needs as intimacy, shared goals, reassurances of social worth, and mutual assistance are better served through friendship ties than through the socially prescribed bonds that cross generational lines.

Source: Vivian Wood and Joan F. Robertson, "Friendship and Kinship Interaction: Differential Effect on the Morale of the Elderly," *Journal of Marriage and the Family* 40 (May, 1978): 367–375.

negative than the psychological realities of aging would indicate. The sense of comfort with the self and society among the aged is shaped by their relatively high levels of social integration; as long as they sustain social attachments, the world appears to be a friendly, responsive, and rewarding place. The marital ties of older people become increasingly important as sources of comfort and support (Atchley, 1977) and friendship becomes increasingly significant as a source of morale and life satisfaction (Wood and Robertson, 1978). Among the very old, the increased sense of loneliness and isolation is primarily due to the reduced opportunities for involvement in intimate relationships. The death of a spouse or a close friend results in the loss of psychological supports and reflects the importance of social attachments for a sense of well-being. (See Box 16.3.)

C. PSYCHOLOGICAL MODERNITY

Basic human concerns have special meanings within the context of modern society. A sense of social purpose, a sense of personal control, and a sense of belonging increasingly depend on deliberate choices and rational decisions. Traditions as blueprints for behavior have been weakened with industrial and technological developments, and new forms of freedom have emerged. If we knew who we were collectively and if we knew where we headed historically, the study of social psychology would be less necessary than it now is. We no longer have a society in which the places of individuals in the broader scheme of social affairs are clear and definite. The stability of social ties that characterized our historical past has been broken, and increases in our freedom of movement have increasingly uprooted us. The result is greater psychological dependence on our individual resources in times of trouble.

Psychological modernity refers to modern forms of consciousness (Berger, Berger, and Kellner, 1973). The concept is not the same as the older idea of social change as progress, or the notion of being up to date. We have no clear gauges for measuring progress; determining what is up to date and hence appropriate is largely a matter of opinion. When we speak of psychological modernity we are referring primarily to the states of mind that have developed in response to contemporary historical circumstances. The growth of cities, the magnitude of bureaucracies, and the pervasiveness of technological environments are among the frameworks of modern social life.

The time dimension of psychological modernity is reflected in knowing how we got to where we are now, knowing where we are now, and knowing where we are going. Coping with the changing conditions of our society, responding to the changes occurring within ourselves, and elaborating on the meaning of social events are among the many aspects of modern awareness. In effect, modernity is the stage or the social setting in which we enact the drama of freedom and control as we seek to invent our futures.

1. Freedom and Control

An emphasis on the voluntaristic element in human conduct is clearly evident in the research of psychologists and sociologists. A great deal of research has been directed toward studies of selective perception, decision making, interpersonal attraction, and the formation of commitments. Clearly people do make many kinds of choices in everyday life; yet the concept of freedom is largely missing from the vocabulary of social psychologists. On purely philosophical grounds, convincing arguments could be made for freedom as an illusion. But from the standpoint of human experiences, people are free if they think they are free, or, correspondingly, freedom is lacking if people feel that they are deprived or that they are prevented from doing the kinds of things they want to do.

BOX 16.4
The Personal Freedom of Living Alone

The 1980 Census indicated that an increased percentage of the adult population is choosing to live alone rather than with a roommate, a spouse, or some other person. In recent years, the percentage living alone has been increasing at an accelerating rate, and at the present time slightly more than one in every five households in the United States is comprised of a person living alone. The research of Michael Hughes and Walter Gove (1981) suggests that the value of personal freedom is an important consideration in the decisions about residential patterns.

Previous research has clearly established that living alone is correlated with several forms of pathological behavior, such as relatively high rates of suicide, psychiatric treatment, physical illness, and mortality. Hughes and Gove maintain that these findings are often accepted uncritically and that they are based primarily on extreme cases of pathology. Drawing on a random sample of 2248 adults in the forty-eight contiguous states, their research on a "normal" population failed to indicate any major psychological disadvantage to living alone as compared to living with others. Taken from several measures of mental well-being, their data show slightly greater positive reports on the quality of life for those living alone in comparison to those living with others.

The preference for living alone appears to be based on the value of personal freedom in the use of leisure, in the organization of a household, and in the development of a lifestyle. Living with others results in exposure to social constraints, commitments, and obligations. The major disadvantages of living alone appear to be the lack of social supports in times of trouble and the lack of remedial action as maladaptive patterns of behavior develop. Hughes and Gove conclude that there are costs and benefits to both living alone and living with others.

Source: Michael Hughes and Walter R. Gove, "Living Alone, Social Integration, and Mental Health," *American Journal of Sociology* 87 (July, 1981): 48–74.

George Hillery and his associates (1971; 1977; 1979) have investigated empirically several aspects of freedom in the experiences of individuals. The primary contribution of their research findings has been to clarify the major forms of freedom by making the distinction between the individual and society and the distinction between personal choices and social constraints. The three main types of freedom to emerge from these research studies are personal freedom, conditional freedom, and disciplined freedom. The forms of freedom are expressed in the perceived options available, the perceived capacities for making choices, and the willingness to make personal sacrifices for attaining what one wants.

Personal freedom is the most unencumbered of all the forms of freedom. It exists under those conditions in which individuals feel free to do what they want to do without any limitations or constraints. Freedom in such cases permits spontaneous behavior and is more likely to be found within the spheres of privacy than within other areas of life (Schwartz, 1968). In many respects personal freedoms are the residuals of social living: they constitute the options that remain after obligations have been fulfilled. The sense of personal freedom frequently reaches its highest level of intensity under those circumstances in which individuals are released from a heavy set of social commitments. The weekend pass for the enlisted soldier during the course of basic training, the time for college students following final exams, and the vacation for the factory worker who does not enjoy his or her job are among the situations sometimes promoting an exhilarating sense of freedom. The popularity of the TGIF (Thank God It's Friday) parties in our society perhaps reflects the lack of intrinsic rewards for many people in the activities of everyday life. (See Box 16.4.)

Conditional freedom stems from group processes and "refers to the notion that other people or things are important in determining the manner in which an individual lives" (Hillery, Dudley, and Morrow, 1977: 694). This form of freedom is conditioned by many circumstances—by the people in the individual's life, by the limits of social resources, and by the perceived capacities of individuals to act in accordance with their wishes. All social groups impose restrictions on their members by setting limits on the range of behavior that they will tolerate or consider appropriate. For example, if you are living in a college dormitory, your own freedoms are likely to be limited by your roommate and by the need to negotiate for the use of physical space. Living in a college dormitory, in a military barrack, or in a commune makes certain options available while precluding others. Being married, working for a corporation, or belonging to a church permits the pursuit of certain valued goals and objectives while preventing the pursuit of certain others. Social life involves making compromises; conditional forms of freedom require aligning personal goals and interests with the objectives of social groups and the rules for regulating conduct. Nearly all social groups provide some latitude for their members while at the same time setting up boundaries around the range of permitted behavior.

The third form of freedom to emerge from the research of Hillery and his associates is **disciplined freedom**. This refers to the willingness of individuals to make sacrifices to attain some desired goal. Getting what we want out of life involves sharing and sacrificing. We make concessions to others and invest personal resources in the attainment of group goals.

The disciplined form of freedom is reflected in personal commitments, in dedication to social causes, and in linkages of self-fulfillment with group accomplishments. The disciplined form of freedom as noted by Hillery in his studies of monasteries, communes, and cooperatives bears an affinity to the earlier observations made by Emile Durkheim (1951) on altruistic suicide. (See Box 16.5.) In extreme cases individuals may seek self-fulfillment through voluntarily sacrificing their lives for a social cause. A well-known historical example is the Japanese Kamikaze fliers of World War II. The pilots volunteered

---

BOX 16.5
The Disciplined Freedom of Monastery Life

Charles Dudley and George Hillery (1979) concentrated on the disciplined form of freedom in their study of monastic life. They made observations of several monasteries over a period of months and conducted interviews with monks who had made personal commitments to the religious life.

Life in a monastery is difficult and demanding. The monks eat, sleep, and pray in places that are separated from the rest of the world. The day begins at 3:15 A.M. with preparations for the morning "office," which includes prayers, devotional readings, and the singing of psalms. Work usually begins about 8:00 A.M. and lasts for about four to six hours, six days a week. The remainder of the time is spent in reading, meditation, prayer, and taking care of personal needs. On becoming a monk, the person takes vows of poverty, chastity, and obedience. The monastic way of life tends to restrict personal freedom while maximizing the opportunity for achieving a disciplined form of freedom.

This sense of freedom is reflected in the monks' integrative experiences with social life: Discipline, personal sacrifices, and group sharing become linked in the promotion of religious values. The monastery makes provisions for the basic requirements of subsistence, places emphasis on sharing, and requires high levels of obedience. It provides places of solitude for the monks to re-create or reconstruct themselves along religious lines. The monks do not feel that they are deprived of freedom as a result of having selected the monastic way of life. Instead, they regard the highest level of self-fulfillment as attainable through submission of the self to a transcendent ideology.

Source: Charles J. Dudley and George A. Hillery, Jr., "Freedom and Monastery Life," *Journal for the Scientific Study of Religion* 18 (March, 1979): 18–28.

for suicide missions knowing fully in advance that their lives would be lost in carrying out the assigned mission. The linkage of self-fulfillment with self-destruction is perhaps the most extreme form of sacrifice possible in the exercise of disciplined freedom. Very few of us would be willing to make the kind of sacrifice made by the Kamikaze pilots; but such an unwillingness is also likely to reflect a lack of strong commitments.

Emotional investments and a sense of commitment are necessary for attaining most of the goals in life; but if the demands become too great or if the sacrifices become too burdensome, we are likely to change our minds and to move in other directions. Pursuing a career, developing a love affair, enhancing the qualities of family life, and acquiring material goods are typical expressions of freedom. For most people, however, such freedoms are likely to take conditional rather than disciplined forms. It is not the type of activity that determines the type of freedom but the emotional investments that social actors make. As noted in Chapter 13, however, extreme commitments are more likely to be found in moral crusades and social movements than in other types of activities. Whatever the case may be, exercises of conditional and disciplined freedom tend to establish social identities and to reflect what it is that people expect to get out of life.

2. Inventing the Future

One of the primary characteristics of the twentieth century is the emphasis in the more highly developed societies on collecting, organizing, and interpreting knowledge in the various forms (Lane, 1966). The modern concerns with advancing new forms of knowledge derive from the recognition that humans shape their own destinies, and that they do so with the information they have at their disposal, however incomplete or inadequate that information may be. The pursuit of knowledge in modern society does not stem from an emphasis on knowledge as something to be valued as an end within itself, but from the concerns for finding solutions to clearly identifiable problems. People extract additional meanings from the world around them in order to enhance basic values and objectives.

The quest for additional knowledge is reflected in the growth of specialized areas of inquiry. For example, a hundred years ago there was no one in the entire world who thought of himself or herself as a social psychologist. Social psychology had not yet been invented as a specialized area of academic inquiry. There were people, of course, who wrote about and reflected on many of the problems about which social psychologists are still concerned. But systematic inquiry into the subject matter of social psychology is primarily an outgrowth of the twentieth century.

It has been said that more than 90 percent of the scientists the world has

The Library on a College Campus
Because of the vast expansion of knowledge in recent years, the library on a college campus requires a much larger building than it did fifty years ago.

ever known are alive today (Heilbronner, 1960), suggesting that we are living in a world in which knowledge is proliferating in many different directions at the same time. Just as we have turned our attention outward to the exploration of space, we also are turning our attention inwardly to examine the subjective qualities of life (Blauner, 1964). Within this context we may reasonably expect a great deal of interest in experimenting with new forms of social organization and social living. To the extent that this is so, humans appear to have the capacity and the freedom to shape their own destinies within certain limits, and these limits may be very broad indeed. Human awareness and intentions enter into the matrix of social causation, along with many other factors, in shaping the course of social events.

While we need not agree with the full implications of Alvin Toffler's (1971) description of social change as future shock, it is clear that many people do view the overall drift of societies as chaotic, unpredictable, and bereft of purpose. Under these conditions it is difficult for the individual to engage in long-range planning with a reasonable degree of confidence. Instead the individual often responds by developing a limited time perspective, by emphasizing the here and now, and by accepting the hedonistic view that one should live for today and let tomorrow take care of itself. To a significant degree, faith in long-term planning of one's life is dependent on being able to see the interrelatedness of events and to make social predictions with a reasonable degree of confidence.

This generation is making a sharp separation between self and society, but it is a separation that cannot be sustained adequately on purely theoretical grounds. The individual is both a producer and a product of social life in its varied forms. The performances that give shape to behavior are in part socially imposed and in part self-generated. Individuals act out of an awareness of others, necessarily take each other into account, and have their own behaviors shaped and modified in the process. Humans are indeed adaptable creatures, and their futures are shaped by the cumulative effects of the decisions made by many people. According to C. Wright Mills (1959: 174),

within an individual's biography and with a society's history, the social task of reason is to formulate choices, to enlarge the scope of human decisions in the making of history. The future of human affairs is not merely some set of variables to be predicted. The future is what is to be decided—within the limits, to be sure, of historical possibility. But this possibility is not fixed; in our time the limits seem very broad indeed.

This quote is a fitting conclusion to our venture into social psychological inquiry. It was selected from Mills' discussion of reason and freedom. In his view, history has not yet completed its exploration of the limits of human nature, nor completed experimentation on the many possible relationships between the individual and society. Mills was essentially correct in this point of view. Realities are constructed at many levels of human action and are always changing in response to changing social conditions. The futures of individuals and societies are created out of hopes and aspirations, out of committed lines of action, and out of the consequences that follow from the decision-making process.

BASIC TERMS

Constructionist perspective
Objectivist perspective
Technological world view
Ethnomethodology

Psychological modernity
Personal freedom
Conditional freedom
Disciplined freedom

REFERENCES

Atchley, Robert C.
   1977 *The Social Forces in Later Life*, Belmont, Calif.: Wadsworth.
Ben-Yehuda, Nachman
   1980 "The European Witch Craze of the 14th to 17th Centuries: A Sociologist's Perspective," *American Journal of Sociology* 86 (July): 1–31.
Berger, Peter, Brigitte Berger, and Hansfried Kellner
   1973 *The Homeless Mind*, New York: Vintage Books.
Blauner, Robert
   1964 *Alienation and Freedom*, Chicago: University of Chicago Press.
Brown, Harrison
   1954 *The Challenge of Man's Future*, New York: Viking Press.
Bullough, Bonnie L.
   1969 *Social Psychological Barriers to Housing Desegregation*, Los Angeles: University of California Press.
Campbell, Angus
   1981 *The Sense of Well-Being in America*, New York: McGraw-Hill.
Campbell, Angus, Philip E. Converse, and Willard L. Rogers
   1976 *The Quality of American Life*, New York: Russell Sage.
Dawe, Alan
   1970 "The Two Sociologies," *British Journal of Sociology* 21:207–218.
Dudley, Charles J.
   1978 "The Division of Labor, Alienation, and Anomie," *Sociological Focus* 11 (April): 97–110.
Dudley, Charles J. and George A. Hillery, Jr.
   1979 "Freedom and Monastery Life," *Journal for the Scientific Study of Religion* 18 (March): 18–28.
Durkheim, Emile
   1951 *Suicide*, Glencoe, Ill.: The Free Press.
Ellul, Jacques
   1964 *The Technological Society*, New York: Vintage Books.
Etzioni, Amitai
   1968 *The Active Society*, New York: The Free Press.
Frankl, Viktor E.
   1965 *Man's Search for Meaning*, New York: Washington Square Press.
Fromm, Erich
   1941 *Escape From Freedom*, New York: Rinehart.
Garfinkel, Harold
   1967 *Studies in Ethnomethodology*, Englewood Cliffs, N.J.: Prentice-Hall.
Gurin, Patricia, Gerald Gurin, Rosina Lao, and Muriel Beattie
   1969 "Internal-External Control in the Motivational Dynamics of Negro Youth," *Journal of Social Issues* 25: 29–53.
Gurin, Patricia, Gerald Gurin, and Betty M. Morrison
   1978 "Personal and Ideological Aspects of Internal and External Control," *Social Psychology* 41 (December): 275–296.
Heft, Harry
   1981 "An Examination of Constructivist and Gibsonian Approaches to Environment Psychology," *Population and Environment* 4 (Winter): 227–245.

Heilbronner, Robert L.
  1960 *The Future as History*, New York: Harper & Row.
Hillery, George A., Jr.
  1971 "Freedom and Social Organization," *American Sociological Review* 36 (February): 51-64.
Hillery, George A., Jr., Charles J. Dudley, and Paula C. Morrow
  1977 "Toward a Sociology of Freedom," *Social Forces* 55 (March): 685-700.
Hillery, George A., Jr., Charles J. Dudley, and Thomas P. Thompson
  1979 "A Theory of Integration and Freedom," *Sociological Quarterly* 20 (Autumn): 551-564.
Hughes, Michael and Walter R. Gove
  1981 "Living Alone, Social Integration, and Mental Health," *American Journal of Sociology* 87 (July): 48-74.
Humphrey, Craig R. and Frederick R. Buttel
  1982 *Environment, Energy, and Society*, Belmont, Calif.: Wadsworth.
Israel, Joachim
  1971 *Alienation: From Marx to Modern Sociology*, Boston: Allyn and Bacon.
Keniston, Kenneth
  1965 *The Uncommitted*, New York: Harcourt, Brace and World.
Lane, Robert E.
  1966 "The Decline of Politics and Ideology in a Knowledgeable Society," *American Sociological Review* 31 (October): 649-662.
Lystad, Mary H.
  1972 "Social Alienation: A Review of Current Literature," *Sociological Quarterly* 13: 90-113.
Mills, C. Wright
  1963 "The Cultural Apparatus," in Irving L. Horowitz (ed.), *Power, Politics, and People*, New York: Ballantine, pp. 405-422.
  1959 *The Sociological Imagination*, New York: Oxford University Press.
  1953 *White Collar*, New York: Oxford University Press.
Moynihan, Daniel P.
  1969 *On Understanding Poverty*, New York: Basic Books.
Neal, Arthur G.
  1971 "Alienation and Social Control," in John P. Scott and Sally F. Scott (eds.), *Social Control and Social Change*, Chicago: University of Chicago Press, pp. 103-136.
Neal, Arthur G., William J. Ivoska, and H. Theodore Groat
  1976 "Dimensions of Family Alienation in the Marital Dyad," *Sociometry* 39 (December): 396-405.
Nisbet, Robert A.
  1962 *Community and Power*, New York: Oxford University Press.
Ogilvy, James
  1979 *Many Dimensional Man*, New York: Harper Colophon Books.
Rotter, Julian B.
  1966 "Generalized Expectancies for Internal Versus External Control of Reinforcements," *Psychological Monographs* 80: 1-28 (whole #609).
Ryan, William
  1976 *Blaming the Victim*, New York: Vintage Books.
Schwartz, Barry

1968 "The Social Psychology of Privacy," *American Journal of Sociology* 73 (May): 741–752.

Seeman, Melvin
1975 "Alienation Studies," *Annual Review of Sociology* 1: 91–124.
1972 "Alienation and Engagement," in Angus Campbell and Philip E. Converse (eds.), *The Human Meaning of Social Change*, New York: Russell Sage, pp. 467–528.

Shepard, Jon M.
1977 "Technology, Alienation, and Job Satisfaction," *Annual Review of Sociology* 3: 1–22.

Tedlock, Dennis and Barbara Tedlock
1975 *Teachings from the American Earth*, New York: Liveright.

Toffler, Alvin
1971 *Future Shock*, New York: Bantam Books.

Weigert, Andrew J.
1981 *Sociology of Everyday Life*, New York: Longman.

Williams, Robin M., Jr.
1970 *American Society*, New York: Knopf.

Wood, Vivian and Joan F. Robertson
1978 "Friendship and Kinship Interaction: Differential Effect on the Morale of the Elderly," *Journal of Marriage and the Family* 40 (May): 367–375.

Author Index

Subject Index